Lecture Notes in Computer Science

Edited by G. Goos, J. Hartmanis, and J. van

Springer
Berlin
Heidelberg
New York
Barcelona
Hong Kong
London
Milan
Paris
Tokyo

Bernd Radig   Stefan Florczyk (Eds.)

Pattern Recognition

23rd DAGM Symposium
Munich, Germany, September 12-14, 2001
Proceedings

Springer

Series Editors

Gerhard Goos, Karlsruhe University, Germany
Juris Hartmanis, Cornell University, NY, USA
Jan van Leeuwen, Utrecht University, The Netherlands

Volume Editors

Bernd Radig
Stefan Florczyk
Technical University Munich
Chair of Image Understanding and Knowledge Based Systems
Orleansstr. 34, 81667 Munich, Germany
E-mail: {radig/florczyk}@in.tum.de

Cataloging-in-Publication Data applied for

Die Deutsche Bibliothek - CIP-Einheitsaufnahme

Pattern recognition : ... DAGM Symposium .... - 23. 2001 -. - Berlin ;
Heidelberg ; New York ; Barcelona ; Hong Kong ; London ; Milan ; Paris ;
Tokyo : Springer, 2001
       (Lecture notes in computer science ; ...)
       Früher u.d.T.: Mustererkennung ...
       23. 2001. Munich, Germany, September 12-14, 2001 : proceedings. - 2001
       (Lecture notes in computer science ; 2191)
       ISBN 3-540-42596-9

CR Subject Classification (1998): I.5, I.4, I.3.5, I.2.10

ISSN 0302-9743
ISBN 3-540-42596-9 Springer-Verlag Berlin Heidelberg New York

Springer-Verlag Berlin Heidelberg New York
a member of BertelsmannSpringer Science+Business Media GmbH

http://www.springer.de

© Springer-Verlag Berlin Heidelberg 2001
Printed in Germany

Typesetting: Camera-ready by author
Printed on acid-free paper   SPIN: 10840606   06/3142   5 4 3 2 1 0

Preface

Sometimes milestones in the evolution of the DAGM Symposium become immediately visible. The Technical Committee decided to publish the symposium proceedings completely in English. As a consequence we successfully negotiated with Springer-Verlag to publish in the international well-accepted series "Lecture Notes in Computer Science". The quality of the contributions convinced the editors and the lectors. Thanks to them and to the authors. We received 105 acceptable, good, and even excellent manuscripts. We selected carefully, using three reviewers for each anonymized paper, 58 talks and posters. Our 41 reviewers had a hard job evaluating and especially rejecting contributions. We are grateful for the time and effort they spent in this task. The program committee awarded prizes to the best papers. We are much obliged to the generous sponsors.

We had three invited talks from outstanding colleagues, namely Bernhard Nebel (Robot Soccer – A Challenge for Cooperative Action and Perception), Thomas Lengauer (Computational Biology – An Interdisciplinary Challenge for Computational Pattern Recognition), and Nassir Navab (Medical and Industrial Augmented Reality: Challenges for Real-Time Vision, Computer Graphics, and Mobile Computing). N. Navab even wrote a special paper for this conference, which is included in the proceedings.

We were proud that we could convince well known experts to offer tutorials to our participants: H.-P. Seidel, Univ. Saarbrücken – A Framework for the Acquisition, Processing, and Interactive Display of High Quality 3D Models; S. Heuel, Univ. Bonn – Projective Geometry for Grouping and Orientation Tasks; G. Rigoll, Univ. Duisburg – Hidden Markov Models for Pattern Recognition and Man-Machine-Communication; G. Klinker, TU München – Foundations and Applications of Augmented Reality; R. Koch, Univ. Kiel – Reconstruction from Image Sequences; W. Förstner, Univ. Bonn – Uncertainty, Testing, and Estimation of Geometric Parameters; K.-H. Englmeier, GSF Munich – Computer Vision and Virtual Reality Applications in Medicine; W. Eckstein and C. Steger, MVTec GmbH, Munich – Industrial Computer Vision.

I appreciate the support of so many persons and institutions who made this conference happen: the generosity and cooperation of the Fachhochschule München and the Technische Universität München, the financial and material contributions by our sponsors, the helpers who did so much excellent work in preparing and realizing this event. Stefan Florczyk, my co-editor, and his team – Ulrike Schroeter, Oliver Bösl – did a great job. With the experience and imagination of my colleagues in the local committee – W. Abmayr, H. Ebner, K.-H. Englmeier, G. Hirzinger, E. Hundt, G. Klinker, H. Mayer – it was a pleasure to create and design this symposium. We all did our best and hope that the participants took their personal advantage of the conference and enjoyed their stay in Munich.

July 2001   Bernd Radig

Conference Committee

Organizer

DAGM e.V.: German Association for Pattern Recognition

General Chairperson:

Prof. Dr. B. Radig   Technical University Munich

List of Referees

Organizing Committee

B. Radig	TU Munich
W. Abmayr	FH Munich
H. Ebner	TU Munich
K.-H. Englmeier	GSF Neuherberg
G. Hirzinger	DLR Oberpfaffenhofen
E. Hundt	Siemens Munich
G. Klinker	TU Munich
H. Mayer	UniBW Munich

Further Members of the Program Committee

J. Buhmann	Univ. Bonn
H. Burkhardt	Univ. Freiburg
D. Fritsch	Univ. Stuttgart
S. Fuchs	TU Dresden
G. Färber	TU Munich
W. Förstner	Univ. Bonn
A. Grün	ETH Zurich, Switzerland
P. Haberäcker	FH Munich
H. Handels	Univ. Lübeck
G. Hartmann	Univ. Paderborn
B. Jähne	Univ. Heidelberg
G. Kropatsch	TU Vienna, Austria
P. Levi	Univ. Stuttgart
C.-E. Liedtke	Univ. Hannover
B. Mertsching	Univ. Hamburg
R. Mester	Univ. Frankfurt
B. Michaelis	Univ. Magdeburg
H.-H. Nagel	Univ. Karlsruhe
H. Ney	RWTH Aachen
H. Niemann	Forwiss Erlangen
E. Paulus	Univ. Braunschweig

Since 1978 the DAGM (German Association for Pattern Recognition) stages annually at different venues a scientific symposium with the aim of envisaging conceptual formulations, ways of thinking, and research results from different areas in pattern recognition, to stimulate the exchange of experience and ideas between the experts, and to further the young generation .

The DAGM e.V. was founded as a registered society in September 1999. Until then the DAGM was constituted from supporter societies which have since then been honorary members of the DAGM e.V.:

DGaO	Deutsche Arbeitsgemeinschaft für angewandte Optik (German Society of Applied Optics)
GMDS	Deutsche Gesellschaft für Medizinische Informatik, Biometrie und Epidemologie (German Society for Medical Informatics, Biometry, and Epidemiology)
GI	Gesellschaft für Informatik (German Informatics Society)
ITG	Informationstechnische Gesellschaft (Information Technology Society)
DGN	Deutsche Gesellschaft für Nuklearmedizin (German Society of Nuclear Medicine)
IEEE	Deutsche Sektion des IEEE (The Institute of Electrical and Electronic Engineers, German Section)
DGPF	Deutsche Gesellschaft für Photogrammetrie und Fernerkundung
VDMA	Fachabteilung industrielle Bildverarbeitung/ Machine Vision im VDMA (Robotics + Automation Division within VDMA)
GNNS	German Chapter of European Neural Network Society
DGR	Deutsche Gesellschaft für Robotik

The

DAGM main prize 2000

endowed with DEM 5000

was awarded to

W. Förstner, A. Brunn, and S. Heuel

University Bonn, Institute of Photogrammetry

for the following contribution:

Statistically Testing Uncertain Geometric Relations.

Further DAGM prices endowed with DEM 1000 for the year 2000 were awarded to

A. Brakensiek, D. Willett, and G. Rigoll

Unlimited Vocabulary Script Recognition Using Character N-Grams

University Duisburg, Germany,
Dept. of Computer Science,
Faculty of Electrical Engineering

M. Felsberg and G. Sommer

A New Extension of Linear Signal Processing for Estimating Local Properties and Detecting Features

University Kiel, Germany,
Institute of Computer Science and Applied Mathematics

C. Knöppel, U. Regensburger,
A. Schanz and B. Michaelis

DaimlerChrysler Research Stuttgart,
Germany,
Department for Driver Assistant Systems

Robuste Erkennung von Straßenfahrzeugen im
Rückraumbereich eines Straßenfahrzeuges

V. Lohweg and D. Müller

Technical University Chemnitz, Germany,
Chair Circuit and System Design

Ein generalisiertes Verfahren zur Berechnung
von translationsinvarianten
Zirkulartransformationen für die Anwendung
in der Signal- und Bildverarbeitung

N. Navab, M. Appel,
Y. Genc, B. Bascle,
V. Kumar and M. Neuberger

Imaging and Visualization,
Siemens Corporate Research, Princeton,
USA,
Siemens Nuclear Power,
Erlangen, Germany,

As-Built Reconstruction Using Images and
Industrial Drawings

Table of Contents

Image Analysis I

Poster

3D-Gathering & Visualization

Poster

Image Processing

Poster

Image Sequence Analysis

Poster

Classification

Poster

Active Vision

Poster

Image Analysis II

3D-Reconstruction

Poster

Interaction Virtual with Real Worlds

Poster

Invited Talk

Model-Based Image Segmentation Using Local Self-Adapting Separation Criteria

Robert Hanek

Lehrstuhl für Bildverstehen und Wissensbasierte Systeme,
Forschungsgruppe Bildverstehen (FG BV),
Technische Universität München, Germany
http://www9.in.tum.de/people/hanek/

Abstract. In this paper we address the problem of model-based image segmentation by fitting deformable models to the image data. From uncertain a priori knowledge of the model parameters an initial probability distribution of the model edge in the image is obtained. From the vicinity of the surmised edge local statistics are learned for both sides of the edge. These local statistics provide locally adapted criteria to distinguish the two sides of the edge even in the presence of spatially changing properties such as texture, shading, or color. Based on the local statistics the model parameters are iteratively refined using a MAP estimation. Experiments with RGB images show that the method is capable of achieving high subpixel accuracy even in the presence of texture, shading, clutter, and partial occlusion.

1 Introduction

Deformable models, also known as snakes or active contours [9], have been proven as an efficient way to incorporate application-specific a priori knowledge into computer vision algorithms. For example, in order to segment a bone in a medical image or in order to visually track a person, models describing the possible contours of the objects of interest are used [11, 10, 2]. The parameters of the models specify object properties such as the pose, size, and shape. The problem of estimating parameters of curve models from images not only has applications in low-level vision such as image segmentation and tracking but also in high-level vision such as 3-D pose estimation, camera calibration, 3-D reconstruction, and object recognition.

In this paper we propose a novel method for estimating the parameters of deformable edge models from image data. This method can also be applied to high-level problems such as 3-D reconstruction and pose estimation. However, here we focus on model-based image segmentation. Due to the high number of publications on image segmentation in the following only a few aspects of the relevant work can be reflected. See our companion paper [7] for a more comprehensive version of this publication.

B. Radig and S. Florczyk (Eds.): DAGM 2001, LNCS 2191, pp. 1–8, 2001.

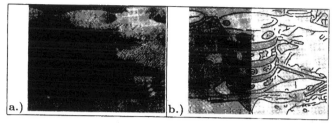

Fig. 1. Mug in front of an inhomogeneous background: a.) color image (see CD), b.) color edges detected by a gradient-based approach (C. Steger [14]). The mug and the background are not well separated due to the edges within both regions.

1.1   Previous Work

The body of work on image segmentation can be roughly classified into three categories: (i) **edge-based segmentation**, (ii) **region-based segmentation**, and (iii) **methods integrating edge-based and region-based segmentation**.

(i) **Edge-based segmentation** relies on discontinuities of image data [1, 12, 3]. The problem of edge-based segmentation is that in practice usually the edge-profile is not known. Furthermore, the profile often varies heavily along the edge caused by e.g. shading and texture. Due to these difficulties usually a simple step-edge is assumed and the edge detection is performed based on a maximum image gradient. In Fig. 1a the color values on either side of the mug's contour are not constant even within a small vicinity. Hence, methods maximizing the image gradient have difficulties to separate the mug and the background, see Fig. 1b.

(ii) **Region-based segmentation** methods such as [16, 5] rely on the homogeneity of spatially localized features (e.g. RGB values). The underlying homogeneity assumption is that the features of all pixels within one region are statistically independently distributed according to the same probability density function. Often this assumption does not hold. In Fig. 1a the distributions of the RGB values of the mug and the background depend on the locations within the image.

(iii) **Integrating methods:** especially in recent years methods have been published which aim to overcome the individual shortcomings of edge-based and region-based segmentation by integrating both segmentation principles [15, 13, 4, 8]. These methods seek a compromise between an edge-based criterion, e.g. the magnitude of the image gradient, and a region-based criterion evaluating the homogeneity of the regions. However, it is questionable whether a compromise between the two criteria yields reasonable results when both the homogeneity assumption and the assumption regarding the edge profile do not hold as in Fig. 1a.

1.2   Main Contributions

The main contributions of this paper are as follows: **1.) Local self-adapting separation criteria** are used in order to distinguish adjacent regions: While other methods use certain fixed criteria (e.g. image gradients, homogeneity criteria, or combinations) to separate adjacent regions, we use local self-adapting separation criteria. These criteria are based on local statistics of pixel features obtained from the vicinity of the surmised curve. These criteria allow to separate the two sides of an edge even in the presence of spatially changing properties, such as changing texture, color, or shading. For the computation of the desired local statistics an efficient method is proposed.

2.) A fit between image data and a 'blurred model' is proposed: in order to increase the capture range, gradient-based methods typically fit the model to a blurred image. We take the opposite approach. We use **non-blurred image data and a 'blurred model'.** Instead of optimizing the relation between blurred image data and a single vector of model parameters we optimize the relation between the non-blurred image data and a probability distribution of model parameters. The advantages are as follows: (i) the capture range is enlarged according to the local uncertainties of the model curve which significantly improves the convergence. (ii) Optimizing the fit between an image and a 'blurred model' is in general computationally cheaper than blurring the image. (iii) High frequency information of the image data can be used.

Overview of the Paper: The reminder of this paper is organized as follows: in section 2 an overview of the here proposed Contracting Curve Density (CCD) algorithm is given. Sections 3 describes the two main steps of the CCD algorithm. Section 4 contains an experimental evaluation and finally in section 5 a conclusion is given.

2 Overview of the Contracting Curve Density (CCD) Algorithm

The here proposed CCD algorithm estimates the parameters of curve models from image data. The CCD algorithm can roughly be characterized as an extension of the EM algorithm [6] using additional knowledge. The additional knowledge consists of: (i) a curve model, which describes the set of possible boundaries between adjacent regions, and (ii) a model of the imaging device. The CCD algorithm, depicted in Fig. 2, performs an iteration of two steps, which roughly correspond to the two steps of the EM algorithm: **1. Local statistics of image data are learned** from the vicinity of the curve. These statistics locally characterize the two sides of the edge curve. **2. From these statistics, the estimation of the model parameters is refined** by optimizing the separation of the two sides. This refinement in turn leads in the next iteration step to an improved statistical characterization of the two sides. During the process, the uncertainty of the model parameters decreases and the probability density of the curve in the image contracts to a single edge estimate. We therefore call the algorithm Contracting Curve Density (CCD) algorithm.

Input: The input of the CCD algorithm consists of the image data I^* and the curve model. The image data are local features, e.g. RGB values, given for each pixel of the image. The curve model consists of two parts: 1.) a differentiable curve function c describing the model edge curve in the image as a function of the

---

Input: image data $\mathbf{I}^*$, differentiable curve function c, mean $\mathbf{m}^*_\Phi$ and covariance Σ^*_Φ
Output: estimate $\mathbf{m}_\Phi$ of model parameters and associated covariance Σ_Φ

Initialization: mean $\mathbf{m}_\Phi = \mathbf{m}^*_\Phi$, covariance $\Sigma_\Phi = c_1 \cdot \Sigma^*_\Phi$
repeat
1. **learn local statistics** of image data from the vicinity of the curve
   (a) compute pixels v in vicinity $\mathcal{V}$ of the image curve from c, $\mathbf{m}_\Phi$ and Σ_Φ
       $\forall v \in \mathcal{V}$ compute vague assignment $\mathbf{a}_v(\mathbf{m}_\Phi, \Sigma_\Phi)$ to the sides of the curve
   (b) $\forall v \in \mathcal{V}$ compute local statistics $\mathbf{S}_v$ of image data $\mathbf{I}^*_\mathcal{V}$
2. **refine estimation** of model parameters
   (a) update mean $\mathbf{m}_\Phi$ by performing one iteration step of MAP estimation:
   $$\mathbf{m}_\Phi = \arg\min_{\mathbf{m}_\Phi} \chi^2(\mathbf{m}_\Phi) \quad \text{with}$$
   $$\chi^2(\mathbf{m}_\Phi) = -2\ln[p(\mathbf{I}_\mathcal{V} = \mathbf{I}^*_\mathcal{V} \mid \mathbf{a}_\mathcal{V}(\mathbf{m}_\Phi, \Sigma_\Phi), \mathbf{S}_\mathcal{V}) \cdot p(\mathbf{m}_\Phi \mid \mathbf{m}^*_\Phi, \Sigma^*_\Phi)]$$
   (b) updated covariance Σ_Φ from Hessian of $\chi^2(\mathbf{m}_\Phi)$
until changes of $\mathbf{m}_\Phi$ and Σ_Φ are small enough
Post-processing: estimate covariance Σ_Φ from Hessian of $\chi^2(\mathbf{m}_\Phi)$
return mean $\mathbf{m}_\Phi$ and covariance Σ_Φ

Fig. 2. The CCD algorithm iteratively refines a Gaussian a priori density $p(\Phi) = p(\Phi \mid \mathbf{m}^*_\Phi, \Sigma^*_\Phi)$ of model parameters to a Gaussian approximation $p(\Phi \mid \mathbf{m}_\Phi, \Sigma_\Phi)$ of the posterior density $p(\Phi \mid \mathbf{I}^*)$.

model parameters Φ, 2.) a Gaussian a priori distribution $p(\Phi) = p(\Phi \mid \mathbf{m}^*_\Phi, \Sigma^*_\Phi)$ of the model parameters Φ, defined by the mean $\mathbf{m}^*_\Phi$ and the covariance Σ^*_Φ. (The superscript $*$ indicates input data.) Depending on the application the quantities $\mathbf{m}^*_\Phi$ and Σ^*_Φ may be obtained for example from a training set, by a human initialization, or from a prediction over time.

Output: The output of the algorithm consists of the estimate $\mathbf{m}_\Phi$ of the model parameters Φ and the covariance Σ_Φ describing the uncertainty of the estimate. The estimate $\mathbf{m}_\Phi$ and the covariance Σ_Φ define a Gaussian approximation $p(\Phi \mid \mathbf{m}_\Phi, \Sigma_\Phi)$ of the posterior density $p(\Phi \mid \mathbf{I}^*)$.

Initialization: The estimate $\mathbf{m}_\Phi$ of the model parameters and the associated covariance Σ_Φ are initialized using the mean $\mathbf{m}^*_\Phi$ and covariance Σ^*_Φ of the a priori distribution. The factor c_1 (e.g. $c_1 = 9$) increases the initial uncertainty and thereby enlarges the capture range of the CCD algorithm.

3   Steps of the CCD Algorithm

The two basic steps of the CCD algorithm, depicted in Fig. 2, are briefly summarized in this section. Due to the space limitation, only the basic concept can be presented here. A more detailed and more mathematical description is given in our companion paper [7].

3.1   Learn Local Statistics (Step 1)

The Gaussian distribution of model parameters $p(\Phi \mid \mathbf{m}_\Phi, \Sigma_\Phi)$ and the model curve function c define a probability distribution of the edge curve in the image.

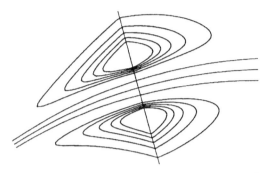

Fig. 3. Contour plot of the windows (weights) used to estimate (learn) local statistics: the three roughly parallel lines describe the surmised position and uncertainty (σ-interval) of the curve. For the pixels on the perpendicular line (straight) local statistics $\mathbf{S}_v$ are computed from the two depicted windows. The windows are adapted in size and shape to the surmised curve and its uncertainty.

This curve distribution vaguely assigns each pixel in the vicinity of the surmised curve to one side of the curve. In **step 1a** the set $\mathcal{V}$ of pixels v in the vicinity of the surmised curve is determined and for the pixels $v \in \mathcal{V}$ the vague side assignments $\mathbf{a}_v(\mathbf{m}_\Phi, \Sigma_\Phi)$ are computed. The components of the assignments $\mathbf{a}_v$ specify to which extent pixel v is expected to belong to the corresponding side. Fig. 4 row b.) depicts for pixels $v \in \mathcal{V}$ the assignments to the lower side of the surmised edge. White pixels indicate a quite certain assignment to the lower side.

In **step 1b** local statistics $\mathbf{S}_v$, i.e. first and second order moments, of the image feature vectors $\mathbf{I}_v^*$ are learned from pixels which are assigned to one side with high certainty. This is done for each of the two sides separated by the curve. In order to obtain the statistics locally adapted windows (weights) are used, see Fig. 3. The windows are chosen such that the local statistics $\mathbf{S}_v$ can be computed recursively. The resulting time complexity of computing $\mathbf{S}_v$ for all pixels $v \in \mathcal{V}$ is $O(|\mathcal{V}|)$, where $|\mathcal{V}|$ is the number of pixels in the vicinity $\mathcal{V}$. Note that the time complexity is independent of the window size along the curve.

3.2   Refine the Estimation of Model Parameters (Step 2)

In the second step, the estimation of the model parameters is refined based on a MAP optimization. **Step 2a** updates the estimate $\mathbf{m}_\Phi$ such that the vague assignments $\mathbf{a}_v(\mathbf{m}_\Phi, \Sigma_\Phi)$ of the pixels $v \in \mathcal{V}$ fit best to the local statistics $\mathbf{S}_v$. The feature vectors $\mathbf{I}_v^*$ of pixels $v \in \mathcal{V}$ are modeled as Gaussian random variables. The mean vectors and covariances are estimated from the local statistics $\mathbf{S}_v$ obtained from the corresponding side of pixel v. The feature vectors of edge pixels are modeled as weighted linear combinations of both sides of the edge. In step 2a, only one iteration step of the resulting MAP optimization is performed. Since the vague assignments $\mathbf{a}_v(\mathbf{m}_\Phi, \Sigma_\Phi)$ explicitly take the uncertainty (the covariance Σ_Φ) of the estimate into account the capture range is enlarged according to

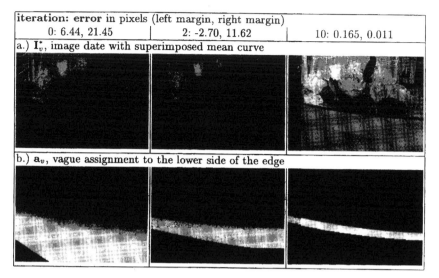

iteration: **error** in pixels (left margin, right margin)		
0: 6.44, 21.45	2: -2.70, 11.62	10: 0.165, 0.011
a.) I_v^*, image date with superimposed mean curve		
b.) a_v, vague assignment to the lower side of the edge		

Fig. 4. a.) Semi-synthetic image showing roses behind a wooden board: the initial error is reduced by more than 99%. **b.)** During the process the uncertainty of the curve is reduced and the vague side assignments a_v become certain.

the local uncertainty in the image. This leads to an individually adapted scale selection for each pixel and thereby to a big area of convergence, see [7]. In **step 2b**, the covariance Σ_Φ of the estimate m_Φ is updated based on the Hessian of the resulting χ^2 objective function.

4   Experiments

In our experiments we apply the proposed CCD algorithm to the segmentation of two fundamental types of image features, namely (i) lines which are radially distorted and (ii) circles. For the sake of a ground truth we first use semi-synthetic images. From two images one combined image is obtained by taking for one side of the curve the content of image one and for the other side of the curve the content of image two. For pixels on the curve the pixel data are interpolated.

(i) **Lines:** Fig. 4 row a.) shows such a semi-synthetic image. For different iterations the estimated curves are superimposed on the image. During the process the initial error is reduced by more than 99%. Fig. 5 contains real image data. The mug has strong internal edges. Shading causes additional variations of the mug's color values. The background contains area of texture as well as strong variations of the illumination. After 11 iterations the estimated curve is aligned to the real curve without any visible deviation.

(ii) **Circles:** Fig. 6 depicts the iteration for a semi-synthetic image. The initial error is reduced by more than 99.8% and the final error is less than 5% of a pixel. However, for real images with similarly complex content we assume that

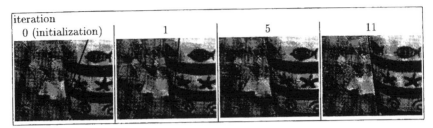

| iteration | | | |
| 0 (initialization) | 1 | 5 | 11 |

Fig. 5. Real image, (sub-image of Fig. 1a.): the initial error of the curve is more than 70 pixels (upper part). After 11 iterations the deviation between the estimated curve and the real curve is not visible.

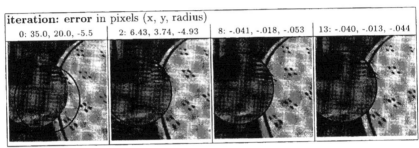

| iteration: error in pixels (x, y, radius) | | | |
| 0: 35.0, 20.0, -5.5 | 2: 6.43, 3.74, -4.93 | 8: -.041, -.018, -.053 | 13: -.040, -.013, -.044 |

Fig. 6. The circle and the background are very inhomogeneous. Furthermore, the circle is only partially visible. Nevertheless, the initial error is reduced by more than 99.8%.

the subpixel accuracy is lower due to different effects, such as unknown blurring caused by the imaging device.

The run time of the algorithm scales roughly linearly to the number of used pixels. Hence, the initial uncertainty has an important impact on the run time. For example on a 500 MHz computer an iteration step using 10.000 pixels (high initial uncertainty) takes about 4s. After about 5 iterations the run time is reduced to less than 1s per iteration.

5   Conclusion

We have proposed a novel method for fitting deformable models to image data. The method iteratively refines the a priori distribution of the model parameters to a Gaussian approximation of the posterior distribution. Locally adapted criteria are used in order to distinguish the two sides of the surmised curve. The separation criteria are learned from local statistics of the curve's vicinity. Pixels which are intersected by the curve are modeled by a mixture of two local distributions corresponding to the two sides of the curve. This locally adapted statistical modeling allows to separate the two sides of the curve with high subpixel accuracy even in the presence of texture, shading, clutter, and partial occlusion.

High robustness, a big area of convergence, is achieved by optimizing the resulting MAP criteria not only for a single vector of model parameters but for a distribution of model parameters. During the process not only the model parameters are refined but also the associated covariance. From the covariance the local uncertainties of the curve are obtained which provide the basis for the automatic and local scale selection. In future work we will apply the proposed CCD algorithm to high-level model-fitting problems such as 3-D pose estimation and 3-D reconstruction.

Acknowledgment: The author would like to thank Michael Beetz, Carsten Steger, and Viswanathan Ramesh for useful discussions during the process of this work.

References

1. BAKER, S., NAYAR, S., AND MURASE, H. Parametric feature detection. *IJCV 27*, 1 (March 1998), 27–50.
2. BLAKE, A., AND ISARD, M. *Active Contours.* Springer-Verlag, Berlin Heidelberg New York, 1998.
3. CANNY, J. A computational approach to edge detection. *PAMI 8*, 6 (November 1986), 679–698.
4. CHAKRABORTY, A., AND DUNCAN, J. Game-theoretic integration for image segmentation. *PAMI 21*, 1 (January 1999), 12–30.
5. CHESNAUD, C., REFREGIER, P., AND BOULET, V. Statistical region snake-based segmentation adapted to different physical noise models. *PAMI 21*, 11 (November 1999), 1145–1157.
6. DEMPSTER, A., LAIRD, N., AND RUBIN, D. Maximum likelihood from incomplete data via the EM algorithm. *J. R. Statist. Soc. B 39* (1977), 1–38.
7. HANEK, R. Model-based image segmentation using local self-adapting separation criteria. Tech. rep., Technische Universität München, 2001. available on **CD DAGM-2001** or at http://www9.in.tum.de/publications/2001/TR-MBI-Hanek.pdf.
8. JONES, T., AND METAXAS, D. Image segmentation based on the integration of pixel affinity and deformable models. In *CVPR98* (1998), pp. 330–337.
9. KASS, M., WITKIN, A., AND TERZOPOULOS, D. Snakes: Active contour models. *IJCV 1*, 4 (January 1988), 321–331.
10. LEVENTON, M., GRIMSON, W., AND FAUGERAS, O. Statistical shape influence in geodesic active contours. In *CVPR00* (2000), pp. I:316–323.
11. MCINERNEY, T., AND TERZOPOULOS, D. Deformable models in medical image analysis: a survey. *Medical Image Analysis 1*, 2 (1996), 91–108.
12. NALWA, V., AND BINFORD, T. On detecting edges. *PAMI 8*, 6 (November 1986), 699–714.
13. PARAGIOS, N., AND DERICHE, R. Coupled geodesic active regions for image segmentation: A level set approach. In *ECCV00* (2000), pp. 224–240.
14. STEGER, C. Subpixel-precise extraction of lines and edges. *International Archives of Photogrammetry and Remote Sensing XXXIII, part B3* (2000), 141–156.
15. THIRION, B., BASCLE, B., RAMESH, V., AND NAVAB, N. Fusion of color, shading and boundary information for factory pipe segmentation. In *CVPR00* (2000), pp. II:349–356.
16. ZHU, S., AND YUILLE, A. Region competition: Unifying snakes, region growing, and bayes/mdl for multiband image segmentation. *PAMI 18*, 9 (September 1996), 884–900.

SIMBA – Search IMages By Appearance

Sven Siggelkow, Marc Schael, and Hans Burkhardt

Institute for Pattern Recognition and Image Processing,
Computer Science Department,
Albert-Ludwigs-Universität Freiburg, Germany
sven.siggelkow@informatik.uni-freiburg.de
http://simba.informatik.uni-freiburg.de

Abstract. In this paper we present SIMBA, a content based image retrieval system performing queries based on image appearance. We consider absolute object positions irrelevant for image similarity here and therefore propose to use invariant features. Based on a general construction method (integration over the transformation group), we derive invariant feature histograms that catch different cues of image content: features that are strongly influenced by color and textural features that are robust to illumination changes. By a weighted combination of these features the user can adapt the similarity measure according to his needs, thus improving the retrieval results considerably. The feature extraction does not require any manual interaction, so that it might be used for fully automatic annotation in heavily fluctuating image databases.

1 Introduction

Content based image retrieval has become a widespread field of research. This is caused by the ever increasing amount of available image data (e.g. via the Internet), which requires new techniques for efficient access. A manual annotation of the images is too time-consuming and cannot keep up with the growth of data. Therefore knowledge from computer vision is exploited to adapt algorithms for this task.

A good overview on content based image retrieval is given in [13]. The features used can be roughly classified into: color with/without layout, texture, shape, combinations thereof, and motion parameters.

The two feature types considered in SIMBA are color and texture: The most simple systems use a color histogram [2], in which, however, all spatial layout information is lost. In [15] and [7] therefore the histogram is refined using layout or smoothness information. Other systems perform a segmentation of the image and compare images based on their features and their absolute or relative locations [14,3]. The segmentation, however, is a crucial problem when considering images of general content. Other authors therefore explicitly restrict to specialized applications, that allow for a robust segmentation like images of museum objects in front of a homogeneous background [2,5].

Texture often is considered in combination with color. Features are diverse, e.g. granularity, contrast, and directionality are used in [2], whereas extended

B. Radig and S. Florczyk (Eds.): DAGM 2001, LNCS 2191, pp. 9–16, 2001.
© Springer-Verlag Berlin Heidelberg 2001

cooccurrence matrices and features like periodicity, directionality, and randomness are considered in [4].

Within this paper *invariant* features are developed to characterize images independently from absolute object positions. These features are thus well suited for image retrieval, as the user will generally consider images similar even if the objects have moved. In general objects are subject to quite complex transformations when projected into an image plane. We are therefore restricted to approximating the real transformations by transformations that can be mathematically treated with reasonable effort. In [1] general methods for the construction of invariant features are explained. Here we focus on invariant features for the group of translations and rotations (Euclidean motion). In addition to their theoretical invariance to global translation and rotation, these features have proven to be robust to independent motion of objects, different object constellations, articulated objects and even to topological deformations. The method does not require error-prone preprocessing of the data (like segmentation) but can be applied directly to the original image data. It is of linear complexity which, however, can be reduced to constant complexity using a Monte-Carlo estimation of the features [12].

In section 2 we briefly summarize the construction of invariant feature histograms. We construct two different kinds of features. One considering color mainly and a second one, considering brightness independent of usual illumination changes. Based on these features we present a system for content based image retrieval called SIMBA in section 3. Then in section 4 we show results of queries performed with that SIMBA. Finally a conclusion is given in section 5.

2   Construction of Invariant Features

We construct invariant features for images $\mathbf{M}$ of size $M \times N$ by integrating over a compact transformation group G [9]:

$$A[f](\mathbf{M}) := \frac{1}{|G|} \int_G f(g\mathbf{M})\, dg. \tag{1}$$

This invariant integral is also known as Haar integral. For the construction of rotation and translation invariant grey scale features we have to integrate over the group of translation and rotation:

$$A[f](\mathbf{M}) = \frac{1}{2\pi NM} \int_{t_0=0}^{N} \int_{t_1=0}^{M} \int_{\varphi=0}^{2\pi} f(g(t_0, t_1, \varphi)\mathbf{M}) d\varphi dt_1 dt_0. \tag{2}$$

Because of the discrete image grid in practice the integrals are replaced by sums, choosing only integer translations and varying the angle in discrete steps applying bilinear interpolation for pixels that do not coincide with the image grid.

For kernel functions f of local support the calculation of the integral generally can be separated into two steps: First for every pixel a local function is evaluated, which only depends on the grey scale intensities in a neighborhood disk according to f. Then all intermediate results of the local computations are summed up.

Instead of summing up the results, a histogram can be calculated, thus keeping more information about the local results. Furthermore different kernel functions f or multiple color layers can be combined into multidimensional (joint) histograms. Instead of using a traditional histogram we apply a fuzzy histogram [1] to get rid of the discontinuous behavior of the traditional histogram.

Kernel functions of monomial type (like $f(\mathbf{M}) = \mathbf{M}(4,0) \cdot \mathbf{M}(0,8)$) in combination with fuzzy histograms have been successfully applied to the task of texture classification [10], texture defect detection [8], and content based image retrieval [11].

In this paper we additionally consider textural features, that are invariant to standard illumination changes. These are constructed using the method above and applying a relational kernel function of type

$$f(\mathbf{M}) = \mathrm{rel}(\mathbf{M}(x_1, y_1) - \mathbf{M}(x_2, y_2)) \tag{3}$$

with the ramp function

$$\mathrm{rel}(\delta) = \begin{cases} 1 & \delta < -\epsilon \\ \frac{1}{2\epsilon}(\epsilon - \delta) & -\epsilon \leq \delta \leq \epsilon \\ 0 & \epsilon < \delta \end{cases} \tag{4}$$

centered at the origin.

Our relational kernel function is motivated by the local binary pattern (LBP). LBP is a well known method for the construction of textural features [6]. This operator maps the relations between the grey scale values of a center pixel and its 3×3 neighborhood pixel onto a binary pattern. The most important property of the LBP is its invariance against strictly increasing grey scale transformations. If we set ϵ to zero we get exactly the comparison function used for the LBP operator.

The problem with a simple comparison, as done by the LBP operator, is the discontinuity of the operator. In the worst case, a small noise within the image results in a big deviation of the feature. If we add a continuous transition ($\epsilon > 0$) we become more robust to noise, but loose a bit of invariance against monotonic grey scale transformations.

Again, equation (2) can be evaluated in two steps: The chosen kernel function f defines a pattern of two pixels that have to be compared with the rel-function. This pattern is rotated around each image pixel (local evaluation) and then translated to all pixel positions (global averaging). Again it is suggestive to do a histogramming instead of the averaging. We thus create a 3-bin histogram for every local evaluation first. Roughly speaking this gives for every image pixel the fractions of pixel pairs with relation 'darker', 'equal', and 'lighter'. By using the fuzzy histogram mentioned above we keep smooth transitions between these three classes. Afterwards an overall joint histogram of these local fractions is constructed from all local evaluations.

As a result we obtain a feature vector characterizing the local activities within the image, which is invariant to image translations and rotations and robust to standard brightness transformations.

3   SIMBA, an Online Prototype for Content Based Image Retrieval

Based on the methods presented above we implemented SIMBA, an appearance based image retrieval system containing nearly 2500 photograph images. The user can combine features that are strongly influenced by the image color (monomial type kernel functions evaluated on each color layer) with the proposed textural features that are calculated from the luminance layer only. By assigning weights to these features the user can adapt his query according to his needs or according to the image content.

SIMBA is constructed as a client-server system, thus providing faster query performance and the possibility of data protection. The search client, which can be located on any computer in the Internet, analyzes the query image and only sends the extracted features to the database server. The query image stays private as it does not leave the client's computer. The database server holds precalculated features of all database images. When a query request from a client arrives it performs a weighted nearest neighbor query (in terms of a histogram intersection) and returns the resulting image names (or URLs) and additional information like the match-value to the client.

Currently SIMBA runs on a SGI O2 MIPS R5000 (web-client) and an IBM RS6000 (server)[1]. But it also runs on Windows as well as various other Unix systems and can be accessed from anywhere in the Internet.

4   Results

We present results obtained with SIMBA using the MPEG-7 test dataset. As told before, the monomial features consider color and thus the results are very intuitive for the user. The texture features based on relational kernel functions are sometimes less intuitive for the user. This is due to the fact, that we do not use a texture database containing several examples of the same texture but use real world images. At least the user might comprehend the results in terms of 'highly textured image parts' or 'homogeneous image parts'.

Figures 1 to 3 show example queries[2]. We oppose results using monomial and relational feature kernels, or combinations thereof. Note, that the examples were intentionally chosen that way, that the results are not satisfying when using monomial kernels only. Often, however, the results using monomial kernels are sufficient already [11].

The query image in figure 1 displays a sunset. There is no sunset image in the database with similar color, thus the result of the monomial kernel functions is not satisfying (first query in figure 1). Applying relational kernel functions the smooth gradient characteristics of different sunsets in the database are caught

---

[1] http://simba.informatik.uni-freiburg.de

[2] We acknowledge Tristan Savatier, Aljandro Jaimes, and the Department of Water Resources, California for providing the displayed images within the MPEG-7 test set.

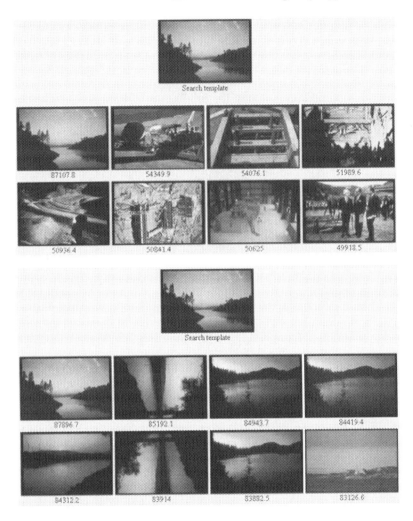

Fig. 1. Query examples from SIMBA. The first query is based on monomial feature kernels only. The next query uses relational kernels only. The upper centered image of each query displays the query template. Below this, the top eight results are shown with the corresponding histogram intersection values.

better (second query in figure 1). The query images in figures 2 and 3 have very characteristic color and texture. The query results using a monomial kernel only are not satisfying (first queries of figures 2 and 3). Combining monomials and relational kernels, however, both color and texture are considered well, so that several images with steel reinforcement resp. railings are found (second queries of figures 2 and 3).

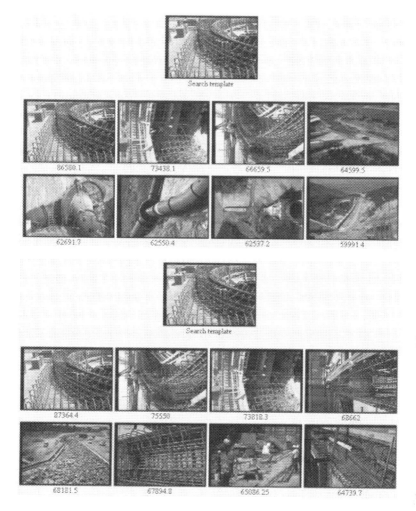

Fig. 2. Query examples from SIMBA. The queries displayed at the top are based on monomial feature kernels only. The second query was performed using an equally weighted combination of monomial and relational kernel functions. The upper centered image of each query displays the query template. Below this, the top eight results are shown with the corresponding histogram intersection values.

5   Conclusion

In this paper we presented a content based image retrieval system based on invariant features. A previous system that paid much attention to color was extended by novel invariant textural features. By weighting these feature types according to the needs or according to the image type, the user is able to improve

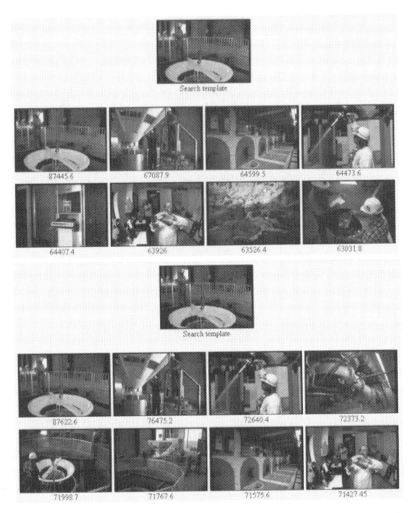

Fig. 3. Query examples from SIMBA. The queries displayed at the top are based on monomial feature kernels only. The second query was performed using an equally weighted combination of monomial and relational kernel functions. The upper centered image of each query displays the query template. Below this, the top eight results are shown with the corresponding histogram intersection values.

the retrieval results considerably. In contrast to many existing image retrieval systems SIMBA does not rely on error-prone preprocessing steps (like segmentation) but derives its features directly from the original image data. All transformations performed are continuous mappings thus ensuring a smooth degradation of the features if the image data is changed moderately. As none of the methods requires manual interaction, the system might also be used for fully automatic generation of annotations in heavily fluctuating image databases.

References

1. H. Burkhardt and S. Siggelkow. Invariant features in pattern recognition – fundamentals and applications. In I. Pitas and C. Kotropoulos, editors, *Nonlinear Model-Based Image/Video Processing and Analysis*, pages 269–307. John Wiley & Sons, 2001.

2. M. Flickner, H. Sawhney, W. Niblack, J. Ashley, Q. Huang, B. Dom, M. Gorkani, J. Hafner, D. Lee, D. Petkovic, D. Steele, and P. Yanker. Query by image and video content: The QBIC system. *IEEE Computer*, 28(9):23–32, September 1995.

3. J. Li, J. Z. Wang, and G. Wiederhold. IRM: Integrated region matching for image retrieval. In *Proceedings of the 2000 ACM Multimedia Conference*, pages 147–156, Los Angeles, October 2000. ACM.

4. F. Liu and R. W. Picard. Periodicity, directionality, and randomness: Wold features for image modeling and retrieval. *IEEE Transactions on Pattern Analysis and Machine Intelligence*, 18(7):722–733, July 1996.

5. A. Lumini and D. Maio. Haruspex: an image database system for query-by-examples. In *Proceedings of the 15th International Conference on Pattern Recognition (ICPR) 2000*, volume 4, pages 258–261, Barcelona, Spain, September 2000.

6. T. Ojala, M. Pietikäinen, and D. Harwood. A comparative study of texture measures with classifications based on feature distributions. *Pattern Recognition*, 29(1):51–59, 1996.

7. G. Pass and R. Zabih. Histogram refinement for content-based image retrieval. In *Proceedings of the 1996 Workshop on the Applications of Computer Vision*, Sarasota, Florida, December 1996.

8. M. Schael and H. Burkhardt. Automatic detection of errors on textures using invariant grey scale features and polynomial classifiers. In M. K. Pietikäinen, editor, *Texture Analysis in Machine Vision*, volume 40 of *Machine Perception and Artificial Intelligence*, pages 219–230. World Scientific, 2000.

9. H. Schulz-Mirbach. Invariant features for gray scale images. In G. Sagerer, S. Posch, and F. Kummert, editors, *Mustererkennung, DAGM 1995*, pages 1–14, Bielefeld, 1995.

10. S. Siggelkow and H. Burkhardt. Invariant feature histograms for texture classification. In *Proceedings of the 1998 Joint Conference on Information Sciences (JCIS)*, Research Triangle Park, North Carolina, USA, October 1998.

11. S. Siggelkow and H. Burkhardt. Fast invariant feature extraction for image retrieval. In H. Burkhardt, H.-P. Kriegel, and R. Veltkamp, editors, *State-of-the-Art in Content-Based Image and Video Retrieval*. Kluwer Academic Publishers, 2001. To appear.

12. S. Siggelkow and M. Schael. Fast estimation of invariant features. In W. Förstner, J. M. Buhmann, A. Faber, and P. Faber, editors, *Mustererkennung, DAGM 1999*, Informatik aktuell, pages 181–188, Bonn, September 1999.

13. A. W. M. Smeulders, M. Worring, S. Santini, A. Gupta, and R. Jain. Content-based image retrieval at the end of the early years. *IEEE Transactions on Pattern Analysis and Machine Intelligence*, 22(12):1349–1380, December 2000.

14. J. R. Smith and S.-F. Chang. Local color and texture extraction and spatial query. In *Proceedings of the 1996 IEEE International Conference on Image Processing (ICIP'96)*, volume III, pages 1011–1014, Lausanne, Switzerland, September 1996.

15. M. Stricker and A. Dimai. Color indexing with weak spatial constraints. In *Storage and Retrieval for Image and Video Databases IV*, volume 2670 of *SPIE Proceedings Series*, pages 29–40, February 1996.

Texture Defect Detection
Using Invariant Textural Features

Marc Schael

Institute for Pattern Recognition and Image Processing,
Computer Science Department,
Albert-Ludwigs-Universität Freiburg, Germany
marc.schael@informatik.uni-freiburg.de
http://lmb.informatik.uni-freiburg.de

Abstract. In this paper we propose a novel method for the construction of invariant textural features for grey scale images. The textural features are based on an averaging over the 2D Euclidean transformation group with relational kernels. They are invariant against 2D Euclidean motion and strictly increasing grey scale transformations. Beside other fields of texture analysis applications we consider texture defect detection here. We provide a systematic method how to apply these grey scale features to this task. This will include the localization and classification of the defects. First experiments with real textile texture images taken from the TILDA database show promising results. They are presented in this paper.

1 Introduction

Among other basic image primitives, e. g. edges, texture is one important cue for image understanding. The lack of an universal, formal definition of texture makes the construction of features for texture analysis hard. Few approaches exist in the literature how texture can be qualitative defined, e. g. [2].

Generally, real world textures underlie transformations which make the construction of textural features difficult. These transformations affect the intensity values, the position, and the orientation of the texture. For texture analysis purposes textural features have to cope with one ore more of these transformations.

In this paper, we propose a novel method for the construction of textural features from grey scale images which are invariant with respect to rotation, translation, and strictly increasing grey scale transformations. Our approach combines two techniques: one for the construction of invariance with respect to 2D Euclidean motion and one for the construction of invariance against strictly increasing grey scale transformations.

Beside other fields of texture analysis applications we consider the texture defect detection (TDD) as an application for our features. The TDD is one important topic of automatic visual inspection. Over the last decade the automatic visual inspection of technical objects has gained increasing importance for industrial application. An extensive review on TDD methods can be found in [11].

B. Radig and S. Florczyk (Eds.): DAGM 2001, LNCS 2191, pp. 17–24, 2001.
© Springer-Verlag Berlin Heidelberg 2001

Song et al. classify the methods for TDD into two categories: local and global ones. According to this classification we provide a local method for the TDD with our textural features, including localization (segmentation of defective regions) and classification of the defects.

This paper is organized as follows: In section 2 we introduce the theory of our textural features. A systematic method for TDD, including localization and classification, is given in section 3. First experiments and results are presented in section 4. A conclusion is given in section 5.

2   Constructing Invariant Textural Features

Schulz-Mirbach proposed a method for the construction of invariant features $A[f]$ for two-dimensional grey scale images $\mathbf{M}^1$ by integrating over a compact transformation group G [7,6]:

$$A[f](\mathbf{M}) := \frac{1}{|G|} \int_G f(g\mathbf{M}) \, dg. \tag{1}$$

The invariant integral is also known as Haar integral. For the construction of rotation and translation invariant grey scale features we have to integrate over the 2D Euclidean transformation group:

$$A[f](\mathbf{M}) = \frac{1}{2\pi NM} \int_{t_x=0}^{W} \int_{t_y=0}^{H} \int_{\varphi=0}^{2\pi} f(g(t_x, t_y, \varphi)\mathbf{M}) \, d\varphi \, dt_x \, dt_y, \tag{2}$$

where $\{t_x, t_y, \varphi\}$ denote the transformation parameter. Because of the discrete image grid in practice the integrals are replaced by sums, choosing only integer translations and varying the angle in discrete steps applying bilinear interpolation for pixels that do not coincide with the image grid.

For kernel functions f of local support the calculation of the integral generally can be separated into two steps: First for every pixel a local function f is evaluated, which only depends on the grey scale intensities in a specific neighborhood[2]. Then all intermediate results of the local computations are summed up.

An alternative approach for the second step of the computation strategy is the usage of fuzzy histograms [1]. The fuzzy histogram (FZH) was created mainly to get rid of the discontinuous behavior of the traditional histogram. The combination of invariant integration with monomials as kernel functions and the FZHs has been successfully applied to the task of texture classification [10], texture defect detection [5], and content based image retrieval [9].

---

[1] The grey scale image is defined as $\mathbf{M} : (x, y) \mapsto [0, D]$, $(x, y) \in [0, W-1] \times [0, H-1]$, where W and H denote the width and heigth, and D denotes the maximum grey scale value of the image.

[2] The neighborhood is on circles around the actually processed pixel, whereby the radius of the circle is defined by f.

However, by using absolute grey scale values for the construction of the invariant feature histograms we are susceptible to inhomogeneous illumination conditions. A local approach for the elimination of illumination influences is the construction of features with local support which are invariant resp. robust against strictly increasing grey scale transformations.

In general we define a relational function rel() which maps the difference δ of two grey scale values to a real number. One simple relational function and its plot is shown in Fig. 1. The grey scale difference δ of two neighbored pixels is mapped to the interval $[0, 1]$.

$$\text{rel}(\delta) = \begin{cases} 1 & \delta < -\epsilon \\ \frac{1}{2\epsilon}(\epsilon - \delta) & -\epsilon \le \delta \le \epsilon \\ 0 & \epsilon < \delta \end{cases}$$

Fig. 1. The definition of the relational function rel() and its plot which maps the grey scale difference δ to $[0, 1]$. D denotes the maximum grey scale value.

The relational kernel function (RKF) is motivated by the local binary pattern (LBP). LBP is a well know method for the construction of textural features [3]. This operator maps the relations between the grey scale values of a center pixel and its 3×3 neighborhood pixel onto a binary pattern. The most important attribute of the LBP is the invariance against strictly increasing grey scale transformations. But, the LBP feature is not rotation invariant. If we are shifting the threshold ϵ of rel() towards zero we get exactly the comparison function used for the LBP.

A simple comparison of adjacent pixels as done by the LBP operator results in an instable property of the feature. In the worst case, a small perturbance of the image results in a big perturbance of the feature. If we add robustness against noise ($\epsilon > 0$) we loose invariance but keep robustness against strictly increasing grey scale transformations. Since we are not using only the values "0" and "1" — like the LBP operator — all δ which are inside the interval $[-\epsilon, \epsilon]$ lead to a continuous result of rel().

Now we formulate the combination of the feature construction technique for rotation and translation invariance with the RKFs. Let $p_i = \{r_i, \phi_i\}, i = 1, 2$ define a parameter set of two circles, where $r_i \in \mathbb{R}_+$ denotes the radius and $\phi_i \in [0, 2\pi[$ defines the phase. We assume a sufficiently high and for all circles equal sampling on all discrete circles. A sufficient heuristic definition of the sample rate is $s = 8 \lceil \max_i\{r_i\} \rceil$. Samples which do not fall onto the image grid must be interpolated, e.g. bilinearly.

The sampling of two circles and the computation of the rel()-function is explained in Fig. 2. The functions m_{p_1} and m_{p_2} denote the interpolated grey scale values on the circles. On all grey scale samples of the circles the difference

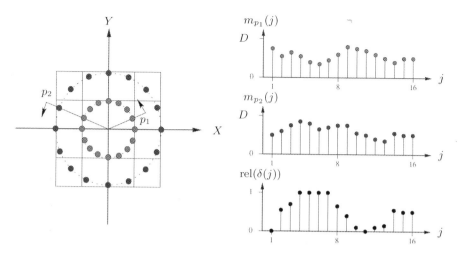

Fig. 2. On the left side two different circles with the parameters $p_1 = \{1, \pi/8\}$ and $p_2 = \{2, 7\pi/8\}$ and the sample rate $s = 16$ are plotted. The upper and the middle diagram on the right show the corresponding grey scale values of the circles, where $j = 1, \ldots, 16$ denotes the sample number. All differences $\delta(j) := m_{p_1}(j) - m_{p_2}(j)$ are mapped with the rel() function to the interval $[0, 1]$. D denotes the maximum grey scale value.

δ is computed. Each grey scale difference is mapped by the function rel() to a value between the interval $[0, 1]$. As a result we obtain a measure for the grey scale relations in the neighborhood of the center pixel.

To achieve invariance against rotation we estimate a FZH on all local rel() results. For each pixel we get a FZH with three bins (with bin centers at 0.0, 0.5, and 1.0). I. e., for each RKF rel() we get three feature maps of the size of the input image minus the support of the RKF. These feature images can be combined by using a three-dimensional joint feature distribution (FD).

3   Texture Defect Detection

We consider a planar textured surface of technical objects of a known texture class (TC), e. g. textile surfaces, and restrict to periodical textures which can be anisotropic. The texture is disturbed by defects of different classes. Orientation and position of the texture and the defects are unknown. Since the distance between the camera and the surface is fixed, we do not need to consider scaling. Furthermore, camera plane and surface are parallel. Thus, there are no projective transformations.

Our method for the texture defect detection is based on the comparison of FDs estimated from the local results of the RKFs. This approach is based on the assumption that a defective region of the texture results in a significant deviation of the FD. In a first step of the supervised training an average reference FD of the defect-free class — the reference class — is estimated. For this step we need a set of defect-free sample images. From all FD results of the samples we compute the average FZH.

For the localization of the defective regions (segmentation of the defects) on the texture we are working with subimages. Depending on the scale of the texture and the size of the texels (texture elements) a subimage size is chosen. Each sample texture is divided into non-overlapping patches. Inside all patches we estimate the three-dimensional FZHs of the local RKF results. Using a FD distance measure, e. g. χ^2, the similarity between the reference FD and the patch FD is calculated. Based on this FD distances we obtain a threshold distance θ which allows the discrimination between the reference and the defect state.

The second step of the training phase comprises of the estimation of the defect models. Again we have to compute the FD for the patches of all defect sample images[3]. A defect is detected if the distance between the patch FD and the reference FD is significant. Since the training is a supervised learning we are able to use the defective patches of a sample image to estimate a defect model FD for this class.

After the training phase we have a model FD of each class. In the following test phase a texture image of unknown state is analyzed. The FDs of all subimages — according to the four different image partitions — are estimated and compared to the reference FD. All χ^2 distances of the subimage FDs and the reference FD were computed. A distance greater than the threshold θ detects a defective subimage. The classification of the subimage is done by a minimum distance classifier. Thus, the minimum χ^2 distance to a defect model FD assigns the defect class. Using different RKFs allows the adaption of the method to different defects.

4   Experimental Results

First experiments were made with real textile images taken from the TILDA[4] database [8]. Two different TCs (*C1R1* and *C2R2*), four defect classes (*E1* to *E4*) and a defect-free reference class (*E0*) were used. The defect classes consist of *E1:* holes, *E2:* oil spots, *E3:* thread errors and *E4:* objects on the surface.

As described in section 3 the training phase was conducted first. The reference FD model for both TCs was estimated with ten image samples. Thereafter, the localization of the defective image regions was performed on the defect images.

---

[3] To ensure that the deviation of the subimage FD to the reference FD is significant we use four different partitions of the image. For each partition the subimage size is equal but the start positions are shifted by the half width or height of the subimage size, respectively.

[4] The textile texture database was developed within the framework of the working group Texture Analysis of the DFG's (Deutsche Forschungsgemeinschaft) major research program "Automatic Visual Inspection of Technical Objects". The database can be obtained on two CD-ROMs on order at the URL http://lmb.informatik.uni-freiburg.de/tilda.

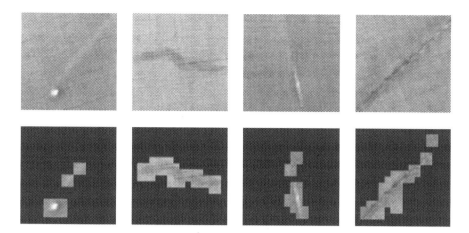

Fig. 3. Segmented defects of texture class *C1R1*.

Examples of the localized defective regions on the images of both TCs are shown in Fig. 3 and Fig. 4. In both figures the defect classes from left to right are *E1* to *E4*. The upper row of both figures shows the selected defect images of size 256×256. Chosen patch sizes for the TC are: *C1R1*: 32×32, and *C2R2*: 40×40. Used parameter sets for the RKF: *C1R1*: $p_1 = \{2,0\}$, $p_2 = \{10,0\}$, $s = 80$, and *C2R2*: $p_1 = \{2,0\}$, $p_2 = \{15,0\}$, $s = 120$. The threshold $\epsilon = 5$ was the same for both TCs.

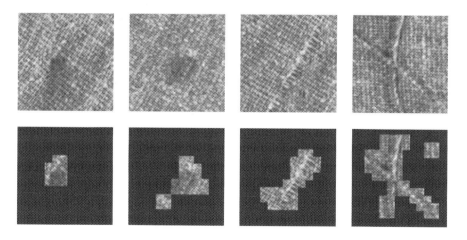

Fig. 4. Segmented defects of texture class *C2R2*.

At this state of the experiments no FD for defect classes were estimated. However, we have computed the inter-class FD distances of the defective image regions by using the Jensen-Shannon (JS) divergence, also known as Jeffrey divergence. This divergence measure was empirically analyzed in [4]. Puzicha et al. achieve good color and texture classification results with the χ^2 and the JS measure. Figure 5 reveals the JS distances of both analyzed TCs *C1R1* and *C2R2*.

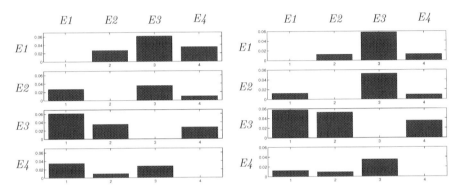

Fig. 5. FD distances between the defect classes *E1* to *E4* measured with the JS-divergence. On the left: results of *C1R1*, on the right results of *C2R2*.

All inter-class FD distances of both texture classes indicate the good discriminative properties of the features. Thus, the classification of the defects using the proposed textural features should be possible.

5   Conclusion

In this paper we presented a novel technique for the construction of textural features which are invariant with respect to 2D Euclidean motion and robust against usual grey scale transformations. A systematic method for the application of the features to the texture defect detection task was given. It includes the localization and classification of the defects. First experiments with our features and the TILDA database show promising results.

The size of the detectable defects depends on the chosen patch size. Thus, the scale of the texture and the patch size must be properly selected. If the spatial extension of a defect is smaller than the patch size, the deviation of the FD might be to small for a detection. However, all defects of the considered texture images from TILDA could be detected. Using suitable RKFs allow the adaption of the method to different defect and texture classes.

In a next step the experiments with the TILDA database must be extended. The proposed textural features are also applicable to the area of content based image retrieval and texture classification.

Acknowledgements. This work was supported by the "Deutsche Forschungs-gemeinschaft" (DFG).

References

1. H. Burkhardt and S. Siggelkow. Invariant features in pattern recognition – fundamentals and applications. In C. Kotropoulos and I. Pitas, editors, *Nonlinear Model-Based Image/Video Processing and Analysis*, pages 269–307. John Wiley & Sons, 2001.
2. R. M. Haralick and L. G. Shapiro. *Computer and Robot Vision*, volume I., chapter 9., Texture, pages 453–494. Addison-Wesley, 1992.
3. T. Ojala, M. Pietikäinen, and D. Harwood. A comparative study of texture measures with classifications based on feature distributions. *Pattern Recognition*, 29(1):51–59, 1996.
4. J. Puzicha, Y. Rubner, C. Tomasi, and J. Buhmann. Empirical evaluation of dissimilarity measures for color and texture. In *Proceedings of the IEEE International Conference on Computer Vision, ICCV'99*, pages 1165–1173, 1999.
5. M. Schael and H. Burkhardt. Automatic detection of errors on textures using invariant grey scale features and polynomial classifiers. In M. K. Pietikäinen, editor, *Texture Analysis in Machine Vision*, volume 40 of *Machine Perception and Artificial Intelligence*, pages 219–230. World Scientific, 2000.
6. H. Schulz-Mirbach. *Anwendung von Invarianzprinzipien zur Merkmalgewinnung in der Mustererkennung*. PhD thesis, Technische Universität Hamburg-Harburg, February 1995. Reihe 10, Nr. 372, VDI-Verlag.
7. H. Schulz-Mirbach. Invariant features for gray scale images. In G. Sagerer, S. Posch, and F. Kummert, editors, *17. DAGM - Symposium "Mustererkennung"*, pages 1–14, Bielefeld, 1995. Reihe Informatik aktuell, Springer. DAGM-Preis.
8. H. Schulz-Mirbach. TILDA - Ein Referenzdatensatz zur Evaluierung von Sichtprüfungsverfahren für Textiloberflächen. Internal Report 4/96, Technische Informatik I, Technische Universität Hamburg-Harburg, 1996.
9. S. Siggelkow and H. Burkhardt. Image retrieval based on local invariant features. In *Proceedings of the IASTED International Conference on Signal and Image Processing (SIP) 1998*, pages 369–373, Las Vegas, Nevada, USA, October 1998. IASTED.
10. S. Siggelkow and H. Burkhardt. Invariant feature histograms for texture classification. In *Proceedings of the 1998 Joint Conference on Information Sciences (JCIS'98)*, Research Triangle Park, North Carolina, USA, October 1998.
11. K. Y. Song, M. Petrou, and J. Kittler. Texture defect detection: A review. In Kevin W. Bowyer, editor, *Applications of Artificial Intelligence X: Machine Vision and Robotics*, volume 1708, pages 99–106. SPIE, March 1992.

Segmentation of Spontaneously Splitting Figures into Overlapping Layers

Amin Massad and Bärbel Mertsching

IMA-Lab, University of Hamburg, Germany
massad@informatik.uni-hamburg.de

Abstract. We describe a method to decompose binary 2-D shapes into layers of overlapping parts. The approach is based on a perceptual grouping framework known as *tensor voting* which has been introduced for the computation of region, curve and junction saliencies. Here, we discuss extensions for the creation of modal/amodal completions and for the extraction of overlapping parts augmented with depth assignments. Advantages of this approach are from a conceptual point of view the close relation to psychological findings about shape perception and regarding technical aspects a reduction of computational costs in comparison with other highly iterative methods.

1 Introduction

The phenomenon of spontaneously splitting figures (Fig. 1) has been discussed in several psychological studies as an example for the existence of perceptual organization in human shape perception. Kellman and Shipley [7], who present a psychologically motivated theory of unit formation in object perception, note that demonstrations have been easier to develop than explanations.

With respect to computer vision, a method for part decompositions studied on spontaneously splitting figures is considered to yield a natural solution for the hard problem of object recognition in the presence of occlusions [1, 6, 11, 15–17]. However, aiming at the decomposition of the input image into disjunct partitions, other segmentation schemes do not provide adequate means for the handling of occlusions and often yield intuitively implausible parts – among them the symmetric axis transform by [2, 3], the transversality principle by [6], process-grammars by [10], and evolving contours by [8, 9]. A detailed discussion may be found in [12]. Here, we intend to merge findings from both disciplines in order to develop a method for the extraction of overlapping forms by the application of a perceptual grouping algorithm.

2 The Tensor Voting Approach

For the development of our unit formation process, we apply different techniques from the *tensor voting* framework, a perceptual saliency theory introduced by Medioni et al. [4, 13]. We consider as the main advantage of this approach over

B. Radig and S. Florczyk (Eds.): DAGM 2001, LNCS 2191, pp. 25–31, 2001.
© Springer-Verlag Berlin Heidelberg 2001

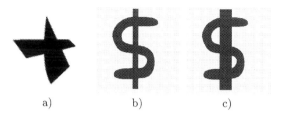

a)   b)   c)

Fig. 1. Spontaneously splitting figures: Despite of the homogenous surface quality, the shapes tend to be seen as two overlapping forms. The figure seen on top of the other is *modally* completed while the other one is *amodally* completed behind the nearer unit. Although the depth ordering may alternate, the units formed remain the same. a) Example from [7]. b), c) Examples used as input images in further demonstrations.

other methods, like [18–21], that the computation is not iterative, i. e. does not require iterations which are necessary for regularization, consistent labeling, clustering, robust methods, or connectionist models. Furthermore, tensor voting does not require manual setting of starting parameters and is highly stable against noise while preserving discontinuities. Multiple curves, junctions, regions, and surfaces are extracted simultaneously without the necessity to define an object model.

To explain the principles of the tensor voting method, let's consider the basic type of input data first which are oriented tokens, edgels $e = [t_x, t_y]^T$, given in a sparse map. In contrast to other vector-based methods – e. g. [5, 14, 21] – the tokens are encoded as second-order symmetric tensors $T = ee^T = [[t_x^2 \ t_x t_y], [t_x t_y \ t_y^2]]$ which in the 2-D case can be interpreted as the covariance matrix of an ellipse. Thus, each token can simultaneously carry two parameters: The degree of orientation certainty encoded by the elongation of the ellipse (i. e. a circle represents maximal uncertainty of orientation which is a feature of a junction) and a saliency measure encoded by the size of the ellipse. Given edgels as input tokens, initially all tensors have maximal elongation and look like sticks. Grouping between the sparse input tokens is deducted from the information propagated by each token into its neighborhood. This interaction is encoded into the layout of an appropriate tensor field, here the stick field depicted in Fig. 2a, which is placed at each input location after a rotational alignment. Then, all fields are combined by a tensor addition. Hence, this voting operation is similar to a convolution. The resulting general tensors carry information about curve saliencies and junction saliencies which are computed by the decomposition $T = (\lambda_1 - \lambda_2)\hat{e}_2\hat{e}_2^T + \lambda_2(\hat{e}_1\hat{e}_1^T + \hat{e}_2\hat{e}_2^T)$ where $\lambda_1 \geq \lambda_2 \geq 0$ denote the eigenvalues of T and $\hat{e}_1$, $\hat{e}_2$ the corresponding normalized eigenvectors. The first term of the sum represents a stick tensor (in direction of the curve orientation) weighted by the curve saliency $\lambda_1 - \lambda_2$ while the second term is a ball tensor weighted by the junction saliency λ_2. Finally, the result of the perceptual grouping is derived by extracting the maxima in the saliency maps, for curves a marching algorithm is

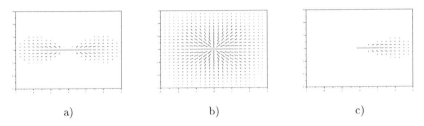

a)   b)   c)

Fig. 2. Voting Fields: a) Stick field encoding the information propagated from an horizontally oriented token (center) into its neighborhood. The field tries to find a continuation with minimal curvature, comparable to the Gestalt law of good continuation. It decreases with growing curvature and distance. b) Ball field for non-oriented data. c) Modified stick field used for voting between junctions.

employed to trace them along their highest saliencies found perpendicularly to the orientations of the stick tensors.

If the input data consists of non-oriented tokens, i. e. points, it can easily be transformed into oriented data by a preceding voting step with a different field, called ball field (Fig. 2b), which is built by integrating the stick field over a 180° rotation.

3   Segmentation of Spontaneously Splitting Figures

Our method for the decomposition of forms into multiple, possibly overlapping layers applies mechanisms of the tensor voting framework at different processing stages as detailed in [12]. First, the binary input images are transformed by application of an isotropic ball field into a boundary saliency map from which contours (including polarity information) and junctions are extracted by application of a stick field.

Motivated by several psychological studies (cf. [7] for a survey), we use the junctions along the contour as seeds for interpolated edges which connect so-called *relatable* edges to form part groupings. This step is implemented as a newly introduced voting between junctions: In search for a continuation of the abruptly ending line segments, each junction sends out votes in the opposite direction of its two incoming edges. The underlying voting field is defined as a semi-lobe of the stick field (Fig. 2c) with a smaller opening angle to emphasize straight continuations and to get a reduced position uncertainty compared to general input domains. Overlapping fields of interacting junctions yield high curve saliencies (Fig. 4b) which are traced by a marching algorithm along the local maxima to form amodal and modal completions of part boundaries, in the following briefly called *virtual contours*. The junctions we have used as seeds are formed by exactly two crossing edges on the real contour because the input is given as a binary image. We will call them L_0-junctions where the index denotes the number of incoming virtual contours.

One important type of junctions, the T-junctions, needs special consideration. These junctions are created by a prior step of junction voting as interactions of voting fields send out by L-junctions with opposite boundary tokens. Then, within the tensor voting framework, T-junctions are extracted as locations of high junction saliencies. For each T-junction its stem is formed by the incoming virtual contour and augmented by a region polarity information deduced from the polarity at the L-junction by which it has been created. Each T-junction will vote into the direction of its stem together with the set of L-junctions which vote as described before. Hence, after two steps of junction voting, we get all possible virtual contours as high curve saliencies which are extracted by a marching algorithm.

For the introduction of a unit formation process, it will be necessary to distinguish between different kinds of junctions as each type indicates distinct shape decompositions. After the extraction of the virtual contours, we reinspect each L_0-junction and look if one or two virtual contours have been generated in their vicinity. In that case the junction is relabeled to an L_1- or L_2- junction, respectively. Then, the T-junctions which are induced by an L_1-junction are relabeled to T_1 and those induced by an L_2-junction to T_2.

The interpretation of an L_0-junction is simply no indication for a decomposition but merely a discontinuity on the contour. Whereas an L_1-junction gives evidence of a decomposition into two disjunct parts with the virtual contour belonging to both outlines. Depending on the part to which it has been assigned, the virtual contour carries one of two opposite polarity vectors. An L_2-junction could be interpreted as the coincidence of two L_1-junctions with each virtual contour carrying two opposite polarities, thus yielding two disjunct parts (Fig. 3a). However, it could also be the case that both virtual contours are formed by two overlapping parts with only one direction of each polarity pair being valid (Fig. 3b). The discrimination between both decompositions is achieved by the walking algorithm described below. Similarly, T_1-junctions (Fig. 3c) indicate a decomposition into two disjunct parts sharing the T-stem with opposite polarity assignments while T_2-junctions (Fig. 3d) imply two overlapping parts which share one half of the T-bar with identical polarity directions.

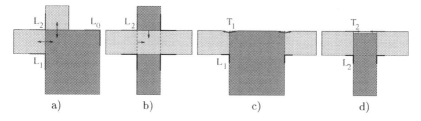

Fig. 3. The different junction types together with the inferred shape decompositions: An L_2-junction with virtual contours belonging to two disjunct (a) and two overlapping parts (b). And a T_1-junction (c) compared to a T_2-junction (d).

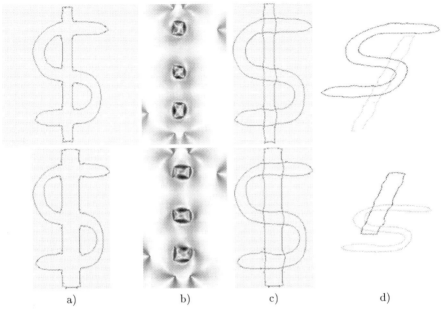

a)   b)   c)   d)

Fig. 4. Results of the part decompositions and depth assignments (see text). Note that, in order to show the depth assignments, the last column (d) depicts a projection of 3-D data with a rotation of approx. 30° about the depth-axis and different gray levels corresponding to the depth values.

As the computations applied up to now are local operations, we have introduced a traversal algorithm, called walking, to collect this local information into a globally consistent shape description. It operates on the adjacency graph of the junctions augmented by their types and an assignment of all potential polarity vectors for each direction meeting at the junctions. L_1- and L_2-junctions initiate as seeds outgoing "walks" into an unvisited direction by sending out a cursor, called walker, which holds information about the current walking direction and region polarity. At the adjacent junction, the incoming direction and polarity is transformed into an outgoing walker based on a set of predefined rules for each junction type. These rules are designed to give a continuation which preserves direction and polarity (details in [12]). If a straight continuation cannot be found, a change in direction together with an adapted polarity vector is inferred from the junction type and entries of already visited contour parts. Cyclic walks are considered as successful part decompositions.

The unit formation process described so far explicitly does not rely on depth information. This independence is in agreement with psychophysical findings. We rather propose to infer depth arrangements after the unit formation by examining the length of the virtual contours. It is known from experiments on spontaneously splitting figures that large parts are perceived to lie closer to the viewer than small parts [7]. Therefore, we inspect the junctions at overlapping shapes and assume parts with short virtual contours – indicated by higher curve saliencies – to lie on top of parts with longer virtual contours. At this point, we can classify the unifiedly named virtual contours as modal or amodal completions, respectively (Fig. 1). Note that an earlier decision, prior to the depth assignments, would have been misleading as it is not required for the unit formation which remains unchanged in case of bistable depth orderings.

4   Results and Conclusion

Figure 4 illustrates the results from this processing on the two examples of Fig. 1b,c. The first column depicts the extracted region boundaries and L_0-junctions (marked by pairs of arrows). The second column shows the curve saliency maps resulting from the junction voting, where higher saliency values are represented by darker pixels. The third column contains the different junction types overlayed with real and virtual contours. The results of the part decomposition and the depth ordering can be found in the last column.

Currently, we are working on extensions of the framework for the realization of bistable depth orderings and the handling of cyclically overlapping shapes. This includes further research to decide whether depth assignments should be global and constant over parts or whether object units can be perceived to stretch across different depths.

References

1. I. Biederman. Recognition by components: A theory of human image understanding. *Psychol. Rev.*, 94:115–147, 1987.
2. H. Blum. A transformation for extracting new descriptors of shape. In W. Wathen-Dunn, editor, *Models for the Perception of Speech and Visual Form*, pages 362–380, Cambride, MA, 1967. MIT Press.
3. H. Blum and R. Nagel. Shape description using weighted symmetric axis features. *Pattern Recognition*, 10(3):167–180, 1978.
4. G. Guy and G. Medioni. Inferring global perceptual contours from local features. *Int. J. Computer Vision*, 20:113–133, 1996.
5. F. Heitger and R. von der Heydt. A computational model of neural contour processing: Figure-ground segregation and illusory contours. In *Proc. IEEE Int. Conf. on Computer Vision*, pages 32–40, 1993.
6. D. Hoffman and W. Richards. Parts of recognition. *Cogn.*, 18:65–96, 1984.
7. P. Kellman and T. Shipley. A theory of visual interpolation in object perception. *Cognitive Psychology*, 23:141–221, 1991.
8. B. Kimia, R. Tannenbaum, and S. Zucker. Shapes, shocks, and deformations I: The components of shape and the reaction-diffusion space. *Int. J. Computer Vision*, 15:189–224, 1995.
9. L. Latecki and R. Lakämper. Conexity rule for shape decomposition based on discrete contour evolution. *CVIU*, 73:441–454, 1999.
10. M. Leyton. A process-grammar for shape. *A.I.*, 34:213–247, 1988.

11. D. Marr and H.K. Nishihara. Representation and recognition of the spatial organization of three-dimensional shapes. In *Proc. R. Soc. Lond.*, volume 200, pages 269–294, 1978.
12. A. Massad and G. Medioni. 2-D shape decomposition into overlapping parts. In *Proc. 4th Int. Workshop on Visual Form (IWVF4)*, pages 398–409, 2001.
13. G. Medioni, M.-S. Lee, and C.-K. Tang. *A computational framework for segmentation and grouping.* Elsevier, Amsterdam, 2000.
14. M. Nitzberg and D. Mumford. The 2.1-D sketch. In *Proc. IEEE Int. Conf. on Computer Vision*, pages 138–144, 1990.
15. A. Pentland. Recognition by parts. In *Proc. IEEE Int. Conf. on Computer Vision*, pages 612–620, London, 1987.
16. K. Rao and R. Nevatia. Computing volume descriptions from sparse 3-d data. *Int. J. of Computer Vision*, 2:33–50, 1988.
17. H. Rom. Part decomposition and shape description. Technical Report IRIS-93-319, Univ. of Southern California, 1993.
18. S. Sarkar and K. Boyer. Integration, inference, and managment of spatial information using bayesian networks: Perceptual organization. *IEEE Trans. Pattern Anal. and Machine Intel.*, 15:256–274, 1993.
19. E. Saund. Perceptual organization of occluding contours of opaque surfaces. *CVIU*, 76:70–82, 1999.
20. A. Sha'ashua and S. Ullman. Structural saliency: the detection of globally salient structures using a locally connected network. In *Proc. IEEE Int. Conf. on Computer Vision*, pages 312–327, 1998.
21. K. Thornber and L. Williams. Analytic solution of stochastic completion fields. *Biol. Cybern.*, 75:141–151, 1996.

Writer Adaptation for Online Handwriting Recognition

Anja Brakensiek, Andreas Kosmala, and Gerhard Rigoll

Dept. of Computer Science, Faculty of Electrical Engineering,
Gerhard-Mercator-University Duisburg, D-47057 Duisburg
{anja, kosmala, rigoll}@fb9-ti.uni-duisburg.de
http://www.fb9-ti.uni-duisburg.de

Abstract. In this paper an on-line handwriting recognition system with focus on adaptation techniques is described. Our Hidden Markov Model (HMM) -based recognition system for cursive German script can be adapted to the writing style of a new writer using either a retraining depending on the maximum likelihood (ML)-approach or an adaptation according to the maximum a posteriori (MAP)-criterion. The performance of the resulting writer-dependent system increases significantly, even if only a few words are available for adaptation. So this approach is also applicable for on-line systems in hand-held computers such as PDAs. This paper deals with the performance comparison of two different adaptation techniques either in a supervised or an unsupervised mode with the availability of different amounts of adaptation data ranging from only 6 words up to 100 words per writer.

Keywords: online cursive handwriting recognition, writer independent, adaptation of HMMs

1   Introduction

During the last years, the significance of on-line handwriting recognition systems, e.g. pen based computers or electronic address books, has increased (compare [1,7,9,11]). Regardless of the considered script type (i. e. cursive script, printed or mixed style), Hidden Markov Models (HMMs, see [10]) have been established because of several important advantages like segmentation-free recognition and automatic training capabilities.

Although the performance of recognition systems increases, the error rate of writer independent recognizers for unconstrained handwriting is still too high - at least for some writer types - for a real application. This problem leads to the implementation of adaptation techniques, which are well known in speech recognition [2,3,4,6]. Apart from some exceptions [12], most of the adaptation techniques are still unestablished in the area of cursive (on-line) handwriting recognition.

An important aspect for a practical usage of adaptation methods is the amount of adaptation data, which is needed to reduce the error rate significantly. It is often impossible and not very user-friendly to select several hundreds

B. Radig and S. Florczyk (Eds.): DAGM 2001, LNCS 2191, pp. 32–37, 2001.

of words from a specific writer, which would be necessary to train a basic recognition system. Thus, the objective should be to conduct a parameter adaptation starting from a general writer independent system by using only a few words. Another aspect is the availability of labeled adaptation data. It could be very useful, when a recognition system can be adapted automatically and unsupervised to a new writing style with unlabeled data, while using the system in the test-mode.

In the following sections our baseline recognition system and some investigated adaptation techniques are described (compare also [5,8,12]). Results are given using the maximum likelihood (ML) retraining and the maximum a posteriori (MAP) adaptation comparing the performance of an unsupervised and supervised adaptation.

2   Baseline Recognition System

Our handwriting recognition system consists of about 90 different linear HMMs, one for each character (upper- and lower-case letters, numbers and special characters like '",:!'). In general the continuous density HMMs consist of 12 states (with up to 11 Gaussian mixtures per state) for characters and numbers and fewer states for some special characters depending on their width. To train the HMMs we use the Baum-Welch algorithm, whereas for recognition, the features are used to find that character sequence by a Viterbi algorithm, which is the most probable for the detected state-probabilities. The presented recognition results refer to a word error rate using a dictionary of about 2200 German words.

2.1   Database

For our experiments we use a large on-line handwriting database of several writers, which is described in the following. The database consists of cursive script samples of 166 different writers, all writing several words or sentences on a digitizing surface. The training of the writer independent system is performed using about 24400 words of 145 writers. Testing is carried out with 4153 words of 21 different writers (about 200 words per writer).

For each of these 21 test writers up to 100 words are available for adaptation and nearly 100 words are used for evaluation of the developed writer dependent system. Some examples of the resampled test-set are shown in Fig.1.

2.2   Feature Extraction

After the resampling of the pen trajectory in order to compensate different writing speeds the script samples are normalized. Normalization of the input-data implies the correction of slant and height. Slant normalization is performed by shearing the pen trajectory according to an entropy-criterion. For height normalization the upper and lower baselines are estimated to detect the coreheight of the script sample, which is independent of ascenders and descenders. These

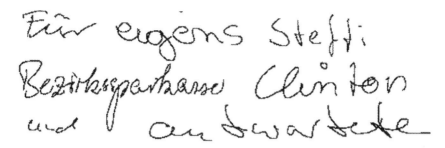

Fig. 1. Some examples of the handwritten database (7 different writers)

baselines are approximated by two straight lines determined by the local minima resp. maxima of the word.

In our on-line handwriting recognition system the following features are derived from the trajectory of the pen input (compare also [11]):

- the angle of the spatially resampled strokes ($\sin \alpha$, $\cos \alpha$)
- the difference angles ($\sin \Delta\alpha$, $\cos \Delta\alpha$)
- the pen pressure (binary)
- a sub-sampled bitmap slid along the pen trajectory (9-dimensional vector), containing the current image information in a 30×30 window

These 14-dimensional feature vectors x are presented to the HMMs (continuous modeling technique) in one single stream for training and testing the recognition system.

3   Adaptation Techniques

For handwriting adaptation we compare two different adaptation approaches, which are well known in speech recognition: a retraining according to the maximum likelihood (ML) criterion using the Baum-Welch algorithm (EM: expectation maximization, compare [10]) and the maximum a posteriori (MAP, see [4]) adaptation.

The goal is to maximize the matching between the Hidden Markov Models trained with the general database of 145 writers and a certain writer (wd: writer dependent) by considering different writing styles. When the amount of training or adaptation data is not sufficient for a robust training of all HMM parameters λ, it is useful to reestimate only the means μ and/or variances c of the Gaussians of the general HMM (wi: writer independent) and to leave the transitions and weights unchanged.

To compare the ML-training (Eq.1) with the MAP algorithm, in the following the objective functions are given in principle.

$$\lambda_{ML} = \operatorname*{argmax}_{\lambda} P(X|\lambda) \quad \Rightarrow \quad \mu_{wi} \overset{EM}{\to} \mu_{ML}, \quad c_{wi} \overset{EM}{\to} c_{ML} \qquad (1)$$

The MAP (or Bayesian) approach (Eq.2) takes the prior probability $P(\lambda)$, which is estimated by the training of the writer independent model, into account. Here, a separate transformation for each Gaussian is performed. The objective function leads to an interpolation between the original mean-vector (per state) and the estimated mean for the special writer depending on the prior probability. The function f_L depends on the occupation likelihood of the adaptation data. A similar transform can also be estimated for the variances c.

$$\lambda_{MAP} = \underset{\lambda}{\mathrm{argmax}}\ P(\lambda|X) \approx \underset{\lambda}{\mathrm{argmax}}\ P(X|\lambda)P(\lambda)$$

$$\Rightarrow \qquad \mu_{MAP} = f_L\ \mu_{wd} + (1 - f_L)\ \mu_{wi} \tag{2}$$

The results in the following section have been achieved in a supervised mode and also in an unsupervised mode using the same parameters.

4   Experiments

In the presented experiments we examine the influence of the adaptation technique and the amount of adaptation data, ranging from 6 to 100 words.

Using the writer independent recognition system (baseline system) a word recognition rate of 86.0% is achieved testing the entire test-set of 4153 words. This test-set is halved for adaptation experiments. So, using the same test-set as for the writer dependent systems, a word recognition rate of 86.3% can be obtained on the half test-set consisting of 2071 words (compare Tab.1 wi). This recognition accuracy results from the fact that the individual accuracies of the writer-independent baseline system for each writer vary from 64.1% to 94.2%.

Tab.1 presents the dependency of the recognition error on the amount of adaptation data and techniques. Again, all experimental results refer to an average recognition rate of 21 different test writers.

The recognition performance increases significantly, as it is expected, when the baseline system is adapted to a new writing style. The error reduction using unlabeled adaptation data is a little bit smaller than in the supervised mode (Tab.1: last 2 columns).

Using a relative large amount of adaptation data (about 100 words), the error is reduced by about 38% relative performing the ML-algorithm (Eq.1), so that a recognition rate of 91.6% is achieved by reestimating the means only (Tab.1: f) in a supervised mode. It can be shown, that the adaptation of the variances is less relevant for recognition performance compared to means-adaptation (Tab.1: g). Using the same database of 100 words for retraining, the accuracy of the baseline system increases to 90.0% by transforming only the variances. Adapting both parameters, means and variances, using the ML-algorithm, the recognition rate decreases to 84.8% (Tab.1: h), indicating that the adaptation dataset is too sparse (100 adaptation words) in order to adapt both parameters simultaneously. So further tests only refer to means-adaptation. A second ML-retraining of the adaptation data leads to a further error reduction (Tab.1: i).

Table 1. Word recognition results (%) for 21 writers comparing different adaptation techniques in a supervised and unsupervised mode

baseline system (**wi**)	86.3	
adaptation technique	supervised	unsupervised
a) MAP: mean, **6 words** for adaptation 1	**87.5**	**87.4**
b) MAP: mean, 6 words for adaptation 2	87.1	87.1
c) MAP: mean, 100 words for adaptation	90.8	90.0
d) ML: mean, 6 words for adaptation 1	86.2	85.8
e) ML: mean, 6 words for adaptation 2	86.0	85.6
f) ML: mean, 100 words for adaptation	91.6	90.4
g) ML: variance, 100 words for adaptation	90.0	88.9
h) ML: mean+variance, 100 words for adaptation	84.8	82.7
i) 2xML: mean, **100 words** for adaptation	**92.0**	**90.8**

Even if only about 6 words are available for adaptation, the error rate can be reduced. To evaluate the recognition results obtained by a 6-word-adaptation, we repeat all these tests with another disjoint adaptation set of (randomly chosen) 6 words (compare Tab.1: a-b and d-e). Here, the best recognition performance is obtained by using the MAP-adaptation technique (Eq.2). The recognition accuracy increases to 87.5% (Tab.1: a; relative error reduction of about 9%) in the supervised mode. Depending on the amount of adaptation data, the MAP-adaptation outperforms a standard ML-retraining when only very few words are available. A ML-reestimation of the means by using only 6 words results in an increase of errors (Tab.1: d,e).

Although the error is reduced significantly by adapting a writer-independent system, the recognition accuracy of a real writer-dependent system, which is trained by about 2000 words of one single writer, is much higher. In this case a recognition rate of about 95% in average (4 writers) is obtained using a 30k dictionary (compare also [11]).

A further question is the use of confidence measures to improve the quality of the adaptation data in the unsupervised mode. One possibility to estimate the confidence score is the evaluation of a n-best recognition. Another interesting aspect is the influence of normalization compared to adaptation on the recognition accuracy. These topics will be evaluated in the future work.

5   Summary

In this paper we presented the comparison of two different adaptation techniques, based on a HMM on-line handwriting recognition system for German cursive script samples. We investigated the performance of an ML-retraining (using the EM-method), optimizing means and/or variances and a MAP-adaptation technique for a database of 21 writers in a supervised mode as well as in an unsupervised mode.

It has been shown that the recognition error can be reduced by using the MAP-adaptation up to 9% relative using only 6 words as adaptation-set. Performing adaptation with a larger database of 100 words the accuracy increases from 86.3% to 92.0%, using a simple ML-reestimation of the means only. Also the unsupervised ML-adaptation leads to a significant error reduction of about 33% relative.

References

1. Y. Bengio, Y. LeCun, C. Nohl, and C. Burges. LeRec: A NN/HMM Hybrid for On-line Handwriting Recognition. *Neural Computation*, 7:1289–1303, Nov. 1995.
2. U. Bub, J. Köhler, and B. Imperl. In-Service Adaptation of Multlingual Hidden-Markov-Models. In *IEEE Int. Conference on Acoustics, Speech, and Signal Processing (ICASSP)*, pages 1451–1454, Munich, Apr. 1997.
3. C. Chesta, O. Siohan, and C.-H. Lee. Maximum A Posteriori Linear Regression for Hidden Markov Model Adaptation. In *6th European Conference on Speech Communication and Technology*, pages 211–214, Budapest, Hungary, Sept. 1999.
4. J.-L. Gauvain and C.-H. Lee. Maximum a Posteriori Estimation for Multivariate Gaussian Mixture Observation of Markov Chains. *IEEE Transactions on Speech and Audio Processing*, 2(2):291–298, Apr. 1994.
5. J. Laaksonen, J. Hurri, E. Oja, and J. Kangas. Comparison of adaptive strategies for online character recognition. In *ICANN 98. Proceedings of the 8th International Conference on Artificial Neural Networks*, volume 1, pages 245–50, London, UK, 1998.
6. C. Leggetter and P. Woodland. Speaker Adaptation of Continuous Density HMMs using Multivariate Linear Regression. In *Int. Conference on Spoken Language Processing (ICSLP)*, Yokohama, Japan, Sept. 1994.
7. S. Manke, M. Finke, and A. Waibel. NPen++: A writer independent, large vocabulary on-line cursive handwriting Recognition System. In *Proceedings of the International Conference on Document Analysis and Recognition (ICDAR)*, Montreal, 1995.
8. P. Natarajan, I. Bazzi, Z. Lu, J. Makhoul, and R. Schwartz. Robust OCR of Degraded Documents. In *5th International Conference on Document Analysis and Recognition (ICDAR)*, pages 357–361, Bangalore, India, Sept. 1999.
9. R. Plamondon and S. Srihari. On-Line and Off-Line Handwriting Recognition: A Comprehensive Survey. *IEEE Transactions on Pattern Analysis and Machine Intelligence (PAMI)*, 22(1):63–84, Jan. 2000.
10. L. Rabiner and B. Juang. An Introduction to Hidden Markov Models. *IEEE ASSP Magazine*, pages 4–16, 1986.
11. G. Rigoll, A. Kosmala, and D. Willett. A Systematic Comparison of Advanced Modeling Techniques for Very Large Vocabulary On-Line Cursive Handwriting Recognition. In S.-W. Lee, editor, *Advances in Handwriting Recognition*, chapter 2, pages 69–78. World Scientific, 1999.
12. A. Senior and K. Nathan. Writer adaptation of a HMM handwriting recognition system. In *IEEE Int. Conference on Acoustics, Speech, and Signal Processing (ICASSP)*, pages 1447–1450, Munich, Apr. 1997.

Blood Vessel Detection in Retinal Images by Shape-Based Multi-threshold Probing

Xiaoyi Jiang* and Daniel Mojon

Department of Neuro-Ophthalmology and Strabismus
Kantonsspital St. Gallen, 9007 St. Gallen, Switzerland
{xiaoyi.jiang, daniel.mojon}@kssg.ch

Abstract. We propose a novel approach to blood vessel detection in retinal images using shape-based multi-threshold probing. On an image set with hand-labeled ground truth our algorithm quantitatively demonstrates superior performance over the basic thresholding and another method recently reported in the literature. The core of our algorithm, classification-based multi-threshold probing, represents a general framework of segmentation that has not been explored in the literature thus far. We expect that the framework may be applied to a variety of other tasks.

1 Introduction

The retina of an eye is an essential part of the central visual pathways that enable humans to visualize the real world. Retinal images tell us about retinal, ophthalmic, and even systematic diseases. The ophthalmologist uses retinal images to aid in diagnoses, to make measurements, and to look for change in lesions or severity of diseases. In particular, blood vessel appearance is an important indicator for many diagnoses, including diabetes, hypertension, and arteriosclerosis. An accurate detection of blood vessels provides us the fundamental for the measurement of a variety of features that can then be applied to tasks like diagnosis, treatment evaluation, and clinical study. In addition the detected vessel network supports the localization of the optic nerve [3] and the multimodal/temporal registration of ocular fundus images [2,14].

In this work we propose a new algorithm for segmenting blood vessels in a retinal image. We systematically probe a series of thresholds on the retinal image. Each threshold results in a binary image in which part of the vessel network is visible. We detect these vessels by a shape-based classification method. Through the combination of the vessels detected from all thresholds we obtain an overall vessel network.

The remainder of the paper begins with a brief discussion of related work. Then, we present our algorithm in Section 3. The results of an experimental evaluation follow in Section 4. Finally, some discussions conclude the paper.

---

* The work was supported by the Stiftung OPOS Zugunsten von Wahrnehmungsbehinderten, St. Gallen, Switzerland.

B. Radig and S. Florczyk (Eds.): DAGM 2001, LNCS 2191, pp. 38–44, 2001.

Fig. 1. A retinal image (left) and thresholding results from two thresholds 60 (middle) and 120 (right), respectively.

2   Related Work

Various approaches have been proposed for blood vessel detection. In [14] the vessel network is detected by a sequence of morphological operations. A two-stage approach is proposed in [10]. A watershed algorithm is applied to produce a highly oversegmented image on which an iterative merge step is performed.

Filter-based methods assume some vessel model and match the model against the surrounding window of each pixel [1,8,9]. As pointed out in [4], however, a simple thresholding of the filter responses generally cannot give satisfactory results. Instead, more sophisticated processing is needed. This is done, for instance, by a multi-threshold region growing in [4].

A number of tracking-based approaches are known from the literature [12, 13,15]. Using start points, either found automatically or specified by the user, these methods utilize some profile model to incrementally step along the vessels. Here it is crucial to start with reliable initial points.

The recent work [4] is of particular interest here. The authors evaluated their vessel detection method on a retinal image set with hand-labeled vessel segmentation. They also made the image material and the ground truth data publically available. We will use these images to quantitatively evaluate and compare the performance of our algorithm.

3   Algorithm

From the methodology point of view our algorithm is very different from the previous ones discussed in the last section. We base the blood vessel detection on thresholding operations. Thresholding is an important segmentation technique and a vast number of approaches are known from the literature; see [5,11] for a survey and comparative performance studies. The nature of retinal images (both nonuniform intensities of vessels and background), however, does not allow a direct use of traditional thresholding techniques. This is illustrated in Figure 1,

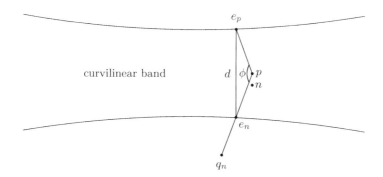

Fig. 2. Quantities for testing curvilinear bands.

where two different thresholds make different parts of the vessel network visible[1]. The fundamental observation here is that a particular part of the vessel network can be well marked by some appropriate threshold which is, however, not known in advance. This motivates us to probe a series of thresholds and to detect vessels in the binary image resulting from the respective threshold. These partial results are then combined to yield an overall vessel network.

Thresholding with a particular threshold T leads to a binary image B_T, in which a pixel with intensity lower than T is marked as potential vessel point. and all other pixels as background. Then, vessels are considered to be *curvilinear structures* in T_B, i.e. lines or curves with some limited width. Our approach to vessel detection in a binary image consists of three steps: a) perform an Euclidean distance transform on B_T to obtain a distance map; b) prune the vessel candidates by means of the distance map to only retain center line pixels of curvilinear bands; c) reconstruct the curvilinear bands from their center line pixels. The reconstructed curvilinear bands give that part of the vessel network that is made visible by the particular threshold T. In the following the three steps are described in some detail.

We apply the fast algorithm for Euclidean distance transform from [6]. For each candidate vessel point the resulting distance map contains the distance to its nearest background pixel and the position of that background pixel.

The pruning operation is the most crucial step in our approach. We use two measures ϕ and d introduced in [7] to quantify the likelihood of a vessel candidate being a center line pixel of a curvilinear band of limited width. The meaning of ϕ and d can be easily understood in Figure 2, where p and n represent a vessel candidate and one of the eight neighbors from its neighborhood N_p, respectively, e_p and e_n are their corresponding nearest background pixel. The two measures

---

[1] Note that retinal images are usually captured in full color. Using a RGB color model, the blue band is often empty and the red band is often saturated. Therefore, we only work with the green band of retinal images.

are defined by:

$$\phi = \max_{n \in N_p} \text{angle}(\overline{pe_p}, \overline{pe_n}) = \max_{n \in N_p} \frac{180}{\pi} \cdot \arccos \frac{\overline{pe_p} \cdot \overline{pe_n}}{||\overline{pe_p}|| \cdot ||\overline{pe_n}||}$$

$$d = \max_{n \in N_p} ||\overline{e_p e_n}||$$

The center line pixels of curvilinear bands typically have high values of ϕ. Therefore, our first pruning operation is based on a limit P_ϕ on ϕ. Since the blood vessels only have a limited width which is approximated by d, we also put a limit P_d on d to only retain thin curvilinear bands.

Applying the two pruning operations above sometimes produces thin curvilinear bands that show only very weak contrast to the surrounding area and are not vessels. For this reason we introduce a third photometric test by requiring a sufficient contrast. The contrast measure is defined by:

$$c = \max_{n \in N_p} \frac{\text{intensity}(q_n)}{\text{intensity}(p)}$$

where q_n ($\overline{pq_n} = P_{fac} \cdot \overline{pe_n}$, $P_{fac} > 1$) represents a pixel of the background in the direction $\overline{pe_n}$. The corresponding pruning operation is based on a limit P_{int} applied to c.

After the three pruning operations we obtain thin curvilinear bands, implicitly defined by their respective center line pixels. Sometimes, however, a few very short structures which are unlikely to be blood vessels are among the detected bands. Therefore, we put an additional size constraint in the following manner. A component labeling is performed on the image containing the center line pixels. Any component smaller than a limit P_{size} is excluded from further consideration.

In summary we totally defined four pruning operations with respect to the properties angle (ϕ), width (d), contrast (c), and size. The remaining center line pixels in the final result, together with their respective distance values can then be used to reconstruct the blood vessels that are made visible by the particular threshold T.

The threshold probing is done for a series of thresholds. A straightforward way is to step through the intensity domain defined by the lowest and the highest intensity of a retinal image at a fixed step T_{step}. In our experimental evaluation described in the next section T_{step} is set to be 2. The results from the different thresholds can be simply merged to form an overall vessel image.

4   Experimental Evaluation

For two reasons we have chosen the set of twenty retinal images used in [4] to evaluate the performance of our algorithm. First, the retinal images have all hand-labeled vessel segmentation and allow therefore quantitative evaluation in an objective manner. Second, the image set contains both normal and abnormal (pathological) cases. In contrast most of the referenced methods have only been

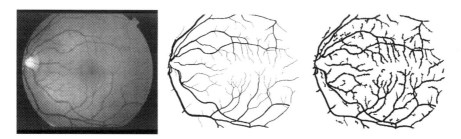

Fig. 3. A retinal image (left), hand-labeling GT (middle), and detected vessels (right).

demonstrated upon normal vessel appearances, which are easier to discern. The twenty images were digitized from retinal fundus slides and are of 605×700 pixels, 24 bits per pixel (standard RGB). We only use the green band of the images.

Given a machine-segmented result image (MS) and its corresponding hand-labeled ground truth image (GT), the performance is measured as follows. Any pixel which is marked as vessel in both MS and GT is counted as a true positive. Any pixel which is marked as vessel in MS but not in GT is counted as a false positive. The true positive rate is established by dividing the number of true positives by the total number of vessel pixels in GT. The false positive rate is computed by dividing the number of false positives by the total number of non-vessel pixels in GT.

Our algorithm has five parameters: P_ϕ, P_d, P_{fac}, P_{int}, P_{size}. We report results using eight sets of parameter values: $P_\phi = 150 - 5k$, $P_d = 6 + k$, $P_{fac} = 2.0$, $P_{int} = 1.07$, $p_{size} = 46 - 3k$, $k = 0, 1, \ldots, 7$. As an example, the detection result for the retinal image in Figure 1, processed at $k = 3$, is given in Figure 3. Figure 4 shows the average performance curve over the twenty images for the eight parameter sets.

For the twenty images there is a second hand-labeling made by a different person available. The first hand-labeling, which is used as ground truth in our evaluation, took a more conservative view of the vessel boundaries and in the identification of small vessels than the second hand-labeling. By considering the second hand-labeling as "machine-segmented result images" and comparing them to the ground truth, we can establish a target performance level. This level is indicated by the isolated circle mark in Figure 4. Our algorithm produces the same number of false positives at a 77% true positive rate as the second set of hand-labeled images at a 90% true positive rate. This suggests room for an improvement of 13% in the true positive rate over our method.

As reference, the average performance curve for the method based on filter response analysis [4] is drawn in Figure 4. We observe similar performance up to approximately 75% true positive rate. For higher true positive rates our approach shows superior performance w.r.t. the false positive rate. In particular, we are able to achieve 90% true positive rate of the second hand-labeling at a false

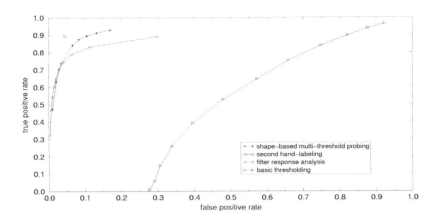

Fig. 4. Average performance over twenty images: our approach vs. other methods.

positive rate which is slightly higher than doubling that of the second hand-labeling, but much lower than that would be required by the approach from [4].

Our multi-threshold probing is motivated by the fact that a single threshold only reveals part of the vessel network and therefore the basic thresholding does not work well. This is quantitatively demonstrated by the average performance curve for the basic thresholding in Figure 4, established for the thresholds $40, 50, 60, \ldots, 150$.

The computation time amounts to about 26 seconds on a Pentium III 600 PC.

5   Conclusion

We have proposed a novel approach to blood vessel detection in retinal images using shape-based multi-threshold probing. On an image set with hand-labeled ground truth our algorithm has quantitatively demonstrated superior performance over the basic thresholding and the method reported in [4].

The core of our algorithm, threshold probing, is independent of the particular shape-based classification of thresholded images into vessel and non-vessel parts. To the knowledge of the authors, such a general framework of classification-based multi-threshold probing has not been explored in the literature thus far. We expect that the framework may be applied to other tasks, such as the detection of pigmented skin lesions and the segmentation of microaneurysms in ophthalmic fluorescein angiograms. These topics are among our current research interests.

Acknowledgments. The authors want to thank A. Hoover at Clemson University for making the retinal image material and the ground truth data publically available.

References

1. S. Chaudhuri, S. Chatterjee, N. Katz, M. Nelson, and M. Goldbaum, Detection of blood vessels in retinal images using two-dimensional matched filters, IEEE Trans. on Medical Imaging, 8(3): 263-269, 1989.
2. W.E. Hart and M. Goldbaum, Registering retinal images using automatically selected control point pairs, Proc. of ICIP, 576–580, 1994.
3. A. Hoover and M. Goldbaum, Fuzzy convergence, Proc. of IEEE Conf. on Computer Vision and Pattern Recognition, 716–721, 1998.
4. A. Hoover, V. Kouznetsova, and M. Goldbaum, Locating blood vessels in retinal images by piece-wise threshold probing of a matched filter response, IEEE Trans. on Medical Imaging, 19(3): 203–210, 2000.
5. S.U. Lee, S.Y. Chung, and R.H. Park, A comparative performance study of several global thresholding techniques for segmentation, Computer Vision, Graphics, and Image Processing, 52: 171–190, 1990.
6. F. Leymarie and M.D. Levine, Fast raster scan distance propagation on the discrete rectangular lattice, CVGIP: Image Understanding, 55(1), 84–94, 1992.
7. G. Malandain and S.F. Vidal, Euclidean skeletons, Image and Vision Computing, 16: 317–327, 1998.
8. F.P. Miles and A.L. Nuttall, Matched filter estimation of serial blood vessel diameters from video images, IEEE Trans. on Medical Imaging, 12(2): 147–152, 1993.
9. T.N. Pappas and J.S. Lim, A new method for estimation of coronary artery dimensions in angiograms, IEEE Trans. on Acoustic, Speech, and Signal Processing, 36(9): 1501–1513, 1988.
10. C. Perra, M. Petrou, and D.D. Giusto, Retinal image segmentation by watersheds, Proc. of IAPR Workshop on Machine Vision Applications, 315–318, Tokyo, 2000.
11. P.K. Sahoo, S. Soltani, A.K.C. Wong, and Y.C. Chen, A survey of thresholding techniques, Computer Vision, Graphics, and Image Processing, 41: 233–260, 1988.
12. S. Tamura, Y. Okamoto, and K. Yanashima, Zero-crossing interval correction in tracing eye-fundus blood vessel, Pattern Recognition, 21(3): 227–233, 1988.
13. Y.A.Tolias and S.M. Panas, A fuzzy vessel tracking algorithm for retinal images based on fuzzy clustering, IEEE Trans. on Medical Imaging, 17(2): 263–273, 1998.
14. F. Zana and J.C. Klein, A multimodal registration algorithm of eye fundus images using vessels detection and Hough transform, IEEE Trans. on Medical Imaging, 18(5): 419–428, 1999.
15. L. Zhou, M.S. Rzeszotarki, L.J. Singerman, and J.M. Chokreff, The detection and quantification of retinopathy using digital angiograms, IEEE Trans. on Medical Imaging, 13(4): 619–626, 1994.

Vehicle Detection in Aerial Images Using Generic Features, Grouping, and Context

Stefan Hinz and Albert Baumgartner

Chair for Photogrammetry and Remote Sensing,
Technische Universität München,
Arcisstr. 21, D-80290 München, Germany
{Stefan.Hinz, Albert.Baumgartner}@bv.tu-muenchen.de
http://www.photo.verm.tu-muenchen.de

Abstract. This paper introduces a new approach on automatic vehicle detection in monocular large scale aerial images. The extraction is based on a hierarchical model that describes the prominent vehicle features on different levels of detail. Besides the object properties, the model comprises also contextual knowledge, i.e., relations between a vehicle and other objects as, e.g., the pavement beside a vehicle and the sun causing a vehicle's shadow projection. In contrast to most of the related work, our approach neither relies on external information like digital maps or site models, nor it is limited to very specific vehicle models. Various examples illustrate the applicability and flexibility of this approach. However, they also show the deficiencies which clearly define the next steps of our future work.

1 Introduction

Motivated from different points of view, automatic vehicle detection in remotely sensed data evolved to an important research issue for more than one decade. In the field of *military reconnaissance*, for instance, intense research on Automatic Target Recognition (ATR) and monitoring systems has been conducted (see [10] for a review), best exemplified by the DARPA RADIUS project during the 90's. The vehicle types to detect by ATR systems have often quite specific and discriminative features, however, these approaches must tackle problems due to noisy data (e.g., RADAR images) or bad viewing conditions. Considering *civil applications*, the growing amount of traffic and the need arising therefrom to (partially) automate the control over traffic flow emphasizes the role of vehicle detection and tracking as substantial part of Intelligent Transportation Systems (ITS; [1]). Matured approaches, e.g., the ones of Nagel and coworkers (cf. [4],[5]) or Sullivan and coworkers (cf. [13],[14]), use vehicle and motion models for the detection and tracking of road vehicles in image sequences taken from stationary cameras. While these systems often incorporate site-model information (e.g., the lanes of a road intersection), approaches related with the *acquisition of geographic data* – including ours – aim to extract or update site-model information (cf. [6],[9],[11]). Here, the use of vehicle detection schemes is motivated by the fact

B. Radig and S. Florczyk (Eds.): DAGM 2001, LNCS 2191, pp. 45–52, 2001.

that, especially in aerial images taken over urban areas, site-model components like roads and parking lots are mainly defined by cars driving or parking there. Hence an important goal of our work is achieving a good overall completeness of the extraction rather than detecting or discriminating specific vehicle types (as, e.g. in [3],[7]).

2   Related Work

As it is argued in [4], one of the key problems of vehicle extraction is the high variability of vehicle types, and thus the intrinsically high dimensional search space. Different attempts have been made to cope with this:

Olson et al. [8] generate 2D templates (the silhouettes of vehicles) by calculating different views on 3D objects. Vehicles are then detected by matching the silhouettes to the binary edge map of the image using a modified Hausdorff measure. In order to increase efficiency, matching is based on a hierarchical tree-like model that classifies the silhouettes according to their similarity. Ruskoné et al. [11] (and also Quint [9]) exploit the contextual knowledge that – especially in urban areas – vehicles are often arranged in collinear or parallel groups. Hence Ruskoné et al. [11] allow a high false alarm rate after the initial steps of vehicle extraction with a neural network classifier. They show that many erroneous detection results can afterwards be eliminated by iteratively grouping collinear and parallel vehicles and rejecting all others. However, the results indicate that a neural network classifier is probably not powerful enough for the task of vehicle detection when applied to the raw image data.

The systems of Chellappa et al. [2] and Quint [9] integrate external information from site-models and digital maps, respectively, which reduces the search for vehicles to certain image regions. Chellappa et al. [2] extend this further by constraining the extraction along the dominant direction of roads and parking lots. Another advantage of this method is the fact that many image regions possibly containing vehicle-like structures as, e.g., chimneys on building roofs, are excluded from the extraction. Thus, less sophisticated vehicle models are sufficient for such systems (these approaches use basically simple rectangular masks). A crucial point when using external information, however, is the need for data consistency. For civil applications site-models are rare, often generalized, possibly outdated, or just not accurately enough registered. Therefore, such approaches are usually less flexible or they have to cope with site-model registration and update in addition.

In order to keep our approach as flexible as possible, we decided to use data stemming from one single source instead of integrating other information, i.e., we use pan-chromatic high resolution aerial images (about 10 cm resolution on the ground) and standard meta-data like calibration and orientation parameters as well as the image capture time.

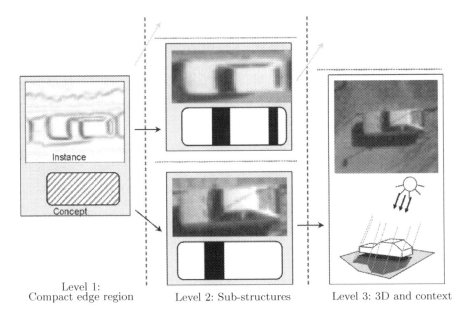

Level 1:
Compact edge region   Level 2: Sub-structures   Level 3: 3D and context

Fig. 1. Hierarchical vehicle model: Increasing detail from left to right

3   Model and Extraction Strategy

The discussion above shows that a reliable vehicle detection scheme must be based on a sophisticated model that focuses on few but prominent features common most of the vehicles types. On the other hand, the extraction strategy should be able to efficiently manage the varying appearance of vehicles even for large images. This leads us to a hierarchical model, that describes the appearance of vehicles at different levels of detail. Other distinctive features closely related to vehicles, though not intrinsic properties, are included by modeling the local context of vehicles (for instance, a vehicle's shadow projection).

3.1   Model

The knowledge about vehicles which is represented by our model is summarized in Fig. 1. Due to the use of aerial imagery, i.e., almost vertical views, the model comprises exclusively features of a vehicle's upper surface and neglects the features of the sides up to now. 3D information is used for predicting the shadow region, though.

At the lowest level of detail (Level 1), we model a vehicle's outline as convex, somewhat compact, and almost rectangular 2D region, possibly showing high edge density inside. This captures nearly all typical vehicles except busses and trucks. At the next level (Level 2), we incorporate basic vehicle sub-structures, e.g., the windshields and uniformly colored surfaces (front, top, and rear) that form a sequence of connected 2D-rectangles — denoted as rectangle sequences in the sequel. This level still describes many types of passenger cars, vans, and small trucks since the rectangles may vary in their size and, what is more, an object instance is not constrained to consist of all of the modeled sub-structures (exemplified by two instances at Level 2 in Fig. 1). The last level (Level 3) contains 3D information and local context of vehicles. Depending on the sub-structures of the previous level different simple height profiles are introduced which enrich the 2D model with the third dimension. As a vehicle's local context we include the bright and homogeneous pavement around a vehicle and a vehicle's shadow projection. Especially the shadow projection has proven to be a reliable feature, since aerial images are only taken under excellent weather conditions — at least for civil applications.

Please note, that the context model needs no external information except ground control points for geo-coding the images. If all image orientation parameters and the image acquisition's date and daytime are known — which is indeed the standard case for aerial imagery — then it is easy to compute the direction of the sun rays and derive therefrom the shadow region projected on the horizontal road surface.

3.2   Extraction Strategy

The extraction strategy is derived from the vehicle model and, consequently, follows the two paradigms *"coarse to fine"* and *"hypothesize and test"*. It consists of following 4 steps: (1) Creation of Regions of Interest (RoIs) which is mainly based on edge voting for convex and compact regions, (2) Hypotheses formation for deriving rectangle sequences from extracted lines, edges, and surfaces, (3) Hypotheses validation and selection which includes the radiometric and geometric analysis of rectangle sequences, and (4) Verification using 3D vehicle models and their local context. See also Fig. 2 for an illustration of the individual steps.

In order to avoid time-consuming grouping algorithms in the early stages of extraction, we first focus on generic image features as edges, lines, and surfaces.

Creation of RoIs: We start with the extraction of edges, link them into contours, and robustly estimate the local direction and curvature at each contour point. Similar to a generalized (i.e., elliptical) Hough-Transform we use direction and curvature as well as intervals for length and width of vehicles for deriving the centers and orientations of the RoIs (Fig. 2 a) and b).

Hypotheses formation: One of the most obvious vehicle features in aerial images is the line-like dark front windshield. Therefore, we extract dark lines of a certain width, length and straightness in the RoIs using the differential geometric approach of Steger [12] and, because vehicles are usually uniformly colored, we select those lines as windshield candidates which have symmetric

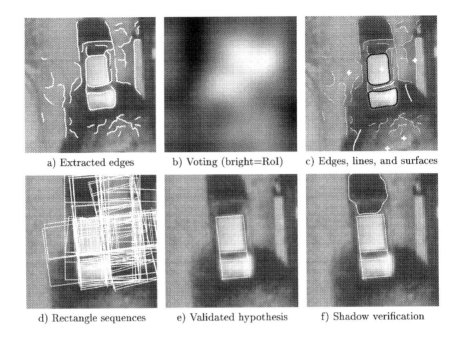

a) Extracted edges   b) Voting (bright=RoI)   c) Edges, lines, and surfaces

d) Rectangle sequences   e) Validated hypothesis   f) Shadow verification

Fig. 2. Individual steps of vehicle detection

contrast on both sides (see bold white lines in Fig. 2 c). Front, top, and rear of a vehicle mostly appear as more or less bright "blob" in the vicinity of a windshield. Thus, we robustly fit a second-order grayvalue surface to each image part adjacent to windshield candidates (apexes are indicated by white crosses in Fig. 2 c) and keep only those blobs whose estimated surface parameters satisfy the condition of an ellipsoidal or parabolic surface. As a side effect, both algorithms for line and surface extraction return the contours of their bounding edges (bold black lines in Fig. 2 c). These contours and additional edges extracted in their neighborhood (thin white lines in Fig. 2 c) are approximated by line segments. Then, we group the segments into rectangles and, furthermore, rectangle sequences. Fitting the rectangle sequences to the dominant direction of the underlying image edges yields the final 2D vehicle hypotheses (Fig. 2 d).

Hypotheses validation and selection: Before constructing 3D models from the 2D hypotheses we check the hypotheses for validity. Each rectangle sequence is evaluated regarding the geometric criteria length, width, and length/width ratio, as well as the radiometric criteria homogeneity of an individual rectangle and gray value constancy of rectangles connected with a "windshield rectangle". The validation is based on fuzzy-set theory and ensures that only promising, non-overlapping hypotheses are selected (Fig. 2 e).

3D model generation and verification: In order to approximate the
3D shape of a vehicle hypothesis, a particular height profile is selected from a
set of predefined profiles. Please note that the hypothesis' underlying rectangles
remain unchanged, i.e., the height values of the profile refer to the image edges
perpendicular to the vehicle direction. The selection of the profiles depends on
the extracted sub-structures, i.e., the shape of the validated rectangle sequence.
We distinguish rectangle sequences corresponding to 3 types of vehicles:
hatch-back cars, saloon cars, and other vehicles such as vans, small trucks, etc.
In contrast to hatch-back and saloon cars, the derivation of an accurate height
profile for the last category would require a deeper analysis of the hypotheses
(e.g., for an unambiguous determination of the vehicle orientation). Hence, in
this case, we approximate the height profile only roughly by an elliptic arc
having a constant height offset above the ground.

After creating a 3D model from the 2D hypothesis and the respective height
profile we are able to predict the boundary of a vehicle's shadow projection on
the underlying road surface. A vehicle hypothesis is judged as verified if a dark
and homogeneous region is extracted besides the shadowed part of the vehicle
and a bright and homogeneous region besides the illuminated part, respectively
(Fig. 2 f).

4   Results and Discussion

Figure 3 shows parts of an aerial image with a ground resolution of 9 cm. The
white rectangle sequences indicate the extracted cars and their sub-structures. In
the image part shown in Fig. 3 a), all cars have been extracted successfully. Due
to the weak contrast, however, the shape of the two cars in the center has not
been recovered exactly. For instance, the corresponding sub-structure of the front
windshield of the upper car is missing. Despite of this, shape and underlying edge
support of the rectangle as well as a successful shadow verification gave enough
evidence to judge this particular hypothesis correctly.

Although three vehicles are successfully detected, the result of the image part
shown in Fig. 3 b) shows more severe failures. The dark vehicle in the upper left
part has been missed because its body, windshields, and shadow region show very
similar gray values. Hence, the system has constructed only one single, over-sized
rectangle which has been rejected during the hypotheses selection phase. While
this kind of error is presumably quite easy to overcome by using color images,
the reason for missing the car in the lower right corner is of more fundamental
nature and strongly related to the specular characteristics of cars. As can be
seen from Fig. 1 (Level 3[1]), due to specularities front and top of the car show
very different average gray values which caused the rejection of this hypothesis.

Hence, we can conclude that the extraction is quite reliable if (at least) some
of the modeled sub-structures are easy to identify. However, the system tends to

---

[1] image has been rotated for display

(a)   (b)

(c)   (d)

Fig. 3. Extraction results on pan-chromatic aerial images (resolution: 9 cm)

miss vehicles due to weak contrast, specularities, and influences of neighboring objects. For addressing these problems, we have to extend our model by relations between individual vehicles and vehicle groupings in order to incorporate more global knowledge like similar orientations and rather symmetric spacing (e.g., a dark "blob" between two previously extracted vehicles is likely to be another vehicle). Further improvements seem possible if color imagery and/or more sophisticated 3D models are used. Last but not least, we plan to integrate this approach into the road extraction system described in [6].

References

1. Bogenberger, K., Ernhofer, O., and Schütte, C., 1999. Effects of Telematic Applications for a High Capacity Ring Road in Munich. In: Proceedings of the 6th World Congress on Itelligent Transportation Systems, Toronto.
2. Chellappa, R., Zheng, Q., Davis, L., Lin, C., Zhang, X., Rodriguez, C., Rosenfeld, A., and Moore, T., 1994. Site model based monitoring of aerial images. In: Image Understanding Workshop, Morgan Kaufmann Publishers, San Francisco, CA, pp. 295–318.
3. Dubuisson-Jolly, M.-P., Lakshmanan, S., and Jain, A., 1996. Vehicle Segmentation and Classification Using Deformable Templates. IEEE Transactions on Pattern Analysis and Machine Intelligence 18(3), pp. 293–308.
4. Haag, M. and Nagel, H.-H., 1999. Combination of Edge Element and Optical Flow Estimates for 3D-Model-Based Vehicle Tracking in Traffic Sequences. International Journal of Computer Vision 35(3), pp. 295–319.
5. Kollnig, H. and Nagel, H.-H., 1997. 3D Pose Estimation by Directly Matching Polyhedral Models to Gray Value Gradients. International Journal of Computer Vision 23(3), pp. 283–302.
6. Hinz, S., Baumgartner, A., Mayer, H., Wiedemann, C., and Ebner, H., 2001. Road Extraction Focussing on Urban Areas. In: Automatic Extraction of Man-Made Objects from Aerial and Space Images (III), Balkema Publishers, Rotterdam (in print).
7. Michaelsen, E. and Stilla, U., 2000. Ansichtenbasierte Erkennung von Fahrzeugen. In: G. Sommer, N. Krüger and C. Perwass (eds), Mustererkennung, Informatik aktuell, Springer-Verlag, Berlin, pp. 245–252.
8. Olson, C., Huttenlocher, D., and Doria, D., 1996. Recognition by Matching With Edge Location and Orientation. In: Image Understanding Workshop.
9. Quint, F., 1997. MOSES: A Structural Approach to Arial Image Understanding. In: A. Gruen, E. Baltsavias and O. Henricsson (eds), Automatic Extraction of Man-Made Objects from Aerial and Space Images (II), Birkhäuser Verlag, Basel, pp. 323–332.
10. Ratches, J., Walters, C., Buser, R., and Guenther, B., 1997. Aided and Automatic Target Recognition Based Upon Sensory Inputs From Image Forming Systems. IEEE Transactions on Pattern Analysis and Machine Intelligence 19(9), pp. 1004–1019.
11. Ruskoné, R., Guiges, L., Airault, S., and Jamet, O., 1996. Vehicle detection on aerial images: A structural approach. In: 13th International Conference on Pattern Recognition, Vol. III, pp. 900–903.
12. Steger, C., 1998. An Unbiased Detector of Curvilinear Structures. IEEE Transactions on Pattern Analysis and Machine Intelligence 20(2), pp. 113–125.
13. Sullivan, G., Worrall, A. and Ferryman, J., 1995. Visual Object Recognition Using Deformable Models of Vehicles. In: IEEE Workshop on Context-based Vision, pp. 75–86.
14. Tan, T., Sullivan, G., and Baker, K., 1998. Model-Based Localisation and Recognition of Road Vehicles. International Journal of Computer Vision 27(1), pp. 5–25.

Reconstruction of Image Structure
in Presence of Specular Reflections

Martin Gröger, Wolfgang Sepp, Tobias Ortmaier, and Gerd Hirzinger

German Aerospace Center (DLR)
Institute of Robotics and Mechatronics
D-82234 Wessling, Germany
http://www.robotic.dlr.de
martin.groeger@dlr.de

Abstract. This paper deals with the reconstruction of original image structure in the presence of local disturbances such as specular reflections. It presents two novel schemes for their elimination with respect to the local image structure: an efficient linear interpolation scheme and an iterative filling-in approach employing anisotropic diffusion. The algorithms are evaluated on images of the heart surface and are suited to support tracking of natural landmarks on the beating heart.

1   Introduction

Glossy surfaces give rise to specular reflection from light sources. Without proper identification specularities are often mistaken for genuine surface markings by computer vision applications such as matching models to objects, deriving motion fields from optical flow or estimating depth from binocular stereo [BB88].

This paper presents two approaches to reconstruct the original image structure in the presence of local disturbances. The algorithms have been developed to enable robust tracking of natural landmarks on the heart surface [GOSH01] as part of the visual servoing component in a minimally invasive robotic surgery scenario [ORS+01]. There specular reflections of the point light source arise on the curved and deforming surface of the beating heart. Due to sudden and irregular occurrence these highlights disturb tracking of natural landmarks on the beating heart considerably [Grö00]. Reconstruction schemes are sufficiently general for application in other fields, where disturbances in images should be eliminated ensuring continuity of local structures.

Previous work mainly investigates specular, together with diffuse, reflection [BB88,Wol94], which aim to suppress the specular component while enhancing the diffuse. This work considers local specular reflections with no detectable diffuse components, which cause total loss of information. Therefore reconstruction can only be guided by surrounding image structures.

The following section introduces robust extraction of image structure by the structure tensor which two schemes for reconstruction are based on: linear interpolation between boundary pixels and anisotropic diffusion within a filling-in scheme. The algorithms are evaluated on video images of the heart with specularities (Sect. 3), before concluding with a summary of results and perspectives.

B. Radig and S. Florczyk (Eds.): DAGM 2001, LNCS 2191, pp. 53–60, 2001.
© Springer-Verlag Berlin Heidelberg 2001

2   Reconstruction

Specularities occur as highlights on the glossy heart surface (Fig. 1). Since their grey values are distinctively high and independent of neighbourhood intensities, simple thresholding can be applied for segmentation. Structure inside specular areas is restored from local structure information determined by the well-known structure tensor. This yields reconstruction which is most likely to correspond to the original area on condition that surface structures possess some continuity. Therefore intensity information mainly from boundary points along the current orientation is used. Results are presented for the mechanically stabilized area of interest of the beating heart (Fig. 1).

Fig. 1. Original image with specularities (detail)

2.1   Structure Detection

The structure tensor provides a reliable measure of the coherence of structures and their orientation, derived from surrounding gradient information. For more details see [Wei98].

Definition 1 (Structure tensor). *For an image f with Gaussian smoothed gradient $\nabla f_\sigma \overset{\text{def}}{=} \nabla(g_\sigma * f)$ the structure tensor is defined as*

$$J_\rho(\nabla f_\sigma) \overset{\text{def}}{=} g_\rho * (\nabla f_\sigma \otimes \nabla f_\sigma) = g_\rho * \begin{pmatrix} (\frac{\partial f_\sigma}{\partial x})^2 & \frac{\partial f_\sigma}{\partial x}\frac{\partial f_\sigma}{\partial y} \\ \frac{\partial f_\sigma}{\partial x}\frac{\partial f_\sigma}{\partial y} & (\frac{\partial f_\sigma}{\partial y})^2 \end{pmatrix} \qquad (1)$$

where g_ρ is a Gaussian kernel of standard deviation $\rho \geq 0$, separately convolved with the components of the matrix resulting from the tensor product $\otimes$.

The *noise scale* σ reduces image noise before the gradient operator is applied, while the *integration scale* ρ adjusts J to the size of structures to be detected. The eigenvalues $\lambda_{1/2}$ of the structure tensor J_ρ measure the average contrast in the direction of the eigenvectors (over some area specified by the integration scale ρ). Since J_ρ is symmetric, its eigenvectors v_1, v_2 are orthonormal [Wei98]. The eigenvector v_1 corresponding to the eigenvalue with greatest absolute value (λ_1) gives the orientation of highest grey value fluctuation. The other eigenvector v_2, which is orthogonal to v_1, gives the preferred local orientation, the *coherence direction*. Moreover, the term $(\lambda_1 - \lambda_2)^2$ is a measure of the local coherence and becomes large for anisotropic structures [Wei98].

The structure tensor J_ρ is used to extract structure orientation for reconstruction. Anisotropic confidence-based filling-in also makes use of the coherence measure $(\lambda_1 - \lambda_2)^2$ for structure dependent diffusion (Sect. 2.3).

2.2   Structure Tensor Linear Interpolation

Specular areas are reconstructed by interpolation between boundary points along the main orientation of the local structure, extracted by the structure tensor.

Extraction of Local Structure. Local orientation is given by the eigenvector v_2 belonging to the minor eigenvalue λ_2 of the structure tensor J_ρ (Sect. 2.1), which is required for every specular pixel. To detect structure in the given heart images appropriate values for noise and integration scale are $\sigma = 1$ and $\rho = 2.8$, corresponding to a catchment area of about 9×9 pixels.

Reconstruction. For each point inside the specular area, search for the two boundary points along the structure orientation associated to it. Linear interpolation between the intensities of the boundary points, weighted according to their relative distances, yields the new value at the current position. Final low-pass filtering ensures sufficient smoothness in the reconstructed area.

2.3   Anisotropic Confidence-Based Filling-In

This reconstruction scheme fills specular areas from the boundary based on local structure information. It employs coherence enhancing anisotropic diffusion.

Coherence Enhancing Anisotropic Diffusion. Diffusion is generally conceived as a physical process that equilibrates concentration without creating or destroying mass. Applied to images, intensity at a certain location is identified with concentration. Thus the diffusion process implies smoothing of peaks and sharp changes of intensity, where the image gradient is strong.

The discussed type of diffusion, designed to enhance the coherence of structures [Wei98], is anisotropic and inhomogeneous. Inhomogeneous means that the strength of diffusion depends on the current image position, e.g. the absolute value of the gradient ∇f. Further, anisotropic diffusion corresponds to non-uniform smoothing, e.g. directed along structures. Thus edges can not only be preserved but even enhanced.

The diffusion tensor $D = D(J_\rho(\nabla f_\sigma))$, needed to specify anisotropy, has the same set of eigenvectors v_1, v_2 as the structure tensor J_ρ (Sect. 2.1), reflecting local image structure. Its eigenvalues λ_1', λ_2' are chosen to enhance coherent structures, which implies a smoothing preference along the coherence direction v_2 with diffusivity λ_2' increasing with respect to the coherence $(\lambda_1 - \lambda_2)^2$ of J_ρ:

$$\lambda_1' \overset{\text{def}}{=} \alpha; \qquad \lambda_2' \overset{\text{def}}{=} \begin{cases} \alpha & \text{if } \lambda_1 = \lambda_2, \\ \alpha + (1-\alpha)\exp\left(\frac{-C}{(\lambda_1 - \lambda_2)^{2m}}\right) & \text{otherwise} \end{cases} \tag{2}$$

where $C > 0, m \in \mathbb{N}, \alpha \in\,]0,1[$, and the exponential function ensures the smoothness of D. For homogeneous regions, α specifies the strength of diffusion. We follow [Wei98] with $C = 1$, $m = 1$, and $\alpha = 0.001$.

Anisotropic Confidence-Based Filling-In. A filling-in scheme for structure driven reconstruction is developed, employing coherence enhancing anisotropic diffusion. The algorithm is an extension of the confidence-based filling-in model of Neumann and Pessoa [NP98], and is described by the following equation:

Definition 2 (Anisotropic confidence-based filling-in). *For an image f, evolving over time as f_t, anisotropic confidence-based filling-in is given by*

$$\frac{\partial f_t}{\partial t} = (1-c)\mathrm{div}(D(J_\rho(\nabla f_0))\nabla f_t) + c(f_0 - f_t) \tag{3}$$

where f_0 is the initial image and $c : \mathrm{dom}(f) \to [0,1]$ is a confidence measure.

In the present work, c maps to $\{0,1\}$, where $c = 0$ refers to unreliable image information, i.e. specularities, and non-specular image points provide reliable information $(c = 1)$. Therefore non-specular regions are not modified, while specular points are processed according to

$$\frac{\partial f_t}{\partial t} = \mathrm{div}(D(J_\rho(\nabla f_0))\nabla f_t) \;. \tag{4}$$

Algorithm. Linear diffusion equations like (4) are commonly solved by relaxation methods. Intensity from boundary pixels is propagated into the specular area, or vice versa, specular intensity is drained from it (source–sink model). In the current implementation reconstruction calculates the dynamic changes of diffusion over time in an iterative approach. In each step diffusion is represented by convolution with space-invariant kernels, shaped according to the diffusion tensor as in [Wei98]. The algorithm runs until the relative change of specular intensity is sufficiently small.

As intensities at the boundary are constant, diffusion corresponds to interpolation between boundary points. Filling-In is related to regularization theory [TA77] in employing a smoothness and a data-related term. The filling-in model discussed here incorporates a linear diffusion scheme. Local structure information for the diffusion process is extracted only from the initial image, which allows efficient implementation of the filling-in process.

3   Evaluation

Reconstruction is required to meet the following criteria:

(R0) Restriction to specular areas
(R1) Smooth reconstruction inside specular areas
(R2) Smooth transition to boundaries
(R3) Continuity of local structures
(A1) Realtime operability

As a basic requirement only specular areas shall be altered (R0). To avoid new artefacts, e.g. edges, smoothness is assessed both inside specular areas (R1) and at the boundary (R2). Structures next to specularities should be continued within reconstructed areas (R3), because uniform filling-in from the boundary may cause new artefacts by interrupted structures. Criterion (A1) is kept in mind to enable realtime application, as required for tracking in a stream of images.

3.1   Reconstruction at Specularities on the Heart Surface

First, quality of reconstruction within structured areas is measured by introducing an artificial disturbance on a horizontal edge, i.e. a 5 × 5 pixel square with intensity similar to specular reflection (Fig. 2, left). The other two images show reconstruction by structure tensor linear interpolation and anisotropic filling-in: The artificial specularity vanishes and original structure is restored.

Since the underlying structure is known, reconstructed areas of both methods can be compared with the original area by the sum of squared differences (SSD), a similarity measure also commonly used for tracking: With intensities between 0 and 255, SSD is 872 for structure tensor interpolation versus 553 for anisotropic filling-in, which is slightly superior as intensities are closer to the original image.

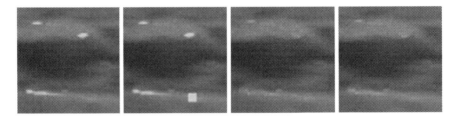

Fig. 2. Elimination of artificial specularity (left to right: original, dto. with artificial specularity (bright square), reconstruction by linear interpolation, and by anisotropic filling-in)

Secondly, reconstruction is considered with real specularities on the heart surface for the area of interest in the original image (Fig. 1). Figures 3 and 4 show reconstruction by linear interpolation and anisotropic filling-in.

Structure Tensor Linear Interpolation. Results of linear interpolation between boundary points are good based on robust orientation information by the structure tensor. Structures are continued (R3), and sufficient smoothness is provided at the boundaries (R2), and within reconstructed areas (R1) by final low-pass filtering.

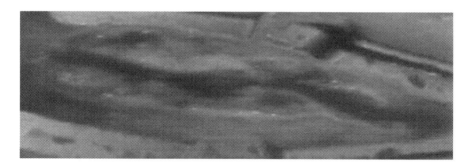

Fig. 3. Image reconstructed by structure tensor interpolation (detail)

Time Complexity. Let n be the image size. To compute the structure tensor, filter operations with the Gaussian derivative to obtain ∇f_σ and applying Gaussians g_ρ to its components each require $\mathcal{O}(n \log n)$, for convolution as complex multiplication in Fourier space using FFT. Including $\mathcal{O}(n)$ for eigenvector computation complexity remains $\mathcal{O}(n \log n)$ for the structure tensor. Reconstruction by linear interpolation follows: assuming without loss a quadratic image there are at most n specular pixels, for each of which search for boundary points takes $\sqrt{n}$ steps. This gives an overall complexity of $\mathcal{O}(\sqrt{n}n)$ including the complexities for the structure tensor and final smoothing ($\mathcal{O}(n \log n)$). Reconstruction of a 720×288 image requires less than two seconds on a 600 MHz Pentium-III Linux workstation, which is a non-optimised upper bound.

Anisotropic Confidence-Based Filling-In. The anisotropic filling-in scheme preserves structure occluded by specular reflections (R3). Inherent smoothness of the diffusion process inside (R1) and at the boundaries of specular reflections (R2) can be visually confirmed (Fig. 4). Specularities can be eliminated if the iteration scheme is applied long enough, but not all intensity from large specular areas may be drained if time is restricted.

Time Complexity. The existence of a steady state and the number of iterations needed depends on the properties of the diffusion equation (4), more closely on its eigenvalues. Each iteration requires convolution with a space-dependent kernel for each specular pixel, yielding $\mathcal{O}(n \log n)$ for an image of size n bounding the number of specular pixels. Additionally the number of iterations required grows

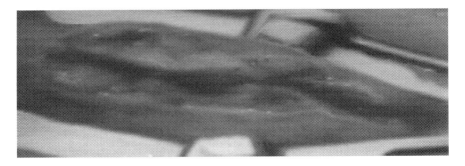

Fig. 4. Image reconstructed by anisotropic filling-in (detail)

with the size of specular areas. Up to 800 iterations are needed to eliminate most specularities on the heart surface, which takes more than one minute for a 720×288 image in the current implementation.

Time performance may be improved by multigrid methods to solve the diffusion equation [PTVF93]. Recent research also indicates speedup by a hierarchical filling-in scheme [SN99] or a neural network approach [FS95] which accelerates the diffusion process by learning changes made by diffusion over a number of iterations.

3.2 Discussion

Both schemes provide good results for reconstruction of specularities, where all criteria (R0)–(R3) can be met: The structure tensor interpolation scheme is fast but does not ensure smoothness within reconstructed areas, which can be compensated easily. Anisotropic filling-in creates inherently smooth areas; it applies a diffusion process depending on both orientation and strength of local structures. However, computational cost is much higher than for the structure tensor which implies worse reconstruction if time is restricted.

Structure information obtained by the structure tensor from the original image is influenced by specularities. Disturbed areas should not be large compared to local structures, since otherwise reasonable reconstruction is not possible: Structure information is distorted and small details cannot be reconstructed.

4   Conclusion and Perspectives

Two novel schemes have been developed to reconstruct original image structure in the presence of local disturbances. Anisotropic confidence-based filling-in employs smoothness constraints to reach an optimum solution for reconstruction. Linear interpolation between boundary points in the coherence direction reaches comparable results with considerably lower computational expense suited for realtime tracking of image structures [GOSH01].

The algorithms have been successfully applied to reconstruct the heart surface in the presence of specular reflections. Further, tracking natural landmarks on the beating heart can be improved greatly, as outliers caused by specularities are compensated [Grö00]. Apart from tracking the algorithms are sufficiently general to reconstruct structured images partially occluded by disturbances.

Acknowledgements. This work was supported partly by the German Research Foundation (DFG) in Collaborative Research Centre SFB 453 on "High-Fidelity Telepresence and Teleaction". The authors thank Dr. D.H. Böhm from the Department of Cardiac Surgery at the University Hospital Grosshadern for video sequences of the beating heart.

References

[BB88]   Gavin Brelstaff and Andrew Blake. Detecting specular reflections using lambertian constraints. In *Proc. 2nd Int'l Conf. on Computer Vision (ICCV)*, pages 297–302. IEEE, 1988.

[FS95]   B. Fischl and E.L. Schwarz. Learning an intergral equation approximation to nonlinear anisotropic diffusion in image processing. Technical Report CAS/CNS-95-033, Boston Univ. Center for Adaptive Systems, Dec. 1995.

[GOSH01]   M. Gröger, T. Ortmaier, W. Sepp, and G. Hirzinger. Tracking local motion on the beating heart. In *FIMH 2001: Int'l Workshop on Functional Imaging and Modeling of the Heart*, Helsinki, Finland, Nov. 2001. submitted.

[Grö00]   Martin Gröger. Robust tracking of natural landmarks of the beating heart. Technical report, German Aerospace Centre (DLR), Institute of Robotics and Mechatronics, 2000.

[NP98]   Heiko Neumann and Luiz Pessoa. Visual filling-in and surface property reconstruction. Technical Report 98-04, Universität Ulm, Fakultät für Informatik, Feb. 1998.

[ORS+01]   T. Ortmaier, D. Reintsema, U. Seibold, U. Hagn, and G. Hirzinger. The DLR minimally invasive robotics surgery scenario. In J. Hoogen G. Färber, editor, *Proceedings of the Workshop on Advances in Interactive Multimodal Telepresence Systems*, pages 135–147, Munich, Germany, March 2001.

[PTVF93]   William H. Press, Saul A. Teukolsky, William T. Vetterling, and Brian P. Flannery. *Numerical Recipes in C: The Art of Scientific Computing*. Cambridge University Press, 2nd edition, 1993.

[SN99]   Wolfgang Sepp and Heiko Neumann. A multi-resolution filling-in model for brightness perception. In *ICANN99: Ninth International Conference on Artificial Neural Networks*, volume 1, pages 461–466. IEE, London, 1999.

[TA77]   Andrey Tikhonov and Vasily Arsenin. *Solution of Ill-Posed Problems*. V. H. Winston & Sons, Washington, D.C., 1977.

[Wei98]   Joachim Weickert. *Anisotropic Diffusion in Image Processing*. B.G. Teubner, Stuttgart, 1998.

[Wol94]   Laurence B. Wolf. On the relative brightness of specular and diffuse reflection. In *Proceedings Conference Computer Vision and Pattern Recognition*, pages 369–376. IEEE, 1994.

Spatio-Temporal Analysis of Human Faces Using Multi-resolution Subdivision Surfaces

Jan Neumann and Yiannis Aloimonos

Center for Automation Research
University of Maryland
College Park, MD 20742-3275, USA
{jneumann,yiannis}@cfar.umd.edu

Abstract. We demonstrate a method to automatically extract spatio-temporal descriptions of human faces from synchronized and calibrated multi-view sequences. The head is modeled by a time-varying multi-resolution subdivision surface that is fitted to the observed person using spatio-temporal multi-view stereo information, as well as contour constraints. The stereo data is utilized by computing the normalized correlation between corresponding spatio-temporal image trajectories of surface patches, while the contour information is determined using incremental background subtraction. We globally optimize the shape of the spatio-temporal surface in a coarse-to-fine manner using the multi-resolution structure of the subdivision mesh. The method presented incorporates the available image information in a unified framework and automatically reconstructs accurate spatio-temporal representations of complex non-rigidly moving objects.

Keywords: Multi-View Stereo, 3D Motion Flow, Motion Estimation, Subdivision Surfaces, Spatio-temporal Image Analysis

1 Introduction

What kind of representation is necessary to understand, simulate and copy an activity of a person or an animal? We need a spatio-temporal representation of the actor in action that captures all the essential shape and motion information that an observer can perceive in a view-independent way. This representation is made up by the 3D spatial structure as well as the 3D motion field on the object surface (also called range flow [13] or scene flow [16]) describing the first order temporal changes of the object surface. Such a representation of the shape and motion of an object would be very useful in a large number of applications. Even for skilled artists it is very hard to animate computer graphics models of living non-rigid objects in a natural way, thus a technique that enables one to recover the accurate 3D displacements would add another dimension to the realism of the animation. Accurate 3D motion estimation is also of great interest to the biomedical field where the motion of athletes or patients is analyzed. The recovery of dense 3D motion fields will also help us to understand the human

B. Radig and S. Florczyk (Eds.): DAGM 2001, LNCS 2191, pp. 61–68, 2001.

representation of action by comparing the information content of 3D and 2D motion fields for object recognition and task understanding.

We present a new algorithm that computes accurately the 3D structure and motion fields of an object solely from image data utilizing silhouette and spatio-temporal image information without any manual intervention. There are many methods in the literature that recover three-dimensional structure information from image sequences captured by multiple cameras. Some example techniques are based on voxel carving [12,19] or multi-base line stereo [18,3], sometimes followed by a second stage to compute the 3D flow [16] from optical flow information. Unfortunately, these approaches usually do not try to compute the motion and structure of the object simultaneously, thereby not exploiting the synergistic relationship between structure and motion constraints. Approaches that recover the motion and structure of an object simultaneously, most often depend on the availability of prior information such as an articulated human model [6,10] or an animation mask for the face [1]. Some of the few examples of combined estimation without domain restricted model assumptions are [20, 8]. But in contrast to our approach the scene is still parameterized with respect to a base view, whereas we use the view-independent object space parameterization. Recently, [17] used a motion and voxel carving approach to recover both motion and structure. They use a fixed 6D-voxel grid to compute the structure and motion, while our subdivision surface representation enables us to optimize the different "frequency bands" of the mesh separately [15] similar to multi-grid methods in numerical analysis.

2   Preliminaries and Definitions

The camera configuration (Figure 1) is parameterized by the camera projection matrices M_k that relate the world coordinate system to the image coordinate system of camera k. The calibration is done using a calibration frame. In the following we assume that the images have already been corrected for radial distortion. We use the conventional pinhole camera model, where the surface point $\mathbf{P} = [x, y, z]^T$ in world coordinates projects to image point $\mathbf{p}_k$ in camera k. The image coordinates and brightness intensity of this point under the assumption of Lambertian reflectance properties for the head are given by

$$\mathbf{p}_k = f \frac{M_k[\mathbf{P}; 1]}{M_k^3[\mathbf{P}; 1]} \tag{1}$$

$$I(\mathbf{p}_k; t) = -c_k \cdot \rho(\mathbf{P}) \cdot [\mathbf{n}(\mathbf{P}; t) \cdot \mathbf{s}(\mathbf{P}; t)] \tag{2}$$

where f is the focal length, M_k^3 is the third row of M_k, $[\mathbf{P}; 1]$ is the homogeneous representation of $\mathbf{P}$, $\rho(\mathbf{P})$ is the albedo of point $\mathbf{P}$, c_k is the constant that describes the brightness gain for each camera, $\mathbf{n}$ is the normal to the surface at $\mathbf{P}$, and $\mathbf{s}$ the direction of incoming light (see [4]). We assume that $\rho(\mathbf{P})$ is constant over time ($d\rho/dt = 0$). In addition, since we record the video sequences with 60Hz, we have $d/dt[\mathbf{n}(\mathbf{P}; t) \cdot \mathbf{s}(\mathbf{P}; t)] = 0$. Thus the brightness of $\mathbf{p}_k$ stays constant over short time intervals.

There are many different ways to represent surfaces in space. For example B-spline surfaces, deformable models, iso-surfaces or level-sets, and polygonal meshes (for an overview see [5]). Subdivision surfaces combine the ease of manipulating polygonal meshes with the implicit smoothness properties of B-spline surfaces. Starting from a control mesh C, we recursively subdivide the mesh according to a set of rules until in the limit we generate a smooth limit surface S. Examples for different subdivision schemes can be found in [11].

A Loop-subdivision surface can be evaluated analytically [14] for every surface point in dependence of its control points. We can express the position of any mesh surface point $\mathbf{s}$ as a linear combination of the subdivision control points $\mathbf{c}_i$, if we denote the limit matrix by L_i, we can write $\mathbf{s} = L_i\,\mathbf{c}_i$. The number of control points determines the degrees of freedom of the mesh. On each level i, we can express the position of the control points $\mathbf{c}_i$ as a linear combination (denoted by the refinement matrices C_i, D_i) of the control points on a coarser level $\mathbf{c}_{i-1}$ and the detail coefficients $\mathbf{d}_{i-1}$ that express the additional degrees of freedom of the new vertices inserted in the refinement step from level $i-1$ to level i. Formally, we can write $\mathbf{s} = L_i c_i = L_i[C_{i-1}D_{i-1}]\begin{bmatrix}\mathbf{c}_{i-1}\\\mathbf{d}_{i-1}\end{bmatrix}$. The decomposition can now be iterated (similar to [9])

$$
\begin{aligned}
s &= L_i c_i = L_i[C_{i-1}D_{i-1}]\begin{bmatrix}\mathbf{c}_{i-1}\\\mathbf{d}_{i-1}\end{bmatrix} \\[2mm]
&= L_i[C_{i-1}D_{i-1}]\begin{bmatrix}C_{i-2} & D_{i-2} & 0\\ 0 & 0 & I_{i-1}\end{bmatrix}\begin{bmatrix}\mathbf{c}_{i-2}\\\mathbf{d}_{i-2}\\\mathbf{d}_{i-1}\end{bmatrix} \\[2mm]
&= L_i[C_{i-1}D_{i-1}]\begin{bmatrix}C_{i-2} & D_{i-2} & 0\\ 0 & 0 & I_{i-1}\end{bmatrix}\cdots\begin{bmatrix}C_0 & D_0 & 0 & \cdots & 0\\ 0 & 0 & I_1 & 0 & 0\\ 0 & 0 & 0 & \ddots & 0\\ 0 & 0 & 0 & 0 & I_{i-1}\end{bmatrix}[\mathbf{c}_0,\mathbf{d}_0,\mathbf{d}_1,\ldots,\mathbf{d}_{i-1}]^T.
\end{aligned}
\tag{3}
$$

This forms the basis of our coarse-to-fine algorithm. Starting from a coarse mesh with only few control points, we find the mesh that optimizes our error criterion. The mesh is then subdivided, thereby increasing the degrees of freedom which enables the algoritm to adapt the mesh resolution according to the complexity of the surface geometry and motion field.

3   Multi-camera Stereo Estimation

We incrementally construct the object silhouettes in each view by modeling the temporal dynamics of the changing foreground pixels and the static background pixels. The intersection of the silhouettes in world space defines the maximal extent of the object. Using information from silhouettes alone, it is not possible to compute more than the visual hull [7] of the object in view. Therefore, to refine our 3D surface estimate of the object, we adapt the vertices of the mesh in consecutive time frames to optimize the following error measure.

Following equation (2), we can assume that the brightness of the projection of $\mathbf{P}$ is the same in all images up to a linear gain and offset, and that it is only changing slowly over time. Each patch $\mathcal{T}$ on the object surfaces traces out a volume in the spatio-temporal image space of each camera. The integration domain is the 1-ring of triangles around each control point. Thus, after determining the visibility of each mesh triangle in all the cameras by a z-buffer algorithm ($\mathcal{V}$ is the set of all pairs of cameras that can both observe the mesh patch), we define the following matching functional in space-time (similar to [2])

$$\mathcal{E}(\mathcal{T}, t) = \sum_{(i,j) \in \mathcal{V}} \mathcal{W}(i,j) \frac{\langle I_i(t), I_j(t) \rangle}{|I_i(t)| \cdot |I_j(t)|} + \sum_i \frac{\langle I_i(t), I_i(t+1) \rangle}{|I_i(t)| \cdot |I_i(t+1)|} \qquad (4)$$

$$+ \sum_{(i,j) \in \mathcal{V}} \mathcal{W}(i,j) \frac{\langle I_i(t+1), I_j(t+1) \rangle}{|I_i(t+1)| \cdot |I_j(t+1)|}$$

$$\langle I_i(t), I_j(t) \rangle = \int_{\mathbf{P} \in \mathcal{T}} (I_i(\mathbf{p}_i(\mathbf{P}, t)) - \overline{I_i(t)}) \cdot (I_j(\mathbf{p}_j(\mathbf{P}, t)) - \overline{I_j(t)}) d\mathbf{P} \qquad (5)$$

$$\overline{I_i(t)} = \int_{\mathbf{P} \in \mathcal{T}} I_i(\mathbf{p}_i(\mathbf{P}, t)) d\mathbf{P}, \quad |I_i(t)|^2 = \langle I_i(t), I_i(t) \rangle \qquad (6)$$

to compare corresponding spatio-temporal image volumes between pairs of cameras. The correspondence hypotheses are based on the current 3D structure and motion estimate given by the position of the mesh control points at time t and $t + 1$. We combine the correlation scores from all the camera pairs by taking a weighted average with the weights $\mathcal{W}(i, j)$ depending on the angles between optical axes of cameras i and j and the surface normal at point $\mathbf{P}$.

The derivatives with respect to the control points can then be computed easily from the derivative of the projection equation (Eq. 1) and the spatio-temporal image derivatives. We use the BFGS-quasi newton method in MATLAB^{TM} Optimization Toolbox to optimize over the control point positions. The upper bounds for their displacement is given by the silhouette boundaries, which we include as inequality constraints in the optimization. The multi-resolution framework improves the convergence of the optimization similar to multi-grid methods in numerical analysis, since the coarser meshes initialize the refined mesh already close to the true solution which allows us to reduce the size of spatio-temporal image volumes we compare, thus increasing efficiency and accuracy.

4   Results

We have established in our laboratory a multi-camera network consisting of sixty-four cameras, Kodak ES-310, providing images at a rate of up to eighty-five frames per second; the video is collected directly on disk. The cameras are

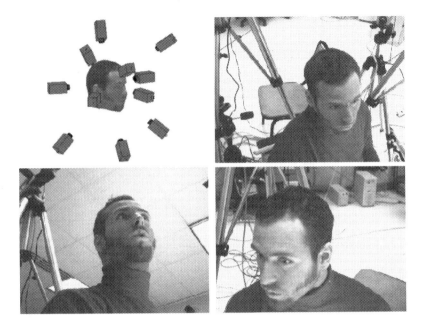

Fig. 1. Calibrated Camera Setup with Example Input Views

connected by a high-speed network consisting of sixteen dual processor Pentium 450s with 1 GB of RAM each which process the data.

For our experiments we used eleven cameras, 9 gray scale and 2 color, placed in a dome-like arrangement around the head of a person who was opening his mouth to express surprise (Figure 1) while turning his head and moving it forward. The recovered spatio-temporal structure enables us to synthesize texture-mapped views of the head from arbitrary viewing directions (Figures 2a-2c). The textures, coming always from the least oblique camera with respect to a given mesh triangle, were not blended together to illustrate the good agreement between adjacent texture region boundaries (note the agreement between the grey-value structures in 2c despite absolute grey-value differences). This demonstrates that the spatial structure of the head was recovered very well.

To separate the non-rigid 3D flow of the mouth gesture from the motion field due to the turning of the head, we fit a rigid flow field to the 3D motion flow field by parameterizing the 3D motion flow vectors by the instantaneous rigid motion $\partial \mathbf{P}/\partial t = \mathbf{v} + \boldsymbol{\omega} \times \mathbf{P}$, where $\mathbf{v}$ and $\boldsymbol{\omega}$ are the instantaneous translation, and rotation ([4]). We use iteratively reweighted least squares to solve for the rigid motion parameters treating the non-rigid motion flow vectors as data outliers. By subtracting the rigid motion flow from the full flow, we extract the non-rigid flow. It can be seen that the motion energy (integrated magnitude of the flow) is concentrated in the non-rigid regions of the face such as the mouth and the jaw as indicated by the higher brightness values in Figure 2d. In contrast, the motion energy on the rigid part of the head (e.g., forehead, nose and ears) is significantly smaller. In the close up view of the mouth region (Figure 2f) we can easily see, how the mouth opens, and the jaw moves down. The brightness values in Figure 2d are increasing proportionally with the magnitude of the motion energy. Although, it is obviously hard to visualize dynamic movement by static imagery, the vector field and motion energy plots (Figures 2d-2f) illustrate that the dominant motion – the opening of the mouth – has been correctly estimated.

5   Conclusion and Future Work

To conclude, we presented a method that is able to recover an accurate 3D spatio-temporal description of an object by combining the structure and motion estimation in a unified framework. The technique can incorporate any number of cameras and the achievable depth and motion resolution depends only on the available imaging hardware. In the future, we plan to explore other surface representations and to study the connection between multi-scale mesh representation and multi-scale structure of image sequences that observe them to increase the robustness of the algorithm even further.

References

1. I.A. Essa and A.P. Pentland. Coding, analysis, interpretation, and recognition of facial expressions. *IEEE Trans. PAMI*, 19:757–763, 1997.
2. O. Faugeras and R. Keriven. Complete dense stereovision using level set methods. In *Proc. Europ. Conf. Computer Vision*, pages 379–393, Freiburg, Germany, 1998.
3. P. Fua. Regularized bundle-adjustment to model heads from image sequences without calibration data. *Int. Journal of Computer Vision*, 38:153–171, 2000.
4. B. K. P. Horn. *Robot Vision*. McGraw Hill, New York, 1986.
5. Andreas Hubeli and Markus Gross. A survey of surface representations for geometric modeling. Technical Report 335, ETH Zürich, Institute of Scientific Computing, March 2000.
6. I.A. Kakadiaris and D. Metaxas. Three-dimensional human body model acquisition from multiple views. *Int. Journal of Computer Vision*, 30:191–218, 1998.
7. A. Laurentini. The visual hull concept for silhouette-based image understanding. *IEEE Trans. PAMI*, 16:150–162, 1994.
8. S. Malassiotis and M.G. Strintzis. Model-based joint motion and structure estimation from stereo images. *Computer Vision and Image Understanding*, 65:79–94, 1997.
9. C. Mandal, H. Qin, and B.C. Vemuri. Physics-based shape modeling and shape recovery using multiresolution subdivision surfaces. In *Proc. of ACM SIGGRAPH*, 1999.
10. R. Plänkers and P. Fua. Tracking and modeling people in video sequences. *Int. Journal of Computer Vision*, 2001. to appear.
11. P. Schröder and D. Zorin. Subdivision for modeling and animation. Siggraph 2000 Course Notes, 2000.

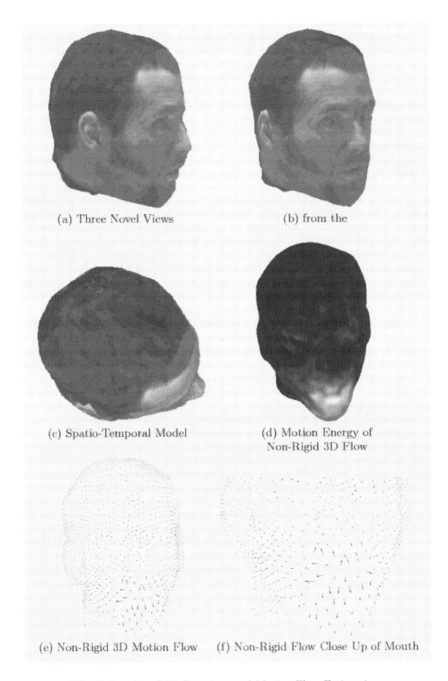

(a) Three Novel Views

(b) from the

(c) Spatio-Temporal Model

(d) Motion Energy of
Non-Rigid 3D Flow

(e) Non-Rigid 3D Motion Flow   (f) Non-Rigid Flow Close Up of Mouth

Fig. 2. Results of 3D Structure and Motion Flow Estimation

12. S. Seitz and C. Dyer. Photorealistic scene reconstruction by voxel coloring. *Int. Journal of Computer Vision*, 25, November 1999.
13. H. Spies, B. Jähne, and J.L. Barron. Regularised range flow. In *Proc. Europ. Conf. Computer Vision*, Dublin, Ireland, June 2000.
14. J. Stam. Evaluation of loop subdivision surfaces. SIGGRAPH'99 Course Notes, 1999.
15. G. Taubin. A signal processing approach to fair surface design. In *Proc. of ACM SIGGRAPH*, 1995.
16. S. Vedula, S. Baker, P. Rander, R. Collins, and T. Kanade. Three-dimensional scene flow. In *Proc. Int. Conf. Computer Vision*, Corfu,Greece, September 1999.
17. S. Vedula, S. Baker, S. Seitz, and T. Kanade. Shape and motion carving in 6d. In *Proc. IEEE Conf. Computer Vision and Pattern Recognition*, Head Island, South Carolina, USA, June 2000.
18. S. Vedula, P. Rander, H. Saito, and T. Kanade. Modeling, combining, and rendering dynamic real-world events from image sequences. In *Proc. of Int. Conf. on Virtual Systems and Multimedia*, Gifu, Japan, November 1998.
19. S. Weik. Passive full body scanner using shape from silhouettes. In *Proc. Int. Conf. on Pattern Recognition*, Barcelona, Spain, 2000.
20. Y. Zhang and C. Kambhamettu. Integrated 3d scene flow and structure recovery from multiview image sequences. In *Proc. IEEE Conf. Computer Vision and Pattern Recognition*, pages II:674–681, Hilton Head, 2000.

3D Anisotropic Diffusion Filtering for Enhancing Noisy Actin Filament Fluorescence Images

Hanno Scharr[1] and Dietmar Uttenweiler[2]

[1] Interdisciplinary Center for Scientific Computing,
Ruprecht-Karls-University, Im Neuenheimer Feld 368, 69120 Heidelberg, Germany
Hanno.Scharr@iwr.uni-heidelberg.de
[2] Institute of Physiology and Pathophysiology, Medical Biophysics,
Ruprecht-Karls-University, Im Neuenheimer Feld 326, 69120 Heidelberg, Germany
Dietmar.Uttenweiler@urz.uni-heidelberg.de

Abstract. We present a PDE-based method for increasing the S/N ratio in noisy fluorescence image sequences where particle motion has to be measured quantitatively. The method is based on a novel accurate discretization of 3-D non linear anisotropic diffusion filtering, where the third dimension is the time t in the image sequence, using well adapted diffusivities. We have applied this approach to fluorescence image sequences of *in vitro* motility assay experiments, where fluorescently labelled actin filaments move over a surface of immobilized myosin. The S/N ratio can be drastically improved resulting in closed object structures, which even allows segmentation of individual filaments in single images. In general this approach will be very valuable when quantitatively measuring motion in low light level fluorescence image sequences used in biomedical and biotechnological applications for studying cellular and subcellular processes and in *in vitro* single molecule assays.

Keywords: Anisotropic Diffusion Filtering, Fluorescence Microscopy, Image Restoration, Image Sequence Processing, Noise.

1   Introduction

Fluorescence imaging techniques have emerged to central quantitative tools in biomedical and biotechnological research. With the high spatial and temporal resolution they are ideally suited to study the spatio-temporal characteristics of cellular, subcellular and molecular processes in a wide variety of applications [8]. This includes the fundamental regulation of cell function by second messengers, e.g. Ca^{2+}-ions, and its pathological alterations associated with many diseases. Further common applications are metabolic pathway analysis for drug design and single molecule studies for the basic understanding of the complex molecular interactions involved in the cellular processes.

However, fluorescence image sequences from dynamic molecular assays pose very high demands on image processing, since the S/N ratio is generally low due to the limited amount of photons available for detection. Therefore the image

B. Radig and S. Florczyk (Eds.): DAGM 2001, LNCS 2191, pp. 69–75, 2001.

sequences obtained from these experiments require special sophisticated methods for image enhancing and a quantitative analysis.

Therefore we have now developed a 3D anisotropic diffusion filter method as an extension of the common 2D anisotropic methods (see e.g. [7], [11]) in order to use the full 3D information of these spatio-temporal datasets for image enhancement. Especially the enhancement and restoration of object features in individual images will be presented, which even allows the reliable segmentation and analysis of individual moving objects.

2   Actin Filament Movement in the *in vitro* Motility Assay

The *in vitro* motility assay originally devised by Kron and Spudich [5] is a typical example, where dynamic molecular behavior is studied with highly sensitive fluorescence imaging (see figure 1). It is routinely used to study the molecular origin of force production and its alterations by various medically relevant modulators, as e.g. volatile anesthetics. The experimental set-up consists of a flow chamber, where isolated actin filaments, which are labelled with the fluorescence indicator rhodamine-phalloidin, move in the presence of adenosine triphosphate (ATP) over a surface of the immobilized motor protein myosin. The chamber is mounted on an epi-fluorescence microscope and a highly sensitive intensified CCD-camera is used to record the fluorescence. Since the fluorescence originates from single fluorescently labelled actin filaments with a diameter of 5 nm, which is much less than the microscopic resolution, the S/N ratio is very low.

In previous work [9] we could show that the structure tensor method [2] can be successfully applied to the quantitative analysis of particle motion in low S/N ratio actin filament fluorescence images, where classical particle tracking approaches fail to produce reliable results due to massive segmentation errors. As a pixel based method the structure tensor is ideally suited to determine the velocity distributions of the moving actin filaments in this experiment. However, if individual particle properties, e.g. path length or filament flexibility, are of interest further analysis has to be carried out.

In the following we will therefore present a new approach for analyzing actin filament motion in these fluorescence image sequences based on a 3D anisotropic diffusion filter method.

3   Anisotropic Diffusion

Every dimension of an image sequence will be treated as a spatial dimension, thus a 2D image sequence is treated as a 3D data set. The original image will be changed by applying anisotropic diffusion, which is expressed by a diffusion time t. Anisotropic diffusion with a diffusion tensor evolves the initial image u under an evolution equation of type

$$\frac{\partial u}{\partial t} = \nabla \cdot (D \nabla u) \qquad (1)$$

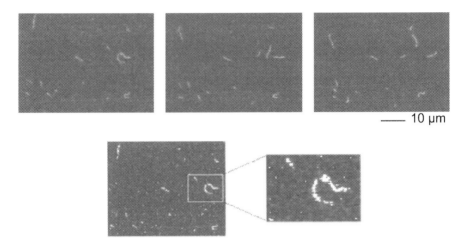

10 μm

Fig. 1. Top row: 3 images from a time series of fluorescence images, where actin filament motion is visible as the displacement of rod-like structures. Bottom row: A standard threshold segmentation of an area of interest from the first image shows, that particle segmentation is difficult in these low S/N ratio image sequences due to the high amount of noise inherent to single molecule fluorescence images. Data from [9].

with the evolving image $u(x, t)$, diffusion time t, 3D derivation vector $\nabla = (\partial_{x_1}, \partial_{x_2}, \partial_{x_3})^T$ and the diffusion tensor D, a positive definite, symmetric 3×3 matrix. It is adapted to the local image structure measured by the structure tensor [2]

$$J_\rho(\nabla u_\xi) = G_\rho * (\nabla u_\xi \nabla u_\xi^T) \tag{2}$$

with convolution $*$, a Gaussian G_ρ with standard deviation ρ, and $u_\xi := G_\xi * u$, a regularized version of u. The normalized eigenvectors e_i of J_ρ give the preferred local orientations, its eigenvalues μ_i give the local contrast along these directions. The structure tensor is highly robust under isotropic additive Gaussian noise [3]. Using a diagonal matrix M with $M_{ii} = \mu_i$, J_ρ can be written

$$J_\rho = (e_1, e_2, e_3)M(e_1, e_2, e_3)^T$$

The diffusion tensor D uses the same eigenvectors e_i. With the directional diffusivities $\lambda_1, \lambda_2, \lambda_3$ and a diagonal matrix Λ with $\Lambda_{ii} = \lambda_i$ it becomes

$$D = (e_1, e_2, e_3)\Lambda(e_1, e_2, e_3)^T . \tag{3}$$

The directional diffusivities λ_i determine the behavior of the diffusion. They shall be high for low values of μ_i and vice versa. In our application we use

$$\lambda_i := \begin{cases} 1 & \text{if } \mu_i \leq \sigma, \\ 1 - (1 - c)\exp(\frac{-d}{(\mu_i - \sigma)^2}) & \text{else,} \end{cases} \tag{4}$$

where $c \in]0,1]$, $d > 0$ and $\sigma > 0$ corresponds with the global absolute noise level. The condition number of D is bounded by $1/c$. Instead of this choice other functions can be used. In comparative tests (see sec. 5.2) we also use nonlinear isotropic diffusion with Tuckey's biweight in 2D and 3D (see e.g.[1]) and edge-enhancing diffusion in 2D ([10]). So far the continuous equations for anisotropic diffusion have been described. We now proceed by describing their discretization.

4   Accurate Discretization Scheme Using Optimized Filters

Eq. (1) can be solved using an Euler forward approximation for $\frac{\partial u}{\partial t}$

$$\frac{u_i^{l+1} - u_i^l}{\tau} = \nabla \cdot D\nabla u_i^l \Leftrightarrow u_i^{l+1} = u_i^l + \tau(\partial_{x_1}, \partial_{x_2}, \partial_{x_3})D(\partial_{x_1}, \partial_{x_2}, \partial_{x_3})^T u_i^l \quad (5)$$

where τ is the time step size and u_i^l denotes the approximation of $u(x,t)$ in the voxel i at (diffusion) time $l\tau$. We use optimized separable first order derivative filters to discretize $\nabla \cdot D_i^l \nabla$ (see [7] for the 2D case). They are composed of a common 1D derivative stencil (e.g. [-1, 0, 1]/2, denoted $\mathcal{D}$) and 1D smoothing kernels (e.g. [3, 10, 3]/16, denoted $\mathcal{B}$) in all other directions

$$\partial_{x_i} = \mathcal{D}_{x_i} * \mathcal{B}_{x_j} * \mathcal{B}_{x_k} \quad (6)$$

where $\{i, j, k\}$ is a permutation of $\{1, 2, 3\}$, lower indices at the brackets give the direction of the kernel and $*$ is a convolution. These filters have been derived in [6,4]. They approximate rotation invariance significantly better than related popular stencils. The following algorithm is repeated for every time step τ:

1. Calculate the structure tensor J (eq. (2)).
2. Get the diffusion tensor D by J (eqs. (3) and (4)).
3. Calculate the flux $j_i := \sum_{m=1}^{n} D_{i,m}\partial_{x_m}u$, $\forall i \in \{1, \ldots, n\}$
4. Calculate $\nabla \cdot (D_i^l \nabla u)$ (eq. (5) by $\nabla \cdot (D_i^l \nabla u) = \sum_{m=1}^{n} \partial_{x_m} j_m$.
5. Update in an explicit way (eq. (5)).

The iteration number is N and the total diffusion time T is $T = \tau N$.

5   Results

5.1   Validation with Synthetic Test Sequences

For the evaluation of image processing methods used for analyzing motility assay data we have created synthetic test data, as described in [9], in order to characterize the algorithms under known conditions. They consist of rod-like objects, which move in x-,y- and diagonal direction or in approximate circles, a basis of all possible displacements. Various amounts of Gaussian noise can be added. As shown in figure 2, the displacement of the objects are 1 pixel/frame for the motion in x,y-direction and for the circular motion and $\sqrt{2}$ pixel/frame for the

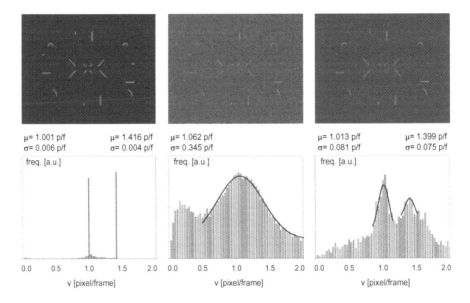

Fig. 2. Synthetic test data used to quantify the accuracy of the velocity reconstruction. The rod-like objects (grey values 200) move in x,y direction, in a 45 degree angle and in approximate circles, respectively, versus a black background. The test pattern with no noise, shown in the left panel, has Gaussian noise with a standard deviation of 60 grey levels added (middle panel). Applying the 3D anisotropic diffusion filtering resulted in the panel shown on the right. The respective velocity histograms as obtained with the structure tensor method, are given below each panel (velocity in pixel/frame or p/f).

diagonal direction. The addition of Gaussian noise with a standard deviation of 60 grey levels leads to the loss of resolution of both peaks and to a broadening of the velocity distribution as described in [9]. Applying the 3D anisotropic diffusion filtering results in a significant improvement of image quality and moreover successfully restores both velocity populations.

Even more important, the spatio-temporal filtering does not introduce significant errors in object velocities, as can be seen from the peaks of Gaussian fits applied to the histograms in figure 2. The error is below 5% for both velocity populations, which is remarkably since the original noisy data can not even be reliably analyzed as shown in the middle panel. Thus the 3D anisotropic diffusion algorithm presented here has both a very high accuracy and restoration power.

5.2   Denoising of Actin Filament Fluorescence Sequences

We applied the 3D anisotropic diffusion filtering to noisy image sequences of actin filament movement in the *in vitro* motility assay and additionally compared the results to commonly used 2D diffusion filtering schemes. From figure 3 it

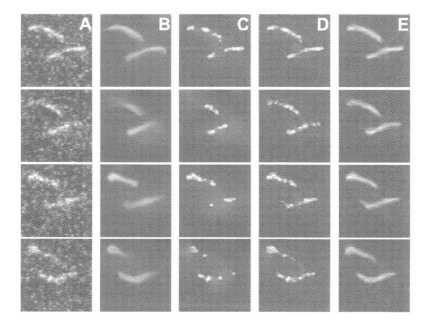

Fig. 3. Example of various diffusion filtering methods for the reconstruction of actin filaments in *in vitro* motility assay image sequences. **A** In the non processed original data the high amount of noise can be seen leading to non closed object structures for the filaments. **B** Edge enhancing diffusion in 2D leads to closed object structures but introduces significant errors at the leading and rear edge of the filaments. Nonlinear isotropic diffusion with Tuckey's biweight in **C** 2D and **D** 3D can not reconstruct closed object structures. **E** The 3D anisotropic diffusion scheme produces closed object structures without morphological changes in filament shape. Original fluorescence data from [9].

is evident, that the successful restoration of actin filaments with closed object structures can only be achieved when using the full spatio-temporal information in the 3D anisotropic diffusion scheme. Even the 2D anisotropic diffusion scheme can not compensate for the heavy degradation of object structures without introducing morphological errors. Therefore the extension of the existing 2D anisotropic diffusion schemes to a full 3D scheme proves to be a major advancement in analyzing noisy image sequences.

6   Summary and Conclusions

In summary we have presented a new approach to enhance noisy image sequences, especially in low light level fluorescence microscopy. The additional use of the temporal information in the anisotropic diffusion filtering enables for the first time a reliable restoration of particle properties, normally not possible with common 2D schemes. Additionally we have validated the method on computer generated test sequences, showing both the very high object restoration power and the very high accuracy in restoring the actual velocities of moving objects. We think that this approach is valuable in many other applications, where low light level dynamic processes have to be quantitatively analyzed by image sequence processing.

Supported by a grant of the Deutsche Forschungsgemeinschaft (FOR240/3-1).

References

[1] M. J. Black, G. Sapiro, D. Marimont, and D. Heeger. Robust anisotropic diffusion. *Trans. Im. Proc., Spec. issue on PDEs and Geom. Driven Diff.*, 7(3):421–432, March 1998.

[2] B. Jähne. Spatio-temporal image processing. In *Lecture Notes in Computer Science*, volume 751. Springer, 1993.

[3] B. Jähne. Performance characteristics of low-level motion estimators in spatiotemporal images. In *DAGM-Workshop Perf. Charact. and Quality of CV Algorithms*, 1997.

[4] B. Jähne, H. Scharr, and S. Körkel. Principles of filter design. In *Handbook on Computer Vision and Applications*, volume 2, pages 125–152. Academic Press, 1999.

[5] S. J. Kron and J. A. Spudich. Fluorescent actin filaments move on myosin fixed to a glass surface. *Proc. Natl. Acad. Sci. USA*, 83:6272–6276, 1986.

[6] H. Scharr. *Optimal Operators in Digital Image Processing*. PhD thesis, Uni. Heidelberg, 2000.

[7] H. Scharr and J. Weickert. An anisotropic diffusion algorithm with optimized rotation invariance. In *DAGM'2000*, September 2000.

[8] D. Uttenweiler and R. H. A. Fink. Dynamic fluorescence imaging. In H. Haußecker B. Jähne and P. Geißler, editors, *Handbook of Computer Vision and Applications*, volume 3, pages 323–346. Academic Press, b edition, 1999.

[9] D. Uttenweiler, C. Veigel, R. Steubing, C. Götz, S. Mann, H. Haussecker, B. Jähne, and R. H. A. Fink. Motion determination in actin filament fluorescence images with a spatio-temporal orientation analysis method. *Biophys. J.*, 78(5):2709–2715, 2000.

[10] J. Weickert. *Anisotropic diffusion in image processing*. Teubner, 1998.

[11] J. Weickert. Nonlinear diffusion filtering. In *Handbook on Computer Vision and Applications*, volume 2, pages 423–450. Academic Press, 1999.

A Point Set Registration Algorithm Using a Motion Model Based on Thin-Plate Splines and Point Clustering

J. Fieres, J. Mattes, and R. Eils

Division Intelligent Bioinformatics, DKFZ Heidelberg, 69 120 Heidelberg, Germany

Abstract. This paper focuses on the problem of ill-posedness of deformable point set registration where the point correspondences are not known a priori (in our case). The basic elements of the investigated kind of registration algorithm are a cost functional, an optimization strategy and a motion model which determines the kind of motions and deformations that are allowed and how they are restricted. We propose a method to specify a shape adapted deformation model based on thin-plate splines and point clustering and oppose it to the annealing of the regularization parameter and to a regular scheme for the warping of space with thin-plate splines. As criteria for the quality of the match we consider the preservation of physical/anatomical corresponding points.

Our natural deformation model is determined by placing the control points of the splines in a way adapted to the superimposed point sets during registration using a coarse-to-fine scheme. Our experiments with known ground truth show the impact of the chosen deformation model and that the shape oriented model recovers constantly very accurately corresponding points. We observed a stable improvement of this accuracy for a increasing number of control points.

1 Introduction

Registration of spatial data is a known problem in computer vision and is of great importance for many applications [12,7]). For instance, in medical image analysis one may want to compare 3-D patient data from a CT scan with an anatomical atlas in order to detect anomalies. Further applications are model-based image segmentation and tracking of deformable objects over time [13].

In order to register (or, "match") two images (or point sets) a parameterized transformation is applied to one of the images (the *sensed* image [12]). The parameters are then adjusted in such a way that the sensed image most accurately resembles the second image (the *reference* image). A classical way of registration comprises three basic elements: a cost functional an optimization strategy and, after rigid and affine registration, the specification of the allowed deformations and their restrictions. We will denote this third element as the *motion model*. The motion model is necessary to overcome the ill-posedness of the optimization problem, i.e. to restrict the solution space for an optimal fit. Physically or

B. Radig and S. Florczyk (Eds.): DAGM 2001, LNCS 2191, pp. 76–83, 2001.

anatomically corresponding points are found implicitly. Approaches extracting critical points in both images explicitly and identifying them thereafter [10,5,6] are very noise sensitive (therefore, [5] proposes a semi-automatic algorithm) and problematical especially for non-rigid registration. Additional image information is lost when defining the transformation just by interpolating or approximating between the extracted corresponding points.

For the registration of raw grey level images progress has been achieved to define a well suited cost functional and appropriate strategies optimizing it. Various so-called iconic similarity measures have been proposed [9]. Slowly converging non-gradient based optimization strategies such as downhill simplex or simulated annealing [8] have to be used. Non-rigid deformations are generally modeled by volume splines defined using a regular grid of control points [7]. On the other hand, methods operating on already extracted and reconstructed surfaces usually define the deformations only on the surfaces itself [13,1]. Approaches using physically based elasticity models have been proposed in this context [1]. In this paper we focus on the non-rigid registration of point sets. To use point set based methods for grey level image registration the application of low-level operators (edge detection, confinement tree extraction [6], etc.) is sufficient. They do not require surface reconstruction. Several cost functionals have been proposed [12,11,4]. The three algorithms we present here minimize in accordance with [12] the sum of the squared least distances of each sensed data point from the reference point set. They differ only in the chosen motion model. Volume deformations are specified by interpolating (as in [12]) between a number of displacement vectors located at certain spots in space. The end points of these vectors (the displacements) are the free parameters to be adjusted, whereas the start points—together with the amount of regularization (e.g., penalization of bending or strain [2]) and a coarse to fine scheme—determine the motion model, i.e. the set of possible deformations of which the best fitting one is chosen. The idea is to place the start points in the best suited way and to interpolate with thin-plate splines in order to be able to place them at any position in space.

We propose a new approach based on this idea. It is adapted to the shapes formed by the point sets. Using a point clustering approach, we place the start points where the discrepancy between the two surfaces is greatest. The two other methods are inspired by previous work. We choose the displacement start points on a rectangular multi-resolution grid similar to that used in [12] (where, however, the non-rigid volume deformations are represented by trilinear B-splines) and either increase the number of control points level by level or we use a fixed number of control points and produce a coarse to fine behavior similar as in [4] by the annealing of the regularization parameter. We compare the three different methods of choosing the motion model in terms of the achievable matching quality. Our criterion for the quality of the match is how good physically/anatomically corresponding points of the two surfaces are brought into registration for a given number of transformation parameters. As will be shown, the motion model can have a strong influence on the matching quality. We do not focus on statistical robustness (e.g., treatment of outlier points) in this work.

2   Problem Formulation and Techniques

For our purpose we state the non-rigid matching problem as follows. Given a reference set $S \subset \mathbb{R}^3$ fixed in space, a set of N (sensed) sample points $\{\mathbf{r}_i \in \mathbb{R}^3 | i = 1 \ldots N\}$, and a deformation $\mathbf{T} : \mathbb{R}^3 \times \Pi \to \mathbb{R}^3$, depending on a set of parameters $P \in \Pi$, with Π being the parameter space. Now find the set of parameters P^*, so that $\mathcal{C}(P^*) = \min_{P \in \Pi} \mathcal{C}(P)$, where

$$\mathcal{C}(P) = \sum_{i=1}^{N} \Big(d\big(\mathbf{T}(P, \mathbf{r}_i), S\big) \Big)^2 \tag{1}$$

is the so-called *cost* or *error functional*. Here, $d(\cdot, S)$ is the Euclidean distance from the surface S:

$$d(\mathbf{x}, S) = \min_{\mathbf{s} \in S} |\mathbf{x} - \mathbf{s}|.$$

The cost functional penalizes the sum of the squared distances of $\mathbf{r}_i$ from S.

To be accurate, the problem is still ill defined. In addition to the requirement that $\mathcal{C}$ is to be minimized we want the deformation to be "reasonable". For example—according to the definition above—the problem would be considered as solved if all sensed points $\mathbf{r}_i$ are mapped to one single point $\mathbf{s}$ on S, which is surely not the intended solution. The additional condition on the transformation is that "logically" corresponding points of the two shapes should be mapped to each other. For this, we specify a motion model in section 2.1 including *regularization* (an additional term in the cost function, which penalizes strong bending; see equation (2)) and stepwise matching from coarser to finer levels. As known, these strategies help to satisfy the correct-mapping criterion.

For representing a non-rigid volumetric deformation $\mathbf{T} : \mathbb{R}^3 \to \mathbb{R}^3, \mathbf{x} \mapsto \mathbf{T}(\mathbf{x})$ we use thin-plate splines. Those are determined by a number of pairs of control points which are mapped to each other (or, equivalently, a set of displacement vectors, located at certain positions in space). We will call the control points in the untransformed volume (resp. the start points of the displacement vectors) *A-landmarks*, or $\mathbf{p}^k$, and their homologs in the transformed volume (resp. the vector end points) *B-landmarks*, or $\mathbf{q}^k$. In the space between the control points the deformation is interpolated by thin-plate splines. Descriptively speaking, one may think of the space as a rubber cube that can be pulled in different directions at certain working points. A precise mathematical description of thin-plate spines in this context is given in *Bookstein, 1989* [3]. For registration, the A-landmarks are fixed using the schemes described in the next section. The positions of the B-landmarks are the free parameters of the deformation: $P = (q_x^1, q_y^1, q_z^1, \ldots, q_x^n, q_y^n, q_z^n)$ with n the total number of control point pairs.

Thin-plate splines are minimally bent while satisfying the interpolation constraints given by the control points ($\mathbf{T}(\mathbf{p}^k) = \mathbf{q}^k$):

$$U_{\text{bend}} = \int_{\mathbb{R}^3} \sum_{i,j,k} \left(\frac{\partial^2 T_i(\mathbf{x})}{\partial x_j \partial x_k} \right)^2 d^3x = \min.$$

The algebra of thin-plate splines allows to compute this quantity easily from the positions of the control points. We add this value to the cost function as as a regularization term, to prevent unintended effects arising from overly bending:

$$\mathcal{C}_{\text{total}} = \mathcal{C} + \alpha U_{\text{bend}}. \tag{2}$$

α is a weighting factor to be chosen (Please note that not the control points but all data points enter in $\mathcal{C}$; therefore equation (2) has not to be confused with work on approximating thin-plate splines [10,4]). The minimizing is done by the Levenberg-Marquardt algorithm, a standard derivative based non-linear mini- mizing method (cf., *Press et al.* [8]). The necessary computation of $\partial \mathcal{C}_{\text{total}}/\partial P$ is straight forward due to the simple algebra of thin-plate splines. For a fast estimation of $d(\mathbf{x}, S)$ and its derivative with respect to $\mathbf{x}$ (also necessary to compute $\partial \mathcal{C}_{\text{total}}/\partial P$) we use a precomputed distance map ("octree spline") as proposed in [12]. Here, the values of $d(\mathbf{x}, S)$ are computed only for the corners of a multi-resolution grid around the reference set, and stored. Then, $d(\mathbf{x}, S)$ can be estimated for an arbitrary point by finding the eight nearest corner values and interpolating between them. Since the interpolating function is differentiable in between the corners the derivative can also be assessed.

2.1   Choosing a Motion Model by Placing the A-Landmarks

While the B-landmarks serve as transformation parameters, being adjusted by the Levenberg-Marquardt algorithm, the positions of the A-landmarks stay con- stant during the matching process and have to be fixed initially. Their placing— together with the amount of regularization—determines the motion model. It turns out that the choice of the positions of the A-landmarks can have a strong impact on the matching quality. In this work we investigate the effects of the chosen motion model, and we evaluate three different approaches, all of which incorporate the coarse-to-fine idea. Approaches A and B are inspired by previous work, method C is the main contribution of this paper.

A: Octree Method (level-by-level). For choosing the positions of the A- landmarks, we employ an octree representation ([12], and see Figure 1) of the untransformed sensed surface. The octree is built as follows. Starting with an initial cube containing the shape of interest, each cube is recursively split into 8 sub-cubes unless a cube doesn't contain parts of the shape, or a pre-set minimum cube size is reached. Obviously, with this process a hierarchical multi-resolution grid is formed, which has a finer resolution close to the shape. We place one A- landmark in the center of each octree cube. In the coarsest step we use a 2-level octree, resulting in 9 A-landmarks (one from the initial cube plus 8 from the 8 sub-cubes of the second octree level). The transformation is initialized with the identity mapping ($\mathbf{q}^k = \mathbf{p}^k$). After running Levenberg-Marquardt, yielding the transformation $\mathbf{T}^{(1)}$, we add more A-landmarks, corresponding to the next finer octree level. The homologous new B-landmarks are initialized with $\mathbf{q}^k = \mathbf{T}^{(1)}(\mathbf{p}^k)$ and another run of Levenberg-Marquardt results in the transformation $\mathbf{T}^{(2)}$. This procedure is repeated until the finest desired level is reached.

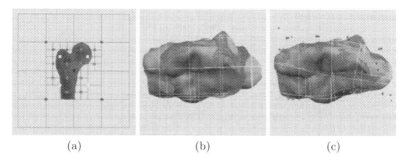

(a)   (b)   (c)

Fig. 1. (a) *5-level octree associated with the shown 3-D surface (orthogonal projection) and corresponding A-landmarks (level 1-4 only), different levels drawn in different colors.* **(b),(c)** *Matching of two cell nuclei. Filled: reference surface; wire-frame: sensed surface. A grid is superimposed to show the occurring volume deformation. (a) After affine registration. (b) after thin-plate spline registration with method A, level 4. The small balls are the B-landmarks.*

B: "Annealing"-Method (octree-based). The coarse-to-fine strategy, necessary to prevent early local deformation which can result in wrong registrations, is incorporated not by increasing the number of control points but by letting the parameter α in (2) decrease stepwise from "infinity" while after each change of α the minimization algorithm is run once. The landmarks are inserted at once for all desired levels of the same octree as in A. The decrease schedule was exponential with five steps, where the minium value of α was the same as in method A. Increasing the number of steps didn't improve matching results (see section 3).

C: Distance Cluster Method. The idea behind this method is to place the A-landmarks where the displacement between the two shapes is strongest. As in method A we follow a coarse to fine scheme by incrementally adding more control points. In each step, the positions of the new A-landmarks are determined as follows: We apply a K-Means clustering on the sensed data points, where the mean of each cluster is computed as a weighted center-of-mass with the "mass" of each data point $\mathbf{r}_i$ being dependent on the distance of $\mathbf{T}^{(n)}(\mathbf{r}_i)$ from the reference surface:

$$\mathrm{CM}_i = \frac{\sum_{j \in \Delta_i} \mathbf{r}_j \cdot d(\mathbf{T}^{(n)}(\mathbf{r}_j), S)^3}{\sum_{l \in \Delta_i} d(\mathbf{T}^{(n)}(\mathbf{r}_l), S)^3},$$

where Δ_i is the set of the indices of data points associated with the ith cluster center. Taking the 3rd power of d is an heuristic proposal. After convergence of the K-means algorithm the CM_i will lie preferably in regions of strong distances $d(\mathbf{T}(\mathbf{r}_i), S)$. The A-landmarks are inserted at the CM_i. As in method A, $\mathbf{T}^{(n)}$ is the identity transformation at the start, and in further steps the current thin-plate spline deformation. Again, the corresponding B-landmarks are initialized according to that transformation.

In the first step, 8 additional landmarks are set on the corners of a bounding box containing the sensed surface, and only one landmark at the CM of the whole shape (K-Means with $k = 1$). How many new landmarks to add in each of the further coarse-to-fine steps is a thing left to be investigated. In our experiments it turned out to be advantageous to add $1 + 3n$ new A-landmarks, where n is the number of steps already taken. In the last step, this rule was trimmed in order to reach the desired number of control points.

3   Experimental Results

We took the surface of a cell nucleus, reconstructed from confocal laser microscopy image data, and deformed it with 9 different random thin-pate-spline deformations. These consisted in 3 successive steps: one coarse deformation (7 random control points, displaced randomly by a relatively large distance), one intermediate step (20 points with moderate displacements), and a fine deformation (40 points, displaced by a relatively small distance). We then matched the deformed cells to the original reference point set, using the 3 different motion models on 3 different levels of fineness (all in all 54 experiments).

To evaluate the matching quality we took the distances of all deformed sensed points from their *corresponding* reference points (difference from ground truth):

$$\Psi = \sum_{i=1}^{N} |T(\mathbf{r}_i) - \mathbf{m}_i|^2,$$

where $\mathbf{r}_i$ are the sensed data points, $\mathbf{m}_i$ are the reference data points, and N is the number of data points. In contrast, the cost function (1) measures the distances of the sensed data points from the *nearest* reference point.

Figure 2 shows the values of Ψ for all the experiments. We can see that the cluster method (C) gives the best quality (low Ψ) on both levels of fineness. This is also true for an even coarser level of 3, resp. 9 landmarks (not shown). The "annealing" method (B) produces higher error values when we get to the finer level. This instability is probably the consequence of early local registrations due to the initially high number of control points. Further refinement of the "annealing rate" didn't improve the results. Methods A and B in contrast produce monotonously better matches with more degrees of freedom.

Another thing to note is that the values Ψ of the cluster method (C) on the coarse level are comparably good as (sometimes better than) method A on the fine level. This suggests that the cluster method is well suited to establish an appropriate motion model using only relatively few adjustable parameters (69 vs. 271 control points). This drastically decreases computation time, since its dependence on the number of control points is approximately quadratic. A low number of transformation parameters is also helpful for the concise description of the deformation and for the comprehension of the mechanisms behind it.

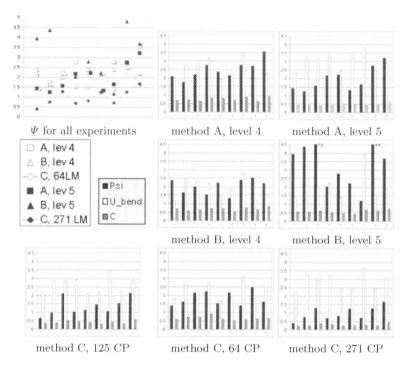

Fig. 2. *9 matches have been executed for each of the three A-landmark placing methods and on two degrees of fineness.* **The diagram in the upper left corner** *displays the values of Ψ (our measure for the matching quality, lower values are better) for all experiments. The symbols representing method C have been connected by lines for emphasis.* **The second column** *shows only the results for the coarse level, corresponding to an octree level of four (64 control points (CP) in average). For the cluster method we took also 64 CP in total. Shown are the values of Ψ, the occurring bending energy U_{bend}, and the cost C.* **The third column** *shows the same data for the fine level, corresponding to an octree level of five, resp. 271 CP in average. For method C, 271 CP, the values of C are way below those for methods A and B. In order to have a better basis—when comparing Ψ—to assess the ability of the methods to find correct associations, we decreased the number to 125, resulting in a value of C similar to methods A and B. The result is shown in the* **lower left corner**.

4   Conclusion

We showed that in deformable registration choosing an appropriate motion model can strongly improve the matching quality and can allow an immense decrease of the number of parameters to be adjusted and hence of computation time. The presented method was able to save 75% of the free transformation parameters in one experiment while preserving matching quality (method C, coarse, 1:25 min average execution time, vs. method A, fine, 64 min; see Figure 2). This permits also a very concise description of the deformation.

Chui and *Rangarajan* [4] proposed a thin-plate spline based point matching algorithm using deterministic annealing as a minimization method. In their approach the coarse-to-fine idea enters by slowly decreasing the regularization parameter, being dependent on the annealing temperature. Our results give strong evidence that doing coarse-to-fine matching solely through regularization is not optimal and especially sensitive to the number of degrees of freedom.

Further work will include the comparison between the use of thin-plate splines (TPS) and of trilinear B-splines to interpolate the volume deformations in the motion model. Therefore, we have to produce ground truth (i.e., synthetic image pairs) using non-TPS transformations for establishing a more objective validation. We will also test the algorithm with natural image pairs. Due to the lack of a ground truth we evaluate matching quality by comparing manually selected corresponding points.

References

1. Amini, A.A., Duncan, J.S.: Bending and stretching models for LV wall motion analysis from curves and surfaces, Image and Vision Comp. **10**(6) (1992) 418–430
2. Bogen, D.K., Rahdert, D.A.: A strain energy approach to regularization in displacement field fits of elastically deforming bodies. IEEE Trans. PAMI **18** (1996) 629-635
3. Bookstein, F.: Principal wraps: Thin-plate splines and the decomposition of deformations. IEEE Trans. PAMI **11** (1989) 567–585
4. Chui, H., Rangarajan, A.: A New Algorithm for Non-Rigid Point Matching. CVPR 2000
5. Frantz, S., Rohr, K., Stiehl, H.S.: Localization of 3D anatomical point landmarks in 3D tomographic images using deformable models. In: MICCAI 2000, Delp, S.L., DiGioia, A.M., Jaramaz, B. (Eds.). LNCS. Springer-Verlag (2000) 492–501
6. Mattes, J. and Demongeot, J.: Structural outlier detection for automatic landmark extraction. In: SPIE Medical Imaging 2001, San Diego, (2001, in press)
7. Meyer, C.R., Boes, J.L., Kim, B., Bland, P.H., Zasadny, K.R., Kison, P.V., Koral, K., Frey, K.A., Wahl, R.L.: Demonstration of accuracy and clinical versatility of mutual information for automatic multimodality image fusion affine and thin-plate spline warped geometric deformations. Med. Image Analysis **1**(3) (1996) 195–206
8. Press, W.H., Teukolsky, S.A., Vetterling, W.T. Flannery, B.P.: Numerical Recipes in C: The Art of Scientific Computing. Cambridge Univ. Press (1992) 2nd edition
9. Roche, A., Malandain, G., Ayache, N., Prima, S.: Towards a better comprehension of similarity measures used in medical image registration. In: MICCAI'99, C. Taylor, A. Clochester (Eds.). LNCS 1679. Springer-Verlag (1999) 555–566
10. Rohr, K.: Image registration based on thin-plate splines and local estimates of anisotropic landmark localization uncertainties. In: MICCAI'98. LNCS 1496. Springer-Verlag (1998) 1174–1183
11. Sclaroff, S., Pentland, A.P.: Modal matching for correspondence and recognition. IEEE Trans. PAMI **17** (1995) 545–561
12. Szeliski, R., Lavallée, S.: Matching 3-D anatomical surfaces with non-rigid deformations using octree-splines. Int. J. of Computer Vision **18(2)** (1996) 171–186
13. Terzopoulos, D., Metaxas, D.: Dynamic models with local and global deformations: Deformable superquadrics. IEEE Trans. PAMI **13**(7) (1991) 703–714

Optimal Camera Orientation from Points and Straight Lines

Marc Luxen and Wolfgang Förstner

Institut für Photogrammetrie, Universität Bonn
Nußallee 15, D-53115 Bonn
Germany
luxen/wf@ipb.uni-bonn.de,
WWW home page: http://www.ipb.uni-bonn.de

Abstract. This paper presents an optimal estimate for the projection matrix for points of a camera from an arbitrary mixture of six or more observed points and straight lines in object space. It gives expressions for determining the corresponding projection matrix for straight lines together with its covariance matrix. Examples on synthetic and real images demonstrate the feasibility of the approach.

1 Introduction

Determining the orientation of a camera is a basic task in computer vision and photogrammetry. Direct as well as iterative solutions for calibrated and uncalibrated cameras are well known, in case only points are used as basic entities. Hartley and Zisserman (cf. [4], pp. 166-169) indicate how to use point and line observations simultaneously for estimating the projection matrix for points. However, they give no optimal solution to this problem.

We present a procedure for optimal estimation of the projection matrix and for determining the covariance matrix of its entries. This can be used to derive the covariance matrix of the projection matrix for lines, which allows to infer the uncertainty of projecting lines and planes from observed points and lines.

The paper is organized as follows: Section 2 presents some basic tools from algebraic projective geometry, gives expressions for the projection of 3D points and lines from object space into the image plane of a camera and explains the determination of the matrix Q for line projection from the matrix P for point projection. Section 3 describes the procedure to estimate P and to derive the covariance matrices of the orientation parameters. Finally we give examples to demonstrate the feasibility of the approach.

2 Basics

We first give the necessary tools from algebraic projective geometry easing the computation of statistically uncertain geometric entities.

B. Radig and S. Florczyk (Eds.): DAGM 2001, LNCS 2191, pp. 84–91, 2001.

2.1   Points, Lines, and Planes and Their Images

Points $\mathbf{x}^\mathsf{T} = (\boldsymbol{x}_0^\mathsf{T}, x_h)$ and lines $\mathbf{l} = (\boldsymbol{l}_h^\mathsf{T}, l_0)$ in the plane are represented with 3-vectors, splitted into their homogeneous part, indexed with h, and non-homogeneous part indexed with 0. Points $\mathbf{X} = (\boldsymbol{X}_0^\mathsf{T}, X_h)$ and planes $\mathbf{A} = (\boldsymbol{A}_h^\mathsf{T}, A_0)$ in 3D space are represented similarly. Lines $\mathbf{L}$ in 3D are represented with their *Plücker coordinates* $\mathbf{L}^\mathsf{T} = (\boldsymbol{L}_h^\mathsf{T}, \boldsymbol{L}_0^\mathsf{T})$. It can be derived from two points $\mathbf{X}$ and $\mathbf{Y}$ by the direction $\boldsymbol{L}_h = Y_h \boldsymbol{X}_0 - X_h \boldsymbol{Y}_0$ of the line and the normal $\boldsymbol{L}_0 = \boldsymbol{X}_0 \times \boldsymbol{Y}_0$ of the plane through the line and the origin. We will need the dual 3D-line $\overline{\mathbf{L}}^\mathsf{T} = (\boldsymbol{L}_0^\mathsf{T}, \boldsymbol{L}_h^\mathsf{T})$ which has homogeneous and non-homogeneous part interchanged. The line parameters have to fulfill the *Plücker constraint* $L_1 L_4 + L_2 L_5 + L_3 L_6 = \boldsymbol{L}_h^\mathsf{T} \boldsymbol{L}_0 = \frac{1}{2} \mathbf{L}^\mathsf{T} \overline{\mathbf{L}} = 0$ which is clear, as $\boldsymbol{L} = Y_h \boldsymbol{X}_0 - X_h \boldsymbol{Y}_0$ is orthogonal to $\boldsymbol{L}_0 = \boldsymbol{X}_0 \times \boldsymbol{Y}_0$. All 6-vectors $\mathbf{L} \neq 0$ fulfilling the Plücker constraint represent a 3D line.

All links between two geometric elements are bilinear in their homogeneous coordinates, an example being the line joining two points in 3D . Thus the coordinates of new entities can be written in the form

$$\boldsymbol{\gamma} = \mathrm{A}(\boldsymbol{\alpha})\boldsymbol{\beta} = \mathrm{B}(\boldsymbol{\beta})\boldsymbol{\alpha} \qquad \frac{\partial \boldsymbol{\gamma}}{\partial \boldsymbol{\beta}} = \mathrm{A}(\boldsymbol{\alpha}) \qquad \frac{\partial \boldsymbol{\gamma}}{\partial \boldsymbol{\alpha}} = \mathrm{B}(\boldsymbol{\beta})$$

Thus the matrices $\mathrm{A}(\boldsymbol{\alpha})$ and $\mathrm{B}(\boldsymbol{\beta})$ have entries being linear in the coordinates $\boldsymbol{\alpha}$ and $\boldsymbol{\beta}$. At the same time they are the Jacobians of $\boldsymbol{\gamma}$.

We then may use error propagation or the propagation of covariances of linear $\boldsymbol{y} = \mathrm{A}\boldsymbol{x}$ functions of $\boldsymbol{x}$ with covariance matrix Σ_{xx} leading to $\Sigma_{yy} = \mathrm{A}\Sigma_{xx}\mathrm{A}^\mathsf{T}$ to obtain rigorous expressions for the covariance matrices of constructed entities $\boldsymbol{\gamma}$,

$$\Sigma_{\gamma\gamma} = \mathrm{A}(\boldsymbol{\alpha})\Sigma_{\beta\beta}\mathrm{A}^\mathsf{T}(\boldsymbol{\alpha}) + \mathrm{B}(\boldsymbol{\beta})\Sigma_{\alpha\alpha}\mathrm{B}^\mathsf{T}(\boldsymbol{\beta})$$

in case of stochastic independence.

We need the line $\mathbf{L}$ as intersection of two planes $\mathbf{A}$ and $\mathbf{B}$

$$\mathbf{L} = \mathbf{A} \cap \mathbf{B} = \begin{pmatrix} X_h \mathrm{I} - \boldsymbol{X}_0 \\ \mathrm{S}_{X_0} \quad 0 \end{pmatrix} \begin{pmatrix} \boldsymbol{B}_h \\ B_0 \end{pmatrix} = \mathsf{\Pi}(\mathbf{A})\mathbf{B} = -\mathsf{\Pi}(\mathbf{B})\mathbf{A}$$

inducing the matrix $\mathsf{\Pi}(\mathbf{A})$ depending on the entries of the plane $\mathbf{A}$. We also need the incidence constraints for points $\mathbf{x}$ and lines $\mathbf{l}$ in 2D, for points $\mathbf{X}$ and planes $\mathbf{A}$ in 3D and for two lines $\mathbf{L}$ and $\mathbf{M}$ in 3D:

$$\mathbf{x}^\mathsf{T}\mathbf{l} = 0 \qquad \mathbf{X}^\mathsf{T}\mathbf{A} = 0 \qquad \mathbf{L}^\mathsf{T}\overline{\mathbf{M}} = 0 \tag{1}$$

2.2   Projection of Points and Lines in Homogeneous Coordinates

Point projection. As explained in [4], the relation between a 3D point in object space and its image point in the image plane can be written as

$$\mathbf{x}' = \mathsf{P}\mathbf{X} \quad \text{with} \quad \mathsf{P}_{3\times4} = \begin{pmatrix} \mathbf{A}^\mathsf{T} \\ \mathbf{B}^\mathsf{T} \\ \mathbf{C}^\mathsf{T} \end{pmatrix} \tag{2}$$

where $\mathbf{X}$ is the homogeneous coordinate vector of a point in object space, $\mathbf{x}'$ the homogeneous coordinate vector representing its image point and P the 3×4-matrix for point projection. Due to the homogeneity of P it only contains 11 independent elements. Its rows $\mathbf{A}^\mathsf{T}$, $\mathbf{B}^\mathsf{T}$ and $\mathbf{C}^\mathsf{T}$ can be interpreted as homogeneous coordinates of the three coordinate planes $x_1' = 0$, $x_2' = 0$ and $x_3' = 0$ intersecting in the projection center $\mathbf{X}_c$ of the camera (cf. [4]). Analogously, the columns of P can be interpreted as the images of the three points at infinity of the three coordinate axes and of the origin.

Line projection. For line projection, it holds (c. f. [2])

$$\mathbf{l}' = \mathsf{Q}\overline{\mathbf{L}} \text{ with } \underset{3\times 6}{\mathsf{Q}} = \begin{pmatrix} \mathbf{U}^\mathsf{T} \\ \mathbf{V}^\mathsf{T} \\ \mathbf{W}^\mathsf{T} \end{pmatrix} = \begin{pmatrix} (\mathbf{B} \cap \mathbf{C})^\mathsf{T} \\ (\mathbf{C} \cap \mathbf{A})^\mathsf{T} \\ (\mathbf{A} \cap \mathbf{B})^\mathsf{T} \end{pmatrix} = \begin{pmatrix} \mathsf{\Pi}(\mathbf{B})\mathbf{C} \\ \mathsf{\Pi}(\mathbf{C})\mathbf{A} \\ \mathsf{\Pi}(\mathbf{A})\mathbf{B} \end{pmatrix} = \begin{pmatrix} -\mathsf{\Pi}(\mathbf{C})\mathbf{B} \\ -\mathsf{\Pi}(\mathbf{A})\mathbf{C} \\ -\mathsf{\Pi}(\mathbf{B})\mathbf{A} \end{pmatrix} \quad (3)$$

where the 6×1 vector $\overline{\mathbf{L}}$ contains the Plücker coordinates of the straight line dual to the line $\mathbf{L}$ and $\mathbf{l}'$ denotes the coordinates of the image of $\mathbf{L}$. As shown in [2], the rows of the 3×6 projection matrix Q for line projection represent the intersections of the planes mentioned above. Therefore they can be interpreted as the Plücker coordinates of the three coordinate axes $x_2' = x_3' = 0$, $x_3' = x_1' = 0$ and $x_1' = x_2' = 0$.

Inversion. Inversion of the projection leads to projection rays $\mathbf{L}'$ for image points $\mathbf{x}'$ and for projection planes $\mathbf{A}'$ for image lines $\mathbf{l}'$

$$\mathbf{L}' = \mathsf{Q}^\mathsf{T}\mathbf{x}' \qquad \mathbf{A}' = \mathsf{P}^\mathsf{T}\mathbf{l}' \quad (4)$$

The expression for $\mathbf{L}'$ results from the incidence relation $\mathbf{x}'^\mathsf{T}\mathbf{l}' = 0$ (cf. (1a)), for all lines $\mathbf{l}' = \mathsf{Q}\overline{\mathbf{L}}$ passing through $\mathbf{x}'$, leading to $(\mathbf{x}'^\mathsf{T}\mathsf{Q})\overline{\mathbf{L}} = \mathbf{L}'^\mathsf{T}\overline{\mathbf{L}} = 0$ using (1c). The expression for $\mathbf{A}'$ results from the incidence relation $\mathbf{l}'^\mathsf{T}\mathbf{x}' = 0$ for all points $\mathbf{x}' = \mathsf{P}\mathbf{X}$ on the line $\mathbf{l}'$, leading to $(\mathbf{l}'^\mathsf{T}\mathsf{P})\mathbf{X} = \mathbf{A}'^\mathsf{T}\mathbf{X} = 0$ using (1b). Especially each point $\mathbf{X}$ on the line $\mathbf{L}$ lies in the projecting plane $\mathbf{A}'$, therefore it holds

$$\mathbf{l}'^\mathsf{T}\mathsf{P}\mathbf{X} = 0. \quad (5)$$

2.3   Determination of Q from P

For a given matrix P together with the covariance matrix $\Sigma_{\beta\beta}$ of its elements $\beta = (\mathbf{A}^\mathsf{T}, \mathbf{B}^\mathsf{T}, \mathbf{C}^\mathsf{T})^\mathsf{T}$ we easily can derive the matrix $\mathsf{Q} = (\mathbf{U}, \mathbf{V}, \mathbf{W})^\mathsf{T}$ using (3). By error propagation we see that the covariance matrix $\Sigma_{\gamma\gamma}$ of $\gamma = (\mathbf{U}, \mathbf{V}, \mathbf{W})^\mathsf{T}$ is given by

$$\Sigma_{\gamma\gamma} = \mathbf{M}\Sigma_{\beta\beta}\mathbf{M}^\mathsf{T}$$

with the 18×12 matrix

$$\mathbf{M} = \begin{pmatrix} 0 & -\mathsf{\Pi}(\mathbf{C}) & \mathsf{\Pi}(\mathbf{B}) \\ \mathsf{\Pi}(\mathbf{C}) & 0 & -\mathsf{\Pi}(\mathbf{A}) \\ -\mathsf{\Pi}(\mathbf{B}) & \mathsf{\Pi}(\mathbf{A}) & 0 \end{pmatrix}.$$

In a similar manner we may now determine the uncertainty of the projecting lines and planes in (4).

3   Estimation of the Projection Matrix P

There are several possibilities to determine the projection matrix P for points from observations of points or straight lines in an image.

For the case that only points are observed, eq. (2) allows us to determine P using the well known DLT algorithm (cf. [4], p. 71). If no points but only straight lines are observed, we might use a similar algorithm based on eq. (3) to determine the matrix Q for lines. Then we need to derive P from Q, which is possible but of course not a very elegant method for determining P. Integrating point and line observations would require a separate determination of P independently estimated from observed points and lines and a fusion of the two projection matrices, which, moreover, would require a minimum of 6 points and 6 lines.

We therefore follow the proposal in [4] and use (2) for points and (5) for lines, as they both are linear in the unknown parameters of the projection matrix P. It only requires at least six pints and lines, however, in an arbitrary mixture. We here give an explicit derivation of the estimation process which not only gives an algebraic solution but a statistically optimal one.

Observations of points. For each observed point $\mathbf{x}'_i = (u'_i, v'_i, w'_i)^\mathsf{T}$, $i = 1, \ldots, I$ it holds (cf. (2))

$$\frac{u'_i}{w'_i} = \frac{\mathbf{A}^\mathsf{T}\mathbf{X}_i}{\mathbf{C}^\mathsf{T}\mathbf{X}_i} \quad \text{and} \quad \frac{v'_i}{w'_i} = \frac{\mathbf{B}^\mathsf{T}\mathbf{X}_i}{\mathbf{C}^\mathsf{T}\mathbf{X}_i}$$

which leads to the two constraints $u'_i\mathbf{C}^\mathsf{T}\mathbf{X}_i - w'_i\mathbf{A}^\mathsf{T}\mathbf{X}_i = 0$ and $v'_i\mathbf{C}^\mathsf{T}\mathbf{X}_i - w'_i\mathbf{B}^\mathsf{T}\mathbf{X}_i = 0$ which are dedicated to estimate the elements of P. In matrix representation, these two constraints can be formulated as bilinear forms

$$\mathsf{A}_i(\mathbf{x}'_i)\boldsymbol{\beta} = \begin{pmatrix} -w'_i\mathbf{X}_i^\mathsf{T} & 0 & u'_i\mathbf{X}_i^\mathsf{T} \\ 0 & -w'_i\mathbf{X}_i^\mathsf{T} & v'_i\mathbf{X}_i^\mathsf{T} \end{pmatrix} \boldsymbol{\beta} = \mathbf{e}_i \qquad \text{resp.} \qquad (6)$$

$$\mathsf{B}_i(\boldsymbol{\beta})\mathbf{x}'_i = \begin{pmatrix} \mathbf{C}^\mathsf{T}\mathbf{X}_i & 0 & -\mathbf{A}^\mathsf{T}\mathbf{X}_i \\ 0 & \mathbf{C}^\mathsf{T}\mathbf{X}_i & -\mathbf{B}^\mathsf{T}\mathbf{X}_i \end{pmatrix} \mathbf{x}_i = \mathbf{e}_i \qquad (7)$$

where the vector $\boldsymbol{\beta}^\mathsf{T} = (\mathbf{A}^\mathsf{T}, \mathbf{B}^\mathsf{T}, \mathbf{C}^\mathsf{T})$ contains all unknown elements of P. Eq. (6) will be used to estimate the $\boldsymbol{\beta}$, (7) will be used for determining the uncertainty of the residuals $\mathbf{e}_i$ by error propagation.

As each observed point $\mathbf{x}'_i$ yields 2 constraints to determine the 11 unknown elements $\boldsymbol{\beta}$, $I \geq 6$ observed points would be needed if only points are observed in the image.

Observations of straight lines. For each observed straight line $\mathbf{l}'_j = (a'_j, b'_j, c'_j)^\mathsf{T}$, $j = 1, \ldots, J$ eq. (5) is valid.

Thus, if $\mathbf{X}_{A,j}$ and $\mathbf{X}_{E,j}$ are two points lying on the 3D line with image $\mathbf{l}'$, one yields the two constraints

$$\mathbf{l}'^\mathsf{T} \mathsf{P} \mathbf{X}_{A,j} = 0 \qquad \text{resp.} \qquad a_j \mathbf{X}_{A,j}^\mathsf{T} \mathbf{A} + b_j \mathbf{X}_{A,j}^\mathsf{T} \mathbf{B} + c_j \mathbf{X}_{A,j}^\mathsf{T} \mathbf{C} = 0 \qquad \text{and}$$

$$\mathbf{l}'^\mathsf{T} \mathsf{P} \mathbf{X}_{E,j} = 0 \qquad \text{resp.} \qquad a_j \mathbf{X}_{E,j}^\mathsf{T} \mathbf{A} + b_j \mathbf{X}_{E,j}^\mathsf{T} \mathbf{B} + c_j \mathbf{X}_{E,j}^\mathsf{T} \mathbf{C} = 0$$

or in matrix representation as bilinear constraints

$$\mathsf{C}_j(\mathbf{l}'_j)\boldsymbol{\beta} = \begin{pmatrix} a_j \mathbf{X}_{A,j}^\mathsf{T} & b_j \mathbf{X}_{A,j}^\mathsf{T} & c_j \mathbf{X}_{A,j}^\mathsf{T} \\ a_j \mathbf{X}_{E,j}^\mathsf{T} & b_j \mathbf{X}_{E,j}^\mathsf{T} & c_j \mathbf{X}_{E,j}^\mathsf{T} \end{pmatrix} \boldsymbol{\beta} = \mathbf{e}_j \qquad \text{resp.} \tag{8}$$

$$\mathsf{D}_j(\boldsymbol{\beta})\mathbf{l}'_j = \begin{pmatrix} \mathbf{X}_{A,j}^\mathsf{T} \mathbf{A} & \mathbf{X}_{A,j}^\mathsf{T} \mathbf{B} & \mathbf{X}_{A,j}^\mathsf{T} \mathbf{C} \\ \mathbf{X}_{E,j}^\mathsf{T} \mathbf{A} & \mathbf{X}_{E,j}^\mathsf{T} \mathbf{B} & \mathbf{X}_{E,j}^\mathsf{T} \mathbf{C} \end{pmatrix} \mathbf{l}'_j = \mathbf{e}_j \tag{9}$$

Again, (8) will be used to determine $\boldsymbol{\beta}$, while (9) will be used for determining the uncertainty of the residuals $\mathbf{e}_j$ by error propagation.

We see that each observation of a straight line in an image yields 2 constraints to determine P. Thus again, if only straight lines are observed, $J \geq 6$ lines are needed.

Note that in the following entities concerning observations of points are indexed with i and entities concerning observations of straight lines are indexed with j.

Parameter estimation. Now we seek an optimal estimate for $\boldsymbol{\beta}$. Due to the homogeneity of P we search for an optimal estimate just under the constraint $|\boldsymbol{\beta}| = 1$. Thus, we optimize

$$\Omega = \sum_i \mathbf{e}_i^\mathsf{T}(\boldsymbol{\beta}) \, \Sigma_{e_i e_i}^{-1}(\boldsymbol{\beta}) \, \mathbf{e}_i(\boldsymbol{\beta}) + \sum_j \mathbf{e}_j^\mathsf{T}(\boldsymbol{\beta}) \, \Sigma_{e_j e_j}^{-1}(\boldsymbol{\beta}) \, \mathbf{e}_j(\boldsymbol{\beta})$$

under the constraint $|\boldsymbol{\beta}| = 1$. In case the observations are normally distributed this is the ML-estimate (under this model).

The solution can be achieved by iteratively solving

$$\boldsymbol{\beta}^{(\nu+1)\mathsf{T}} \Big[\sum_i \mathsf{A}_i^\mathsf{T}(\widehat{\mathbf{x}}_i'^{(\nu)}) \Big(\mathsf{B}_i(\boldsymbol{\beta}^{(\nu)}) \Sigma_{x_i' x_i'} \mathsf{B}_i^\mathsf{T}(\boldsymbol{\beta}^{(\nu)}) \Big)^{-1} \mathsf{A}_i(\mathbf{x}_i')$$

$$+ \sum_j \mathsf{C}_j^\mathsf{T}(\widehat{\mathbf{l}}_j'^{(\nu)}) \Big(\mathsf{D}_j(\boldsymbol{\beta}^{(\nu)}) \Sigma_{l_j l_j} \mathsf{D}_j^\mathsf{T}(\boldsymbol{\beta}^{(\nu)}) \Big)^{-1} \mathsf{C}_j(\mathbf{l}_j) \Big] \boldsymbol{\beta}^{(\nu+1)} \underset{|\boldsymbol{\beta}^{(\nu+1)}|=1}{\longrightarrow} \min \tag{10}$$

(cf. [6]). Observe, this is the solution of an ordinary eigenvalue problem with a non-symmetric matrix, as the left factor, e. g. $\mathsf{A}_i^\mathsf{T}(\widehat{\mathbf{x}}_i'^{(\nu)})$ uses the fitted observations $\widehat{\mathbf{x}}_i'^{(\nu)}$, whereas the right factor $\mathsf{A}_i(\mathbf{x}_i')$ uses the observed values.

The covariance matrices of $\mathbf{e}_i$ and $\mathbf{e}_j$ are given by $B_i(\boldsymbol{\beta}^{(\nu)})\Sigma_{x'_i x'_i}B_i{}^{\mathsf{T}}(\boldsymbol{\beta}^{(\nu)})$ and $D_i(\boldsymbol{\beta}^{(\nu)})\Sigma_{l'_i l'_i}D_i{}^{\mathsf{T}}(\boldsymbol{\beta}^{(\nu)})$, so that they have to use the previous estimate $\boldsymbol{\beta}^{(\nu)}$.

The procedure is initiated with $\Sigma_{e_i e_i} = \Sigma_{e_j e_j} = \mathbf{I}$ and using the observed values $\widehat{\mathbf{x}}'_i$ and $\widehat{\mathbf{l}}'_j$ as initial values $\widehat{\mathbf{x}}'^{(0)}_i$ and $\widehat{\mathbf{l}}'^{(0)}_j$ for the fitted observations. This leads in the first step to the classical algebraic solution (cf. [1], p. 332, p. 377) and no approximate values are needed.

The estimated observations $\widehat{\mathbf{x}}'^{(\nu)}_i$ and $\widehat{\mathbf{l}}'^{(\nu)}_j$ needed in (10) can be calculated by (cf. [6])

$$\widehat{\mathbf{x}}'^{(\nu)}_i = \left(\mathbf{I} - \Sigma_{x'_i x'_i}B_i{}^{\mathsf{T}}(\boldsymbol{\beta}^{(\nu)})\left(B_i(\boldsymbol{\beta}^{(\nu)})\Sigma_{x'_i x'_i}B_i{}^{\mathsf{T}}(\boldsymbol{\beta}^{(\nu)})\right)^{-1}B_i(\boldsymbol{\beta}^{(\nu)})\right)\mathbf{x}'_i \quad (11)$$

$$\widehat{\mathbf{l}}'^{(\nu)}_j = \left(\mathbf{I} - \Sigma_{l'_j l'_j}D_j{}^{\mathsf{T}}(\boldsymbol{\beta}^{(\nu)})\left(D_j(\boldsymbol{\beta}^{(\nu)})\Sigma_{l'_j l'_j}B_j{}^{\mathsf{T}}(\boldsymbol{\beta}^{(\nu)})\right)^{-1}D_j(\boldsymbol{\beta}^{(\nu)})\right)\mathbf{l}'_j \quad (12)$$

With the final weight matrix $\Sigma^+_{ee} = \mathrm{Diag}(\mathrm{Diag}(\Sigma^+_{e_i e_i}), \mathrm{Diag}(\Sigma^+_{e_j e_j}))$ of the contradictions $\mathbf{e}_i$ and $\mathbf{e}_j$ the covariance matrix

$$\Sigma_{ll} = \mathrm{Diag}(\mathrm{Diag}(\Sigma_{x'_i x'_i}), \mathrm{Diag}(\Sigma_{l'_j l'_j}))$$

of the observations, the covariance matrix of the estimated values is given by

$$\Sigma_{\widehat{\beta}\widehat{\beta}} = M^+ \quad \text{with} \quad M = \sum_i A_i{}^{\mathsf{T}}(\widehat{\mathbf{x}}'_i)\left(B_i(\widehat{\boldsymbol{\beta}})\Sigma_{x'_i x'_i}B_i{}^{\mathsf{T}}(\widehat{\boldsymbol{\beta}})\right)^{-1}A_i(\widehat{\mathbf{x}}'_i)$$

$$+ \sum_j C_j{}^{\mathsf{T}}(\widehat{\mathbf{l}}'_j)\left(D_j(\widehat{\boldsymbol{\beta}})\Sigma_{l'_j l'_j}D_j{}^{\mathsf{T}}(\widehat{\boldsymbol{\beta}})\right)^{-1}C_j(\widehat{\mathbf{l}}'_j)$$

The pseudo inverse M^+ can be determined exploiting the fact that $\widehat{\boldsymbol{\beta}}$ should be the null-space of M^+. We obtain an estimate for the unknown variance factor $\widehat{\sigma}^2 = \Omega/R$ with $R = \mathrm{rk}(\Sigma_{ee}) - 11$ with the redundancy R and the weighted sum of squared residuals of the constraints Ω. The redundancy results form the fact that we effectively have $\mathrm{rk}(\Sigma_{ee})$ constraints which have to determine 11 unknown independent parameters of P. Therefore the estimated covariance matrix of the estimated parameters is given by

$$\widehat{\Sigma}_{\widehat{\beta}\widehat{\beta}} = \widehat{\sigma}^2 \Sigma_{\widehat{\beta}\widehat{\beta}}$$

4   Examples

4.1   Synthetic Data

The presented method was applied on a synthetical image, only using straight lines as observations. The straight lines used connect all point pairs of a synthetic cube. The cube has size 2 [m] and is centered at the origin, the projection center is $(10, -3, 4)^{\mathsf{T}}$ [m] and therefore has a distance of approx. 11.2 [m]. The principal distance is 500 [pel], the assumed accuracy for the observed lines is 1 [pel], which

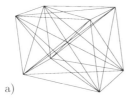 

a)   b)

Fig. 1. Synthetic test data. (**a**) Ideal observations of lines in an image of a synthetic Cube. (**b**) Erroneous observations, assuming an accuracy of 1[pel] referring to the end points.

refers to the two end points. The cube appears with a diameter of approx. 200 [pel], thus the viewing angle is approx. 23° and the measuring accuracy is approx. 1 : 200. The figure shows the image of the ideal cube and the image of the erroneous lines. The estimated projection matrix, determined from 28 observed lines, differs from the ideal one by 0.6 %, an accuracy which is to be expected.

4.2   Real Data

The presented method to determine P was also applied on real data, again using only observations of straight lines. The test object has the shape of an un-symmetric T with a height of 12 cm and a width of 14.5 cm (cf. Fig. 4.2). It is not very precise, so that object edges are not very sharp. Object information was gained manually by measuring the lengths of the object edges, supposing that the object edges are orthogonal. An image of the test object was taken (cf. Fig. 4.2a) using a digital camera SONY XC77 CE with a CCD chip of size 750 × 560 pixel. From the image straight lines were extracted automatically using the feature extraction software FEX (cf. [3]), leading to the results shown in Fig. 4.2b.

 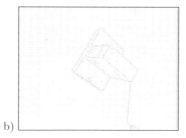

a)   b)

Fig. 2. Real test data. (**a**) Image of the test object. (**b**) Results of the feature extraction with FEX.

With revised data (short and spurious lines were thrown out) the parameter estimation delivered the estimate

$$
\widehat{P} = \begin{pmatrix} 0.00295953 & -0.00320425 & -0.00106391 & 0.564433 \\ 0.00397216 & 0.00257314 & 0.0003446 & 0.743515 \\ 0.00000259 & 0.00000141 & -0.0000050 & 0.00246196 \end{pmatrix}
$$

with the relative accuracies $\widehat{\sigma}_{P_{ij}}/\widehat{P}_{ij}$ given in the following table:

(i,j)	1	2	3	4
1	0.883 %	0.598 %	1.711 %	0.116 %
2	0.964 %	1.492 %	9.504 %	0.068 %
3	3.013 %	8.218 %	1.393 %	0.049 %

The relative accuracies indicate that most elements of P are determined with good precision, particularly in view of the fact that the object information we used is not very precise and that the observed object edges are not very sharp. Obviously, the relative accuracy of some of the elements of P is inferior to the others. This is caused by the special geometry of the view in this example and not by the estimation method applied.

5   Conclusion

The examples demonstrate the feasibility of the presented method to estimate the projection matrix P for points. The method is practical, as it needs no approximate values for the unknown parameters and statistically optimal, as it leads to the maximum likelihood estimate. Therefore we think that it could be frequently used in computer vision and photogrammetry.

References

1. Duda, R. O., Hart, P. E.: Pattern Classification and Scene Analysis. Wiley (1973)
2. Faugeras, O, Papadopoulo, T.: Grassmann-Caley Algebra for Modeling Systems of Cameras and the Algebraic Equations of the Manifold of Trifocal Tensors, Trans. of the ROYAL SOCIETY A 356, (1998) 1123 – 1152
3. Fuchs, C.: Extraktion polymorpher Bildstrukturen und ihre topologische und geometrische Gruppierung, DGK, Bayer. Akademie der Wissenschaften, Reihe C, Heft 502
4. Hartley, R. Zisserman, A.: Multiple View Geometry in Computer Vision, Cambridge University Press (2000)
5. Förstner, W., Brunn, A., Heuel, S.: Statistically Testing Uncertain Geometric Relations, In G. Sommer, N. Krüger and Ch. Perwass, editors, *Mustererkennung 2000*, pp. 17-26. DAGM, Springer, September 2000.
6. Förstner, W.: Algebraic Projective Geometry and Direct Optimal Estimation of Geometric Entities, In Stefan Scherer, editor, *Computer Vision, Computer Graphics and Photogrammetry - a Common Viewpoint*, pp. 67-86. ÖAGM/AAPR, Österreichische Computer Gesellschaft (2001)

Points, Lines, and Planes
and Their Optimal Estimation

Stephan Heuel

Institut für Photogrammetrie, Universität Bonn
Nussallee 15, D-53115 Bonn
heuel@ipb.uni-bonn.de

Abstract. We present a method for estimating unknown geometric entities based on identical, incident, parallel or orthogonal observed entities.
These entities can be points and lines in 2D and points, lines and planes
in 3D. We don't need any approximate values for the unknowns. The
entities are represented as homogeneous vectors or matrices, which leads
to an easy formulation for a linear estimation model. Applications of the
estimation method are manifold, ranging from 2D corner detection to
3D grouping.

1   Introduction

Constructing geometric entities such as points, lines and planes from given entities is a frequent task in Computer Vision. For example, in an image we may
want to construct a junction point from a set of intersecting line segments (*corner detection*) or construct a line from a set of collinear points and line segments
(*grouping*). In 3D, a space point can be reconstructed by a set of image points
(*forward intersection*); as a last example, one may want to construct a polyhedral
line given incident, parallel or orthogonal lines and planes (*3D-grouping*).

These geometric constructions can be described as an estimation task, where
an unknown entity has to be fitted to a set of given observations in the least-
squares sense. Unfortunately the underlying equations are nonlinear and quite
difficult to handle in the Euclidean case. Because of the non-linearity, one needs
approximate values for the unknowns, which are not always obvious to obtain.

This article presents a general model for estimating points, lines and planes
without knowing approximate values. We propose to use algebraic projective
geometry in 2D and 3D together with standard estimation methods. We first
explore possible representations for geometric entities, obtaining a vector and a
matrix for each entity. Then we express relations between the entities by simple,
bilinear functions using the derived vectors and matrices. These relations can be
directly used in a parameter estimation procedure, where the initial value can be
obtained easily. We show possible applications and some test results validating
the performance of the proposed method.

The proposed estimation model is based on (i) algebraic projective geometry,
which has been has been extensively promoted in Computer Vision in the last
decade (cf. [2],[6]) and (ii) integration of statistical information to the projective
entities. Kanatani [7] presented a similar approach though he does not make full
use of the elegant projective formulations, leading to complex expressions.

B. Radig and S. Florczyk (Eds.): DAGM 2001, LNCS 2191, pp. 92–99, 2001.
© Springer-Verlag Berlin Heidelberg 2001

2 Representation of Geometric Entities

Assuming that both our observations and unknowns could be points, lines and planes in 2D and 3D, we first want to explore possible representations for these entities.

2.1 Vector Representation

Following the conventions in [4], points and lines in 2D are represented as homogeneous vectors $\mathbf{x}$, $\mathbf{y}$ and $\mathbf{l}$, $\mathbf{m}$; in 3D we have $\mathbf{X}$, $\mathbf{Y}$ for points, $\mathbf{L}$, $\mathbf{M}$ for lines and $\mathbf{A}$, $\mathbf{B}$ for planes. Euclidean vectors will be denoted with italic bold letters like $\boldsymbol{x}$ for a Euclidean 2D point, cf. the first column in table 1. Furthermore we will use the canonical basis vectors $\mathbf{e}_i, \mathbf{E}_i = (0, ..., \underset{i}{1}, ..., 0)$ for points, lines or planes depending on the context.

For the geometric entities, each homogeneous vector contains a Euclidean part, indexed with a zero, and a homogeneous part, indexed with an h. This is chosen such that the distance of an element to the origin can be expressed as the norm of the Euclidean part divided by the norm of the homogeneous part, e.g. the distance of a plane to the origin is given by $d_{A,0} = |A_0|/|A_h|$. The uncertainty of an entity can be described by the covariance matrix of this vector. Note that a line $\mathbf{L} = (\mathbf{L}_h^\mathsf{T}, \mathbf{L}_0^\mathsf{T})$ is a 6-vector which has to fulfill the Plücker condition $\overline{\mathbf{L}}^\mathsf{T}\mathbf{L} = 0$ with the dual line $\overline{\mathbf{L}} = (\mathbf{L}_0^\mathsf{T}, \mathbf{L}_h^\mathsf{T})$.

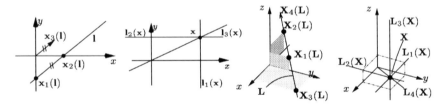

Fig. 1. (a) A line $\mathbf{l}$ and the three common points $\mathbf{x}_i(\mathbf{l})$ with the three lines $\mathbf{e}_i$. (b) A point $\mathbf{x}$ and the three lines $\mathbf{l}_i(\mathbf{x})$ incident to $\mathbf{x}$ and the points $\mathbf{e}_i$. (c) A line $\mathbf{L}$ and the four common points $\mathbf{X}_i(\mathbf{L})$ with the four lines $\mathbf{E}_i$. (d) A point $\mathbf{X}$ and the four lines $\mathbf{L}_i(\mathbf{X})$ incident to $\mathbf{X}$ and the points $\mathbf{E}_i$.

2.2 Matrix Representation

An entity is represented by a vector using its coordinates, but one can also use another representation: for example, a 2D line can be represented by its three homogeneous coordinates (a, b, c), or implicitly by two points $\mathbf{x}_1(\mathbf{l})$ and $\mathbf{x}_2(\mathbf{l})$ on the x- resp. y-axis, see fig. 1(a). Additionally, one can choose the infinite point $\mathbf{x}_3(\mathbf{l})$, which lies in the direction of the line and is undefined, thus $(0, 0, 0)^\mathsf{T}$, if the line is at infinity. These three points can be constructed by $\mathbf{x}_{1...3}(\mathbf{l}) = \mathbf{l} \cap \mathbf{e}_{1...3}$. Writing $\mathbf{x}_{1...3}(\mathbf{l})$ in a 3×3 matrix yields the skew-symmetric matrix $\mathsf{S}(\mathbf{l})$ as defined in the second row of the table 1.

The same argument can be used to derive a skew-symmetric matrix $\mathsf{S}(\mathbf{x})$, which contains three lines $\mathbf{l}_{1...3}(\mathbf{x})$ incident to the point $\mathbf{x}$, see fig. 1(b). These

Table 1. *Points, lines and planes in 2D and 3D represented as homogeneous vectors* $\mathbf{x}$, $\mathbf{l}$ *and matrices* $\mathsf{S}(\mathbf{x})$, $\mathsf{S}(\mathbf{l})$, *resp in 3D represented as homogeneous vectors* $\mathbf{X}$, $\mathbf{L}$, $\mathbf{A}$ *and matrices* $\mathsf{\Pi}^{\mathsf{T}}(\mathbf{X}), \mathsf{\Gamma}(\mathbf{L}), \overline{\mathsf{\Pi}}^{\mathsf{T}}(\mathbf{A})$. *Each row of a homogeneous matrix represents a vector of the other entity. All three row entities of a matrix in turn define the given entity, see text for details.*

2D	vector	matrix
point	$\mathbf{x}^{\mathsf{T}} = (\boldsymbol{x}_0^{\mathsf{T}}, x_h) =$ $(u, v; w)$	$\mathsf{S}(\mathbf{x}) = \begin{pmatrix} 0 & -w & v \\ w & 0 & -u \\ -v & u & 0 \end{pmatrix} = \begin{pmatrix} \mathbf{l}_1(\mathbf{x})^{\mathsf{T}} \\ \mathbf{l}_2(\mathbf{x})^{\mathsf{T}} \\ \mathbf{l}_3(\mathbf{x})^{\mathsf{T}} \end{pmatrix} = \begin{pmatrix} (\mathbf{l} \cap \mathbf{e}_1)^{\mathsf{T}} \\ (\mathbf{l} \cap \mathbf{e}_2)^{\mathsf{T}} \\ (\mathbf{l} \cap \mathbf{e}_3)^{\mathsf{T}} \end{pmatrix}$
line	$\mathbf{l}^{\mathsf{T}} = (\boldsymbol{l}_h^{\mathsf{T}}, l_0) = (a, b; c)$	$\mathsf{S}(\mathbf{l}) = \begin{pmatrix} 0 & -c & b \\ c & 0 & -a \\ -b & a & 0 \end{pmatrix} = \begin{pmatrix} \mathbf{x}_1(\mathbf{l})^{\mathsf{T}} \\ \mathbf{x}_2(\mathbf{l})^{\mathsf{T}} \\ \mathbf{x}_3(\mathbf{l})^{\mathsf{T}} \end{pmatrix} = \begin{pmatrix} (\mathbf{l} \wedge \mathbf{e}_1)^{\mathsf{T}} \\ (\mathbf{l} \wedge \mathbf{e}_2)^{\mathsf{T}} \\ (\mathbf{l} \wedge \mathbf{e}_3)^{\mathsf{T}} \end{pmatrix}$

3D	vector	matrix
point	$\mathbf{X}^{\mathsf{T}} = (\boldsymbol{X}_0^{\mathsf{T}}, X_h) =$ $(U, V, W; T)$	$\mathsf{\Pi}^{\mathsf{T}}(\mathbf{X}) = \begin{pmatrix} X_h \mathbb{I} & \mathsf{S}(\boldsymbol{X}_0) \\ -\boldsymbol{X}_0^{\mathsf{T}} & \mathbf{0}^{\mathsf{T}} \end{pmatrix} = \begin{pmatrix} T & 0 & 0 & 0 & W & -V \\ 0 & T & 0 & -W & 0 & U \\ 0 & 0 & T & V & -U & 0 \\ -U & -V & -W & 0 & 0 & 0 \end{pmatrix}$
line	$\mathbf{L}^{\mathsf{T}} = (\boldsymbol{L}_h^{\mathsf{T}}, \boldsymbol{L}_0^{\mathsf{T}}) =$ $(L_1, L_2, L_3; L_4, L_5, L_6)$	$\mathsf{\Gamma}(\mathbf{L}) = \begin{pmatrix} -\mathsf{S}(\boldsymbol{L}_h) & -\boldsymbol{L}_0 \\ \boldsymbol{L}_0^{\mathsf{T}} & 0 \end{pmatrix} = \begin{pmatrix} 0 & L_3 & -L_2 & -L_4 \\ -L_3 & 0 & L_1 & -L_5 \\ L_2 & -L_1 & 0 & -L_6 \\ L_4 & L_5 & L_6 & 0 \end{pmatrix}$
		$\overline{\mathsf{\Gamma}}(\mathbf{L}) = \mathsf{\Gamma}(\overline{\mathbf{L}}) = \begin{pmatrix} -\mathsf{S}(\boldsymbol{L}_0) & -\boldsymbol{L}_h \\ \boldsymbol{L}_h^{\mathsf{T}} & 0 \end{pmatrix} = \begin{pmatrix} 0 & L_6 & -L_5 & -L_1 \\ -L_6 & 0 & L_4 & -L_2 \\ L_5 & -L_4 & 0 & -L_3 \\ L_1 & L_2 & L_3 & 0 \end{pmatrix}$
plane	$\mathbf{A}^{\mathsf{T}} = (\boldsymbol{A}_h^{\mathsf{T}}, A_0) =$ $(A, B, C; D)$	$\overline{\mathsf{\Pi}}^{\mathsf{T}}(\mathbf{A}) = \begin{pmatrix} -\mathsf{S}(\boldsymbol{A}_h) & A_0\mathbb{I} \\ -\boldsymbol{A}_h^{\mathsf{T}} & \mathbf{0}^{\mathsf{T}} \end{pmatrix} = \begin{pmatrix} 0 & C & -B & D & 0 & 0 \\ -C & 0 & A & 0 & D & 0 \\ B & -A & 0 & 0 & 0 & D \\ -A & -B & -C & 0 & 0 & 0 \end{pmatrix}$

matrices have rank 2, because only two rows in the matrix $\mathsf{S}(\bullet)$ are needed to construct the third one.

In a similar manner we can define matrices for points, lines and planes in 3D: for example, a point $\mathbf{X}$ can be defined by a set of four intersecting lines $\mathbf{L}_{1\ldots4}(\mathbf{X})$, where three lines are each parallel to one axis and the fourth line intersects the origin, see fig. 1(d). Since a line is represented by a 6-vector, we obtain a 4×6 matrix $\mathsf{\Pi}^{\mathsf{T}}(\mathbf{X}) = (\mathbf{L}_1(\mathbf{X})^{\mathsf{T}} \ldots \mathbf{L}_4(\mathbf{X})^{\mathsf{T}})$ as a representation of a point $\mathbf{X}$. Note that the six columns of $\mathsf{\Pi}^{\mathsf{T}}(\mathbf{X})$ can be interpreted as six planes, which are incident to the point $\mathbf{X}$ and to the six space lines $\mathbf{E}_i$.

A space line can be determined by four points $\mathbf{X}_{1\ldots4}(\mathbf{L})$, three of them are on the axis-planes $\mathbf{E}_{1\ldots3}$, the fourth one lies on the infinite plane $\mathbf{E}_4$ in direction of the line, see fig. 1(c). These four points define 4×4 skew-symmetric matrix $\overline{\mathsf{\Gamma}}(\mathbf{L})$. Only two rows of the matrix $\overline{\mathsf{\Gamma}}(\mathbf{L})$ are linearly independent, the selection of the rows depend on the position and direction of the line. As a space line can also be represented by four planes $\mathbf{A}_{1\ldots4}(\mathbf{L})$, we can define a line matrix based on these for planes, yielding $\mathsf{\Gamma}(\mathbf{L})$, cf. table 1. In the literature, $\mathsf{\Gamma}(\mathbf{L})$ and $\overline{\mathsf{\Gamma}}(\mathbf{L})$ are referred as Plückermatrices, e.g. in [6].

The matrix of a plane can be defined dually to the matrix of a point by $\overline{\mathsf{\Pi}}^{\mathsf{T}}(\mathbf{A})$, as in table 1, right column, last row. Note that $\mathsf{S}(\mathbf{x})$, $\mathsf{S}(\mathbf{l})$, $\mathsf{\Pi}(\mathbf{X})$, $\mathsf{\Gamma}(\mathbf{L})$, $\mathsf{\Pi}(\mathbf{A})$ are not only representations of points, lines and planes, but also the Jacobians for constructing elements by join $\wedge$ and intersection $\cap$, see [4].

3 Relations between Unknown and Observed Entities

When estimating an unknown entity, all the observations are related to the unknown in some way. In this work we assume the relations to be either *incidence*, *equality*, *parallelity* and *orthogonality*; for example an unknown space line $\mathbf{M}$ may have a list of incident points $\mathbf{X}_i$, incident lines $\mathbf{L}_i$ and parallel planes $\mathbf{A}_i$ as observed entities. In this section we want to derive algebraic expressions for a relation between two entities.

First we want to focus on incidence and equality relations in 3D: the simplest incidence relation is a point-plane incidence, since it is only the dot product of the two vectors: $\mathbf{X}^\mathsf{T}\mathbf{A} = 0$. Furthermore, the incident relation of two lines can be expressed by a dot product: $\overline{\mathbf{M}}^\mathsf{T}\mathbf{L} = 0$. From $\mathbf{X}^\mathsf{T}\mathbf{A}$ and $\overline{\mathbf{M}}^\mathsf{T}\mathbf{L}$ we can derive all other possible incidence and equality relations: for example, if two lines $\mathbf{L}$ and $\mathbf{M}$ are equal, each of the four points $\mathbf{X}_{1\ldots4}(\mathbf{M})$ must be incident to each of the four planes $\mathbf{A}_{1\ldots4}(\mathbf{L})$. Therefore the matrix product of $\overline{\mathsf{\Gamma}}(\mathbf{L})\,\mathsf{\Gamma}(\mathbf{M}) = 0$ must be zero. Another example is a line $\mathbf{L}$ which is incident to plane $\mathbf{A}$ if the four lines $\mathbf{L}_{1\ldots4}(\mathbf{A})$ are incident to the line $\mathbf{L}$. All possible incidence and equality relations between unknowns and observations are listed in table 3.

Table 2. *Possible incidence, equality, parallelity and orthogonality relations between lists of observed points $\mathbf{x}_i$ and of lines $\mathbf{l}_i$ and unknown points $\mathbf{y}$ and lines $\mathbf{m}$.*

obs.→	$\mathbf{x}_i$		$\mathbf{l}_i$	
↓ unk.	relation	constraint	relation	constraint
$\mathbf{y}$	$\mathbf{x}_i \equiv \mathbf{y}$	$\mathsf{S}(\mathbf{x}_i)\,\mathbf{y} = \mathbf{0}$	$\mathbf{l}_i \ni \mathbf{x}_i$	$\mathbf{l}_i^\mathsf{T}\mathbf{y} = 0$
$\mathbf{m}$	$\mathbf{x}_i \ni \mathbf{m}$	$\mathbf{x}_i^\mathsf{T}\mathbf{m} = 0$	$\mathbf{l}_i \equiv \mathbf{m}$	$\mathsf{S}(\mathbf{l}_i)\mathbf{m} = \mathbf{0}$
			$\mathbf{l}_i \parallel \mathbf{m}$	$(\mathbf{l}^\perp)\mathbf{m} = 0$
			$\mathbf{l}_i \perp \mathbf{m}$	$\mathbf{l}_i^t\mathbf{m} = 0$

Table 3. *Possible incidence and equality relations $\in, \equiv$ between lists of observed space points $\mathbf{X}_i$, lines $\mathbf{L}_i$, and planes $\mathbf{A}_i$ and unknown space points $\mathbf{Y}_i$, lines $\mathbf{M}_i$ and planes $\mathbf{B}_i$ and their corresponding algebraic constraint.*

o.→	$\mathbf{X}_i$		$\mathbf{L}_i$		$\mathbf{A}_i$	
↓u.	relation	constraint	relation	constraint	relation	constraint
$\mathbf{Y}$	$\mathbf{X}_i \equiv \mathbf{Y}$	$\mathsf{\Pi}(\mathbf{X}_i)\,\mathbf{Y} = 0$	$\mathbf{L}_i \ni \mathbf{Y}$	$\mathsf{\Gamma}(\mathbf{L}_i)\,\mathbf{Y} = 0$	$\mathbf{A}_i \ni \mathbf{Y}$	$\mathbf{A}_i^\mathsf{T}\mathbf{Y} = 0$
$\mathbf{M}$	$\mathbf{X}_i \in \mathbf{M}$	$\overline{\mathsf{\Pi}}^\mathsf{T}(\mathbf{X}_i)\,\mathbf{M} = 0$	$\mathbf{L}_i \equiv \mathbf{M}$	$\overline{\mathsf{\Gamma}}(\mathbf{L}_i)\,\mathsf{\Gamma}(\mathbf{M}) = 0$	$\mathbf{A}_i \ni \mathbf{M}$	$\mathsf{\Pi}^\mathsf{T}(\mathbf{A}_i)\,\mathbf{M} = 0$
			$\mathbf{L}_i \cap \mathbf{M}_i \neq \emptyset$	$\overline{\mathbf{L}}_i^\mathsf{T}\mathbf{M} = 0$		
$\mathbf{B}$	$\mathbf{X}_i \in \mathbf{B}$	$\mathbf{X}_i^\mathsf{T}\mathbf{B} = 0$	$\mathbf{L}_i \in \mathbf{B}$	$-\overline{\mathsf{\Gamma}}(\mathbf{L}_i)\,\mathbf{B} = 0$	$\mathbf{A}_i \equiv \mathbf{B}$	$\mathsf{\Pi}(\mathbf{A}_i)\mathbf{B} = 0$

Parallelity and orthogonality relations refer to the homogeneous parts of the vectors: in 3D we have to test whether the (Euclidean) direction $\mathbf{L}_h$ of the line $\mathbf{L}$ is perpendicular resp. parallel to the plane normal $\mathbf{A}_h$. In general, these relations can be expressed by the dot product or by the cross product of the two vectors, where the cross product can be written using the skew-symmetric matrix S; the relations are listed in table 4.

Two things are important to note: (i) all algebraic constraints for the relations and 2D and 3D (for 2D, see table 2) are bilinear with respect to each entity, cf. [4]. (ii) We do not have to compute every dot product relevant for a specific relation. It is sufficient to select as many as the degree of freedoms of the relation: for example, the incidence of a point $\mathbf{X}$ and a line $\mathbf{L}$ has two degrees of freedom, therefore we can select two rows $\mathbf{A}_{j,k}^{\mathsf{T}}(\mathbf{L})$ out of $\Gamma(\mathbf{L})$ and compute the dot product $\mathbf{A}_j^{\mathsf{T}}(\mathbf{L})\,\mathbf{X} = 0$ and $\mathbf{A}_k^{\mathsf{T}}(\mathbf{L})\,\mathbf{X} = 0$. The selection depends on the coordinates L_j of line $\mathbf{L}$, it is numerically safe to take the two rows with the largest $|L_{j,k}|$.

Table 4. *Possible orthogonality and parallelity relations* $\perp, \parallel$ *between observed list of lines* $\mathbf{L}_i$ *and list of planes* $\mathbf{A}_i$ *and unknown lines* $\mathbf{M}$ *and* $\mathbf{A}$. *The lower index* h *indicates the use of the homogeneous part of an entity, cf. table 1.*

obs.→	$\mathbf{L}_i$		$\mathbf{A}_i$	
↓ unk.	relation	constraint	relation	constraint
$\mathbf{M}$	$\mathbf{L}_i \parallel \mathbf{M}$	$\mathsf{S}(\mathbf{L}_{i_h})\,\mathbf{M}_h = 0$	$\mathbf{A}_i \parallel \mathbf{M}$	$\mathbf{A}_{i_h}^{\mathsf{T}}\mathbf{M}_h = 0$
	$\mathbf{L}_i \perp \mathbf{M}$	$\mathbf{L}_{i_h}^{\mathsf{T}}\mathbf{M}_h = 0$	$\mathbf{A}_i \perp \mathbf{M}$	$\mathsf{S}(\mathbf{A}_{i_h})\mathbf{M}_h = 0$
$\mathbf{B}$	$\mathbf{L}_i \parallel \mathbf{B}$	$\mathbf{L}_{i_h}^{\mathsf{T}}\,\mathbf{B}_h = 0$	$\mathbf{A}_i \parallel \mathbf{B}$	$\mathsf{S}(\mathbf{A}_{i_h})\mathbf{B}_h = 0$
	$\mathbf{L}_i \perp \mathbf{B}$	$\mathsf{S}(\mathbf{L}_{i_h})\,\mathbf{B}_h = 0$	$\mathbf{A}_i \perp \mathbf{B}$	$\mathbf{A}_{i_h}^{\mathsf{T}}\mathbf{B}_h = 0$

4   Estimation of an Unknown Entity

We now have the relations between an unknown entity $\boldsymbol{\beta}$ and a list of observation entities $\boldsymbol{\gamma}_i$ expressed as an implicit form $\boldsymbol{g}_i(\boldsymbol{\beta};\boldsymbol{\gamma}_i) = \mathbf{0}$.

Taking this equation, we can use the Gauss-Helmert model for estimating the unknown $\boldsymbol{\beta}$, cf. [8] or [9]. Since the Gauss-Helmert model is a linear estimation model, we need the Jacobians $\partial\boldsymbol{g}_i(\boldsymbol{\beta};\boldsymbol{\gamma}_i)/\partial\boldsymbol{\gamma}_i$ and $\partial\boldsymbol{g}_i(\boldsymbol{\beta};\boldsymbol{\gamma}_i)/\partial\boldsymbol{\beta}$. We already have given them in sec. 3 because all our expressions were bilinear: in the tables 2,3 and 4 the Jacobians $\partial\boldsymbol{g}_i(\boldsymbol{\beta};\boldsymbol{\gamma}_i)/\partial\boldsymbol{\beta}$ are given for each combination of unknown $\boldsymbol{\beta}$ and observation $\boldsymbol{\gamma}_i$[1].

As the estimation is iterative, we need an initial value for the unknown $\boldsymbol{\beta}$. Since we do not need the observations, we can minimize the algebraic distance Ω (cf. [1], p. 332 & 377):

$$\Omega = \sum_i \boldsymbol{g}_i^{\mathsf{T}}\boldsymbol{g}_i = \boldsymbol{\beta}^{\mathsf{T}}\left(\sum_i \mathsf{A}_i\mathsf{A}_i^{\mathsf{T}}\right)\boldsymbol{\beta} \qquad \text{with } \mathsf{A}_i = \frac{\partial\boldsymbol{g}_i(\boldsymbol{\beta};\boldsymbol{\gamma}_i)}{\partial\boldsymbol{\beta}}$$

This leads to an eigenvector problem for the matrix $\sum_i \mathsf{A}_i\mathsf{A}_i$: the smallest normalized eigenvector gives the approximate value for the unknown $\boldsymbol{\beta}$.

In section 3 we have seen that the Jacobians A_i may not have full rank, which leads to a singular covariance matrix Σ_{gg} inside the Gauss-Helmert model. One can either compute the pseudoinverse as in [4], or select the rows of the Jacobians, so that the Jacobian has the same rank number as the number of degrees of freedom for the relation.

---

[1] for equality relations, one can also use a different Jacobian as proposed in [4]

5 Example Tasks

We have implemented the proposed estimation as a unique generic algorithm with all 2D and 3D entities and all proposed onstraints. The input of the algorithm is the type of the unknown and an arbitrary set of observations . We will denote observations with their corresponding constraint types $\in, \equiv, \|, \perp$ as upper index; e.g. if an unknown point $\mathbf{y}$ should lie on a set of lines observation, we have $\boldsymbol{g}(\mathbf{y}; \mathbf{l}_i^{\ni}) = 0 \Leftrightarrow \mathbf{l}_i^{\ni} \ni \mathbf{y}$, denoting the observed lines $\mathbf{l}_i^{\ni}$ with upper index $\ni$, since they are incident to the point $\mathbf{y}$.

Using the same estimation algorithm, we can e.g. solve the following tasks among many others (the third and the fourth task will be evaluated in sec. 6):

- *Corner detection in 2D.* We have an unknown point $\mathbf{y}$ and a set of observed lines $\mathbf{l}_i^{\ni}$ for which the unknown is incident, $\mathbf{l}_i^{\ni} \ni \mathbf{y}$. The implicit functional model is $\boldsymbol{g}(\mathbf{y}; \mathbf{l}_i^{\ni}) = \mathbf{0}$, the Jacobians are $\mathsf{S}(\mathbf{y})$ and $\mathsf{S}(\mathbf{l}_i^{\ni})$.
- *Grouping in 2D.* We have an unknown line $\mathbf{m}$ and the following lists of observations: (1) incident points $\mathbf{x}_i^{\in}$, (2) collinear (i.e. equal) lines $\mathbf{l}_i^{\equiv}$, (3) parallel lines $\mathbf{l}_i^{\|}$, (4) orthogonal lines $\mathbf{l}_i^{\perp}$. The implicit functional model is $\boldsymbol{g}(\mathbf{y}; \mathbf{x}_i^{\in}, \mathbf{l}_i^{\equiv}, \mathbf{l}_i^{\|}, \mathbf{l}_i^{\perp}) = \mathbf{0}$. The Jacobians for $\partial \boldsymbol{g}(\mathbf{m}; \boldsymbol{\gamma}_i)/\partial \mathbf{m}$ are listed in table 2.
- *Forward intersection.* We want to construct a 3D point $\mathbf{Y}$ out of a set of points $\mathbf{x}_j$ and lines $\mathbf{l}_{i,j}$ in n images $j \in \{1 \ldots n\}$. Inverting the projections P_j, we can obtain 3D lines $\mathbf{L}(\mathbf{x}_j)$ and planes $\mathbf{A}(\mathbf{l}_{i,j})$, see [2]. and [3]. We can now estimate the unknown 3D point $\mathbf{M}$: the implicit functional model is $\boldsymbol{g}(\mathbf{Y}; \mathbf{L}(\mathbf{x}_j), \mathbf{A}(\mathbf{l}_{i,j})) = \mathbf{0}$. The Jacobians used here are $\Gamma(\mathbf{L}(\mathbf{x}_j))$, $\overline{\Pi}^{\mathsf{T}}(\mathbf{Y})$, $\mathbf{A}(\mathbf{l}_{i,j})^{\mathsf{T}}$ and $\mathbf{Y}^{\mathsf{T}}$. Note that we can also construct 3D lines from sets of 2D points and lines by forward intersection, see also sec. 6.
- *Grouping in 3D.* A 3D line representing one edge of a cube is unknown, the observed entities are: (1) incident points $\mathbf{X}_i^{\in}$, (2) incident lines $\mathbf{L}_i^{\cap}$, (3) collinear (i.e. equal) lines $\mathbf{L}_i^{\equiv}$, (4) parallel lines $\mathbf{L}_i^{\|}$, (5) orthogonal lines $\mathbf{L}_i^{\perp}$, (6) incident planes $\mathbf{A}_i^{\ni}$, (7) parallel planes $\mathbf{A}_i^{\|}$ and (8) orthogonal planes $\mathbf{A}_i^{\perp}$. All observed entities can be derived by the other 9 edges, 8 corners and 6 surfaces of the cube. We have $\boldsymbol{g}(\mathbf{M}; \mathbf{X}_i^{\in}, \mathbf{L}_i^{\cap}, \mathbf{L}_i^{\equiv}, \mathbf{L}_i^{\|}, \mathbf{L}_i^{\perp} \mathbf{A}_i^{\ni}, \mathbf{A}_i^{\|}, \mathbf{A}_i^{\perp}) = \mathbf{0}$ and the Jacobians listed in table 3 and 4. In the same manner we can also construct a point representing a cube corner or a plane representing a cube surface.

6 Experimental Results

Artificial Data. To validate our algorithm, we have tested it for the previously described 3D grouping task in section 5 using artificial data and applying all proposed constraints. Artificial data provides ground-truth which is necessary for validating an estimation method. We estimated a 3D point, line and plane being part of translated and rotated cubes of size 1. For each of the 6 corners, 12 edges and 6 surfaces of the cube, 5 observations have been generated randomly with a Gaussian error of 0.1% and 1%. When taking into account all possible constraints, the redundancy of the estimations are 57 for the unknown point,

176 for the unknown line and 162 for the unknown plane. We drew 1000 sample cubes and then estimated 1000 points, lines and planes. In fig. 2, the first row shows the cumulative histogram for the estimated $\widehat{\sigma}_0^2$ for the points $\widehat{\mathbf{Y}}$, $\widehat{\mathbf{M}}$ and planes $\widehat{\mathbf{B}}$, over all estimates we get an average of $\overline{\widehat{\sigma}_0^2} = 0.988$. The second row depicts the scatter diagram for the estimated point $\widehat{\mathbf{Y}}$, projected onto the three principal planes. Furthermore, the χ^2–test on bias was not rejected.

For the given datasets, all estimations converged within 3 to 4 iterations. The stopping criteria for the iteration was defined as follows: the corrections to the values of β should be less than 1% with respect to its standard deviation. The algorithm was implemented in the scripting language Perl and takes about 1 [sec] for 50 point resp. plane observations with a factor 1.5 slower for lines.

Real Data. We have tested the task of forward intersection of 3D lines using corresponding points and lines from four overlapping aerial images. Interactively we specified sets of 2D points and line segments which correspond to the same 3D edges. The 2D features were automatically extracted by a polymorphic point-feature extraction method called FEX, cf. [5]. FEX also gives covariance matrices for the extracted points and lines. The projection matrices were fixed though one can include statistical information here, too. For one scene we estimated 16 3D-lines corresponding to object edges, on average we used 4 point- and 4 line observation for each 3D line. The endpoints of the 2D line segments defined the endpoints of the 3D line segments. The length of the line segments were between 2 [m] and 12 [m], the average standard deviation at the line endpoints orthogonal to the 3D line segments were between 0.02 [m] and 0.16 [m], cf. fig. 3.

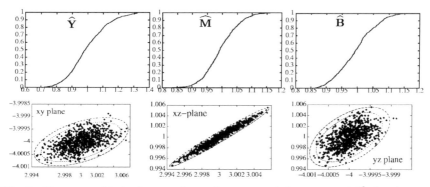

Fig. 2. *First row: this is the cumulative histogram of the estimated $\widehat{\sigma}_0^2$ for the estimated point, line and plane resp. Second row: scatter diagram of the estimated point $\widehat{\mathbf{Y}}$ projected on the $xy-$, $xz-$, yz–planes. The inner confidence ellipse is averaged over all 1000 estimated ellipses, the outer one is the empirical confidence ellipse based on all estimated points and is approx. larger by a factor 1.2*

7   Conclusions

We proposed a generic estimation method for estimating points, lines and planes from identical,incident, parallel or equal points, lines and planes. It can be used

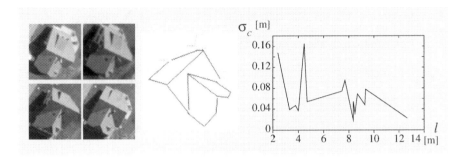

Fig. 3. *From four aerial image patches (left) we manually matched 2D features of 16 roof edges (middle). The average cross error σ_c at the endpoints of estimated 3D line segment doesn't exceed 0.17 [m], the length l of the line segments varied between 2 and 14 [m], see text for details.*

in a wide variety of applications and does not need any approximate values for the unknowns. The implementation has been tested on a large artificial dataset to validate its correctness. Future work includes among other topics: (i) The estimation of polyhedral structures like polygons on a plane or cuboid elements. (ii) Additional constraints like metric constraints, e.g. fixed distance between entities. (iii) The estimation method could be embedded in a robust estimation scheme like RANSAC.

References

1. R. Duda and P. Hart. Pattern classification and scene analysis, 1973.
2. O. Faugeras and T. Papadopoulo. Grassmann-cayley algebra for modeling systems of cameras and the algebraic equations of the manifold of trifocal tensors. In *Trans. of the ROYAL SOCIETY A, 365*, pages 1123–1152, 1998.
3. W. Förstner. On Estimating 2D Points and Lines from 2D Points and Lines. In *Festschrift anläßlich des 60. Geburtstages von Prof. Dr.-Ing. Bernhard Wrobel*, pages 69 – 87. Technische Universität Darmstadt, 2001.
4. W. Förstner, A. Brunn, and S. Heuel. Statistically testing uncertain geometric relations. In G. Sommer, N. Krüger, and Ch. Perwass, editors, *Mustererkennung 2000*, pages 17–26. DAGM, Springer, September 2000.
5. C. Fuchs. *Extraktion polymorpher Bildstrukturen und ihre topologische und geometrische Gruppierung*. DGK, Bayer. Akademie der Wissenschaften, Reihe C, Heft 502, 1998.
6. R.I. Hartley and A. Zisserman. *Multiple View Geometry*. Cambridge University Press, 2000.
7. K. Kanatani. *Statistical Optimization for Geometric Computation: Theory and Practice*. Elsevier Science, 1996.
8. E. M. Mikhail and F. Ackermann. *Observations and Least Squares*. University Press of America, 1976.
9. B. Steines and S. Abraham. Metrischer Trifokaltensor für die Auswertung von Bildfolgen. In W. Förstner, J.M. Buhmann, A. Faber, and P. Faber, editors, *Mustererkennung '99*, LNCS, 1999.

A Probabilistic Approach to Simultaneous Segmentation, Object Recognition, 3D Localization, and Tracking Using Stereo

Georg von Wichert

Siemens AG, Corporate Technology, Information and Communications, 81730 Munich, Germany

Abstract. Vision systems for service robotics applications have to cope with varying environmental conditions, partial occlusions, complex backgrounds and a large number of distractors (clutter) present in the scene. This paper presents a new approach targeted at such application scenarios that combines segmentation, object recognition, 3D localization and tracking in a seamlessly integrated fashion. The unifying framework is the probabilistic representation of various aspects of the scene. Experiments indicate that this approach is viable and gives very satisfactory results.

1   Introduction

Vision systems for service robotics applications have to cope with varying environmental conditions, partial occlusions, complex backgrounds and a large number of distractors (clutter) present in the scene. Systems mounted on mobile platforms additionally have to incorporate ego-motions and therefore have to solve the real-time tracking problem. Conventional vision systems generally perform the necessary segmentation and recognition as well as possibly 3D-localization and tracking in a pipelined, sequential way, with a few exceptions like [7] who integrate recognition and segmentation in a closed loop fashion.

However, one can imagine several ways in which different parts of the image processing pipeline could profit from each other. Service robots for example will in most cases be allowed observe their environment for short time periods to take advantage of the information present in image streams. Moving scenes will show the objects under observation from changing view points and this can be exploited to maintain and improve existing object recognition and localization hypotheses, provided that those are tracked over time. In a similar way, object recognition can profit from successful segmentation and segmentation in turn can benefit from depth information, if available. These possible synergies are currently not exploited by most systems.

This paper presents a new approach that combines segmentation, recognition, 3D-localization and tracking in a seamlessly integrated fashion. We aim at developing vision algorithms which will reliably work in real everyday environments. To reach this goal it is mandatory to take advantage of the synergies between the different stages of the conventional processing pipeline. Our approach is to eliminate the pipeline structure and simultaneously solve the segmentation, object recognition, 3D localization and tracking

B. Radig and S. Florczyk (Eds.): DAGM 2001, LNCS 2191, pp. 100–107, 2001.

problems. The unifying framework is the probabilistic representation of various aspects of the scene.

2   Method

Our method, as currently implemented and described in section 2.3, takes advantage of previous work in two major areas. First of all object recognition methods based on probabilistic models of the objects appearance have recently been presented by many research groups (see [9,11] among many others) and have shown promising results with respect to robustness against varying viewpoints, lighting and partial occlusions. In addition these models can be trained from demonstrated examples. Thus, the model acquisition process does not necessarily require a skilled operator, which is a nice property for the application of such a system in the service robotics field.

The second major contribution onto which the current implementation of our approach is built is the condensation algorithm by Isaard and Blake [4]. It is used for the probabilistic representation and tracking of our object hypotheses (recognition and localization) over time. A short overview of probabilistic object recognition and the condensation algorithm is given in sections 2.1 and 2.2. As mentioned before, our goal is to integrate segmentation, object recognition, 3D localization and tracking in order to take advantage of synergies among them. The probabilistic approach to object recognition is the framework that enables us to do so.

2.1   Probabilistic Object Recognition

Probabilistic approaches have received significant attention in various domains of robotics reaching from environmental map building [6] to mobile robot localization [1,13] and active view planning [10,14,8]. This is mainly due to the absolute necessity for explicit models of environmental uncertainty as a prerequisite for building successful robot systems.

For a probabilistic recognition of an object o from a image measurement m, we are interested in the conditional probability $p(o|m)$. This is called posterior probability for the object o given the measurement m. The optimal decision rule for deciding whether the object is present, is to decide based on which probability is larger $p(o|m)$ or $p(\overline{o}|m) = 1 - p(o|m)$ with $\overline{o}$ referring to the absence of the object. This decision rule is optimal in the sense of minimizing the rate of classification errors [2].

It is practically not feasible to fully represent $p(o|m)$, but using the Bayes rule we can calculate it according to

$$p(o|m) = \frac{p(m|o)p(o)}{p(m)} \tag{1}$$

with

- $p(o)$ the a priori probability of the object o
- $p(m)$ the a priori probability of the measurement m

– $p(m|o)$ the conditional probability of the measurement m given the presence of the object o

These probabilities can be derived from measurement histograms computed from training data. In case of a simple object detection problem, the decision rule $p(o|m) > p(\overline{o}|m)$ can be rewritten as a likelihood test. We decide that the object is present if

$$\frac{p(m|o)}{p(m|\overline{o})} > \frac{p(\overline{o})}{p(o)} = \lambda \tag{2}$$

Here λ can be interpreted as a detection threshold, which in many cases will be set arbitrarily, since the a priori probabilities of the objects depend upon the environmental and application context and are difficult to obtain. Having k *independent* measurements m_k (e.g. from a region R belonging to the object) the decision rule becomes

$$\frac{\prod_k p(m_k|o)}{\prod_k p(m_k|\overline{o})} > \frac{p(\overline{o})}{p(o)} = \lambda \tag{3}$$

If the m_k are measurement results of local appearance characteristics like color or local edge energy (texture), the resulting recognition systems tend to be comparatively robust to changes in viewing conditions [9,11,8]. However, this is not the main subject of this article.

The appearance based object recognition approach solves only one part of our problem. Furthermore, it theoretically requires, that the scene is properly segmented since equation 3 assumes that all measurements m_k come from the same object. A proper segmentation of complex cluttered scenes is known to be a difficult task. Depth information would be extremely helpful. Object boundaries generally will be easier to detect in depth images, but these are computationally expensive when computed over full frames. The depth recovery could be done more efficiently, if we already had a position hypothesis $\underline{x}$ for the object to be recognized at the current time step t. Section 2.3 will show how all these synergies can be exploited, without the need for extensive stereo correspondence search.

2.2   A Short Introduction to the Condensation Algorithm

The goal of using the condensation algorithm is to efficiently compute and track our current belief $p(\underline{x}, t)$ of the object position $\underline{x}$, i.e. the probability that the object is at $\underline{x}$ at time t. While one could represent this belief distribution in a regular grid over the 3D-space of interest as done by Moravec [5], it is evident that this requires huge amounts of memory and is computationally expensive. Additionally, in the context of object pose tracking most of the space is *not* occupied by the object(s) being tracked. Therefore those grid cells will have uniformly low values. Closed form (e.g. Gaussian) unimodal representations of the belief distribution are generally not suitable in cluttered scenes, since the belief will be multi-modal. Isard and Blake propose factored sampling to represent such non-gaussian densities. They developed the Condensation Algorithm for tracking belief distributions over time, based on a dynamic model of the process and observations from image sequences. Details of their method can be found in [4].

For the context of this paper it is important, that it is an iterative method in which the density is represented as a weighted set $\{s^{(n)}\}$ of N samples from the state space of the dynamic system (in our case from the 3D space of possible position hypotheses). The samples are drawn according to the prior belief distribution $p(\underline{x})$ and assigned weights $\pi^{(n)} = p(z|\underline{x} = s^{(n)})$ and z being an observation. The $\pi^{(n)}$ are normalized to sum up to 1. The subsequent distribution is predicted using a dynamic model $p(\underline{x}_t|\underline{x}_{t-1})$. The weighted set $\{s^{(n)}, \pi^{(n)}\}$ represents an approximation of the posterior density $p(\underline{x}|z)$ which is arbitrarily close for $N \to \infty$. Accordingly the observation density has to be evaluated at $\underline{x} = s^{(n)}$ only. Thus, only small portions of the images have to be processed. The number of samples N determines the computational effort required in each time step.

2.3 Simultaneous Solution to the Segmentation, Object Recognition, 3D Localization, and Tracking Problems

Our approach is to use Condensation for representing and tracking the belief $p(\underline{x})$ of the object of interest being at $\underline{x}$. The state space used in our implementation is the three-dimensional vector $\underline{x}$ describing the object position in space. The current system does not model object rotations. As can be seen from the short description of the Condensation algorithm given in section 2.2 we have to model our objects dynamics $p(\underline{x}_t|\underline{x}_{t-1})$. The "dynamic" model currently used is a simple three-dimensional random walk with a Gaussian conditional density. Of course, this will be extended in the future. Having specified the very simple dynamic model, we have to define the evaluation procedure of the observation density $p(z|\underline{x})$, i.e. the probability for the observation z, given that the object is at $\underline{x}$.

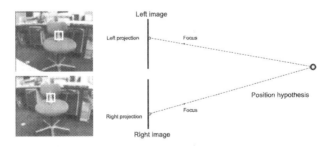

Fig. 1. A simple stereo setup.

We use a calibrated stereo setup. Therefore we are able to project each position hypothesis $\underline{x}$ into both images (see figure 1). A hypothesis is probable, if the local image patches centered at the projected points in both images satisfy two constraints:

Consistency Constraint: First of all both patches have to depict the same portion of the object, i.e. look nearly the same after being appropriately warped to compensate for the different viewpoints. This is implemented by computing the normalized correlation of both patches. The constraint is satisfied if the correlation result exceeds an empirically determined threshold. The satisfaction of this constraint implicitly contains a range based segmentation of the scene.

Recognition Constraint: In addition both patches should depict portions of the object the system is looking for. Here we use a probabilistic recognition system that currently takes color as the local appearance feature. Our measurements m_k used by equation 3 are 16 different colors obtained by an unsupervised vector quantization (using the K-Means algorithm on characteristic images) of the UV-sub-space of the YUV-color-space. The constraint is satisfied if the likelihood ratio of equation 3 is bigger than the detection threshold $\lambda = 150$. The recognition part of our algorithm is thus similar to those presented in [12] and [3].

If both constraints are satisfied, the observation density $p(z|\underline{x})$ is computed as follows

$$p(z|\underline{x}) = \prod_k p(m_k(\underline{x}_i^l)|o) \prod_k p(m_k(\underline{x}_i^r)|o)$$

where $m_k(\underline{x}_i^{l,r})$ is the local appearance measurement computed at the projection $x_i^{l,r}$ of the position hypothesis $\underline{x}$ into the left and right images. The object position is computed as the first moment of $p(z|\underline{x})$, which in turn is approximated by the weighted sample set[1].

3   Experimental Results

The combined object recognition, localization and tracking method presented in the previous sections has been implemented and evaluated using real world data. The task in the experiments was to discover and track a known object (bottle of orange juice) under realistic environmental conditions (complex background, dynamic scene). Object model ($p(m_k|o)$) and background model ($p(m_k|\overline{o})$) were estimated from training images. The the position belief distribution $p(\underline{x})$ was initialized to be uniform inside the field of view up to a distance of $5m$.

Fig. 2 shows that only 14 iterations are required to initially recognize and localize the object in a distance of $1.5m$. It is obvious, that this initial phase could not be represented using a uni-modal Gaussian model of the belief distribution. The approximation used by the Condensation Algorithm is able to represent the belief with only 1000 samples. After the initial discovery of the object, the samples are concentrated in a very small portion of the search space and cover only one quarter of the image. The computation of the feature values has to be performed in this portion of the images only. It has to be noted, that there is *no* expensive search for stereo correspondence in the disparity space.

The experimental setup selected for this paper ensures that the object recognition part of the problem can reliably be solved, the features used are "appropriate" for the

---

[1] This is based on the assumption of a single object being tracked.

problem. The experiment shows, that if this is the case, the integrated approach presented in this paper can segment the scene as well as recognize, localize and track the object of interest.

The image sequence shown in fig. 2 has a duration of $1.5s$ after which the object was found and localized. On our Pentium II/400 computer we can compute around 10 iterations per second and our implementation still has room for significant optimizations.

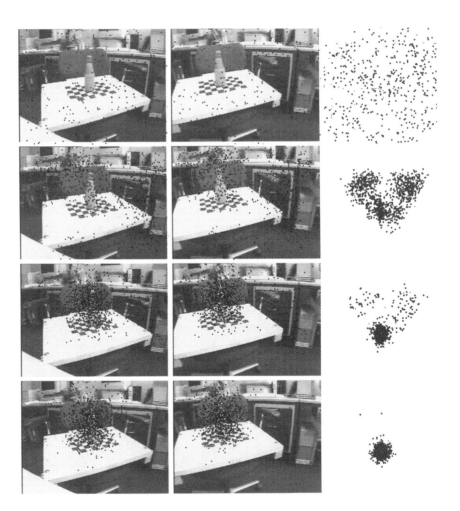

Fig. 2. The convergence of sampled belief approximation after 0, 5, 10 and 14 iterations on a static scene. The images show the sample ($N = 1000$) set projected onto left and right image and the floor plane.

After the convergence of the belief distribution, the object can reliably be tracked by the system. Fig. 3 depicts the trace of a tracking experiment, where the bottle was manually moved, (approximately) on a straight line. The images show the scene before the author's hand enters it. The small dots depict the center of mass of the belief distribution, estimated from the samples at each iteration during the experiment. Even with our slow cycle of only $10Hz$ the tracker locks onto the object robustly. This is due to the tight coupling with the object recognition, which from the tracking point of view provides a sharp object-background separation.

Fig. 3. The trace of a short tracking experiment.

4   Conclusions

We have presented a novel and very efficient approach for a probabilistic integration of recognition, 3D-localization and tracking of objects in complex scenes. Experiments indicate that this approach is viable and gives very satisfactory results. It is important to note, that the single components of our system are still very simple. The probabilistic model does not account for spatial dependencies among the image measurements m_k (and thus prohibits the estimation of object rotations), the color features we use will not be sufficient for more complex objects and finally the underlying dynamic model of the condensation tracker is extremely limited. But these limitations can easily be overcome using more advanced and well known algorithms especially for feature extraction and object modeling (see for example [11] for wavelet features incorporating spatial dependencies). Future work will focus on these improvements and other new features as the incorporation of multiple objects. In addition the system will be integrated on our mobile manipulation test-bed MobMan [15].

References

[1] Wolfram Burgard, Dieter Fox, Daniel Henning, and Timo Schmidt. Estimating the absolute position of a mobile robot using position probability grids. Technical report, Universität Bonn, Institut für Informatik III, 1996.

[2] Keinosuke Fukunaga. *Introduction to Statistical Pattern Recognition.* Computer Science and Scientific Computing. Academic Press, Inc., 2 edition, 1990.

[3] Brian V. Funt and Graham D. Finlayson. Color constant color indexing. *IEEE Transactions on Pattern Analysis and Machine Intelligence*, 17(5):522–529, 1995.

[4] M. Isard and A. Blake. Condensation – conditional density propagation for visual tracking. *Intern. Journal on Computer Vision*, 29(1):5–28, 1998.

[5] Hans P. Moravec. Robot spatial perception by stereoscopic vision and 3d evidence grids. Technical Report CMU-RI-TR-96-34, Carnegie Mellon University, Robotics Institute, Pittsburgh, USA, 1996.

[6] Hans P. Moravec and Alberto Elfes. High resolution maps from wide angle sonar. In *Intern. Conf. on Robotics and Automation*, pages 19–24, 1985.

[7] J. Peng and B. Bhanu. Closed-loop object recognition using reinforcement learning. *IEEE Transactions on Pattern Analysis and Machine Intelligence*, 20(2):139–154, 1998.

[8] M. Reinhold, F. Deinzer, J. Denzler, D. Paulus, and J. Pösl. Active appearance-based object recognition using viewpoint selection. In B. Girod, G. Greiner, H. Niemann, and H.-P. Seidel, editors, *Vision, Modeling, and Visualization 2000*, pages 105–112. infix, Berlin, 2000.

[9] Bernt Schiele and James Crowley. Probabilistic object recognition using multidimensional receptive field histograms. In *Proc. of the Intern. Conf. on Pattern Recognition (ICPR'96)*, pages 50–54, 1996.

[10] Bernt Schiele and James Crowley. Where to look next and what to look for. In *Proc. of the Conf. on Intelligent Robots and Systems (IROS'96)*, pages 1249–1255, 1996.

[11] Henry Schneiderman and Takeo Kanade. A statistical model for 3d object detection applied to faces and cars. In *IEEE Conference on Computer Vision and Pattern Recognition*. IEEE, June 2000.

[12] M. J. Swain and D. H. Ballard. Color indexing. *International Journal on Computer Vision*, 7(1):11–32, 1991.

[13] S. Thrun, D. Fox, and W. Burgard. Monte carlo localization with mixture proposal distribution. In *Proc. of the Seventh National Conference on Artificial Intelligence (AAAI)*, 2000.

[14] Sebastian B. Thrun. A baysian approach to landmark discovery and active perception in mobile robot navigation. Technical Report CMU-CS-96-122, School of Computer Science, Carnegie Mellon University, Pittsburgh, USA, 1996.

[15] Georg von Wichert, Thomas Wösch, Steffen Gutmann, and Gisbert Lawitzky. MobMan – Ein mobiler Manipulator für Alltagsumgebungen. In R. Dillmann, H. Wörn, and M. von Ehr, editors, *Autonome Mobile Systeme 2000*, pages 55–62. Springer, 2000.

Improving the Robustness in Extracting 3D Point Landmarks Based on Deformable Models

Manfred Alker[1], Sönke Frantz[1], Karl Rohr[2], and H. Siegfried Stiehl[1]

[1] Universität Hamburg, FB Informatik, AB Kognitive Systeme, Vogt-Kölln-Str. 30,
D-22527 Hamburg, {alker,frantz,stiehl}@kogs.informatik.uni-hamburg.de
[2] International University in Germany, D-76646 Bruchsal, rohr@i-u.de

Abstract. Existing approaches to extracting 3D point landmarks based on deformable models require a good model initialization to avoid local suboptima during model fitting. To overcome this drawback, we propose a generally applicable *novel hybrid optimization algorithm* combining the advantages of both conjugate gradient (cg-)optimization (known for its time efficiency) and genetic algorithms (exhibiting robustness against local suboptima). We apply our algorithm to 3D MR and CT images depicting tip-like and saddle-like anatomical structures such as the horns of the lateral ventricles in the human brain or the zygomatic bones as part of the skull. Experimental results demonstrate that the robustness of model fitting is significantly improved using hybrid optimization compared to a purely local cg-method. Moreover, we compare an *edge strength-* to an *edge distance-based fitting measure*.

Keywords: 3D landmark extraction, deformable models, robustness, hybrid optimization, conjugate gradient method, genetic algorithm

1 Introduction

Extracting 3D point landmarks from 3D tomographic images is a prerequisite for landmark-based approaches to 3D image registration, which is a fundamental problem in computer-assisted neurosurgery. While earlier approaches exploit the local characteristics of the image data using differential operators (e.g., [16],[11]), in [5] an approach based on parametric deformable models has recently been proposed that takes into account more global image information and allows to localize 3D point landmarks more accurately. However, since local optimization is employed for model fitting, a good model initialization is required to avoid local suboptima. To overcome this drawback, we propose a new, generally applicable *hybrid optimization algorithm* combining the computational efficiency of the (local) conjugate gradient (cg-)optimization method with the robustness of (global) genetic algorithms. Existing optimization algorithms for fitting parametric deformable models to image data are either purely local (e.g., [13],[18],[1],[5]) or strictly global (e.g., [4],[17]). Moreover, we compare an *edge strength-* (e.g., [18]) with an *edge distance-based fitting measure* (cf., e.g., [1]). We apply our fitting algorithm in order to extract salient surface loci (curvature extrema) of *tip-* and *saddle-like structures* such as the tips of the ventricular horns or the saddle points at the zygomatic bones (see Fig. 1(a),(b)). For representing such structures, we use globally deformed quadric surfaces (Sect. 2). The fitting measures

B. Radig and S. Florczyk (Eds.): DAGM 2001, LNCS 2191, pp. 108–115, 2001.

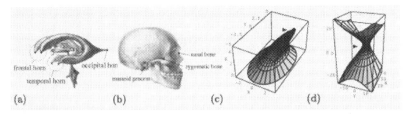

Fig. 1. (a),(b): Ventricular horns of the human brain (from [12]) and the human skull (from [2]). Examples of 3D point landmarks are indicated by dots. **(c),(d)**: Quadric surfaces as geometric models for tips ((c): tapered and bended half-ellipsoid) and for saddle structures ((d): hyperboloid of one sheet). The landmark positions are indicated by a dot.

for model fitting are then described in Sect. 3, while our hybrid algorithm for optimizing a fitting measure w.r.t. the model parameters is outlined in Sect. 4. Experimental results of studying the robustness of model fitting are presented in Sect. 5. In particular, we analyze the landmark localization accuracy of our new approach and compare it with that of purely local cg-optimization.

2 Modeling Tip- and Saddle-Like Structures with Quadrics

In the literature, a variety of 3D surface models has been used for different applications, e.g., for segmentation, registration, and tracking (e.g., [13],[15], [4],[18],[1]; see [9] for a survey). To extract 3D point landmarks, we here use quadric surfaces as geometric models for tip- and saddle-like structures ([5]) since they well represent the anatomical structures of interest here, but only have a small number of model parameters. In addition, it is advantageous here that they may be represented by both a parametric and an implicit defining function. Tapered and bended ellipsoids are utilized for representing 3D tip-like structures such as the ventricular horns, whereas hyperboloids of one sheet are used for 3D saddle-like structures such as the zygomatic bones (see Fig. 1(c),(d)). For tip-like structures, the *parametric form* of our model is obtained by applying linear tapering [4] and quadratic bending [4] as well as a rigid transformation, resp., to the parametric form of an ellipsoid:

$$\boldsymbol{x}_{tip}(\theta,\phi) = \boldsymbol{R}_{\alpha,\beta,\gamma} \begin{pmatrix} a_1\cos\theta\cos\phi/(\rho_x\sin\theta+1)+\delta\cos\upsilon(a_3\sin\theta)^2 \\ a_2\cos\theta\sin\phi/(\rho_y\sin\theta+1)+\delta\sin\upsilon(a_3\sin\theta)^2 \\ a_3\sin\theta \end{pmatrix} + \boldsymbol{t}, \qquad (1)$$

where $0 \leq \theta \leq \pi/2$ and $-\pi \leq \phi < \pi$ are the latitude and longitude angle parameters, resp. Further on, $a_1, a_2, a_3 > 0$ are scaling parameters, $\rho_x, \rho_y \geq 0$ denote the tapering strengths in x- and y-direction, and δ, υ determine the bending strength and direction, resp. For the rigid transformation, α, β, γ denote the Eulerian angles of rotation and $\boldsymbol{t}^T = (X, Y, Z)$ is the translation vector of the origin. Hence, the model is described by the parameter vector $\boldsymbol{p} = (a_1, a_2, a_3, \delta, \upsilon, \rho_x, \rho_y, X, Y, Z, \alpha, \beta, \gamma)$. The landmark position is then given by $\boldsymbol{x}_l = \boldsymbol{x}_{tip}(\pi/2, 0) = \boldsymbol{R}_{\alpha,\beta,\gamma}(\delta\cos\upsilon\, a_3^2, \delta\sin\upsilon\, a_3^2, a_3)^T + \boldsymbol{t}$. The *parametric form* of hyperboloids of one sheet is the same as the one given in [5].

3   Model Fitting with Edge-Based Fitting Measures

In order to fit the geometric models from Sect. 2 to the image data, a fitting measure is optimized w.r.t. the model parameters. Here, we consider an *edge strength-* and an *edge distance-based fitting measure*. For the *edge strength-based measure* M_{ES} (e.g., [18]), [14]), the edge strength e_g is integrated over the model surface M:

$$M_{ES}(\boldsymbol{p}) = -\int_M e_g(\boldsymbol{x})dF = -\int\int_{\theta,\phi} e_g(\boldsymbol{x}(\theta,\phi;\boldsymbol{p})) \left\| \frac{\partial \boldsymbol{x}}{\partial \theta} \times \frac{\partial \boldsymbol{x}}{\partial \phi} \right\| d\theta d\phi \to \text{Min!},$$
(2)

where $e_g(\boldsymbol{x}) = \|\nabla g(\boldsymbol{x})\|$ is the gradient magnitude of the intensity function g and $\boldsymbol{x}$ is a point on the model surface M which is parameterized by θ, ϕ. The vector of model parameters is denoted by $\boldsymbol{p}$. To emphasize small surfaces, we additionally apply a *surface weighting factor* to the fitting measure (2) which then takes the form $M_{ES} = -\frac{\int_M e_g(\boldsymbol{x})dF}{\sqrt{\int_M dF}}$.

The *edge distance-based fitting measure* M_{ED} used here is written as (cf., e.g., [13],[1],[17])

$$M_{ED}(\boldsymbol{p}) = \sum_{i=1}^{N} e_g(\boldsymbol{\xi}_i) \; \rho\left(\frac{1 - \hat{F}(\boldsymbol{\xi}_i, \boldsymbol{p})}{\|\nabla \hat{F}(\boldsymbol{\xi}_i, \boldsymbol{p})\|} \right) \to \text{Min!}$$
(3)

The sum is taken over all N image voxels $\boldsymbol{\Xi} = \{\boldsymbol{\xi}_1, \dots, \boldsymbol{\xi}_N\}$ which – in order to eliminate the influence of neighbouring structures – lie within a *region-of-interest (ROI)* and whose edge strength $e_g(\boldsymbol{\xi}_i)$ exceeds a certain threshold value. Further on, we use $\rho(x) = |x|^{1.2}$ for all $x \in \mathbb{R}$ as a distance weighting function to reduce the effect of outliers ([19]). The argument of ρ is a first order distance approximation between the image voxel with coordinates $\boldsymbol{\xi}_i$ and the model surface ([17]), where $\hat{F}$ denotes the *inside-outside function* of the tapered and bended quadric surface after applying a rigid transform (cf., e.g., [13],[4],[1]). The *inside-outside function* F of an undeformed ellipsoid can be written as

$$\text{F}(\boldsymbol{\xi}) := \left(|x/a_1|^2 + |y/a_2|^2 + |z/a_3|^2 \right)^{1/2},$$
(4)

where $\boldsymbol{\xi} = (x, y, z)^t$. Since ellipsoids have a closed surface, there is a simple interpretation of the *inside-outside function* that explains its name:

$$\begin{cases} \text{If} & \text{F}(\boldsymbol{\xi}) = 1, & \boldsymbol{\xi} \text{ is on the surface,} \\ \text{if} & \text{F}(\boldsymbol{\xi}) > 1, & \boldsymbol{\xi} \text{ is outside, and} \\ \text{if} & \text{F}(\boldsymbol{\xi}) < 1, & \boldsymbol{\xi} \text{ is inside.} \end{cases}$$
(5)

Due to inaccuracies of the first order distance approximation that is used in (3), the edge distance-based fitting measure (3) is not suitable for hyperboloids of one sheet.

Also, a volume factor is used in conjunction with (3) to emphasize small volumes. This factor has been chosen as $1 + \frac{a_1 a_2 a_3}{a_{1,est} a_{2,est} a_{3,est}}$, where the weighting factor $a_{1,est} a_{2,est} a_{3,est}$ is coarsely estimated to a value of $10^3 \; vox^3$ (*vox* denotes the spatial unit of an image voxel). For volume weighting factors (or size factors), see also, e.g., [13].

4   A Novel Hybrid Optimization Algorithm

Most optimization algorithms considered in the literature for model fitting are *local* algorithms such as the *conjugate gradient (cg-)method* (e.g., [13],[18],[1],[5]). The cg-method combines problem specific search directions of the *method of steepest descent* with optimality properties of the method of *conjugate directions* (e.g., [6]). However, since it is a purely local method, it is prone to run into local suboptima. On the other hand, global optimization methods such as genetic algorithms (GAs; e.g., [7]) have been proposed to avoid local suboptima (e.g., [4],[17]), but are plagued with slow convergence rates. We here propose a *hybrid algorithm* which combines the advantages of both methods. Similar to GAs, we consider a whole *population* of parameter vectors, but we differ in the *mutation strategy* since we do not use *bit-flips* and *crossovers* to imitate natural mutation ([7]). By contrast, we use several most promising local optima resulting from a *line search* after each cg-step as candidate solutions. In order to obtain a generally applicable strategy, we adapt the population size to the complexity of the problem at hand by increasing the maximal population size each time a candidate solution converges to a local optimum, i.e. when its objective function value does not improve for a given number of cg-iterations. Consequently, several parameters can be adapted to the specific optimization problem at hand:

- the maximum population size that must not be exceeded (here: 20),
- the number of cg-iterations after which the least successful population members (measured by their value of the fitting measure) are discarded (here: 5),
- the minimum number of population members that are retained after each such 'survival of the fittest' step (here: 5),
- the number of cg-iterations with no significant improvement of the value of the fitting measure after which a population member is marked convergent and is not subject to further cg-iterations (here: 80), and
- a difference threshold for two parameter vectors of the deformable model below which they are considered as being equal.

The mentioned parameters have been used in all our experiments. Except for the need of adjusting these parameters, the optimization strategy presented here is a general-purpose method for poorly initialized nonlinear optimization problems and its applicability is not confined to model fitting problems in medical image analysis. Only one example of *hybrid optimization* in image analysis is known to us: In [8], discontinuity preserving visual reconstruction problems, e.g. sparse data surface reconstruction and image restoration problems, are described as coupled (binary-real) optimization problems. An informed GA is applied to the binary variables (describing the discontinuities), while a cg-method is applied to the real variables for a given configuration of the binary variables visited by the GA. By contrast, in our approach the local and the global part are treated uniformly.

5   Experimental Results for 3D Tomographic Images

Scope of experiments. In our experiments, the deformable models were fitted to tip-like and saddle-like anatomical structures and our hybrid optimization algorithm has been compared to purely local cg-optimization w.r.t. poorly initialized model parameters using

- different *types of image data*: two 3D T1-weighted MR images and one 3D CT image of the human head,
- different *types of landmarks*: frontal/occipital horn of the left/right lateral ventricle, left/right zygomatic bone as part of the skull,
- different *fitting measures*: edge distance-based and edge strength-based, and
- different sizes of the *region of interest (ROI)* for model fitting: ROI radius of 10 *vox* and 15 *vox* (*vox*: spatial unit of an image voxel).

Experimental strategy. For each 3D MR and 3D CT image, an initial good fit is determined by repeated model fittings and visual inspection of the fitting results. For obtaining poor initial estimates for model fitting, the parameter values of the initial good fit are varied by adding Gaussian distributed random numbers with zero mean and large variances. In order to determine the landmark localization error e, the landmark positions calculated from the fitted deformable models are compared to ground truth positions that were manually specified in the 3D images in agreement with up to four persons. In addition, to measure the model fitting accuracy, we consider the root-mean-squared distance between edge points of the image and the model surface, e_{RMS}, using a Euclidean distance map ([10]) from the image data after applying a 3D edge detection algorithm based on [3]. This procedure is iterated sufficiently often (here: 100 times) with different, randomized model initializations. The mean values and RMS estimates of the resulting values of e and e_{RMS} are tabulated then. For evaluating the fitting measures (2),(3), the derivatives of the intensity function are computed numerically using cubic B-spline interpolation and Gaussian smoothing (see [5]).

General results. Common to all experiments is that the final value of the fitting measure is better by about 10-50% for hybrid optimization than for purely local cg-optimization. In most cases, the landmark localization and the model fitting accuracy also improve significantly. Thus, hybrid optimization turns out to be superior to purely local cg-optimization at the expense of an increase in computational costs of a factor of 5-10 (30s–90s for local cg-optimization and 150s–900s for hybrid optimization on a SUN SPARC Ultra 2 with 300MHz CPU).

The edge distance-based fitting measure in (3) turns out to be more suitable for 3D MR images of the ventricular horns with high signal-to-noise ratio since it incorporates *distance* approximations between the image data and the model surface (*long* range forces, cf. [15]). However, in comparison to (2), it is relatively sensitive to noise. Moreover, it is not suitable for hyperboloids of one sheet due to inaccuracies of the first order distance approximation associated with it.

Results for the ventricular horns. The tips of the frontal and occipital horns of the lateral ventricles are considered here. Typical examples of successful model fitting, which demonstrate the robustness of model fitting, are given in Fig. 2. Here, contours of the model initialization are drawn in black and the results of model fitting using purely local cg-optimization are drawn in grey, while the results of model fitting using our new hybrid optimization algorithm are drawn in white. The ground truth landmark positions are indicated by a $\oplus$-symbol. As can be seen from the averaged quantitative results in Table 1, hybrid optimization is superior to purely local cg-optimization and yields in most cases better model fitting (e_{RMS}) and landmark localization (e) results (cf. also Figs. 2(a), (b)). Note that rather coarsely initialized model parameters have been used ($\overline{e}_{initial} \approx 7 \ldots 9\,vox$), and thus some unsuccessful fitting results – particularly in the case of the less pronounced occipital horns – deteriorate the average accuracy of model fitting as shown in Table 1.

Table 1. Fitting results averaged over 100 model fittings with randomized poor model initializations for 3D MR images of the *frontal/occipital* ventricular horns using *13 model parameters* ($\overline{e}$: mean landmark localization error (in vox), $\overline{e}_{RMS}$: RMS distance between deformable model and image data (in vox), voxel size $= 0.86 \times 0.86 \times 1.2 \mathrm{mm}^3$).

		Model initialization	Edge dist.-b. fitt. meas.		Edge strength-b. fitt. meas.	
			local cg-opt.	hybrid opt.	local cg-opt.	hybrid opt.
Frontal	$\overline{e}$	7.71 ± 3.16	3.28 ± 2.99	1.40 ± 1.18	3.54 ± 2.18	2.49 ± 2.21
horn (left)	$\overline{e}_{RMS}$	2.22 ± 1.10	1.00 ± 0.63	0.65 ± 0.22	1.04 ± 0.31	0.87 ± 0.35
Frontal	$\overline{e}$	6.57 ± 3.18	3.87 ± 2.16	3.15 ± 2.18	6.55 ± 3.53	5.19 ± 3.70
horn (right)	$\overline{e}_{RMS}$	2.12 ± 1.11	1.05 ± 0.60	0.78 ± 0.25	1.56 ± 1.26	1.28 ± 0.79
Occipital	$\overline{e}$	9.08 ± 4.42	6.90 ± 3.89	6.68 ± 3.93	4.74 ± 4.33	4.61 ± 4.31
horn (right)	$\overline{e}_{RMS}$	3.00 ± 1.40	2.06 ± 0.93	2.04 ± 0.87	1.34 ± 0.87	1.29 ± 0.78

Results for the zygomatic bones. All results for the zygomatic bones were obtained with the edge strength-based fitting measure (2). Model fitting for the saddle points at the zygomatic bones (e.g., Fig. 2(c)) in general is not as successful as it is for the tips of the ventricular horns since our geometric primitive does not describe the anatomical structure at hand with comparable accuracy. However, the mean landmark localization error $\overline{e}$ can be reduced from initially $\overline{e}_{initial} = 6.4 \ldots 6.9\,vox$ to $\overline{e} = 2.5 \ldots 3.2\,vox$ and the accuracy of model fitting is $\overline{e}_{RMS} = 1.5 \ldots 1.8\,vox$ (voxel size $= 1.0 \mathrm{mm}^3$).

6   Conclusion

In this paper, landmark extraction based on deformable models has been investigated in order to improve the stability of model fitting as well as of landmark localization in the case of poorly initialized model parameters. To this end, a generally applicable novel hybrid optimization algorithm has been introduced and edge strength- and edge distance-based fitting measures have been compared. Experimental results have demonstrated the applicability of our hybrid algorithm as well as its increased robustness as compared to a purely local cg-method. However, the experimental results do not clearly favour one fitting measure. For the frontal ventricular horns, our edge distance-based fitting measure is more successful, while for the less pronounced occipital horns and for the zygomatic bones, the edge strength-based fitting measure is more suitable.

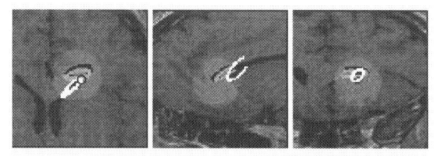

(a) 3D MR image of the *frontal* horn of the *left* lateral ventricle, edge *distance-based* fitting measure, ROI size 15.0 *vox*

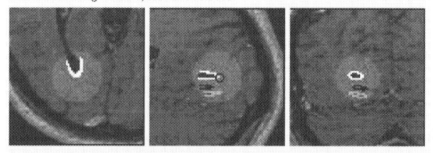

(b) 3D MR image of the *occipital* horn of the *right* lateral ventricle, edge *strength-based* fitting measure, ROI size 15.0 *vox*

(c) 3D CT image of the *left* zygomatic bone, edge *strength*-based fitting measure, ROI size 15.0 *vox*

Fig. 2. Examples of successfully fitting tapered and bended half-ellipsoids to 3D MR images of the frontal and occipital horns of the lateral ventricles (Fig. 2(a–b)) as well as of fitting a half-hyperboloid with no further deformations to a 3D CT image of the zygomatic bone (Fig. 2(c)). Contours of the model surfaces in axial, sagittal, and coronal planes are depicted here (from left to right). *Black*: model initialization, *grey*: fitting result for local cg-optimization, and *white*: fitting result for our hybrid optimization algorithm. The ground truth landmark positions are indicated by a ⊕-sign.

References

1. E. Bardinet, L.D. Cohen, and N. Ayache. Superquadrics and Free-Form Deformations: A Global Model to Fit and Track 3D Medical Data. *Proc. CVRMed'95*, LNCS 905, pp. 319–326. Springer, 1995.
2. R. Bertolini and G. Leutert. *Atlas der Anatomie des Menschen. Band 3: Kopf, Hals, Gehirn, Rückenmark und Sinnesorgane.* Springer, 1982.
3. J.F. Canny. A Computational Approach to Edge Detection. *PAMI*, 8(6):679–698, 1986.
4. K. Delibasis and P.E. Undrill. Anatomical object recognition using deformable geometric models. *Image and Vision Computing*, 12(7):423–433, 1994.
5. S. Frantz, K. Rohr, and H.S. Stiehl. Localization of 3D Anatomical Point Landmarks in 3D Tomographic Images Using Deformable Models. *Proc. Int. Conf. on Medical Image Computing and Computer-Assisted Intervention (MICCAI 2000)*, LNCS 1935, pp. 492–501, Springer, 2000.
6. G.H. Golub and C.F. Van Loan. *Matrix Computations.* Johns Hopkins University Press, 1996.
7. D. Goldberg. Genetic Algorithms in Search, Optimization and Machine Learning. Addison Wesley, 1989.
8. S.H. Lai and B.C. Vemuri. Efficient hybrid-search for visual reconstruction problems. *Image and Vision Computing*, 17(1):37–49, 1999.
9. T. McInerney and D. Terzopoulos. Deformable Models in Medical Image Analysis: A Survey. *Medical Image Analysis*, 1(2):91–108, 1996.
10. D.W. Paglieroni. A Unified Distance Transform Algorithm and Architecture. *Machine Vision and Applications*, 5(1):47–55, 1992.
11. K. Rohr. On 3D differential operators for detecting point landmarks. *Image and Vision Computing*, 15(3):219–233, 1997.
12. J. Sobotta. *Atlas der Anatomie des Menschen. Band 1: Kopf, Hals, obere Extremität, Haut.* Urban & Schwarzenberg, 19th edition, 1988.
13. F. Solina and R. Bajcsy. Recovery of Parametric Models from Range Images: the Case for Superquadrics with Global Deformations. *PAMI*, 12(2):131–147, 1990.
14. L.H. Staib and J.S. Duncan. Model-Based Deformable Surface Finding for Medical Images. *IEEE Trans. Med. Imag.*, 15(5):720–731, 1996.
15. D. Terzopoulos and D. Metaxas. Dynamic 3D Models with Local and Global Deformations: Deformable Superquadrics. *PAMI*, 13(7):703–714, 1991.
16. J.-P. Thirion. New Feature Points based on Geometric Invariants for 3D Image Registration. *Internat. Journal of Computer Vision*, 18(2):121–137, 1996.
17. V. Vaerman, G. Menegaz, and J.-P. Thiran. A Parametric Hybrid Model used for Multidimensional Object Representation. *Proc. ICIP'99*, vol. 1, pp. 163–167, 1999.
18. B.C. Vemuri and A. Radisavljevic. Multiresolution Stochastic Hybrid Shape Models with Fractal Priors. *ACM Trans. on Graphics*, 13(2):177–207, 1994.
19. Z. Zhang. Parameter Estimation Techniques: A Tutorial with Application to Conic Fitting. *INRIA Rapport de recherche*, No. 2676, 1995.

Efficient 3D Vertex Detection in Range Images Acquired with a Laser Sensor

Dimitrios Katsoulas and Lothar Bergen

Institute for Pattern Recognition and Image Processing,
Computer Science Department,
Albert-Ludwigs-Universität Freiburg, Germany
dkats@informatik.uni-freiburg.de,
http://lmb.informatik.uni-freiburg.de

Abstract. In many branches of industry, piled box-like objects have to be recognized, grasped and transferred. Unfortunately, existing systems only deal with the most simple configurations (i.e. neatly placed boxes) effectively. It is known that the detection of 3D-vertices is a crucial step towards the solution of the problem, since they reveal essential information about the location of the boxes in space. In this paper we present a technique based on edge detection and robust line fitting, which efficiently detects 3D-vertices. Combining this technique with the advantages of a time of flight laser sensor for data acquisition, we obtain a fast system which can operate in adverse environments independently of lighting conditions.

1 Introduction

This paper addresses the depalletizing problem (or bin picking problem) in the context of which a number of objects of arbitrary dimensions, texture and type must be automatically located, grasped and transferred from a pallet (a rectangular platform), on which they reside, to a specific point defined by the user. The need for a robust and generic automated depalletizing system stems primarily from the car and food industries. An automated system for depalletizing is of great importance because it undertakes a task that is very monotonous, strenuous and sometimes quite dangerous for humans. More specifically, we address the construction of a depalletizer dealing with cluttered configurations of boxes as shown in Fig. 1.

Existing systems can be classified as follows: systems incorporating no vision at all and systems incorporating vision. The latter group can be further divided into systems based on intensity or range data. For an in depth discussion of existing systems the reader is referred to [7], where the superiority of systems employing range imagery is discussed as well.

One of the fastest and conceptually closest systems to the one we propose, is the one of Chen and Kak [2]. A structured light range sensor is used for data acquisition. A region based technique is used to segment the range image into surfaces. Since a completely visible vertex in the scene provides the strongest

B. Radig and S. Florczyk (Eds.): DAGM 2001, LNCS 2191, pp. 116–123, 2001.
© Springer-Verlag Berlin Heidelberg 2001

Fig. 1. Intensity image

constraints for calculating hypotheses about the position of an object in the scene, vertices are detected by intersecting surfaces acquired from the segmentation. The main disadvantage of this approach is that since a vertex is computed as the intersection of three surfaces, the objects should expose three surfaces to the imaging source. In many cases this is not true, which results in a small number of localized objects per scan. In the extreme case of neatly placed objects of the same height, for example, no vertices can be detected at all. A second disadvantage originates from the fact that, according to [5], the region based segmentation methods of range data are time consuming operations. A third drawback, common to almost all the systems in the literature, is the usage of structured light techniques for range data acquisition. Since it is desirable for the projected light to be the only illumination source for the scene, they certainly perform better than camera based systems, but they still can not be used in uncontrolled industrial environments. Furthermore, they require time-consuming calibration.

This paper, in which a sub part of a depalletizing system is described, is organized as follows.

Initially, we describe the scene data acquisition module, which is capable of operating in a variety of environmental conditions, even in complete darkness. The description of a fast and accurate edge detector for object border extraction based on scan line approximation follows. The presentation of an algorithm for detecting vertices in a fast and robust manner is then given. This technique requires only two lines for vertex detection (as opposed to three surfaces) and therefore provides richer information about the objects and, as will be seen, at a low computational cost. Finally, a paragraph summarizing the system's advantages and outlining future work concludes.

2   Data Acquisition

The system comprises an industrial robot, namely the model KR 15/2 manufactured by KUKA GmbH, a square vacuum-gripper and a time of flight laser sensor (model LMS200, manufactured by SICK GmbH). The output of the laser sensor is a set of two-dimensional points, which are defined as the intersection

of the objects with the sensor's scanning plane [4]. This set of planar points
acquired from the laser sensor will be hereinafter referred to as scan line. The
sensor is integrated on the gripper, and the latter is seamlessly attached to the
robot's flange, as in [7]. In this way, we take full advantage of the flexibility for
viewpoint selection made possible by a six degrees of freedom robot.

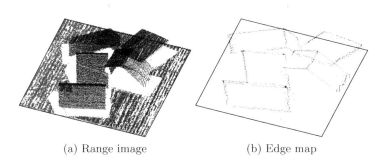

(a) Range image   (b) Edge map

Fig. 2. Jumbled boxes

Due to the fact that we plan the robot to grasp objects in a top-to-bottom
approach, we perform a linear scanning of the upper part of the pallet. The
robot is programmed to execute a linear movement, the end points of which are
the mid points of the two opposite sides of the rectangular pallet. The scanning
plane of the sensor is always perpendicular to the direction of the movement
and the sensor faces the upper side of the pallet. The set of scan-lines collected
during the movement of the sensor is our 2.5D image.

One of the most salient problems of range imagery based on time of flight
laser sensors, is the occurrence of noisy points caused by range or reflectance
changes [1]. In order to discard these noisy points, before further processing, we
apply the noise attenuation method described in [1] to the scan-lines of our range
image. An acquired range image with attenuated noise is depicted in Fig. 2(a).

3   Edge Detection

The adopted scan line approximation algorithm, proposed in [6], splits a scan
line into segments which are later approximated by model functions. With the
help of these functions, edge strength values are computed for each pair of endpoints of neighboring segments. To illustrate, the edge strength value definition
for the two segments, approximated with the functions $f_1(x)$ and $f_2(x)$, which
a linear in our case (Fig. 3(a)), but could be curves in general, is defined as

$$\text{JumpEdgeStrength} = |f_1(\overline{x}) - f_2(\overline{x})|,$$
$$\text{CreaseEdgeStrength} = \cos^{-1} \frac{(-f_1'(\overline{x}), 1)(-f_2'(\overline{x}), 1)^T}{\|(-f_1'(\overline{x}), 1)\| \|(-f_2'(\overline{x}), 1)\|},$$

where $\overline{x} = \frac{x_1 + x_2}{2}$. The scan-line splitting technique [3] is illustrated in Fig. 3(b). If we suppose that our scan line comprises the points with labels A-E, a linear segment is initially estimated from the end points and the maximum distance of the line to every point of the scan line is calculated. If no point has a distance greater than a predetermined threshold T_{split} from the approximation curve, then the process stops for the particular scan line segment, since it is satisfactorily approximated. If the maximum distance is bigger than T_{split}, the whole process is repeated recursively (e.g. for the scan-lines AC and CE). This process is illustrated in Fig. 3(b). The approximating functions are defined on the segments originating from the splitting by means of a least square fitting.

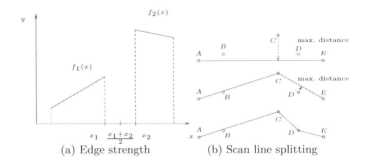

(a) Edge strength   (b) Scan line splitting

Fig. 3. Edge detection

The splitting algorithm is controlled by only one parameter T_{split}. Scan-line over-segmentation problems are solved when this threshold is increased. However, the arbitrary increase of T_{split} produces an under-segmentation phenomenon. In order not to lose edge information, we set a low value in the threshold and we applied the fast segment-merging technique suggested in [10]. This is where our detector differs from [6]. In each of the fitted segments, a significance measure (SM) is assigned as

$$SM = \frac{L}{e},$$

where L is the length of the segment and e is the approximation error of the least square fitting. The significance measure is based on a pseudo-psychological measure of perceptual significance, since it favors long primitives, provided they fit reasonably well. According to the merging procedure each segment is combined sequentially with the previous, the next and both the previous and next segments and for each combination a SM is computed. If one of the combinations results in a bigger SM than the one of the candidate segment, the corresponding segments are merged.

An initial version of this algorithm applied on scan-lines is presented in [7], where a discussion concerning the algorithm's accuracy is also presented. The application of the algorithm to the range data shown in Fig. 2(a) is depicted in Fig. 2(b). The edge map was created by applying the detector to every row and column of the range image and by retaining the edge points with high jump edge strength values and crease edge strength values around 90 degrees. The time needed for the creation of the edge map in the input range image comprising 424 rows and 183 columns was about 2.8 seconds on an Intel Pentium III, 600MHz processor.

4   3D Vertex Detection

As discussed in the introduction, the use of lines as low-level features provides us with rich information about the scene at a low computational cost. In the following section we shall demonstrate how line segments can be fitted robustly to the edge data. We then point out how a-priori knowledge about the objects can be used to obtain vertices from the line segments.

4.1   Line Detection in 3D

For the line fitting we have chosen the Hough transform (HT) for it's robustness with respect to noisy, extraneous or incomplete data. Unfortunately, the computational complexity and memory requirements of the standard Hough transform (SHT) rise exponentially with the number of parameters under detection. Therefore, the SHT is unsuitable for 3D-line detection involving four parameters.

An attempt to reduce the number of parameters by applying the SHT to the projection of edge data to the planes defined by the coordinate axis proved unsuccessful due to the high line density.

The probabilistic Hough transforms (PHTs) (cf. [9]) offer another approach to reduce the computational complexity by calculating and accumulating feature parameters from sampled points. While this reduces the computational complexity of the accumulation to some extent, the complexity of the peak detection and the memory requirements remain unchanged.

Leavers developed the dynamic generalized Hough transform (DGHT) (cf. [8]), a technique which allows for the use of one-dimensional accumulators if a coarse segmentation of the objects can be obtained and if the features under detection can be suitably parameterized. This technique, which belongs to the group of PHTs, reduces the memory requirements from R^n to nR, where R is the resolution of the parameters space and n the number of parameters. Inspired by the DGHT, we have developed a technique for 3D-line fitting, which will be described in the remainder of this section.

Initially, the connected components (CCs) of the projection of the edges onto the ground plane are detected and sorted according to their size. Line fitting is performed by iterating three steps: coarse segmentation of the edge points using the biggest CC as seed, robust line parameter estimation and removal of edge points in the vicinity of the robustly estimated line. In the coarse segmentation step a 3D-line is fitted in the least square sense to the points of the CC. Points within a certain distance of this line are used as input to robust parameter estimation. In the robust parameter estimation step the parameters of the line consisting of the direction vector d and the starting point p are calculated. Pairs of points are sampled, their difference vectors normalized and the components of the normalized vectors accumulated in three one-dimensional accumulators. The maxima of the three accumulators yield the components of the direction vector n. The data points are then projected on to the plain through the origin whose normal vector is d. The 2D coordinates of the data points in the plane are then accumulated in two one-dimensional accumulators and provide us with the point p.

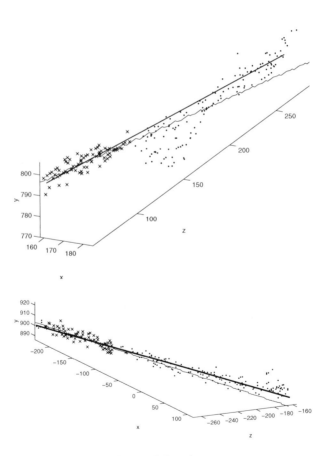

Fig. 4. 3D-line fitting

Figure 4 shows the results of our robust fitting technique for two segments: each CC is represented with crosses, the edge points with dots, the result of the least square fitting with a thin line and the final result with a thick line.

Due to the sparseness of the edge data in 3D-space, the precision of the lines fitted to the CC is largely sufficient for the segmentation of the edge data. The robustness with respect to outliers and the precision required for vertex detection is guaranteed by the parameter estimation with the one-dimensional accumulators and is clearly illustrated in Fig. 4.

4.2   Vertex Reconstruction

3D-vertices can now be obtained from close lines forming near 90 degree angles. The vertices can then be used in a hypothesis generation and verification step (cf. the system described in [2]) to accurately localize the boxes.

5   Conclusion

We have presented an efficient technique for the detection of 3D-vertices in range images. The joint use of edge detection and a technique inspired by the dynamic generalized Hough transform renders this technique fast and robust. This technique will be part of a real-time depalletizer for cardboard boxes. Due to the fact that vertices are obtained as the intersection of two lines (as opposed to the intersection of three planes), a rich set of hypotheses about the location of the boxes is generated. This increases the probability of grasping several objects per scan. Moreover, if the dimensions of the boxes are known it may be possible to achieve complete scene understanding. Another key feature of the depalletizer is the use of a laser sensor, which allows the system to be used in adverse environments and independent of the lighting conditions.

In the future, we plan to complete the construction of the system by adding a box location hypothesis generation and verification step.

Acknowledgments. This work was supported for the first author by the German ministry of economy and technology under the PRO INNO program, Grant No. KF 0185401KLF0. We also wish to thank Nikos Canterakis for the fruitful discussions.

References

1. M. D. Adams. Amplitude modulated optical range data analysis in mobile robotics. In Lisa Werner, Robert; O'Conner, editor, *Proceedings of the 1993 IEEE International Conference on Robotics and Automation: Volume 2*, pages 8–13, Atlanta, GE, May 1993. IEEE Computer Society Press.
2. C. H. Chen and A. C. Kak. A robot vision system for recognizing 3-D objects in low-order polynomial time. *IEEE Transactions on Systems, Man, and Cybernetics*, 19(6):1535–1563, November-December 1989.

3. Richard Duda and Peter Hart. *Pattern Recognition and Scene Analysis.* John Wiley and Sons, 1973.

4. SICK GmbH. *Measurement Software Tool (MST) technical description.*

5. A. Hoover. An experimental comparison of range image segmentation algorithm. *IEEE Trans. PAMI, 18(7):637–689, 1996.*, 1996.

6. Xiaoyi Jiang and Horst Bunke. Edge detection in range images based on scan line approximation. *Computer Vision and Image Understanding: CVIU*, 73(2):183–199, February 1999.

7. D.K. Katsoulas and D.I. Kosmopoulos. An efficient depalletizing system based on 2D range imagery. In *Proceedings of the IEEE International Conference on Robotics and Automation (ICRA-2001), Seoul, Korea*, pages 305–312. IEEE Robotics and Automation Society, May 21–26 2001.

8. V. F. Leavers. *Shape Detection in Computer Vision Using the Hough Transform.* Springer-Verlag, London, 1992.

9. V. F. Leavers. Which Hough transform? *CVGIP: Image understanding*, 58(2):250–264, 1993.

10. P. Rosin and G. West. Nonparametric segmentation of curves into various representations. *IEEE Trans. on Pattern Analysis and Machine Intelligence, Vol. 17, No. 12, 1995.*, 1995.

Scale Adaptive Filtering Derived from the Laplace Equation

Michael Felsberg and Gerald Sommer*

{mfe,gs}@ks.informatik.uni-kiel.de

Abstract. In this paper, we present a new approach to scale-space which is derived from the 3D Laplace equation instead of the heat equation. The resulting lowpass and bandpass filters are discussed and they are related to the monogenic signal. As an application, we present a scale adaptive filtering which is used for denoising images. The adaptivity is based on the local energy of spherical quadrature filters and can also be used for sparse representation of images.

Keywords: scale-space, quadrature filters, adaptive filters, denoising

1 Introduction

In this paper, we present a new approach to scale-space. In the classical case, the heat equation leads to a homogeneous linear scale-space which is based on convolutions with Gaussian lowpass filters [8]. This method has been extended into several directions, in order to obtain more capable methods for low level vision. Perona and Malik introduce a diffusion constant which varies in the spatial domain controlling the grade of smoothing [9]. In his approach, Weickert substitutes the scalar product in the controlling term by the outer product yielding a method for anisotropic diffusion [12]. Sochen et. al. chose a more general point of view by considering the image intensity as a manifold [10] where the metric tensor controls the diffusion. This list is far from being complete, but what is important in this context is that all mentioned approaches have three things in common. At first, they are all based on the heat equation which can be seen as a heuristic choice from a physical model. In [13] however, several approaches for deriving the Gaussian scale-space as the unique solution of some basic axioms are presented. From our point of view, there is at least one PDE besides the diffusion equation that also generates a linear scale-space[1]. Second, all approaches try to control the diffusion by some information obtained from the image which are mostly related to partial derivatives and a measure for edges. Therefore, structures with even and odd symmetries are not weighted in the same way. Thirdly, all mentioned diffusions have theoretically infinite duration which means that

* This work has been supported by German National Merit Foundation and by DFG Graduiertenkolleg No. 357 (M. Felsberg) and by DFG Grant So-320-2-2 (G.Sommer).

[1] At least our new approach *seems* to fulfil all axioms of Iijima [13]. If it really does, this would imply that there must be an error in the proof of Iijima.

B. Radig and S. Florczyk (Eds.): DAGM 2001, LNCS 2191, pp. 124–131, 2001.
© Springer-Verlag Berlin Heidelberg 2001

the diffusion has to be stopped at a specific time. The stopping of the diffusion process is crucial for the result.

Our new method differs with respect to all three aspects from the classical ones. At first, it is based on the 3D Laplace equation which yields besides a smoothing kernel the monogenic signal, a 2D generalisation of the analytic signal [4]. Extending the properties of the analytic signal to 2D, the monogenic signal is well suited for estimating the local energy of a structure independently if it has an even or odd symmetry. Hence, if the smoothing is controlled by the energy, it is independent of the local symmetry. The energy of a local structure differs with the considered scale and in general it has several local maxima. These local maxima correspond to the partial local structures which form the whole considered structure. Our approach does not control the smoothing process itself but builds up a linear scale-space and applies an appropriate post-processing. Depending on the application, a coarsest scale and a minimal local energy are chosen, which determine an appropriate 2D surface in the 3D scale-space.

2 Theory

In this paper, images are considered as 2D real signals $f(x, y)$, whereas the scale-space is a 3D function defined over the spatial coordinates x and y and the scale parameter s. The commonly used signal model of scale-space is a stack of images, or from the physical point of view, a heat distribution at a specific time. Our model is quite different and it is motivated by two points of view. On the one hand, 1D signal processing and especially the Hilbert transform are closely related to complex analysis and holomorphic functions. On the other hand, holomorphic functions can be identified with *harmonic vector fields*, i.e., zero-divergence gradient fields. Indeed, the Hilbert transform emerges from postulating such a field in the positive half-plane $y > 0$ and by considering the relation between the components of the field on the real line [5]. Motivated by this fact, we introduce the following *signal model* (see Fig. 1). In the 3D space (x, y, s), the signal is embedded as the s-component of a 3D zero-divergence gradient field in the plane $s = 0$. For $s > 0$ the s-component is given by smoothed versions of the original image, so that the s-component corresponds to the classical scale-space. For $s = 0$ the other two components turn out to be the 2D equivalent of the Hilbert transform [5] and for $s > 0$ they are the generalised Hilbert transforms of the smoothed image. Hence, the most fundamental function in this embedding is the underlying *harmonic potential* p, i.e., p fulfils the Laplace-equation (see below). Due to the embedding, the Fourier transform is always performed wrt. x and y only, with the corresponding frequencies u and v. Accordingly, convolutions are also performed wrt. x and y only.

As already mentioned in the introduction and according to the signal model, we derive the non-Gaussian linear scale-space from the 3D Laplace equation ($\Delta_3 = \partial_x^2 + \partial_y^2 + \partial_s^2$ indicating the 3D Laplace operator)

$$\Delta_3 p(x, y, s) = 0 \ . \tag{1}$$

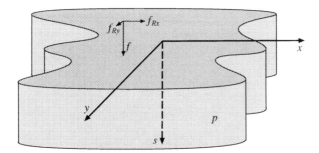

Fig. 1. Signal model for 2D signals, the scale-space, and the generalised analytic signal. The signal f is given by the s-derivative of the harmonic potential p. The other two derivatives ($f_{Rx} = h_x * f$ and $f_{Ry} = h_y * f$) are the generalised Hilbert transforms of f

The fundamental solution is given by $p(x, y, s) = c(x^2 + y^2 + s^2)^{-1/2}$ (the Newton potential) [1] where c is a constant that we choose to be $-(2\pi)^{-1}$. Since derivative operators commute, the partial derivatives of $p(x, y, s)$ are also solutions of (1) (comparable to the fact that the real part and the imaginary part of a holomorphic function are harmonic functions). Therefore, we obtain the (conjugated) Poisson kernels as further solutions [11]

$$g(x, y, s) = \frac{\partial}{\partial s} \frac{-1}{2\pi(x^2 + y^2 + s^2)^{1/2}} = \frac{s}{2\pi(x^2 + y^2 + s^2)^{3/2}} \tag{2}$$

$$h_x(x, y, s) = \frac{\partial}{\partial x} \frac{-1}{2\pi(x^2 + y^2 + s^2)^{1/2}} = \frac{x}{2\pi(x^2 + y^2 + s^2)^{3/2}} \tag{3}$$

$$h_y(x, y, s) = \frac{\partial}{\partial y} \frac{-1}{2\pi(x^2 + y^2 + s^2)^{1/2}} = \frac{y}{2\pi(x^2 + y^2 + s^2)^{3/2}} . \tag{4}$$

By taking the limit $s \to 0$, g is the delta-impulse $\delta_0(x)\delta_0(y)$ (representing the identity operator) and $(h_x, h_y)^T$ are the kernels of the Riesz transforms, so that $(g, h_x, h_y)^T * f$ is the monogenic signal of the real signal f [4]. Quite more interesting in this context is the fact that for $s > 0$ $(g, h_x, h_y)^T * f$ is the monogenic signal of the lowpass filtered signal $g * f$. This follows immediately from the transfer functions corresponding to (2–4) ($q = \sqrt{u^2 + v^2}$):

$$G(u, v, s) = \exp(-2\pi q s) \tag{5}$$

$$H_x(u, v, s) = i\, u/q \, \exp(-2\pi q s) \tag{6}$$

$$H_y(u, v, s) = i\, v/q \, \exp(-2\pi q s) . \tag{7}$$

Besides, the Laplace equation (1) can also solved by separating (x, y) and s giving two factors: one is the kernel of the 2D Fourier transform $\exp(-i2\pi(ux + vy))$ and the other one is $G(u, v, s)$ see [6]. Hence, instead of forming the scalar valued scale-space by $g(x, y, s) * f(x, y)$, we build a *vector field* **f**:

$$\mathbf{f}(x, y, s) = (\, g(x, y, s) \; h_x(x, y, s) \; h_y(x, y, s) \,)^T * f(x, y) \tag{8}$$

which is not only a family of monogenic signals (for different values of s) but also a solenoidal and irrotational field (which means that divergence and rotation are both zero), or, in terms of Geometric Algebra, a monogenic function [3] (monogenic: nD generalisation of holomorphic).

3   A New Linear Scale-Space

Now, getting from the mathematical background to interpretation, we firstly consider the shape of the derived lowpass filter g and the transfer function of the difference of two lowpass filters with different values of s, see Fig. 2. All four

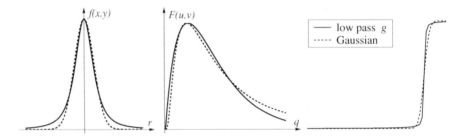

Fig. 2. Left: impulse response of lowpass filter g (solid line) and impulse response of Gaussian lowpass filter (dotted line). Middle: transfer function of the difference of two lowpass filters for different scales s and s' (solid line) and transfer function of the lognormal bandpass (dotted line). Right: lowpass filters applied to a step edge

filters are isotropic and hence, they are plotted wrt. to the radial coordinate $r = \sqrt{x^2 + y^2}$ and the radial frequency q, respectively. The impulse response of g has a sharper peak than the one of the Gaussian lowpass. On the other hand, it decreases slower with increasing r. Accordingly, steps in the image are changed according to Fig. 2 (right). While the curvature is smoother in the case of the filter g, the slope of the edge is more reduced by the Gaussian filter. Adopting the idea of the Laplacian pyramid [2], we use the difference of two lowpass filters to obtain a bandpass filter. It has a zero DC component and is similar to the lognormal bandpass, but it has a singularity in the first derivative for $q = 0^2$. Hence, low frequencies are not damped as much as in the lognormal case, but for high frequencies, the transfer function G decreases faster.

Considering the uncertainty relation, the lowpass filter g is slightly worse than the Gaussian lowpass (factor $\sqrt{1.5}$) which means that the localisation in phase space is not far from being optimal. In contrast to the lognormal bandpass filter, the spatial representation of the new bandpass filter is given analytically, so that it can be constructed in the spatial domain more easily. What is even more important, is that the linear combination of lowpass filtered monogenic

---

[2] Note that this is not valid for the transfer functions (6) and (7).

signals is again a monogenic signal. Therefore, the difference of two of these signals is a *spherical quadrature filter* (see also [3]). The last property of the new lowpass / bandpass filters which is important in the following, is the energy. The DC-component of the lowpass filter is one by definition (5). The bandpass filters for a multi-band decomposition are constructed according to

$$B_k(u,v) = \exp(-2\pi\sqrt{u^2+v^2}\lambda^k) - \exp(-2\pi\sqrt{u^2+v^2}\lambda^{k-1}) \qquad (9)$$

for $\lambda \in (0;1)$ which means that the maximal energy of the bandpass filter is independent of k.

4   Scale Adaptive Filters

The described scale-space approach can be used to denoise images or to reduce the number of features in an image (to *sparsify* it). Our algorithm behaves as follows: the scale-space is calculated up to a maximal smoothing s_M which is sufficient to remove nearly all the noise. For each scale, the monogenic signal is calculated and an index function is defined by the finest scale with a local maximum of the local magnitude

$$\text{index}(x,y) = \begin{cases} s_m & \text{if } \exists \epsilon > 0 : |f_M(x,y,s_m)| \geq |f_M(x,y,s)| \; \forall s < s_m + \epsilon \\ & \wedge \quad s_m < s_M \quad \wedge \quad |f_M(x,y,s_m)|^2 \geq E_T \\ s_M & \text{else} \end{cases} \qquad (10)$$

where the coarsest scale s_M is chosen if the maximal energy is lower than a threshold E_T. Using this index function, a denoised image is constructed, where at each position the lowpass is chosen by the index. The algorithm is motivated by the fact that the response of the monogenic signal shows local maxima when it is applied in the 'correct' scale, where in general we have more than one maximum. Since it is not reasonable to consider the image on arbitrary coarse scales (e.g. averaging of one quarter of the image), the range of scale is reduced and we mostly have only one maximum, see Fig. 3. The threshold of the energy at the maximum suppresses weak textures by setting the index function to maximal smoothing. Additionally, we apply median filters to the index functions, in order to denoise the latter. It is not reasonable to have an arbitrarily changing scale index since the scale is depending on the local neighbourhood.

   In our first experiment, we applied the algorithm to the test images in Fig. 3 and Fig. 4. The images were both processed with the same threshold and the same maximal scale. In both cases, a 3x3 median filter was applied to the scale index obtained from (10). The dark shadows at the top and left border of the smoothed house-image are artifacts resulting from performing the convolutions in the frequency domain. Obviously, textures with low energy are removed while edges and other structures with high energy are preserved. If a structure is preserved or not depends on the choice of the parameter E_T. In the case of noisy images, this energy threshold can be estimated according to a Rayleigh distribution (see [7]).

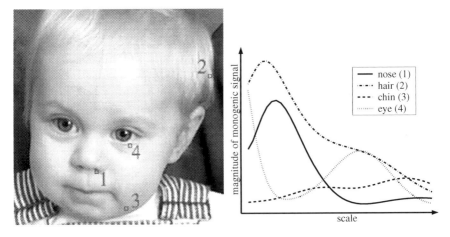

Fig. 3. Test image (left). The energy of the monogenic signal at four positions (indicated in the left image) for varying scale can be found in the plot on the right

In our second experiment, we added Gaussian noise to the image in Fig. 3 (see Fig. 5, left) and applied the standard method of isotropic Gaussian diffusion to it. The result can be found in the middle image in Fig. 5. The typical behaviour of Gaussian diffusion can be seen well: near the edges the noise is still present. Our approach results in the image on the right in the same figure. Except for some singular points the noise has been removed completely. The energy threshold was chosen by the method mentioned in the previous paragraph. In contrast to the diffusion algorithm, our method tends to over-smooth slightly those region boundaries where the energy of the edge is lower than the energy of the noise (see upper left corner).

The algorithm can also be used to sparsify images. Instead of constructing the denoised image from lowpass filtered versions using the scale index, the filter response of the monogenic signal is kept for local maxima of the energy only. That means that for the 'else' case in (10) the result is set to zero (nothing is stored). The amount of the remaining information can be estimated by the dark areas in the index images in Fig. 4. The representation which is obtained includes information of the monogenic signal only at positions with high local energy at an appropriate scale.

5   Conclusion

We have presented a new approach to scale-space which is not based on the heat equation but on the 3D Laplace equation. The resulting lowpass and bandpass filters have been shown to work properly and a relation to spherical quadrature filters and the monogenic signal has been established. Using the energy of the monogenic signal for different scales, a scale adaptive denoising algorithm has

Fig. 4. Upper row, left to right: scale index for first test image, second test image, corresponding scale index, relative difference between original and smoothed version. Below: smoothed images

been presented which can also be adopted for a sparse representation of features. The results are comparable to those of isotropic Gaussian diffusion. The denoising based on the Laplace equation shows less noise in the neighbourhood of edges, but low-energy edges are not preserved as well as in the Gaussian case. The new approach can easily be extended to anisotropic denoising by introducing a 2×2 scaling matrix instead of the real scale parameter s. The behaviour for low-energy edges is supposed to be better in that case.

References

1. BURG, K., HAF, H., AND WILLE, F.: *Höhere Mathematik für Ingenieure, Band IV Vektoranalysis und Funktionentheorie.* Teubner Stuttgart, 1994.
2. BURT, P.J., AND ADELSON, E.H.: The Laplacian pyramid as a compact image code. *IEEE Trans. Communications 31,* 4 (1983) 532–540.
3. FELSBERG, M., AND SOMMER, G.: The multidimensional isotropic generalization of quadrature filters in geometric algebra. In *Proc. Int. Workshop on Algebraic Frames for the Perception-Action Cycle, Kiel* (2000), G. Sommer and Y. Zeevi, Eds., vol. 1888 of *Lecture Notes in Computer Science,* Springer-Verlag, Heidelberg, pp. 175–185.

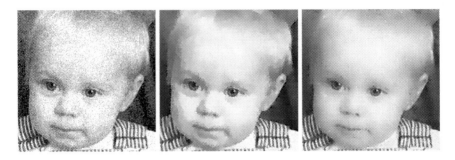

Fig. 5. Test image with noise (left), variance: $6e + 3$. Isotropic diffusion (parameters: contrast $\lambda = 3$, noise scale $\sigma = 2$, time step $\Delta t = 0.2$, and 50 iterations) yields the result in the middle, variance: $4.5e + 3$. The image on the right shows the result of our approach, variance: $3.5e + 3$

4. FELSBERG, M., AND SOMMER, G.: A new extension of linear signal processing for estimating local properties and detecting features. In *22. DAGM Symposium Mustererkennung, Kiel* (2000), G. Sommer, Ed., Springer-Verlag, Heidelberg, pp. 195–202

5. FELSBERG, M., AND SOMMER, G.: The monogenic signal. Tech. Rep. 2016, Institute of Computer Science and Applied Mathematics, Christian-Albrechts-University of Kiel, Germany, May 2001.

6. FELSBERG, M., AND SOMMER, G.: The structure multivector. In *Applied Geometrical Algebras in Computer Science and Engineering* (2001), Birkhäuser. to be published.

7. KOVESI, P.: Image features from phase information. *Videre: Journal of Computer Vision Research 1*, 3 (1999).

8. LINDEBERG, T.: *Scale-Space Theory in Computer Vision.* The Kluwer International Series in Engineering and Computer Science. Kluwer Academic Publishers, Boston, 1994.

9. PERONA, P., AND MALIK, J.: Scale-space and edge detection using anisotropic diffusion. *IEEE Trans. Pattern Analysis and Machine Intelligence 12*, 7 (1990), 629–639.

10. SOCHEN, N., KIMMEL, R., AND MALLADI, R.: A geometrical framework for low level vision. *IEEE Trans. on Image Processing, Special Issue on PDE based Image Processing 7*, 3 (1998), 310–318.

11. STEIN, E.M.: *Harmonic Analysis.* Princeton University Press, New Jersey 1993.

12. WEICKERT, J.: *Anisotropic Diffusion in Image Processing.* PhD thesis, Faculty of Mathematics, University of Kaiserslautern, 1996.

13. WEICKERT, J., ISHIKAWA, S., AND IMIYA, A.: Scale-space has first been proposed in japan. *Mathematical Imaging and Vision* (1997).

One-Sided Stability of Medial Axis Transform

Sung Woo Choi and Hans-Peter Seidel

Max Planck Institute for Computer Science
Stuhlsatzenhausweg 85
66123 Saarbrücken, Germany
E-mail: {swchoi,hpseidel}@mpi-sb.mpg.de

Abstract. Medial axis transform (MAT) is very sensitive to the noise, in the sense that, even if a shape is perturbed only slightly, the Hausdorff distance between the MATs of the original shape and the perturbed one may be large. But it turns out that MAT is stable, if we view this phenomenon with the one-sided Hausdorff distance, rather than with the two-sided Hausdorff distance. In this paper, we show that, if the original domain is weakly injective, which means that the MAT of the domain has no end point which is the center of an inscribed circle osculating the boundary at only one point, the one-sided Hausdorff distance of the original domain's MAT with respect to that of the perturbed one is bounded linearly with the Hausdorff distance of the perturbation. We also show by example that the linearity of this bound cannot be achieved for the domains which are not weakly injective. In particular, these results apply to the domains with the sharp corners, which were excluded in the past. One consequence of these results is that we can clarify theoretically the notion of extracting "the essential part of the MAT", which is the heart of the existing pruning methods.

1 Introduction

The *medial axis* (**MA**) of a plane domain is defined as the set of the centers of the maximal inscribed circles contained in the given domain. The *medial axis transform* (**MAT**) is defined as the set of all the pairs of the medial axis point and the radius of the corresponding inscribed circle. Because of the additional radius information, **MAT** can be used to reconstruct the original domain. More explicitly, the medial axis transform **MAT**(Ω) and the medial axis **MA**(Ω) of a plane domain Ω is defined by **MAT**$(\Omega) = \{ (p, r) \in \mathbb{R}^2 \times [0, \infty) \,|\, B_r(p) :$ maximal ball in $\Omega \}$, **MA**$(\Omega) = \{p \in \mathbb{R}^2 \,|\, \exists r \geq 0, \text{ s.t. } (p, r) \in \textbf{MAT}(\Omega)\}$.

Medial axis (transform) is one of the most widely-used tools in shape analysis. It has a natural definition, and has a graph structure which preserves the original shape homotopically [2], [3]. But the medial axis transform has one weak point; It is not stable under the perturbation of the domain [12], [5], [1]. See Figure 6. Even when the domain in (b) is slightly perturbed to the domain in (a) (that is, the Hausdorff distance between the domains in (a) and (b) is small), the **MAT** (**MA**) changes drastically, which results in a large value of the Hausdorff distance between the **MAT**s (**MA**s) of the domains in (a) and (b).

B. Radig and S. Florczyk (Eds.): DAGM 2001, LNCS 2191, pp. 132–139, 2001.
© Springer-Verlag Berlin Heidelberg 2001

This seemingly unplausible phenomenon can produce a lot of problems, especially in the recognition fields, since the data representing the domains have inevitable noises. So there has been many attempts to reduce the complexity of the **MAT** by "pruning" out what is considered less important, or considered to be caused by the noise [11], [13], [9].

One important observation that can be made from Figure 6 is that the **MAT** (**MA**) in (b) is contained approximately in the **MAT** (**MA**) in (a). In other words, although the two-sided Hausdorff distance of the **MAT**s in (a) and (b) is large, the *one-sided* Hausdorff distance of the **MAT** in (b) with respect to that in (a) is still small.

In this paper, we analyze this phenomenon, and show that **MA** and **MAT** are indeed stable, if we measure the change by the one-sided Hausdorff distance instead of the two-sided Hausdorff distance. We will show that, when a plane domain Ω satisfies a certain smoothness condition which we call the *weak-injectivity*, then the one-sided Hausdorff distance of $\mathbf{MA}(\Omega)$ (*resp.*, $\mathbf{MAT}(\Omega)$) with respect to $\mathbf{MA}(\Omega')$ (*resp.*, $\mathbf{MAT}(\Omega')$) has an upper bound which is *linear* with the Hausdorff distances between Ω, Ω' and between $\partial\Omega$, $\partial\Omega'$ for arbitrary domain Ω'. In particular, the weak-injectivity is shown to be essential for having the linear bound. This result extends the previous one for the *injective* domains [5]; We now can allow the sharp corners in the domains for which the linear one-sided stability is valid.

It turns out that the coefficient of the linear bound grows as the angle θ_Ω (See Section 2) characteristic to a weakly injective domain Ω decreases. An important consequence of this is that we can approximately measure the degree of the "detailed-ness" of a domain Ω by the value θ_Ω. Along with this, we will discuss about the relation between our result and the pruning of **MAT**.

2   Preliminaries

2.1   Normal Domains

Contrary to the common belief, $\mathbf{MAT}(\Omega)$ and $\mathbf{MA}(\Omega)$ may not be graphs with finite structure, unless the original domain Ω satisfies the following rather strong condition [3]: Ω is compact, or equivalently, Ω is closed and bounded, and the boundary $\partial\Omega$ of Ω is a (disjoint) union of finite number of simple closed curves, each of which in turn consists of finite number of real-analytic curve pieces. So we will consider only the domains satisfying this condition, which we call *normal*.

Let Ω be a normal domain. Then, except for some finite number of the special points, the maximal ball $B_r(p)$ for every $P = (p, r) \in \mathbf{MAT}(\Omega)$ has exactly two contact points with the boundary $\partial\Omega$. It is well known that $\mathbf{MA}(\Omega)$ is a C^1 curve around such p in $\mathbb{R}^2$. See Figure 1. We will denote the set of all such *generic* points in $\mathbf{MA}(\Omega)$ by $G(\Omega)$, and, for every $p \in G(\Omega)$, define $0 < \theta(p) \leq \frac{\pi}{2}$ to be the angle between $\overline{pq_1}$ (or equivalently $\overline{pq_2}$) and $\mathbf{MA}(\Omega)$ at p, where q_1, q_2 are the two contact points.

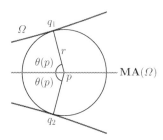

Fig. 1. Local geometry of **MA** around a generic point

Now, for every normal domain Ω, we define $\theta_\Omega = \inf \{\theta(p) : p \in G(\Omega)\}$. Note that $0 \leq \theta_\Omega \leq \frac{\pi}{2}$. We also define $\rho_\Omega = \min \{r : (p, r) \in \mathbf{MAT}(\Omega)\}$, that is, ρ_Ω is the smallest radius of the maximal balls contained in Ω.

We call an end point of **MA** a 1-*prong point*. There are exactly three kinds of the 1-prong points in **MA**, which are depicted in Figure 2; Type (a) is the center of a maximal circle with only one contact point at which the circle osculates the boundary. Type (b) is a sharp corner. Type (c) is a 1-prong point with a contact arc. It is easy to see that $\theta_\Omega = 0$, if and only if $\mathbf{MA}(\Omega)$ has a 1-prong point of the type (a), and $\rho_\Omega = 0$, if and only if $\mathbf{MA}(\Omega)$ has a 1-prong point of the type (b).

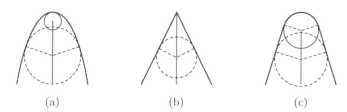

(a)   (b)   (c)

Fig. 2. Three types of 1-prong points

We call a normal domain Ω *injective*, if $\theta_\Omega > 0$ and $\rho_\Omega > 0$, and *weakly injective*, if $\theta_\Omega > 0$. Thus, Ω is injective, if and only if every end point of $\mathbf{MA}(\Omega)$ is of the type (c), and it is weakly injective, if and only if $\mathbf{MA}(\Omega)$ does not have the end points of the type (a). Note that a weakly injective domain may have a sharp corner (*i.e.*, the type (b)), while an injective domain may not.

For more details on the properties of the medial axis transform, see [2], [3], [10].

2.2   Hausdorff Distance: Euclidean *vs.* Hyperbolic

Although sometimes it might be misleading [6], the Hausdorff distance is a natural device to measure the difference between two shapes. Let A and B be two (compact) sets in $\mathbb{R}^2$. The *one-sided Hausdorff distance* of A with respect to B, $\mathcal{H}(A|B)$, is defined by $\mathcal{H}(A|B) = \max_{p \in A} d(p, B)$, where $d(\cdot, \cdot)$ is the usual Euclidean distance. The *(two-sided) Hausdorff distance* between A and B, $\mathcal{H}(A, B)$, is defined by $\mathcal{H}(A, B) = \max\{\mathcal{H}(A|B), \mathcal{H}(B|A)\}$. Note that, whereas the two-sided Hausdorff distance measures the difference between two sets, the one-sided Hausdorff distance measures how approximately one set is contained in another set.

Though the Hausdorff distance is intuitively appealing, it cannot capture well the seemingly unstable behaviour of **MAT** under the perturbation. Recently, there has been the introduction of a new measure called the *hyperbolic Hausdorff distance*, so that **MAT** (and **MA**) becomes stable, if the difference between two **MAT**s is measured by this measure [6] (See Proposition 1 below).

Let $P_1 = (p_1, r_1)$, $P_2 = (p_2, r_2)$ be in $\mathbb{R}^2 \times \mathbb{R}_{\geq 0}$, where we denote $\mathbb{R}_{\geq 0} = \{x \in \mathbb{R} \mid x \geq 0\}$. Then the *hyperbolic distance* $d_h(P_1|P_2)$ from P_1 to P_2 is defined by $d_h(P_1|P_2) = \max\{0, d(p_1, p_2) - (r_2 - r_1)\}$. Let M_1, M_2 be compact sets in $\mathbb{R}^2 \times \mathbb{R}_{\geq 0}$. Then the *one-sided hyperbolic Hausdorff distance* $\mathcal{H}_h(M_1|M_2)$ of M_1 with respect to M_2 is defined by $\mathcal{H}_h(M_1|M_2) = \max_{P_1 \in M_1} \{\min_{P_2 \in M_2} d_h(P_1|P_2)\}$, and the *(two-sided) hyperbolic Hausdorff distance* between M_1 and M_2 is defined by $\mathcal{H}_h(M_1, M_2) = \max\{\mathcal{H}_h(M_1|M_2), \mathcal{H}_h(M_2|M_1)\}$.

Now we have the following result which plays an important role in showing the main result (Theorem 1) of this paper.

Proposition 1. ([6]) *For any normal domains Ω_1 and Ω_2, we have*

$$\max\{\mathcal{H}(\Omega_1, \Omega_2), \mathcal{H}(\partial\Omega_1, \partial\Omega_2)\} \leq \mathcal{H}_h(\mathbf{MAT}(\Omega_1), \mathbf{MAT}(\Omega_2)),$$
$$\mathcal{H}_h(\mathbf{MAT}(\Omega_1), \mathbf{MAT}(\Omega_2)) \leq 3 \cdot \max\{\mathcal{H}(\Omega_1, \Omega_2), \mathcal{H}(\partial\Omega_1, \partial\Omega_2)\}.$$

3 Perturbation of Weakly Injective Domain

We first review the previous result for the injective domains.

Proposition 2. (Infinitesimal Perturbation of Injective Domain, [5], [7]) *Let Ω be an injective domain. Then we have*

$$\mathcal{H}(\mathbf{MA}(\Omega)|\mathbf{MA}(\Omega')) \leq \frac{2}{1 - \cos\theta_\Omega} \cdot \epsilon + o(\epsilon),$$
$$\mathcal{H}(\mathbf{MAT}(\Omega)|\mathbf{MAT}(\Omega')) \leq \frac{\sqrt{4 + (3 - \cos\theta_\Omega)^2}}{1 - \cos\theta_\Omega} \cdot \epsilon + o(\epsilon),$$

for every $\epsilon \geq 0$ and normal domain Ω' with $\max\{\mathcal{H}(\Omega, \Omega'), \mathcal{H}(\partial\Omega, \partial\Omega')\} \leq \epsilon$.

We show that, infinitesimally, the one-sided Hausdorff distance of **MAT** (and **MA**) of a weakly injective domain is bounded linearly by the magnitude of the perturbation. Define a function $g : (0, \pi/2] \to \mathbb{R}$ by $g(\theta) = 3\left(1 + \frac{2\sqrt{1+\cos^2\theta}}{1-\cos\theta}\right)$.

Theorem 1. (Infinitesimal Perturbation of Weakly Injective Domain)
Let Ω be a weakly injective domain. Then we have

$$\mathcal{H}(\mathbf{MAT}(\Omega)|\mathbf{MAT}(\Omega')), \mathcal{H}(\mathbf{MA}(\Omega)|\mathbf{MA}(\Omega')) \leq g(\theta_\Omega) \cdot \epsilon + o(\epsilon),$$

for every $\epsilon \geq 0$ and normal domain Ω' with $\max\{\mathcal{H}(\Omega, \Omega'), \mathcal{H}(\partial\Omega, \partial\Omega')\} \leq \epsilon$.
Proof. See [7].

Example 1. Let Ω be a weakly injective domain with a sharp corner P_1 depicted as in Figure 3. Let Ω' be the domain obtained by smoothing Ω near P_1 so that $\mathbf{MAT}(\Omega) = \overline{P_2P_3}$. Let $P_i = (p_i, r_i)$ for $i = 1, 2, 3$. Note that $\mathcal{H}(\Omega, \Omega') = \mathcal{H}(\partial\Omega, \partial\Omega') = \epsilon$, and $\mathcal{H}(\mathbf{MA}(\Omega)|\mathbf{MA}(\Omega')) = d(p_1, p_2) = \frac{1}{1-\cos\theta_\Omega} \cdot \epsilon$, $\mathcal{H}(\mathbf{MAT}(\Omega)|\mathbf{MAT}(\Omega')) = d(P_1, P_2) = \frac{\sqrt{1+\cos^2\theta_\Omega}}{1-\cos\theta_\Omega} \cdot \epsilon$.

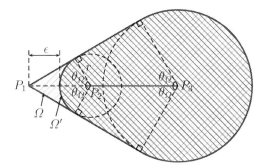

Fig. 3. One-sided stability for weakly injective domain

This example shows that the factor $\frac{1}{1-\cos\theta_\Omega}$ in $g(\theta_\Omega)$, which blows up as $\theta_\Omega \to 0$, is indeed unavoidable. One important consequence is that the class of the weakly injective domains is the largest possible class for which we have a linear bound for the one-sided Hausdorff distance of $\mathbf{MAT}$ (and $\mathbf{MA}$) with respect to the perturbation.

4   Illustrating Examples

Now we will consider a few examples, and calculate explicitly the constants θ_Ω and $g(\theta_\Omega)$ for each of them.

Example 2. Consider an equilateral triangle and a star-shaped domain depicted respectively as in Figure 4 (a) and (b). Note that $\theta_\Omega = \frac{\pi}{3}$ for (a), and $\theta_\Omega = \frac{\pi}{5}$ for (b). So $g(\theta_\Omega) = 3(1 + 2\sqrt{5}) = 16.416408\ldots$ for (a), and $g(\theta_\Omega) = 43.410203\ldots$ for (b).

Example 3. Consider the rectangular domains with the constant widths depicted as in Figure 5. Note that $\theta_\Omega = \frac{\pi}{4}$, and hence $g(\theta_\Omega) = 3\left(1 + 2\sqrt{3}(1 + \sqrt{2})\right) = 28.089243\ldots$ for all cases.

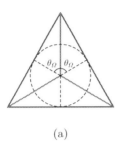
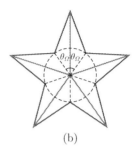

(a)   (b)

Fig. 4. (a) Equilateral triangle; $\theta_\Omega = \frac{\pi}{3}$ and $g(\theta_\Omega) = 16.416408\ldots$, (b) five-sided star; $\theta_\Omega = \frac{\pi}{5}$ and $g(\theta_\Omega) = 43.410203\ldots$.

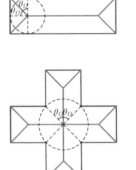

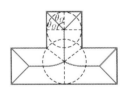

Fig. 5. Rectangular domains with the constant widths; For all cases, we have $\theta_\Omega = \frac{\pi}{4}$ and $g(\theta_\Omega) = 28.089243\ldots$.

5   The Essential Part of the MAT: Relation to Pruning

Theorem 1 together with Example 1 says that the angle θ_Ω is an important quantity reflecting the degree of the "detailed-ness" of a domain Ω. The smaller θ_Ω becomes, the finer approximation, that is, the smaller $\max\{\mathcal{H}(\Omega,\Omega'),\mathcal{H}(\partial\Omega,\partial\Omega')\}$ is needed for $\mathbf{MAT}(\Omega')$ and $\mathbf{MA}(\Omega')$ of another domain Ω' to contain (approximately) $\mathbf{MAT}(\Omega)$ and $\mathbf{MA}(\Omega)$ respectively.

Suppose we perturb a weakly injective domain with domains which are also weakly injective. In this case, $\mathbf{MAT}$ and $\mathbf{MA}$ become stable under the "two-sided" Hausdorff distance. In particular, we have the following corollary:

Corollary 1. (Approximation by Weakly Injective Domains) *Let Ω be a normal domain, and let Ω_1 and Ω_2 be two weakly injective domains such that $\max\{\mathcal{H}(\Omega_i,\Omega),\mathcal{H}(\partial\Omega_i,\partial\Omega)\} \leq \epsilon$ for $i = 1,2$. Let $\theta = \min\{\theta_{\Omega_1},\theta_{\Omega_2}\}$. Then we have $\mathcal{H}\left(\mathbf{MAT}(\Omega_1),\mathbf{MAT}(\Omega_2)\right),\mathcal{H}\left(\mathbf{MA}(\Omega_1),\mathbf{MA}(\Omega_2)\right) \leq 2g(\theta)\cdot\epsilon + o(\epsilon).$*

Thus, the effects on **MAT** and **MA** which arise from the choice of the weakly injective domains to approximate a normal domain is relatively small. So the **MAT** and the **MA** of an approximating weakly injective domain may be considered as a common part among all the other approximations with the same θ_Ω, and hence, an essential part of the original **MAT** and **MA** with the fine details determined by the value of θ_Ω. This suggests that, by approximating a given normal domain with the weakly injective domains, it is possible to extract approximately the most essential part of the original **MAT** and **MA**, which is the main objective of the existing pruning methods.

For example, Let Ω' be the original domain as shown in Figure 6 (a), whose **MA** has much unilluminating parts due to its noisy boundary. We approximate Ω' by a weakly injective domain Ω shown in Figure 6 (b), which has relatively simpler **MA**.

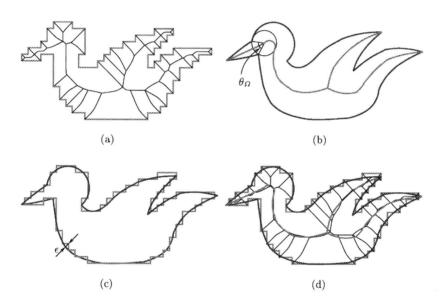

(a)   (b)

(c)   (d)

Fig. 6. Pruning **MAT**: (a) The original normal domain Ω' with its **MA**; (b) The approximating weakly injective domain Ω with its **MA**. Note that the sharp corners are allowed; (c) The Hausdorff distance between Ω and Ω', Here, $\epsilon = \max\{\mathcal{H}(\Omega, \Omega'), \mathcal{H}(\partial\Omega, \partial\Omega')\}$; (d) Comparison of **MA**(Ω) and **MA**(Ω'). Note that **MA**(Ω) captures an essential part of **MA**(Ω'), while simplifying **MA**(Ω').

By Theorem 1, we can get a bound on how approximately **MA**(Ω) is contained in **MA**(Ω'), or how faithfully **MA**(Ω) approximates parts of **MA**(Ω'), from the constant θ_Ω. Moreover, from Corollary 1, we see that **MA**(Ω) is *the* *essential part* of $\mathbf{MA}(\Omega')$ up to the bound in Corollary 1. In overall, by computing the much simpler $\mathbf{MA}(\Omega)$, we can get the essential part (within the bounds) of $\mathbf{MA}(\Omega')$ without ever computing $\mathbf{MA}(\Omega')$ at all. See [4] for the computation of $\mathbf{MAT}$ for domains with the free-form boundaries.

Of course, there still remains the problem of how to approximate/smooth the original noisy boundary. But we claim that, whatever method is used, our bounds can serve as a theoretical guarantee of the correctness of the approximation/pruning, which is absent in most of the existing pruning schemes.

One notable advance from [5] is that we can now allow the sharp corners for the approximating domain. For the discussion of using the general normal domains for the approximation, See [8].

References

1. J. August, K. Siddiqi and S. W. Zucker, "Ligature instabilities and the perceptual organization of shape," *Computer Vision and Image Understanding*, vol. 76, no. 3, pp. 231–243, Dec. 1999.
2. H. Blum, "A transformation for extracting new descriptors of shape," *Proc. Symp. Models for the Perception of Speech and Visual Form* (W.W. Dunn, ed.), MIT Press, Cambridge, MA, pp. 362–380, 1967.
3. H. I. Choi, S. W. Choi and H. P. Moon, "Mathematical theory of medial axis transform," *Pacific J. Math.*, vol. 181, no. 1, pp. 57–88, Nov. 1997.
4. H. I. Choi, S. W. Choi, H. P. Moon and N.-S. Wee, "New algorithm for medial axis transform of plane domain," *Graphical Models and Image Processing*, vol. 59, no. 6, pp. 463–483, 1997.
5. S. W. Choi and S.-W. Lee, "Stability analysis of medial axis transform," *Proc. 15th ICPR*, (Barcelona, Spain), vol 3, pp. 139–142, Sept. 2000.
6. S. W. Choi and H.-P. Seidel, "Hyperbolic Hausdorff distance for medial axis transform," Research Report, MPI-I-2000-4-003, 2000.
7. S. W. Choi and H.-P. Seidel, "Linear one-sided stability of MAT for weakly injective domain," Research Report, MPI-I-2001-4-004, 2001.
8. S. W. Choi and H.-P. Seidel, "One-sided stability of MAT and its applications," *preprint*, 2001.
9. M. P. Deseilligny, G. Stamon and C. Y. Suen, "Veinerization: A new shape descriptor for flexible skeletonization," *IEEE Trans. PAMI*, vol. 20, no. 5, pp. 505–521, May 1998.
10. P. J. Giblin and B. B. Kimia, "On the local form and transitions of symmetry sets, medial axes, and shocks," *Proc. 7th ICCV*, (Kerkyra, Greece), pp. 385–391, Sept. 1999.
11. F. Mokhtarian and A. K. Mackworth, "A theory of multiscale, curvature-based shape representation for planar curves," *IEEE Trans. PAMI*, vol. 14, no. 8, pp. 789–805, Aug. 1992.
12. U. Montanari, "A method for obtaining skeletons using a quasi-Euclidean distance," *J. of the ACM*, vol. 18, pp. 600–624, 1968.
13. D. Shaked and A. M. Bruckstein, "Pruning medial axes," *Computer Vision and Image Understanding*, vol. 69, no. 2, pp. 156–169, Feb. 1998.

Robust Line Detection in Historical Church Registers

M. Feldbach and K.D. Tönnies

Computer Vision Group, Department of Simulation and Graphics,
Otto-von-Guericke University, P.O. Box 4120, D-39016 Magdeburg, Germany,
{feldbach, klaus}@isg.cs.uni-magdeburg.de

Abstract. For being able to automatically acquire information recorded in church registers and other historical scriptures, the text of such documents needs to be segmented prior to automatic reading. Segmentation of old handwritten scriptures is difficult for two main reasons. Lines of text in general are not straight and ascenders and descenders of adjacent lines interfere. The algorithms described in this paper provide ways to reconstruct the path of the lines of text using an approach of gradually constructing line segments until an unique line of text is formed. The method was applied to church registers. They were written by different people in different styles between the 17th and 19th century. Line segmentation was found to be successful in 95% of all samples.

Keywords: Handwriting recognition, text line detection, document image processing

1 Introduction

Many historical documents that exist in libraries and various archives could be exploited electronically. Among those documents, church registers contain information on birth, marriage and death of the local population. Digital processing of such data requires automatic reading of this text. We present an approach for automatic line detection which is an important preprocessing step of this.

Most line detection methods assume that the image of the text does not change much and that lines are well separated [6,1]. Church registers, however, were written with lines of text being close to each other, with type, size and shape of the handwriting changing between different registers and with text of a given line possibly reaching into adjoining lines. Even methods that deal with line segmentation of such unconstrained data [9] often require separation of the text with sufficient space between lines [4,8], straightness of the lines [7] or only a single line [5]. As none of these constraints are given in our case, other knowledge needs to be exploited for giving evidence of text lines. We followed a strategy that is independent of gaps between lines of text and straightness of text lines. Evidence stems from local minima defining locally straight baselines. Local straightness is ascertained from gradually creating larger and larger line segments and removing those segments that do not follow horizontal and vertical

B. Radig and S. Florczyk (Eds.): DAGM 2001, LNCS 2191, pp. 140–147, 2001.

Fig. 1. Part of an entry in a church register of the county of Wegenstedt in 1812 and the reconstructed baselines and centre lines.

continuity constraints. The algorithm reconstructs baselines and centre lines in cases such as shown in Fig. 1 from a chaincode representation of the skeleton which is derived from the text in a preprocessing stage using modules from the VECTORY Software [3]. It automatically reconstructs the base lines and the centre lines [2].

The algorithm was tested on texts from church registers of the county of Wegenstedt that span a range of 300 years.

2   Line Detection

Four different "ledger" lines, the ascender line, the descender line, the baseline and the centre line bound the characters in a line of text. The baseline is the most pronounced line in the church registers. The location of the centre line can be deduced from the baseline and corrected based on evidence from the pen strokes. The ascender line and the descender line are not well pronounced because ascenders and descenders occur too infrequently and their height has a large variance. Thus, we restrict our search to that of the baseline and the centre line.

The set of connected chaincode elements forms foreground objects which are called *continua*. The baseline is found based on the local minima of all continua in y-direction. They are assumed to be locally straight even though lines of text curve over the complete width of the page. Local minima indicate, for the most part, points on the baseline and on the descender line with the majority stemming from baseline minima. Thus, the only line stretching over the whole width of the page and being made up of local minima from continua that are close enough together and locally straight, should be the baseline. To a lesser extent, the same argument holds for finding the centre line based on the local maxima of the chaincode of the continua. Finding baseline and centre line is carried out in four steps: *(1)* Potential baseline segments (pBLSs) are found that are segments of straight lines through local minima of the chaincode. *(2)* Baseline segments (BLSs) are selected or constructed from the pBLSs. *(3)* Baselines are created by joining BLSs which represent the same baseline. *(4)* Centre lines are created based on the local maxima of the chaincode and on the assumption that they run approximately in parallel to adjacent baselines.

The robustness of parameter settings that are used for the processes described below are reported in section 3. In the following h_{sc} stands for the average height of small characters (distance between baseline and centre line), w_c means the average width of a character.

2.1   Detection of Potential Baseline Segments (pBLSs)

The pBLSs are created from local minima of all continua on the page. Local minimum vertices v_{min}^i are marked. A pBLS consists of a direction α and an ordered list of at least four vertices. Let $d_{x,max}^v = 3.4 \cdot w_c$ and $d_{y,max}^v = 0.2 \cdot h_{sc}$. Adjacent vertices in this list must not be further apart than $d_{x,max}^v$. None of the vertices may vary by more than $d_{y,max}^v$ from the straight line connecting these vertices and defined by the direction α.

pBLSs are created independently for each v_{min}^i and for each direction at increments of $1°$ within $\pm 20°$ (we found this range to be sufficient). New vertices v_{min}^j are added that lie in direction α constrained by the above-mentioned distance and deviation tolerances. The search for a pBLS terminates when no new vertices can be added.

2.2   Creating Baseline Segments (BLSs)

After finding all possible pBLSs, each vertex may belong to more than one pBLS. First, pBLS are excluded that devide by more than $\pm 7°$ from the main direction of all pBLS. This direction is estimated from the histogram of directions of all pBLS. The threshold of $\pm 7°$ was found experimentally.

The remaining set of pBLSs still contains wrong segments. The next step creates a subset of baseline segments (BLSs) from the set of pBLSs. BLSs are selected according to the following rules:

- The number of strokes above the BLS must be larger than that below it.
- The BLS must not be completely contained in another pBLS in an adjacent direction with a smaller vertical deviation of the included vertices.
- The BLS must not be intersected by a longer pBLS that includes it in horizontal direction.

A special case arises if two pBLS cover the same part of the baseline but with conflicting interpretations. This is the case if the vertex lists p_1 and p_2 of two crossing pBLSs exist with $p_1 = \left\{ v_{min}^a, \ldots, v_{min}^i, \ldots, v_{min}^j, \ldots, v_{min}^m \right\}$ and $p_2 = \left\{ v_{min}^b, \ldots, v_{min}^i, \ldots, v_{min}^j, \ldots, v_{min}^n \right\}$ (shown in Fig. 2).

Such line segments are separated into three subsets. The middle part is the set of vertices $v_{min}^i, \ldots, v_{min}^j$ that is contained in p_1 as well as in p_2. One subset on the left side and one subset on the right side is chosen. In order to come to a decision between the subsets $v_{min}^a, \ldots, v_{min}^i$ and $v_{min}^b, \ldots, v_{min}^i$ and between the subsets $v_{min}^j, \ldots, v_{min}^m$ and $v_{min}^j, \ldots, v_{min}^n$, the one is chosen that contains the larger number of vertices.

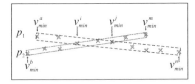
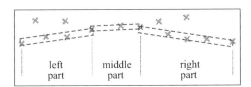

(a) Crossing BLSs with vertex   (b) Three resulting, new BLSs
    lists p_1 and p_2

Fig. 2. Solving a special case of crossing BLSs.

2.3   Creating Baselines

Elements of the set of BLSs are joined in order to form baselines. The process starts with the leftmost and uppermost BLS that is not part of a baseline and attempts to create a baseline by adding the next BLS. Let $d^s_{x,max} = 7 \cdot w_c$ and $d^s_{y,max} = 1.6 \cdot h_{sc}$. The joint is possible if the next BLS is with its leftmost vertex not further away than $d^s_{x,max}$ from the right most vertex of the current BLS and if the vertical distance difference is less than $d^s_{y,max}$. The process proceeds until no more BLS can be added. It is repeated for new baselines until no BLS exists that is not part of a baseline.

It may happen that false baselines are created from combining local minima, lying off the baseline, from artefacts caused by ascenders and descenders and even true local minima at the baseline (the latter because a tolerance of $\pm 7°$ is still large). For the removal of false baselines a quality measure is computed from total length of the baseline l_{total} and the percentage of strokes s_{above} immediately above the baseline as compared to all strokes as $q_{bl} = l_{total} \cdot s_{above}$. If two potential baselines intersect, the one baseline with lower q_{bl} value will be deleted.

Wrong baselines may also be located between lines of text. They are generally shorter than true baselines. They may be detected because of these facts. Let l_{av} be the average length of all baselines. The average vertical distance d_v between adjacent base lines is computed from all baselines with $l_{total} < 0.8 \cdot l_{av}$. The latter excludes wrong baselines from the computation. Let d_{prev} be the distance of a baseline to the previous one, d_{next} the distance to the next one. The baselines with $min(d_{prev}, d_{next}) < 0.6 \cdot d_{av}$ will be removed.

2.4   Computing the Centre Line

The centre line could be computed in a similar fashion from local maxima of the skeleton of the continua as the baseline, but the local maxima give a much weaker support for the line segments. However, the path of the baseline is known. Given the assumption that the centre line is approximately parallel to the baseline and given the assumption that the distance between centre line and baseline is less than 50% of the distance between two adjacent baselines, the centre line can be reconstructed.

Based on the position and direction of a BLS, a centre line segment (CLS) is searched by calculating the average vertical offset of the local maximum vertices being situated above the BLS and below the previous baseline (see Fig. 3). The horizontal distance constraint is not used because the existence of this CLS is known and only its position is searched.

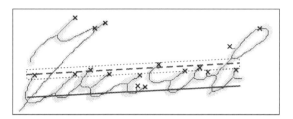

Fig. 3. Chain-code of writing, BLS (solid line), CLS (dashed line) with tolerance space (dashed rectangle) for the maxima (crosses).

3   Results

Line detection for church chronicles needs to be robust because even on a single page the style of the script may vary due to the time range of several days during which the page was written. This aim is achieved by the utilization of redundant information in the geometrical arrangement. For example a BLS can be reconstructed even if not all involved local minima are included or a baseline can be built even if one BLS is missing. The detection algorithm should perform well without requiring parameter adaptation unless the script differs widely. Parameters should only depend on features that can be easy deduced from the script.

Parameters depending on w_c or h_{sc} were adapted to three different scripts from 1649, 1727 and 1812 showing in Fig. 4. We found the optimal value by changing a parameter step by step and counting the resulting errors (see Fig. 5 (a)). By calculating factors from these values and the basic features of the script, we have the possibility to adapt the parameters $d^v_{x,max}$, $d^v_{y,max}$ (see subsection 2.1) and $d^s_{x,max}$, $d^s_{y,max}$ (see subsection 2.3) to another script.

The robustness of the algorithm can be seen from the wide range in which parameters may vary without significant increase of error (shown, e. g., for $d^v_{y,max}$ in Fig. 5 (a); results for $d^v_{x,max}$, $d^s_{x,max}$ and $d^s_{y,max}$ were similar). Other parameters like the range of directions during detection of pBLS affects the results scarcely and are set constant.

Robustness was tested by deliberately varying w_c and h_{sc} from their optimal setting and recording the error. Results can be seen in Fig. 6.

$h_{sc} = 2.0\,mm$ $h_{sc} = 2.6\,mm$ $h_{sc} = 1.9\,mm$

$w_c = 2.4\,mm$ $w_c = 4.5\,mm$ $w_c = 3.0\,mm$

Fig. 4. Samples of script from 1649, 1727 and 1812 and the basic parameters.

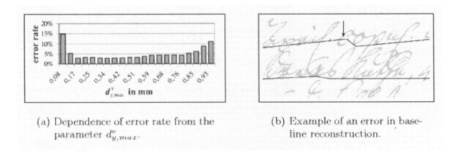

(a) Dependence of error rate from the   (b) Example of an error in base-
parameter $d^v_{y,max}$.   line reconstruction.

Fig. 5. Example of a test result using script from 1812 and a example of an error.

The error rate was defined as the percentage of words with wrong or without reconstructed base or centre lines (see example in Fig. 5 (b)).

We tested entries in church registers with overall 1161 words and five different handwritings (from 1649, 1727, 1812, 1817 and 1838). The error rates of all handwritings are between 3 and 5 percent; only the script from 1727 causes a error rate of 9 percent because there are many interferences like underlines and single words between the lines of text. Nonetheless the total result is 49 errors in 1161 words (4.2%).

4   Conclusions

We presented a robust approach for detection of baselines and centre lines of text which are the most important lines for an automatic text reading. Thereby, the procedure enables line recognition under the complex conditions caused by the style of script. It is done by gradually building up evidence for text lines based on local minima. It requires only an approximate adaptation of parameters to basic features of script. Thus, the algorithm will find textlines with high accuracy without additional adaptations although the style of writing may change even on a single page.

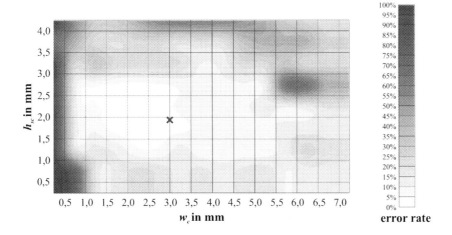

Fig. 6. Dependence of error rate of the two script features h_{sc} and w_c was tested on a paragraph from 1812. The Location of the estimated values for h_{sc} and w_c is shown as 'x'.

Further improvement could come from a previous analysis of distance values of local extrema in oder to get information about the script features. Serious interferences could be eliminated if underlines are recognized.

However, a 100% error-free reconstruction without preceding recognition of text itself will be impossible. This is the case because local straightness, horizontal continuity of lines and vertical continuity of distances between lines must allow for some variation. Cases can be constructed where this variation will lead to wrong selection of line segments.

References

1. A. El-Yacoubi, M. Gilloux, R. Sabourin, and C. Y. Suen. An HMM-Based Approach for Off-Line Unconstrained Handwritten Word Modeling and Recognition. *IEEE Transactions on Pattern Analysis and Machine Intelligence*, 21(8):752–760, August 1999.
2. M. Feldbach. Generierung einer semantischen Repräsentation aus Abbildungen handschriftlicher Kirchenbuchaufzeichnungen. Diploma thesis, Otto-von-Guericke University of Magdeburg, 2000.
3. Graphikon Gesellschaft für Bildverarbeitung und Computergraphik mbH. Mandelstraße 16, D-10409 Berlin, Germany. URL: www.graphikon.com. Software: VECTORY, Version 4.0.
4. G. Kim, V. Govindaraju, and S. N. Srihari. An Architecture for Handwritten Text Recognition Systems. *International Journal on Document Analysis and Recognition*, 2(1):37–44, February 1999.
5. S. Madhvanath and V. Govindaraju. Local Reference Linies for Handwritten Phrase Recognition. *Pattern Recognition*, 32:2021–2028, 1999.

6. S. Madhvanath, E. Kleinberg, and V. Govindaraju. Holistic Verification of Hand-written Phrases. *IEEE Transactions on Pattern Analysis and Machine Intelligence*, 21(12):1344–1356, December 1999.
7. Y. Pu and Z. Shi. A Natural Learning Algorithm Based on Hough Transform for Text Lines Extraction in Handwritten Documents. In *Proceedings of the Sixth International Workshop on Frontiers of Handwriting Recognition (IWFHR VI), Taejon, Korea*, pages 637–646, 1998.
8. M. Shridar and F. Kimura. Segmentation-Based Cursive Handwriting Recognition. In H. Bunke and P. S. P. Wang, editors, *Handbook of Character Recognition and Document Image Analysis*, pages 123–156. World Scientific, February 1997.
9. P. Steiner. Zwei ausgewählte Probleme zur Offline-Erkennung von Handschrift. Diploma thesis, University of Bern, August 1995.

Similarity Measures for Occlusion, Clutter, and Illumination Invariant Object Recognition

Carsten Steger

MVTec Software GmbH
Neherstraße 1, 81675 München, Germany
Phone: +49 (89) 457695-0, Fax: +49 (89) 457695-55
steger@mvtec.com

Abstract. Novel similarity measures for object recognition and image matching are proposed, which are inherently robust against occlusion, clutter, and nonlinear illumination changes. They can be extended to be robust to global as well as local contrast reversals. The similarity measures are based on representing the model of the object to be found and the image in which the model should be found as a set of points and associated direction vectors. They are used in an object recognition system for industrial inspection that recognizes objects under Euclidean transformations in real time.

1 Introduction

Object recognition is used in many computer vision applications. It is particularly useful for industrial inspection tasks, where often an image of an object must be aligned with a model of the object. The transformation (pose) obtained by the object recognition process can be used for various tasks, e.g., pick and place operations or quality control. In most cases, the model of the object is generated from an image of the object. This 2D approach is taken because it usually is too costly or time consuming to create a more complicated model, e.g., a 3D CAD model. Therefore, in industrial inspection tasks one is usually interested in matching a 2D model of an object to the image. The object may be transformed by a certain class of transformations, depending on the particular setup, e.g., translations, Euclidean transformations, similarity transformations, or general 2D affine transformations (which are usually taken as an approximation to the true perspective transformations an object may undergo).

Several methods have been proposed to recognize objects in images by matching 2D models to images. A survey of matching approaches is given in [3]. In most 2D matching approaches the model is systematically compared to the image using all allowable degrees of freedom of the chosen class of transformations. The comparison is based on a suitable similarity measure (also called match metric). The maxima or minima of the similarity measure are used to decide whether an object is present in the image and to determine its pose. To speed up the recognition process, the search is usually done in a coarse-to-fine manner, e.g., by using image pyramids [10].

The simplest class of object recognition methods is based on the gray values of the model and image itself and uses normalized cross correlation or the sum of squared

B. Radig and S. Florczyk (Eds.): DAGM 2001, LNCS 2191, pp. 148–154, 2001.

or absolute differences as a similarity measure [3]. Normalized cross correlation is invariant to linear brightness changes but is very sensitive to clutter and occlusion as well as nonlinear contrast changes. The sum of gray value differences is not robust to any of these changes, but can be made robust to linear brightness changes by explicitly incorporating them into the similarity measure, and to a moderate amount of occlusion and clutter by computing the similarity measure in a statistically robust manner [6].

A more complex class of object recognition methods does not use the gray values of the model or object itself, but uses the object's edges for matching [2,8]. In all existing approaches, the edges are segmented, i.e., a binary image is computed for both the model and the search image. Usually, the edge pixels are defined as the pixels in the image where the magnitude of the gradient is maximum in the direction of the gradient. Various similarity measures can then be used to compare the model to the image. The similarity measure in [2] computes the average distance of the model edges and the image edges. The disadvantage of this similarity measure is that it is not robust to occlusions because the distance to the nearest edge increases significantly if some of the edges of the model are missing in the image.

The Hausdorff distance similarity measure used in [8] tries to remedy this shortcoming by calculating the maximum of the k-th largest distance of the model edges to the image edges and the l-th largest distance of the image edges and the model edges. If the model contains n points and the image contains m edge points, the similarity measure is robust to $100k/n\%$ occlusion and $100l/m\%$ clutter. Unfortunately, an estimate for m is needed to determine l, which is usually not available.

All of these similarity measures have the disadvantage that they do not take the direction of the edges into account. In [7] it is shown that disregarding the edge direction information leads to false positive instances of the model in the image. The similarity measure proposed in [7] tries to improve this by modifying the Hausdorff distance to also measure the angle difference between the model and image edges. Unfortunately, the implementation is based on multiple distance transformations, which makes the algorithm too computationally expensive for industrial inspection.

Finally, another class of edge based object recognition algorithms is based on the generalized Hough transform [1]. Approaches of this kind have the advantage that they are robust to occlusion as well as clutter. Unfortunately, the GHT requires extremely accurate estimates for the edge directions or a complex and expensive processing scheme, e.g., smoothing the accumulator space, to determine whether an object is present and to determine its pose. This problem is especially grave for large models. The required accuracy is usually not obtainable, even in low noise images, because the discretization of the image leads to edge direction errors that already are too large for the GHT.

In all of the above approaches, the edge image is binarized. This makes the object recognition algorithm invariant only against a narrow range of illumination changes. If the image contrast is lowered, progressively fewer edge points will be segmented, which has the same effects as progressively larger occlusion. The similarity measures proposed in this paper overcome all of the above problems and result in an object recognition strategy robust against occlusion, clutter, nonlinear illumination changes, and a relatively large amount of defocusing. They can be extended to be robust to global as well as local contrast reversals.

2 Similarity Measures

The model of an object consists of a set of points $p_i = (x_i, y_i)^T$ with a corresponding direction vector $d_i = (t_i, u_i)^T$, $i = 1, \ldots, n$. The direction vectors can be generated by a number of different image processing operations, e.g., edge, line, or corner extraction, as discussed in Section 3. Typically, the model is generated from an image of the object, where an arbitrary region of interest (ROI) specifies that part of the image in which the object is located. It is advantageous to specify the coordinates p_i relative to the center of gravity of the ROI of the model or to the center of gravity of the points of the model.

The image in which the model should be found can be transformed into a representation in which a direction vector $e_{x,y} = (v_{x,y}, w_{x,y})^T$ is obtained for each image point (x, y). In the matching process, a transformed model must be compared to the image at a particular location. In the most general case considered here, the transformation is an arbitrary affine transformation. It is useful to separate the translation part of the affine transformation from the linear part. Therefore, a linearly transformed model is given by the points $p_i' = A p_i$ and the accordingly transformed direction vectors $d_i' = A d_i$, where

$$A = \begin{pmatrix} a_{11} & a_{12} \\ a_{21} & a_{22} \end{pmatrix} .$$

As discussed above, the similarity measure by which the transformed model is compared to the image must be robust to occlusions, clutter, and illumination changes. One such measure is to sum the (unnormalized) dot product of the direction vectors of the transformed model and the image over all points of the model to compute a matching score at a particular point $q = (x, y)^T$ of the image, i.e., the similarity measure of the transformed model at the point q, which corresponds to the translation part of the affine transformation, is computed as follows:

$$s = \frac{1}{n} \sum_{i=1}^{n} \langle d_i', e_{q+p'} \rangle = \frac{1}{n} \sum_{i=1}^{n} t_i' v_{x+x_i', y+y_i'} + u_i' w_{x+x_i', y+y_i'} . \tag{1}$$

If the model is generated by edge or line filtering, and the image is preprocessed in the same manner, this similarity measure fulfills the requirements of robustness to occlusion and clutter. If parts of the object are missing in the image, there are no lines or edges at the corresponding positions of the model in the image, i.e., the direction vectors will have a small length and hence contribute little to the sum. Likewise, if there are clutter lines or edges in the image, there will either be no point in the model at the clutter position or it will have a small length, which means it will contribute little to the sum.

The similarity measure (1) is not truly invariant against illumination changes, however, since usually the length of the direction vectors depends on the brightness of the image, e.g., if edge detection is used to extract the direction vectors. However, if a user specifies a threshold on the similarity measure to determine whether the model is present in the image, a similarity measure with a well defined range of values is desirable. The following similarity measure achieves this goal:

$$s = \frac{1}{n} \sum_{i=1}^{n} \frac{\langle d_i', e_{q+p'} \rangle}{\|d_i'\| \cdot \|e_{q+p'}\|} = \frac{1}{n} \sum_{i=1}^{n} \frac{t_i' v_{x+x_i', y+y_i'} + u_i' w_{x+x_i', y+y_i'}}{\sqrt{t_i'^2 + u_i'^2} \cdot \sqrt{v_{x+x_i', y+y_i'}^2 + w_{x+x_i', y+y_i'}^2}} . \tag{2}$$

Because of the normalization of the direction vectors, this similarity measure is additionally invariant to arbitrary illumination changes since all vectors are scaled to a length of 1. What makes this measure robust against occlusion and clutter is the fact that if a feature is missing, either in the model or in the image, noise will lead to random direction vectors, which, on average, will contribute nothing to the sum.

The similarity measure (2) will return a high score if all the direction vectors of the model and the image align, i.e., point in the same direction. If edges are used to generate the model and image vectors, this means that the model and image must have the same contrast direction for each edge. Sometimes it is desirable to be able to detect the object even if its contrast is reversed. This is achieved by:

$$s = \left| \frac{1}{n} \sum_{i=1}^{n} \frac{\langle d_i', e_{q+p'} \rangle}{\|d_i'\| \cdot \|e_{q+p'}\|} \right| . \tag{3}$$

In rare circumstances, it might be necessary to ignore even local contrast changes. In this case, the similarity measure can be modified as follows:

$$s = \frac{1}{n} \sum_{i=1}^{n} \frac{|\langle d_i', e_{q+p'} \rangle|}{\|d_i'\| \cdot \|e_{q+p'}\|} . \tag{4}$$

The above three normalized similarity measures are robust to occlusion in the sense that the object will be found if it is occluded. As mentioned above, this results from the fact that the missing object points in the instance of the model in the image will on average contribute nothing to the sum. For any particular instance of the model in the image, this may not be true, e.g., because the noise in the image is not uncorrelated. This leads to the undesired fact that the instance of the model will be found in different poses in different images, even if the model does not move in the images, because in a particular image of the model the random direction vectors will contribute slightly different amounts to the sum, and hence the maximum of the similarity measure will change randomly. To make the localization of the model more precise, it is useful to set the contribution of direction vectors caused by noise in the image to zero. The easiest way to do this is to set all inverse lengths $1/\|e_{q+p'}\|$ of the direction vectors in the image to 0 if their length $\|e_{q+p'}\|$ is smaller than a threshold that depends on the noise level in the image and the preprocessing operation that is used to extract the direction vectors in the image. This threshold can be specified easily by the user. By this modification of the similarity measure, it can be ensured that an occluded instance of the model will always be found in the same pose if it does not move in the images.

The normalized similarity measures (2)–(4) have the property that they return a number smaller than 1 as the score of a potential match. In all cases, a score of 1 indicates a perfect match between the model and the image. Furthermore, the score roughly corresponds to the portion of the model that is visible in the image. For example, if the object is 50% occluded, the score (on average) cannot exceed 0.5. This is a highly desirable property because it gives the user the means to select an intuitive threshold for when an object should be considered as recognized.

A desirable feature of the above similarity measures (2)–(4) is that they do not need to be evaluated completely when object recognition is based on a threshold $s_{\min}$ for the similarity measure that a potential match must achieve. Let s_j denote the partial sum of the dot products up to the j-th element of the model. For the match metric that uses the sum of the normalized dot products, this is:

$$s_j = \frac{1}{n} \sum_{i=1}^{j} \frac{\langle d_i', e_{q+p'} \rangle}{\|d_i'\| \cdot \|e_{q+p'}\|} \quad . \tag{5}$$

Obviously, all the remaining terms of the sum are all ≤ 1. Therefore, the partial score can never achieve the required score s_{min} if $s_j < s_{min} - 1 + j/n$, and hence the evaluation of the sum can be discontinued after the j-th element whenever this condition is fulfilled. This criterion speeds up the recognition process considerably.

3   Object Recognition

The above similarity measures are applied in an object recognition system for industrial inspection that recognizes objects under Euclidean transformations, i.e., translation and rotation, in real time. Although only Euclidean transformations are implemented at the moment, extensions to similarity or general affine transformations are not difficult to implement. The system consists of two modules: an offline generation of the model and an online recognition.

The model is generated from an image of the object to be recognized. An arbitrary region of interest specifies the object's location in the image. Usually, the ROI is specified by the user. Alternatively, it can be generated by suitable segmentation techniques. To speed up the recognition process, the model is generated in multiple resolution levels, which are constructed by building an image pyramid from the original image. The number of pyramid levels l_{max} is chosen by the user.

Each resolution level consists of all possible rotations of the model, where thresholds ϕ_{min} and ϕ_{max} for the angle are selected by the user. The step length for the discretization of the possible angles can either be done automatically by a method similar to the one described in [2] or be set by the user. In higher pyramid levels, the step length for the angle is computed by doubling the step length of the next lower pyramid level.

The rotated models are generated by rotating the original image of the current pyramid level and performing the feature extraction in the rotated image. This is done because the feature extractors may be anisotropic, i.e., the extracted direction vectors may depend on the orientation of the feature in the image in a biased manner. If it is known that the feature extractor is isotropic, the rotated models may be generated by performing the feature extraction only once per pyramid level and transforming the resulting points and direction vectors.

The feature extraction can be done by a number of different image processing algorithms that return a direction vector for each image point. One such class of algorithms are edge detectors, e.g, the Sobel or Canny [4] operators. Another useful class of algorithms are line detectors [9]. Finally, corner detectors that return a direction vector, e.g., [5], could also be used. Because of runtime considerations the Sobel filter is used in the current implementation of the object recognition system. Since in industrial inspection the lighting can be controlled, noise does not pose a significant problem in these applications.

To recognize the model, an image pyramid is constructed for the image in which the model should be found. For each level of the pyramid, the same filtering operation that was used to generate the model, e.g., Sobel filtering, is applied to the image. This returns a direction vector for each image point. Note that the image is not segmented, i.e., thresholding or other operations are not performed. This results in true robustness to illumination changes.

To identify potential matches, an exhaustive search is performed for the top level of the pyramid, i.e., all precomputed models of the top level of the model resolution hierarchy are used to compute the similarity measure via (2), (3), or (4) for all possible poses of the model. A potential match must have a score larger than a user-specified threshold s_{min} and the corresponding score must be a local maximum with respect to neighboring scores. As described in Section 2, the threshold s_{min} is used to speed up the search by terminating the evaluation of the similarity measure as early as possible.

After the potential matches have been identified, they are tracked through the resolution hierarchy until they are found at the lowest level of the image pyramid. Various search strategies like depth-first, best-first, etc., have been examined. It turned out that a breadth-first strategy is preferable for various reasons, most notably because a heuristic for a best-first strategy is hard to define, and because depth-first search results in slower execution if all matches should be found.

Once the object has been recognized on the lowest level of the image pyramid, its position and rotation are extracted to a resolution better than the discretization of the search space, i.e., the translation is extracted with subpixel precision and the angles with a resolution better than the angle step length. This is done by fitting a second order polynomial (in the three pose variables) to the similarity measure values in a $3 \times 3 \times 3$ neighborhood around the maximum score. The coefficients of the polynomial are obtained by convolution with 3D facet model masks. The corresponding 2D masks are given in [9]. They generalize to arbitrary dimensions in a straightforward manner.

4   Examples

Figure 1 displays an example of recognizing multiple objects. To illustrate the robustness against nonlinear illumination changes, the model image in Figure 1(a) was acquired using back lighting. Figure 1(b) shows that all three cog wheels have been recognized correctly despite the fact that front lighting is used and that a fourth cog wheel occludes two of the other cog wheels.

5   Conclusions

A new class of similarity measures for object recognition and image matching, which are inherently robust against occlusion, clutter, nonlinear illumination changes, and global as well as local contrast reversals, have been proposed. The similarity measures are used in an object recognition system for industrial inspection that is able to recognize objects under Euclidean transformations in video frame rate. The system is able to achieve an accuracy of 1/22 pixel and 1/12 degree on real images.

(a) Image of model object   (b) Found objects

Fig. 1. Example of recognizing multiple objects. To illustrate the robustness against illumination changes, the model image uses back lighting while the search image uses front lighting.

Future work will focus on extending the object recognition system to handle at least similarity transformations and possibly general affine transformations.

References

1. D. H. Ballard. Generalizing the Hough transform to detect arbitrary shapes. *Pattern Recognition*, 13(2):111–122, 1981.
2. Gunilla Borgefors. Hierarchical chamfer matching: A parametric edge matching algorithm. *IEEE Transactions on Pattern Analysis and Machine Intelligence*, 10(6):849–865, November 1988.
3. Lisa Gottesfeld Brown. A survey of image registration techniques. *ACM Computing Surveys*, 24(4):325–376, December 1992.
4. John Canny. A computational approach to edge detection. *IEEE Transactions on Pattern Analysis and Machine Intelligence*, 8(6):679–698, June 1986.
5. Wolfgang Förstner. A framework for low level feature extraction. In Jan-Olof Eklundh, editor, *Third European Conference on Computer Vision*, volume 801 of *Lecture Notes in Computer Science*, pages 383–394, Berlin, 1994. Springer-Verlag.
6. Shang-Hong Lai and Ming Fang. Robust and efficient image alignment with spatially varying illumination models. In *Computer Vision and Pattern Recognition*, volume II, pages 167–172, 1999.
7. Clark F. Olson and Daniel P. Huttenlocher. Automatic target recognition by matching oriented edge pixels. *IEEE Transactions on Image Processing*, 6(1):103–113, January 1997.
8. William J. Rucklidge. Efficiently locating objects using the Hausdorff distance. *International Journal of Computer Vision*, 24(3):251–270, 1997.
9. Carsten Steger. An unbiased detector of curvilinear structures. *IEEE Transactions on Pattern Analysis and Machine Intelligence*, 20(2):113–125, February 1998.
10. Steven L. Tanimoto. Template matching in pyramids. *Computer Graphics and Image Processing*, 16:356–369, 1981.

Affine Point Pattern Matching

K. Voss and H. Suesse

Friedrich-Schiller-University Jena, Department of Computer Science
Ernst-Abbe-Platz 1-4
D-07743 Jena, Germany
{nkv,nbs}@uni-jena.de
http://pandora.inf.uni-jena.de

Abstract. This paper presents a general solution for the problem of affine point pattern matching (APPM). Formally, given two sets of two-dimensional points (x,y) which are related by a general affine transformation (up to small deviations of the point coordinates and maybe some additional outliers). Then we can determine the six parameters a_{ik} of the transformation using new Hu point-invariants which are invariant with respect to affine transformations. With these invariants we compute a weighted point reference list. The affine parameters can be calculated using the method of the least absolute differences (LAD method) and using linear programming. In comparison to the least squares method, our approach is very robust against noise and outliers. The algorithm works in $O(n)$ average time and can be used for translation and/or rotations, isotropic and non-isotropic scalings, shear transformations and reflections.

1 Introduction

Point pattern matching (PPM) is an important problem in image processing. Cox and Jager have given already in 1993 an overview with respect to different types of transformations and methods [6].

The here presented method describes a general solution for the problem of affine point pattern matching in $O(n)$ time where the point attachment will be performed in the space of the so called Hu invariants, see [11]. In the original literature the Hu invariants are only invariant with respect to similarity transformations. In the present paper we develop Hu invariants which are even affinely invariant using the ideas of normalization. With the help of these invariants, a list of weighted point references can be calculated. Following an idea of Ben-Ezra [3] the affine transformation can be calculated by the least absolute differences (so called LAD method) using linear programming. The algorithm is numerically stable against noise of the points and outliers.

B. Radig and S. Florczyk (Eds.): DAGM 2001, LNCS 2191, pp. 155–162, 2001.
© Springer-Verlag Berlin Heidelberg 2001

2   Affine Invariants

2.1   Affine Normalization of Discrete Point Sets

Formally, given an affine transformation and two discrete sets of points. We use the method of normalization well known in the theory of affine invariants for planar objects, see ([2,13]). As features we use the discrete moments instead of the area moments. Therefore, at the beginning we define the discrete moments $M_{j,k}$ of a finite point set P. Here is $M_{0,0} = n$ the number of points, and $(\overline{x}, \overline{y})$ is the center of gravity for the given point set. Now the central moments $m'_{j,k}$ are given by a translation $x' = x - \overline{x}$ and $y' = y - \overline{y}$, so that we have $m'_{1,0} = 0$ and $m'_{0,1} = 0$ in the first normalization step. In the second step we perform with $x'' = x' + \alpha y'$ and $y'' = y'$ a shearing (or "stretching") in x direction. By this, the old central moments $m'_{j,k}$ are transformed in new moments $m''_{j,k}$. We obtain especially for $m''_{1,1}$ with the simple requirement $m''_{1,1} = 0$, the parameter α is determined as $\alpha = -m'_{1,1}/m'_{0,2}$. Now we can calculate all new moments $m''_{j,k}$ with given normalization values for $(m''_{1,0}, m''_{0,1}, m''_{1,1}) = (0,0,0)$.

Finally, a general anisotrope scaling $x''' = \beta x''$ and $y''' = \gamma y''$ yields the moments $m'''_{j,k}$. The moments $m'''_{2,0}$ and $m'''_{0,2}$ shall be normalized to 1 so that the parameters β and γ have to be $\beta = \frac{1}{\sqrt{m''_{2,0}}}$, $\gamma = \frac{1}{\sqrt{m''_{0,2}}}$. Note, that there are differences between these expressions and the expressions using the normalization of the area moments, see [13,17].

Now, the five lowest order moments are normalized to the canonical values: $(m'''_{1,0}, m'''_{0,1}, m'''_{1,1}, m'''_{2,0}, m'''_{0,2}) = (0,0,0,1,1)$.

2.2   Hu Invariants with Respect to Affine Transformations

A stable normalization of the rotation is not posssible. For that reason, we try to find numerically stable expressions which are invariant against rotations. Such numerically stable expressions are introduced by Hu (see [11]). Hu has been derived 7 invariants $H_1, H_2, ..., H_7$ including one to third order moments. For our purpose we need additional Hu invariants including up to fourth order moments. These invariants can be easily derived using the so called complex moments, see [2,16]. Some of the classical Hu invariants and the new Hu invariants are given in table 1. All other Hu invariants up to order 4 vanish because of our normalizations $m'''_{20} = m'''_{02} = 1$ and $m'''_{11} = 0$. Note, that the so called algebraic moment-invariants (see [7]) are numerically too sensitive against noise because there are values of a power of the moments until 11.

2.3   Hu Invariants of Single Points

We put the origin of the coordinate system in each of the points $p \in P$ and compute the affine Hu invariants $H_k(p)$ now depending on this point p. That means, we needn't to normalize the moments to the centroid because p is itself the origin. It follows, that we receive for every point p affine Hu invariants. Now, we can search for any point $p \in P$ the corresponding point $q \in Q$ with the same (or at least similar) Hu invariants.

Table 1. Affine Hu invariants up to 4-th order moments

order		Hu invariant
2	H_2	$m_{20}''' + m_{02}''' = 2$
3	H_3	$\left(m_{30}''' - 3m_{12}'''\right)^2 + \left(3m_{21}''' - m_{03}'''\right)^2$
3	H_4	$\left(m_{30}''' + m_{12}'''\right)^2 + \left(m_{21}''' + m_{03}'''\right)^2$
4	H_8	$\left(m_{40}''' - m_{04}'''\right)^2 + 4\left(m_{31}''' + m_{13}'''\right)^2$
4	H_9	$\left(m_{40}''' + m_{04}'''\right)^2 + 16\left(m_{31}''' - m_{13}'''\right)^2 - 12m_{22}'''\left(m_{04}''' - 3m_{22}''' + m_{40}'''\right)$
4	H_{11}	$m_{40}''' + 2m_{22}''' + m_{04}'''$

Table 2. Affine discrete Hu invariants $H_k(p)$ for every point from a point set of 10 points

point p	$H_3(p)$	$H_4(p)$	$H_8(p)$	$H_9(p)$	$H_{11}(p)$
(164,320)	0.014	0.645	0.084	0.134	0.755
(422,314)	0.127	0.531	0.042	0.104	0.609
(150,425)	0.232	0.687	0.020	0.182	0.732
(89,75)	0.345	0.544	0.081	0.123	0.670
(242,398)	0.324	0.855	0.033	0.505	0.897
(324,434)	0.288	0.776	0.049	0.399	0.851
(91,189)	0.334	0.609	0.117	0.200	0.721
(339,417)	0.184	0.739	0.045	0.297	0.834
(263,355)	0.242	0.693	0.031	0.481	0.877
(448,112)	0.323	0.483	0.037	0.107	0.561

3   Determination of the Affine Transformations

3.1   Next Neighbor Search in the Hu Space

First of all we have to calculate in the space of all Hu point invariants a list of reference points $(p_i = (x_i, y_i), q_i = (x_i', y_i'), w_i), i = 1, ..., n$. For a point $p_i \in P$ it is to find a reference point $q_i \in Q$ with a weight or probability w_i. In our experiments we have used a simple nearest neighbor classificator to find a corresponding point. The weight w_i can be calculated using the classificator, where there is an unique correspondence or not and can depending on the distance of the corresponding points. There are some heuristics in finding a good measure for the weights.

In Table 2 it can be seen the numerical range of the affine Hu invariants of a point set.

3.2   Estimators for the Affine Parameters

The next step is now the calculating of the affine transformation from the weighted correspondence list. This can be done in a common way by the least squares estimator using the L_2-metric. An advantage of this estimator is that we have to solve only a linear system of 6 equations with 6 variables. But it is also well known that the least squares method is very sensitive to outliers. That is the reason why we need a good initial guess for an iterative reweighted least-squares algorithm. It is also well-known that the L_1-metric is much more robust than the L_2-metric. For example, if we have the two one-dimensional problems $L_2^2 = \sum_{i=1}^n (a_i - \mu)^2 \to min!$ and $L_1 = \sum_{i=1}^n |a_i - \nu| \to min!$ then the median ν minimizes the L_1 metric, and the centroid μ minimizes the L_2 metric.

Because of that we are using instead of the least squares method (L_2-metric) the method of the least absolute differences (LAD, L_1-metric):

$$L_1 = \sum_{i=1}^n w_i|x_i' - a_{11}x_i - a_{12}y_i - a_{13}| + w_i|y_i' - a_{21}x_i - a_{22}y_i - a_{23}| \to minimum!$$

The next question is to find a good numerical procedure for solving this problem. It is not possible to find the solution from $\nabla L_1 = 0$, but if we use the relation $|x| = \sqrt{x^2}$ it is possible to form the gradient in any point excluding $x = 0$. Starting with an arbitrary initial value for the 6 affine parameters, a sequence for the parameters can be calculated using the gradient method. It is simple to show that this sequence converges towards the global minimum. We have only a 6-dimensional optimization problem, but this problem is nonlinear and difficult to handle. An another very good idea is to form a linear programming problem with the disadvantage that the number of variables increases. But the handling of a linear programming problem is very simple.

3.3   Linear Programming

To form a linear programming problem we follow an idea from [3] and solve this optimization problem with a linear optimization technique - the wellknown simplex method, see [12]. But first of all we have to translate the L_1 optimization problem into a linear optimization problem. Let $d_i = f(x_i, y_i)$ be the residual of a function $f(x, y)$ for the point (x_i, y_i). We introduce two new nonnegative variables with $d_i = d_i^+ - d_i^-$, $d_i^+ \geq 0$, $d_i^- \geq 0$. Now we consider the absolute value

$$|d_i| = |d_i^+ - d_i^-| = \begin{cases} d_i^+ , if\ d_i^- = 0 \\ d_i^- , if\ d_i^+ = 0 \end{cases} ,$$

and construct the following optimization problem

$$min_{value} = min \left\{ \sum_{i=1}^N (d_i^+ + d_i^-) \right\} .$$

It is easy to see that $min_{value} = min \left\{ \sum_{i=1}^N |d_i| \right\}$ because it is necessary that at the minimum at least one of the variables d_i^+ or d_i^- vanishes. In our problem we have for every point two residuals or defects $d1_i = x_i' - a_{11}x_i - a_{12}y_i - a_{13}$, $d2_i = y_i' - a_{21}x_i - a_{22}y_i - a_{23}$. This provides us the basic idea for a linear programming solver.

The standard form of a linear optimization problem (LOP) is:

$$\mathbf{c}^{\mathrm{T}}\mathbf{x} \to minimum \text{ subject to } \mathbf{D}\mathbf{x} = \mathbf{b}, \; x_k \geq 0 \; \forall k \;.$$

$\mathbf{D}$ is a $(m \times n)$ matrix, m is the number of constraint equations and n is the number of variables with $n > m$.

Because of that, we have to form all affine variables as differences of non-negative variables $a_{ij} = a_{ij}^+ - a_{ij}^-, a_{ij}^+ \geq 0, a_{ij}^- \geq 0$. Following the remarks at the beginning of this chapter this is also to do for the residuals d_i using slack variables $z_k = z_k^+ - z_k^-, z_k^+ \geq 0, z_k^- \geq 0$. The constraint equations are now

$$a_{11}^+ x_i - a_{11}^- x_i + a_{12}^+ y_i - a_{12}^- y_i + a_{13}^+ - a_{13}^- + z1_i^+ - z1_i^- = x_i'$$
$$a_{21}^+ x_i - a_{21}^- x_i + a_{22}^+ y_i - a_{22}^- y_i + a_{23}^+ - a_{23}^- + z2_i^+ - z2_i^- = y_i'$$
$$i = 1, ..., N \quad .$$

A problem in solving this LO-problem is that the set of all feasible solutions is unbounded due to the differences of nonnegative variables $a_{ij} = a_{ij}^+ - a_{ij}^-, a_{ij}^+ \geq 0, a_{ij}^- \geq 0$ and $z_k = z_k^+ - z_k^-, z_k^+ \geq 0, z_k^- \geq 0$. This implies difficulties using the simplex method. To overcome these difficulties we introduce an additional bounding constraint:

$$\sum_{k,l} a_{kl}^+ + \sum_{k,l} a_{kl}^- + \sum_{i=1}^{N} z1_i^+ + \sum_{i=1}^{N} z1_i^- + \sum_{i=1}^{N} z2_i^+ + \sum_{i=1}^{N} z2_i^- + s = limit \;.$$

Here, $s \geq 0$ is an additional slack variable and $limit$ is a given, very large and positive constant. The parameters of the affine transformation can be determined by solving the following minimization problem:

$$\sum_{i=1}^{N} w_i (z1_i^+ + z1_i^- + z2_i^+ + z2_i^-) \to minimum!$$

If we have a point list with N corresponding points then our LO-problem contains $2N + 1$ constraint equations and $12 + 4N + 1$ variables including all slack variables. The average complexity of the simplex method is polynomial in the number of constraints $2N+1$, which is in a fixed relation to the number N of correspondences. In most practical cases, however, the average complexity is known to be nearly linear, see [12]. We can decrease the complexity decomposing the system in two systems estimating the parameters a_{11}, a_{12}, a_{13} and a_{21}, a_{22}, a_{23} separately.

4   Experimental Results for Synthetic Data Sets

Three types of evaluation procedures were performed: (i) testing the L_1-metric and the L_2-metric using known point correspondences, (ii) testing the new affine

Hu invariants to detect correct point correspondences, (iii) comparison of the L_1-metric and the L_2-metric using the affine Hu-invariants. The tests were applied to different types of outliers and different standard deviations of noise. The coordinates of all points were in the interval $0 \leq x_i, y_i \leq 400 \; \forall i$.

4.1   Noise of the Coordinates

The noise scenario test can be seen in Fig. 1. The relative errors of the affine parameters are be displayed. It can be seen the robustness of the method against noise of the point coordinates.

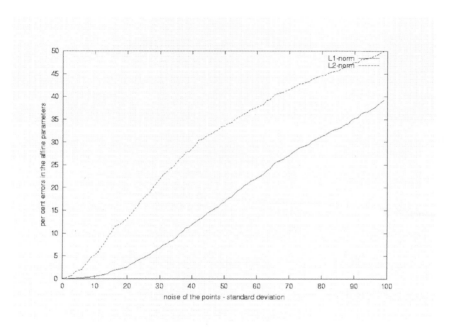

Fig. 1. Errors of the affine parameters in dependence of all noisy pixels

4.2   Outliers

In Fig. 2 the dependence of the errors from (per cent) outliers are demonstrated. The outliers have a standard deviation of 100. In Fig. 2 the extreme robustness using the L_1-metric and the affine Hu-invariants is very surprisingly.

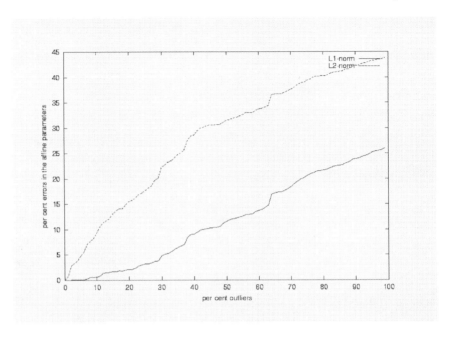

Fig. 2. Errors of the affine parameters in dependence of outliers using the whole system

4.3   Real-Time Performance

In Fig. 3 it can be seen the complexity of the method in practical applications. The computation time are in seconds done on a 500 MHz PC. It can be seen that the complexity is nearly linear.

References

1. S.Abraham, K.Voss, H.Suesse: Affines matching planarer Punktmengen mittels Normalisierung über diskrete Momente. *Proc. 18. DAGM-Symposium*, Heidelberg 1996, Springer-Verlag, pp. 315-322
2. Y.S. Abu-Mostafa and D.Psaltis, Image Normalization by Complex Moments, *PAMI 7* (1985) 46-55.
3. M. Ben-Ezra, S. Peleg, and M. Werman: Real-time motion analysis with linear programming. *CVIU 78*(1999) 32-52
4. M. Carcassoni, E.R. Hancock: Point pattern matching with robust spectral correspondence. *Proceedings CVPR*(2000) 649-655
5. Chang, S.H., Cheng, F.H., Hsu, W.H., Wu, G.Z.: Fast algorithm for point pattern-matching: Invariant to translations, rotations and scale changes. *PR 30*(1997) 311-320
6. G.S.Cox, G.DeJager: A survey of point pattern matching techniques and a new approach to point pattern recognition.*Proc. of South African Symposium on Communications and Signal Processing 1993*,pp. 243-248

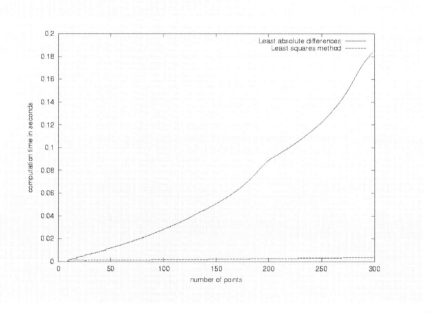

Fig. 3. Real-time performance of the system

7. Flusser J., T. Suk: Pattern recognition by affine moment invariants. *PR 26*(1993) 167-174

8. S. Gold, A. Rangarajan, C.-P. Lu, S. Pappu, E. Mjolsness: New algorithms for 2D and 3D point matching: Pose estimation and correspondence. *PR 31*(1998) 1019-1031

9. M. Hagedoorn, and R.C. Veltkamp: Reliable and efficient pattern matching using an affine invariant metric. *IJCV 31* (1999) 203-225

10. J.Hong, X.Tan: A new approach to point pattern matching. *Proc. of 9th International Conference on Pattern Recognition* 1988, Vol.1, pp.82.84

11. M.K.Hu: Visual pattern recognition by moment invariants.*IT* 8 (1962) 179-187

12. H. Karloff: Linear Programming. *Birkhauser Verlag,*Basel 1991.

13. I.Rothe, H.Suesse, K. Voss: The method of normalization to determine invariants. *IEEE Trans. PAMI 18* (1996) 366-377

14. J. Sprinzak, M. Werman: Affine point matching. *PRL 15* (1994) 337-339

15. K.Voss, H.Suesse: A new one-parametric fitting method for planar objects. *IEEE Trans. PAMI* 21 (1999) 646-651

16. K.Voss, H.Suesse: Adaptive Modelle und Invarianten für zweidimensionale Bilder. *Shaker-Verlag,*Aachen 1995

17. K.Voss, H.Suesse: Invariant fitting of planar objects by primitives. *IEEE Trans. PAMI* 19 (1997) 80-84

18. P.B. van Wamelen, Z. Li, S.S. Iyengar: A fast algorithm for point pattern matching problem. *appear in PAMI*

Surface Expansion from Range Data Sequences

Hagen Spies[1], Bernd Jähne[1], and John L. Barron[2]

[1] Interdisciplinary Center for Scientific Computing,
University of Heidelberg, INF 368, 69120 Heidelberg, Germany,
{Hagen.Spies,Bernd.Jaehne}@iwr.uni-heidelberg.de
[2] Dept. of Comp. Science, University of Western Ontario,
London, Ontario, N6A 5B7 Canada,
barron@csd.uwo.ca

Abstract. We compute the range flow field, i.e. the 3D velocity field, of a moving deformable surface from a sequence of range data. This is done in a differential framework for which we derive a new constraint equation that can be evaluated directly on the sensor data grid. It is shown how 3D structure and intensity information can be used together in the estimation process. We then introduce a method to compute surface expansion rates from the now available velocity field. The accuracy of the proposed scheme is assessed on a synthetic data set. Finally we apply the algorithm to study 3D leaf motion and growth on a real range sequence.

Keywords. Range flow, expansion rates, range data sequences.

1 Introduction

We denote the instantaneous velocity field that describes the motion of a deformable surface as *range flow*. The term range flow is used as we derive this velocity field from sequences of range data sets. Together with the 3D structure the range flow field can be used to study the dynamic changes of such surfaces. One interesting question is whether the surface area changes during the motion. This can for example be used to study growth processes in biological systems such as leaves or skin.

The same displacement vector field has also been called scene flow when computed directly from stereo image sequences [11]. We present range flow estimation in a differential framework that is related to optical flow algorithms. Other approaches that use deformable models have been reported before [10,12].

The contribution of this paper is twofold. First we introduce a new version of the constraint equation for range flow estimation that can be evaluated directly on the sensor grid. Second we show how a change in the surface area can be determined locally from range flow fields.

2 Range Flow

We now restate the concept of range flow estimation and introduce a new formulation of the range flow motion constraint equation.

B. Radig and S. Florczyk (Eds.): DAGM 2001, LNCS 2191, pp. 163–169, 2001.

2.1   Motion Constraint

The observed surface can be described by its depth as a function of space and time $Z = Z(X, Y, t)$. The total derivative with respect to time then directly yields the range flow motion constraint equation [4,12,9]:

$$Z_X U + Z_Y V - W + Z_t = 0 \ . \tag{1}$$

Here $(U, V, W)^T$ is the range flow and indices denote partial derivatives. In order to evaluate this equation we need to compute these partial derivatives of the depth function with respect to world coordinates. However typical range sensors sample the data on a sensor grid, e.g. that of a CCD camera.

While it is possible to compute derivatives from a surface fit, we rather use convolutions. This allows to draw on the well established linear filter theory and can be implemented very efficiently. Towards this end we notice that a range sensor produces one data set for each of X,Y and Z on its grid ($X = X(x, y, t)$ etc.). Here sensor coordinates are denoted by (x,y). The three components of the range flow field are the total derivatives of the world coordinates with respect to time ($U = \frac{\mathrm{d}X}{\mathrm{d}t}$ etc.). This can be expressed in the following equations:

$$U = \partial_x X \, \dot{x} + \partial_y X \, \dot{y} + \partial_t X \ , \tag{2}$$

$$V = \partial_x Y \, \dot{x} + \partial_y Y \, \dot{y} + \partial_t Y \ , \tag{3}$$

$$W = \partial_x Z \, \dot{x} + \partial_y Z \, \dot{y} + \partial_t Z \ . \tag{4}$$

The total time derivative is indicated by a dot. As we are not interested in the rates of change on the sensor coordinate frame we eliminate $\dot{x}$ and $\dot{y}$ to obtain the range flow motion constraint expressed in sensor coordinates:

$$\frac{\partial(Z, Y)}{\partial(x, y)} U + \frac{\partial(X, Z)}{\partial(x, y)} V + \frac{\partial(Y, X)}{\partial(x, y)} W + \frac{\partial(X, Y, Z)}{\partial(x, y, t)} = 0 \ , \tag{5}$$

where $\frac{\partial(Z,Y)}{\partial(x,y)}$ is the Jacobian of Z,Y with respect to x,y. Notice that the Jacobians are readily computed from the derivatives of X,Y,Z in the sensor frame obtained by convolving the data sets with derivative kernels.

In practice many sensors have aligned world and sensor coordinate systems which implies $\partial_y X = \partial_x Y = 0$. Yet Eq. (5) poses the general constraint independent of a particular sensor.

2.2   TLS Solution

Equation (5) poses only one constraint in the three unknowns U,V,W. This manifestation of the aperture problem has been examined in more detail before [7]. In order to get an estimate we pool the constraints in a local neighbourhood and assume the flow to be constant within this area.

As all data terms in Eq. (5) are bound to contain errors it is reasonable to use total least squares estimation as opposed to standard least squares. To do so we rewrite Eq. (5) as $d^T p = 0$ with a data vector d given by the Jacobians. In order to avoid the trivial solution we require that $|p| = 1$. It is straightforward to show that the solution is given by the eigenvector corresponding to the smallest eigenvalue of the so called structure tensor [7]:

$$J_{ij} = B * (d_i \cdot d_j) , \quad i, j = 1 \ldots 4 . \tag{6}$$

The local integration is computed here via convolution with an averaging mask B, typically a Binomial. From the thus estimated parameter vector we can recover the range flow as:

$$f = (U\, V\, W)^T = \frac{1}{p_4}(p_1\, p_2\, p_3)^T . \tag{7}$$

The smallest eigenvalue gives the residual of the attempted fit. This can be used to define a confidence measure based on a threshold τ [9]:

$$\omega = \begin{cases} 0 & \text{if } \lambda_4 > \tau \\ \left(\frac{\tau - \lambda_4}{\tau + \lambda_4}\right)^2 & \text{else} \end{cases} . \tag{8}$$

It is quite possible that the neighbourhood does not contain enough information to compute a full flow estimate. This can be somewhat amended by using the intensity data as well, how this is done is described next.

2.3   Including Intensity

The usage of intensity data in addition to the range data can improve both the accuracy and density of the estimated range flow significantly [8]. We assume that the intensity does not change with moderate depth changes. Thus, like for optical flow, we attribute all changes in intensity to motion. This yields another constraint equation:

$$0 = \partial_x I\, \dot{x} + \partial_y I\, \dot{y} + \partial_t I . \tag{9}$$

Combined with (2) and (3) we obtain an additional constraint on U and V:

$$\frac{\partial(I, Y)}{\partial(x, y)} U + \frac{\partial(X, I)}{\partial(x, y)} V + \frac{\partial(X, Y, I)}{\partial(x, y, t)} = 0 . \tag{10}$$

This can also be written as $d'^T p = 0$, where we simply set $d'_3 = 0$. The intensity constraint (10) results in another structure tensor J' constructed following Eq. (6). The sum of the two tensors yields a combined tensor from which the solution is then found by the analysis described above.

In order to ensure no a priori bias between intensity and depth we also require that the two data channels have been scaled such that their values are in the same order of magnitude. This can be done by subtracting the mean and adjusting the data to have the same variance. Additionally we can use a weight factor on the intensity tensor J' to account for different signal to noise ratios.

2.4   Dense Flow Fields

Even the usage of intensity data does not ensure a unique solution in every local neighbourhood. Because of the need to compute derivatives of both the range data and range flow they are required to vary smoothly. We employ normalized averaging to obtain the required smoothness. This averaging is a special case of normalized convolution and is computed as follows [3]:

$$\bar{f} = \frac{B * (\Omega \cdot f)}{B * \Omega} .$$ (11)

Ω contains a confidence value for each estimated flow according to Eq. (8). The range data is smoothed in the same way where the certainty of the range measurement is used as confidence values.

3   Expansion Rates

There are a number of applications where one wants to determine whether the movement and deformation of an observed surface changes its surface area. Examples are the study of the effects of temperature changes or mechanical stress on materials and the observation of growth rates in biological systems.

The surface area of a regular surface can be defined as the integral over the area of tangential parallelograms [2]:

$$A = \int |\partial_x r(x,y) \times \partial_y r(x,y)| \, dxdy .$$ (12)

Hence we can define a local area element as $|\partial_x r \times \partial_y r|$. The relative change in the local surface area caused by the displacement vector $\Delta r = \Delta t f$ is then given by:

$$dA = \frac{|\partial_x(r + \Delta r) \times \partial_y(r + \Delta r)|}{|\partial_x r \times \partial_y r|} .$$ (13)

We are now ready to define the relative expansion rate as:

$$e = (dA - 1) \cdot 100 \, \% .$$ (14)

This quantity can again be computed from derivatives, obtained via convolution, of both the range data and range flow arrays.

Because of the need to compute derivatives of both the range data and range flow they are required to vary smoothly and should be on the same scale. Thus we employ the same normalized averaging on the range data as on the range flow, see Sect. 2.4.

4   Experiments

In the following all derivatives are computed using 5-tap derivative filters that have been designed to give an optimal direction estimation [5]. For the integration in the structure tensor, see Eq. (6), we use a 9×9 Binomial. The threshold on the smallest eigenvalue is set to $\tau = 0.1$ and averaging in Eq. (11) is done by computing the second level of the Gaussian pyramid.

4.1   Synthetic Data

The synthetic data used here to test the introduced algorithm consists of an expanding sphere. The sensor is taken to use a pinhole camera, as is the case for structured lighting or stereo systems. The radius of the sphere is initially 150mm and its centre is located at $(0, 0, 300)^T \, mm$. The focal length is set to 20mm and sensor elements (CCD pixel) are placed at 0.05mm in both directions. We apply an intensity texture to each surface element based on the spherical angles $I = I(\theta, \phi)$:

$$I = \begin{cases} 100 & \text{if } \theta < 0.5° \\ 100 + 50 \sin(\frac{2\pi\theta}{1°}) + 50 \sin(\frac{2\pi\phi}{30°}) & \text{else} \end{cases} . \tag{15}$$

Surface expansion is modelled by a change in radius. We use a sequence with an expansion rate of 1% per frame, this corresponds to multiplying the radius with a factor of 1.00499 between successive frames. Additionally the whole sphere is moving with a constant velocity of $(0.01, 0.02, 0.03)^T \, [mm/frame]$.

Sensible values for the noise in the range data with a viewing distance around 150mm are given by $\sigma_Z = 0.1mm$ [1]. For the error in X and Y coordinates we assume a noise around $\sigma_{X,Y} = 0.01mm$ and the intensity noise lies in the range of $\sigma_I = 1.0$.

The following table gives the mean values for the relative error in the expansion rate E_e, the relative error in the range flow magnitude E_m and the mean absolute angle deviation between correct and estimated 3D velocity E_d:

$\sigma_{X,Y}$	σ_Z	σ_I	E_e [%]	E_m [%]	E_d [°]
0.00	0.0	0.0	1.02	0.001	0.01
0.01	0.0	0.0	1.35	0.002	0.02
0.00	0.1	0.0	1.10	0.001	0.01
0.00	0.0	1.0	3.24	0.003	0.05
0.02	0.0	0.0	2.03	0.003	0.04
0.00	0.2	0.0	1.55	0.001	0.02
0.00	0.0	2.0	6.32	0.004	0.10
0.01	0.1	1.0	3.11	0.003	0.05
0.02	0.2	2.0	6.89	0.005	0.10

First we conclude that the range flow field is very accurate even for slightly higher noise levels. However the estimation of expansion rates depends strongly

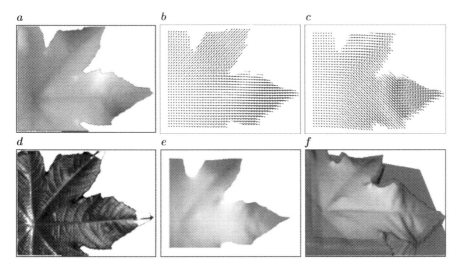

Fig. 1. Real castor bean leaf: **a** depth (Z) data, **b** U,V-component and **c** U,W-component of the range flow field. **d** Intensity data. Growth in the range from -2% to 3% per hour: **e** as map and **f** as texture on the 3D structure.

on the noise. For a standard deviation of 0.1mm in the Z coordinate we can compute accurate expansion rates. This accuracy can be achieved with current sensor technology.

4.2   Leaf Growth

An application that requires the evaluation of expansion rates is the study of growth in leaves. As an example we investigate a moving and growing castor bean leaf. The 3D structure is captured using a structured light range sensor. We sample the leaf every 2 minutes to obtain a sequence of range data sets. Figure 1a,d show the depth and intensity data for the frame where we compute range flow. The flow field is given in Fig. 1b,c. We see that there is considerable motion of the leaf in particular in Z direction. Clearly a lot of this motion does not stem from growth alone. The obtained growth rate in % per hour are given in Fig. 1e,f. In accordance with previous findings from leaves that have been confined to a plane we see that growth diminishes as we move from the base to the tip of the leaf [6].

5   Conclusion

We introduced a new version of the range flow motion constraint equation that can be evaluated directly on the sensor grid. In particular there is no need to fit a surface model to the range data. A formula for the computation of expansion rates from the thus computed range flow fields has been given. We could demonstrate that our method is capable to compute accurate range flow and surface expansion rates on both synthetic and real data.

References

[1] J. Beraldin, S. F. El-Hakim, and F. Blais. Performance evaluation of three active vision systems built at the national research council of canada. In *Conf. on Optical 3D Measurement Techniques III*, pages 352–361, Vienna, Austria, October 1995.

[2] M. P. do Carmo. *Differential Geometry of Curves and Surfaces*. Prentice-Hall, Englewood Cliffs, NJ, 1976.

[3] G. H. Granlund and H. Knutsson. *Signal Processing for Computer Vision*. Kluwer Academic, Dordrecht, The Netherlands, 1995.

[4] B. K. P. Horn and J. Harris. Rigid body motion from range image sequences. *CVGIP*, 53(1):1–13, January 1991.

[5] B. Jähne, H. Scharr, and S. Körkel. Principles of filter design. In *Handbook of Computer Vision and Applications*. Academic Press, 1999.

[6] D. Schmundt, M. Stitt, B. Jähne, and U. Schurr. Quantitative analysis of local growth rates of dicot leaves at high temporal and spatial resolution, using image sequence analysis. *Plant Journal*, 16:505–514, 1998.

[7] H. Spies, H. Haußecker, B. Jähne, and J. L. Barron. Differential range flow estimation. In *DAGM*, pages 309–316, Bonn, Germany, September 1999.

[8] H. Spies, B. Jähne, and J. L. Barron. Dense range flow from depth and intensity data. In *ICPR*, pages 131–134, Barcelona, Spain, September 2000.

[9] H. Spies, B. Jähne, and J. L. Barron. Regularised range flow. In *ECCV*, pages 785–799, Dublin, Ireland, June/July 2000.

[10] L. Tsap, D. Goldgof, and S. Sarkar. Multiscale combination of physically-based registration and deformation modeling. In *CVPR*, pages 422–429, June 2000.

[11] S. Vedula, S. Baker, P. Rander, R. Collins, and T. Kanade. Three-dimensional scene flow. In *ICCV*, pages 722–729, Pittsbrugh, PA, September 2000.

[12] M. Yamamoto, P. Boulanger, J. Beraldin, and M. Rioux. Direct estimation of range flow on deformable shape from a video rate range camera. *PAMI*, 15(1):82–89, January 1993.

Illumination-Invariant Change Detection Using a Statistical Colinearity Criterion

Rudolf Mester[1], Til Aach[2], and Lutz Dümbgen[3]

[1] Institute for Applied Physics, University of Frankfurt
Robert-Mayer-Str. 2–4, D-60054 Frankfurt, Germany
[2] Institute for Signal Processing, University of Lübeck
[3] Institute for Mathematics, University of Lübeck
Ratzeburger Allee 160, D-23538 Lübeck, Germany
mester@iap.uni-frankfurt.de, aach@isip.mu-luebeck.de,
duembgen@math.mu-luebeck.de

Abstract. This paper describes a new algorithm for illumination-invariant change detection that combines a simple multiplicative illumination model with decision theoretic approaches to change detection. The core of our algorithm is a new statistical test for linear dependence (colinearity) of vectors observed in noise. This criterion can be employed for a significance test, but a considerable improvement of reliability for real-world image sequences is achieved if it is integrated into a Bayesian framework that exploits spatio-temporal contiguity and prior knowledge about shape and size of typical change detection masks. In the latter approach, an MRF-based prior model for the sought change masks can be applied successfully. With this approach, spurious spot-like decision errors can be almost fully eliminated.

1 Introduction

In many computer vision applications, the detection and accurate delineation of moving objects forms an important first step. Many video surveillance systems, especially those employing a static or quasi-static camera, use processing algorithms that first identify regions where at least potentially a motion can be observed, before these regions are subject to further analysis steps, which might be, for instance, a quantitative analysis of motion. By this procedure, the available processing power of the system can be focused on the relevant subareas of the image plane. In applications such as traffic surveillance or video-based security systems, this focusing on the moving parts of the image typically yields a reduction of the image area to be processed in more detail to about 5-10 percent. Obviously, such a strategy is very advantageous compared to applying costly operations such as motion vector estimation to the total area of all images.

In order to let a change detection scheme be successful, an utmost level of robustness against different kinds of disturbances in typical video data is required (a very low false alarm rate), whereas any truly relevant visual event should be detected and forwarded to more sophisticated analysis steps (high sensitivity). Obviously, this presents change detection as a typical problem that should be dealt with by statistical decision and detection theory. Some early papers [2,4] stress the importance of selecting the most

B. Radig and S. Florczyk (Eds.): DAGM 2001, LNCS 2191, pp. 170–177, 2001.

efficient test statistic, which should be both adapted to the noise process and to a suitably chosen image model. A certain boost in performance has been introduced in the early nineties by employing prior models for the *typical shape and size* of the objects to be detected; this can be achieved very elegantly using *Gibbs-Markov random fields* [9,5,6]. These models reduce very strongly the probability of false positive and false negative alarms due to the usage of spatio-temporal context. They are superior to any kind of change mask post-processing (e.g. by morphological filters), since both the shape *and* the strength of observed signal anomaly is used. Such algorithms are in the meantime widely accepted as state of the art and integrated in multimedia standard proposals such as [11].

Despite all these advancements, certain problematic situations remain in real-life video data, and possibly the most important ones are *illumination changes*. A rapid change in illumination does cause an objectively noticeable signal variation, both visually and numerically, but it is very often not regarded as a *relevant* event. Therefore, recent investigations [10,12,13] have put emphasis on the desired feature of *illumination invariance*. In contrast to earlier work, the present paper aims at integrating illumination invariance in a framework that is as far as possible based on decision theory and statistical image models.

2   The Image Model, Including Illumination Changes and Superimposed Noise

We model the recorded image brightness as the product of illumination and reflectances of the surfaces of the depicted objects. We furthermore assume that the illumination is typically a spatially slowly varying function (cf. [1]).

For change detection, we compare for two subsequent images the grey levels which lie in a small sliding window[1]. Due to the spatial low-frequency behaviour of illumination, we can assume that illumination is almost constant in each small window. Thus, if no structural scene change occurs within the window, temporal differences between observed grey levels in the window can be caused only

1. by a positive multiplicative factor k which modulates the signal and accounts for illumination variation
2. and secondly by superimposed noise which can be modelled as i.i.d. Gaussian or Laplacian noise.

Let us consider the case that this *null hypothesis* H_0 is true: if we order the grey values from the regarded windows $\mathcal{W}_1$ and $\mathcal{W}_2$ into column vectors $\mathbf{x}_1$ and $\mathbf{x}_2 \in \mathrm{IR}^N$, these are related by $\mathbf{x}_1 = \mathbf{s} + \epsilon_1$ and $\mathbf{x}_2 = k \cdot \mathbf{s} + \epsilon_2$, where ϵ_i, $i = 1, 2$, are additive noise vectors,

$$\mathsf{E}[\epsilon_1] = \mathsf{E}[\epsilon_2] = \mathbf{0}, \qquad \mathsf{Cov}[\epsilon_1] = \mathsf{Cov}[\epsilon_2] = \sigma_d^2 \cdot \mathbf{I}_N \qquad (1)$$

and $\mathbf{s}$ is a signal vector. Unfortunately, the signal vector $\mathbf{s}$ is unknown. In such situations it might on the first glance appear reasonable to employ some kind of signal model

---

[1] or a fixed block raster, if detection and speed is of primary interest, and not so much the spatial accuracy of the detection masks

(e.g. using cubic facets). However, considering the extremely variable local structure of real video scenes, especially for outdoors applications, it is certainly not advantageous to model the signal blocks as e.g. low-pass signals, since the algorithm would work worse in this locations where the signal model incidentally differs strongly from the true signal such as in highly textured areas. In an ideal noise free case, $\mathbf{x}_1$ and $\mathbf{x}_2$ are parallel given H_0. We thus formulate change detection as testing whether or not $\mathbf{x}_1$ and $\mathbf{x}_2$ can be regarded as degraded versions of colinear vectors, with factor k and the true signal vector $\mathbf{s}$ being unknown entities (so-called *nuisance parameters*).

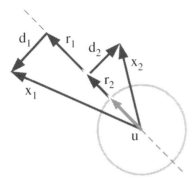

Fig. 1. Geometrical interpretation of testing the colinearity of two vectors $\mathbf{x}_1, \mathbf{x}_2$.

2.1   Derivation of the Colinearity Test Statistic

Earlier (and simpler) approaches to the task of testing the colinearity concentrated either on the difference between the two observed vectors $\mathbf{x}_i$ or on regarding the *angular differ- ence* between the $\mathbf{x}_i$. It is clearly not advisable to normalize both vectors prior to further processing, since this irreversibly suppresses statistically significant information. With a certain noise level σ_d^2 given, it makes a *significant* difference whether an certain angular difference is found for 'long' or 'short' signal vectors – it is simply much easier to change the direction of a 'short' signal vector. Therefore, basing the change detection decision on the angle between the observed vectors (e.g. by using the normalized correlation coefficient) cannot be recommended.

The approach we propose instead aims as much as possible on preserving any bit of statistical information in the given data. Fig. 1 illustrates the derivation of the test statistic. Given the observations $\mathbf{x}_i$, $i = 1, 2$ and assuming i.i.d. Gaussian noise, a maximum likelihood (ML) estimate of the true signal 'direction' (represented by a unit vector $\mathbf{u}$) is given by minimizing the sum $D^2 = |\mathbf{d}_1|^2 + |\mathbf{d}_2|^2$ of the squared distances $\mathbf{d}_i$ of the observed vectors $\mathbf{x}_i$ to the axis given by vector $\mathbf{u}$. Clearly, if $\mathbf{x}_1$ and $\mathbf{x}_2$ are colinear, the difference vectors and hence the sum of their norms are zero[2]. The projections $\mathbf{r}_i$,

---

[2] Note that $\mathbf{s}$, $k\mathbf{s}$, ϵ_1, ϵ_2 are unknown entities, and $\mathbf{r}_1$, $\mathbf{r}_2$, $\mathbf{d}_1$, $\mathbf{d}_2$ are only their estimates.

$i = 1, 2$ are ML estimates of the corresponding signal vectors. Obviously, we have

$$|\mathbf{d}_i|^2 = |\mathbf{x}_i|^2 - |\mathbf{r}_i|^2 \qquad \text{for} \quad i = 1, 2$$

$$|\mathbf{r}_i| = ||\mathbf{x}_i| \cdot \cos\varphi_i| = |\mathbf{x}_i^T \cdot \mathbf{u}| \qquad (|\mathbf{u}| = 1!)$$

$$\implies \quad |\mathbf{d}_i|^2 = |\mathbf{x}_i|^2 - |\mathbf{x}_i^T \cdot \mathbf{u}|^2$$

$$\implies \quad D^2 \stackrel{def}{=} |\mathbf{d}_1|^2 + |\mathbf{d}_2|^2 = |\mathbf{x}_1|^2 + |\mathbf{x}_2|^2 - |\mathbf{x}_1^T \cdot \mathbf{u}|^2 - |\mathbf{x}_2^T \cdot \mathbf{u}|^2$$

Let us now form the $2 \times N$ matrix $\mathbf{X}$ with

$$\mathbf{X} \stackrel{def}{=} \begin{pmatrix} \mathbf{x}_1^T \\ \mathbf{x}_2^T \end{pmatrix} \qquad\qquad \mathbf{X} \cdot \mathbf{u} = \begin{pmatrix} \mathbf{x}_1^T \cdot \mathbf{u} \\ \mathbf{x}_2^T \cdot \mathbf{u} \end{pmatrix}$$

$$\implies \quad |\mathbf{X} \cdot \mathbf{u}|^2 = \mathbf{u}^T \cdot \mathbf{X}^T \cdot \mathbf{X} \cdot \mathbf{u} = |\mathbf{x}_1^T \cdot \mathbf{u}|^2 + |\mathbf{x}_2^T \cdot \mathbf{u}|^2$$

So it turns out that

$$D^2 = |\mathbf{d}_1|^2 + |\mathbf{d}_2|^2 = |\mathbf{x}_1|^2 + |\mathbf{x}_2|^2 - \mathbf{u}^T \cdot \mathbf{X}^T \cdot \mathbf{X} \cdot \mathbf{u}$$

and the vector $\mathbf{u}$ that minimizes D^2 is the same vector that maximizes

$$\mathbf{u}^T \cdot \mathbf{X}^T \cdot \mathbf{X} \cdot \mathbf{u} \longrightarrow \max \qquad \text{with } |\mathbf{u}| = 1$$

which is obviously an eigenvalue problem[3] with respect to matrix $\mathbf{X}^T \cdot \mathbf{X}$. Due to the special way it is constructed from just two vectors, $\mathbf{X}^T \cdot \mathbf{X}$ has maximum rank 2 and thus has only two non-vanishing eigenvalues. We are only interested in the value of the test statistic D^2, and fortunately it can be shown that D^2 is identical to the smallest non-zero eigenvalue of matrix $\mathbf{X}^T \cdot \mathbf{X}$. Beyond that, it can be shown (e.g. quite illustratively by using the *singular value decomposition* (SVD) of matrix $\mathbf{X}$) that the non-zero eigenvalues of $\mathbf{X}^T \cdot \mathbf{X}$ and $\mathbf{X} \cdot \mathbf{X}^T$ are identical. Thus, the sought eigenvalue is identical to the smaller one of the two eigenvalues of the 2×2 matrix $\mathbf{X} \cdot \mathbf{X}^T$, which can be computed in closed form without using iterative numerical techniques. So the minimum value for D^2 can be determined without explicitly computing the 'signal direction unit vector' $\mathbf{u}$. This whole derivation is strongly related to the Total Least Squares (TLS) problem (cf. [14]) and matrix rank reduction tasks in modern estimation theory.

2.2   The Distribution of Test Statistic D^2

In order to construct a mathematically and statistically meaningful decision procedure, the distribution of the test statistic D^2 must be known at least for the null hypothesis H_0 (= colinearity). The asymptotic distribution of the test statistic D^2 can be derived on the basis of some mild approximations. For the case that the norm of the signal vector $\mathbf{s}$ is significantly larger than the expected value for the noise vector norm (which

---

[3] The matrix $\mathbf{X}^T \cdot \mathbf{X}$ can also be regarded as a (very coarse) estimate of the correlation matrix between the vectors $\mathbf{x}_i$, but this does not provide additional insight into the task of optimally testing the colinearity.

should hold true in almost all practical cases), it can be shown that the sum $|\mathbf{d}_1|^2 + |\mathbf{d}_2|^2$ is proportional to a χ^2 variable with $N - 1$ degrees of freedom with a proportionality factor σ_d^2 according to eg. (1).

$$D^2 \quad \sim \quad \sigma_d^2 \cdot \chi_{N-1}^2 \tag{2}$$

This result can be intuitively understood: assuming that the probability density function of the additive noise for each pixel is a zero-mean i.i.d. Gaussian with the same variance for all N pixels, the difference vectors $\mathbf{d}_i$ reside in a $N - 1$-dimensional subspace of IR^N which is determined by the direction vector $\mathbf{u}$. If the length $|\mathbf{s}|$ of the signal vector is large, the direction $\mathbf{u}$ is independent of the additive noise vectors ϵ_i. The components of $\mathbf{d}_i$ retain the property of being zero-mean Gaussians.

It might be surprising that the actual value of the multiplicative factor k does not influence the distribution of D^2, at least as long as the assumption of $|\mathbf{s}| \gg |\epsilon_i|$ holds. This makes this decision invariant against (realistic) multiplicative illumination changes, which is of course exactly what it has been developed for.

The distribution which has been theoretically derived and described above was also exactly what we found in a set of Monte Carlo simulations for the test statistic D^2 for N varying between 4 and 64 and factor k varying between 0.2 and 5 (which corresponds, in fact, already to a quite strong multiplicative change of illumination). Figures 2 and 3 show examples of the empirical distributions obtained by these simulations.

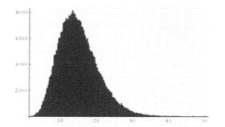

Fig. 2. Empirical distribution of D^2 for $\sigma_d^2 = 1$, $N = 16$, 100000 realizations. These empirical distributions do not noticeably change when k varies with $0.2 < k < 5$.

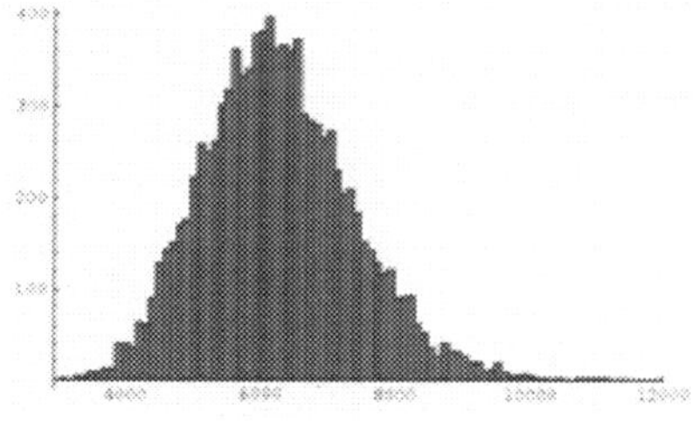

Fig. 3. Empirical distribution of D^2 for $\sigma_d^2 = 100$, $N = 64$, 10000 realizations. Note the conformity to the predicted scaling of $D^2 \sim \sigma_d^2 \cdot \chi_{N-1}^2$

Testing the null hypothesis H_0 (= colinearity) can be expressed as testing whether or not D^2 can be explained by the given noise model. On the basis of the now known distribution of D^2 under the null hypothesis, a significance test can be designed, which boils down to testing D^2 against a threshold t which has been determined in such a way that the conditional probability $Prob[D^2 > t \mid H_0] = \alpha$ with the *significance level* α.

3   Integration of the Colinearity Test Statistic into a Bayesian MRF-Based Framework

To improve the (already very good) performance of this test even further, we have integrated the new test statistic into the Bayesian framework of earlier, illumination sensitive change detection algorithms [6,8]. The Bayesian approach draws its power from using Gibbs/Markov random fields (MRF) for expressing the prior knowledge that the objects or regions to be detected are mostly compactly shaped. For integrating the new test, the conditional distribution $p(D^2|H_1)$ of the test statistic D^2 under the alternative hypothesis (H_1) has to be known at least coarsely. The resulting algorithm compares the test statistic D to an adaptive context dependent threshold, and is non-iterative. Thereby, the new approach is a illumination-invariant generalization of the already very powerful scheme [6,8] which already was an improvement over the iterative proposal [4,5].

Under the alternative hypothesis H_1 (vectors $\mathbf{x}_1$ and $\mathbf{x}_2$ are *not* colinear), we model the conditional pdf $p(D^2|H_1)$ by

$$p(D^2|H_1) = \left(\frac{1}{\sqrt{2\pi}\sigma_c} \right)^N \cdot \exp \left(-\frac{D^2}{2 \cdot \sigma_c^2} \right) \tag{3}$$

with $\sigma_c^2 \gg \sigma_d^2$ (for detail cf. [5,8]). The assumption that this density is Gaussian does not matter very much; it is just important that the variance σ_c^2 is significantly larger than σ_d^2 and that the distribution is almost flat close to the origin. Furthermore, we model the sought change masks by an MRF such that the detected changed regions tend to be compact and smoothly shaped. From this model, *a priori* probabilities $\text{Prob}(c)$ and $\text{Prob}(u)$ for the labels c (changed) and u (unchanged) can be obtained. The *maximum a priori* (MAP) decision rule – given the labels in the neighbourhood of the regarded block – is then

$$\frac{p(D^2|H_1)}{p(D^2|H_0)} \overset{c}{\underset{u}{\gtrless}} \frac{\text{Prob}(u)}{\text{Prob}(c)} \tag{4}$$

A little algebraic manipulation yields the context adaptive decision rule

$$D^2 \overset{c}{\underset{u}{\gtrless}} T + (4 - \nu_c) \cdot B \tag{5}$$

where D^2 is the introduced test statistic, and T a fixed threshold which is modulated by an integer number ν_c. The parameter ν_c denotes the number of pixels that carry the label c and lie in the 3×3-neighbourhood of the pixel to be processed (see figure). These labels are known for those neighbouring pixels which have already been processed while scanning the image raster (causal neighbourhood), as symbolized by the gray shade in the illustration.

For the pixels which are not yet processed we simply take the labels from the previous change mask (anticausal neighbourhood). Clearly, the adaptive threshold on the right hand side of (5) can only take the nine different values $\nu_c = 0, 1, \ldots, 8$. The parameter

B is a positive cost constant. The adaptive threshold hence is the lower, the higher the number ν_c of adjacent pixels with label c. It is obvious that this behaviour favours the emergence of smoothly shaped changed regions, and discourages noise-like decision errors. The nine different possible values for the adaptive threshold can be precomputed and stored in a look-up table, so this procedure needs only slightly more computational effort than just applying a fixed threshold.

4   Results

Figure 4 shows some typical experimental results obtained by using the described technique. In the used image sequence there is true motion (a toy train) and a visually and numerically strong illumination change obtained by waving a strong electric torch across the scene. A comparison of image c), where a conventional change detection technique is employed, versus image d) (illumination invariant change detection) shows the advantages of the new technique very clearly.

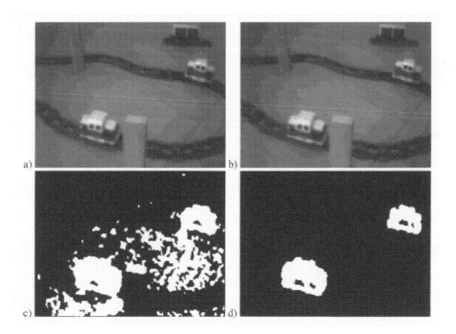

Fig. 4. a), b): Subsequent original frames from a sequence with moving toy trains. A beam of light crosses this scene quickly from left to right. c) Result of the illumination sensitive change detection algorithm in [8], mixing illumination changes with the moving locomotives. d) Result of the new illumination invariant change detection. The locomotives have been safely detected, and all erroneous detection events due to illumination changes are suppressed.

5   Conclusions

We consider the illumination-invariant change detection algorithm presented here as a significant step forward compared to earlier (already quite well performing) statistics-based approaches. For the near future, a comparison to competing approaches using homomorphic filtering (cf. [13]) remains to be performed. Furthermore, it appears to be very promising to extend the discussed approaches to change detection towards the integrated processing of more than 2 subsequent frames. We are convinced that – if again statistical modeling and reasoning is employed – a further improvement compared to the *state of the art* can be achieved.

References

1. A. V. Oppenheim, R. W. Schafer, T. G. Stockham Jr: Nonlinear filtering of multiplied and convolved signals. *Proc. IEEE* 56(8):1264–1291, 1968.
2. Y. Z. Hsu, H.-H. Nagel, G. Rekers: New likelihood test methods for change detection in image sequences. *Comp. Vis. Grap. Im. Proc* 26:73–106, 1984.
3. K. Skifstad, R. Jain: Illumination independent change detection for real world image sequences. *Computer Vision, Graphics, and Image Processing,* 46, pp. 387–399, 1989.
4. T. Aach, A. Kaup, R. Mester: A statistical framework for change detection in image sequences. *13ième Colloque GRETSI*, pp. 1149–1152, Juan-Les-Pins, France, Sept. 1991.
5. T. Aach, A. Kaup, R. Mester: Statistical model-based change detection in moving video. *Signal Processing* 31(2), pp.165–180, 1993.
6. T. Aach, A. Kaup, R. Mester: Change detection in image sequences using Gibbs random fields. *IEEE Internal. Works. Intell. Signal Processing Com. Sys.*, pp. 56–61, Sendai, Japan, Oct. 1993.
7. G. Tziritas, C. Labit: *Motion Analysis for Image Sequence Coding.* Elsevier, 1994.
8. T. Aach, A. Kaup: Bayesian algorithms for change detection in image sequences using Markov random fields. *Signal Processing: Image Communication* 7(2): pp. 147–160, 1995.
9. A. Mitiche, P. Bouthemy: Computation and analysis of image motion: A synopsis of current problems and methods. *Inl. Jour. Comp. Vis.* 19(1):29–55, 1996.
10. S.-Z. Liu, C.-W. Fu, S. Chang: Statistical change detection with moments under time-varying illumination. *IEEE Trans. Image Processing* 7(9), pp. 1258–1268, 1998.
11. ISO/IEC JTC 1/SC 29/WG 11 N2502, Final Draft International Standard, Annex F, Information Technology - Very-low bitrate audio-visual coding - Part 2: Visual, Atlantic City, 1998.
12. E. Durucan, T. Ebrahimi: Robust and illumination invariant change detection based on linear dependence for surveillance application. Proc. *EUSIPCO 2000*, pp. 1041–1044, Tampere, Finland, Sept. 3-8, 2000.
13. D. Toth, T. Aach, V. Metzler: Bayesian spatio-temporal motion detection under varying illumination European Signal Processing Conference (EUSIPCO), Tampere, Finland, 4.-8.9.2000 (M. Gabbouj, P. Kuosmanen, eds.), 2081-2084.
14. R. Mester, M. Mühlich: Improving Motion and Orientation Estimation Using an Equilibrated Total Least Squares Approach. IEEE Intern. Conf. Image Proc. 2001 (ICIP 2001) , Thessaloniki, Greece, Oktober 2001.

Memorizing Visual Knowledge for Assembly Process Monitoring

Christian Bauckhage, Jannik Fritsch, and Gerhard Sagerer

Technische Fakultät, AG Angewandte Informatik
Bielefeld University, P.O. Box 100131, 33501 Bielefeld, Germany
{cbauckha}@techfak.uni-bielefeld.de

Abstract. Machine learning is a desirable property of computer vision systems. Especially in process monitoring knowledge of temporal context speeds up recognition. Moreover, memorizing earlier results allows to establish qualitative relations between the stages of a processes. In this contribution we present an architecture that learns different visual aspects of assemblies. It is organized hierarchically and stores prototypical data from different levels of image processing and object recognition. An example underlines that this *memory* facilitates assembly recognition and recognizes structural relations among complex objects.

1 Introduction and Related Work

The use of computer vision in automatic manufacturing ranges from control, supervision, and quality assessment to understanding of events in an assembly cell [13]. Concerning intelligent man-machine interaction in robotic assembly the latter is of special relevance. Usual robotic assembly is a step by step procedure of building complex objects from simpler ones. The resulting artifacts are called *mechanical assemblies* and are composed of *subassemblies*. As subassemblies may as well consist of simpler units, objects resulting from construction processes often show a hierarchical composition. Knowledge of structure and temporal evolution of assemblies enables to deduce what is going on in a construction cell. This, however, requires techniques for automatic recognition and structural analysis as well as a facility to capture information derived at earlier stages of construction.

This contribution presents an approach that copes with these requirements. We introduce a system that stores and relates results from visual assembly recognition. It realizes a learning mechanism which speeds up recognition and accumulates useful information throughout an assembly process.

Over the last years, interest in visual assembly monitoring has increased significantly. Khawaja et al. [6] report on quality assessment based on geometric object models. Dealing with visual servoing Nelson et al. [12] apply feature based

---

* This work has been supported by the DFG within SFB 360.

B. Radig and S. Florczyk (Eds.): DAGM 2001, LNCS 2191, pp. 178–185, 2001.
© Springer-Verlag Berlin Heidelberg 2001

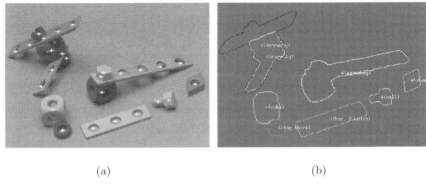

(a)   (b)

Fig. 1. 1(a) Examples of objects and assemblies dealt with by our system shown with calculated positions of mating features. 1(b) Results of object recognition and structural assembly analysis for this example.

object recognition to cope with misplaced parts. Miura and Ikeuchi [11], Tung and Kak [15], and Lloyd et al. [9] introduce methods to learn assembly sequences from observation. However, the latter contributions either are not purely based on vision or they only deal with simple block world objects.

Abstracting from detailed geometry we presented syntactic methods to describe assembled objects and to generate assembly plans from image data [2,3]. Implemented as a semantic network our method examines images of bolted assemblies (s. Fig. 1(a)) and yields hierarchical assembly structures (s. Fig. 1(b)). As assembly structures and assembly sequences are tightly related, we integrated structural analysis and visual action detection to increase the reliability of process monitoring [1]. A module for event perception registers which objects are taken or put into the scene. Based on observed event sequences it deduces what kind of constructions are carried out. If a new cluster of objects appears in the scene, it triggers a syntactical analysis to decide whether the cluster depicts an assembly and corresponds to the recent sequence of events.

2   Concept of a Memory Storing Visual Cues

Whenever the assembly detection component of our integrated system is called, it performs an analysis by means of a semantic network. This, in fact, is rather time consuming if it is done ignoring knowledge derived earlier. Kummert et al. [7] proposed information propagation through time to speed up semantic object recognition. Due to the complex structure of assemblies their approach is hardly applicable to assembled objects. Furthermore, hierarchical descriptions of assemblies usually are not unique. This complicates assembly *recognition* since matching hierarchical descriptions is burdensome. In the following we propose a solution to both these problems.

Our method to detect assembly structures analyzes the topology of clusters of labeled image regions resulting from elementary object recognition [7]. In order to determine details of objects connections positions of *mating features* are calculated from the regions and their topological relations are examined [3]. Mating features are necessary to interconnect objects; in Fig. 1(a) calculated positions of mating features are indicated by white crosses.

Experiments suggested that the appearance of a cluster of regions or the 2D distribution of mating feature are characteristic features of individual assemblies and might be used for recognition.

This led to the idea of a database-like memory to store information from different levels of image processing and associate it with corresponding assembly structures. Its conceptual layout is sketched in Fig. 2. The memory consists of several tables, called *dimensions*, storing data. There is an implicit hierarchy of dimensions since higher level data is computed from lower level data. Each dimension comes along with a specialized function to compare entities of its content.

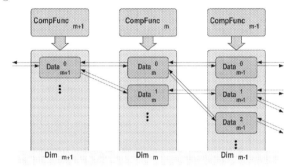

Fig. 2. Concept of a memory to store and relate information for assembly recognition. Data from different stages of processing is stored in different tables Dim_m, $m \in \mathbb{N}$. A function $CompFunc_m$ is associated with each table to compare corresponding datasets. Datasets from different tables that represent the same assembly are related via pointers.

Here our approach differs from classical databases: since visual assembly recognition is a pattern recognition task data which is to be stored in the memory might be similar to but usually not identical with earlier stored one. Thus we need sophisticated functions computing similarities instead of key comparisons known from databases. Data from different dimensions representing the same assembly is connected via pointers so that it is possible to retrieve information concerning an assembly given just a certain aspect. Note that these functions can be chosen freely. The concept sketched in Fig. 2 is modular and facilitates the exchange of pattern recognition techniques.

Based on this concept, assembly recognition is done as follows:

1. Compute the lower most type of information from an image and check whether similar one is contained in the lowest dimension. If this is the case trace the pointers to the highest dimension, report the information found there and stop. If similar information can not yet be found in the lowest dimension register it and continue with 2.

2. Continue image processing. If similar data can be found in the corresponding hierarchical level interconnect this entity and the recently registered data from the previous level, trace the pointers to the highest dimension and

stop. If similar information has not yet been stored in the current dimension store it and draw pointers to the corresponding data in the level below.

3. Continue with 2. until the highest level of information is reached.

3   Implementational Issues and a Performance Example

In the actual implementation of the memory we realized 4 dimensions. These are used to store clusters of regions, sets of 2D mating feature positions (called interest points in the following), syntactic assembly structures, and names assigned to an assembly by a user interacting with the system. To compare two clusters of labeled regions the number and types of objects comprised in the clusters and the compactness and exentricity of the merged regions are considered. This is a rather coarse approach basically suited to recognize assemblies that do not change their position and orientation over time. More effort was spent in matching interest points. Out of the many known approaches to point set matching (cf. e.g. [10,5] and the references therein) we chose two fast ones for our scenario: calculating the Hausdorff-distance between two sets and computing an affine transformation between point sets optimized by means of a gradient descent method.

Besides its 2D image coordinates each interest point is assigned the type of mating feature it represents. Thus an interest point is a tuple $p = (\boldsymbol{x}, t)$ with $\boldsymbol{x} \in \mathbb{R}^2$ and $t \in Type$ where $Type = \{BoltThread, BarHole, CubeHole, \ldots\}$.

Defining a distance $d(p, p') = ||\boldsymbol{x} - \boldsymbol{x}'|| + d_{Type}(t, t')$ where we choose

$$d_{Type}(t, t') = \begin{cases} 0 & \text{, if } t = t' \\ \frac{\sqrt{2}}{2} & \text{, otherwise} \end{cases}$$

$\mathbb{R}^2 \times Type$ becomes a metric space and methods to measure distances between sets of interest points are available. To determine the distance from a point set P_0 to a point set P_1 by optimizing an affine transformation the coordinates $\boldsymbol{x}$ of all points in both sets are normalized to the unit square. Then two points $p_1^0 = (\boldsymbol{x}_1^0, t_1^0)$ and $p_2^0 = (\boldsymbol{x}_2^0, t_2^0)$ are chosen from P_0 such that

$$||\boldsymbol{x}_1^0 - \boldsymbol{x}_2^0|| = \max_{p, p' \in P_0} ||\boldsymbol{x} - \boldsymbol{x}'||.$$

Likewise a pair of points (p_1^1, p_2^1) is chosen from P_1 with types corresponding to t_1^0 and t_2^0. An affine operator $\boldsymbol{A}$ mapping $(\boldsymbol{x}_1^1, \boldsymbol{x}_2^1)$ to $(\boldsymbol{x}_1^0, \boldsymbol{x}_2^0)$ is estimated and applied to the coordinates of all points in P_1. Subsequently, we compute the number of elements of equal types. Therefore the two sets P_0 and P_1 are projected to the corresponding multi sets (cf. [8]) of types, i.e. $P_i \rightarrow P_{Type,i} = \{t_j | (\boldsymbol{x}, t)_j \in P_i \wedge t_j = t\}$. Given the multi set intersection $P_{Type} = P_{Type,0} \bigcap P_{Type,1}$, its size $n = |P_{Type}|$ yields the number of elements of equal types in P_0 and P_1. Then a bijective assignment of type equivalent points $p_i^0 \leftrightarrow p_i^1$, $p_i^0 \in P_0, p_i^1 \in P_1$, $i \in \{1, \ldots, n\}$ is computed such that the distance

$$E = \frac{1}{2n} \sum_i ||\boldsymbol{x}_i^0 - \boldsymbol{A}\boldsymbol{x}_i^1||^2$$

is minimal. Afterwards $\boldsymbol{A} = [a_{ij}]$ is iteratively updated according to $a_{ij}(\tau+1) = a_{ij}(\tau) - \frac{\partial E(\tau)}{\partial a_{ij}(\tau)}$ until E falls below a certain threshold or a maximum number of iterations is reached. The two sets are called equivalent if E is smaller than the threshold. For details and variations of this method please refer to [4].

The Hausdorff distance between two point sets P_0 and P_1 depends on a method to measure the distance between individual points. Considering the distance $d : (\mathbb{R}^2 \times Type) \times (\mathbb{R}^2 \times Type) \to \mathbb{R}$ as defined above the Hausdorff distance between P_0 and P_1 is given as $H(P_0, P_1) = \max(h(P_0, P_1), h(P_1, P_0))$ where

$$h(P_0, P_1) = \max_{p \in P_0} \min_{p' \in P_1} d(p, p').$$

To test the equivalence of two sets of interest point the image coordinates $\boldsymbol{x}$ of all points in the sets are transformed to principle axes coordinates and the Hausdorff distance is computed. If it is smaller than a threshold estimated from test samples, the sets are said to represent the same object. Again, for details please refer to [4].

It turned out that the methods tended to yield different results when applied to the same data. We thus realized a simple majority voting scheme (cf. [14]) to increase the reliability of results from point set matching.

As computing the distance between point sets by means of an affine operator mainly considers image coordinates while computing the Hausdorff distance considers image coordinates and mating feature types, we decided to compute another cue that first of all regards point types. Given two point sets P_0 and P_1 with sizes $n_0 = |P_0|$ and $n_1 = |P_1|$ we again look at their multi sets of types and compute the corresponding intersection P_{Type}. Without loss of generality let us assume that $n_0 \leq n_1$. If $n = |P_{Type}| \geq 0.7n_0$ then P_0 and P_1 are said to be equal.

Now there are enough cues for majority voting. Two sets of interest points represent the same entity if at least two of the described methods vote accordingly, i.e. if at least two methods yield that P_0 and P_1 are equivalent.

As Fig. 3 indicates, matching interest points against earlier derived ones is beneficial in terms of computational effort. The figure sketches the average time needed to process images of assemblies comprising an increasing number of bolts, i.e. images of increasing complexity. Obviously, the amount of time required for syntactical assembly analysis grows exponentially. This is due to the fact that syntactic methods examine local

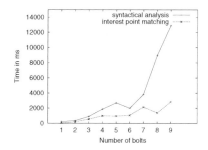

Fig. 3. Computational costs for visual assembly processing.

properties of patterns. In our case, local adjacency relations within clusters of objects are analyzed to derive assembly structures. The more adjacencies there are the more derivations are possible. If a chosen alternative fails to yield a good

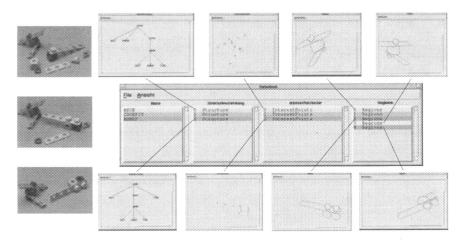

Fig. 4. A series of images depicting the course of a construction and screen shots indicating the internal state of the memory after monitoring this sequence.

explanation (because many objects in the cluster do not fit into the current structure) it has to be discarded and another description must be considered. Interest point matching, in contrast, deals with global properties of assemblies. It does not aim at explaining local relations between parts but regards distances between sets of features of parts. If these sets, as in our case, are of reasonable size (an assembly with e.g. nine bolts typically has about 40 interest points) combinatorial explosions can be avoided.

In terms of recognition accuracy voted point matching reaches an average of 82%. This seems a rather poor performance, however, user interaction can defuse this problem. If neither region based matching nor interest point matching detect a correspondence to a known assembly, a new syntactical description is computed and the regions, the interest points, and the syntactic structure are related and stored in the memory. A user then can assign a name to this structure. If he chooses a name already contained in the memory, the system has *learned* another prototypical description of the respective assembly. The following discussion of an exemplary interaction with the system should illustrate this mechanism.

Figure 4 depicts a series of construction steps and screenshots of the state of the memory resulting from the process. Initially, the scene contained two assemblies. The corresponding region clusters were computed and stored in the memory. Sets of interest points were calculated and stored as well. Furthermore, syntactical descriptions of both assemblies were generated and a user assigned names to these structures. One was called HECK, the other was referred to as COCKPIT. A series of mating operations resulted in the second scene. As the HECK did not change its appearance in the image no new information concerning it was stored. The new assembly was called RUMPF and corresponding data was registered. In the final scene HECK and RUMPF were rearranged and new clusters of regions were stored in the memory. However, new sets of interest point did not have to be stored since the system found correspondences to the already known ones. The large window in the middle of Fig. 4 depicts the contents of the memory. Clicking on the entry RUMPF caused all the corresponding facts to be highlighted in dark grey. Moreover, as point set matching yielded that COCKPIT is a subassembly of RUMPF (cf. [4]) all entries belonging to COCKPIT were highlighted in lighter grey.

4   Summary

This contribution described a system to store and associate different types of information from visual assembly process monitoring. This memory is multidimensional since it registers data from different levels of image processing. If new information is drawn from image processing it is stored and related to earlier derived facts. By this the memory dynamically learns prototypical features for assembly recognition. Is is scalable since new dimensions can easily be integrated into the architecture and it is modular because methods to compare data of a certain dimension can be exchanged.

The implemented version of the memory facilitates intelligent man-machine interaction in an assembly scenario. Using shape and point matching techniques speeds up visual assembly recognition and allows to detect assembly-subassembly relationships. If the system fails to recognize an assembly properly by comparing earlier derived data, a user can correct its conclusions and the system can use this correction to further extend its knowledge.

References

1. C. Bauckhage, J. Fritsch, and G. Sagerer. Erkennung von Aggregaten aus Struktur und Handlung. *Künstliche Intelligenz*, 3:4–11, 1999.
2. C. Bauckhage, S. Kronenberg, F. Kummert, and G. Sagerer. Grammars and Discourse Theory to Describe and Recognize Mechanical Assemblies. In *Advances in Pattern Recognition*, Lecture Notes in Computer Science 1876, pages 173–182. Springer-Verlag, 2000.
3. C. Bauckhage, F. Kummert, and G. Sagerer. Learning Assembly Sequence Plans Using Functional Models. In *Proc. IEEE International Symposium on Assembly and Task Planning (ISATP'99)*, pages 1–7, 1999.
4. N. Esau and L. Steinborn. Konzeption und Realisierung eines Aggregatgedächtnisses zur Analyse von Konstruktionsprozessen. Dipl. Arbeit, Universität Bielefeld, Feb. 2001. available at: www.TechFak.Uni-Bielefeld.DE/techfak/ ags/ai/publications/master-theses/Esau_Steinborm2001.ps.gz.
5. K. Fries, J. Meyer, B. Lindemann, and H. Hagen. Correspondence Analysis: The Matching of 3-Dimensional Sets of Points. In *Proc. Vision, Modelling, and Visualization 2000*, pages 399–406. infix, 2000.
6. K.W. Khawaja, A.A. Maciejewski, D. Tretter, and C. Bouman. A Multiscale Assembly Inspection Algorithm. *IEEE Robotics & Automation Magazine*, 3(2):15–22, 1996.

7. F. Kummert, G.A. Fink, and G. Sagerer. Schritthaltende hybride Objektdetektion. In E. Paulus and F.M.Wahl, editors, *Mustererkennung 97, 19. DAGM-Symposium Braunschweig, Informatik-Fachberichte*, pages 137–144. Springer-Verlag, 1997.

8. C. L. Liu. *Elements of Discrtete Mathematics*. McGraw-Hill, 1977.

9. J.E. Lloyd, J.S. Beis, D.K. Pai, and D.G. Lowe. Programming Contact Tasks Using a Reality-Based Virtual Environment Integrated with Vision. *IEEE Transactions on Robotics and Automation*, 15(3):423–434, 1999.

10. B. Luo and E.R. Hancock. Alignment and Correspondence Using Singular Value Decomposition. In *Advances in Pattern Recognition*, Lecture Notes in Computer Science 1876, pages 226–235. Springer-Verlag, 2000.

11. J. Miura and K. Ikeuchi. Task Oriented Generation of Visual Sensing Strategies in Assembly Tasks. *IEEE Transactions on Pattern Analysis and Machine Intelligence*, 20(2):126–138, 1998.

12. B.J. Nelson, N.P. Papanikolopoulos, and P.K. Khosla. Robotic Visual Servoing and Robotic Assembly Tasks. *IEEE Robotics & Automation Magazine*, 3(2):23–31, 1996.

13. J.A. Noble. From inspection to process understanding and monitoring: a view on computer vision in manufacturing. *Image and Vision Computing*, 13(3):197–214, 1995.

14. B. Parhami. Voting Algorithms. *IEEE Transactions on Reliability*, 43(4):617–629, 1994.

15. C.-P. Tung and A.C. Kak. Integrating Sensing, Task Planning and Execution for Robotic Assembly. *IEEE Transactions on Robotics and Automation*, 12:187–201, 1996.

Wavelet Subspace Method
for Real-Time Face Tracking

Volker Krüger[1] and Rogerio S. Feris[2]

[1] Center for Automation Research
University of Maryland
College Park, MD 20740
tel: +1-301-405-1756
fax: +1-301-314-9115
email: vok@cfar.umd.edu
[2] Department of Computer Science
University of São Paulo
Rua do Matão, 1010, 05508-900 São Paulo-SP, Brazil
email: rferis@ime.usp.br

Abstract. In this article we present a new method for visual face tracking that is carried out in wavelet subspace. Firstly, a wavelet representation for the face template is created, which spans a low dimensional subspace of the image space. The wavelet representation of the face is a point in this wavelet subspace. The video sequence frames in which the face is tracked are orthogonally projected into this low-dimensional subspace. This can be done efficiently through a small number of local projections of the wavelet functions. All further computations are then performed in the low-dimensional subspace. The wavelet subspace inherets its invariance to rotation, scale and translation from the wavelets; shear invariance can also be achieved, which makes the subspace invariant to affine deformations.

Keywords: face tracking, wavelet decomposition, wavelet network

1 Introduction

In this paper we study how wavelet subspaces can be used to increase efficiency in image computation for affine object tracking. A wavelet subspace is a vector space that is dual to an image subspace spanned by a set of wavelets. Any set of wavelets can be understood as spanning a subspace in the image space. An image in imagespace can be orthogonally projected into the image subspace and the vector of the wavelet coefficients defines a point in the dual wavelet subspace. The image subspace (and consequentely the wavelet spacespace) may be low dimensional. In order to estabilish tracking, the basic idea is to deform the image subspace (or the wavelet subspace, respectively) to let it imitate the affine deformation of the input image. When tracking is successful, the weight vector in the wavelet subspace should be constant. To be precise, let us assume

B. Radig and S. Florczyk (Eds.): DAGM 2001, LNCS 2191, pp. 186–193, 2001.

that at a certain time instance, tracking was successful and the object is indeed mapped onto a certain "correct" point in wavelet subspace. As the object moves in space, its weak projection into imagespace undergoes a possebly affine deformation. Clearly, the new affinely deformed image, if orthogonally projected into the image subspace, will not anymore map onto the same (correct) point in the wavelet subspace. However, when the wavelet subspace undergoes the same affine deformation as the image, then the image will map again onto the correct point, i.e. and tracking is successful.

Finding the correct deformation is in general a very complex operation. Therefore, instead of deforming the wavelet subspace directly, we deform the dual image subspace, that is the space spanned by the wavelets. The fact that rotation, dilation and translation are intrinsic parameters of wavelets further simplifies matters. Indeed, only a small set of local projections of the wavelets is needed to compute the unknown deformation parameters.

We will use the notion of *Wavelet Network* (WN) in order to formalize the above ideas. WNs are a generalization of the Gabor Wavelet Networks, as introduced in [6,4].

In section 2 we will give an short introduction to WNs and establish the needed properties. In section 3, we will introduce our subspace tracking approach, discuss the details and conclude the paper with the experiments in section 4 and concluding remarks.

In the reminder of this paper, we will limit the discussion to face tracking, as faces appear to be of large research interest [5,2,1,7,9]. In [2] an efficient, general tracking framework is presented. The efficiency of that approach outperforms our approach as it uses a discrete template for track. In our approach, we use a continuous template, composed by continuous wavelets. Large scale changes pose a major problem to discrete approach while it can handled more easily by the continuous wavelet template.

In [1] a stochastic mean-shift approach us used for robust tracking. The emphasis of this approach is robustness on the expense of precision.

In [7] a stochastic approach for simultanious tracking and verification has been presented. The employed method uses sequential importance sampling (SIS). As templates, discrete gray value templats or bunch graphs are used.

In [9] Gabor wavelets and bunch graphs were used for tracking faces. Because of the large number of used wavelets, this approach was able to run with approximately one Hz.

In [5] tracking method is presented that is based on Gabor wavelet networks. The method presented here is a generalization of [5] and outperforms that tracking method in terms of efficiency.

2   Introduction to Wavelet Networks

To define a WN, we start out, generally speaking, by taking a family of N wavelet functions $\Psi = \{\psi_{\mathbf{n}_1}, \ldots, \psi_{\mathbf{n}_N}\}$, where $\psi_{\mathbf{n}}(\mathbf{x}) = \psi(\mathbf{SR}(\mathbf{x} + \mathbf{c}))$, with $\mathbf{n} = (c_x, c_y, \theta, s_x, s_y)^T$. ψ is called *motherwavelet* and should be *admissible*. Here,

Fig. 1. *Face images reconstructed with different number of wavelets. As the mother-wavelet ψ, the odd Gabor function has been used.*

c_x, c_y denote the translation of the wavelet, s_x, s_y denote the dilation and θ denotes the orientation. The choice of N is arbitrary and may be related to the degree of desired representation precision of the network (see fig. 1). In order to find a good WN for a function $f \in \mathbb{L}^2(\mathbb{R}^2)$ (f dc-free, w.l.o.g.) the energy functional

$$E = \min_{\mathbf{n}_i, w_i \text{ for all } i} \|f - \sum_i w_i \psi_{\mathbf{n}_i}\|_2^2 \tag{1}$$

is minimized with respect to the weights w_i and the wavelet parameter vector $\mathbf{n}_i$. The two vectors $\Psi = (\psi_{\mathbf{n}_1}, \dots, \psi_{\mathbf{n}_N})^T$ and $\mathbf{w} = (w_1, \dots, w_N)^T$ define then the *wavelet network* $(\Psi, \mathbf{w})$ for function f.

From the optimized wavelets Ψ and weights $\mathbf{w}$ of the WN, the function f can be (closely) reconstructed by a linear combination of the weighted wavelets:

$$\hat{f} = \sum_{i=1}^N w_i \psi_{\mathbf{n}_i} = \Psi^T \mathbf{w} . \tag{2}$$

This equation shows that the quality of the image representation and reconstruction depends on the number N of wavelets and can be varied to reach almost any desired precision.

2.1   Direct Calculation of Weights

The weights w_i of a WN are directly related to the local projections of the wavelets $\psi_{\mathbf{n}_i}$ onto the image. Wavelet functions are not necessarily orthogonal, thus implying that, for a given family Ψ of wavelets, it is not possible to calculate a weight w_i by a simple projection of the wavelet $\psi_{\mathbf{n}_i}$ onto the image. In fact, a family of dual wavelets $\tilde{\Psi} = \{\tilde{\psi}_{\mathbf{n}_1} \dots \tilde{\psi}_{\mathbf{n}_N}\}$ has to be considered. The wavelet $\tilde{\psi}_{\mathbf{n}_j}$ is the dual wavelet of the wavelet $\psi_{\mathbf{n}_i}$ iff $\langle \psi_{\mathbf{n}_i}, \tilde{\psi}_{\mathbf{n}_j} \rangle = \delta_{i,j}$. With $\tilde{\Psi} = (\tilde{\psi}_{\mathbf{n}_1}, \dots, \tilde{\psi}_{\mathbf{n}_N})^T$, we can write $\left[\langle \Psi, \tilde{\Psi} \rangle \right] = \mathbb{1}$. In other words, given $g \in \mathbb{L}^2(\mathbb{R}^2)$ and a WN $\Psi = \{\psi_{\mathbf{n}_1}, \dots, \psi_{\mathbf{n}_N}\}$, the optimal weights for g that minimize the energy functional are given by $w_i = \langle g, \tilde{\psi}_{\mathbf{n}_i} \rangle$. It can be shown that

$$\tilde{\psi}_{\mathbf{n}_i} = \sum_j \left(\Psi^{-1} \right)_{i,j} \psi_{\mathbf{n}_j} , \text{ where } \Psi_{i,j} = \langle \psi_{\mathbf{n}_i}, \psi_{\mathbf{n}_j} \rangle . \tag{3}$$

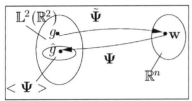

Fig. 2. *A function* $g \in \mathbb{L}^2(\mathbb{R}^2)$ *is mapped by the linear mapping* $\tilde{\Psi}$ *onto the vector* $\mathbf{w} \in \mathbb{R}^N$ *in the wavelet subspace. The mapping of* $\mathbf{w}$ *into* $\mathbb{L}^2(\mathbb{R}^2)$ *is achieved with the linear mapping* Ψ. *Both mappings constitute an orthogonal projection of a function* $g \in \mathbb{L}^2(\mathbb{R}^2)$ *into the image subspace* $< \Psi > \subset \mathbb{L}^2(\mathbb{R}^2)$.

3   Face Tracking in Wavelet Subspace

The wavelet representation described in the previous section can be used effectively for affine face tracking. Basically, this task is achieved by affinely deforming a WN so that it matches the face image in each frame of a video sequence. The affine deformation of a WN is carried out by considering the entire wavelet network as a single wavelet, which is also called *superwavelet* [5]. Let $(\Psi, \mathbf{w})$ be a WN with $\Psi = (\psi_{\mathbf{n}_1}, \ldots, \psi_{\mathbf{n}_N})^T$ and $\mathbf{w} = (w_1, \ldots, w_N)^T$. A superwavelet $\Psi_{\mathbf{n}}$ is defined as a linear combination of the wavelets $\psi_{\mathbf{n}_i}$ such that

$$\Psi_{\mathbf{n}}(\mathbf{x}) = \sum_i w_i \psi_{\mathbf{n}_i}(\mathbf{SR}(\mathbf{x} - \mathbf{c})) , \tag{4}$$

where the vector $\mathbf{n} = (c_x, c_y, \theta, s_x, s_y, s_{xy})^1$ defines the dilation matrix $\mathbf{S}$, the rotation matrix $\mathbf{R}$ and the translation vector $\mathbf{c}$, respectively. The affine face tracking is then achieved by deforming the superwavelet $\Psi_{\mathbf{n}}$ in each frame J, so that its parameters $\mathbf{n}$ are optimized with respect to the energy functional

$$E = \min_{\mathbf{n}} \| J - \Psi_{\mathbf{n}} \|_2^2 . \tag{5}$$

Clearly, this method performs a typical pixel-wise pattern matching in image space, where the template corresponds to the wavelet representation, which is affinely distorted to match the face in each frame. Obviously, the wavelet weights w_i are constant under the deformation of the template. Therefore, the affine deformation is captured only by the deformation of the wavelets, while the weight vector remains invariant.

We thus claim that the "tracking in image space" described above may also be achieved in the wavelet subspace $\mathbb{R}^N$, which is isomorphic to the image subspace $< \Psi >$, as illustrated by fig. 2. As it can be seen there, both spaces are related through the matrices Ψ and $\tilde{\Psi}$. As the first step, consider a WN $(\Psi, \mathbf{v})$ that is optimized for a certain face image. As previously mentioned, the optimal weight vector $\mathbf{v}$ is obtained by an orthogonal projection of the facial image into the closed linear span of Ψ. Hence, we say that the face template was mapped into the weights $\mathbf{v} \in \mathbb{R}^N$, which we will call *reference weights*.

We mentioned before that the wavelet template gets affinely deformed in order to tracking in image space. Analogously, the tracking in wavelet subspace is performed by affinely deforming the subspace $< \Psi >$, until the weight vector $\mathbf{w} \in \mathbb{R}^N$, obtained by the orthogonal mapping of the current frame into this

---

[1] To include the shear in the parameter set of the wavelets, see [5].

subspace, is closest to the reference weight vector **v**. In fact, this procedure performs roughly the same pattern matching as before, but this is done efficiently in the low-dimensional wavelet subspace $\mathbb{R}^N$.

The mapping of images into $\mathbb{R}^N$ is carried out with low computational cost through a small number of local filtrations with the wavelets. Recall from section 2.1 that $w_i = \langle I, \tilde{\psi}_{\mathbf{n}_i} \rangle$, where $\tilde{\psi}_{\mathbf{n}_i} = \sum_j \left(\Psi^{-1}\right)_{i,j} \psi_{\mathbf{n}_j}$. This is equal to the following equation:

$$w_i = \sum_j \left(\Psi^{-1}\right)_{i,j} \langle I, \psi_{\mathbf{n}_j} \rangle. \tag{6}$$

Thus, the optimal weights w_i are derived from a linear combination of wavelet filtrations, where the coefficients are given by the inverse of matrix $\Psi_{i,j} = \langle \psi_{\mathbf{n}_i}, \psi_{\mathbf{n}_j} \rangle$. It can be shown that the matrix $\Psi_{i,j}$ is, except for a scalar factor, invariant with respect to affine transformations of the wavelet network. It can therefore be computed off-line and beforehand. Hence, the weights w_i are computed efficiently with eq. (6) through a local application $\langle I, \psi_{\mathbf{n}_i} \rangle$ of each of the N wavelets $\psi_{\mathbf{n}_i}$, followed by a $N \times N$ matrix multiplication.

Let $\mathbf{n} = (c_x, c_y, \theta, s_x, s_y, s_{xy})$ be an affine parameter vector which configures a parameterization for subspace $< \Psi >$. As we described before, tracking in wavelet subspace is achieved by gradually changing these parameters until the projection of the current frame J onto $\mathbf{w} \in \mathbb{R}^N$ is closest to the reference weights **v**. In other words, we must optimize the parameters **n** with respect to the energy functional:

$$E = \min_{\mathbf{n}} \|\mathbf{v} - \mathbf{w}\|_\Psi \text{ with } w_i = \sum_j \frac{1}{s_x \cdot s_y} \left(\Psi^{-1}\right)_{i,j} \langle J, \psi_{\mathbf{n}_j} \left(\mathbf{SR}\left(\mathbf{x} - \mathbf{c}\right)\right)\rangle \tag{7}$$

where **S** is the dilation matrix, **R** is the rotation matrix and **c** is the translation vector, all defined through the vector $(c_x, c_y, \theta, s_x, s_y, s_{xy})$. During tracking, this optimization is done for each successive frame. As there is not much difference between adjacent frames, the optimization is fast. To minimize the energy functional (7), the Levenberg-Marquardt algorithm was used. For this, the continuous derivatives of functional (7) with respect to each degree of freedom were computed.

In equation (7) the notation $\|\mathbf{v} - \mathbf{w}\|_\Psi$ refers to the distance between vectors **v** and **w** in the wavelet subspace $\mathbb{R}^N$. We define the difference $\|\mathbf{v} - \mathbf{w}\|_\Psi$ as the Euclidean distance between the two corresponding images $\hat{f}$ and $\hat{g}$:

$$\|\mathbf{v} - \mathbf{w}\|_\Psi = \|\sum_{i=1}^N v_i \psi_{\mathbf{n}_i} - \sum_{j=1}^N w_j \psi_{\mathbf{n}_j}\|_2 \tag{8}$$

Various transformations lead to

$$\|\mathbf{v} - \mathbf{w}\|_\Psi = \left[\sum_{i,j} (v_i - w_i)(v_j - w_j)\langle \psi_{\mathbf{n}_i}, \psi_{\mathbf{n}_j}\rangle\right]^{\frac{1}{2}} = (\mathbf{v} - \mathbf{w})^t \, \Psi_{i,j} \, (\mathbf{v} - \mathbf{w}). \tag{9}$$

The matrix of pairwise scalar products $\Psi_{i,j} = \langle \psi_{\mathbf{n}_i}, \psi_{\mathbf{n}_j}\rangle$ is the same matrix as the one in section 2.1 and eq. (6). Note that if the wavelets $\{\psi_{\mathbf{n}_i}\}$ were orthogonal, then Ψ would be the unity matrix and eq. (9) would describe the same

Fig. 3. *Sample frames of our wavelet subspace tracking. Note that the tracking method is robust to facial expressions variations as well as affine deformations of the face image.*

distance measure as proposed in [10]. Compared to tracking in image space, the method presented here poses a considerable enhancement in terms of efficiency, as it provides a great data reduction, considering that tracking is performed in the low dimensional wavelet subspace. Moreover, it spares out the computationally demanding template reconstruction and pixel-wise sum-of-squared-difference computation required in the image-based tracking.

4   Experiments

The proposed approach for affine face tracking was successfully tested on various image sequences. All test sequences showed a person in motion, more or less frontal to the camera, so that the facial features were always visible. The face undergoes slight out-of-plane rotation, in-plane rotation, scaling and gesture changes. The experiments were carried out offline, see fig. 3 for sample images[2].

On the face of the person, a WN with 116 wavelets was optimized and used to estimate the "ground truth" affine parameters in each frame. To analyze how tracking precision is related to the number N of used wavelets, we used different WN and chose the largest 51, 22 and 9 wavelets, sorted according to decreasing normalized weights. The graphs in fig. 4 depict the estimation of the face parameters x-position, y-position and angle θ as well as the ground-truth in each frame. It shows how tracking precision increases with the number N of wavelets. N can be chosen task dependent and can be changes dynamically. The tracked inner-face region had a size of 50x65 pixels. Using only 9 wavelets, the computing time for each Levenberg-Marquardt cycle was 15ms on a 1GHz Linux-Athlon. Higher performance is achieved for smaller face regions, or fewer parameters (e.g. just translation and rotation).

In comparison to the method in [5] we observed in our experiments a speedup of a factor two for each single Levenberg-Marquardt cycle, but with a slight increase in the number of needed cycles. However, we do believe that the use of other algorithms, such as the Condensation method [3] or the Sequential Importance Sampling (SIS) method [8], will increase efficiency.

---

[2] see http://www.ime.usp.br/~rferis to view one of the test sequences

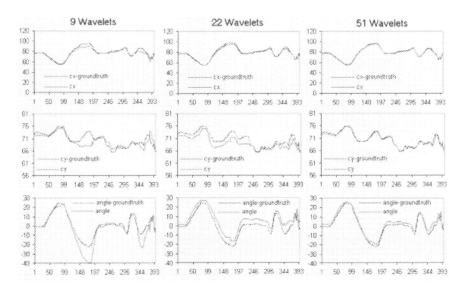

Fig. 4. *Estimation of the face parameters x-position, y-position and angle θ in each frame, using WNs with 9, 22 and 51 wavelets. The ground-truth is depicted to illustrate the decrease of precision when considering few wavelets.*

5   Conclusions

In this paper we have presented a tracking method, that is carried out in wavelet subspace. Since wavelets are invariant to affine deformations they leave the reference vector of a template face constant. Furthermore, the direct relationship between the wavelet coefficients and the wavelet filter responses, which is widely used for multi-resolution analysis and for motion estimation, allows to map an image into the low-dimensional wavelet subspace $\mathbb{R}^N$, where all subsequent computations can be carried out.

The method has the further advantage, that its precision and computation time can be adapted to the needs of a given task. When fast and only approximate tracking is needed, a small number of filtrations is usually sufficient to realize tracking. When high precision tracking is needed, the number of wavelets can be gradually increased. This implies on the one hand more filtrations, but ensures on the other hand a higher precision, as we have shown in the experimental section.

Very many tracking algorithms have difficulties dealing with large scale changes. We think that the use of continuous wavelets and the possibility of dynamically changing the number of used wavelets could simplify matters.

So far, the optimization of the wavelet networks has been done with a Levenberg-Marquardt algorithm. We think that a combination with Condensation or Sequential Importance Sampling (SIS) could help to further decrease computational complexity. This will be evaluated in future work.

Acknowledgements. Volker Krüger is supported by the Human ID Grant program under the ONR Grant N00014-00-1-0908; Rogerio Feris is grateful to FAPESP (99/01487-1).

References

1. Dorin Comaniciu, Visvanathan Ramesh, and Peter Meer. Real-time tracking of non-rigid objects using mean shift. In *Proc. IEEE Conf. on Computer Vision and Pattern Recognition*, volume 2, pages 142–149, Hilton Head Island, SC, June 13-15, 2000.
2. G. Hager and P. Belhumeur. Efficient region tracking with parametric models of geometry and illumination. *IEEE Trans. Pattern Analysis and Machine Intelligence*, 20:1025–1039, 1998.
3. M. Isard and A. Blake. Condensation – conditional density propagation for visual tracking. *Int. J. of Computer Vision*, 29:5–28, 1998.
4. V. Krüger, S. Bruns, and G. Sommer. Efficient head pose estimation with gabor wavelet networks. In *Proc. British Machine Vision Conference*, Bristol, UK, Sept. 12-14, 2000.
5. V. Krüger and G. Sommer. Affine real-time face tracking using gabor wavelet networks. In *Proc. Int. Conf. on Pattern Recognition*, Barcelona, Spain, Sept. 3-8, 2000.
6. V. Krüger and G. Sommer. Gabor wavelet networks for object representation. In *Tag. Bd. Deutsche Arbeitsgemeinschaft für Mustererkennung*, 22. DAGM-Symposium, Kiel, Sept. 13-15, 2000.
7. B. Li and R. Chellappa. Simultanious tracking and verification via sequential posterior estimation. In *Proc. IEEE Conf. on Computer Vision and Pattern Recognition*, Hilton Head Island, SC, June 13-15, 2000.
8. Baoxin Li. Human and object tracking and verification in video. Technical Report CS-TR-4140, Center for Automation Research, University of Maryland, May 2000.
9. T. Maurer and C. v.d. Malsburg. Tracking and learning graphs on image sequences of faces. In *Proc. of the Int. Conf. on Artificial Neural Networks, ICANN*, pages 323–328, Bochum, Germany, Jul. 16-19. C. v.d. Malsburg, W. v. Seelen, J. Vorbrüggen, B. Sendhoff (eds.), Springer-Verlag, Berlin, 1996.
10. L. Wiskott, J. M. Fellous, N. Krüger, and C. v. d. Malsburg. Face recognition by elastic bunch graph matching. *IEEE Trans. Pattern Analysis and Machine Intelligence*, 19:775–779, 1997.

Reliable Estimates of the Sea Surface Heat Flux from Image Sequences

Christoph S. Garbe[1,2] and Bernd Jähne[1,2]

[1] Institut für Umweltphysik
Im Neuenheimer Feld 229
D-69120 Heidelberg
[2] Interdisciplinary Center for Scientific Computing,
Im Neuenheimer Feld 368,
D-69120 Heidelberg,
Germany
{Christoph.Garbe,Bernd.Jaehne}@iwr.uni-heidelberg.de

Abstract. We present a new technique for estimating the sea surface heat flux from infrared image sequences. Based on solving an extension to the standard brightness change constraint equation in a total least squares (TLS) sense, the total derivative of the sea surface temperature with respect to time is obtained. Due to inevitable reflexes in field data the TLS framework was further extended to a robust estimation based on a Least Median of Squares Orthogonal Distances (LMSOD) scheme. From this it is possible for the first time to compute accurate heat flux densities to a high temporal and spatial resolution. Results obtained at the Heidelberg Aeolotron showed excellent agreement to ground truth and field data was obtained on the GasExII experiment.

1 Introduction

The net sea surface heat flux j is a crucial parameter for quantitative measurements of air-sea gas exchange rates, as well as for climate models and simulations. Meteorological estimates currently employed to measure j have poor spatial resolution and need to average for several minutes to produce results.

There exists strong experimental evidence that surface renewal is an adequate model for heat transfer at the air-sea interface ([10], [3]). In this model a fluid parcel is transported from the bulk to the surface were it equilibrates by a mechanism akin to molecular diffusion. It has been shown that based on this model assumption, it is feasible to compute j by measuring the temperature difference ΔT across the thermal sub layer and its total derivative with respect to time $\mathrm{d}/\mathrm{d}t\Delta T$ [3]. ΔT can be derived from infra-red images alone [6]. In the present work we will show how the total derivative can be estimated from IR image sequences and thus heat flux measurements be made to a high spatial resolution at the frame rate of the IR-Camera.

B. Radig and S. Florczyk (Eds.): DAGM 2001, LNCS 2191, pp. 194–201, 2001.
© Springer-Verlag Berlin Heidelberg 2001

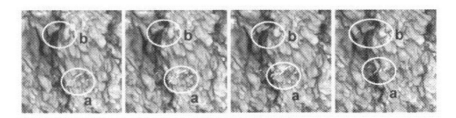

Fig. 1. A typical sequence as taken with an infrared camera at 100Hz. While the reflexes in region **a** are quite easy to detect, the reflexes in region **b** and in the left top corner of the images are hard to detect in the still frames. However, they introduce significant errors in the estimation of the heat flux density j.

In an IR-Camera the sea surface temperature (SST) is mapped as a grey value g onto the image plane. As the SST changes due to physical processes, the brightness conservation does not hold. Therefore the brightness change constraint equation (BCCE) commonly used in optical flow computations has to be extended to be applicable in the context of this work. The extended BCCE can then be solved in a local neighborhood in a total least squares (TLS) sense akin to the structure tensor. This is shown in section 2.1. Due to reflections in the image data from field experiments the proposed model of the extended BCCE is violated. This problem can be overcome by embedding the TLS framework in a robust estimator. In the context of this work a random sampling approach was chosen that is based on the Least Median of Squares Orthogonal Distances (LMSOD) scheme [1]. This will be outlined in section 3. In section 4 the actual results of the estimate of j with the proposed algorithm are displayed.

2   The Total Derivative from Image Sequences

The total derivative of ΔT with respect to time is readily given by

$$\frac{\mathrm{d}}{\mathrm{d}t}\Delta T = \frac{\partial}{\partial t}\Delta T + (\boldsymbol{u}\boldsymbol{\nabla})\,\Delta T, \qquad (1)$$

where $\boldsymbol{u} = [u_1, u_2, u_3]^\top$ is the three dimensional velocity of the fluid parcel.

To determine $\mathrm{d}/\mathrm{d}t\,\Delta T$ of a fluid parcel in equation (1) by digital image processing, it is not sufficient to extract the change of temperature $\partial T/\partial t$ at a fixed position of the image, which is quite trivial. Moreover an exact estimate of the velocity $\boldsymbol{u}$ has to be found. In the following sections a means for deriving $\mathrm{d}/\mathrm{d}t\,\Delta T$ directly from an image sequence will be presented.

2.1   The Extended Brightness Model

A very common assumption in optical flow computations is the BCCE [7]. It states that the image brightness $g(\boldsymbol{x}, t)$ at the location $\boldsymbol{x} = (x_1, x_2)^\top$ should change only due to motion [2], that is, the total derivative of its brightness has to vanish:

$$\frac{dg}{dt} = \frac{\partial g}{\partial t} + \frac{\partial g}{\partial x}\frac{dx}{dt} + \frac{\partial g}{\partial y}\frac{dy}{dt} = g_t + (\boldsymbol{f}\boldsymbol{\nabla})g = 0, \tag{2}$$

with the optical flow $\boldsymbol{f} = (dx/dt, dy/dt)^\top = (u, v)^\top$, the spacial gradient $\boldsymbol{\nabla}g$ and the partial time derivative $g_t = \partial g/\partial t$.

When using an infrared camera for acquiring image sequences, the temperature T of a three dimensional object is mapped as a grey value g onto the image plane. Thru camera calibration the parameters of this transformation are known. From comparing the two equations (1) and (2) it is evident that the BCCE does not hold in the context of this work. In order to satisfy this constraint, the temperature change we seek to measure would have to be equal to zero.

It is known that the BCCE can be generalized to incorporate linear and nonlinear brightness changes based on the differential equation of the physical processes involved [4]. Thus, the BCCE is generalized by adding a linear term c [8],[9]:

$$g_t + (\boldsymbol{f}\boldsymbol{\nabla}g) - c = (g_x, g_y, -1, g_t) \cdot (u, v, c, 1)^\top = \boldsymbol{d}^\top \boldsymbol{p} = 0, \tag{3}$$

where c is a constant, which is proportional to $d/dt\Delta T$. The data vector $\boldsymbol{d} = (g_x, g_y, -1, g_t)^\top$ is given by the partial derivatives of the image data, which are denoted by subscripts. Equation (3) poses an underdetermined system of equations, as there is only one constraint with the three unknowns $\boldsymbol{f} = (u, v)^\top$ and c. Assuming constant optical flow $\boldsymbol{f}$ over a small spatio-temporal neighborhood surrounding the location of interest containing n pixels, the problem consists of n equations of the form of equation (3). With the data matrix $\boldsymbol{D} = (\boldsymbol{d_1}, \ldots, \boldsymbol{d_n})^\top$ the TLS problem can be reformulated as an extension of the structure tensor [5], that is

$$\|\boldsymbol{Dp}\|_2 = \boldsymbol{p}^\top \boldsymbol{D}^\top \boldsymbol{Dp} = \boldsymbol{p}^\top \boldsymbol{Fp} \longrightarrow \min. \tag{4}$$

with $\boldsymbol{p}^\top \boldsymbol{p} = 1$ to avoid the trivial solution $\boldsymbol{p} = 0$. The eigenvector $\boldsymbol{e} = (e_1, e_2, e_3, e_4)^\top$ to the smallest eigenvalue λ of the generalized structure tensor

$$\boldsymbol{F} = \boldsymbol{D}^\top \boldsymbol{D} = \begin{pmatrix} <g_x \cdot g_x> & <g_x \cdot g_y> & <g_x> & <g_x \cdot g_t> \\ <g_y \cdot g_x> & <g_y \cdot g_y> & <g_y> & <g_y \cdot g_t> \\ <g_x> & <g_y> & <1> & <g_t> \\ <g_t \cdot g_x> & <g_t \cdot g_y> & <g_t> & <g_t \cdot g_t> \end{pmatrix} \tag{5}$$

represents the sought after solution to the problem [5]. In this notation local averaging using a binomial filter is represented by $< \cdot >$. In the case of full flow, that is no aperture problem present, the parameter vector $\boldsymbol{p}$ is given by $\boldsymbol{p} = 1/e_4(e_1, e_2, e_3)^\top$. Due to the inherent structure of the infrared image sequences an aperture problem seldom exists and only full flow needs to be considered.

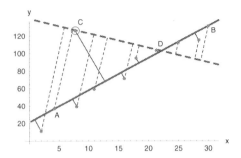

Fig. 2. An Illustration of the LMSOD estimator. The solid line representing the correct estimate (connecting point A and B) has a much smaller sum of squared residuals than the wrong estimate (the dotted line connecting point C and D). The wrong estimate is therefore rejected.

3   Parameter Estimation in a Robust Framework

In controlled laboratory experiments reflexes on the water surface from objects of a different temperature can be greatly suppressed, as is the case in the dedicated Heidelberg wind wave facility, the Aeolotron. However, in field experiments reflexes stemming from different sources are inevitable. These reflexes vary greatly in appearance. They can, however, be viewed as non gaussian noise on the image data. TLS approaches exhibit very favorable properties in the case of gaussian noise but are very susceptible to outliers in the data. In the case of reflexes, the ratio of outliers in the data to that to inliers can be as high as 50%. If undetected, the reflexes are bound to introduce significant errors in the estimation of the net heat flux, often rendering results useless. Therefore their detection is paramount. It would of course be favorable if the data at the reflexes would not only been cast away, but could be corrected and used in subsequent data analysis.

The parameter estimation based on TLS is made robust by means of LMSOD [1]. This is a random sampling scheme were a number of m subsamples are drawn for which equation (3) is solved exact. The subsample for which the median of the residuals to the rest of the data set is smallest is chosen as a preliminary estimate. From this estimate the inliers are selected and a TLS performed. An illustration of this algorithm is displayed in figure 2.

In more detail the algorithm can be described as follows: First, a subsample $\hat{D}_J = (d_1, \cdots, d_k)^\top$ of k observations is drawn, were k is equal to the number of parameters to be estimated, that is $k = 4$ for equation (3). From such a subsample $\hat{D}_J$, an exact solution for the parameters can be found, which is equal to solving a linear system of k equations. The result is the trial estimate vector p_J. It is of course very likely that these trial estimates will stray far from the sought of estimate. Therefore, the residuum r_i for the trial estimate is calculated from every observation $i \in \{1, \ldots, n - k\}$, leaving out the subsample J, that is $r_i = \boldsymbol{d}_i^\top \boldsymbol{p}_J$. These trial residuums make up the residuum vector $\boldsymbol{r}_J = (r_1, \ldots, r_{n-k})^\top$ to a given subsample $\hat{\boldsymbol{D}}_J$. In a next step the median of $\boldsymbol{r}_J$ is computed. The whole process is repeated for a number of subsamples $J \in \{1, \ldots, m\}$ and the trial estimate with the minimal median $\boldsymbol{r}_J$ retained. Central to this estimator is the question, of how many subsamles one has to draw to converge to the right solution. A number of random selections for subsamples has to be drawn, such that the probability of at least one of the m subsample equating to the right estimate is almost 1. Assuming that n/p is a large number, this probability $\varPi$ is given by

$$\varPi = 1 - (1 - (1 - \epsilon)^p)^m \quad \Rightarrow \quad m = \frac{\ln(1 - \varPi)}{\ln(1 - (1 - \epsilon)^p)}, \tag{6}$$

where ϵ is the fraction of contaminated data [11]. This equation shows that the number of subsamples that have to been drawn is significantly less compared to sampling every possible combination of points, which is given by $m = n!/((n - p)! \cdot p!)$.

The LMSOD estimator has one debilitating drawback, namely its lack of efficiency ($n^{-1/3}$ convergence), which is exactly the big advantage of maximum likelihood estimators like the TLS. Therefore the LMSOD estimate is used to find inliers on which the TLS estimator is then applied.

3.1   Detection and Elimination of Outliers

Outliers in the data set can of course be characterized by their big residual r as compared to the inliers. This residual has of course to be scaled according to the rest of the data in order to be thresholded it in a meaningful way. One possible way of calculating the scale factor is given in [11]. First an initial scale estimate s^o is computed, according to

$$s^o = 1.4826 \cdot \left(1 + \frac{5}{n - k}\right) \sqrt{\mathrm{median}\ r_i^2} \tag{7}$$

The median of the squared residuals in equation (7) is the same value by which the final estimate was chosen which makes the computation of s^o very efficient.

The preliminary scale estimate s^o is then used to determine a weight w_i for the ith observation, that is

$$w_i = \begin{cases} 1 \text{ if } |r_i/s^o| \leq 2.5 \\ 0 \text{ otherwise} \end{cases} \tag{8}$$

By means of these weights a final scale estimate S independent of outliers is calculated by

$$S = \sqrt{\frac{\sum_{i=1}^{n} w_i r_i^2}{\sum_{i=1}^{n} w_i - k}}. \tag{9}$$

a   b   c

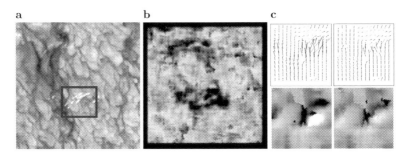

Fig. 3. a) An image from the IR-sequence, **b)** The number of weights as computed by LMSOD. Black areas indicate fewer weights which corresponds to reflexes. **c)** The flow field and the linear parameter for TLS and LMSOD inside the box in **a**. Black regions indicate where no parameters could be estimated.

The final weights are chosen similarly to equation (8) with the preliminary scaling factor s^o being replaced by the final scale factor S. With these final weights a weighted total least squares estimate (WTLS) is computed. Since the weights are binary (either 0 or 1) this is the same as using a TLS solemnly on the inliers.

4   Results

The field data presented in figures 1 and 3 was taken during the GasExII experiment at the equatorial pacific this spring. Therefore only preliminary analyses have been performed. As can be seen in figure 3, the robust estimator detects the reflexes and adjusts the weights accordingly. Even reflexes that are hard to see in the single frame are detected and can be removed. Subsequently the flow field is not affected as the one computed from TLS alone, nor is the total derivative of ΔT with respect to time. The use of a robust estimator with its higher computational cost is thus justified by the results.

In order to verify the approach presented in this paper, laboratory experiments have been performed at the Heidelberg Aeolotron, a dedicated wind wave facility that exhibits excellent thermal properties. The experimental set-up as well as some results can be seen in figure 4. In experiments at different wind speeds, relative humidity, as well as air and water temperatures are recorded to a high accuracy. From these physical quantities the net heat flux can be calculated [3]. There is excellent agreement between the two estimates. Our technique exhibits heat flux measurements on space and timescales that were never before attainable. Therefore fluctuations that are correlated to wave motions have been measured for the first time.

a
b

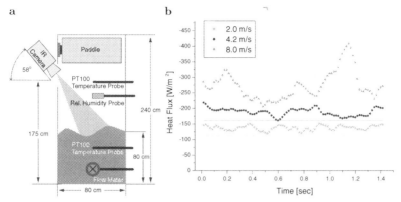

Fig. 4. a) The basic experimental set-up for experiments at the Heidelberg Aeolotron. Wind is generated by paddles and the temperatures of air and water, as well as relative humidity are recorded, as are wind speed and the velocity of the water. **b)** Comparison of heat flux measurements from the proposed technique with that calculated from conventional means. Fluctuations are not errors, but are correlated to wave motion.

5   Conclusion

A novel technique for measuring the net heat flux at the sea surface was presented. The BCCE was extended to include a term for linear brightness change to account for temperature changes in the IR sequences due to heat dissipation. This extended BCCE can be solved in a TLS framework, similar to the structure tensor in optical flow computations. This technique was made robust by means of LMSOD in order to account for reflexes, common in field data. It was shown that reflexes can be detected and correct parameters estimated. The validity of our technique could also be shown in laboratory experiments. In the future interesting phenomena uncovered with this technique for the first time will be investigated further.

References

[1]   Bab-Hadiashar, A., D. Suter, Robust Optic Flow Computation, in *International Journal of Computer Vision*, *29*,(1):59-77, 1998.
[2]   Fennema, C. and Thompson, W., *Velocity determination in scenes containing several moving objects*, Computer Graphics and Image Processing, vol. 9, pp. 301-315, 1979
[3]   Garbe, C., H. Haußecker, B. Jähne, Measuring the Sea Surface Heat Flux and Probability Distribution of Surface Renewal Events, in *Gas Transfer at Water Surfaces*, AGU, in press, 2001.
[4]   Haußecker, H., C. Garbe, H. Spies, and B. Jähne, A total least squares framework for low-level analysis of dynamic scenes and processes, in *21.Symposium für Mustererkennung DAGM 1999*, pp. 240–249, 1999.

[5] Haußecker, H., and H. Spies, *Handbook of Computer Vision and Applications*, vol. 2, chap. 13. Motion, pp. 309–396, Academic Press, 1999.

[6] Haußecker, H., C. Garbe, U. Schimpf, B. Jähne, Physics from ir image sequences: Quantitative analysis of transport models and parameters of air-sea gas transfer, in *Gas Transfer at Water Surfaces*, AGU, in press, 2001.

[7] Horn, B.K.P. and Schunk, B.G.,*Determining optical flow*, Artificial Intelligence, 17:185-204

[8] Nagel, H.-H.,*On a constraint equation for the estimation of displacement rates in image sequences*, IEEE PAMI, 11(1), 13-30, 1989

[9] Negahdaripour, S., *Revised definition of optical flow: integration of radiometric and geometric clues for dynamic scene analysis*, IEEE PAMI, 20(9), 961-979, 1998

[10] Rao, K. N., R. Narasimah, and M. B. Narayanan, The 'bursting' phenomenon in a turbulent boundary layer, *Journal of Fluid Mechanic*, *48*, 339–352, 1971.

[11] Rousseeuw, P, and Leroy, A., *Robust regression and outlier detection*, Wiley, 1987.

[12] Soloviev, A. V., and P. Schlüssel, Parameterization of the cool skin of the ocean and of the air-ocean gas transfer on the basis of modeling surface renewal, *Journal of Physical Oceanography*, *24*, 1339–1346, 1994.

Axel Techmer

Infineon Technologies AG, Corporate Research, 81730 Munich
axel.techmer@infineon.com

Abstract. The detection of approaching vehicles in traffic lanes is an essential processing step for a driver assistant or a visual traffic monitoring system. For this task a new motion based approach is presented, which allows processing in real-time without the need of special hardware. Motion estimation was processed along contours and restricted to the observed lane(s). Due to the lane based computation vehicles were segmented by evaluation of the motion direction only. The contour tracking algorithm allows a robust motion estimation and a temporal stabilisation of the motion based segmentation. The capabilities of our approach are demonstrated in two applications: a overtake checker for highways and a visual traffic monitoring system.

Introduction

ation about vehicles in traffic lanes is essential in systems for driver assistance or visual traffic
ring. Robustness against changes in illumination, real-time processing and the use of low-cost hardware
uirements, which will affect the commercial success of such a vision system.

n is a fundamental information for the understanding of traffic sequences. Unfortunately motion estimation
puter-tionally expensive. To reach real-time without a sophisticated and therefore expensive hardware,
i estimation is only done at significant points ([1],[2],[3]) or constraints about the expected motion are
[4]). In [1],[2] and [3] feature points like corners are used as significant points. Motion estimation at
points leads to a sparse motion field, which makes it difficult to detect complete objects. Taniguchi ([4])
ts a vehicle detection for the observation of the rear and lateral view. He uses the assumption, that passing
me out from the focus of expansion (FOE) while the background drains into the FOE. However, this
ption is only true at straight lanes. Also a possible offset, caused by vibrations of the observing vehicle, is
nsidered. Due to the vehicle dynamic and unevenness of the roadway these vibrations occur permanently.
aper presents a new approach for motion estimation in real-time applications. Motion is computed via a
al tracking of contours. Instead of using single feature points, which leads to a sparse motion field,
rs are a good compromise between data reduction and motion information. Because visible vehicle
aries are described by contours, grouping contours will lead to a complete vehicle segmentation.
onally contours can be tracked by evaluating shape only. This makes motion estimation more robust
changes in illumination. Motion computation based on local operators suffers form the aperture problem
his will be reduced by the evaluation of contours.
ver, contour extraction produces failures: one contour can be separated in parts; or not related contour parts
connected. In order to overcome this problem, contour tracking is not solved via the direct evaluation of
al successive contours. Instead the optimal correspondence between the actual contours and the previous
nage is computed via a correlation based approach.
i estimation is only done inside the observed lane(s). This reduces the time for computation and
onally simplifies the motion based segmentation. Contour tracking leads to a robust motion estimation and
the temporal stabilization of the motion based segmentation. Chapter 2 explains the motion based vehicle
on. In chapter 3 the possible applications of the presented approach are demonstrated in two examples.
per ends with a summary in chapter 4.

Motion Based Vehicle Segmentation

ain processing steps of the proposed motion based vehicle detection are shown in fig. 1. $I(x,y,t)$ denotes
ual camera image. An example for a rear and lateral observation on highways is given (see image a of fig.
r the presented vehicle segmentation knowledge about the observed lane is assumed. In case of a static
ation area this information can be predefined or in the other case the results of a lane detection module are
n the example of fig. 1 a predefined observation area is indicated. The first processing step is a lane based
rmation, which projects the observation area on a rectangle, denoted as $M(u,v,t)$. Vehicles are detected

The result of this step is illustrated in image c of fig. 1. The motion information at the contour points are sa
$\mathbf{m}^N(t)$. The results of the temporally stabilized motion segmentation are stored in a binary mask, $Mask($
(see image e in fig. 1). From this mask the corresponding bounding box can easily be extracted. The positi
the vehicle is then projected back in the camera image (see image a in fig. 1). Details of the single proce
steps are presented below.

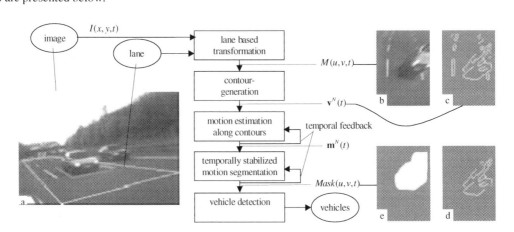

Fig. 1. The figure illustrates the processing steps of the proposed vehicle detection.

2.1 Lane based transformation

The goal of this processing step is to transform the observed lane area from a camera image to a rectangle
principle of this transformation is illustrated in fig. 2.

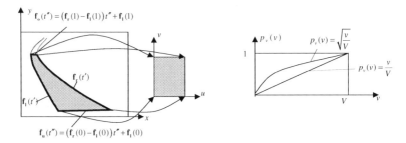

Fig. 2. The left part of the figure illustrates the principle of the lane based transformation. The observed area is given b
parametric functions, which specify the left and right boundary, $\mathbf{f}_l(t)$ and $\mathbf{f}_r(t)$. The right part illustrates two p
choices for $t = p_u(v)$ (explained below).

The result of the proposed transformation is similar to a birdview generated from inverse persp
transformation. In contrast to other methods (e.g. [9] no camera parameters are used. The transformation
only two functions, $\mathbf{f}_l(t)$ and $\mathbf{f}_r(t)$, which specify the left and right boundary of the observed lane.

The transformation should map an observation area in the camera image to an rectangle, which is formula
$I(x(u,v), y(u,v)) \rightarrow M(u,v)$. The ranges of the image coordinates are given by $x \in [0, X]$ and $y \in [0, Y]$ f
camera image and $u \in [0, U]$ and $v \in [0, V]$ for the mapped image. The two boundary functions are given a
dimensional polynomial functions, $\mathbf{f}_l(t) = [f_{lx}(t), f_{ly}(t)]^T$ and $\mathbf{f}_r(t) = [f_{rx}(t), f_{ry}(t)]^T$, where t lies in the ran
$t \in [0,1]$. So the upper boundary can be described by $\mathbf{f}_o(t') = (\mathbf{f}_r(1) - \mathbf{f}_l(1))t' + \mathbf{f}_l(1)$ and the lower bounda
$\mathbf{f}_o(t') = (\mathbf{f}_r(0) - \mathbf{f}_l(0))t' + \mathbf{f}_l(0)$ with $t' \in [0,1]$. Now $x(u,v)$ and $y(u,v)$ result from the substitution $t = p_u(u$
$t' = p_v(v)$:

$$x(u,v) = \left(f_{xr}(p_v(v)) - f_{xl}(p_v(v)) \right) p_u(u) + f_{xl}(p_v(v)) \tag{1}$$

$$y(u,v) = \left(f_{yr}(p_v(v)) - f_{yl}(p_v(v)) \right) p_u(u) + f_{yl}(p_v(v)) \ .$$

s of the functions $p_v(v)$ and $p_u(u)$ must lie in the range of $p_v(v), p_u(u) \in [0,1]$. One possible choice could be
$= v/V$ and $p_u(u) = u/U$ (see fig. 2). This leads to a linear sampling of the observation area.

ne-based transformation offers some advantages:
oresenting the observed area in a rectangle is computational efficient. Saving and processing of not
erved areas is reduced.
icles move along lanes. Therefore motion reduces to a quasi one-dimensional vector.
uitably choice of $p_v(v)$, e.g. $p_v(v) = \sqrt{v/V}$ (see fig. 2), reduces the influence of the camera perspective.
ecially the differences between motion in near and far image areas can be compensated. This leads to
ller search areas in the motion estimation process. Additionally the dimension of the mapped image can
significantly reduced. In the presented examples of chapter 3 a dimension of 120 rows to 80 columns was
ficient.

Contour Generation

cond processing step in fig. 1 is contour generation. This step is necessary because motion is computed by
our tracking. Contours have to be extracted form the gray-value image, $M(u,v,t)$. Our approach uses the
detection method described in [6] and the edge linking method described in [7]. The output of the contour
tion is a contour structure denoted as $v^N(t)$ (see fig. 1).

Motion Estimation

n estimation is solved by contour tracking. An extended version of this approach can be found in [5]. The
diagram of fig. 3 shows an overview of the necessary processing steps.

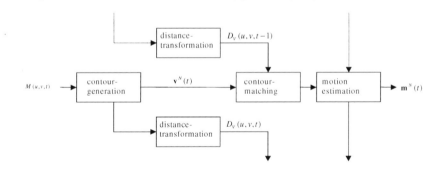

Fig. 3. Block diagram for contour based motion estimation

rst task is to find some correspondence between contours in temporal successive images, which is called
r matching in fig. 3. The extracted contours at time t are denoted as $v^N(t) = \{v_0(k,t),...,v_{N-1}(k,t)\}$. To
one contour $v_i(k,t)$ over time an optimal transformation has to be determined, which transforms a part of
to a corresponding part of $v_j(l,t-1)$. Due to the processing of contours, which are generated from
s, no knowledge of the complete contours $v_i(k,t)$ and $v_j(l,t-1)$ can be assumed. This situation is
istrated in fig. 4.

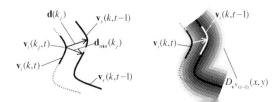

dotted parts indicate missing contour information. The right part illustrates the principle of the contour matching form in equation (2). The white vector indicates the optimal translation $\mathbf{d}_{ij}$. To show the distance image the minimal distance expressed as intensities.

This optimal transformation is computed at every contour point and it is assumed that it can be modeled simple translation. For every contour point the following task has to be solved: Find the best match between actual contour part $\mathbf{v}_i(k_j,t)$ surround each single point and the previous contour points, $\mathbf{v}^N(t-1)$. To measure best match the previous contour points are processed by a distance transformation. This step leads to a dis image, where every image pixel is set to the minimal distance to a point of $\mathbf{v}^N(t-1)$ (see Fig. 4. (right) example of this distance image). The actual contour part is then moved over the distance image. For translation the distance values along the contour part are summed up. The optimal translation is the trans leading to the lowest sum of distance values. More formally, for a contour point $\mathbf{v}_i(k_j,t)$ the optimal trans $\mathbf{d}_{ij}$, is found by minimizing the following energy:

$$E(\mathbf{d}_{ij}) = \sum_{k=0}^{K-1} D_{\mathbf{v}^{N'}(t-1)}\left(\mathbf{v}_i(k,t) + \mathbf{d}_{ij}\right). \tag{2}$$

$D_{\mathbf{v}^{N'}(t-1)}(u,v,t-1)$ denotes a distance image, which is generated by a distance transformation based on extracted contours at time $t-1$, $\mathbf{v}^{N'}(t-1)$ and is expressed as

$$D_{\mathbf{v}^{N'}(t-1)}(u,v,t-1) = \min \left\| [u,v]^T - \mathbf{v}^{N'}(t-1) \right\|. \tag{3}$$

Efficient algorithms (parallel or sequential) of the distance transformation can be found in [8]. Fig. 4 illus the contour matching formulated in equation (2).

To track contour points over several images, it is necessary to find a temporal predecessor for every Therefore equation (2) has to be modified:

$$E(\mathbf{d}_{ij}) = \begin{cases} \sum_{k=0}^{K-1}\left(D_{\mathbf{v}'(t)}\left(\mathbf{v}_i(k,t) + \mathbf{d}_{ij}\right)\right)^2 & \text{if } D_{\mathbf{v}'(t)}\left(\mathbf{v}_i(k_j,t) + \mathbf{d}_{ij}\right) = 0 \\ \text{MAX\_VAL} & \text{else} \end{cases} \tag{4}$$

This formulation enforces that only translations are possible, which move the contour point $\mathbf{v}_i(k_j,t)$ expl one point on $\mathbf{v}^{N'}(k,t-1)$.

The presented contour matching allows the tracking of contour points over several images. This is u integrate the motion vectors over time, which leads to a temporal stabilized motion estimation. The stab motion vectors at every contour point are denoted as $\mathbf{m}^N(t)$.

For images of the dimension 184 columns to 128 rows the presented motion estimation implemented Pentium III (600 MHz) is running in real-time (< 40 msec).

2.4 Temporal Stabilization of Motion Segmentation

In this processing step vehicles are detected based on their motion. The contour tracking, developed previous section, allows a temporal stabilization of the motion based segmentation. Because of the tem correspondence of contour points it is also possible to track how often a contour point was selected before information is stored in an image called $Age(u,v,t)$.

Temporal stabilization needs the actual contour structure, $\mathbf{v}^N(t)$, the corresponding motion vector, $\mathbf{m}^N(t)$ explicit assignment of the predecessors, $\mathbf{d}^N(t)$ and the $Age(u,v,t-1)$ as input. The algorithm consists following steps:

1. Select all contour points with a negative motion component in v direction. This simple motion segmenta possible because of the lane based transformation. These selected points are treated as potential contour of a vehicle. This is illustrated in fig. 1 d. The selected points are denoted as $\mathbf{p}^M(t)$. M specifies the num selected points. Additionally, at the selected points the explicit assignment of the predecessors are deno $\mathbf{d}^M(t)$.

2. If a selected point, $\mathbf{p}_i$, was also detected at time $t-1$, increment the age of the point by 1, else initiali age with 1. Formally, this can be expressed as follows: first, at every pixel $Age(u,v,t)$ is set to 0; seco

$$Age(p_{ui}, p_{vi}, t) = Age(p_{ui} - a_{ui}, p_{vi} - a_{vi}, t-1) + 1 \ . \tag{5}$$

selected points, which are older than a given threshold are treated as true contour points of a vehicle.
se true points are marked in the mask image, $Mask(u,v,t)$:

$$Mask(u,v,t) = \begin{cases} 1 & \text{if} \quad Age(u,v,t) > age_{thresh} \\ 0 & \text{else} \end{cases} \tag{6}$$

$sk(u,v,t)$ is then dilated to generate closed vehicle masks. The results of this processing step is illustrated
g. 1 e.
icles are finally detected in $Mask(u,v,t)$. This is achieved by finding the corresponding bounding box.

Applications

chapter two applications of the proposed vehicle detection are presented. The first application was already
ted in fig. 1. The observation of the rear and lateral lane on highways is for example necessary for an
ke checker. The motion based vehicle detection, presented in the previous chapter can be used directly for
plication. The left part of fig. 5 shows the results of the vehicle detection for the overtake checker. The left
1 contains the detected vehicles in the camera image. The right column shows the corresponding
rmed images: the transformed camera image; the extracted contours; the selected contour points and the
ally stabilized motion masks. Additionally the bounding boxes, extracted form the mask image, are
ed. The dimension of the transformed images are 120 rows by 80 columns. On a Pentium III (600 MHz)
"-implementation of the proposed vehicle detection takes about 10 msec. The exact processing times
s on the number of contour points.
cond application is a visual traffic monitoring system. Results of the motion based segmentation are
in the right part of fig. 5. At six successive instants the transformed image, the extracted contours with
vectors and the generated motion masks are displayed. The time index is written in the left upper corner
transformed camera image. Index 300 shows the situation of the beginning of a red period (the first
is already waiting), index 400 during a red period, and index 900 at the beginning of a new green period.
e overlap of the vehicles in the upper lane area, moving vehicles are detected as one group. Single
s are only detected as they approach to the camera.
demonstrates that the proposed vehicle segmentation is robust under different lighting conditions and
ndent to different vehicle types.

Summary

aper presents a new approach for the detection of vehicles. Segmentation is based on motion only. The
on of the processing to the observed lane(s) and a new concept for contour tracking, allows processing in
ne. On a Pentium III processor (600 MHz) a pure "C"-implementation requires 10 msec. The dimension
ransformed images is set to 120 rows by 80 columns.
ir tracking, explained in chapter 2, leads to a robust motion estimation. Additionally, it allows the
al stabilization of the motion segmentation. Vehicles, are detected reliable and errors of motion
station are rejected. The proposed approach allows also contour tracking over a long time period. It is
e to track single contours from their entry to their leaving of the observation area. The transition time can
l to measure the effective velocity or waiting time at a traffic light.
esented contour tracking allows the use of motion as basic information in real-time applications. It is
e to combine motion information with other approaches, e.g. stereo processing or model based
ches, for a further improvement of robustness.

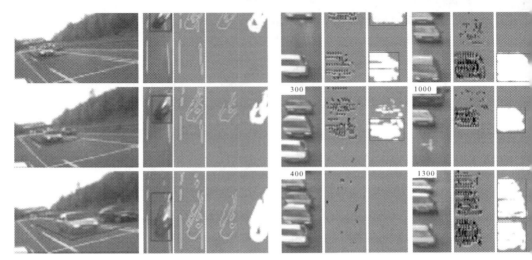

Fig. 5. Results of the motion based vehicle detection for the overtake checker (left) and visual traffic monitoring (rig

Fig. 6. Vehicle segmentation is robust under sunny conditions (left) and independent of vehicles types (right).

References

1 W. Enkelmann, V. Gengenbach, W. Krüger, S. Rössle, W. Tölle, *Obstacle Detection by Real-Time Optica Evaluation*, Intelligen Vehicles '94, 97-102, 1994

2 S. M. Smith, *ASSET-2: Real-Time Motion Segmentation and Shape Tracking*, IEEE Transactions on Pattern Analy Machine Intelligence, 17, 8, 814-820, 1995

3 D. Beymer, P. McLauchlan et al., *A Real-Time Computer Vision System for Measuring Traffic Parameters*, CV 1997

4 Y. Taniguchi, K. Okamoto, *Automatic Rear and Side Surveillance System*, 6th Annual World Congress on IST, 199

5 A. Techmer, *Contour-based motion estimation and object tracking for real-time applications*, accepted for ICIP 200

6 J. Canny, *A Computational Approach to Edge Detection*, IEEE Transactions on Pattern Analysis and M Intelligence, **8**, 6, 679-698, 1986,

7 R. Nevatia, K. R. Babu, *Linear Feature Extraction and Description*, Computer Graphics and Image Processing, 1 269, 1980

8 G. Borgefors, *Distance Transformation in Digital Images*, Computer Vision, Graphics and Image Processing, 3 371, 1986

9 S. Bohrer, *Visuelle Hinderniserkennung durch Auswertung des optischen Flusses in inversperspektivischen* Fakultät für Elektrotechnik, Ruhr-Universität Bochum, 1993

10 D. Marr, S. Ullmann, *Directional Selectivity and its Use in Early Visual Processing*, Proceedings of the Royal S 1981

Detection and Tracking of Moving Objects for Mosaic Image Generation

Birgit Möller[1] and Stefan Posch[2]

[1] Technische Fakultät, AG Angewandte Informatik, University of Bielefeld
P.O. Box 100 131 , 33501 Bielefeld
bimoelle@Techfak.uni-bielefeld.de
[2] University of Halle, posch@informatik.uni-halle.de

Abstract. Mosaic images provide an efficient representation of image sequences and simplify scene exploration and analysis. However, the application of conventional methods to generate mosaics of scenes with moving objects causes integration errors and a loss of dynamic information. In this paper a method to compute mosaics of dynamic scenes is presented addressing the above mentioned problems. *Moving pixels* are detected in the images and not integrated in the mosaic yielding a consistent representation of the static scene background. Furthermore, dynamic object information is extracted by tracking *moving regions*. To account for unavoidable variances in region segmentation topologically neighboring regions are grouped into sets before tracking. The regions' and objects' motion characteristics are described by trajectories. Along with the background mosaic they provide a complete representation of the underlying scene which is ideally suited for further analysis.

1 Introduction

An important topic in computer based scene exploration is the analysis of image sequences, since motion within the scene cannot be extracted using single images only. However, the resulting amount of data to be processed usually limits the application area of image sequences. One possibility to reduce the amount of data is to create mosaic images. In doing so a sequence is integrated in one single mosaic image thus removing redundancies within the sequence. Applying conventional methods to generate mosaics to sequences with moving objects yields integration errors and a loss of dynamic information (see e.g. [1]). In the works of Mégret [6] and Davis [3] moving areas within a sequence are therefore detected and omitted for integration. Thus integration errors can be avoided but dynamic information still is lost. Cohen [2] suggests tracking of moving regions based on dynamic templates, however, if the shapes of objects change significantly templates are not sufficient. In Irani [4] tracking is realized by temporal integration, but no explicit data extraction is suggested.

---

* This work has been supported by the German Research Foundation (DFG) within SFB 360.

B. Radig and S. Florczyk (Eds.): DAGM 2001, LNCS 2191, pp. 208–215, 2001.
© Springer-Verlag Berlin Heidelberg 2001

The method presented in this paper is based on a two-step strategy for each image to process resulting in a mosaic of the static scene background and trajectories describing the object motion. In the first step pixels belonging to projections of moving objects, in the following referred to as *moving pixels*, are detected resulting in a motion map and omitted during subsequent integration of greylevel information to generate the background mosaic. In the second step regions, referred to as *moving regions*, are first extracted from the motion maps. They are subsequently grouped into connected components and matched against the components of the previous image. Thus temporal correspondences can be established and trajectories are derived.

The paper is organized as follows. In section 2 a brief introduction to image alignment and detection of moving pixels is given. Section 3 outlines the temporal correspondence analysis based on moving regions by which dynamic scene information is extracted. Results of applying the algorithms to various image sequences are presented in section 4, and finally a conclusion is given.

2   Motion Detection

To detect moving objects in an image sequence many methods have been proposed in the literature. Most algorithms rely on the analysis of pixel based intensity differences between the images after an alignment step in case of a non-static camera. In our approach the images are aligned using *perspective flow* developed by [5] and implemented in [8], where the current background mosaic serves as reference. The alignment is based on an underlying motion model describing the global motion between both images induced by the active camera. We chose a projective transformation, which yields correct global transformation e.g. for camera rotation around the optical centers (no translation) and arbitrary static scenes, while projections of moving objects result in violations of this model. These errors are subsequently detected either computing the average intensity difference or the mean magnitude of the local normal flow $\boldsymbol{n}(x,y)$ for each pixel (x,y) within a neighborhood μ, as illustrated in equation 1 for the mean normal flow $N(x,y)$. Taking neighboring pixels into account yields more robust classification results as the influence of image noise is reduced.

$$N(x,y) = \frac{1}{|\mu|} \cdot \sum_{(x',y') \in \mu} \| \boldsymbol{n}(x',y') \| \tag{1}$$

The classification of moving pixels itself is acomplished thresholding the resulting pixelwise motion measure. Thus detection of motion is achieved except for image regions where motion does not cause any changes in intensity. However, the resulting motion maps are often fragmented and are therefore smoothed applying a dilatation operator of size 7 x 7 to the thresholded motion maps. Hence moving areas become more compact and small gaps in between are closed.

The resulting motion information is used to integrate the current image into the mosaic where only static pixels are taken into account yielding a consistent representation of the static scene background. Further temporal correspondence analysis is based on this data as presented in the next section.

3   Temporal Correspondence Analysis

The resulting motion information is sufficient to generate mosaics of the static scene background. As a next step we aim at explicitly representing the dynamic information of the image sequence contained in the already calculated motion maps. Therefore in our approach moving regions resulting from region labelling the thresholded and dilated motion maps are tracked and trajectories describing their motions are generated to represent the dynamic information.

3.1   Tracking of Moving Regions

Tracking is based on moving regions. The matching criterion for tracking will now be developed for these regions, but subsequently applied for sets of regions (section 3.2).

Each moving region needs to be characterized by several features which allow us to match corresponding regions of consecutive images. When selecting appropriate features it has to be taken into account that due to variances within the segmentation process and because of scene events like object decompositions or collisions, the moving regions' shape and size may vary significantly even for consecutive images. Furthermore regions often do not show homogeneous intensity values since generally moving regions contain projections from different objects or surfaces. Of course, also regions resulting from one object may be of inhomogenous gray values. Due to these limitations features need to be chosen which are mainly invariant against scaling and changes in shape and which preserve an adequate description of the regions' pixel values. This is true for the histogram of the pixel values and the centroid. Based on these features robust detection of correspondences between regions of consecutive images is possible: Two regions are considered as corresponding if the distance between their centroids is smaller than a given threshold θ_d, usually set to 60 pixel, and if the distributions of their intensity values are similar. This is checked by computing the overlapping area F of the two normalized histograms, whereas the minima of the entries a_i or b_i in all cells i are summed up:

$$F = \sum_i \min(a_i, b_i) \tag{2}$$

The resulting intersection area F is required to exceed a given percentage θ_p for establishing a match. θ_p is usually chosen between 0.75 and 0.85. For robust region tracking the sizes A and B of both regions given by the number of pixels are compared in addition. However, only if large differences between A and B occure a match is rejected due to the region expansion induced by the dilatation operator which has to be taken into account explicitly. The difference in size between to areas is regarded too large if the following condition holds:

$$\frac{|A - B|}{A + B} \geq 0.2 \qquad (3)$$

3.2 Tracking Components

Matching all pairs of moving regions from two consecutive images is not very efficient due to the combinatorics. Additionally regions frequently decompose or merge in the course of the image sequence induced by variances of the segmentation results (see e.g. motion maps in fig. 2) or events within the scene. In such cases correspondences cannot be established due to significant differences in the regions' histograms or size or too large distances between their centroids. Therefore we propose to track connected components instead, which are referred to as *components* subsequently, similarly as in [7] for color segmentation. In [7], regions are considered as neighboring, if they are spatially adjacent and similar with respect to their color features. In our case regions are assumed to be neighboring, if their minimum point distance is smaller than a given threshold. As mentioned, matching of connected components is based on the same criteria as developed to match moving regions (section 3.1) where the features can be derived directly from the features of the underlying regions. Searching for correspondences between these components reduces complexity, and variances within the segmentation can be handled since it is not required that components contain the same number of regions. Rather each component is treated as a single region. Using this strategy objects or parts of objects can be tracked robustly in most cases. However, in some cases correspondences cannot be established due to a changing arrangement of the regions within the components during the tracking process. To cope with these situations for each unmatched component all subsets of constituting moving regions are considered in a final step. Between all subsets of all components from consecutive images the best match is searched iteratively where the same match criteria as for components are applied. Matched subsets are removed from the sets and search continues until no more matches can be established or all given subsets have been matched.

3.3 Trajectories

As a result of tracking, correspondences between components of consecutive images have been established. To extract the dynamic information, in the present context given by the motion direction, trajectories for all tracked components are generated. The position of each component in an image is given by its centroid. A concatenation of the centroids of matched components, and matched subcomponents as well, yields a trajectory describing the objects' motions within the image sequence. In the case of translational motion this is sufficient to characterize the object motion. Future work will focus on a more detailed analysis of the trajectories, which may serve as a starting point to apply more sophisticated motion models. Furthermore they can be used to detect discontinuities of object motion and components incorrectly classified as moving in the later case. Trajectory points of these components show little variance which should make it possible to distinguish them from moving ones (see figure 4). Finally, based on the trajectories a reconstruction of homogenous objects which cannot be detected as a whole is possible. Different moving components belonging to one object show similar trajectories and could be grouped to reconstruct the object.

4   Results

The proposed algorithms for detection and tracking of moving objects have been tested on various image sequences. All sequences were aquired using an active camera which scanned the scene by pan and/or tilt movements. For the first three examples presented in this article the mosaics of the static scene background are shown along with the reconstructed trajectories. On the left side of each figure several images of the underlying sequence are depicted while in the lower half motion maps for different points of time within the sequence are shown. The last example illustrates the possibilities for false alarm detection and elimination of initial object positions (see below) based on trajectory analysis.

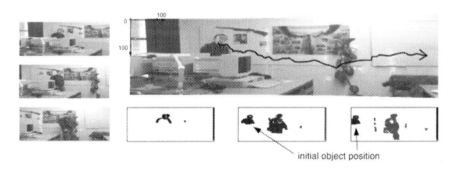

Fig. 1. Results of tracking a person: although the shape of the regions changes (maps below the mosaic) the motion trajectory (black line) can be reconstructed correctly

In figure 1 the person's motion is reconstructed correctly (using intensity difference for detection) despite the fact that the shape of the detected regions and their sizes vary significantly over time (as can be seen in the motion maps). The position of the person can be reconstructed almost completely and no parts of it are integrated so that a consistent representation of the static scene background results. However, it needs to be mentioned that the initial position of the person remains in the mosaic. It is integrated at the beginning of the sequence because it initially belongs to the static background. After the person has left his initial position, the beforehand occluded background becomes visible and results in large intensity differences at this image region, which consequently is detected as a "moving" region. Therefore at this position new intensity information can never be integrated. However, the centroid of this virtually moving region is nearly constant and the analysis of trajectory data is a promising starting point to correct this error in the future.

The second example (fig. 2) shows a mosaic image of a scene containing several pens. A pencil enters the scene from the top left corner and stops moving after hitting one of the other pens in the scene. Its trajectory (reconstructed using normal flow detection) is drawn black whereas the white arrow indicates the real motion direction. Especially at the beginning of the tracking process the motion given by the trajectory differs significantly from the true one. This originates from the fact that initially only parts of the pencil are visible. As new parts become visible a displacement of the centroid results and the reconstructed translation direction is distorted accordingly. As soon as the pencil is completely visible this divergences disappear and the centroids' displacements are caused by real object motions only, allowing a correct reconstruction of direction.

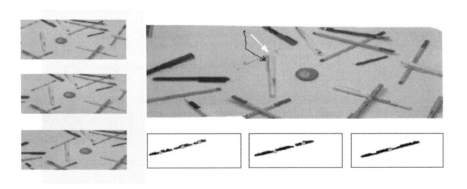

Fig. 2. Mosaic and reconstructed trajectory (black) of an object within a desk scenario. The motion maps show great variances (centroids of moving regions marked grey).

Figure 3 illustrates the mosaic and extracted trajectories of another desk scenario. The match box in the upper half of the four images on the left is opened and its two parts are moving in opposite directions afterwards. As in the first example, the initial box position remains part of the static mosaic whereas the following positions are omitted within the integration process. However, the object parts cannot be detected completely computing the intensity difference due to lack of contrast between the image background and the object parts. Especially the box top moving to the left causes integration errors due to incomplete object detection. Still the reconstructed trajectories describe the object motion almost correctly. Even the decomposition of the box (which forces the moving regions to be split up multiple times, see motion maps in figure 3) is identified correctly. Due to the fact that the regions resulting from the decomposition are grouped into one component they can be matched to the single region of the previous image. With increasing distance, however, they are eventually arranged into different components (points of time indicated by white circles within the figure). This causes a significant change within their centroids' positions (white arrows). However, the existing correspondences can be detected correctly and the scene events represented exactly.

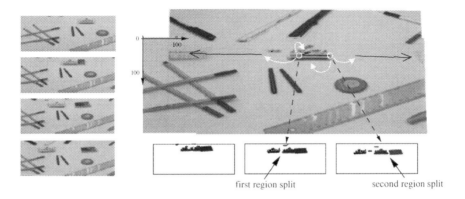

Fig. 3. Detection and tracking of an object decomposing in two parts

Concluding, the last example in figure 4 illustrates the former mentioned possibilities to detect false classified regions by trajectory analysis. The images of the sequence and the related mosaic depict several objects of the construction scenario of the SFB 360 where the dark ring in the center of the images moves to the right. Its initial position remains part of the mosaic. However, the plot of trajectory points at the bottom shows, that variance within these points is quite small and should be sufficient to identify this region as false classified. Hence the mosaic image can be corrected lateron by integrating local information from the current image although the region had been classified as moving beforehand.

5   Conclusion

In this paper an approach to generate mosaics of image sequences containing moving objects has been presented. A mosaic of the static scene background is generated and in parallel trajectories representing the dynamic information are extracted. To this end moving regions within the sequence are segmented

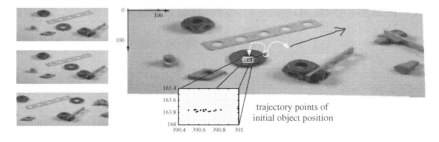

Fig. 4. The static initial position of the moving ring remains part of the mosaic. However, analysing the trajectory points indicates low variance suitable for identification.

based on pixelwise normal flow or intensity difference between two images. Subsequently the regions are grouped into sets of topologically neighboring regions tracking is based on. In this manner variances within the segmentation process and object decompositions can be handled. The components and if necessary subsets of them are robustly tracked over time by comparing their intensity histograms and centroid positions. Future work will focus on removing initial object positions from the mosaics and on detecting false alarms. As pointed out trajectory data as computed yield an ideal starting point to solve these problems.

References

1. Bergen, J., Anandan, P., Irani, M.: Efficient Representation of Video Sequences and Their Applications. Signal Processing : Image Communication (1996) (8):327–351
2. Cohen, I., Medioni, G.: Detection and Tracking of Objects in Airborne Video Imagery. CVPR Workshop on Interpretation of Visual Motion (1998)
3. Davis, J.: Mosaics of Scenes with Moving Objects. CVPR **1** (1998) 97-100
4. Irani, M., Rousso, B., Peleg, S.: Computing Occluding and Transparent Motions. International Journal of Computer Vision (IJCV) **12:1** (1994) 5-16
5. Mann, S., Picard, R. W.: Video Orbits of the Projective Group: A New Perspective on Image Mosaicing. M.I.T. Media Laboratory Perceptual Computing Section Technical Reports, No. 338 (1996)
6. Mégret, R., Saraceno, C.: Building the background mosaic of an image sequence. Tech. Report PRIP-TR-060, TU Wien (1999)
7. Rehrmann, V.: Object Oriented Motion Estimation in Color Image Sequences. Proc. of 5th ECCV (1998) 704-719
8. Sypli, D., Tappe, H.: Konstruktion von Mosaikbildern für die Bildanalyse. Masterthesis, University of Bielefeld (1999)

Acquiring Robust Representations for Recognition from Image Sequences

Christian Wallraven and Heinrich Bülthoff

christian.wallraven@tuebingen.mpg.de

Max Planck Institute for Biological Cybernetics

Spemannstr. 38

72076 Tübingen

Abstract. We present an object recognition system which is capable of on-line learning of representations of scenes and objects from natural image sequences. Local appearance features are used in a tracking framework to find 'key-frames' of the input sequence during learning. In addition, the same basic framework is used for both learning and recognition. The system creates sparse representations and shows good recognition performance in a variety of viewing conditions for a database of natural image sequences.

Keywords: object recognition, model acquisition, appearance-based learning

1 Introduction

Many computer vision recognition systems typically followed Marr's approach to vision in building three-dimensional (3D) representations of objects and scenes. The appearance-based or view-based approach, however, has recently gained much momentum due to its conceptual simplicity and strong support from studies on human perception. In this approach, an object is represented by viewer-centered 'snapshots' instead of an object-centered 3D model.

In recent years appearance-based vision systems based on local image descriptors have demonstrated impressive recognition performance ([1,4,2,8]). These systems normally work on a pre-defined database of objects (in the case of [8] more than 1000 images). However, one problem these approaches have not yet addressed is how to acquire such a database. When considering an active agent which has to learn and later recognize objects, the visual input the agent receives consists of a sequence of images. The temporal properties of the visual input thus represent another source of information the agent can exploit ([5]).

In this work, we therefore want to go one step further and move from a database of static images to image sequences. We present a recognition system which is capable of building on-line appearance-based scene representations for recognition from real world image sequences. These sequences are processed by the system to find 'key-frames' - frames where the visual change in the scene is high (related to the idea of 'aspect-graphs' from [3]). These key-frames are then characterized by local image descriptors on multiple scales which are used in the learning and recognition stages. The system uses the same framework for learning and for recognition which leads to an efficient and simple implementation. It was tested in a variety of different real world viewing situations and demonstrated very good recognition performance.

B. Radig and S. Florczyk (Eds.): DAGM 2001, LNCS 2191, pp. 216–222, 2001.

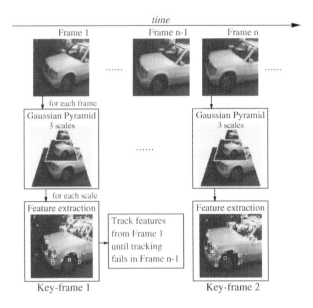

Fig. 1. Overview of the learning stage.

2   Overview

The system consists of two parts which share the same architecture: the learning part and the recognition part. In the learning part (see Fig.1), the input consists of an image sequence, which is processed on-line. First, each incoming frame is embedded in a Gaussian pyramid to provide a multi-scale representation. In the first frame features are extracted, which are then tracked in the subsequent frames. Once tracking fails, a new key-frame is found and a new set of features is extracted in this key-frame, and the whole process repeats until the sequence ends. The model of the sequence then consists of a number of key-frames, which contain visual features on multiple scales. The second part is the recognition stage: Here, the test image (taken under different viewing conditions) is compared to the already learned models by using the same procedural steps. Local features are extracted and matched against the key-frames in all learned models. In the next sections, we describe the two parts of the system in more detail.

3   The Learning Stage

3.1   Feature Extraction

We decided to use corners as visual features, since these were found to be good and robust features under many viewing conditions in numerous other works. In order to extract corners we modified a standard algorithm [10] to integrate information about all three color channels since this further improved robustness in the color image sequences we processed. Corners are found by inspecting the structure in a 9x9 neighborhood $\mathcal{N}$ of each pixel in the following way:

$$\mathbf{H} = \begin{pmatrix} \sum_{\mathcal{N}} \left\langle \frac{\partial \mathbf{I}}{\partial x}, \frac{\partial \mathbf{I}}{\partial x} \right\rangle & \sum_{\mathcal{N}} \left\langle \frac{\partial \mathbf{I}}{\partial x}, \frac{\partial \mathbf{I}}{\partial y} \right\rangle \\ \sum_{\mathcal{N}} \left\langle \frac{\partial \mathbf{I}}{\partial x}, \frac{\partial \mathbf{I}}{\partial y} \right\rangle & \sum_{\mathcal{N}} \left\langle \frac{\partial \mathbf{I}}{\partial x}, \frac{\partial \mathbf{I}}{\partial x} \right\rangle \end{pmatrix}$$

with $<,>$ as dot-product and $\mathbf{I}$ as the vector of RGB-values such that an element of $\mathbf{H}$ is e.g. $H(1,2) = \sum \frac{\partial I_r}{\partial x}\frac{\partial I_r}{\partial y} + \frac{\partial I_g}{\partial x}\frac{\partial I_g}{\partial y} + \frac{\partial I_b}{\partial x}\frac{\partial I_b}{\partial y}$. The smaller of the two eigenvalues λ_2 of $\mathbf{H}$ yields information about the structure of the neighborhood. We use a hierarchical clustering algorithm to cluster the values of λ_2 into two sets and use the one with the higher mean-value as the feature set. Using a clustering algorithm has the advantage that one does not need to specify a hard-coded threshold for the values of λ_2 for each image.

The whole procedure results in about 200 features over all three scales.

3.2   Tracking Visual Features

After extraction of feature positions, these features are then tracked over the image sequence. For this purpose, we are looking for corners in the image at time $t + 1$ in the vicinity of corners found at time t. The actual matching of the corners is done with an algorithm that is based on [7] (where it was used for stereo matching) and pioneered by [9], which we shortly summarize as it provides an elegant solution to feature matching and is also used later on in the recognition stage.

The algorithm constructs a matrix $\mathbf{A}$ with each entry $A(i,j)$ defined by

$$A(i,j) = e^{\frac{1}{2\sigma_{\text{dist}}^2}(-\text{dist}(f_{i,t+1},f_{j,t}))} \cdot e^{\frac{1}{2\sigma_{\text{NCC}}^2}(1-\text{NCC}(f_{i,t+1},f_{j,t}))}$$

with $f_{i,t+1}$ is the position of a corner at time $t + 1$ and $f_{j,t}$ another corner at time t in the previous image and i, j indexing all feature pairs in the two images.

The first term measures the distance (dist) from feature i to feature j with σ_{dist} set to small values (in our implementation $\sigma_{\text{dist}} = 8, 16, 32$ pixels for each of the three scales of the Gaussian pyramid) thus giving a tendency toward close matches in distance. The second term measures the normalized cross-correlation (NCC) of the neighborhoods from features i and j, with σ_{NCC} set to a value of 0.4, thus biasing the results toward features that are similar in appearance. Based on the Singular Value Decomposition of $\mathbf{A}$ ($\mathbf{A} = \mathbf{U} \cdot \mathbf{V} \cdot \mathbf{W}^{\mathbf{T}}$), the matching algorithm uses the modified SVD of this matrix, defined by $\mathbf{A}' = \mathbf{U} \cdot \mathbf{I} \cdot \mathbf{W}^{\mathbf{T}}$ where $\mathbf{I}$ is the identity matrix. Features are matched if they have both the highest entrance in the column and row of $\mathbf{A}'$ and if the NCC exceeds a given threshold (in our case $th_{\text{NCC}} > 0.6$). This method effectively provides a least-square mapping and at the same time ensures that there is a one-to-one mapping of features[1].

The resulting algorithm is capable of tracking under affine feature transformations between two images ensuring reliable and flexible tracking even for larger feature displacements between frames. Tracking could thus even be implemented in real-time since for normal camera and object velocities the tracker does not need to run at full framerate as it is able to cope with larger displacements.

---

[1] Note, that the feature mapping can occur between sub-sets of features.

The tracking procedure is followed until more than 75 percent of the initial features are lost at any one scale. This type of 'tracking through survival' effectively excludes false matches since these tend not to be stable across the whole image sequence. Once tracking fails, a new key-frame is inserted, new features are extracted and the process repeats until the sequence ends.

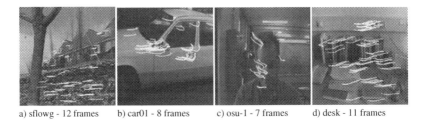

a) sflowg - 12 frames   b) car01 - 8 frames   c) osu-1 - 7 frames   d) desk - 11 frames

Fig. 2. Examples of feature tracking. The first (brightness reduced) frame of the sequence together with trajectories of the tracked features from all scale levels is shown.

We tested the performance of the tracker using various sequences available on the internet and also using sequences taken with a digital video-camera; some results are shown in Fig.2. All sequences are color sequences[2], Figs.2b,d are taken with an off-the-shelf camcorder. Fig.2a,d primarily show translational camera movement, while Fig.2b,c show mixtures of both translational and rotational components. In addition, the shaky path of the hand-held camera is clearly visible in Fig.2b,d. In Fig.2c the head makes a complicated movement while getting nearer to the camera, which is again accurately captured by the tracking algorithm. This example also shows the capability of the algorithm to track features even under non-rigid transformations (facial movements on static background) in the image.

In the end, the model of the sequence consists of a number of key-frames with features at several scales. We then save the pixel values in a 11x11 pixel window around each feature point which could be tracked between key-frames. Depending on the amount of visual change in the sequence this approach thus results in a high compression rate since we are using only a small amount of local features but still retain some actual pixel information.

Fig.3 shows examples for key-frames for three sequences of our database of car sequences. The database consists of 10 video sequences of cars which were recorded by walking with a video-camera around a car under daylight lighting conditions. No effort was made to control shaking or distance to the car. For all experiments we took only four frames per second from the sequences resulting in about 70-80 frames for the whole sequence. Note that the models consist of similar amounts of key-frames and that the viewpoints of the key-frames are roughly the same.

---

[2] The `sflowg` and `osu-1` sequences are available at
http://sampl.eng.ohio-state.edu/~sampl/data/motion.

Fig. 3. Key-frames for three car sequences.

4   Recognition of Images

For recognition we use the same framework as for learning. For this we change the parameters of the tracking algorithm to allow for greater image distances with $\sigma_{dist} = 40, 80, 160$ pixels while at the same time also increasing σ_{NCC} and th_{NCC} to 0.7. This ensures that only features with a high support both from global feature layout and from local feature similarity will be matched. Since we are using only a small amount of features (≈ 40 over all scales), matching can be done very fast for all key-frames even in a larger database.

In the following we will describe two types of recognition experiments. The first experiment was done with a variety of image degradations to test the stability of the system under controlled conditions - for this, we also used the sflowg, osu-1 and desk sequences. For the second experiment we took pictures of five cars with a digital camera under a variety of different viewing conditions such as different background, different lighting, occlusion, etc.

4.1   Recognition Results

Experiment 1 (image degradations): We used 7 types of image degradations, which are listed in Table 1. Two random images out of 14 test sequences were degraded and then matched against all other images in the sequence; for this, matching was done on all three scales and the mean percentage of matches recorded. Also shown in Table 1 is the mean percentage of the best matching frame and the recognition rate for 28 test images. Recognition failures occurred only in the shear, zoom and occlusion conditions, where feature distances were sometimes closer to neighboring frames due to the geometric transformations. To demonstrate the limits of the feature-based approach, we randomly superimposed 12x12pixel squares in the occlusion condition over the images so that 15% of the image was occluded. This led to a drastic reduction in recognition rate due to the almost destroyed local image statistics. Fig.4a shows one correctly recognized test image from condition 8.

Experiment 2 (recognition of novel images): We took 20 more images of five of the cars with a digital camera (and thus with different camera optics) in different viewing conditions to test how the system behaves in more realistic

Table 1. Image degradations

type	percentage matched	recognition rate
1. brightness +60%	66.4%	85.7%
2. contrast +60%	65.6%	85.7%
3. noise +40%	57.6%	92.9%
4. equalized color	53.3%	85.7%
5. shear	31.9%	78.6%
6. zoom x 1.5	32.9%	82.1%
7. occlude 15%	5.8%	46.4%
8. all of 1,2,3,4,5	28.3%	75%

Table 2. Recognition of novel images

condition	percentage model	percentage frame (false matches)	recognition rate
1. lighting changed	7.5%	22.3% (9.4%)	80%
2. viewing distances	9.3%	24.8% (8.2%)	90%
3. occlusion	10.2%	35.2% (9.2%)	100%

conditions. These included changes in lighting conditions (Fig.4b), two different viewing distances (Fig.4c) and occlusion by other objects (Fig.4d). Table 2 lists the percentage of matched features for the best matching model, which was obtained by summing up match percentages for each key-frame and dividing by the number of key-frames. A closer analysis of the match percentages shows that nearly all the matches are concentrated around the best matching key-frame, which demonstrates the robustness of the matching process. This is also shown by the much higher percentage of matched features for the best matching key-frame in the second column. The percentage of false matches, which we determined by visual inspection, is also indicated in Table 2 in brackets. Mismatches were mostly due to similar features on the background in the testing frames[3]. The nearest key-frame was chosen for 18 out of 20 frames even with sometimes drastically different backgrounds. However, in *all* cases the test image was assigned to the correct model and in only one case was the best matching frame more than two frames away from the right key-frame.

Some test images are shown in the upper row of Fig.4b-f together with their best matching key-frame in the lower row.

Fig. 4. Recognition results with a) degraded and b)-f) novel images. Test images are depicted in the upper row.

---

[3] Note, that a false match rate of 10% in most cases means not more than 2 false matches.

5   Conclusion and Outlook

We have presented a recognition system which is capable of on-line learning of sparse scene representations from arbitrary image sequences. It uses a simple and efficient framework both for learning and recognition. Recognition performance on a small database (which we plan to extend also to other object classes) showed that even this simple implementation is capable of recognition under a variety of different viewing conditions. Approaches such as [11] for feature characterization could even further improve the recognition results. Another by-product of recognition by key-frames is an approximate pose-estimation which could for example be beneficial for active agents in navigation and interaction with objects.

An extension of this system would be to use the feature trajectories *in between* key-frames in a structure from motion framework to recover a (necessarily) coarse 3D structure of the scene. This could further help with recognition of objects under larger changes in object orientation in the scene.

Since the system uses no segmentation, the resulting models will include information about the object and the surroundings. In an active vision paradigm an attention module could actively select the features belonging to one particular object, while the others are discarded and not tracked. In addition, we want to move the system from closed-loop (i.e. presenting pre-cut sequences for learning) to open-loop, where it decides autonomously when to begin a new model. For this, we are currently investigating the use of other types of features (such as color or texture - see e.g. [6]), which can be evaluated on a more global scale.

References

1. A. Baerveldt, "A vision system for object verification and localization based on local features", *Robotics and Autonomous Systems*, 34(2-3): 83-92, 2001.
2. D. Jugessur, G. Dudek, "Local Appearance for Robust Object Recognition", *In Proc. CVPR'00*, 834-839, 2000.
3. J. Koenderink, A. van Doorn, "The internal representation of solid shape with respect to vision", *Biological Cybernetics*, 32, 1979.
4. D. Lowe, "toward a Computational Model for Object Recognition in IT Cortex", *In Proc. BMCV'00*, 20-31, 2000.
5. A. Massad, B. Mertsching, and S. Schmalz, "Combining multiple views and temporal associations for 3-D object recognition", *In Proc. ECCV'98*, 699-715, 1998.
6. B. Mel, "SEEMORE: Combining color, shape, and texture histogramming in a neurally-inspired approach to visual object recognition", *Neural Computation*, 9:777–804, 1997.
7. M. Pilu, "A direct method for stereo correspondence based on singular value decomposition", *In Proc. CVPR'97*, 261-266, 1997.
8. C. Schmid, R. Mohr, "Local Greyvalue Invariants for Image Retrieval", *IEEE TPAMI*, 19(5):530-535, 1997.
9. G. Scott, H. Longuet-Higgins, "An algorithm for associating the features of two images", *In Proc. Royal Society of London*, B(244):21–26, 1991.
10. C. Tomasi, T. Kanade, "Detection and tracking of point features", *Carnegie-Mellon Tech Report CMU-CS-91-132*, 1991.
11. T. Tuytelaars, L. van Gool, "Content-based image retrieval based on local affinely invariant regions", *In Proc. Visual '99*, 493-500, 1999.

Image Sequence Analysis of Satellite NO$_2$ Concentration Maps

M. Wenig[1,2], C. Leue[1,2], S. Kraus[1], T. Wagner[2], U. Platt[2], and B. Jähne[1,2]

[1] Interdisciplinary Center for Scientific Computing (IWR), Heidelberg University,
INF 368, 69120 Heidelberg, Germany
[2] Institute for Environmental Physics, Heidelberg University, INF 229, 69120
Heidelberg, Germany

Abstract. Here we describe a new method for the quantification of a
global NO$_x$ budget from image sequences of the GOME instrument on
the ERS-2. The focus of this paper is on image processing techniques
to separate tropospheric and stratospheric NO$_2$-colums using *normalized convolution* with *infinite impulse response filters* (IIR) to interpolate
gaps in the data and average the cloud coverage of the earth, the estimation the NO$_2$ life time and the determination of regional NO$_x$ source
strengths.

1   Introduction

In April 1995 the ERS-2 satellite was launched by the *European Space Agency*
(ESA). The satellite carries besides other instruments the *Global Ozone Monitoring Experiment* (GOME), an instrument that allows to measure trace gas
concentrations in the atmosphere using the *Differential Optical Absorption Spectroscopy* (DOAS) [4].

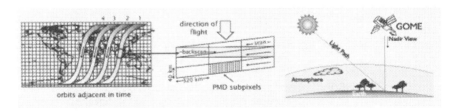

Fig. 1. Scanning geometry of the GOME instrument and visualization of the measured
slant column densities (SCD).

The GOME instrument consists of four spectrometers which monitor the
earth in nadir view with a ground pixel size of 320x40 km. It records a spectrum
every 1.5 seconds and needs about 3 days to completely scan the whole earth.
Measured trace gas concentrations are integrated along a light path through the
whole atmosphere (see Fig. 1). Since these paths are usually not vertical they are

B. Radig and S. Florczyk (Eds.): DAGM 2001, LNCS 2191, pp. 223–230, 2001.

called *slant column densities* (SCD). To obtain column density data which are independent from the viewing geometry the SCDs are transformed into *vertical column densities* (VCD) using the so called *Air Mass Factor* (AMF), which is in particular dependent of the solar zenith angle (SZA), ground albedo and the cloud cover. Evaluation of the DOAS spectra is done using a nonlinear fit algorithm to match reference spectra of trace gases against the measured spectrum and hence determine the specific concentration. [3] made major improvement regarding to evaluation speed, using *B-spline* interpolation [5] and reducing the number of iteration steps, so long time analysis can be done in acceptable time.

To estimate NO_x source strengths at first a separation of the tropospheric and stratospheric NO_2 concentrations as shown in Section 2 has to be done. Further more in Section 3 a new technique to determine the NO_2 life time is presented. Combining these results in Section 4 a estimation of regional NO_x source strengths can be done.

2   Separation of Stratosphere and Troposphere

First step in the subsequent analysis is the separation of the stratospheric and the tropospheric contribution to the total NO_2 column as we are only interested in the tropospheric NO_2 emissions.

Fig. 2 **(a)** shows the typical distribution of the vertical column density (VCD) of NO_2 for 9 September 1998. On this map the basic assumptions to discriminate troposphere and stratosphere can be observed:

The stratospheric contribution to the total column varies on a much larger scale than the tropospheric fraction, due to the longer life time of nitric oxides in the stratosphere and the fact that the tropospheric emissions are mainly caused by punctual emissions of industrial sources or biomass burning events.

It can be observed that the stratospheric distribution is less variable in longitudinal direction than in latitudinal direction where apparently a typical latitudinal profile is established. This is mainly due to the wind system in the stratosphere.

As described in [6] clouds hide parts of the visible NO_2 column which lay below the cloudy layer (in the troposphere). As a result the NO_2 column observed over cloudy regions will mainly consist of stratospheric contributions. If such a condition happens to appear over the ocean the effect becomes even more important since due to the low earth albedo the tropospheric contribution is attenuated relative to the stratospheric one. Therefore cloudy pixels over sea should represent the stratospheric NO_2 column.

2.1   Cloud Detection

These considerations will now be exploited to estimate the stratospheric NO_2 distribution. First land regions are masked out to avoid errors in the stratospheric signal due to tropospheric contributions. On the remaining pixels the stratospheric proportion of the total column will dominate. For further limitation cloud free pixels are masked out as well. This is done using the cloud detection algorithm introduced by [6] which is able to deduce a cloud fraction for each GOME pixel. Using a threshold we segment pixels with a cloud fraction of at least 50% and apply the resulting mask on the trace gas map. This procedure yields an image of NO$_2$ column densities with pixels that very likely represent the stratospheric NO$_2$ column but contain large gaps due to the masking process.

2.2   Interpolation by Normalized Convolution

These gaps have to be interpolated in order to estimate the stratosphere. So for this purpose the procedure of interest is the concept of *Normalized Convolution* by [2]. If g denotes the original image, where g(x,y) is the NO$_2$ concentration, m the mask for each pixel in the intervall $[0, 1]$, which is given by $1/\sigma_g^2$ and is 0 for the gaps, then the interpolated image g' is given by: $g' = \frac{\mathcal{B}(g \cdot m)}{\mathcal{B}(m)}$, with the lowpass filter operator $\mathcal{B}$ which can be of different size in any coordinate direction. The advantage of this filter type lies in its efficiency and the fact that it combines interpolation and averaging. The resulting numerical errors are dependent of the size of the gaps and are typically between 3.0% and 20.0%, the resulting stratospheric NO$_2$-VCDs range from $1 \cdot 10^{15}$ to $4 \cdot 10^{15} \frac{molecules}{cm^2}$ (see Fig. 2).

For $\mathcal{B}$ we chose the IIR (*infinite impulse response*) Deriche filter (see [1]): $\mathcal{B}(x) = k(\alpha|x| + 1)e^{-\alpha|x|}$, with $x \in \mathbf{Z}$ the coordinate of one dimension, standardisation k and $\alpha \in \mathbb{R}^{\geq 0}$ as a steering parameter. This filter is similar to a Gaussian filter but has the advantage of recursive implementation. This is extremely important because the use of FIR (*finite impulse response*) filters on a 3D image (latitude, longitude and time) is very time consuming. The Deriche filter is a second order recursive filter with causal and anticausal proportions $(g'(x) = \mathcal{B}(x) = g_1(x) + g_2(x))$:

$$g_1(x) = \underbrace{k(g(x) + e^{-\alpha}(\alpha - 1)g(x - 1))}_{FIR} + \underbrace{2e^{-\alpha}g_1(x - 1) - e^{-2\alpha}g_1(x - 2)}_{IIR} \quad (1)$$

$$g_2(x) = \underbrace{kg(x + 1)(e^{-\alpha}(\alpha + 1) - e^{-2\alpha})}_{FIR} + \underbrace{2e^{-\alpha}g_2(x + 1) - e^{-2\alpha}g_1(x + 2)}_{IIR} \quad (2)$$

This means 8 multiplications and 7 additions per pixel and dimension for a given steering parameter α. The different variability of the NO$_2$ maps in each direction can be exploited by the use of different values for α in latitudinal and longitudinal direction.

The result of the interpolation is now defined as representing the stratospheric background of the total NO$_2$ column (see Fig. 2). The tropospheric contribution can now be estimated by forming the difference between the original image and the estimated stratosphere. The resulting image has to be multiplied by a correction image which is the quotient of the stratospheric and tropospheric air mass

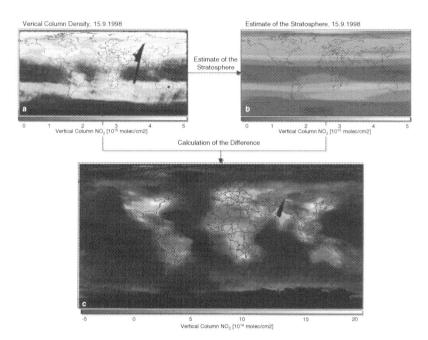

Fig. 2. Visualization of the discrimination algorithm. Starting with map (**a**) we mask out land masses and cloud free pixels and estimate the stratosphere (**b**) using Normalized Convolution. The tropospheric residual (**c**) can then be estimated calculating the difference between (**a**) and (**b**). It shows pronounced maxima in industrialized regions (please note the different scales of the maps).

factors and these factors are dependent on the actual solar zenith angle and the ground albedo. In the resulting image Fig. 2-(**c**) we see that localized emission sources appear pronounced, whereas the global stratospheric trend could be suppressed nearly completely.

Additional corrections have to be made in order to convert the NO_2 concentrations in NO_x concentrations and to consider the influence of clouds. The first is implemented using the *Leighton* ratio which is dependent of the Ozone concentration $[O_3]$, the NO_2-photolysis frequency $J(NO_2)$ and the rate coefficient of the reaction of O_3+NO_2, $k = 1.7 \cdot 10^{-12} \cdot \exp(\frac{-1310}{T})\frac{cm^3}{molec\ s}$. The factor which corrects for the influence of clouds is determined statistically by analyzing the annual average of NO_2 concentrations for different cloud covers.

3   Estimation of the Mean NO_2 Life Time

For the determination of the mean NO_2 source strength from the tropospheric maps the knowledge of the NO_2 life time τ is necessary. Fig. 3 (**e**) shows increased NO_2 columns over the ocean near coasts in wind direction whereas in the opposite direction no such feature can be found. This behavior is due to the chemical decay of NO_2 over the ocean where there is no net production but only chemical decay

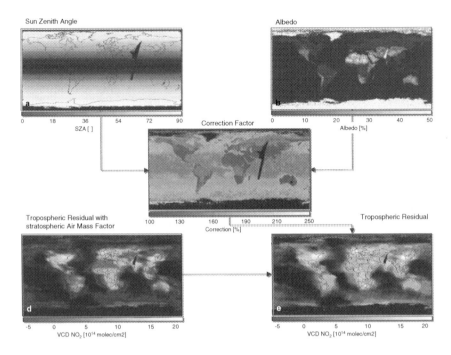

Fig. 3. Illustration of the correction process for the tropospheric residual with the tropospheric Air Mass Factor. The correction factor (**c**) is calculated from the SZA (**a**) and the ground albedo (**b**) which we estimate directly from the GOME PMD (Polarization Monitoring Device, part of the GOME Spectrometer) data. Applying (**c**) to the original tropospheric residual (**d**) we gain the corrected tropospheric NO$_2$ column in (**e**).

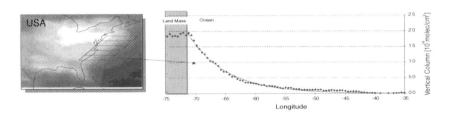

Fig. 4. Example for the decay curve along a latitudinal section through a NO$_2$ plume at the eastern shore of the US. The 1/e width of the curve can be calculated by a nonlinear regression with an exponential function. Combined with the average wind speed ($6.0 \pm 0.5 m/s$) an average NO$_2$-lifetime of 27 ± 3 hours is derived.

(see Fig. 4). From this decay curve we estimate the mean NO_2 life time from a case study in North America.

The basic assumption for the method is that in the annual mean the wind speed u and the life time τ can be substituted by their mean values and that the chemical decay can be described by a linear model (first order decay). The decay curve of NO_2 then shows a static behavior and can be expressed by the following equation (in x-direction): $\frac{dc}{dt} = 0 = u_x \frac{\partial c}{\partial x} + \frac{1}{\tau}c$ with the NO_2 concentration c. From integration it follows directly: $c(x) = c_0 \exp\left(-x(u_x\tau)^{-1}\right)$. The mean NO_2 life time τ over one year can thus be calculated by the determination of the $\frac{1}{e}$ width of the decay curve.

From a nonlinear fit the $\frac{1}{e}$ width is found to be $x_e = 670 \pm 75\,km$. This fit has been done for every dataline of the marked area (see Fig.4) and the variation of the results has been used to determine the error for x_e. The average wind speed was $u_x = 6.8 \pm 0.5\,\frac{m}{s}$ for the lower troposphere (from `ftp://zardoz.nilu.no`). From this information we calculate a resulting life time τ of $\tau \approx 98000$ s $= 27 \pm 3$ h which corresponds well to values found in literature of approximately one day.

4   Estimation of the Mean NO_x Source Strength

The estimation of the source strength (production rate) λ can now be done from the data of the annual mean image of the tropospheric NO_2 residual considering the correction factor mentioned above. Assuming that the production rate is constant over the year as well as the life time τ. The temporal development of the NO_2 concentration is then described by

$$\frac{dc}{dt} = \lambda - \frac{1}{\tau}c \Rightarrow c_T = \frac{1}{T}\int_0^T c(t)dt = \frac{\lambda}{T}(\tau T + \tau^2(e^{-\frac{t}{\tau}} - 1)) \approx \lambda\tau \quad (3)$$

with the mean concentration c_T for the time period T. By comparison with the measured values c_T (see Fig. 3 (e)) and the life time τ from 3 we can now estimate the global nitrogen budget and the mean production rate λ over one year.

Results of the determination of the global source strength and nitrogen budget are presented in Fig. 5. It shows that the global emission strength derived with this algorithm is (48 ± 20) Tg N yr^{-1}, which is in good agreement with reference values from literature (All values are in units of [Tg N yr^{-1}]): Logan et al. (JGR 88:10,785-807) 1983: 25-99, IPCC Report Cambridge 1990: 16-55, Hough (JGR 96:7325-7362) 1991: 42.0, Penner et al. (JGR 96:959-990) 1991: 42.2, Müller (JGR 97:3787-3804) 1992: 21.6, IPCC Report Cambridge 1992: 35.1-78.6, IPCC Report Cambridge 1995: 52.5, Olivier et al. Rep. no. 771060002 Bilthoven 1995: 31.2 and Lee et al. (Atm.Env.31(12):1735-1749) 1997: 23-81.

Whereas the absolute values contain still uncertainties of approximately a factor of 2 at least their relations show the order of the regions emitting most nitrogen. It is shown that Africa emits most nitrogen though it is only a poorly industrialized region. This is most likely due to biomass burning and soil emissions. A more detailed description of the used algorithms and interpretation of the results can be found in [6].

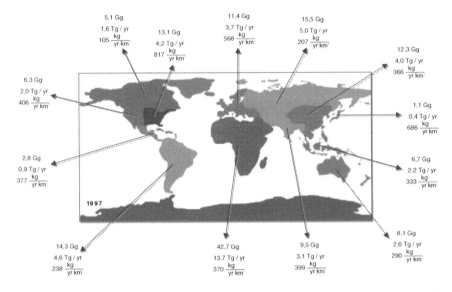

Fig. 5. Estimate of the mean NO$_x$-burden (in 10^9g nitrogen) and emission (in 10^{12}g nitrogen per year and in kg nitrogen/km^2 and year) for 1997 for different parts of the world.

5   Conclusions

Our new method to discriminate the tropospheric and stratospheric NO$_2$ contributions to the vertical NO$_2$ column from GOME satellite data only uses intrinsic image information and can thus be applied self consistently to each global NO$_2$ map of an image sequence (see Section 2). From the tropospheric NO$_2$ images information about the mean NO$_2$ life time can be obtained by analyzing its decay behavior in coastal regions (see Section 3). The estimated life time of 27±3 h corresponds very well to values found in literature of about one day. This leads to a first estimation of the mean NO$_x$ budget for the year 1997 and the calculations also will be done for the following years. The errors can be decreased by better knowledge about clouds and aerosols which allow a more precise calculation of the air mass factors. Though the errors are relatively high this method is a good alternative to the traditional ground based measurements.

We realize that in each of the evaluation steps described above substantial improvements are possible and necessary. While work is under way in our institution to make these improvements, this manuscript is focussed on presenting preliminary results which, nevertheless, clearly demonstrate the power of this new technology, and to make them available to the scientific community. Examples, where uncertainties and systematic errors can be significantly reduced include better characterization of the effect of clouds and aerosol on the tropospheric NO$_2$ column seen by GOME. Also the estimate of the NO$_x$- lifetime can clearly be improved beyond our simple assumption of a global average value.

References

1. R. Deriche. Fast algorithms for low-level vision. *IEEE Transactions on Pattern Analysis and Machine Intelligence*, 12(1):78–87, January 1990.
2. H. Knutsson and C.F. Westin. Normalized and differential convolution, methods for interpolation and filtering of incomplete and uncertain data. *IEEE Transactions on Pattern Analysis and Machine Intelligence*, 3:515–523, 1993.
3. Carsten Leue. *Detektion der troposphärischen NO2 Daten anhand von GOME*. PhD thesis, Universität Heidelberg, 1999.
4. U. Platt. Differential Optical Absorption Spectroscopy (DOAS). In W.M. Sigrist, editor, *Air Monitoring by Spectrometric Techniques*, volume 127. John Wiley & Sons, Inc., 1994.
5. M. Unser, A. Aldroubi, and M. Eden. Fast B-spline transforms for continuous image representation and interpolation. *IEEE Transactions on Pattern Analysis and Machine Intelligence*, 13(3):277–285, March 1991.
6. M. Wenig. *Satellite Measurement of Long-Term Global Tropospheric Trace Gas Distributions and Source Strengths - Algorithm Development and Data Analysis*. PhD thesis, University of Heidelberg, July 2001.
7. M. Wenig, C. Leue, B. Jähne, and U. Platt. Cloud classification using image sequences of GOME data. In *European Symposium on Atmospheric Measurements from Space*. ESA, February 1999.

Root Growth Measurements in Object Coordinates

Norbert Kirchgeßner[1], Hagen Spies[1], Hanno Scharr[1], and Uli Schurr[2]

[1] Interdisciplinary Center for Scientific Computing, University of Heidelberg, INF
368, 69120 Heidelberg, Germany
[2] Institute of Botany, University of Heidelberg, INF 360, 69120 Heidelberg, Germany
Norbert.Kirchgessner@IWR.Uni-Heidelberg.De

Abstract. We show a framework for growth analysis of plant roots in
object coordinates which is one requirement for the botanical evaluation
of growth mechanisms in roots. The method presented here is appliable
on long image sequences up to several days, it has no limit for the sequence length. First we estimate the displacement vector field with the
structure tensor method. Thereafter we determine the physiological coordinates of the root by active contours. The contours are first fitted on the
root boundary and yield the data for the calculation of the middle line as
the object coordinate axis of the root. In the third step the displacement
field is sampled at the position of the middle line and projected onto it.
The result is an array of tangential displacement vectors along the root
which is used to compute the spatially resolved expansion rate of the
root in physiological coordinates. Finally, the potential of the presented
framework is demonstrated on synthetic and real data.

1 Introduction

Plant expansion growth can be mapped to a high spatial and temporal resolution
by using optical flow techniques [Schmundt and Schurr, 1999], [Schurr et al.,
2000]. However, not only the magnitude, but also the location of growth zones
on the biological object are required. Therefore it is necessary to project maps
detected by low-level analysis to feature-based coordinates of the plant.

In the growing root the relevant physiological coordinate axis is the middle
line originating at the root tip: cells that have been formed at the root tip expand
along this axis.

The common method for measuring root growth is, to put ink markers or
other tracers on the root [Beemster and Baskin, 1998] [Walter et al, 2000]. The
growth rate (GR) is then determined by observing the change of their position
over time. This technique has only a coarse temporal and spatial resolution,
the number of markers is limited and it is very inconvenient to evaluate the
sequences.

Root growth occurs only in the region near the root tip [Walter et al., 2000].
Therefore we only observe this area. Optimal resolution is obtained in a setup,
when most of the image is taken by the root. However, then the expansion

B. Radig and S. Florczyk (Eds.): DAGM 2001, LNCS 2191, pp. 231–238, 2001.
© Springer-Verlag Berlin Heidelberg 2001

process moves the root out of the imaged frame. For long term observations (over several days) we follow the tip by moving the camera on an x-y-stage. For studying diurnal rhythms during light and dark an illumination in the near IR is used.

The described algorithm has three components. At the outset the displacement vector field on the root (v_x, v_y) is calculated in image coordinates by the structure tensor method. Afterwards the object coordinate axis is extracted by an active contour model (sec. 3). The last step projects the displacement vector field on the coordinate axis (sec. 4). This results in the tangential displacements v_t along the root axis. We get the growth distribution by computing the divergence of v_t. In sec. 5 we apply the method on real and synthetic data.

2   Displacement Vector Field

We calculate the displacement vector field (DVF) with the so called structure tensor method. The assumption that any brightness change is due to movement directly guides to the optical flow constraint equation [Horn and Schunk, 1981].

$$\frac{\mathrm{d}g}{\mathrm{d}t} = \frac{\partial g}{\partial x}\frac{\mathrm{d}x}{\mathrm{d}t} + \frac{\partial g}{\partial y}\frac{\mathrm{d}y}{\mathrm{d}t} + \frac{\partial g}{\partial t} = \boldsymbol{v}^T \nabla g \overset{!}{=} 0 \tag{1}$$

where we use $\nabla^T = (\frac{\partial}{\partial x}, \frac{\partial}{\partial y}, \frac{\partial}{\partial t})$, $\boldsymbol{v}^T = (\frac{\mathrm{d}x}{\mathrm{d}t}, \frac{\mathrm{d}y}{\mathrm{d}t}, 1) = (v_x, v_y, 1)$ and g as grey value. For further details we refer to [Haußecker and Jähne, 1997, Haußecker and Spies, 1999].

The structure tensor method provides a confidence measure ζ which indicates the positions of a possible displacement estimation (the DVF can only be estimated at regions with sufficient texture). In the later evaluation ζ is taken into account by computing a fillfactor (sec. 5.2). This is the ratio of the number of reliable estimations with $\zeta \geq 0,8$ and the number of pixels which belong to the root.

This step yields the DVF of the root which is later sampled at the middle line positions and then used to calculate the growth distribution.

3   Physiological Root Coordinates

The aim of this work is to do biological meaningful measurements of root growth. For this purpose one requirement is, to calculate the growth rates in a physiological coordinate system. As cells emerge at the very root tip and expand along the root axis, the distance from the root tip, measured along the middle line of the root, defines the coordinate axis. The determination of this line as a b-spline is done as follows: The b-spline representation is a continuous mathematical description of the curve. The run of the b-spline is defined by a number of fulcrums and one can pass along the line by varying a parameter value continuously. The entire numbered indexes correspond to the fulcrum positions of the b-spline.

a   b

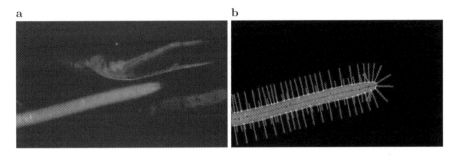

Fig. 1. **a** Original root image **b** Preprocessed image with fitted root boundary, normals for position estimation of the boundary and extracted middle line.

In a first step, the root boundaries are extracted and represented by an active contour method (a b-spline with the ability to fit its position to image contents [Blake and Isard, 1998]) and used in the second step to determine the middle line as another b-spline (sec. 3.2). Subsequently we sample the DVF at the positions of the middle line at distances of one pixel. As we know the tangent direction of a b-spline at any position, we can easily project the DVF on the middle line (sec. 4).

3.1   Root Boundary

To extract the boundary of the observed root by an active contour we first preprocess the sequence to prevent that the contour is pulled off the root boundary by e.g. air bubbles in the image (see Fig 1**a**). A global threshold is applied and the biggest segmented area is used as the root mask. Applying this mask on the original image removes all but the root.

A pixel line of the boundary is obtained by eroding the root mask by one pixel and subtracting the erosion result. Along this pixel line we take 45 evenly spaced points as initial fulcrums for the active contour. The active contour adjusts itself to the root image by replacing each fulcrum position by the position of the maximal gradient in normal direction to the spline (see Fig 1**b**). At the position where the spline is too far away because of missing fulcrums, new ones are introduced.

The above procedure is applied to each image of the sequence and gives us the root boundary in the form of a b-spline S_b which is used in the next section to extract the middle line.

3.2   Middle Line

The b-spline S_b of the root boundary is now used to get the middle line of the root in form of a b-spline S_m. We search for fulcrums of the middle line S_m by applying the following method to each fulcrum of the boundary S_b.

First originating from the fulcrum position we search in normal direction to S_b for the root boundary on the other side of the root (see Fig. 1b for the normals). The other side of the root is detected by mirroring the gradient filter which is applied on the normals of S_b for finding the exact root boundary in 3.1. The convolution returns a maximum at an edge in the other direction, that means on the other side of the root. In the middle of the new point and its corresponding fulcrum of S_b the new fulcrum of the middle line S_m is positioned.

In the region of the root tip this procedure gives no result because the normals on which the other side of the root is searched do not intersect with the root boundary (see Fig. 1b). Here we extrapolate S_m linearly and intersect the boundary S_b with this extrapolation to obtain the fulcrum of the middle line.

Now the axis of the physiological root coordinates is available as a b-spline S_m, thus a continuous mathematical description with its direction at every position which is needed for the projection of the DVF on S_m.

4   Projection of the DVF

At this point we combine the DVF as calculated with the structure tensor (section 2) and the middle line S_m extracted with an active contour (section 3) in each image of the sequence.

In order to separate movements of the whole root from motion caused by growth we project the DVF on S_m. The projection of the DVF is calculated at intervals of 1 pixel starting from the root tip. This way we get an array of the tangential displacements along S_m. At each position the following steps are done.

First we determine the indices of S_m of the sampling positions. There a bilinear interpolation of the DVF is done. For stabilization the DVF is averaged in normal direction to S_m over 21 positions. This value is finally projected on S_m to get the tangential displacement $v_t(x)$) of the root.

This yields an one-dimensional array for each image which contains the tangential displacements $v_t(x)$ along the middle line of the root at intervals of 1 pixel. The relative GR distribution of the root $g(x)$ is computed as the slope of this array for each time step.

5   Experiments

The presented framework was tested with artificial and real data to show its accuracy and suitability for real botanical measurements.

5.1   Synthetic Data

The synthetic data on which we apply our method was made to estimate its accuracy at different speeds of the root tip and the influence of noise. The artificial root (see Fig. 2) consists of gaussian spots which are displaced in x-direction with 0.5, 1.0 and 1.5 pixel/frame at the root tip and a sinusoidal decrease (see Fig. 3a, c, e). Normal distributed noise with a standard deviation of 1, 2 and 3 grey values was added on the 8 bit images, which approximately corresponds to the noise level of the applied cameras. The estimated displacements are shown in Fig. 3a, c and e, they are systematically lower than the real displacements. The maximum estimation error of the displacement occurs at the position of high displacement decrease because there the assumption of a homogene displacement is violated. Nevertheless the resultant GR distribution is close to the real one. This resolution fullfils the requirements of the botanical application.

a   b

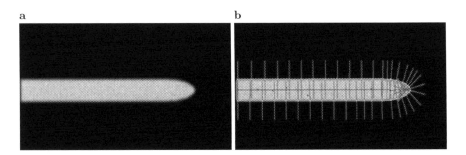

Fig. 2. Synthetic image. **a** original **b** preprocessed with extracted boundary, position estimation normals and middle line.

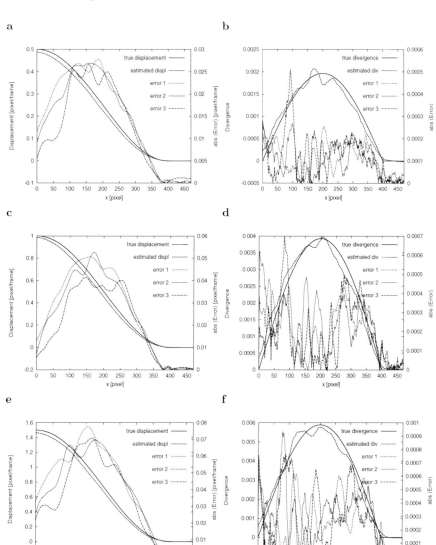

Fig. 3. Results of the synthetic data at different root tip displacements and noise levels. Gaussian noise with a standart deviation σ of 1, 2 and 3 grey values was added on each sequence. The estimated DVF/divergence is only shown for noise with $\sigma = 1$. For the other noise levels only the estimation error is shown **a** DVF at a tip displacement v_t of 0.5 pixel and errors for different noise / frame **b** Divergence $v_t = 0.5$ pixel / frame **c** DVF at a tip displacement v_t of 1.0 pixel / frame **d** Divergence $v_t = 1.0$ pixel / frame **e** DVF at a tip displacement v_t of 1.5 pixel / frame **f** Divergence $v_t = 1.5$ pixel / frame

5.2   Real Data

The real data was recorded at the Botanical Institute of the University Heidelberg. The images were taken on maize roots in intervals of 5 minutes with a resolution of 640x480 pixel, the middle line was extracted (see Fig. 4a, b). As the results scatter rather strongly (see Fig. 4c) we compute an average DVF (see Fig. 4d). For this purpose each DVF is rejected which has a fillfactor (sec. 2) less than 0.2.

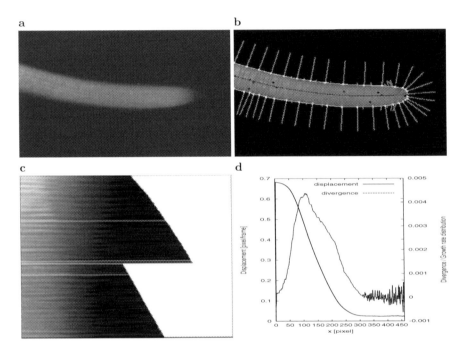

Fig. 4. a Recorded image of a maize root. b Preprocessed image with extracted boundary and middle line. c Diagram of t (y-axis) over the projected DVF $v(x)_t$ x-axis). The root tip is located on the left. High resp. low displacements are represented bright resp. dark. The length of the DVF increases as the root grows. The step in the middle is caused by the camera tracking of the root tip, where no displacement estimation is possible. d Averaged DVF $v(x)_t$ and spatial resolved growth rate distribution $\frac{\partial v_t(x)}{\partial x}$ of the root. The root tip is located in the origin.

6   Conclusion and Acknowledgements

We show a framework for root growth measurements in physiological coordinates. We combine the estimation of the DVF with a technique that samples the estimations along the middle line S_m of the root and projects the DVF on S_m. This enables biologists to measure directly in the relevant coordinate system. In future work this method will be extended to more complicated coordinate systems such as the vein system on plant leaves. Part of this work has been funded under the DFG research unit "Image Sequence Analysis to Investigate Dynamic Processes" (For240).

References

G. T. S. Beemster and T. I. Baskin. Analysis of cell division and elongation underlying the developmental acceleration of root growth in arabidopsis. *Plant Physiology*, 116: 1515–1526, 1998.

A. Blake and M. Isard. *Active Contours*. Springer, 1998.

H. Haußecker and B. Jähne. A tensor approach for precise computation of dense displacement vector fields. In F.M. Wahl E. Paulus, editor, *Mustererkennung 97*, pages 199–208, Braunschweig, September 1997. Springer.

H. Haußecker and H. Spies. Motion. In B. Jähne, H. Haußecker, and P. Geißler, editors, *Handbook of Computer Vision and Applications*, volume 2, pages 309–396. Academic Press, 1999.

B.K. Horn and B.G. Schunk. Determining optical flow. In *Artificial Intelligence*, volume 17, pages 185–204, 1981.

D. Schmundt and U. Schurr. Plant leaf growth studied by image sequence analysis. In B. Jähne, H. Haußecker, and P. Geißler, editors, *Computer Vision and Applications Volume 3*, pages 719–735. Academic Press, San Diego, New York, Boston, London, Sydney, Tokyo, Toronto, 1999.

U. Schurr, U. Heckenberger, K. Herdel, A. Walter, and R. Feil. Leaf develompent in ricinus communis during drought stress: dynamics of growth processes, of cellular structure and of sink-source transition. *Journal of Experimental Botany*, 51(350): 1515–1529, 2000.

A. Walter, W. Silk, and U. Schurr. Effect of soil ph on growth and cation deposition in the root tip of zea mays l. *Journal of Plant Growth Regulation*, 19:65–76, 2000.

On Fusion of Multiple Views for Active Object Recognition

Frank Deinzer*, Joachim Denzler, and Heinrich Niemann

Chair for Pattern Recognition, Department of Computer Science,
Universität Erlangen-Nürnberg, Martensstr. 3, 91058 Erlangen
{deinzer,denzler}@informatik.uni-erlangen.de
http://www.mustererkennung.de

Abstract. In the last few years the research in 3–D object recognition has focused more and more on active approaches. In contrast to the passive approaches of the past decades where a decision is based on one image, active techniques use more than one image from different viewpoints for the classification and localization of an object. In this context several tasks have to be solved. First, how to choose the different viewpoint and how to fusion the multiple views.

In this paper we present an approach for the fusion of multiple views within a continuous pose space. We formally define the fusion as a recursive density propagation problem and we show how to use the CONDENSATION algorithm for solving it.

The experimental results show that this approach is well suited for the fusion of multiple views in active object recognition.

Keywords. Active Vision, Sensor Data Fusion

1   Introduction

Active object recognition has been investigated in detail recently [4,8,1,7,2]. The main motivation is that recognition can be improved if the right viewpoint is chosen. First, ambiguities between objects can be avoided that make recognition difficult or impossible at all. Second, one can prevent to present views to the classifier where in the mean worse results are expected. Those views depend on the classifier and can be recognized right after training, when the first tests are performed.

One important aspect in active object recognition — besides the choice of the best viewpoint — is the fusion of the classification and localization results of a sequence of viewpoints. Not only for ambiguous objects, for which more than one view might be necessary to resolve the ambiguity (examples are presented in the experimental sections), the problem arises how to fuse the collected views to finally return a classification and localization result. Also a sequence of views will improve recognition rate in general if a decent fusion scheme is applied. In this paper we present of a fusion scheme based on the CONDENSATION algorithm [5]. The reason for applying the CONDENSATION algorithm is

---

* This work was partially funded by the German Science Foundation (DFG) under grant SFB 603/TP B2. Only the authors are responsible for the content.

B. Radig and S. Florczyk (Eds.): DAGM 2001, LNCS 2191, pp. 239–245, 2001.

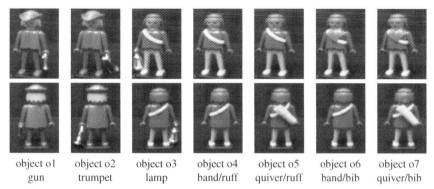

object o1	object o2	object o3	object o4	object o5	object o6	object o7
gun	trumpet	lamp	band/ruff	quiver/ruff	band/bib	quiver/bib

Fig. 1. Examples of the seven toy manakins used for the experiments. Please note that objects o4 to o7 cannot be classified with one view due to the complex ambiguities

threefold: first, inherently one has to deal with multimodal distributions over the class and pose space of the objects. Second, moving the camera from one viewpoint to the next will add uncertainty in the fusion process, since the movement of the camera will always be disturbed by noise. Thus, in the following fusion process of the classification and localization results acquired so far with the results computed from the current image, this uncertainty must be taken into account. Third, it is not straight forward to model the involved probability distributions in closed form, especially if multiple hypothesis, i.e. multimodal distributions, shall be handled. These three aspects let us believe, that the CONDENSATION algorithm is perfectly suited for the fusion of views in active object recognition. Especially, the ability to handle dynamic systems is advantageous: in viewpoint fusion the dynamics is given by the known but noisy camera motion between two viewpoints.

In the next section we summarize the problem and propose our sensor data fusion scheme based on the CONDENSATION. The performed experiments and an introduction to the classifier used in the experiments are resented in Section 3 to show the practicability of our method. Finally, a conclusion is given in Section 4.

2   Fusion of Multiple Views

In active object recognition object classification and localization of a static object is based on a sequence or series of images. These images shall be used to improve the robustness and reliability of the object classification and localization. In this active approach object recognition is not simply a task of repeated classification and localization for each image, but in fact a well directed combination of a funded fusion of images and an active viewpoint selection.

This section deals with the principles of the fusion of multiple views. Approaches for active viewpoint selection will be left out in this paper. They have been presented in [3,2].

2.1   Density Propagation with the Condensation Algorithm

Given an object, a series of observed images $f_n, f_{n-1}, \ldots, f_0$ and the camera movements $a_{n-1}, \ldots, a_0$ that lead to these images, one wants to draw conclusions from these observation for the non-observable state q_n of the object. This state q_n contains the *discrete* class and the *continuous* pose of the object

In the context of a Bayesian approach, the knowledge on the object's state is given in form of the a posteriori density $p(q_n|f_n, a_{n-1}, f_{n-1}, \ldots, a_0, f_0)$. This density can be calculated from

$$p(q_n|f_n, a_{n-1}, \ldots, a_0, f_0) = \frac{1}{k_n} p(q_n|a_{n-1}, f_{n-1}, \ldots, a_0, f_0)p(f_n|q_n) \quad (1)$$

with the normalizing constant

$$k_n = p(f_n, a_{n-1}, \ldots, a_0, f_0). \quad (2)$$

The density $p(q_n|a_{n-1}, f_{n-1}, \ldots, a_0, f_0)$ can be written as

$$p(q_n|a_{n-1}, f_{n-1}, \ldots, a_0, f_0) =$$
$$\int_{q_{n-1}} p(q_n|q_{n-1}, a_{n-1})p(q_{n-1}|a_{n-1}, f_{n-1}, \ldots, a_0, f_0)dq_{n-1} \quad (3)$$

with the Markov assumption $p(q_n|q_{n-1}, a_{n-1}, \ldots, q_0, a_0) = p(q_n|q_{n-1}, a_{n-1})$ for the state transition. This probability depends only on the camera movement a_{n-1}. The inaccuracy of the camera movement is modeled with a normally distributed noise component so that the state transition probability can be written as $p(q_n|q_{n-1}, a_{n-1}) = \mathcal{N}(q_{n-1} + a_{n-1}, \Sigma)$ with the covariance matrix Σ of the inaccuracy of the camera movement. If one deals with *discrete* states q_n, the integral in equation (3) simply becomes a sum

$$p(q_n|f_{n-1}, \ldots, f_0) = \sum_{q_{n-1}} p(q_n|q_{n-1}, a_{n-1})p(q_{n-1}|f_{n-1}, \ldots, f_0) \quad (4)$$

that can easily be evaluated in an analytical way. For example, to classify an object Ω_κ in a sequence of images with $q_n = (\Omega_\kappa)$, $p(q_n|q_{n-1}, a_{n-1})$ degrades to

$$p(q_n|q_{n-1}, a_{n-1}) = \begin{cases} 1 & \text{if } q_n = q_{n-1} \\ 0 & \text{otherwise} \end{cases} \quad (5)$$

since the object class does not change if the camera is moved, and consequently equation (4) must have an analytically solution.

But we want to use the fusion of multiple view for our viewpoint selection approach [3,2] where we have to deal with localization of objects in continuous pose spaces and consequently states q_n with continuous pose parameters. For that reason it is no longer possible to simplify equation (3) to equation (4).

The classic approach for solving this recursive density propagation is the well-known Kalman Filter [6]. But in computer vision the necessary assumptions for the Kalman

Filter, e.g. $p(f_n|q_n)$ being normally distributed, are often not valid. In real world applications this density $p(f_n|q_n)$ usually is not normally distributed due to object ambiguities, sensor noise, occlusion, etc. This is a problem since it leads to a distribution which is not analytically computable. An approach for the complicated handling of such multimodal densities are the so called particle filters. The basic idea is to approximate the a posteriori density by a set of weighted particles. In our approach we use the CONDENSATION algorithm (CONditional DENSity propAATION) [5]. It uses a sample set $C_n = \{c_1^n, \ldots, c_K^n\}$ to approximate the multimodal probability distribution in equation (1). Please note that we do not only have a continuous state space for q_n but a *mixed* discrete/continuous state space for object class and pose as mentioned at the beginning of this section. The practical procedure of applying the CONDENSATION to the fusion problem is illustrated in the next section.

2.2   Condensation Algorithm for Fusion of Multiple Views

In this section we want to show, how to use the CONDENSATION algorithm for the fusion of multiple views.

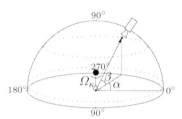

Fig. 2. Experimental setup and the possible pose space

As we want to classify and localize objects, we need to include the class and pose of the object into our state q_n. In our experimental setup we move our camera on a hemisphere around the object (see Fig. 2). Consequently, the pose of the object is modeled as the viewing position on a hemisphere (azimuthal and colatitude angles). This leads to the following definitions of the state $q_n = (\Omega_\kappa \ \alpha^n \ \beta^n)^T$ and the samples $c_i^n = (\Omega_\kappa \ \alpha_i^n \ \beta_i^n)^T$ with the class Ω_κ, the azimuthal $\alpha \in [0°; 360°)$ and the colatitude $\beta \in [0°; 90°]$. In Fig. 2 the pose space is illustrated. The camera movements are defined accordingly as $a_n = (\Delta\alpha_n \ \Delta\beta_n)^T$ with $\Delta\alpha_n$ and $\Delta\beta_n$ denoting the relative azimuthal and colatitude change of the viewing position of the camera

In the practical realization of the CONDENSATION, one starts with an initial sample set $C^0 = \{c_1^0, \ldots, c_K^0\}$ with samples distributed uniformly over the state space. For the generation of a new sample set C^n, samples c_i^n are

1. drawn from C^{n-1} with probability

$$\frac{p(f_{n-1}|c_i^{n-1})}{\sum\limits_{j=1}^{K} p(f_{n-1}|c_j^{n-1})} \tag{6}$$

2. propagated with the sample transition model

$$c_i^n = c_i^{n-1} + \begin{pmatrix} 0 \\ r_\alpha \\ r_\beta \end{pmatrix} \quad \text{with} \quad \begin{matrix} r_\alpha \sim \mathcal{N}(\Delta\alpha_n, \sigma_\alpha) \\ r_\beta \sim \mathcal{N}(\Delta\beta_n, \sigma_\beta) \end{matrix} \tag{7}$$

Table 1. Recognition rates for different sizes K of the sample set. The transition noise parameters are set to $\sigma_\alpha = 1.8°$ and $\sigma_\beta = 1.5°$. N denotes the number of fusioned images

Object	$N=1$	$N=2$	$N=5$	$N=10$
o1	32%	16%	16%	16%
o2	48%	84%	92%	92%
o3	16%	36%	60%	60%
o4	24%	56%	64%	68%
o5	64%	88%	88%	92%
o6	24%	52%	76%	80%
o7	40%	80%	88%	88%
ϕ	35%	59%	69%	71%

Table header spanning: $K = 43400$

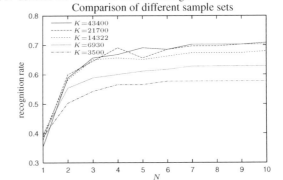

and the variance parameters σ_α and σ_β of the azimuthal and colatitude Gaussian noise $\mathcal{N}(\Delta\alpha_n, \sigma_\alpha)$ and $\mathcal{N}(\Delta\beta_n, \sigma_\beta)$. They model the inaccuracy of the camera movement under the assumption that the error of the azimuthal and colatitude movements of the camera are independent of each other.

3. evaluated in the image by $p(f_n|c_i^n)$.

For a detailed explanation on the theoretical background of the approximation of equation (1) by the sample set C^N cf. [5].

It is important to note that it is absolutely necessary to include the class Ω_κ into the object state q_n (and therewith also into the samples c_i^n). An obvious idea that would omit this is to set up several sample sets – one for each object class – and perform the CONDENSATION separately on each set. But this would not result in an integrated classification/localization, but in separated localizations on each set under the assumption of observing the corresponding object class. No fusion of the object class over the sequence of images would be done in that case.

3   Experiments

For the experiments presented in this section we have decided for an appearance based classifier using the Eigenspace approach in a statistical variation similar to [1]. As already proposed the CONDENSATION algorithm is independent of the used classifier as long as the classifier is able to evaluate $p(f_n|q_n)$. Our classifiers projects an image f_n into the three-dimensional Eigenspace and evaluates the resulting feature vector for the trained normal distribution with pose parameters that are closest to the given pose. The intention of three-dimensional Eigenspace is to force big importance to the fusion aspect as the chosen low dimensional Eigenspace of course is not suited to produce optimal feature vectors.

Our data set consists of the seven toy manikins shown in Fig. 1. The objects have been selected in a way that they are strongly ambiguous from some viewpoints. The objects o4 to o7 even cannot be classified with one view so that a fusion of multiple views is essential. The evaluation of our fusion approach was done with 25 sequences of

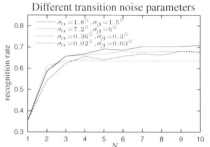

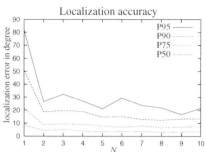

Fig. 3. Recognition rates for different settings of the transition noise parameters σ_α and σ_β. The size of the sample set is $K=43400$. N denotes the number of fusioned images

Fig. 4. Accuracy of localization for percentile values of 95% (P95), 90% (P90), 75% (P75), 50% (P50). Size of sample set $K=43400$, transition noise parameters $\sigma_\alpha=1.8°$, $\sigma_\beta=1.5°$

10 images each per object. The camera movements a were chosen *randomly* from the – within the mechanical limits of $0.03°$ – continuous space of possible movements.

In Table 1 we show the recognition rates for different sizes K of the sample set. As expected, the quality of classification increases with the number N of fused images. It also turns out that the size of the sample set has a noticeable influence on the recognition rates as the approximation of equation (1) is more accurate for larger sample sets.

Another important point we investigated was the influence of the noise parameters σ_α and σ_β from equation (7) on the recognition rate. In Fig. 3 the recognition rates for different transition noise settings are shown. As it can be seen, too much transition noise (large σ_α and σ_β) performs better than insufficient transition noise. The reason for that is that small σ_α and σ_β cause the samples in the sample set to be clustered at a very "narrow" area with the consequence that errors in the camera movement and localization are not sufficiently compensated. In contrast, too much noise spreads the samples too far.

The results of the experiments for the localization accuracy are shown in Fig. 4. The accurateness is given with the so called *percentile* values, which describe the limits of the localization error if the classification is correct and only the X% best localizations are taken into account. For example, the percentile value P90 expresses the largest localization error within the 90% most accurate localizations. As it can be seen in Fig. 4, the P90 localization error drops from $50°$ in the first image down to $13°$ after ten images.

The computation time needed for one fusion step is about 1.8 seconds on a LINUX PC (AMD Athlon 1GHz) for the sample set with $K = 43400$ samples. As the computational effort scales linear to the size of the sample set, we are able to fuse 7 images per second for the small sample set with $K = 3500$ samples which already provides very reasonable classification rates. We also want to note that the CONDENSATION algorithm can be parallelized very well so that even real-time applications can be realized using our approach.

4   Conclusion

In this paper we have presented a general approach for the fusion of multiple views for active object recognition. Using the CONDENSATION algorithm we are independent of the chosen statistical classifier. Other advantages of our approach are its scalability of the size of the sample set and possibility to parallelize the CONDENSATION algorithm. In the experiments we have shown that our approach is well suited for the fusion of multiple views as we were able to double the overall classification rate from 35% to 71% and increase of the classification rate for single objects of up to 233%.

Presently we use randomly chosen views for our fusion. But we expect that far better classification rates will be reached after fewer views if we combine our fusion approach with our viewpoint selection [3,2]. The combination of these two approaches for the selection of views and their fusion will result in a system that is still independent of the used classifier and well-suited for the given task of classifying ambiguous objects.

Open questions in our approach are the minimal necessary size of the sample set and the optimal parameters for the noise transition models. Furthermore other sample techniques are to be evaluated.

References

1. H. Borotschnig, L. Paletta, M. Prantl, and A. Pinz. Appearance based active object recognition. *Image and Vision Computing*, (18):715–727, 2000.
2. F. Deinzer, J. Denzler, and H. Niemann. Classifier Independent Viewpoint Selection for 3-D Object Recognition. In G. Sommer, N. Kr"uger, and Ch Perwass, editors, *Mustererkennung 2000*, pages 237–244, Berlin, September 2000. Springer.
3. F. Deinzer, J. Denzler, and H. Niemann. Viewpoint Selection - A Classifier Independent Learning Approach. In *IEEE Southwest Symposium on Image Analysis and Interpretation*, pages 209–213, Austin, Texas, USA, 2000. IEEE Computer Society, California, Los Alamitos.
4. J. Denzler and C.M. Brown. Information theoretic sensor data selection for active object recognition and state estimation. *IEEE Transactions on Pattern Analysis and Machine Intelligence (in press)*, 2001.
5. M. Isard and B. Andrew. CONDENSATION—conditional density propagation for visual tracking. *International Journal of Computer Vision*, 29(1):5–28, 1998.
6. R.E. Kalman. A new approach to linear filtering and prediction problems. *Journal of Basic Engineering*, pages 35–44, 1960.
7. L. Paletta, M. Prantl, and A. Pinz. Learning temporal context in active object recognition using bayesian analysis. In *International Conference on Pattern Recognition*, volume 3, pages 695–699, Barcelona, 2000.
8. B. Schiele and J.L. Crowley. Transinformation for active object recognition. In *Proceedings of the Sixth International Conference on Computer Vision*, Bombay, India, 1998.

Probabilistic Discriminative Kernel Classifiers for Multi-class Problems

Volker Roth

University of Bonn
Department of Computer Science III
Roemerstr. 164
D-53117 Bonn
Germany
roth@cs.uni-bonn.de

Abstract. Logistic regression is presumably the most popular representative of probabilistic discriminative classifiers. In this paper, a kernel variant of logistic regression is introduced as an iteratively re-weighted least-squares algorithm in kernel-induced feature spaces. This formulation allows us to apply highly efficient approximation methods that are capable of dealing with large-scale problems. For multi-class problems, a pairwise coupling procedure is proposed. Pairwise coupling for "kernelized" logistic regression effectively overcomes conceptual and numerical problems of standard multi-class kernel classifiers.

1 Introduction

Classifiers can be partitioned into two main groups, namely *informative* and *discriminative* ones. In the informative approach, the classes are described by modeling their structure, i.e. their generative statistical model. Starting from these class models, the posterior distribution of the labels is derived via the Bayes formula. The most popular method of informative kind is classical *Linear Discriminant Analysis* (LDA). However, the informative approach has a clear disadvantage: modeling the classes is usually a much harder problem than solving the classification problem directly.

In contrast to the informative approach, discriminative classifiers focus on modeling the decision boundaries or the class probabilities directly. No attempt is made to model the underlying class densities. In general, they are more robust as informative ones, since less assumptions about the classes are made. The most popular discriminative method is *logistic regression* (LOGREG), [1]. The aim of logistic regression is to produce an estimate of the posterior probability of membership in each of the c classes. Thus, besides predicting class labels, LOGREG additionally provides a probabilistic confidence measure about this labeling. This allows us to adapt to varying class priors.

A different approach to discriminative classification is given by the *Support Vector* (SV) method. Within a maximum entropy framework, it can be viewed as the discriminative model that makes the least assumptions about the estimated model parameters,

B. Radig and S. Florczyk (Eds.): DAGM 2001, LNCS 2191, pp. 246–253, 2001.

cf. [2]. Compared to LOGREG, however, the main drawback of the SVM is the absence of probabilistic outputs.[1]

In this paper, particular emphasis is put on a nonlinear "kernelized" variant of logistic regression. Compared to kernel variants of Discriminant Analysis (see [5,6]) and to the SVM, the kernelized LOGREG model combines the conceptual advantages of both methods:

1. it is a discriminative method that overcomes the problem of estimating class conditional densities;
2. it has a clear probabilistic interpretation that allows us to quantify a confidence level for class assignments.

Concerning multi-class problems, the availability of probabilistic outputs allows us to overcome another shortcoming of the SVM: in the usual SVM framework, a multi-class problem with c classes is treated as a collection of c "one-against-all-others" subproblems, together with some principle of combining the c outputs. This treatment of multi-class problems, however, bears two disadvantages, both of a conceptual and a technical nature: (i) separating one class from all others may be an unnecessarily hard problem; (ii) all c subproblems are stated as quadratic optimization problems over the *full* learning set. For large-scale problems, this can impose unacceptably high computational costs.

If, on the other hand, we are given posterior probabilities of class membership, we can apply a different multi-class strategy: instead of solving c one-against-all problems, we might solve $c(c-1)/2$ pairwise classification problems, and try to couple the probabilities in a suitable way. Methods of this kind have been introduced in [7] and are referred to as *pairwise coupling*. Since kernelized LOGREG provides us with estimates of posterior probabilities, we can directly generalize it to multi-class problems by way of "plugging" the posterior estimates into the pairwise coupling procedure.

The main focus of this paper concerns pairwise coupling methods for *kernel classifiers*[2]. For kernel-based algorithms in general, the computational efficiency is mostly determined by the number of training samples. Thus, pairwise coupling schemes also overcome the numerical problems of the one-against-all strategy: it is much easier to solve $c(c-1)/2$ small problems that to solve c large problems. This leads to a reduction of computational costs that scales linear in the number of classes. We conclude this paper with performance studies for large-scale problems. These experiments effectively demonstrate that kernelized LOGREG attains a level of accuracy comparable to the SVM, while additionally providing the user with posterior estimates for class membership. Moreover, concerning the computational costs for solving multi-class problems, it outperforms one of the best SVM optimization packages available.

---

[1] Some strategies for approximating SVM posterior estimates in a post-processing step have been reported in the literature, see e.g. [3,4]. In this paper, however, we restrict our attention to fully probabilistic models.

[2] A recent overview over kernel methods can be found in [8].

2   Kernelized Logistic Regression

The problem of classification formally consists of assigning observed vectors $x \in R^d$ into one of c classes. A *classifier* is a mapping that assigns labels to observations. In practice, a classifier is trained on a set of observed i.i.d. data-label pairs $\{(x_i, y_i)\}_{i=1}^N$, drawn from the unknown joint density $p(x, y) = p(y|x)p(x)$. For convenience in what follows, we define a *discriminant function* for class k as

$$g_k(x) = \log \frac{P(y = k|x)}{P(y = c|x)}, \quad k = 1, \ldots, c - 1. \tag{1}$$

Assuming a *linear* discriminant function leads us to the logistic regression (LOGREG) model: $g_k(x) = w_k^T x.$[3]

Considering a **two-class** problem with labels $\{0, 1\}$, it is sufficient to represent $P(1|x)$, since $P(0|x) = 1 - P(1|x)$. Thus, we can write the "success probability" in the form

$$\pi_w(x) := P(1|x) = \frac{1}{1 + \exp\{-(w^T x)\}}. \tag{2}$$

For discriminative classifiers like LOGREG, the model parameters are chosen by maximizing the *conditional log-likelihood*:

$$l(w) = \sum_{i=1}^N [y_i \log \pi_w(x_i) + (1 - y_i) \log(1 - \pi_w(x_i))]. \tag{3}$$

In order to find the optimizing weight vector w, we wish to solve the equation system $\nabla_w l(w) = 0$. Since the $\pi_i := \pi_w(x_i)$ depend nonlinearly on w, however, this system cannot be solved analytically and iterative techniques must be applied. The *Fisher scoring* method updates the parameter estimates w at the r-th step by

$$w_{r+1} = w_r - \{E[H]\}^{-1} \nabla_w l(w), \tag{4}$$

with H being the Hessian of l.[4] The scoring equation (4) can be restated as an *Iterated Reweighted Least Squares* (IRLS) problem, cf. [10]. Denoting with X the design matrix (the rows are the input vectors), the Hessian is equal to $(-X^T W X)$, where W is a diagonal matrix:

$$W = \mathrm{diag}\,\{\pi_1(1 - \pi_1), \ldots, \pi_N(1 - \pi_N)\}.$$

The gradient of l (the scores) can be written as $\nabla_w l(w) = X^T W e$, where e is a vector with entries $e_j = (y_j - \pi_j)/W_{jj}$. Forming a variable

$$q_r = X w_r + e,$$

---

[3] Throughout this paper we have dropped the constant b in the more general form $g(x) = w^T x + b$. We assume that the data vectors are augmented by an additional entry of one.

[4] For LOGREG, the Hessian coincides with its expectation: $H = E[H]$. For further details on Fisher's method of scoring the reader is referred to [9].

the scoring updates read

$$(X^T W_r X) w_{r+1} = X^T W_r q_r. \tag{5}$$

These are the normal form equations of a least squares problem with input matrix $W_r^{1/2} X$ and dependent variables $W_r^{1/2} q_r$. The values W_{ii} are functions of the actual w_r, so that (5) must be iterated.

Direct optimization of the likelihood (3), however, often leads to severe overfitting problems, and a preference for smooth functions is usually encoded by introducing *priors* over the weights w. In a regularization context, such prior information can be interpreted as adding some *bias* to maximum likelihood parameter estimates in order to reduce the estimator's variance. The common choice of a spherical Gaussian prior distribution with covariance $\Sigma_w \propto \lambda^{-1} I$ leads to a *ridge regression* model, [11]. The regularized update equations read

$$(X^T W_r X + \lambda I) w_{r+1} = X^T W_r q_r. \tag{6}$$

The above equation states LOGREG as a regularized IRLS problem. This allows us to extend the linear model to nonlinear kernel variants: each stage of iteration reduces to solving a system of linear equations, for which it is known that the optimizing weight vector can be expanded in terms of the input vectors, cf. [5]:

$$w = \sum_{i=1}^{N} x_i \alpha_i = X^T \alpha. \tag{7}$$

Substituting this expansion of w into the update equation (6) and introducing the dot product matrix $(K)_{ij} = (x_i \cdot x_j)$, $K = X X^T$, we can write

$$(K W_r K + \lambda K) \alpha_{r+1} = K W_r q'_r, \tag{8}$$

with $q'_r = K \alpha_r + e$. Equation (8) can be simplified to

$$(K + \lambda W_r^{-1}) \alpha_{r+1} = q'_r. \tag{9}$$

With the usual kernel trick, the dot products can be substituted by kernel functions satisfying Mercer's condition. This leads us to a nonlinear generalization of LOGREG in kernel feature spaces which we call **kLOGREG**.

The matrix $(K + \lambda W_r^{-1})$ is symmetric, and the optimizing vector α_{r+1} can be computed in a highly efficient way by applying approximative *conjugate gradient* inversion techniques, see cf. [12], p. 83. The availability of efficient approximation techniques from the well-studied field of numerical linear algebra constitutes the main advantage over a related approach to kLOGREG, presented in [13]. The latter algorithm computes the optimal coefficients α_i by a sequential approach. The problem with this on-line algorithm, however, is the following: for each new observation x_t, $t = 1, 2, \ldots$ it imposes computational costs of the order $\mathcal{O}(t^2)$. Given a training set of N observations in total, this accumulates to an $\mathcal{O}(N^3)$ process, for which to our knowledge no efficient approximation methods are known.

3   Pairwise Coupling for Multi-class Problems

Typically two-class problems tend to be much easier to learn than multi-class problems. While for two-class problems only one decision boundary must be inferred, the general c-class setting requires us to apply a strategy for coupling decision rules. In the standard approach to this problem, c two-class classifiers are trained in order to separate each of the classes against all others. These decision rules are then coupled either in a probabilistic way (e.g. for LDA) or by some heuristic procedure (e.g. for the SVM).

A different approach to the multi-class problem was proposed in [7]. The central idea is to learn $c(c-1)/2$ pairwise decision rules and to couple the pairwise class probability estimates into a joint probability estimate for all c classes. It is obvious, that this strategy is only applicable for pairwise classifiers with probabilistic outputs.[5] From a theoretical viewpoint, pairwise coupling bears some advantages: (i) jointly optimizing over all c classes may impose unnecessary problems, pairwise separation might be much simpler; (ii) we can select a highly specific model for each of the pairwise subproblems.

Concerning *kernel classifiers* in particular, pairwise coupling is also attractive for practical reasons. For kernel methods, the computational cost are dominated by the size of the training set, N. For example, conjugate gradient approximations for kLOGREG scale as $\mathcal{O}(N^2 \cdot m)$, with m denoting the number of conjugate-gradient iterations. Keeping m fixed leads us to a $\mathcal{O}(N^2)$ dependency as a lower bound on the real costs.[6] Let us now consider c classes, each of which contains N_c training samples. For a one-against-all strategy, we have costs scaling as $\mathcal{O}(c(cN_c)^2) = \mathcal{O}(c^3(N_c)^2)$. For the pairwise approach, this reduces to $\mathcal{O}(1/2\,c(c-1)(2N_c)^2) = \mathcal{O}(2(c^2 - c)(N_c)^2)$. Thus, we have a reduction of computational costs inverse proportional to the number of classes. Pairwise coupling can be formalized as follows: considering a set of events $\{A_i\}_{i=1}^{c}$, suppose we are given probabilities $r_{ij} = \mathrm{Prob}\,(A_i|A_i\text{ or }A_j)$. Our goal is to couple the r_{ij}'s into a set of probabilities $p_i = \mathrm{Prob}\,(A_i)$. This problem has no general solution, but in [7] the following approximation is suggested: introducing a new set of auxiliary variables $\mu_{ij} = \frac{p_i}{p_i+p_j}$, we wish to find $\hat{p}_i$'s such that the corresponding $\hat{\mu}_{ij}$'s are in some sense "close" to the observed r_{ij}'s. A suitable closeness measure is the Kullback-Leibler divergence between r_{ij} and $\hat{\mu}_{ij}$

$$\mathcal{D}^{KL} = \sum_{i<j} r_{ij} \log \frac{r_{ij}}{\hat{\mu}_{ij}} + (1 - r_{ij}) \log \frac{1 - r_{ij}}{1 - \hat{\mu}_{ij}}. \tag{10}$$

The associated score equations read

$$\sum_{j \neq i} \hat{\mu}_{ij} = \sum_{j \neq i} r_{ij}, \quad i = 1, \dots, c, \quad \text{subject to} \sum_i p_i = 1. \tag{11}$$

---

[5] In a former version of [7], available as Tech. Rep. at the University of Toronto, it has been suggested to apply "approximative" pairwise coupling to the SVM. However, we feel that this approach is not very promising since it lacks a clear probabilistic interpretation.

[6] For the SVM, the situation is more difficult and heavily depends on implementation details. As an example, the popular LOQO package [14], has even $\mathcal{O}(N^3)$ complexity, due to a Cholesky decomposition of a $N \times N$ matrix. Subset methods are usually much more efficient, but their performance is problem-dependent, and thus difficult to analyze.

Starting with an initial guess for the $\hat{p}_i$ and corresponding $\hat{\mu}_{ij}$, we can compute the $\hat{p}_i$'s that minimize (10) by iterating

- $\hat{p}_i \leftarrow \hat{p}_i \cdot \left(\sum_{j \neq i} r_{ij} \right) / \left(\sum_{j \neq i} \hat{\mu}_{ij} \right)$
- renormalize the $\hat{p}_i$'s and recompute the $\hat{\mu}_{ij}$.

Suppose, we have successfully trained all pairwise kLOGREG classifiers. Then, we can predict the class membership of a new observation x_* as follows:

---

1. Evaluate the $c(c-1)/2$ classification rules to obtain

$$r_{ij}(x_*) = \text{Prob}\left(x_* \in \text{class } i \,|\, x_* \in \text{class } i \text{ or } x_* \in \text{class } j \right),$$

and initialize $\hat{\mu}_{ij} = r_{ij}$.
2. Starting with an initial guess for the $\hat{p}_i$'s, run the above iterations.
3. We finally obtain the posterior probabilities for class membership of pattern x_*.

---

4   Experiments

Here we present results for the "MPI chairs", and "Isolet" datasets.[7] In both cases the number of classes is relatively high: the chair dataset consists of downscaled images from 25 different classes of chairs; the Isolet dataset contains spoken names of all 26 letters of the alphabet. We compared both the prediction accuracy and the computational costs of a "state-of-the-art" SVM package[8] and kLOGREG. The results are summarized in table 1. We conclude, that pairwise coupled kLOGREG attains a level of prediction accuracy comparable to the SVM, while imposing significantly lower computational costs. Concerning the training times, the reader should notice that we are comparing the highly tuned *SVMTorch* optimization package with our straight-forward kLOGREG implementation, which we consider to yet possess ample opportunities for further optimization.

Table 1. Test error rates (e) and computation times (t) on the **MPI chair** and the **Isolet** database. c = number of classes, N_c = number of samples per class, $Idim$ = input dimension, N_T = size of test set. The training times (t) are measured on a 500 MHz PC.

Dataset		c	N_c	$Idim$	N_T	SVM		kLOGREG	
Chairs Images		25	89	256	2500	e = 1.48%	t = 152 s	e = 1.52%	t = 53 s
	Images + edges	25	89	1280	2500	e = 0.80%	t = 19 min	e = 0.84%	t = 3:05 min
Isolet		26	240	617	1560	e = 3.0%	t = 21 min	e = 3.0%	t = 18 min

---

[7] Available via `ftp://ftp.mpik-tueb.mpg.de/pub/chair_dataset` and
`http://www.ics.uci.edu/~mlearn/MLRepository.html` respectively.
[8] We used the *SVMTorch II* V1.07 implementation, see [15].

5   Conclusion

In this paper we have presented a new approach to multi-class classification with kernel methods. In particular, we have focused on a kernelized variant of classical logistic regression, which we name *kLOGREG*. The kLOGREG classifier combines the advantages of related versions of kernel methods: it is a *discriminative* classifier that overcomes the problem of estimating class models, and it has a clear *probabilistic interpretation*. We have stated kLOGREG as an iteratively re-weighted least-squares problem in kernel feature spaces. The real payoff of this algorithmic formulation is the applicability of highly efficient approximation techniques from the well-studied field of numerical linear algebra.

Concerning multi-class problems, we can use the kLOGREG classifier as a building block in a *pairwise coupling* procedure. The main idea of pairwise coupling is to couple all pairwise decision rules into an estimate for the posterior probability of class membership. Besides of conceptual advantages over classical ways of handling multi-class problems, this technique additionally has a clear numerical advantage: for a fixed number of training patterns, the computational costs reduce linearly in the number of classes.

Experiments for large-scale problems with many classes have effectively demonstrated that kLOGREG attains a level of accuracy comparable to the SVM. Moreover, concerning the computational costs, our straight-forward implementation which basically uses routines from *Numerical Recipes*, [12], outperformed one of the best SVM packages available. We thus conclude that kLOGREG is a highly suited method for dealing with multi-class problems that require us to quantify the uncertainty about the predicted class labels.

Acknowledgments. The author wishes to thank J. Buhmann, M. Braun and L. Hermes for fruitful discussions. Thanks for financial support go to German Research Council (DFG).

References

1. D.R. Cox and E. J. Snell. *Analysis of Binary Data.* Chapman & Hall, London, 1989.
2. T. Jaakkola, M. Meila, and T. Jebara. Maximum entropy discrimination. In S.A. Solla, T.K. Leen, and K.-R. Müller, editors, *Advances in Neural Information Processing Systems,* volume 12, pages 470–476. MIT Press, 1999.
3. P. Sollich. Probabilistic methods for support vector machines. In S.A. Solla, T.K. Leen, and K.-R. Müller, editors, *Advances in Neural Information Processing Systems,* volume 12, pages 349–355. MIT Press, 1999.
4. L. Hermes, D. Frieauff, J. Puzicha, and J. Buhmann. Support vector machines for land usage classification in Landsat TM imagery. In *Proc. of the IEEE 1999 International Geoscience and Remote Sensing Symposium,* volume 1, pages 348–350, 1999.
5. V. Roth and V. Steinhage. Nonlinear discriminant analysis using kernel functions. In S.A. Solla, T.K. Leen, and K.-R. Müller, editors, *Advances in Neural Information Processing Systems,* volume 12, pages 568–574. MIT Press, 1999.

6. S. Mika, G. Rätsch, J. Weston, B. Schölkopf, and K.-R. Müller. Fisher discriminant analysis with kernels. In Y.-H. Hu, J. Larsen, E. Wilson, and S. Douglas, editors, *Neural Networks for Signal Processing IX*, pages 41–48. IEEE, 1999.
7. Trevor Hastie and Robert Tibshirani. Classification by pairwise coupling. In Michael I. Jordan, Michael J. Kearns, and Sara A. Solla, editors, *Advances in Neural Information Processing Systems*, volume 10. The MIT Press, 1998.
8. K.-R. Müller, S. Mika, G. Rätsch, K. Tsuda, and B. Schölkopf. An introduction to kernel-based learning algorithms. *IEEE Transactions on Neural Networks*, 12(2): 181–201, March 2001.
9. M.R. Osborne. Fisher's method of scoring. *Internat. Statistical Review*, 60: 99–117, 1992.
10. I. Nabney. Efficient training of RBF networks for classification. Technical Report NCRG/99/002, Aston University, Birmingham, UK., 1999.
11. A.E. Hoerl and R.W. Kennard. Ridge regression: Biased estimation for nonorthogonal problems. *Technometrics*, 12: 55–67, 1970.
12. W.H. Press, S.A. Teukolsky, W.T Vetterling, and B.P. Flannery. *Numerical Recipes in C.* Cambridge University Press, 1992.
13. T. Jaakkola and D. Haussler. Probabilistic kernel regression models. In David Heckerman and Joe Whittaker, editors, *Procs. 7th International Workshop on AI and Statistics.* Morgan Kaufmann, 1999.
14. R. J. Vanderbei. LOQO: An interior point code for quadratic programming. *Optimization Methods and Software*, 11: 451–484, 1999.
15. Ronan Collobert and Samy Bengio. Support vector machines for large-scale regression problems. Technical Report IDIAP-RR-00-17, IDIAP, Martigny, Switzerland, 2000.

Appearance-Based Statistical Object Recognition by Heterogeneous Background and Occlusions

Michael Reinhold*, Dietrich Paulus, and Heinrich Niemann

Chair for Pattern Recognition, University Erlangen-Nürnberg
Martensstr. 3, 91058 Erlangen, Germany
reinhold@informatik.uni-erlangen.de,
http://www5.informatik.uni-erlangen.de

Abstract. In this paper we present a new approach for the localization and classification of 2-D objects that are situated in heterogeneous background or are partially occluded. We use an appearance-based approach and model the local features derived from wavelet multiresolution analysis by statistical density functions. In addition to the object model we define a new model for the background and a function that assigns the single feature vectors either to the object or to the background. Here, the background is modelled as uniform distribution, therefore we need for all possible backgrounds only one density function. Experimental results show that this model is well suited for this recognition task.

Keywords: object recognition, statistical modelling, background model

1 Introduction

There are several approaches for object recognition. Since the approaches that use the results of a segmentation process like lines or vertices suffer from segmentation errors and the loss of information, we use an appearance-based approach; i. e. the image data, e. g. the pixel intensities, are used directly without a previous segmentation process. One appearance-based approach is the "eigenspace" introduced by [5] that use principal component analysis and encode the data in so-called "eigen-images". Other authors apply histograms; the most well-known approach are the "multidimensional receptive field histograms" of [8] which contain the results of local filtering, e. g. by Gaussian derivative filters. [2] use a statistical approach for the recognition and model the features by Gaussian mixtures. We use and extend the statistical model of [6]: local feature vectors are calculated by the coefficients of the multiresolution analysis using Johnston-Wavelets. The object features are modelled statistically as normal distributions by parametric density functions. As we will show in the experiments this approach is very insensitive to changes in the illumination.

For the recognition in real environments very often the objects reside not in the homogeneous background of the training, but in cluttered background and some parts of the objects are occluded. For this purpose [4], who use the eigenspace approach, try to find

---

* This work was funded by the German Science Foundation (DFG) Graduate Research Center 3-D Image Analysis and Synthesis. Only the authors are responsible for the content.

B. Radig and S. Florczyk (Eds.): DAGM 2001, LNCS 2191, pp. 254–261, 2001.

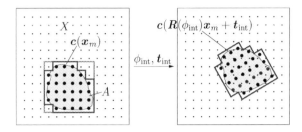

Fig. 1. *Left:* Image covered by a grid, the object is enclosed by a tight boundary (black line); the respective old rectangular box is plotted in gray, because of its form it enclose not only object features but also background features. *right:* For movements of the object inside the image plane the object grid is transformed with the same internal rotation ϕ_{int} and internal translation t_{int} as the object

n object features in the image that are neither affected by the background nor occluded. For this reason they generate pose hypotheses and select the n best fitting features. In contrast other authors explicitly model the background and assign the features to the object or to the background. For example, [3], who use vertices as features, assume a uniform distribution for the position of the background features and model a probabilistic weighted assignment. Whereas in [1] the features are assigned neither to the object nor to the background. Since medical radiographs were classified, the background model has a constant gray value of zero. Also for our approach a background model was presented in [6] and [7]: the known background was trained as Gaussian distribution and a weighted assignment was applied. We propose a new model for this approach: the background is modelled as uniform distribution over the possible values of the feature vectors, therefore we are independent of the current background. We define a assignment function that assigns each of the local feature vectors either to the object or to the background, depending whether the calculated value of the object density or of the background density is higher for this local feature vector. The recognition is performed hierarchically by a maximum likelihood estimation, whereby an accelerated algorithm is used for the global search.

In the following section we shortly outline the object model for homogeneous background and in section 3 we describe our new model for heterogeneous background and occlusions. In section 4 the experiments and the results are presented. Finally we end with a summary of the results and the future work in section 5.

2   Object Model for Homogenous Background

A grid with the sampling resolution r_s, whereby s is the index for the scale, is laid over the square image f as one can see in figure 1. These grid locations will be summarized in the following as $X_s = \{x_{m,s}\}_{m=0,\ldots,M-1}, x_{m,s} \in \mathbb{R}^2$. On each grid-point a local feature vector $c_s(x_{m,s})$ with two components is calculated by the coefficients of the multiresolution analysis using discrete Johnston 8-TAP wavelets and is interpreted as random variable for the statistical model. Thereby the randomness among others is the noise of the image sampling process and changes in the lighting conditions. To simplify the notation, the index s is omitted in the following.

For the object model a close boundary is laid around the object. In [6] only a rectangular box was implemented and it was positioned manually. In contrast now the form of the boundary is arbitrary so that it enclose the object much better (see left image of figure 1). Besides it is calculated automatically during the training, wherefore only one image of the object in front of a dark background is necessary. During the recognition this trained form of the bounded region A is used. We assume that the feature vectors $c_{A,m}$ inside the bounded region $A \subset X$ belong to the object, and are statistically independent from the feature vectors $c_{X \setminus A,k}$ outside the bounded region $X \setminus A$. Therefore, for the object model we only need to consider the (object) feature vectors $c_{A,m}$, concatenated written as vector c_A. Now, the object can be described by the density function $p(c_A | B, \phi, t)$ depending on the learned model parameter set B, the rotation $\phi = \phi_{\mathrm{int}}$ and the translation $t = t_{\mathrm{int}}$.

Further we assume that the features are normally distributed. In [6] a statistical dependency between adjacent feature vectors in a row was modelled, but for arbitrary objects the results is worse than for statistical independency. Therefore we assume that the single feature vectors are statistically independent from each other. So the density functions can be written as

$$p(c_A | B, \phi, t) = \prod_{x_m \in A} p(c_{A,m} | \mu_m, \Sigma_m, \phi, t) \quad , \tag{1}$$

whereby μ_m is the mean vector and Σ_m the covariance matrix of the m-th feature vector. Because of the statistically independence Σ_m is a diagonal matrix.

For the localization we perform a maximum likelihood estimation over all possible rotations $\phi = \phi_{\mathrm{int}}$ and transformations $t = t_{\mathrm{int}}$:

$$(\phi, t) = \underset{(\phi,t)}{\mathrm{argmax}}\, p(c_A | B_\kappa, \phi, t) \quad , \tag{2}$$

and for the classification an additional maximum likelihood estimation over all possible classes κ:

$$(k, \phi, t) = \underset{\kappa}{\mathrm{argmax}}\, \underset{(\phi,t)}{\mathrm{argmax}}\, p(c_A | B_\kappa, \phi, t) \quad . \tag{3}$$

For accelerating the localization, first a rough localization is conducted on a rough resolution, followed by a refinement on a finer resolution. For further details see [6].

3   Model for Heterogenous Background and Occlusions

For occlusions the assumption that all the feature vectors inside the region A belong to the object is wrong. Besides for heterogeneous background the features vectors at the border of the object that cover not only the object but also partially the background are modified. Therefore [4] try to find n of the totally N object features that are not affected by the heterogeneous background and the occlusion [4]. But for this approach there is a risk to confuse similarly looking objects - like the two matchboxes in figure 3 (below). For this purpose, we consider all local feature vectors $c_{A,m}$ in the bounded region A and define a background model and a assignment function $\zeta \in \{0,1\}^N$. Whereby the m-th component ζ_m of ζ assigns the local feature vector $c_{A,m}$ to the object ($\zeta_m = 1$) or to the background ($\zeta_m = 0$). So the density function

$$p(c_A|B, \phi, t) = \sum_{\zeta} p(c_A, \zeta|B, \phi, t) \qquad (4)$$

also includes the assignment function ζ and becomes a mixture density. Now B includes the learned parameters B_1 of the object as well the learned parameters B_0 of the background. In [6] and [7] the background has to been known already during the training and was trained as a normal distribution, i. e. for each different background an own background density has to been trained. Besides statistically dependencies between the feature vectors in a row were modelled. For some experiments also for the assignment function a row-dependency was modelled [7], whereas for other experiments statistically independence of the assignments was supposed [6]. Thereby weighted assignments were modelled, i. e. a local feature vector $c_{A,m}$ belongs with a probability $p(\zeta_m = 1)$ to the object and $p(\zeta_m = 0)$ to the background. This leads to a very complex model.

To be independent from the current background and handle every possible background by only one background density, we model the background as a uniform distribution over the possible values of the feature vectors. So nothing has to be known about the background a priori; the background density depends only on chosen feature set, e. g. the wavelet type for filtering. Additionally, it is identical for all feature vectors and therefore it is independent from the transformations t_{int} and ϕ_{int}. As in section 2 we assume statistically independence of the features and also of the assignments, so the density function in (4) can be transformed to

$$p(c_A|B, \phi, t) = \sum_{\zeta} \prod_{x_m \in A} p(c_{A,m}, \zeta_m|B, \phi, t)$$

$$= \prod_{x_m \in A} \sum_{\zeta_m} p(c_{A,m}, \zeta_m|B, \phi, t)$$

$$= \prod_{x_m \in A} \sum_{\zeta_m} p(\zeta_m)\, p(c_{A,m}|\zeta_m, B, \phi, t) \qquad . \qquad (5)$$

This is a much simpler expression than (4): now we no longer have a marginalization about all possible assignments ζ for all features c_A, but for each single feature vector $c_{A,m}$ a marginalization about the single assignments ζ_m.

The assignment ζ_m is a hidden information. For example we do not know, how much of an object is occluded. So we set the a priori probability that a local feature vector $c_{A,m}$ belongs to the object or to the background as equal. Further we model ζ_m as a (0,1)-decision, i. e. a feature vector $c_{A,m}$ belongs either to the object or to the background. The decision is taken during the localization process. Thereby ζ is chosen so that the density value $p(c_A|B, \phi, t)$ is maximized. That is the density value for each feature

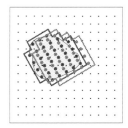 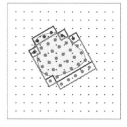

Fig. 2. *Left:* for each possible internal transformation all the feature vectors have to been interpolated, *right:* for the same rotation only another translation the most feature vectors can be reused

vector $c_{A,m}$ (see (5))

$$\sum_{\zeta_m} p(\zeta_m)\, p(c_{A,m}|\zeta_m, \boldsymbol{B}, \phi, \boldsymbol{t}) \tag{6}$$

has to be maximized. This can be done by the assignment ζ_m

$$\zeta_m = \underset{\zeta_m}{\mathrm{argmax}}(p(c_{A,m}|\zeta_m = 1, \boldsymbol{B}_1, \phi, \boldsymbol{t}), p(c_{A,m}|\zeta_m = 0, \boldsymbol{B}_0)) \quad, \tag{7}$$

and setting the probability $p(\zeta_m)$ for the respective assignment to one, the probability for the other assignment to zero.

For example, for the Johnston wavelets used in the experiments of section 4 the object density $p(c_{A,m}|\zeta_m = 1, \boldsymbol{B}_1, \phi, \boldsymbol{t})$ for a not occluded feature vector $c_{A,m}$ lays typically between e^{-1} and e^1. For occlusion it becomes very low: between e^{-100} and e^{-10}. In this case the feature vector $c_{A,m}$ is assigned to the background and the background density $p(c_{A,m}|\zeta_m = 0, \boldsymbol{B}_0) = e^{-3.5}$ (that is the value for the used Johnston wavelets) is chosen for this feature vector $c_{A,m}$.

For the localization and classification a maximum likelihood estimation is performed as described in (2) and (3). We also tested a heuristic measurement in section 4 for the classification. The single objects differ in their size, i. e. also in the number N of their local object feature vectors $c_{A,m}$ inside the bounded region A. Since non fitting object features are assigned to the background and the background density value is used, there are some misclassification caused by the different size of the objects. Therefore we normalize the density before the maximum likelihood estimation by the number N of local object feature vectors $c_{A,m}$:

$$(k, \phi, \boldsymbol{t}) = \underset{\kappa}{\mathrm{argmax}}\, \underset{(\phi, \boldsymbol{t})}{\mathrm{argmax}}\, \sqrt[N]{p(c_A|\boldsymbol{B}_\kappa, \phi, \boldsymbol{t})} \quad. \tag{8}$$

Because of the statistical independence (see (5)) the expression in (8) is the geometric mean of the density values $p(c_{A,m}|\zeta_m, \boldsymbol{B}, \phi, \boldsymbol{t})$ of all feature vectors $c_{A,m}$ with the respective assignments ζ_m.

Further we speed up the first step of the localization process that starts with a global search over all possible internal rotations ϕ_{int} and translations $\boldsymbol{t}_{\mathrm{int}}$ on a rough resolution.

Fig. 3. The 5 objects in the different environments: box on the training background, matchbox 1 on the black background, matchbox 2 on the heterogenous background, car 1 with 25% black occlusion, car 2 with 50% heterogeneous occlusion

Although we evaluate the density function only at discrete points of this transformation space, we have to calculate the density value for 225 possible internal translations t_{int} each with 36 possible internal rotations ϕ_{int}. For each of the altogether 8100 possible transformations we have to interpolate about the 80 feature vectors as one can see in the left image of figure 2.

Since the interpolation is computationally expensive, we change this algorithm. We interpolate the required area of the grid for each rotation ϕ_{int} only once and then translate the object grid according to the rotated coordinates axes in steps respective to the resolution r_s. As visible in the right image of figure 2 each interpolated feature vector can be used for many transformations.

4   Experiments and Results

For the experiments we used the five objects in figure 3. The images were 256 pixels in square. For the training, 18 images of each object in different poses with the same illumination were taken, the background was nearly homogeneous with a pixel intensity about 60. We took 17 further images of each object in other positions for the tests. For the experiments with heterogeneous background we cut out the objects and pasted them in an absolute black background as well as in front of a mouse pad (see figure 3). For the occlusions we blacked out 25% respectively 50% of the object in the test images, as well as we covered the objects in the image with a part of the mouse pad. It has

Table 1. Error rate in percent for only object density no background model, the old background model [6], the new background model without and with normalization (see eq. 8); for each model 3*170 localization and classification experiments are performed, *left:* error rate for the localization, *middle:* for the classification, *right:* average computation time for one localization on a Pentium III 800 MHz

one illumination	localization			classification			
	het. back.	25% occl.	50% occl.	het. back.	25% occl.	50% occl.	time
only object dens.	22,9%	69,4%	82,4%	25,3%	62,4%	70,6%	0,8 s
background m. [6]	6,5%	24,1%	51,7%	20,1%	21,2%	50,0%	6,5 s
new background m.	0,0%	0,0%	7,1%	0,0%	0,0%	4,7%	1,3 s
the same with norm.				0,0%	0,0%	2,3%	1,3 s

to be mentioned that a absolute black background or occlusion is a big difference to the training, because the first component of the local feature vectors is the logarithmic low-pass value of the wavelet analysis. So we got for each model 170 localization and 170 classification experiments for heterogeneous background, 25% occlusion and 50% occlusion. For the background model [6] two background classes were trained and used: the absolute black background and the mouse pad.

For the recognition we used for the rough localization a resolution of $r_s = 8$ pixels and for the refinement a resolution of $r_s = 4$ pixels. The objects were searched in the whole image for all internal rotations and translations. Thereby a localization is counted as wrong if the rotation error is bigger than $7°$ respectively the translation error bigger than 7 Pixels.

As one can see in table 1 the simple object model for homogeneous background (section 2) could handle heterogenous background, but failed very often for occlusion. The old background model [6] is better than the simple object model, but it is very slow and for 50% occlusion the error rate was about 50%. Whereas the new background model is much better and faster: for heterogeneous background and 25% occlusion there were no errors, and even for 50% occlusion the error rate was small. Further, by the normalization the classification error rate for 50% occlusion could be reduced from 4,7% to 2,3%. Additionally, the new model is five times faster than the old background model.

For testing the robustness of this approach we also performed experiments with two different illuminations. We trained each object with 9 images taken with illumination 1 and 9 images taken with illumination 2, where one of the three spotlights was switched off. Also for the test images we used these two illuminations. For the new background model the localization and classification error rate for heterogenous background and 25% occlusion was still very small, only for 50% occlusion it increased. But it could be reduced to 4,8% by the normalization.

5   Conclusions and Outlook

In this paper we presented a new efficient background model for object recognition. The background is modelled as uniform distribution and therefore independent from

Table 2. Error rates in percent for two illuminations: for only object density no background model, the old background model [6], the new background model without and with normalization (see eq. 8); for each model 3∗170 localization and classification experiments are performed, *left:* error rate for the localization; *right:* for the classification, the average computation time is nearly the same as in table (1)

two illuminations	localization			classification		
	het. back.	25% occl.	50% occl.	het. back.	25% occl.	50% occl.
only object dens.	11,4%	60,0%	77,7%	26,4%	50,0%	70,0%
background m. [6]	6,8%	32,4%	54,7%	7,7%	23,9%	61,2%
new background m.	0,0%	3,0%	24,2%	0,0%	4,7%	18,9%
the same with norm.				0,0%	0,0%	4,8%

the current used background, i. e. all possible backgrounds can be handled by only one background density function. We defined a assignment function that assigns each local feature vector either to the object or to the background. With this model we improved the recognition rate to nearly 100% for heterogeneous background and 25% occlusion and to nearly 95% for occlusion of 50%, even if two different lighting conditions are used.

In the future we will extend the background model to 3-D objects. For this purpose we have to model the so far fix size of the bounded region as a function of the out of image plane transformations. This is necessary because the appearance and the size of the objects vary with these external transformations. In addition the assignment function is a good basis for multi object recognition.

References

1. J. Dahmen, D. Keysers, M. Motter, H. Ney, T. Lehmann, and B. Wein. An automatic approach to invariant radiograph classification. In H. Handels, A. Horsch, T. Lehmann, and H.-P. Meinzer, editors, *Bildverarbeitung für die Medizin 2001*, pages 337–341, L"ubeck, March 2001. Springer Verlag, Berlin.
2. J. Dahmen, R. Schlüter, and H. Ney. Discriminative training of gaussian mixtures for image object recognition. In W. Förstner, J. Buhmann, A. Faber, and P. Faber, editors, *21. DAGM Symposium Mustererkennung*, pages 205–212, Bonn, September 1999. Springer Verlag, Berlin.
3. J. Hornegger. *Statistische Modellierung, Klassifikation und Lokalisation von Objekten*. Shaker Verlag, Aachen, 1996.
4. A. Leonardis and H. Bischof. Dealing with occlusions in the eigenspace approach. In *Proceedings of the IEEE Computer Vision and Pattern Recognition (CVPR)*, pages 453–458, San Francisco, 1996.
5. H. Murase and S. K. Nayar. Visual learning and recognition of 3-D objects from appearance. *International Journal of Computer Vision*, 14:5–24, 1995.
6. J. Pösl. *Erscheinungsbasierte statistische Objekterkennung*. Shaker Verlag, Aachen, 1998.
7. J. Pösl and H. Niemann. Object localization with mixture densities of wavelet features. In *International Wavelets Conference*, Tanger, Marokko Tangier, Marocco, April 1998. INRIA.
8. B. Schiele and J. Crowley. Object recognition using multidimensional receptive field histograms. In *Fourth European Conference on Computer Vision (ECCV)*, pages 610–619, Cambridge, UK, April 1996. Springer, Heidelberg.

Combining Independent Component Analysis and Self-Organizing Maps for Cell Image Classification

Tanja Kämpfe, Tim W. Nattkemper, and Helge Ritter

Neuroinformatics Group, Faculty of Technology,
University of Bielefeld, P.O. Box 100 131,
D-33501 Bielefeld
{tkaempfe,tnattkem,helge}@techfak.uni-bielefeld.de

Abstract. We consider the task of cell classification in fluorescent micrographs. We combine the use of Independent Component analysis as a preprocessing step and a Self-organizing Map for the resulting ICA feature space to classify image patches into cell and noncell images and to investigate the features of image patches in the vicinity of the classification border. We compare the classification performance of ICA bases of different size, generated from applying the infomax algorithm to image eigenspaces of different dimensionalities. We find an optimal performance for intermediate dimensionalities, characterized by the ICA basis patterns exhibiting salient features of an "idealized" cell shape, and we achieve classification results comparable to a previous approach based on PCA features.

Keywords. independent component analysis, self organizing maps, image classification, feature computation

1 Introduction

In recent years, automation of sample preparation and imaging led to an increased number of digitized microscope images in microbiological research, refered to as micrographs. The evaluation of micrographs by human experts is an expensive, tiresome and error-prone task. Thus the development of efficient image based classification algorithms for a full-automatic micrograph evaluation or for decision support in cell classification is potentially extremely valuable to the biological and medical researchers. However, the development of suitable algorithms is a delicate task [9], because the cell images are usually severely degraded by factors such as out of focus blur, non-uniform illumination and highly irregular object structures.

In the present paper we consider the use of ICA features in conjunction with a Self-organizing Map (SOM) for the identification of cell bodies in micrographs of fluorescent cells. This approach is part of a larger effort towards the development of a highly scalable system for segmentation of fluorescence micrographs in high throughput [8].

Our current system uses PCA features as a first step after which a neural network classifies image patches whether they are occupied by a fluorescent cell or not. Since the training of the system is based on data labelled by human experts, and since the decision

B. Radig and S. Florczyk (Eds.): DAGM 2001, LNCS 2191, pp. 262–268, 2001.
© Springer-Verlag Berlin Heidelberg 2001

whether an image feature is a cell body or not is even difficult for human experts, we want to assist the development of improved classifiers with an analysis which image features may be particularly important for the expert's decision. However, as is well known, PCA features tend to bear little resemblance to the objects from which they are derived. Therefore, we here investigate as an alternative approach the use of ICA features, which tend to be more localized and more amenable to human interpretation. To visualize the distribution of cells and noncells in feature space, we use a Self-organizing Map. Besides the usefulness of the combined method approach for visualization, we also find that it achieves classification results which are comparable to the previous system.

2 Independent Component Analysis of Images

ICA theory [4] is originated in the field of blind source separation on audiosignals. Its use for dimension reduction is also motivated by neuron response properties found in the visual system of mammals [10]. The goal of ICA is to find a set of statistically independent components that span the space of the input images.

Each input image of D pixel is treated as a row vector of a $N \times D$-matrix $\mathbf{X}$ (N is the number of given images) $\mathbf{x}_i \in \mathbb{R}^D$. In the following, we always use centered data ($\langle \mathbf{X} \rangle = 0$). The given images are supposed to be a linear combination of K source images $\mathbf{s}_i \in \mathbb{R}^D$ which are considered as the rows of a $K \times D$ matrix $\mathbf{S}$:

$$\mathbf{X} = \mathbf{AS} \tag{1}$$

The matrix $\mathbf{A} \in \mathbb{R}^{N \times K}$ is called mixing matrix. An approach to find the $\mathbf{s}_i$ is to compute a so called decorrelation matrix $\mathbf{W}$ such that $\mathbf{U} = \mathbf{WX}$ yields a $K \times D$ matrix whose rows are - up to scaling and permutation - equivalent to the K source images. We set $\mathbf{S} = \mathbf{U}$ and thus $\mathbf{WA} = \mathbf{I}$. Figure 1 illustrates the described model by the example of image patches extracted from a micrograph.

Various approaches for computing the decorrelation matrix $\mathbf{W}$ exist. Most of that restrict $\mathbf{W}$ to a square matrix. The algorithm used in this application is based on the infomax-algorithm introduced by Sejnowski and Bartlett in [3] and [2]. The idea is to maximize the entropy of the distribution $P(y)$ of an auxiliary variable $y = g(\mathbf{WX})$ where g is a sigmoid squashing function. When $\mathbf{W}$ is such that $P(y)$ approaches a uniform density (which is characterized by a maximal entropy), it factorizes and so does the corresponding density for the linearly transformed variables $\mathbf{WX}$. Gradient ascent on the entropy yields the learning rule which can be put into a computationally more advantageous form by using the "natural gradient" [1]:

$$\triangle \mathbf{W} \propto (1 + (1 - 2\mathbf{y}) \cdot \mathbf{x}^T) \cdot \mathbf{W} \tag{2}$$

While application of (2) for the training images $\mathbf{x}_i$ would be feasable, it has been observed in [2] and [5] that replacement of the $\mathbf{x}_i$ by a subset of the eigenvectors $\tilde{\mathbf{x}}_j, \quad j = 1, \ldots, K$ of the covariance matrix $\langle \mathbf{XX}^T \rangle$ leads to better learning performance. Geometrically, this means that the ICA components are sought in a subspace that captures the data variation except for a small part that corresponds to the neglected

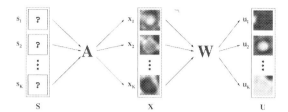

Fig. 1. The ICA-model applied on image patches of micrographs: Statistically independent source images **S** transformed by an unknown mixing matrix **A** form the observed images **X**. The decorrelation matrix **W** such that **WA** = **I** applied on **X** yields independent components **U** with **U** = **S**.

eigenvalues. At the same time, this offers a simple approach to compute only a limited number K of independent components from a much larger number N of image patches.

3   ICA of Micrograph Image Patches

We applied the ICA-algorithm to a set of 15×15 pixel subimages of a 658×517 pixel micrograph showing muscle tissue with fluorescence labeled lymphocyte cells. For the input matrix $\mathbf{X} \in \mathbb{R}^{K \times D}$ of the infomax-algorithm we chose the first K principal components of 131 image patches classified (by the human expert) as containing a cell.

Most of the computed independent components resemble fragments of an "idealized" cell image whose shape can be described as a centered circle with clearly distinguishable inner region and surround. For some components, the fragment is picked from one of the image corners, others show a "banana-like" part along the cell border or a fragment of the inner region fitting to the cell border (see fig. 2 third row on the right). Each fragment is clearly distinguishable from the background with properties making it suitable as an edge detector.

For a small number of input images, for example the five principal components with the largest eigenvalues, the computed independent components resemble the eigencells. With an increasing number of ICA components, these break down into smaller pieces; ultimately, for K values approaching the number of image pixels, this leads to almost meaningless, pixel-sized components (see fig. 2 right) approximating the unit vectors along the pixel directions.

4   Classification of Cell Images Using Self-Organizing Maps

A Self-organizing Map (SOM) [6] is a widely used tool for visualizing and exploring n-dimensional data. It projects n-dimensional input data on a two dimensional grid of prototype vectors. Therefore it visualizes the distribution of the images in the feature space. Furthermore, a trained SOM can be used for classifying the input data. We take advantage of these attributes for analysing the usability of ICA computed features.

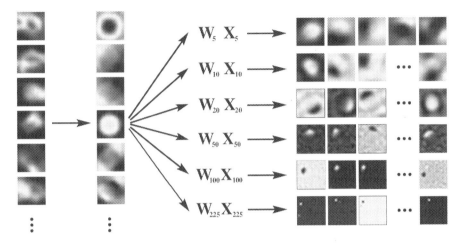

Fig. 2. Based on an arbitrary number of image patches (first column) a varying number K of principal components is computed (second column). These form the rows of the matrix $\mathbf{X}_K$ which is used to compute the corresponding weight matrix $\mathbf{W}_K$. The resulting independent components are shown on the right for various values of K. Small values of K yield more "holistic" features; for large K-values the features become more and more fragmented down to an approximation of the pixel unit vectors (bottom row).

One point of interest in analysing ICA for feature extraction is how to determine the number of independent components, and thereby the dimensionality of the feature space an image patch is projected to. For an experimental study, sets of 5, 10, 20 and 50 independent components are computed from the described training set. The resulting filters are used to map the image patches to feature vectors: $\boldsymbol{f}_k(\mathbf{x}_i) = \mathbf{U}\mathbf{x}_i, \quad i = 1, \ldots, N$ and $\mathbf{U} \in \mathbb{R}^{K \times D}$ leads to $\boldsymbol{f}_k(\mathbf{x}_i) \in \mathbb{R}^K$, $K \in \{5, 10, 20, 50\}$. Subsets of the resulting independent components are shown in figure 2. A SOM with varying parameters is applied to the features $\boldsymbol{f}_k(\mathbf{x}_i)$ and the resulting distribution of the image patches on the nodes is obtained as well as the classification result.

For training and testing the SOM we use a set of about 660 image patches. 131 of them are labeled as being occupied by a cell, following called *cell*, the remaining ones as not, called *noncell*. The further set is equivalent to the set of image patches which has been used to compute the ICA filters $\mathbf{U}$. The image set is divided in three sets of about 220 image patches each. Two sets are combined to the training set and the third is used for testing. After training the nodes are labeled as "cell-matching" and "noncell-matching" nodes by the prevailing label of the matching image patches. Figure 3 shows two SOMs of different dimensions. For each node the label is represented as well as one image patch arbitrarily chosen from the respective set of matching image patches. Comparing the labels of the image patches with the node labels averaged by cross validation on exchanging sets yields the misclassification rate. The following table shows the received rates by various feature dimensions and SOM architectures with exponential decreasing learning rate and neighborhood radius.

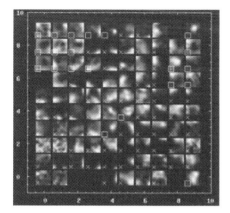 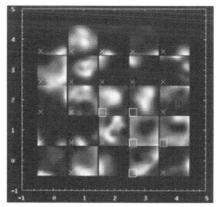

Fig. 3. Two Self-organizing Maps (SOM) with image patches and node labels after training. The represented image patches are chosen arbitrarily from the respective set of matching image patches. □ denotes a cell-matching node and × a noncell-matching node.

dimension SOM	misclassification rate				rate of uncertain nodes			
	dimension of feature				dimension of feature			
	5	10	20	50	5	10	20	50
5×5	0.0909	0.0894	0.0606	0.0758	0.55	0.49	0.48	0.51
10×10	0.0863	0.0712	**0.0545**	0.0697	0.19	0.17	0.15	0.17
15×15	0.0894	0.0939	0.0878	0.0924	0.07	0.06	0.04	0.05

On varying SOM architectures we observed that features based on 20 independent components are most useful for classification. A misclassification rate of 0.0545 is the best result we obtained using a 10×10 SOM.

A SOM allows to inspect the label statistics and image patches associated to a selected node. Thereby a deeper understanding of the classification performance can be obtained. Although labeled different, the image patches matching the same node look similar (see fig. 4 top right). Therefore, some of the SOM nodes are hard to label as "ʹcell-matching"ʹ or "ʹnoncell-matching"ʹ nodes because after training cells match them as well as noncells. First we do not regard the proportion of cells and noncells at the uncertain nodes but only the fact that they are uncertain. The fraction by the number of nodes in the SOM is listed in the table above.

Disregarded the misclassification rate, we observed that the dominating factor influencing the number of uncertain nodes is the size of the SOM. This can be explained by the various proportions of the number of nodes on the border line between a cell-matching region and a noncell-matching region to the number in the regions themself. But comparing the rate of uncertain nodes for equivalent SOM dimensions yields in favoriting 20 dimensional feature vectors $f_{20}(x_i)$ because the labeling in those cases is most certain.

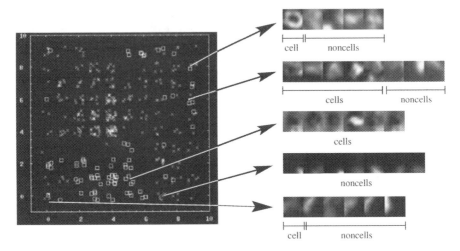

Fig. 4. A 10×10 SOM with image patches matching selected nodes. □ denotes a cell which matchs a node, × denotes noncell. Image patches matching selected nodes are reproduced on the right.

5 Discussion

We explored a feature extraction approach based on the ICA-theory for the task of classifying cell micrograph image patches. We found ICA features that – unlike PCA features – can be interpreted in terms of geometric cell features when the number K of extracted ICA features falls in some intermediate range (well below the number of pixels in an image patch). Using a SOM for classification of image patches into cell and noncell images, we found a non-monotonous dependence of the classification performance on the number K of extracted ICA components, with an optimum classification performance correlated with the K-range for which the resemblance of ICA-components into subparts of an "idealized" cell is most salient. This optimum K-range seems to tag the border beween principal component like filters and independent components splitted to unspecific shreds.

The achieved misclassification rate of 0.05 is comparable to that of a PCA-based cell classification system [7] and makes the current approach a competitive alternative to the PCA-based classifier. While the use of a SOM as a classifier is known to be not optimal [6], it provides its classification together with a visualization of the feature space. Thereby it allows also to visually explore the classification border and to inspect the features characterizing image patches that are most easily confused by the system as well as by human experts. This, together with the use of ICA-features with their observed, better visual interpretability as compared to PCA can help to improve the design of more specialized feature extraction schemes for cell micrograph classification or similarly difficult visual classification tasks characterized by a high amount of degradation.

This work was partially funded by the BMBF under contract 01IB 001B.

References

1. S. Amari, A. Cichocki, and H.H. Yang. A new learning algorithm for blind signal separation. Advances in Neural Information Precessing Systems 8, 1996. MIT Press.
2. Marian Stewart Bartlett, H. Martin Lades, and Terrence J. Sejnowski. Independent Component Representation for Face Recognition. In *Proceedings of the SPIE*, volume 3299: Conference on Human Vision and Electronic Imaging III, pages 528–539, 1998.
3. Anthony J. Bell and Terrence J. Sejnowski. An Information-Maximization Approach to Blind Separation and Blind Deconvolution. *Neural Computation*, 6:1129–1159, 1995.
4. Pierre Comon. Independent component analysis, A new concept? *Signal Processing*, 36:287–314, 1994.
5. T. Kämpfe. Independent Component Analysis zur Merkmalsextraktion in der Bildverarbeitung, 2000. masterthesis.
6. T. Kohonen. *Self-Organizing Map*. Springer Verlag, 2 edition, 1997.
7. T. W. Nattkemper, H. Ritter, and W. Schubert. A neural classificator enabling high-throughput topological analysis of lymphocytes in tissue sections. *IEEE Trans. on Inf. Techn. in Biomed.*, 5(2), 2001. in press.
8. T. W. Nattkemper, H. Wersing, W. Schubert, and H. Ritter. A neural network architecture for automatic segmentation of fluorescence micrographs. In *Proc. of the 8th Europ. Symp. on Art. Neur. Netw. (ESANN)*, pages 177–182, Bruges, Belgium, 2000.
9. S. H. Ong, X. C. Jin, Jayasooriah, and R. Sinniah. Image analysis of tissue sections. *Comput. Biol. Med.*, 26(3):269–279, 1996.
10. J.H. van Hateren and A. van der Schaaf. Independent component filters of natural images compared with simple cells in primary visual cortex. *Proc.R.Soc.Lond.*, 265:359–366, 1998.

Nonlinear Shape Statistics via Kernel Spaces

Daniel Cremers, Timo Kohlberger, and Christoph Schnörr

Computer Vision, Graphics and Pattern Recognition Group
Department of Mathematics and Computer Science
University of Mannheim, 68131 Mannheim, Germany
{cremers, tiko, schnoerr}@uni-mannheim.de
http://www.cvgpr.uni-mannheim.de

Abstract. We present a novel approach for representing shape knowledge in terms of example views of 3D objects. Typically, such data sets exhibit a highly nonlinear structure with distinct clusters in the shape vector space, preventing the usual encoding by linear principal component analysis (PCA). For this reason, we propose a nonlinear Mercer-kernel PCA scheme which takes into account both the projection distance and the within-subspace distance in a high-dimensional feature space. The comparison of our approach with supervised mixture models indicates that the statistics of example views of distinct 3D objects can fairly well be learned and represented in a completely unsupervised way.

Keywords: Nonlinear shape statistics, Mercer kernels, nonlinear density estimation, shape learning, variational methods, kernel PCA

1 Introduction

One of the central questions in computer vision is how to model the link between external visual input and internally represented, previously acquired knowledge. For the case of image segmentation, prior information on the shape of expected objects can drastically improve segmentation results [9,10]. A conceptually attractive way of incorporating prior information is given by a variational approach in which external image information and statistically acquired knowledge about the shape of expected objects are combined in a single cost functional [6]:

$$E = E_{image} + E_{shape}. \tag{1}$$

The present paper is concerned with the question of how to construct such a shape energy, which measures the similarity of a given shape to a set of training shapes. We focus on encoding views of distinct objects in an unsupervised way.

In most of the models of shape variability it is assumed that the training shapes define some linear subspace of the shape space [4]. Though quite powerful in many applications, this assumption only has limited validity if the observed deformations are more complex. It fully breaks down once shapes of different classes are included in the training set, such as those corresponding to different objects or just different views of a single 3D object. An example is given in

B. Radig and S. Florczyk (Eds.): DAGM 2001, LNCS 2191, pp. 269–276, 2001.
© Springer-Verlag Berlin Heidelberg 2001

Figure 1, which shows a sampling along the first principal component for a set of 10 hand shapes containing right and left hands: the assumption of a linear distribution obviously results in an unwanted mixing up of the two classes.

Fig. 1. Mixing of two classes in a Gaussian model: Sampling along the first principal component around the mean (center) for a training set of 10 hands, comprising both left and right hands. Shapes of different classes are *morphed* in an undesirable way.

Several approaches have been undertaken to model nonlinear shape variability. They often suffer from certain drawbacks, namely they assume some prior knowledge about the structure of the nonlinearity [8], or the number of underlying classes [3], or they involve an intricate model construction [2].

An elegant and promising way to avoid these drawbacks is to employ feature spaces induced by *Mercer kernels* [1], in order to indirectly model a nonlinear transformation $\Phi(x)$ of the original data from a space X into a potentially infinite-dimensional space Y, aspiring a simpler distribution of the mapped data in Y. The search for an appropriate nonlinearity Φ is replaced by the search for an appropriate kernel function $k(x, y)$ defining the scalar product on Y:

$$k(x, y) = (\Phi(x), \Phi(y)). \tag{2}$$

With great success, this Mercer kernel approach has been used for the purpose of *classification* [5]. By contrast, our aim in the present paper is that of constructing a similarity measure by *probability density estimation*. We therefore propose to approximate the nonlinearly mapped data points $\Phi(x)$ by a Gaussian probability density *in the high-dimensional space Y*. It turns out that this can be done in the framework of Mercer kernels, i.e. all nonlinearities Φ can be expressed in terms of scalar products.

The resulting nonlinear density estimate in the original space X does not assume any prior information about the number of classes. Comparison with a supervised mixture model on simulated 2D data and its application to silhouettes of various 3D objects reveals that our estimate captures the essential nonlinear structure in the original (shape) space, although being fully unsupervised.

Our method of density estimation is related to the so-called *kernel PCA*, which shall therefore be reviewed in the next section.

2   Kernel Principal Component Analysis

In [13] a method to perform nonlinear principal component analysis is proposed. This is done by assuming an appropriate nonlinear transformation $\Phi(x_i)$ of the training data $\{x_i\}_{i=1,\dots,\ell}$ into a space Y and performing a linear principal component analysis of the transformed data in Y (after centering it in Y). It is shown that the nonlinearity Φ enters the relevant expressions only in terms of scalar products (2). Therefore the choice of an appropriate nonlinear transformation Φ corresponds to the choice of an appropriate kernel $k(x, y)$. The eigenvectors in Y can be expressed as linear combinations of the mapped training data:

$$V_k = \sum_{i=1}^{\ell} \alpha_i^k \Phi(x_i), \tag{3}$$

with known coefficients α_i^k. The projection of a mapped point $\Phi(z)$ on the eigenvector V_k is therefore given by:

$$\beta_k := (V_k, \Phi(z)) = \sum_{i=1}^{\ell} \alpha_i^k k(x_i, z). \tag{4}$$

In [12] this kernel PCA is applied to pattern reconstruction. To this end the authors propose to minimize the distance

$$\rho(z) = ||P_r \Phi(z) - \Phi(z)||^2 \tag{5}$$

of a mapped sample point to its projection onto the subspace spanned by the first r eigenvectors:

$$P_r \Phi(z) = \sum_{k=1}^{r} \beta_k V_k. \tag{6}$$

The distance (5) can be expressed in terms of the kernel function (2). For a suitable kernel, a corrupted pattern z is reconstructed by minimizing (5).

3   Density Estimation in Kernel Space

In the present paper we deviate from the kernel PCA formulation above, namely we propose to perform a nonlinear probability density estimation by exploiting kernel spaces. We model the statistical distribution of the *nonlinearly mapped* data by a Gaussian distribution in Y. After centering, the covariance matrix in Y is given by

$$\Sigma_\Phi := \sum_{i=1}^{\ell} \Phi(x_i)\, \Phi(x_i)^t. \tag{7}$$

Let $\{\lambda_i\}_{i=1,\dots,r}$ be the nonzero eigenvalues of Σ_Φ and V the matrix containing the respective eigenvectors V_K. In general Σ_Φ is not invertible and needs to be appropriately regularized (cf. [7]), for example by replacing all zero eigenvalues by the smallest non-zero eigenvalue λ_r. The inverse of this matrix is:

$$\Sigma_\Phi^* = V \begin{pmatrix} \lambda_1^{-1} & & & \\ & \lambda_2^{-1} & & \\ & & \ddots & \\ & & & \lambda_r^{-1} \end{pmatrix} V^t + \lambda_r^{-1} \cdot \left(I - V V^t \right). \tag{8}$$

Approximating the distribution of mapped points in Y by a Gaussian density

$$\mathcal{P}(z) \propto \exp\left(-\frac{1}{2}\Phi(z)^t \, \Sigma_\Phi^* \, \Phi(z)\right), \qquad (9)$$

corresponds (up to scaling) to an energy of the form:

$$E(z) = \Phi(z)^t \, \Sigma_\Phi^* \, \Phi(z). \qquad (10)$$

Using definition (8), the energy is split into two terms:

$$E(z) = \sum_{k=1}^{r} \lambda_k^{-1} \, (V_k, \Phi(z))^2 \;\; + \;\; \lambda_r^{-1} \left(|\Phi(z)|^2 - \sum_{k=1}^{r} (V_k, \Phi(z))^2\right). \qquad (11)$$

Inserting expansion (3) of the eigenvectors V_k and the kernel (2) we get:

$$E(z) = \sum_{k=1}^{r} \left(\sum_{i=1}^{\ell} \alpha_i^k \, k(x_i, z)\right)^2 \cdot \left(\lambda_k^{-1} - \lambda_r^{-1}\right) + \lambda_r^{-1} \cdot k(z, z). \qquad (12)$$

Again, the nonlinearity Φ only appears in terms of the kernel function. Starting from a shape vector z, minimization of (12) increases its similarity to the training data $\{x_i\}$.

How and why does energy (10) differ from distance (5) proposed in [12]? The second term in (11), weighted by λ_r^{-1}, is identical with (5). It corresponds to the distance of a mapped point $\Phi(z)$ to the feature space F, which is the subspace of Y spanned by the mapped training data. Following an analogous derivation in the linear setting [11], we call this term *distance from feature space* (DFFS). The first term in (11) is called *distance in feature space* (DIFS). Both of these distances are visualized in Figure 2: the original data is mapped from the space $\mathbb{R}^n$ to a (generally higher dimensional) space Y by the nonlinear mapping Φ. The space Y is the direct sum of F and its orthogonal complement $\bar{F}$ in Y.

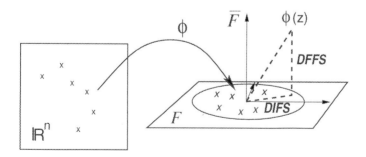

Fig. 2. Nonlinear mapping into $Y = F \oplus \bar{F}$ and the distances DIFS and DFFS.

In order to measure how similar a point z is to the training data $\{x_i\}$, both distances – DIFS *and* DFFS – need to be included. The DFFS by itself is not sufficient: it completely ignores how the mapped training data is distributed in F. Moreover, one can easily imagine the mapped test point $\Phi(z)$ to be far away from the mapped training data, while still being at exactly the same DFFS.

Including the DIFS as proposed in (11) accounts for the distance of the projection $P_r\Phi(z)$ *within* F from the mapped training data $\{\Phi(x_i)\}_{i=1,\ldots,\ell}$. It is the Mahalanobis distance in the feature subspace F. Therefore, (11) is a more reliable measure of the similarity of a test point z to the training data $\{x_i\}$.

4   Numerical Results

4.1   Unsupervised Density Estimation via Kernel Spaces versus Supervised Mixture Models

Given the information which class each training point belongs to, one can construct a mixture model of Gaussian distributions as a nonlinear extension of PCA. For each class i one calculates mean m_i and covariance matrix Σ_i. The total probability is the sum of the probabilities for each class. The corresponding energy is given by:

$$E(z) = -\frac{1}{\beta} \log \left[\sum_i c_i \exp(-\beta E_i(z)) \right] , \quad \text{where } c_i := |2\pi \Sigma_i|^{-1/2} \quad (13)$$

and

$$E_i(z) = \frac{1}{2}(z - m_i)^t \, \Sigma_i^{-1} \, (z - m_i). \quad (14)$$

The additional parameter β is introduced to allow smoothing. For small values of β one obtains the weighted sum of the single class energies (14):

$$E(z) \approx \frac{1}{\sum_i c_i} \sum_i c_i E_i(z) + \text{const} \quad \text{for } \beta \ll 1. \quad (15)$$

The limit $\beta \to \infty$ gives their minimum: $\lim_{\beta\to\infty} E(z) = \min_i E_i(z) + \text{const}.$

We compared our approach (12) for a Gaussian radial basis function kernel[1]

$$k(x, y) = \exp\left(-\frac{||x - y||^2}{2\sigma^2} \right) \quad (16)$$

to the supervised case (13) on an artificial training set of 2D points, which were sampled from three different Gaussian distributions. The training data and the level-lines of the respective energies are depicted in Figure 3.

The comparison shows several advantages of our method. The kernel space approach is *unsupervised*: The class membership of a training point is neither known, nor determined beforehand. Even the knowledge that the data of each class is sampled from a Gaussian distribution is not taken into account. Yet, the qualitative comparison shows that the data distribution is approximated better than by the mixture model, which is based on the valid assumption of Gaussian distributions and which does imply the knowledge about the class membership of each point. Accordingly, the density estimate obtained by the mixture model is always restricted to ellipse-like level lines.

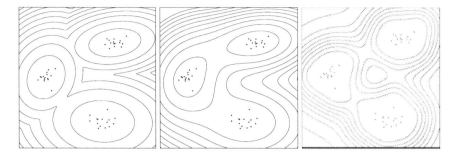

Fig. 3. Level-lines of the energies corresponding to a supervised mixture model (13) for $\beta = 1$ (**left**) and $\beta = 0.02$ (**center**) and the unsupervised density estimate via kernel spaces (10) for $\sigma = 1.5$ (**right**). These figures illustrate that our approach captures nonlinear data distributions without the need to classify the training data beforehand.

4.2   Nonlinear Shape Statistics in Kernel Space

In order to apply our distance measure (10) to realistic shapes, we parameterized the silhouettes of binarized training objects by closed spline curves. The spline curves were aligned with respect to Euclidean transformations and cyclic renumbering of the control points – see Figure 4. We used 100 control points

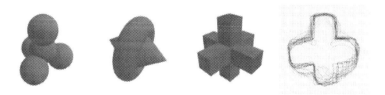

Fig. 4. 3D sample objects, and aligned silhouettes for several views of these objects. Applying linear PCA to the training set on the right would not produce an accurate description of the shape variability.

in order to assure a sufficiently detailed contour description. The control point vectors were then used as training data to construct the energy (12), again using the kernel (16). In order to visualize the energy we projected the control point vectors of the training contours onto the first two principal components of a linear PCA[1]. The data points and the respective level lines of energy (12) are shown in Figure 5. The projection shows that our density estimate works well even in higher dimensions[2] and for distributions which are not necessarily

---

[1] Note that linear PCA is only used as a coordinate frame for *visualization* of the high-dimensional data!

[2] Due to the 2D projection, Figure 5 is merely a *crude visualization* of how the data distribution is approximated in the original 200-dimensional space.

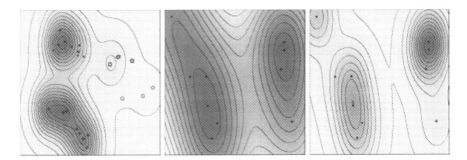

Fig. 5. Training shapes and level lines corresponding to the shape density estimate in kernel space (12), projected onto the first two principal components of a linear PCA. **Left:** Different views of objects 1 (○), 2 (+) and 3 (●) in Figure 4 for $\sigma = 0.04$. **Center:** Left hands (+) and right hands (●) (used in Figure 1) for $\sigma = 0.1$. **Right:** Hands for $\sigma = 0.04$. Clusters in high-dimensional shape space are estimated in variable detail.

Gaussian – see Figure 5. Compared to linear PCA (elliptical level lines) the true data distribution is approximated much better. This is crucial since the different shapes can be quite similar – see Figure 4, right side. Moreover, the construction of the shape energy is fully unsupervised, i.e. it does not involve the number of objects nor the number of clusters, in which the different views of one object can be separated. By changing the parameter σ in (16), one can choose how detailed the approximation of the data should be – see Figure 5, middle and right.

Note that we are *not* interested in *classification* of the objects, we merely want a measure of how *similar* an object is to a set of training objects given their 2D projections. It is therefore irrelevant whether all projections of *one 3D object* can be associated with *one cluster*. Rather we expect to obtain several clusters corresponding to the stable views of each object.

5   Conclusion

We presented a method to perform nonlinear density estimation in the framework of kernel spaces. A set of training points is mapped to a higher dimensional space Y by a nonlinear mapping Φ. The distribution of mapped points is then approximated by a Gaussian distribution in Y. Back projection to the original space allows a visualization of the estimated density. Comparison to supervised mixture models shows the advantages of our approach – namely that it is fully unsupervised and that the data distribution is approximated more appropriately. An application of this density estimation to silhouettes of 3D objects shows that the density estimate via kernel spaces seems to be well suited for high-dimensional and highly nonlinear data distributions. We argued that the distance measure corresponding to the density estimation in kernel spaces is more reliable than that obtained in kernel PCA [12].

Ongoing work focuses on ways to automatically estimate the optimal size of the parameter σ and on the application of the proposed density estimation to image segmentation [6].

Acknowledgments. We thank H. G. Schuster, J. C. Claussen, C. Kervrann, J. Keuchel, H.H. Bülthoff and J. Denzler for stimulating discussions.

References

1. B. E. Boser, I. M. Guyon, and V. N. Vapnik. A training algorithm for optimal margin classifiers. In D. Haussler, editor, *Proc. of the 5th Annual ACM Workshop on Computational Learning Theory*, pages 144–152, Pittsburgh, PA, 1992. ACM Press.
2. B. Chalmond and S. C. Girard. Nonlinear modeling of scattered multivariate data and its application to shape change. *IEEE Trans. Patt. Anal. Mach. Intell.*, 21(5):422–432, 1999.
3. T.F. Cootes and C.J. Taylor. A mixture model for representing shape variation. *Image and Vis. Comp.*, 17(8):567–574, 1999.
4. T.F. Cootes, C.J. Taylor, D.M. Cooper, and J. Graham. Active shape models – their training and application. *Comp. Vision Image Underst.*, 61(1):38–59, 1995.
5. V. Cortes, C. and Vapnik. Support vector networks. *Machine Learning*, 20:273–297, 1995.
6. D. Cremers, C. Schnörr, and J. Weickert. Diffusion–snakes: Combining statistical shape knowledge and image information in a variational framework. In *IEEE Workshop on Variational and Level Set Methods*, Vancouver, Canada, Jul. 13, 2001. To appear.
7. D. Cremers, C. Schnörr, J. Weickert, and C. Schellewald. Diffusion–snakes using statistical shape knowledge. In G. Sommer and Y.Y. Zeevi, editors, *Algebraic Frames for the Perception-Action Cycle*, volume 1888 of *Lect. Not. Comp. Sci.*, pages 164–174, Kiel, Germany, Sept. 10–11, 2000. Springer.
8. T. Heap and D. Hogg. Automated pivot location for the cartesian-polar hybrid point distribution model. In *Brit. Machine Vision Conference*, pages 97–106, Edinburgh, UK, Sept. 1996.
9. C. Kervrann and F. Heitz. A hierarchical markov modeling approach for the segmentation and tracking of deformable shapes. *Graphical Models and Image Processing*, 60:173–195, 5 1998.
10. M.E. Leventon, W.E.L. Grimson, and O. Faugeras. Statistical shape influence in geodesic active contours. In *Proc. Conf. Computer Vis. and Pattern Recog.*, volume 1, pages 316–323, Hilton Head Island, South Carolina, June 13–15, 2000.
11. B. Moghaddam and A. Pentland. Probabilistic visual learning for object representation. *IEEE Trans. Patt. Anal. Mach. Intell.*, 19(7):696–710, 1997.
12. B. Schölkopf, S. Mika, Smola A., G. Rätsch, and Müller K.-R. Kernel PCA pattern reconstruction via approximate pre-images. In L. Niklasson, M. Boden, and T. Ziemke, editors, *Internat. Conf. on Art. Neural Networks ICANN*, pages 147–152, Berlin, Germany, 1998. Springer.
13. B. Schölkopf, A. Smola, and K.-R. Müller. Nonlinear component analysis as a kernel eigenvalue problem. *Neural Computation*, 10:1299–1319, 1998.

Normalization in Support Vector Machines

Arnulf B.A. Graf[1,2] and Silvio Borer[1]

[1] arnulf.graf@tuebingen.mpg.de
Swiss Federal Institute of Technology Lausanne
Laboratory of Computational Neuroscience, DI-LCN
1015 Lausanne EPFL, Switzerland
[2] Max Planck Institute for Biological Cybernetics
Spemannstrasse 38, 72076 Tübingen, Germany

Abstract. This article deals with various aspects of normalization in the context of Support Vector Machines. We consider fist normalization of the vectors in the input space and point out the inherent limitations. A natural extension to the feature space is then represented by the kernel function normalization. A correction of the position of the Optimal Separating Hyperplane is subsequently introduced so as to suit better these normalized kernels. Numerical experiments finally evaluate the different approaches.

Keywords. Support Vector Machines, input space, feature space, normalization, optimal separating hyperplane

1 Introduction

Support Vector Machines (SVMs) have drawn much attention because of their high classification performance [1]. In this article, they are applied in a computer vision problem, namely the classification of images. SVMs are often combined with a preprocessing stage to form pattern recognition systems. Moreover, it turns out to be intrinsically necessary for the SV algorithm (see [1]-[4]) to have data which is preprocessed. It has been shown [5] that *normalization* is a preprocessing type which plays an important role in this context. Theoretical considerations on the kernel interpretation of normalization and an adaptation of the SV algorithm to normalized kernel functions will be developed in this paper in order to shed new light on such pattern recognition systems.

In this study, we deal with normalization aspects in SVMs. First, normalization in the input space is considered in Sec. 2 and a resulting problem related to SV classification is outlined. A possible solution, namely the normalization of the kernel functions in the feature space, is then subsequently presented. A modification of the SV algorithm is then presented in Sec. 3. This modification takes into account the properties of the normalized kernels and amounts to a correction of the position of the Optimal Separating Hyperplane (OSH). The corresponding numerical experiments are reported in Sec. 4 and Sec. 5 concludes the paper.

B. Radig and S. Florczyk (Eds.): DAGM 2001, LNCS 2191, pp. 277–282, 2001.

2   Normalization in the Input and Feature Space

The normalization of the vectors of the input space can be considered as the most basic type of preprocessing. Assume $\boldsymbol{x} \in \mathbb{R}^N$ is an input vector, the corresponding normalized vector $\tilde{\boldsymbol{x}}$ may be expressed as:

$$\tilde{\boldsymbol{x}} = \frac{\boldsymbol{x}}{\|\boldsymbol{x}\|} \in \mathbb{R}^N \tag{1}$$

where $\|\boldsymbol{x}\|^2 = \sum_{i=1}^{N} x_i^2$. This vector lies on a unit hypersphere of $\mathbb{R}^N$. Thus, if the input vectors are images, normalization in the input space amounts to rescaling the intensity of the pixels of the images since such a preprocessing only changes the norm of the image vector. The SV algorithm is constructed to find the OSH in the feature space, the latter being obtained by a non-linear mapping from the normalized input space. When considering the effect of such a mapping on the normalized input vectors, it appears, in most cases, to cause a loss of normalization or a scale problem as shown in figure 1. This may create a

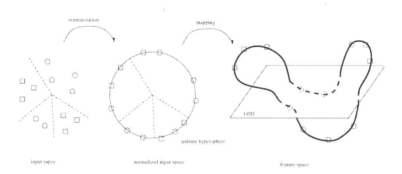

Fig. 1. Normalization in the input space and its representation in the feature space

problem for the SV algorithm since the latter mainly needs "input" vectors in the feature space which are in some way "scaled". As suggested in [5], normalization in the feature space presents a solution to this problem.

Normalization in the feature space is not strictly-speaking a form of preprocessing since it is not applied directly on the input vectors but can be seen as a kernel interpretation of the preprocessing considered above, i.e., an extension to the feature space of the normalization of the input vectors. Normalization in the feature space essentially amounts to redefining the kernel functions of the SVM as it is applied to the unprocessed input vectors. Moreover, since the non-linear mapping is not known, this normalization only makes use of the kernel functions. Assume $K(\boldsymbol{x}, \boldsymbol{y})$ is the kernel function representing a dot product in the feature space. Normalization in the feature space then amounts to defining a new kernel function $\tilde{K}(\boldsymbol{x}, \boldsymbol{y})$ as follows:

$$\tilde{K}(\boldsymbol{x}, \boldsymbol{y}) = \frac{K(\boldsymbol{x}, \boldsymbol{y})}{\sqrt{K(\boldsymbol{x}, \boldsymbol{x}) K(\boldsymbol{y}, \boldsymbol{y})}} \in \mathbb{R} \tag{2}$$

We clearly have $\tilde{K}(\boldsymbol{x}, \boldsymbol{x}) = 1$. Notice that this is always true for RBF kernels $K(\boldsymbol{x}, \boldsymbol{y}) = exp(-\frac{\|\boldsymbol{x}-\boldsymbol{y}\|^2}{c})$. Thus, all vectors in the feature space lie on a unit hyper-sphere. For monomial kernels $K(\boldsymbol{x}, \boldsymbol{y}) = (\boldsymbol{x} \cdot \boldsymbol{y})^p$, normalization in the input space is equivalent to normalization in the feature space. Indeed, we have: $K(\tilde{\boldsymbol{x}}, \tilde{\boldsymbol{y}}) = (\tilde{\boldsymbol{x}} \cdot \tilde{\boldsymbol{y}})^p = \left(\frac{\boldsymbol{x} \cdot \boldsymbol{y}}{\|\boldsymbol{x}\|\|\boldsymbol{y}\|}\right)^p = \tilde{K}(\boldsymbol{x}, \boldsymbol{y})$. When the kernel function is replaced by the dot product in the input space $(p = 1)$, equation (2) reduces to equation (1). Moreover, note that $\tilde{K}(\boldsymbol{x}, \boldsymbol{y}) = \tilde{\varphi}(\boldsymbol{x}) \cdot \tilde{\varphi}(\boldsymbol{y})$ where $\tilde{\varphi}(\boldsymbol{x}) = \frac{\varphi(\boldsymbol{x})}{\|\varphi(\boldsymbol{x})\|} = \frac{\varphi(\boldsymbol{x})}{\sqrt{K(\boldsymbol{x}, \boldsymbol{x})}}$ stands for the "normalized" mapping and thus the expression above satisfies the conditions of Mercer's theorem.

When considering single-class SVMs as introduced in [6], the normalized kernel functions play a predominant role. We consider dealing with data rescaled such that it lies in the positive orthant i.e. in $[0, \infty)^N$. The normalized kernels then place the datapoints on a portion of the unit hypersphere in the feature space allowing them to be separated from the origin by a hyperplane.

3 Adaptation of the SV Algorithm in a Normalized Feature Space

Normalization in the feature space changes the kernel functions, and thus also the SV optimization problem. We shall here study the implications of a normalized feature space, i.e. of normalized kernel functions, on the SV algorithm. The latter determines the OSH defined by its normal vector $\boldsymbol{w}$ and its position b. By construction, the margins of separation are symmetric around the OSH since both lie at a distance $\delta = \frac{1}{\|\boldsymbol{w}\|}$ from the OSH. However, all the datapoints lie on a unit hypersphere in the normalized feature space. It would thus be more accurate to do classification not according to an OSH computed such that the margins are symmetric around it, but according to an OSH determined such that the margins define equal distances *on* the hypersphere. This may be done by adjusting the value of b. The margins, and thus $\boldsymbol{w}$, are unchanged since the problem is symmetric around $\boldsymbol{w}$. In other words, the separating hyperplane is translated. In order to compute the correction to the value of b, consider figure 2. The intersection of the two margin hyperplanes with the unit hyper-sphere are represented by the angles α_1 and α_2 defined by $cos(\alpha_1) = b - \delta$ and $cos(\alpha_2) = b + \delta$. The bisection of the angle formed by α_1 and α_2 is represented by the angle φ and can be computed as $\varphi = \frac{\alpha_1 + \alpha_2}{2} = \frac{arccos(b-\delta) + arccos(b+\delta)}{2}$. Moreover, we set $cos(\varphi) = b'$ where b' stands for the new position of the OSH. Finally we get the following expression:

$$b'(b, \boldsymbol{w}) = cos\left(\frac{arccos(b - \frac{1}{\|\boldsymbol{w}\|}) + arccos(b + \frac{1}{\|\boldsymbol{w}\|})}{2}\right) \tag{3}$$

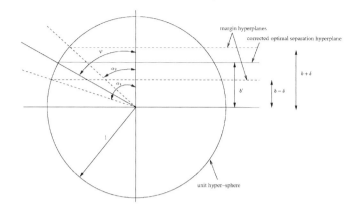

Fig. 2. Normalization in a two-dimensional feature space and computation of b'

From the above equation, we see that $b \neq b'$. The correction of b mentioned here leads to a new optimal separating hyperplane defined by $(\boldsymbol{w}, b')$. This method is valid regardless of the kernel function as long as it is normalized according to equation 2. The value of $b'(b, \boldsymbol{w})$ can be computed from equation 3 once the optimal parameters of the separating hyperplane $(\boldsymbol{w}, b)$ are found by the SV algorithm. The correction is not applied *while* the optimization process is running since this would create convergence problems.

4   Numerical Experiments

Here, we construct a pattern recognition system formed by a SVM with either input space normalization, feature space normalization or the latter combined with the correction of the position of the OSH.

Database. The Columbia Object Image Library (COIL-100) which can be down-loaded from *http://www.cs.columbia.edu/CAVE/* was chosen as in [7] but for different training and testing protocols (see underneath). The latter is composed of 100 different objects, each one being represented by 72 color images (one perspective of the object every 5 degrees) of size 128x128 pixels. These images were first converted to greyscale images and reduced to 32x32 pixels images using averages over square pixel patches of size 4x4 pixels. The database was separated into a *training* and a *testing* dataset. For each object the perspectives 0-30-60-. . . -330 went into the training set and the perspectives 15-45-75-. . . -345 into the testing set. In other words, both datasets are composed of regularly-spaced non-overlapping perspectives of each object. We are thus confronted with a multi-class classification problem and the choices mentioned below are made for the training and for the classification protocols.

Training. For each object $i = 1, \ldots, 100$, a classifier C_i is generated by assigning a target $+1$ to the training images of the object i and a target -1 to the training images of all the remaining objects. We thus choose a "one against all" strategy. The regularisation parameter is set *a priori* to 1000.

Classification. Each testing image z is presented to each of the classifiers and is assigned to class i where $C_i(z) \geq C_k(z) \quad \forall k \neq i$ according to a "winner take all" strategy. As shown in [8], this approach is computationally very efficient for feedforward neural networks with binary gates such as those encountered in SVMs. Since the class of the testing images is known, an error is computed for each test image. The *classification error* for the experiment is then the average of all the individual errors for each C_i and the corresponding variance over the objects is also computed.

Polynomial kernel functions $K(x, y) = (1 + xy)^p$ are particularly well suited for the considered studies. The results are presented in Figure 3. When considering

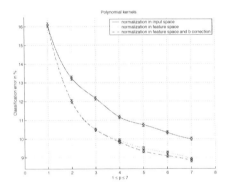

Fig. 3. Classification error and variance with normalization in the input space, in the feature space or in the feature space with correction of b

the results, we notice that the three error curves are monotonically decreasing and none are crossing each other. This seems to reflect the good generalization ability of the considered algorithms. The experiments clearly point out that the normalization in the feature space outperforms the normalization in the input space for all the considered degrees except for $p = 1$. Indeed, for linear kernels, input and feature space normalizations are of the same order of magnitude for large values of the input vectors. This is the case here since the latter represent vectors of size 1024 with values ranging between 0 and 255. Thus, for higher values of p (more sensitive the kernel functions), the difference between these two normalizations gets more pronounced, yielding a bigger difference in the classification performance. Furthermore, the correction of the position of the OSH for normalized kernels decreases the classification error further (albeit not significantly) for the four most sensitive kernels. Again, the linear case is left unchanged since both normalizations are then almost identical. The correction brought to the value of b by the previously-introduced method can be measured as being $\frac{|b-b'|}{b} \simeq 5\%$.

5   Conclusions

When considering a classification machine in computer vision, the preprocessing stage is of crucial importance. In particular when dealing with SVMs, this stage can influence dramatically the results of the classification. In this article, we mentioned that considering the preprocessing stage can be equivalent to studying the kernel functions of SVMs. In this perspective, we discussed one of the most basic types of preprocessing, namely normalization. Normalization was first considered in the input space and it was noticed that this preprocessing was not appropriate when considering SVMs. A natural extension is to move into the feature space by considering normalization of the kernel functions. Since classification is performed in this space, a correction of the position of the OSH was introduced to better suit the normalized kernels. This novel algorithm is shown to have the same optimal solutions for w as the standard SV algorithm, but the considered correction is introduced in the final computation of the position of the OSH. Numerical experiments corroborated that normalization in the feature space outperformed the one in the input space and that the correction of the SV algorithm was revealed to be most effective.

Acknowledgments. The fruitful discussions with W. Gerstner, who has introduced me to this subject while staying at the EPFL, are highly appreciated. Reading of the last version was done by B. Schölkopf to whom the author expresses his thanks.

References

[1] B. Schölkopf. *Support Vector Learning*. R. Oldenburg Verlag, Munich, 1997.
[2] B. Schölkopf, C.J.C. Burges & A.J. Smola. *Advances in Kernel Methods*. The MIT Press, MA, 1999.
[3] C. Cortes & V. Vapnik. *Support-Vector Networks*. Machine Learning, Kluwer Academic Publishers, 273-297, 1995.
[4] S. Haykins. *Neural Networks: a Comprehensive Approach*. Prentice Hall, 1999.
[5] R. Herbrich & T. Graepel. *A PAC-Bayesian Margin Bound for Linear Classifiers: Why SVMs work*. Advances in Neural Information System Processing 13, 2001 (in press).
[6] B. Schölkopf, J. C. Platt, J. Shawe-Taylor, A. Smola & R. C. Williamson. *Estimating the Support of a High-Dimensional Distribution*. Technical Report MSR-TR-99-87, 2000.
[7] M. Pontil & A. Verri. *Support Vector Machines for 3D Object Recognition*. IEEE Transactions on Pattern Analysis and Machine Intelligence 20, 637-646, 1998.
[8] W. Maass. *On the Computational Power of Winner-Take-All*. Neural Computation 12, 2519-2535, 2000.

Solving Multi-class Pattern Recognition Problems with Tree-Structured Support Vector Machines

Friedhelm Schwenker

University of Ulm
Department of Neural Information Processing
D-89069 Ulm
schwenker@informatik.uni-ulm.de
http://www.informatik.uni-ulm.de/ni/Mitarbeiter/FSchwenker.html

Abstract. Support vector machines (SVM) are learning algorithms derived from statistical learning theory. The SVM approach was originally developed for binary classification problems. In this paper SVM architectures for multi-class classification problems are discussed, in particular we consider binary trees of SVMs to solve the multi-class problem. Numerical results for different classifiers on a benchmark data set of handwritten digits are presented.

1 Introduction

Statistical learning theory developed by V. Vapnik formalizes the task of learning from examples and describes it as a problem of statistics with finite sample size [1]. Originally, the SVM approach was developed for two-class or binary classification. The N-class classification problem is defined as follows: Given a set of M training vectors $(x^\mu, y^\mu)_{\mu=1}^M$, with input vector $x^\mu \in \mathbb{R}^d$ and with $y^\mu \in \{1, \ldots, N\}$ as the class label of input x^μ. Find a decision function $F : \mathbb{R}^d \to \{1, \ldots, N\}$ mapping an input x to a class label y. Multi-class classification problems (where the number of classes N is larger than 2) are often solved using voting schemes based on the combiniation of binary decision functions. One approach is constructing N binary classifiers (e.g. a SVM network), one for each class, together with a maximum detection across the classifier outputs to classifiy an input vector x. This *one-against-rest* strategy is widely used in the pattern recognition literatur. Another classification scheme is the *one-against-one* strategy, where $\binom{N}{2}$ binary classifiers are constructed—separating each pair of classes, together with a majority voting scheme to classify the input vectors. A different approach to solve a N-class pattern recognition problem is to build a hierachy or tree of binary classifiers. Each node of the graph is a classifier performing a predefined classification subtask. In this procedure the hierarchy of subtasks has to be determined before the classifiers are trained.

2 Support Vector Learning

In this section we briefly review the basic ideas of support vector learning and present four multi-class classification techniques which may be applied to SVMs.

B. Radig and S. Florczyk (Eds.): DAGM 2001, LNCS 2191, pp. 283–290, 2001.

SVMs were initially developed to classify data points of linear separable data sets [6,9]. In this case a training set consisting of M examples (x^μ, y^μ), $x^\mu \in \mathbb{R}^d$, and $y^\mu \in \{-1,1\}$ can be divided up into two sets by a separating hyperplane. Such a hyperplane is determined by a weight vector $b \in \mathbb{R}^d$ and a bias or threshold $\theta \in \mathbb{R}$ satisfying the separating contraints

$$y^\mu(\langle x^\mu, b\rangle + \theta) \geq 1 \quad \mu = 1, \ldots, M.$$

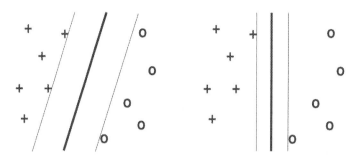

(a) Optimal separating hyperplane with a large margin.

(b) Separating hyperplane with a smaller margin.

Fig. 1. Binary classification problem. The examples of the two different classes are linear separable.

The distance between the separating hyperplane and the closed data points of the training set is called the margin. The separating hyperplane with maximal margin is unique and can be expressed by a linear combination of those training examples (so-called support vectors) lying exactly at the margin has the form

$$H(x) = \sum_{\mu=1}^{M} \alpha_\mu^* y^\mu \langle x, x^\mu\rangle + \alpha_0^*.$$

Here $\alpha_1^*, \ldots, \alpha_M^*$ is the solution optimizing the functional

$$Q(\alpha) = \sum_{\mu=1}^{M} \alpha_\mu - \frac{1}{2} \sum_{\mu,\nu=1}^{M} \alpha_\mu \alpha_\nu y^\mu y^\nu \langle x^\mu, x^\nu\rangle$$

subject to the constraints $\alpha_\mu \geq 0$ for all $\mu = 1, \ldots, M$ and $\sum_{\mu=1}^{M} \alpha_\mu y^\mu = 0$. Then a training vector x^μ is a support vector if the corresponding coefficient $\alpha_\mu^* > 0$. Then it is $b = \sum_{\mu=1}^{M} \alpha_\mu x^\mu$ and the bias α_0^* is determined by a single support vector (x^s, y^s): $\alpha_0^* = y^s - \langle x^s, b\rangle$.

The SVM approach can be extended to the nonseparable situation and to the regression problem. In most applications (regression or pattern recognition problems) linear solutions are insufficient, so it is common to define an appropriate set of nonlinear mappings $g := (g_1, g_2, \ldots)$, transforming the input vectors x^μ into a vector $g(x^\mu)$ which is element of a new feature space $\mathcal{H}$. Then the separating hyperplane can be constructed in the feature space $\mathcal{H}$. Provided $\mathcal{H}$ is a Hilbert space, the explicit mapping $g(x)$ does not need to be known since it can implicitly defined by a kernel function $K(x, x^\mu) = \langle g(x), g(x^\mu) \rangle$ representing the inner product of the feature space. Using a kernel function K satisfying the condition of Mercer's theorem (see [9]), the separating hyperplane is given by

$$H(x) = \sum_{\mu=1}^{M} \alpha_\mu y^\mu K(x, x^\mu) + \alpha_0.$$

The coefficients α_μ can be found by solving the optimization problem

$$Q(\alpha) = \sum_{\mu=1}^{M} \alpha_\mu - \frac{1}{2} \sum_{\mu,\nu=1}^{M} \alpha_\mu \alpha_\nu y^\mu y^\nu K(x^\mu, x^\nu)$$

subject to the contraints $0 \leq \alpha_\mu \leq C$ for all $\mu = 1, \ldots, M$ and $\sum_{\mu=1}^{M} \alpha_\mu y^\mu = 0$ where C is a predefined positive number. An important kernel function satisfying Mercers condition is the Gaussian kernel function (also used in this paper)
$$K(x, y) = e^{-\frac{\|x-y\|_2^2}{2\sigma^2}}.$$

3   Multi-class Classification

In many real world applications, e.g. speech recognition, or optical character recognition, a multi-class pattern recognition problem has to be solved. The SVM classifier is a binary classifier. Various approaches have been developed in order to deal with multi-class classification problems. The following strategies can be applied to build N-class classifiers utilizing binary SVM classifiers.

One-against-rest classifiers. In this method N different classifiers are constructed, one classifier for each class. Here the l-th classifier is trained on the whole training data set in order to classify the members of class l against the rest. For this, the training examples have to be re-labeled: Members of the l-th class are labeled to 1; members of the other classes to -1. In the classification phase the classifier with the maximal output defines the estimated class label of the current input vector.

One-against-one classifiers. For each possible pair of classes a binary classifier is calculated. Each classifier is trained on a subset of the training set containing only training examples of the two involved classes. As for the *one-against-rest* strategy the training sets have to be re-labeled. All $N(N-1)/2$ classifiers are combined through a majority voting scheme to estimate the final classification [2,3]. Here the class with the maximal number of votes among all $N(N-1)/2$ classifiers is the estimation.

Hierarchies/trees of binary SVM classifiers. Here the multi-class classification problem is decomposed into a series of binary classification sub-problems organised in a hierarchical scheme; see Figure 2. We discuss this approach in the next section.

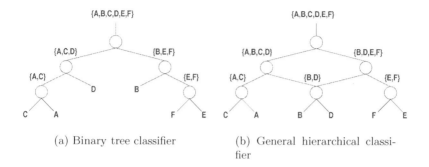

| (a) Binary tree classifier | (b) General hierarchical classifier |

Fig. 2. Two examples of hierarchical classifiers. The graphs are directed acyclic graphs with a single root node at the top of the graph and with terminal nodes (leaves) at the bottom. Individual classes are represented in the leaves, and the other nodes within the graph are classifiers performing a binary decision task, which is defined through the annotations of the incoming and the outgoing edges.

Weston and Watkins proposed in [10] an extension of the binary SVM approch to solve the N-class classification problem directly.

4   Classifier Hierarchies

4.1   Confusion Classes

One of the most important problems in multi-class pattern recognition problems is the existence of confusion classes. A confusion class is a subset of the set of the classes $\{1, \ldots, N\}$ where the feature vectors are very similar and a small amount of noise in the measured features may lead to misclassifications. For example, in OCR the measured features for members of the classes o, O, 0 and Q are typically very similar, so usually {o, O, 0, Q} defines a confusion class. The major idea of hierarchical classification is first to make a coarse discrimination between confusion classes and then a finer discrimination within the confusion classes [5].

In Figure 2 examples of hierarchical classifiers are depicted. Each node within the graph represents a binary classifier discriminating feature vectors of a confusion class into one of two smaller confusion classes or possibly into individual classes. The terminal nodes of the graph (leaves) represent these individual classes, and the other nodes are classifiers performing a binary decision task, thus these nodes have exactly two children. Nodes within the graph may have more than one incoming edge. Figure 2a shows a tree-structured classifier, where each node has exactly one incoming edge. In Figure 2b a more general classifier structure defined through a special directed acyclic graph is depicted. In the following we restrict our considerations to tree structured SVMs.

4.2   Building Classifier Trees by Unsupervised Clustering

The classification subtask is defined through the annotations of the incoming and outgoing edges of the node. Let us consider for example the SVM classifier at the root of the tree in Figure 2a. The label of the incoming edge is $\{A, \ldots, F\}$, so for this (sub-)tree a 6-class classification task is given. The edges to the children are annotated with $\{A, C, D\}$ (left child) and $\{B, E, F\}$ (right child). This means that this SVM has to classify feature vectors into confusion class $\{A, C, D\}$ or $\{B, E, F\}$. To achieve this, all members of the six classes $\{A, \ldots, F\}$ have to be re-labeled: Feature vectors with class labels A, C, or D get the new label -1 and those with class label B, E, or F get the new label 1. After this re-labeling procedure the SVM is trained as described in the previous section. Note, that re-labeling has to be done for each classifier training.

We have not answered the question how to construct this subset-tree. One approach to construct such a tree is to divide the set of classes K into disjoint subsets K_1 and K_2 utilizing clustering. In clustering and vector quantization a set of representative prototypes $\{c_1, \ldots, c_k\} \subset \mathbb{R}^d$ is determined by unsupervised learning from the feature vectors x^μ, $\mu = 1, \ldots, M$ of the training set. For each prototype c_j the Voronoi cells R_j and clusters C_j are defined by

$$R_j := \{x \in \mathbb{R}^d \ : \ \|c_j - x\|_2 = \min_i \|c_i - x\|_2\}$$

and

$$C_j := R_j \cap \{x^\mu \ : \ \mu = 1, \ldots, M\}.$$

The relative frequency of members of class i in cluster j is

$$p_{ij} := \frac{|\Omega_i \cap C_j|}{|C_j|}.$$

For class i the set Ω_i is define by

$$\Omega_i = \{x^\mu \ : \ \mu = 1, \ldots, M, \ y^\mu = i\}.$$

The k-means clustering with $k = 2$ cluster centers c_1 and c_2 define hyperplane in the feature space $\mathbb{R}^d$ separating two sets of feature vectors. From the corresponding clusters C_1 and C_2 a partition of the classes K into two subsets K_1 and K_2 can be achieved through the following assignment:

$$K_j := \{i \in K \ : \ j = \mathrm{argmax}\ \{p_{i1}, p_{i2}\}\}, \quad j = 1, 2.$$

Recursively applied, this procedure leads to a binary tree as depicted in Figure 2.

5   Application and Conclusion

The data set used for evaluating the performance of the classifier consists of 20,000 handwritten digits (2,000 samples per class). The digits, normalized in height and width, are represented by a 16×16 matrix (g_{ij}) where $g_{ij} \in \{0, \dots, 255\}$ is a value from a 8 bit gray scale (for details concerning the data set see [4]). The whole data set has been divided into a set of 10,000 training samples and a set of 10,000 test samples. The training set has been used to design the classifiers, and the test set for testing the performance of the classifiers.

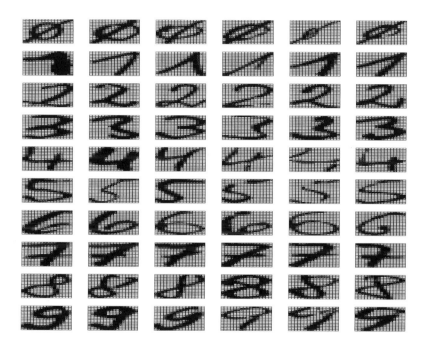

Fig. 3. Exampels of the handwritten digits.

Results for the following classifiers and training procedures are given:

MLP: Multilayer perceptrons with a single hidden layer of sigmoidal units (Fermi transfer function) trained by standard backpropagation; 100 training epoches; 200 hidden units.

1NN: 1-nearest neighbour classifier.

LVQ: 1-nearest neighbour classifier trained with Kohonen's software package with OLVQ1 and LVQ3; 50 training epoches; 500 prototypes.

RBF: RBF networks with a single hidden layer of Gaussian RBFs trained by standard backpropagation with 50 epoches training the full parameter set; 200 hidden units each with a single scaling parameter.

SVM-1-R: SVM with Gaussian kernel function; *one-against-rest* strategy; NAG library for optimisation.

SVM-1-1: As **SVM-1-R** but with the *one-against-one* strategy.

SVM-TR: Binary tree of SVM networks. The classifier tree has been build by k-means clustering with $k = 2$. In Figure 4 a representative tree is depicted which was found by clustering experiments and which was used for the training of the tree of SVMs.

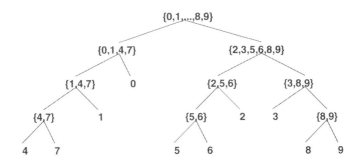

Fig. 4. Tree of subclasses for the handwritten digits data set.

For this data set further results may be found in the final `StatLog` report (see p. 135-138 in [4] and in [8]). The error rates for **1NN**, **LVQ**, and **MLP** classifiers are similar in both studies. The **1NN** and **LVQ** classifiers perform well. RBF networks trained by backpropagation learning and support vector learning show the best classification performance. A significant difference between the different multi-class classification strategies *one-against-rest*, *one-against-one*, and the binary SVM classifier tree could not be found.

Table 1. Results for the handwritten digits.

Classifier	MLP	1NN	LVQ	RBF	SVM-1-R	SVM-1-1	SVM-TR
error [%]	2.41	2.34	3.01	1.51	1.40	1.37	1.39

We have presented different strategies for the N-class classification problem utilising the SVM approach. In detail we have discussed a novel tree structured SVM classifier architecture. For the design of binary classifier trees we introduced unsupervised clustering or vector quantisation methods. We have presented numerical experiments on a benchmark data set. Here, the suggested SVM tree model shows remarkable classification results which were in the range of other classifier schemes. Similar resluts have been found for the recognition of 3D objects (see [7]), but further evaluation of this method experiments with different multi-class problems (data sets with many classes) have to be made.

References

1. C. Cortes and V. Vapnik. Support vector networks. *Machine Learning*, 20:273–297, 1995.
2. J.H. Friedman. Another approach to polychotomous classification. Technical report, Stanford University, Department of Statistics, 1996.
3. U. Kreßel. Pairwise classification and support vector machines. In B. Schölkopf, C. Burges, and A. Smola, editors, *Advances in Kernel Methods*, chapter 15, pages 255–268. The MIT Press, 1999.
4. D. Michie, D.J. Spiegelhalter, and C.C. Taylor. *Machine Learning, Neural and Statistical Classification*. Ellis Horwood, 1994.
5. M. Nadler and E.P. Smith. *Pattern Recognition Engineering*. John Wiley & Sons Inc. 1992.
6. A. Schölkopf, C. Burges, and A. Smola. *Advances in Kernel Methods — Support Vector Learning*. MIT Press, 1998.
7. F. Schwenker, H.A. Kestler, S. Simon, , and G. Palm. 3D Object Recognition for Autonomous Mobile Robots Utilizing Support Vector Machines. In *Proceedings of the 2001 IEEE International Symbosium on Comutational Intelligence in Robotics and Automation*. 2001 (in press).
8. F. Schwenker, H.K. Kestler, and G. Palm. Three Learning Phases for Radial Basis Function Networks. *Neural Networks*, 14:439–458, 2001.
9. V.N. Vapnik. *Statistical Learning Theory*. John Wiley and Sons, 1998.
10. J. Weston and C. Watkins. Multi-class support vector machines. Technical Report CSD-TR-98-04, Royal Holloway, University of London, Department of Computer Science, 1998.

Facial Expression Recognition with Pseudo-3D Hidden Markov Models

Frank Hülsken, Frank Wallhoff, and Gerhard Rigoll

Dept. of Computer Science, Faculty of Electrical Engineering,
Gerhard-Mercator-University Duisburg, D-47057 Duisburg,
{huelsken,wallhoff,rigoll}@fb9-ti.uni-duisburg.de,
WWW home page: http://www.fb9-ti.uni-duisburg.de

Abstract. We introduce a novel approach to gesture recognition, based on Pseudo-3D Hidden Markov Models (P3DHMMs). This technique is capable of integrating spatially and temporally derived features in an elegant way, thus enabling the recognition of different dynamic face-expressions. Pseudo-2D Hidden Markov Models have been utilized for two dimensional problems such as face recognition. P3DHMMs can be considered as an extension of the 2D case, where the so-called super-states in P3DHMM encapsulate P2DHMMs. With our new approach image sequences can efficiently and successfully be processed. Because the 'ordinary' training of P3DHMMs is time expensive and can destroy the 3D approach, an improved training is presented in this paper. The feasibility of the usage of P3DHMMs is demonstrated by a number of experiments on a person independent database, which consists of different image sequences of 4 face-expressions from 6 persons.

1 Introduction

The recognition of facial expression is a research area with increasing importance for human computer interfaces. There are a number of difficulties due to the variation of facial expression across the human population and to the context-dependent variation even for the same individual. Even for humans, it is often difficult to recognize the correct facial expression (see [2]), especially on a still image.

An automatic facial expression recognition system can be generally decomposed into three parts. First the detection and location of faces in a scene, second the facial expression feature extraction and the facial expression classification.

The first part has been already studied by many researchers and because of the difficulties to find faces in a cluttered scene, it seems that the most successful systems are based on neutral networks as presented in [7]. In this paper, we do not address the face detection problem.

Facial expression feature extraction deals with the problem of finding features for the most appropriate representation of the face images for recognition. There are mainly two options to deal with the images. On the one hand a geometric feature-based system is used, as for e.g. in [1]. These features are robust to variation in scale, size, head orientation and location of the face in an image,

B. Radig and S. Florczyk (Eds.): DAGM 2001, LNCS 2191, pp. 291–297, 2001.
© Springer-Verlag Berlin Heidelberg 2001

but the computation is very expensive. The second approach for extracting features is to deal with the entire pixel image. For this purpose one can use signal processing methods such as Discrete Cosine Transformation (DCT) or Garbor Transformation (see [9]), to obtain another representation of the image.

The facial expression classification module computes the result of the recognized expression. In many recognition systems, neural networks are used. In this paper the classification part is realized by means of Hidden Markov Models (HMMs). A good overview is given in [6]. Because our task is to recognize facial expressions on image sequences instead of a single picture, the use of Pseudo-3D Hidden Markov Models (P3DHMMs) is practicable. For image recognition Pseudo-2D Hidden Markov Models were applied with excellent results (see [3], [8], [4]). P3DHMMs have been previously utilized by Müller et al. [5] for image sequence recognition on a crane signal database consisting of 12 different predefined gestures.

2   Data Set and System Overview

For the training and test database we recorded video sequences with 25 frames per second with a resolution of 320×240 pixels. The camera was adjusted in the way that the head was almost in front pose. Original images have been rescaled and cropped such that the eyes are roughly at the same position (resolution: 196×172 pixels) The database contains 96 takes of 6 persons. Each sequence has 15 frames. The image sequence starts with a neutral facial expression and changes to one of the 4 categories of expression which are anger, surprise, disgust and happiness. Fig. 1 shows the different expressions in our database. It shall be pointed out again here that these expressions are *dynamic* expressions, where the real meaning of the expressions can be only identified after the complete sequence has been observed. The still images in Fig.1 are frames captured mostly at the end of each sequence. The complexity of the recognition task is largely resulting from the fact that each person has a different personal way of performing each expression and that some individuals in the test database preferred a more moderate rather than an expressive way of performing the face gestures, where even human observers had difficulties of identifying these expressions correctly on the spot.

Fig. 1. Facial expression database: Examples for anger, surprise, disgust and happiness, from left to right

The recognition system consists of three processing levels: preprocessing, feature extraction and statistical classification. The best results achieved we with the following system. Starting with the original image sequence of the face expression, the preprocessing calculates the difference image sequence. The feature extraction uses DCT-transformation to produce a vector for each frame of the difference image sequence. A P3DHMM based recognition module classifies the face expression, represented by the feature vector sequence. The output of the system is the recognized expression.

2.1 Preprocessing

The difference image sequence is calculated by subtracting the pixel value at the same position (x,y) of adjacent frames of the original image sequence.

$$D'(x, y, t) = P(x, y, t) - P(x, y, t - 1) \tag{1}$$

Thus the difference image contains positive and negative pixel values. In order to reduce noise we apply a threshold operation to the difference image. Every pixel with an absolute value smaller than the threshold is set to zero.

$$D(x, y, t) = \begin{cases} 0 & : \|D'(x, y, t)\| < S\| \\ D'(x, y, t) & : \|D'(x, y, t)\| \geq S\| \end{cases} \tag{2}$$

Obviously, the size of the grey values of the difference image in such a frame indicates the intensity of the motion for each spatial position (x,y) of the image. If one imagine the pixel values of the difference image as a "mountain area" of elevation D(x,y) at point (x,y), then this mountain area can be approximately considered as a distribution of the movement over the image space in x- and y-direction.

2.2 Feature Extraction

Each image of a sequence is scanned with a sampling window from top to bottom and from left to right. The pixels in the sampling window of the size $N \times N$ are transformed using a ordinary DCT according to Eq.3.

$$C(u, v) = \alpha(u)\alpha(v) \sum_{x=0}^{N-1} \sum_{y=0}^{N-1} f(x, y) \cdot \cos\left(\frac{(2x + 1)u\pi}{2N}\right) \cos\left(\frac{(2y + 1)v\pi}{2N}\right) \tag{3}$$

The sampling window is shifted so that we have a certain overlapping to a previous frame. To reduce the size of the feature vector only the first few coefficients, located on the left top triangle of the transformed image block, are taken, because these coefficients contain the most important information of the image.

2.3   Statistical Classification

The recognition of image sequences can be considered as a 3-dimensional pattern recognition problem, where the first 2 dimensions are characterized by the horizontal and vertical components of each image frame and the 3rd dimension is the time. Due to very encouraging results we obtained recently on other related problems in that area (see [5]), we favored the use of Pseudo-3D Hidden Markov Models for this demanding task. P3DHMMs can be considered as a very new paradigm in image sequence processing and have been mainly pioneered by our research group for image sequence recognition problems, where time-varying as well as static information is of crucial importance for the recognition performance. The reason that facial expression recognition is a problem that falls exactly under this category can be explained in the following way: As already previously mentioned, one possible approach to facial expression recognition would be the localization of facial cues such as eye brows or lips in order to use these parameters as descriptors for typical expressions. This would have firstly resulted into enormous problems in detecting the correct cues (especially in person-independent mode) and it would have been secondly very difficult to evaluate a dynamic sequence of these cues. By investigating the entire face image as is done in our approach, basically all face areas are used as cues and we do not have the problem to miss any of these cues, either in defining or detecting them. On the other hand, processing the entire face includes also the danger that the system degenerates to a face recognition system instead of a facial expression recognition system. An unknown template might for instance been assigned to a reference pattern not because it contains the right expression but because the overall face is close to the face represented in the reference pattern. Additionally, the facial expression can be only correctly identified if the change over time is taken into account. Therefore, timing as well as static information (in our case the cues implicitly included in an image frame) has to be evaluated for high performance facial expression recognition and exactly this is our motivation for the usage of P3DHMMs. Fig.2 shows the principal structures of P2DHMMs and P3DHMMs.

HHMs are finite non-deterministic state machines with a fixed number of states N with a N-dimensional associated output density functions b as well as transition probabilities, described by a $N \times N$-dimensional transition matrix $a_{i,j}$.

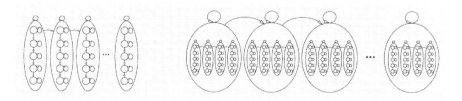

Fig. 2. General structures of P2DHMM and P3DHMM

So a HMM $\lambda(\boldsymbol{\pi}, \boldsymbol{a}, \boldsymbol{b})$ is fully described by

$$
\begin{array}{lll}
S = \{s_1, s_2, ..., s_N\} & & \text{State set} \\
V = \{v_1, v_2, ..., v_M\} & & \text{Possible output set} \\
(a_{i,j}) = P[q_{t+i} = s_j \mid q_t = s_i] & , 1 \leq i, j \leq N & \text{State transition probability} \\
b_i(k) = P[v_k \text{ at } t \mid q_t = s_i] & , 1 \leq i \leq N, 1 \leq k \leq N & \text{Output density function} \\
\pi_i = P[q_1 = s_i] & , 1 \leq i \leq N & \text{Initial start distribution}
\end{array}
\tag{4}
$$

where q_t denotes the the actual state at time t. After training the different models λ with the Baum-Welch algorithm, the probability $P(O \mid \lambda)$ for a given observation sequence $O = O_1 O_2 \cdots O_T$ (with $O_i \in V$) can be evaluated with the Viterbi algorithm. The model with the highest probability is assigned with the observation. For a detailed explanation see [6].

A P2DHMM is an extension of the one-dimensional HMM paradigm, which has been developed in order to model two-dimensional data. The state alignment of adjacent columns is calculated independently of each other, thus the model is called pseudo 2-dimensional. The states in horizontal direction are called superstates, and each superstate encapsulates a one-dimensional HMM in vertical direction. By applying this encapsulation principle a second time to the 2D HMMs, we can obtain the P3DHMM structure with superstates that can be interpreted as start-of-image states. Each superstate now consists of a P2DHMM. Samaria shows in [8], that a P2DHMM can be transformed into an equivalent one-dimensional HMM by inserting special start-of-line states and features. Consequently, it is also possible to transform P3DHMMs into 1D linear HMMs, which is a crucial procedure for the feasibility of the training and recognition process associated with HMMs.

Fig.3 shows an equivalent 1D-HMM of a $4 \times 3 \times 2$ P3DHMM with start-of-line states. These states generate a high probability for the emission of start-of-

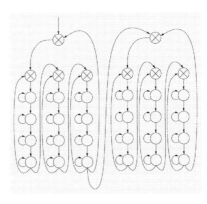

Fig. 3. Augmented $4 \times 3 \times 2$ P3DHMM with transitions(arrows), states(circle) and superstates(crossed)

line features. To distinguish the start-of-line features from all possible ordinary features, the features of these have to be set to completely different values. Also the feature vectors have to be edited, so that the assignment for the states works correctly. Values for the superstates have to be inserted after each line for the start-of-line states and after each picture for the start-of-image states. The major advantage of this transformation is the fact that it is possible to train these models with the standard Baum-Welch algorithm and to use the well-known Viterbi algorithm for recognition.

3   Experiments and Results

The recognition system was tested on different sizes for the HMMs and different feature extraction parameters. The best results were achieved with a DCT block with a size of 16×16 pixels with 75% overlapping. The feature vectors consisted of the first 10 coefficients of the DCT block matrix. For the recognition, four superstates with (4×4) P2DHMMs per superstate have been used as configuration of the P3DHMMs. A single P3DHMM is trained for each face expression using 3 sequences at a time of 6 different persons.

Because the full training of P3DHMMs is very expensive in time, a novel improved training approach is introduced here: Since a P3DHMM contains P2DHMMs, the training of the models can be broken down into two parts: First all image sequences representing one facial expression are subdivided into sections, more or less equally distributed over the length of the sequence. Thus our P3DHMM contains 4 P2DHMMs, we use 4 sections. Since one can expect that the outcome of the P3DHMM learning procedure is that roughly each quarter of the sequence will be assigned to a corresponding P2DHMMs of the 4 superstates in the P3DHMM, each isolated P2DHMM was first separately trained on the corresponding quarter of the image sequence. Afterwards the trained P2DHMMs were combined to a P3DHMM. That can be done very easily. Between the start-of-image states the states of the P2DHMMs can be inserted. Only the transitions have to be modified, especially the transition to the end state of the P2DHMM have to be redirected to the next start-of-image state and so to the beginning of the next P2DHMM. For initialization, the P3DHMM is trained with the complete sequences. The total time saving of the training is about 50% of the normal training. Another advantage of that kind of training is the initialization of the time structure into the P3DHMM.

Table 1 shows the recognition rates achieved in the experiments and displays the improvement through the use of multiple Gaussian mixtures. For this the probability density function becomes a sum of several Gaussian mixtures so that the feature vectors are devided into statistically independent streams. Also here the training could be done faster, if the containing P2DHMMs mixed up separately, before the combined P3DHMM is trained. in Section 2, we believe that the person-independent recognition of the facial expressions with an accuracy of close to 90% is an already very respectable result. We expect even further improvements in the near future.

Table 1. Recognition rates achieved in the experiments

rec.rate	1 Mixture	2 Mixture	3 Mixture	4 Mixture	5 Mixture
on rank 1	70.83%	75.00%	79.17%	87.50%	87.50%
on rank 2	79.17%	87.50%	87.50%	95.83%	95.83%
on rank 3	95.83%	100.00%	100.00%	100.00%	100.00%

4 Summary

Facial expression recognition based on pseudo three-dimensional Hidden Markov Models has been presented. This modeling technique achieved very good recognition rates with simple pre-processing methods, due to the powerful classification capabilities of the novel P3DHMM paradigm. The problem of the time intensive training effort for the P3DHMMs has be elegantly solved due to our new initialization and partial training techniques. The advantage of P3DHMMs mainly lies in the integration of spatial and temporally derived features, and their joint warping capabilities. Thus, we strongly believe that this novel approach has clear advantages over other, more traditional approaches in such a special area as facial expression recognition, where we need exactly the capabilites provided by P3DHMMs. Our results seem to confirm and underpin this assumption.

References

1. R. Chellappa, C. Wilson, and S. Sirohey. Human and Machine Recognition of Faces: A Survey. *Proceedings of IEEE*, 83(5):705–740, May 1995.
2. P. Ekmann and W. Friesen. Unmasking the face: A guide to recognizing emotions from facial expressions. *Consulting Psychologists Press CA*, 1975.
3. S. Kuo and O. Agazzi. Keyword Spotting in Poorly Printing Documents Using Pseudo 2D-Hidden Markov Models. *IEEE Trans. on Pattern Recognition and Machine Intelligence*, 16(8):842–848, Apr 1994.
4. S. Müller, S. Eickeler, and G. Rigoll. High Performance Face Recognition Using Pseudo 2D-Hidden Markov Models. In *Proc. European Control Conference*, Karlsruhe, Germany, Aug. 1999.
5. S. Müller, S. Eickeler, and G. Rigoll. Pseudo 3-D HMMs for Image Sequence Recognition. In *IEEE Intern. Conference on Image Processing*, Kobe, Japan, Oct. 1999.
6. L. Rabiner. A Tutorial on Hidden Markov Models and Selected Applications in Speech Recognition. *Proc. of the IEEE*, 77(2):257–285, Feb 1989.
7. H. Rowley, S. Baluja, and T. Kanade. Neural Network-Based Face Detection. *IEEE Transactions on Pattern Analysis and Machine Intelligence*, 20(1):23–38, Jan 1998.
8. F. Samaria. *Face Recognition Using Hidden Markov Models*. PhD thesis, Engineering Department, Cambridge University, Cambridge, Oct 1994.
9. Z. Zhang, M. Lyons, M. Schuster, and S. Akamatsu. Comparison Between Geometry-Based and Gabor-Wavelets-Based Facial Expression Using Multi-Layer Perceptron. *Proceedings of the IEEE*, Apr 1998.

Towards Online Pose Measurement for Robots

Jan Böhm, Jürgen Hefele, and Dieter Fritsch

email: first.last@ifp.uni-stuttgart.de
Institute for Photogrammetry
University of Stuttgart
Geschwister-Scholl-Str. 24, 70174 Stuttgart, Germany

Abstract. We present a photogrammetric system for on-line pose measurement of a robot. The system is based on photogrammetric measurement techniques, namely resection. We describe the theoretical foundations of our approach as well as early details of our implementation and hardware set-up. The results achieved are compared to those of a commercial ball-bar system.

1 Introduction

While industrial robots typically can achieve a repeatability of $0.1\ mm$ or less, their absolute accuracy can be in the range of only $1\,mm$ or worse. Many new applications in robotics, including flexible optical measurement, require improved absolute accuracy. Photogrammetry has been used for several years to perform off-line calibration in order to increase accuracy. However when operating a robot under shop-floor conditions the accuracy is expected to decrease again over time. Clearly an on-line pose correction is desirable. We present a system for the on-line pose measurement based on photogrammetry.

2 Photogrammetric System

Photogrammetric measurement is based on the classical collinearity equations defining the condition, that the projection center, a point in object space and its corresponding point on the image plane are on a straight line. Let c be the principal distance of the camera, (X_0, Y_0, Z_0) the principal point, (X, Y, Z) the coordinates of the object point and (x, y) the coordinates of the corresponding image point. Then the collinearity equation is (see [7])

$$x = x_0 - c\frac{(X-X_c)r_{11}+(Y-Y_c)r_{12}+(Z-Z_c)r_{13}}{(X-X_c)r_{31}+(Y-Y_c)r_{32}+(Z-Z_c)r_{33}} = x_0 - c\frac{Z_x}{N}$$
$$y = y_0 - c\frac{(X-X_c)r_{21}+(Y-Y_c)r_{22}+(Z-Z_c)r_{23}}{(X-X_c)r_{31}+(Y-Y_c)r_{32}+(Z-Z_c)r_{33}} = y_0 - c\frac{Z_y}{N}$$

with the condition that r_{ij} are the elements of a 3-D orthogonal rotation matrix. For many applications in photogrammetry the rotation matrix R is parameterized using Cardan angles ω, ϕ, κ. However, it has shown to be favorable

B. Radig and S. Florczyk (Eds.): DAGM 2001, LNCS 2191, pp. 298–304, 2001.

(see [10]) to use a parameterization using quaternions. We use Hamilton normalized quaternions to describe a rotation matrix:

$$R = (I + S)(I - S)^{-1}, \ S = \begin{bmatrix} 0 & -c & b \\ c & 0 & -a \\ -b & a & 0 \end{bmatrix}$$

2.1   Camera Model

While the basic camera model in photogrammetry is the pin-hole camera, additional parameters are used for a more complete description of the imaging device. The following parameters are based on the physical model of D. C. Brown ([1]). We follow the notation for digital cameras presented by C. S. Fraser ([3]). Three parameters K_1, K_2 and K_3 are used to describe the radial distortion. Two parameters P_1 and P_2 describe the decentring distortions. Two parameters b_1 and b_2 describe a difference in scale between the x- and y-axis of the sensor and shearing. To obtain the corrected image coordinates (x, y) the parameters are applied to the distorted image coordinates (x', y') as follows

$$
\begin{aligned}
\overline{x} &= x' - x_0 \\
\overline{y} &= y' - y_0 \\
\triangle x &= \overline{x}r^2 K_1 + \overline{x}r^4 K_2 + \overline{x}r^6 K_3 + (2\overline{x}^2 + r^2)P_1 + 2P_2\overline{xy} + b_1\overline{x} + b_2\overline{y} \\
\triangle y &= \overline{y}r^2 K_1 + \overline{y}r^4 K_2 + \overline{y}r^6 K_3 + 2P_1\overline{xy} + (2\overline{y}^2 + r^2)P_2 \\
x &= \overline{x} + \triangle x \\
y &= \overline{y} + \triangle y
\end{aligned}
$$

Where (x_0, y_0) is the principal point and $r = \sqrt{\overline{x}^2 + \overline{y}^2}$ is the radial distance from the principal point. The camera's parameters are determined in a bundle adjustment using a planar test field. The bundle adjustment process is carried out before-hand.

2.2   Resection

The problem of (spatial) resection involves the determination of the six parameters of the exterior orientation of a camera station. We use a two-stage process to solve the resection problem. A closed-form solution using four points gives the initial values for an iterative refinement using all control points.

Closed-form Resection. Several alternatives for a closed form solution to the resection problem were given in literature. We follow the approach suggested by Fischler et. al. [2]. Named the "Perspective 4 Point Problem" their algorithm solves for the three unknown coordinates of the projection center when the coordinates of four control points lying in a common plane are given. Because the control points are all located on a common plane the mapping in-between image- and object points is a simple plane-to-plane transformation T. The location of the projection center can be extracted from this transformation T when the principal distance of the camera is known. For a detailed description of the formulas please refer to the original publication.

To complete the solution of the resection problem we also need the orientation of the camera in addition to its location. Kraus [8] gives the solution for determining the orientation angles when the coordinates of the projection center are already known. The algorithm makes use of only three of the four points.

Iterative Refinement. The closed-form solution makes use of only four control points. Usually much more control points are available and the solution is more accurate if all observations are used in a least squares adjustment. For an iterative solution, the collinearity equations have to be linearized. This is standard in photogrammetry. While most of the partial derivatives of the classical bundle adjustment remain the same, the elements for rotation have changed because of our use of quaternions . Six new partial derivatives replace the common $\frac{\partial \xi}{\partial \omega}, \frac{\partial \xi}{\partial \phi}, \dots$:

$$\frac{\partial \xi}{\partial b} = \frac{-2f}{N^2 D}(-Z_x^2 + cZ_xZ_y - aZ_yN - N^2)$$
$$\frac{\partial \xi}{\partial a} = \frac{-2f}{N^2 D}(cZ_x^2 + Z_xZ_y + bZ_yN + cN^2)$$
$$\frac{\partial \xi}{\partial c} = \frac{-2f}{N^2 D}(-aZ_x^2 - bZ_xZy + Z_yN - aN^2)$$
$$\frac{\partial \eta}{\partial b} = \frac{-2f}{N^2 D}(-Z_xZ_y + aZ_xN + cZ_y^2 + cN^2)$$
$$\frac{\partial \eta}{\partial a} = \frac{-2f}{N^2 D}(cZ_xZ_y - bZ_xN + Z_y^2 + N^2)$$
$$\frac{\partial \eta}{\partial c} = \frac{-2f}{N^2 D}(-aZ_xZ_y - Z_xN - bZ_y^2 - bN^2)$$

Using the results from the closed-form solution as described above, we can now iteratively refine the solution for all control points available.

Simulated Results. Simply using the formulas given above and applying error propagation we can now do a simulation of the resection to predict the expected errors in resection. Assuming a focal length of $12\,mm$ and with a standard pixel size of 6.7 μm, the expected errors in x, y and z for a certain error in image measurement are given in table 1.

3   Implementation

The algorithms described above were implemented in an on-line pose measurement system. The systems components, both mechanical and electronic are described below. In addition the test configuration using an industrial robot is described.

3.1   Hardware

The optical sensor we are using is a Basler A113 camera, with a Sony CCD chip, which has a resolution of 1300×1030 pixels. The camera provides a digital output according to IEEE standard RS644. A frame-grabber is integrated into a standard PC. The digital camera system is superior to an analog camera system since it does not exhibit line jitter problems thus enabling more precise measurements. Schneider-Kreuznach lenses with $12mm$ focal length are mounted onto the camera.

To maximize the signal intensity we use retro-reflective targets and a ring light on the camera. To minimize the effects of external light sources we use near-infrared LEDs as light source and a filter on the lens. (see figure 1, left)

The control points are fixed onto a plane, also used as a calibration plate. We use coded targets to achieve automated identification of the targets. The circular center of the target is used for sub-pixel precise measurement of the targets position. A circular code surrounding the center carries a binary representation of the unique identifier. (see figure 1, center)

The set-up for our experiments consists of a Kuka KR15 robot. It is a six axis robot with a maximum payload of 15 kg at maximum range of 1570 mm. The robot is specified with a repeatability of ± 0.1 mm. The absolute accuracy is not specified.

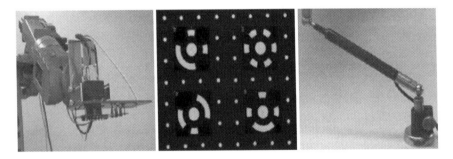

Fig. 1. Left: camera and ring LED mounted onto the robot. Center: part of the test field. Right: Ball-bar tester.

3.2   Image Processing

Image processing is performed on a standard PC. The images are first binarized using an optimal thresholding algorithm introduced by Otsu (see [9]). Then a consistent component labeling is performed to find targets. We discriminate the circular centers from all other 'blobs' by size and a simple shape-test. Since the targets can be smaller than 10 pixels in diameter we do not perform ellipse fitting (see [4]). The center of the target is computed as the weighted centroid.

In addition the elliptic axes and the pose angle are computed. The center, the axes and the angle are used to determine the code ring. The code ring is read with six-times oversampling. The acyclic redundant code provides unique identifiers for up to 352 targets.

In addition to the coded target much smaller uncoded targets were added to the test field. After the closed-form resection has been computed using the coded targets, the approximate position of these targets can be projected onto the image since their three-dimensional location is known from calibration. Thus these additional targets can be easily identified through their position.

3.3   Results

The sensor delivers a frame rate of about 12 frames per second. The implemented system is capable to process a single image in $420ms$. A typical image will contain about 30 coded and about 200 uncoded targets. This gives us a processing speed of 500 targets per second including all image processing steps and the resection. The standard deviations obtained in a first test run are given in table 1.

Table 1. Standard deviations of resection.

standard deviations	simulation		test-run
image measurement	$\frac{1}{5}$pixel	$\frac{1}{10}$pixel	...
resection in x	$0.06\,mm$	$0.03\,mm$	$0.2\,mm$
resection in y	$0.06\,mm$	$0.03\,mm$	$0.2\,mm$
resection in z	$0.02\,mm$	$0.009\,mm$	$0.06\,mm$

4   Circular Test

ISO 230-4 [6] describes the "Circular tests for numerically controlled machine tools". While these test were originally designed for the simultaneous movement of only two axes, they also have valid implications for other machines. When the test is carried out the robot performs a circular motion and a measurement system detects any deviation from the ideal path. The parameters of the test include

1. diameter of the nominal path
2. contouring feed
3. machine axes moved to produce the actual path

The results of the test include the radial deviation F, which is defined as the deviation between the actual path and the nominal path, where the center of the nominal path can be determined either by manual alignment or by least squares adjustment.

4.1   Ball-Bar System

There exist several commercial systems to perform the circular test. We chose as a reference system the Renishaw ball-bar system. The system consists mainly of a linear displacement sensor which is placed between two ball-mounts, one near the tool center point (TCP) of the machine and one in the center of the circular path. The displacement sensor continually measures the distance of the two balls and thereby measures any deviations in the radius of the circular path. (see figure 1, right)

The device has a length of 150 mm, a measurement resolution of 0.1 μm, an approximate accuracy of 1 μm and a measurement range of ±1 mm. It is able to measure the deviation at a frequency of 300 Hz.

For the actual test we programmed a circular path of 149.9 mm to ensure the system will stay within its measurement range. The contouring feed was 10 mm/s. Because the TCP orientation was programmed to be constant, all six axes of the robot were moved to produce the path.

4.2   Photogrammetric Test

For the test of our own system we used exactly the same circular path of the robot. The calibration plate was placed on the floor, the camera looking down onto it. The circular path, the calibration plate and the image plane were all approximately parallel to each other. Our online system continuously records the six parameters of the exterior orientation. The projection center coordinates are used to compute the least squares adjustment of the circular path to determine the center and radius of the ideal path, as suggested by ISO 230-4. The deviation of the measured coordinates of the projection center to the ideal path is the radial deviation. The deviations in the rotation angle is also recorded. This feature is not available in the ball-bar test.

4.3   Results

Figure 2 shows the results of the circular test. We see that currently we are unable to achieve the same accuracies as the commercial ball-bar system. The deviations in rotation mentioned above are significant since the camera is mounted onto the robot with a certain distance (~ 100 mm) from the TCP. Therefore the deviations in the projection center not only represent deviations in the position of the TCP but also in its rotation. We can clearly see from figure 2(c) how extreme deviations in orientation correspond to extreme deviations in position. Since the ball-mount of the ball-bar tester is located much closer (~ 10 mm) to the true TCP, it is less sensitive to errors in rotation.

5   Summary

The implemented system is an improvement of our off-line system published earlier [5]. It has proven to be quite flexible and we believe it can be easily integrated into many application in robotics, especially applications in optical measurement. Currently the accuracies do not compare well to those of a commercial ball-bar system. However the deviations are mostly due to an error in

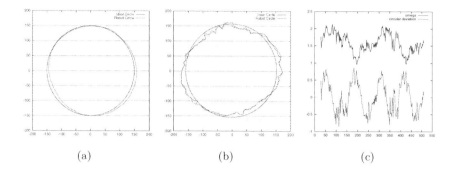

(a)　　　　　　　　　(b)　　　　　　　　　(c)

Fig. 2. Results of the circular test (a) for the ball-bar system the movement of the ball-mount center is shown)and (b) for the photogrammetric system the movement of the camera's projection center is shown in mm. Deviations are magnified by a factor of 25. (c) Angular deviation and radial deviation.

the robots TCP orientation. For future work the deviations measured at the projection center should be re-transformed to the TCP from the known hand-eye calibration matrix. To achieve on-line pose correction the obtained pose information has to be passed directly to the robot control unit.

References

1. Duane C. Brown. Close-range camera calibration. *Photogrammetric Engineering*, 37(8):855–866, 1971.
2. M. A. Fischler and R. C. Bolles. Random sample consensus: A paradigm for model fitting with applications to image analysis and automated cartography. *Communications of the ACM*, 24(6):381–393, June 1981.
3. Clive S. Fraser. Digital camera self-calibration. *ISPRS Journal of Photogrammetry and Remote Sensing*, 52:149–159, 1997.
4. Clive S. Fraser and Juliang Shao. An image mensuration strategy for automated vision metrology. In A. Gruen and H. Kahmen, editors, *OPtical 3-D Measurement techniques IV*, pages 187–197. Wichmann, September 1997.
5. Juergen Hefele and Claus Brenner. Robot pose correction using photogrammetric tracking. In *Machine Vision and Three-Dimensional Imagin Systems for Inspection and Metrology*. SPIE, SP, November 2000.
6. ISO. *Test code for machine tools - Part 4: Circular tests for numerically controlled machine tools*, August 1996.
7. K. Kraus. *Photogrammetrie Band 1*. Dümmler, 1984.
8. K. Kraus. *Photogrammetrie Band 2*. Dümmler, 1996.
9. N. Otsu. A threshold selection method from grey-level histograms. *SMC*, 9:62–66, January 1979.
10. Senlin Zhang. Anwendungen der drehmatrix in hamilton normierten quaternionen bei der bündelblockausgleichung. *ZfV*, 4:203–210, 1994.

Optimal Camera Parameter Selection for State Estimation with Applications in Object Recognition

J. Denzler[1], C.M. Brown[2], and H. Niemann[1]

[1] Chair for Pattern Recognition, Department of Computer Science
Universität Erlangen-Nürnberg, Martensstr. 3, 91058 Erlangen
denzler@informatik.uni-erlangen.de
http://www.mustererkennung.de
[2] Computer Science Department
University of Rochester, USA
brown@cs.rochester.edu
http://www.cs.rochester.edu

Abstract. In this paper we introduce a formalism for optimal camera parameter selection for iterative state estimation. We consider a framework based on Shannon's information theory and select the camera parameters that maximize the mutual information, i.e. the information that the captured image conveys about the true state of the system. The technique explicitly takes into account the a priori probability governing the computation of the mutual information. Thus, a sequential decision process can be formed by treating the a posteriori probability at the current time step in the decision process as the a priori probability for the next time step. The convergence of the decision process can be proven.

We demonstrate the benefits of our approach using an active object recognition scenario. The results show that the sequential decision process outperforms a random strategy, both in the sense of recognition rate and number of views necessary to return a decision.

1 Introduction

State estimation from noisy image data is one of the key problems in computer vision. Besides the inherent difficulties with developing a state estimator that returns decent results in most situation, one important question is whether we can optimize state estimation by choosing the right sensor data as input. It is well known that the chosen sensor data has a big influence on the resulting state estimation. This general contiguity has been discussed in detail in dozens of papers in the area of active vision where the main goal was to select the right sensor data to solve a given problem.

In our paper we tackle the problem of optimal sensor data selection for state estimation by adjusting the camera parameters. The optimal camera parameters are found by minimizing the uncertainty and ambiguity in the state estimation process, given the sensor data. We will present a formal information theoretic metric for this informal characterization later on. We do not restrict the approach to acquiring sensor data once. The approach cycles through an action selection and sensor data acquisition stage where the sensor data decided for depends on the state estimation up to the current time step. One

B. Radig and S. Florczyk (Eds.): DAGM 2001, LNCS 2191, pp. 305–312, 2001.
© Springer-Verlag Berlin Heidelberg 2001

important property of the proposed sequential decision process is that its convergence can be proven and that it is optimal in the sense of the reduction in uncertainty and ambiguity. We will demonstrate our approach in an active object recognition scenario.

The general problem of optimal sensor data acquisition has been discussed before. Examples can be found in the area of active robot localization [6] and active object recognition [1], where a similar metric has been used, but the sequential implementation is missing. The most related approach, not only from the application point of view, but also from a theoretical point of view is the work of [11]. The commonness, differences and improvements to this work are discussed later on. Similarities can also be found to the work of [2,10], where a Bayesian approach [2] as well as an approach using reinforcement learning [10] has been presented for optimally selecting viewpoints in active object recognition. Our approach can be seen as a theoretically justifiable extension to this work. Interesting related work from the area of control theory are [9,7].

The paper is structured as follows. In the next section we describe the problem in a formal manner and introduce the metric that is optimized during one step of the sequential decision process. In Section 3 we build up the sequential decision process and give a sketch of the convergence proof which can be found in detail in [4]. The active object recognition scenario is described in Section 4. The experimental results are summarized in Section 5. The paper concludes with a summary and an outlook to future work.

2   Formal Problem Statement

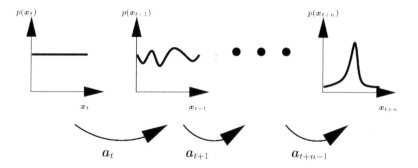

Fig. 1. General principle: reduce uncertainty and ambiguity (variance and multiple modes) in the pdf of the state x_t by choosing appropriate information-acquisition actions a_t.

The problem and the proposed solution are depicted in Fig. 1. A sequence of probability density functions (pdf) $p(x_t)$, $x_t \in \mathcal{S}$ over the state space $\mathcal{S}$ is shown. The sequence starts with a uniform distribution, i.e. nothing is known about the state of the system.

Certain actions a_t are applied that select the sensor data at time step t. The following state estimation process results in a new probability distributions $p(x_{t+1})$ over the state space. Finally, after n steps one should end up with a unimodal distribution with small variance and the mode close to the true state of the system. The problem now is twofold: first how to measure the success of a chosen action, i.e. how close the pdf is to a unimodal distribution with small variance. And second, how do we compute the action, that brings us closer to such a distribution.

The first question can be answered by using information theoretic concepts. In information theory the *entropy* of a pdf

$$H(x_t) = - \int_{x_t} p(x_t) \log(p(x_t)) dx_t$$

is defined which measures the amount of uncertainty in the outcome of a random experiment. The more unpredictable the outcome the larger the entropy is. It reaches its maximum for a uniform pdf and its minimum at zero for a delta function, i.e. for an unambiguous outcome.

The answer to the second question can also be found in information theory. Assume the following setting: the system is in state x_t. The state itself cannot be observed but an observation o_t related with the state by a pdf $p(o_t|x_t, a_t)$. The pdf is also conditioned on the action a_t. In information theory the concept *mutual information* (MI) gives us a hint on which action a_t shall be chosen. The MI

$$I(x_t; o_t|a_t) = \int_{x_t} \int_{o_t} p(x_t)p(o_t|x_t, a_t) \log \left(\frac{p(o_t|x_t, a_t)}{p(o_t|a_t)} \right) do_t dx_t \qquad (1)$$

is the difference between the entropy $H(x_t)$ and the conditional entropy $H(x_t|o_t, a_t)$. It describes how much uncertainty is reduced in the mean about the true state x_t after the observation. Since we introduced the dependency on the action a_t we can influence the reduction in uncertainty by selecting that action a_t^* that maximizes the MI

$$a_t^* = \underset{a_t}{\operatorname{argmax}} \ I(x_t; o_t|a_t) \quad . \qquad (2)$$

All we need is the likelihood function $p(o_t|x_t, a_t)$ and the a priori probability $p(x_t)$.

In [11] a similar approach has been proposed in an active object recognition application, with the exception that the a priori information has been assumed to be uniform in any case. In the next section we extend this approach to a sequential decision process which convergence can be proven. The important difference is that we explicitly take into account the inherently changing prior. The prior changes, since new sensor data changes the information available about the true state.

3   Optimal Iterative Sensor Data Selection

From the previous section we know which action a_t to select to get the sensor data o_t that best reduces the uncertainty in the state estimation. From the definition of MI it is

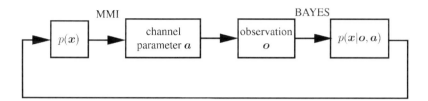

Fig. 2. Sequential decision process of maximum mutual information (MMI) for camera parameter selection and Bayesian update of $p(x|o, a)$ based on the observed feature o.

obvious that the reduction will only be reached in the mean. As a consequence there might be observations under action a_t that result in an increase of the uncertainty. Another, more serious problem is, that there might be more than one sensor data acquisition step necessary to resolve all ambiguity. An example is presented later on in the experimental section in the area of object recognition.

One way to deal with these problems is to form a sequential decision process and to take into account the information acquired so far, when selecting the next action. The sequential decision process consists of two steps: the selection of the best action a_t based on the maximum of the mutual information (MMI) and the application of the Bayes rule to compute the a posterior probability when the observation has been made. The posterior is then fed back and used as prior for the next time step. This is justified by the fact that the posterior contains all information acquired to far, i.e. sensor data fusion is implicitly done during this step. In Fig. 2 the whole sequential decision process is depicted.

By definition the iterative decision process is optimal since each step is optimal with respect to the prior of the state x_t. Since the posterior is used as prior for the next time step we assure that the next action is selected considering the knowledge acquired so far. More important is the fact that this sequential decision process converges, i.e. the pdf $p(x)$ over the state space will converge towards a certain distribution. Only a sketch of the proof is given in the following.

The key point of the convergence proof is that a irreducible Markov chain can be defined representing the sequential decision process [4]. Two corrolaries give us the proof of convergence. The first one is that the Kullback–Leibler distance between two distribution on a Markov chain will never increase over time. The second one is that the Kullback–Leibler distance between a distribution on a Markov chain and a stationary distribution on a Markov chain decreases over time. If there are more than one stationary distributions the convergence will be against the distribution with minimum Kullback–Leibler distance to all stationary distribution. Since each irreducible Markov chain has at least one stationary distribution we end up with a convergence toward a certain distribution over the Markov chain. This distribution is difficult to compute. But by this result we know that the sequential decision process will converge. This convergence is important for practical considerations, i.e. when to stop the whole process.

In practice this convergence can also be observed. In many of our experiments in the area of active object recognition the distribution converges to the optimum distribution with respect to minimum entropy. Note, that it depends on the accuracy of the likelihood functions whether the resulting distribution will identify the right state. If the likelihood function, i.e. the relationship between state and observation, is erroneous, the sequential decision process cannot improve state estimation at all. On the one hand this might be seen as a drawback, since the state estimator is not optimized but only the sensor data provided for state estimation. On the other hand it is a big advantage, since any Bayesian state estimator at hand can be combined with the proposed sequential decision process. The more ambiguous the observations are the more the state estimation will be improved by our method.

Due to lack of space we have restricted us here to the description on the main principles. A more detailed discussion on the underlying information theoretic concepts as well as on the evaluation of the differential mutual information by Monte Carlo techniques can be found in [5]. There the reader will also find error bounds for the estimation of the mutual information.

4 Active Object Recognition Using Viewpoint Selection

To apply our proposed method we have chosen an object recognition scenario. We have selected a statistical Eigenspace approach which has been introduced in [2]. Here we apply it as the state estimator for classification.

The key idea is that the projection $c = \Phi_{\Omega_\kappa} f$ of an image f into the Eigenspace of a class Ω_κ is assumed to be normally distributed, i.e. $p(c|f, \Omega_\kappa) \sim N(\mu_\kappa, \Sigma_\kappa)$. Classification is then done not by computing the minimum distance in Eigenspace between a projected test image f and the manifold of a certain class [8] but by maximizing the a posteriori probability $\frac{1}{c} p(c|f, \Omega_\kappa) p(\Omega_\kappa)$. As a consequence the prior can be explicitly taken into account and one does not get only the best class hypotheses but also a statistical measure for the match. For viewpoint selection the likelihood functions $p(c|f, a, \Omega_\kappa)$ for each viewpoint a have to be estimated during training. In our case a maximum likelihood estimation of the parameters of the Gaussian is performed. Due to lack of space only a coarse summary of the method could be given. More details are found in [2,4,5].

5 Experiments and Results

Five toy manikins form the data set (cf. Fig. 3). There are only certain views from which the objects can be distinguished. The main differences in the objects are the small items that the manikins carry (band, lamp, quiver, gun, trumpet).

The experimental setup consists of a turntable and a robot arm with a camera mounted that can move around the turntable. The actions $a = (\phi, \theta)^T$ define the position of the camera on the hemisphere around the object. The statistical eigenspace approach is used as classifier. The state x is the class of the object.

We compared our viewpoint planning with a random strategy for viewpoint selection. Table 1 summarizes the results. The planning based on maximum mutual information outperforms a random strategy, in both recognition rate and number of views necessary for classification. In most cases the object can be recognized within three views at the

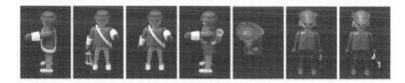

Fig. 3. The first view is ambiguous with respect to the objects in image two and three. The second and third view allow for a distinction of objects two and three but not to distinguish object one from four (the objects with and without quiver on the back). Similar arguments hold for the two objects shown in the last three images.

latest. Also the maximum a posteriori probability after the decision for one class is larger in the mean for the viewpoint planning, indicating more confidence in the final decision (for example, object trumpet: 0.97 vs. 0.65). In contrast to other viewpoint selection approaches, for example based on reinforcement learning [3], we do not need to train the optimal sequence. All necessary information is already encoded in the likelihood functions, which are provided by the Bayesian classifier.

Table 1. Results for viewpoint planning and random viewpoint control (100 trials per object): Recognition rate, mean number of views, and the mean of the maximum a posteriori probability for the right class after the decision.

object	planned viewpoint control			random viewpoint control		
	rec. rate	mean no. views	mean max. a poster. prob.	rec. rate	mean no. views	mean max. a poster. prob.
band	86	1.13	0.98	77	4.28	0.95
lamp	97	1.14	0.98	93	4.94	0.96
quiver	99	1.05	0.99	95	3.09	0.97
gun	90	2.19	0.97	80	8.96	0.69
trumpet	99	2.29	0.97	70	8.89	0.65
average	94.2	1.56	0.97	83.0	6.03	0.84

In Fig. 4 (left) the MI is shown at the beginning of the sequential decision process, i.e. the prior is assumed to be uniform. The x– and y–axis are the motor-steps for moving the turntable and the robot arm, to select positions of the camera on the hemisphere. The motor-step values correspond to a rotation between 0 and 360 degree for the turntable and -90 to 90 degree for the robot arm. The MI is computed by Monte Carlo simulation [5]. The maximum in this 2D function in the case of viewpoint selection defines the best action (viewpoint) to be chosen. In Fig. 4 (right) the corresponding view of the object is shown (for one of the objects as an example). This viewpoint is plausible, since the presence of the quiver as well as the lamp can be determined, so that three of the five objects can already be distinguished.

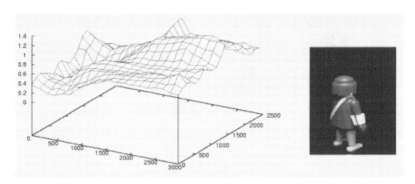

Fig. 4. Left: MI in the viewpoint selection example assuming a uniform prior (computed by Monte Carlo evaluation). The x and y are the motor-steps for the turntable and robot arm, respectively. Along the z axis the MI is plotted. Right: best view a decided by the maximum in the MI ($a = (2550, 1500)$). As example, object band is shown.

In general the computation time depends linearly on the number of actions and the number of classes. In practice, for viewpoint selection less than one second is needed on a Pentium II/300 for the computation of the best action using 1000 samples, 5 classes and a total of 3360 different actions (positions on the hemisphere).

6   Conclusion

We have presented a general framework for sensor data selection in state estimation. The approach has been applied to the optimal selection of camera parameters (viewpoint) in active object recognition. It is worth noting that the approach is not restricted to camera parameter selection but can be applied in any situation where the sensor acquisition process can be influenced. One examples is gaze control, where the pan/tilt/zoom parameters of a camera are changed [5]. Another example might be the adaptive change of illumination to enhance relevant features.

The approach presented in this paper is independent from the state estimator at hand. The only requirement is that the state estimator must provide likelihood functions for the observation given the state. The big advantage of this fact is, that any state estimator can be improved by our method as long as the state estimator does not return systematically wrong results.

Compared to previously published work our approach forms a sequential decision process and its convergence can be proven. In contrast to reinforcement learning approaches [3] for active object recognition we do not need to train the optimal sequence. Thus, the typical tradeoff between exploitation and exploration in reinforcement learning does not exist for our framework. All relevant information necessary to decide for an optimal action is already encoded in the likelihood functions and the prior. The prior is computed step by step during the recognition process and the likelihood functions are assumed to be provided by the state estimator. Experiments showed that the framework works in an object recognition scenario with a state of the art classifier and outperforms a random strategy.

In our current work we extended this approach to state estimation of dynamic systems and we will modify the algorithms in a way that also continuous actions spaces can be handled.

References

1. T. Arbel and F.P. Ferrie. Viewpoint selection by navigation through entropy maps. In *Proceedings of the Seventh International Conference on Computer Vision*, Kerkyra, Greece, 1999.
2. H. Borotschnig, L. Paletta, M. Prantl, and A. Pinz. Appearance based active object recognition. *Image and Vision Computing*, (18):715–727, 2000.
3. F. Deinzer, J. Denzler, and H. Niemann. Classifier Independent Viewpoint Selection for 3-D Object Recognition. In G. Sommer, N. Kr"uger, and Ch Perwass, editors, *Mustererkennung 2000*, pages 237–244, Berlin, September 2000. Springer.
4. J. Denzler and C. Brown. Optimal selection of camera parameters for state estimation of static systems: An information theoretic approach. Technical Report TR–732, Computer Science Department, University of Rochester, 2000.
5. J. Denzler and C.M. Brown. Information theoretic sensor data selection for active object recognition and state estimation. *IEEE Transactions on Pattern Analysis and Machine Intelligence (in press)*, 2001.
6. D. Fox, W. Burgard, and S. Thrun. Active markov localization for mobile robots. Technical report, Carnegie Mellon University, 1998.
7. J.M. Manyika and H.F. Durran-Whyte. On sensor management in decentralized data fusion. In *Proceedings of the Conference on Decision and Control*, pages 3506–3507, 1992.
8. H. Murase and S. Nayar. Visual Learning and Recognition of 3–D Objects from Appearance. *International Journal of Computer Vision*, 14:5–24, 1995.
9. C.A. Noonan and K.J. Orford. Entropy measures of multi–sensor fusion performance. In *Proceedings of the IEE Colloqium on Target Tracking and Data Fusion*, pages 15/1–15/5, 1996.
10. L. Paletta, M. Prantl, and A. Pinz. Learning temporal context in active object recognition using bayesian analysis. In *International Conference on Pattern Recognition*, volume 3, pages 695–699, Barcelona, 2000.
11. B. Schiele and J.L. Crowley. Transinformation for active object recognition. In *Proceedings of the Sixth International Conference on Computer Vision*, Bombay, India, 1998.

View Planning for Unknown Indoor Scenes Based on a Cost Benefit Analysis

Konrad Klein[1]* and Vítor Sequeira[2]

[1] Fraunhofer Institut Graphische Datenverarbeitung
Rundeturmstr. 6, D-64283 Darmstadt, Germany, `konrad.klein@igd.fhg.de`
[2] European Commission – Joint Research Centre
TP 270, 21020 Ispra (Va), Italy, `vitor.sequeira@jrc.it`

Abstract. From the task of automatically reconstructing real world scenes using range images, the problem of planning the image acquisition arises. Although solutions for small objects in known environments are already available, these approaches lack scalability to large scenes and to a high number of degrees of freedom. In this paper, we present a new planning algorithm for initially unknown, large indoor environments. Using a surface representation of seen and unseen parts of the environment, we propose a method based on the analysis of occlusions. In addition to previous approaches, we take into account both a quality criterion and the cost of the next acquisition. Results are shown for two large indoor scenes – an artificial scene and a real world room – with numerous self occlusions.

Keywords: view planning, active vision, range image fusion, 3d reconstruction, modelling from reality, autonomous exploration.

1   Introduction

In recent years a number of approaches to the reconstruction of real world scenes from range images have been proposed. However, the acquisition of the required range images is a time-consuming process which human operators usually cannot perform efficiently. Alternatively, the acquisition step can be automated. While the necessary robots are available for a range from small objects to large scale environments, there is no sufficiently scalable algorithm to determine the acquisition parameters of the range images. Thus, an appropriate view planning technique is crucial e.g. for the fast and cost effective generation of virtual reality models, as-built analysis of architectural and industrial environments, and remote inspection of hazardous environments.

In this paper, we address the problem of view planning with an initially unknown geometry of the scene and a given set of parameters for the first view. The parameter sets for the subsequent views are planned iteratively within the acquisition cycle, which can be outlined in four steps:

1. Image acquisition.

---

* The work presented here was done while Konrad Klein was with the EC-Joint Research Centre, funded by the European Commission's TMR network "CAMERA", contract number ERBFM-RXCT970127.

B. Radig and S. Florczyk (Eds.): DAGM 2001, LNCS 2191, pp. 313–320, 2001.
© Springer-Verlag Berlin Heidelberg 2001

2. Integration of the newly acquired image into the reconstructed model using an appropriate representation of unseen parts of the object.
3. *View Planning:* Determination of the parameters for the next acquisition or termination if the result is not improved by further acquisitions.
4. Moving the acquisition system to the next capture point.

The majority of approaches previously proposed is based on the analysis of the boundary surface of the visible volume. Conolly [2] proposes an octree-based ray-casting approach of which the rationale is a discretisation of the problem using a spherical discretisation map for the searched viewing parameters, and an occupancy-grid representation for the object. Maver and Bajcsy [4] aim to completely acquire an object's surface from one single direction using a camera-laser triangulation system based on the analysis of occlusions. This approach relies on triangulation based scanners and is thus unsuitable for the use in large scenes. Pito [5] proposes an approach based on the analysis of both the measured and the "void surface", which bounds unseen parts of the visible volume. The optimisation of the parameter set for the next view is performed in two steps, of which the first reduces the search space by computing possible optima positions without taking occlusions into account. Some authors [6,7,8] consider the occlusion surfaces discretely, thereby avoiding an exhaustive evaluation of the search space. These approaches are best suitable when a pre-existing CAD-model can be used in the planning step, while the high number of occlusion surfaces in noisy real world data render these approaches unusable.

This paper presents a novel method for view planning in large, complex indoor environments with an acquisition system providing eight degrees of freedom (3D position, viewing direction, field of view, and resolution). The core component of the method is our innovatory objective function, which quantifies the cost-benefit ratio of an acquisition. This function is subject to a global optimisation method in order to determine the set of parameters for the following image acquisition. The aim of the overall planning algorithm is a complete surface model measured with a predefined sampling density in each point.

2   View Planning

The parameters to be determined for each view mainly depend on the acquisition system. A typical range acquisition system is based on a laser range finder mounted on a pan-and-tilt unit with variable field of view and resolution, which can be freely positioned using a tripod or a mobile robot (Fig. 1). Consequently, eight parameters have to be determined which are the 3D position, the viewing direction (two angles), the horizontal and vertical field of view, and the resolution.

When determining the set of parameters of the next view, the following partly competitive goals are pursued:

– Maximise the visible volume by resolving occluded volumes.
– Maximise the area of the surface measured with sufficient sampling density.
– Minimise the resources needed to reconstruct the scene with a predefined quality.

Fig. 1. Tripod and mobile acquisition robot (Autonomous Environmental Sensor for Telepresence AEST [9]).

These goals are incorporated in an objective function G which evaluates a parameter set for a given scene description based on the previously taken images. The view planning problem is then addressed by solving a constrained continuous global optimisation problem for the search space $D \subset \mathbb{R}^8$ limited by the constraints formulated in Section 2.3. Besides the first range image, the algorithm requires the desired sampling density as an input parameter.

2.1 Iterative Surface Construction

Following Pito [5] we use a binary partition of space into the visible volume, which is located between any of the capture positions and the surface measured from that position, and the invisible volume, which is unseen in the images already acquired because it is located outside all fields of view or because it is occluded by measured surfaces. The invisible volume consists of the object volume and additional *void* volume. Accordingly, the surface **S** of the visible volume is partitioned into a measured part and the unmeasured *void* surface (Fig. 2).

This partition is described for acquisition step i by the volume v_i visible in the acquired image, the measured surface m_i, and the unmeasured (*void*) surface u_i of the visible volume, so that the surfaces m_i and u_i together completely enclose the volume v_i. For the integration of multiple range images into a single surface description, we denote the surface already measured in step $1 \ldots i$ by M_i, and the *void* surface that has not been resolved in step $1 \ldots i$ by U_i. While these surfaces are initially $M_1 := m_1$ and $U_1 := u_1$, we iteratively construct the new representation in each step by

$$U_{i+1} := U_i \cap v_{i+1} \ \cup \ u_{i+1} \cap (v_1 \cup \ldots \cup v_i)$$
$$M_{i+1} := M_i \cup m_{i+1} \tag{1}$$

so that the results of the previous iteration of the acquisition cycle can be re-used. Both the measured surface M_i and the void surface U_i are represented by a triangle mesh.

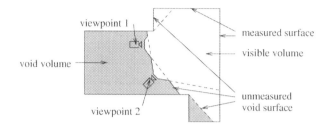

Fig. 2. The visible volume and its surface

The union of two meshes is implemented using a mesh zippering approach, while the intersection between a mesh and a volume is implemented by clipping the triangles against the volume. Standard methods of mesh simplification [1] can be used to reduce the number of triangles.

2.2 Objective Function

When planning views to an partly unknown environment, one has to assess possible views such that the unknown environment is captured within the planned sequence of views. It is reasonable to achieve this by additional measurements towards a void surface because the void volume decreases and the area of measured surface increases in this manner. However, the effect cannot be quantitatively predicted. Instead, we treat the void surface like an unmeasured object surface and plan the next view accordingly.

When evaluating a set of parameters, we take into account the field of view, the viewing direction, and the resolution of the next view. These values are expressed by the variables ϑ_h and ϑ_v for the horizontal and vertical field of view, φ_a and φ_e for the azimuth and elevation angle of the sensor, and m for the resolution as a factor in reference to a standard resolution. Using these definitions, the visibility of the point $\mathbf{p}$ from point $\mathbf{x}$ is expressed by the weight $w_v(\mathbf{p}, \mathbf{x}, \varphi_a, \varphi_e, \vartheta_h, \vartheta_v)$, which is 1 if the point $\mathbf{p}$ is visible in the evaluated view and 0 otherwise.

For the incorporation of a quality criterion we define a function $\beta : \mathbf{S} \longrightarrow \mathbb{R}$ which yields the sampling density for a given point on the surface $\mathbf{S}$. Points on void surfaces yield a function value of 0. Additionally, we associate each point $\mathbf{p}$ on $\mathbf{S}$ with a desired sampling quality $\beta_{\max}(\mathbf{p})$.

Accordingly, we define a function $F : \mathbf{S} \times \mathbb{R}^8 \longrightarrow \mathbb{R}$, which expresses the expected sampling density yielded at a point on the surface $\mathbf{S}$ when viewed with the evaluated set of parameters. With the solid angle A_{patch} covered by one pixel at the position in the image grid in standard resolution[1] onto which the point $\mathbf{p} \in \mathbf{S}$ is projected, the function

---

[1] The size of one pixel on the unit sphere (the solid angle) can be computed for every grid position $(u, v) \in \mathbb{R}^2$ in the field of view and for every resolution > 0 using the Jacobian matrix of the mapping from the image grid to Cartesian coordinates. We assume the size of a pixel to be linear in the resolution factor m.

F is formulated by

$$F(\mathbf{p}, \mathbf{x}, \varphi_a, \varphi_e, \vartheta_h, \vartheta_v, m) := m \cdot \frac{n(\mathbf{p} - \mathbf{x})}{d^3 \cdot A_{\text{patch}}} \tag{2}$$

where n is the normal of the surface $\mathbf{S}$ in point $\mathbf{p}$ and $d = |\mathbf{p} - \mathbf{x}|$ is the distance between the capture point $\mathbf{x}$ and $\mathbf{p}$.

In order to avoid a high number of small images or a high number of data points the costs of an image acquisition with the evaluated set of parameters have to be taken into account as well. To meet these demands, we express the objective function as a cost-benefit ratio which has to be minimised, thereby taking the number of pixels N and the costs c_A of each acquisition into account. The benefit depends on the parts of the scene actually seen from point $\mathbf{x}$ and is thus integrated over the visible area of the surface $\mathbf{S}$. Summarising the geometric parameter vector by $(\mathbf{x}, \varphi_a, \varphi_e, \vartheta_h, \vartheta_v) =: \tau$ the objective function can finally be expressed by the cost-benefit ratio

$$G(\tau, m) := \frac{m \cdot N + c_A}{\displaystyle\iint\limits_{(\mathbf{p} \in \mathbf{S})} w_v(\mathbf{p}, \tau) \cdot (\min\{\beta_{\text{max}}(\mathbf{p}), F(\mathbf{p}, \tau, m)\} - \min\{\beta_{\text{max}}(\mathbf{p}), \beta(\mathbf{p})\}) \, \mathrm{d}S} \tag{3}$$

where the value of c_A has to be chosen empirically and is in the order of magnitude of the number of pixels in a typical image. Considering the predefined desired quality $\beta_{\text{max}}(\mathbf{p})$ ensures that redundant measurements do not increase the computed benefit.

2.3   Implementation

We compute the objective function defined in Eq. 3 efficiently using an image-based-rendering approach where the results of the expensive visibility determination can be re-used for multiple evaluations of the function with a constant viewpoint $\mathbf{x}$ [3]. Consequently, an appropriate method of global optimisation is required which allows for an efficient order of evaluated parameter sets and is robust in the presence of noise caused by the computation in image precision. We meet these demands by a simple uniform grid search algorithm.

During the global optimisation, two different constraints have to be taken into account, of which the first allows for the operational range of the acquisition device and the necessary distance to obstacles. The second constraint is an overlap criterion which ensures the registration of the newly acquired image with the model reconstructed so far. Our experiments showed an overlapping share of 20% of the pixels to be sufficient.

When automatically reconstructing a scene, the acquisition cycle requires a termination criterion, as which we use the improvement of the sampling density with respect to the desired sampling density: If the area of the surface reconstructed with the desired sampling density does not increase by an acquisition step, the algorithm terminates.

3   Results

When evaluating the results of the planning technique, two main criteria can be distinguished, of which the first is the percentage of the scene volume reconstructed at a given iteration. As the presence of obstacles in an invisible volume cannot be decided on, the percentage of the reconstructed volume is crucial for automatic path planning with an autonomous mobile acquisition robot. The second criterion is the amount of surface area represented at a given resolution. We evaluate the percentage of the surface area represented with the desired sampling density as well as the percentage represented with lower densities (75%, 50%, 25% of the desired resolution, and the percentage visible at all). By analysing both criteria as functions of the iteration number the quality of the reconstruction in each iteration can be estimated.

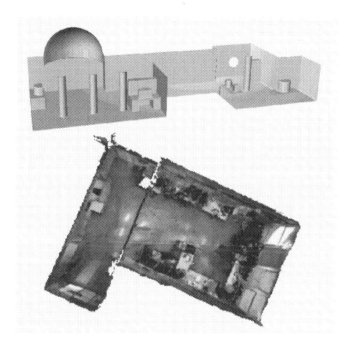

Fig. 3. Rendered, backface-culled view of the artificial scene (top) and reconstruction result after 10 automatically planned image acquisitions for a real world scene (bottom).

We present two complex scenes to demonstrate the practical usability of the method. The first test scene is an artificial model of 20m × 7m × 5.3m shown in Fig. 3 which is used with an acquisition simulator. Surfaces which cannot be measured by the acquisition system are simulated by three holes in the model, so that these areas remain undefined in all range images.

The sensor geometry and the constraints match the data for our laser scanner (approximately polar coordinate system from a pan-and-tilt unit): height between 0.9 m and 2.0 m, viewing direction 0° to 360° (azimuth angle) and −60° to 60° (elevation angle), horizontal field of view 38° to 278°, vertical field of view 30° to 60°. The maximal angular resolution is 0.1° per pixel in both directions, while the desired sampling density β_{max} is 1600 samples per m^2 (corresponding to a 2.5 cm grid). Fig. 4 shows the proposed criteria for a sequence of 20 views. While the reconstructed volume quickly reaches 99% of the final volume (iteration 12), the desired sampling density requires significantly more iterations: although 95% of the surface area are depicted in one of the 20 images, only 37.4% are represented with the desired sampling density. This is mainly due to the complicated geometry which requires a high number of views from a close distance.

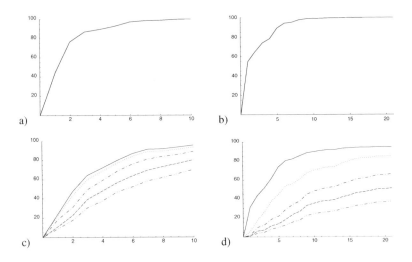

Fig. 4. Results for the real world scene (left) and the artificial scene (right): Percentage of reconstructed volume (top) and percentage of surface area represented with given sampling densities (bottom) for each iteration.

The second test scene is a typical complex laboratory environment (10m × 6m ×4.3m), which serves as a complicated real world scene. All technical parameters are identical to those from the experiment with the artificial scene, except for the desired sampling density of 625 samples per m^2 (corresponding to a 4 cm grid), and the maximum angular resolution of 0.5° per pixel (both directions). Fig. 4 shows the evaluation data from 10 views. While some occlusions have not been resolved, the algorithm yields a sufficient density in more than 70% of the reconstructed surface area. This demonstrates the efficiency of the method with limited resources. Failures in the registration due to an insufficient overlap did not occur in our experiments.

4   Conclusion and Future Work

We present a technique of planning the range image acquisition for the reconstruction of large, complex indoor scenes which incorporates both cost and benefit of the image acquisition. The practical usability is demonstrated in the automated reconstruction of two large scenes. Future work will address the use of information from previous iterations of the acquisition cycle.

References

1. M.-E. Algorri and F. Schmitt. Mesh Simplification. In *Eurographics Proceedings*, volume 15, 1996.
2. C. I. Conolly. The determination of next best views. In *International Conference on Robotics and Automation*, pages 432–435. ICRA-85, 1985.
3. Konrad Klein and Vítor Sequeira. The view-cube: An efficient method of view planning for 3d modelling from range data. In *Proceedings 5th IEEE Workshop on Applications of Computer Vision (WACV 2000)*, pages 186–191, 2000.
4. Jasna Maver and Ruzena Bajcsy. Occlusions as a guide for planning the next view. *IEEE Trans. Pattern Analysis and Machine Intelligence*, 15(5):417–433, May 1993.
5. Richard Pito. A sensor based solution to the next best view problem. In *Int. Conference on Pattern Recognition*, pages 941–945, Vienna, Austria, August 1996.
6. Michael K. Reed and Peter K. Allen. Constraint-based sensor planning for scene modeling. *IEEE Trans. Pattern Analysis and Machine Intelligence*, 22(12):1460–1467, December 2000.
7. D. R. Roberts and A. D. Marshall. Viewpoint selection for complete surface coverage of three dimensional objects. In *British Machine Vision Conference*, pages 740–750, 1998.
8. Vítor Sequeira, João G. M. Gonçalves, and M. Isabel Ribeiro. Active view selection for efficient 3d scene reconstruction. In *Proc. ICPR'96 - 13th International Conference on Pattern Recognition*, pages 815–819, Vienna, Austria, 1996.
9. Vítor Sequeira, Kia Ng, Erik Wolfart, João G. M. Gonçalves, and David Hogg. Automated reconstruction of 3d models from real world environments. *ISPRS Journal of Photogrammetry and Remote Sensing*, (54):1–22, 1999.

Cooperative Probabilistic State Estimation for Vision-Based Autonomous Soccer Robots

Thorsten Schmitt, Robert Hanek, Sebastian Buck, and Michael Beetz

TU München, Institut für Informatik, Orléansstrasse 34, 81667 München, Germany

{schmittt,hanek,buck,beetzm}@in.tum.de

http://www9.in.tum.de/agilo

Abstract. With the services that autonomous robots are to provide becoming more demanding, the states that the robots have to estimate become more complex. In this paper, we develop and analyze a probabilistic, vision-based state estimation method for individual, autonomous robots. This method enables a team of mobile robots to estimate their joint positions in a known environment and track the positions of autonomously moving objects. The state estimators of different robots cooperate to increase the accuracy and reliability of the estimation process. This cooperation between the robots enables them to track temporarily occluded objects and to faster recover their position after they have lost track of it. The method is empirically validated based on experiments with a team of physical robots.

1 Introduction

Autonomous robots must have information about themselves and their environments that is sufficient and accurate enough for the robots to complete their tasks competently. Contrary to these needs, the information that robots receive through their sensors is inherently uncertain: typically the robots' sensors can only access parts of their environments and their sensor measurements are inaccurate and noisy. In addition, control over their actuators is also inaccurate and unreliable. Finally, the dynamics of many environments cannot be accurately modeled and sometimes environments change nondeterministically.

Recent longterm experiments with autonomous robots [13] have shown that an impressively high level of reliability and autonomy can be reached by explicitly representing and maintaining the uncertainty inherent in the available information. One particularly promising method for accomplishing this is *probabilistic state estimation*. Probabilistic state estimation modules maintain the probability densities for the states of objects over time. The probability density of an object's state conditioned on the sensor measurements received so far contains all the information which is available about an object that is available to a robot. Based on these densities, robots are not only able to determine the most likely state of the objects, but can also derive even more meaningful statistics such as the variance of the current estimate.

Successful state estimation systems have been implemented for a variety of tasks including the estimation of the robot's position in a known environment, the automatic learning of environment maps, the state estimation for objects with dynamic states (such as doors), for the tracking of people locations, and gesture recognition [12].

With the services that autonomous robots are to provide becoming more demanding, the states that the robots have to estimate become more complex. Robotic soccer provides a good case in point. In robot soccer (mid-size league) two teams of four autonomous robots play soccer against each other. A probabilistic state estimator for competent robotic soccer players should provide the

B. Radig and S. Florczyk (Eds.): DAGM 2001, LNCS 2191, pp. 321–328, 2001.
© Springer-Verlag Berlin Heidelberg 2001

action selection routines with estimates of the positions and may be even the dynamic states of each player and the ball.

This estimation problem confronts probabilistic state estimation methods with a unique combination of difficult challenges. The state is to be estimated by multiple mobile sensors with uncertain positions, the soccer field is only partly accessible for each sensor due to occlusion caused by other robots, the robots change their direction and speed very abruptly, and the models of the dynamic states of the robots of the other team are very crude and uncertain.

In this paper, we describe a state estimation module for individual, autonomous robots that enables a team of robots to estimate their joint positions in a known environment and track the positions of autonomously moving objects. The state estimation modules of different robots cooperate to increase the accuracy and reliability of the estimation process. In particular, the cooperation between the robots enables them to track temporarily occluded objects and to faster recover their position after they have lost track of it.

The state estimation module of a single robot is decomposed into subcomponents for self-localization and for tracking different kinds of objects. This decomposition reduces the overall complexity of the state estimation process and enables the robots to exploit the structures and assumptions underlying the different subtasks of the complete estimation task. Accuracy and reliability is further increased through the cooperation of these subcomponents. In this cooperation the estimated state of one subcomponent is used as evidence by the other subcomponents.

The main contributions of this paper are the following ones. First, we show that image-based probabilistic estimation of complex environment states is feasible in real time even in complex and fast changing environments. Second, we show that maintaining trees of possible tracks is particularly useful for estimating a global state based on multiple mobile sensors with position uncertainty. Third, we show how the state estimation modules of individual robots can cooperate in order to produce more accurate and reliable state estimation.

In the remainder of the paper we proceed as follows. Section 2 describes the software architecture of the state estimation module and sketches the interactions among its components. Section 3 provides a detailed description of the individual state estimators. We conclude with our experimental results and a discussion of related work.

2   Overview of the State Estimator

Fig. 1a shows the components of the state estimator and its embedding into the control system. The subsystem consists of the perception subsystem, the state estimator itself, and the world model. The perception subsystem itself consists of a camera system with several feature detectors and a communication link that enables the robot to receive information from other robots. The world model contains a position estimate for each dynamic task-relevant object. In this paper the notion of position refers to the x- and y-coordinates of the objects and includes for the robots of the own team the robot's orientation. The estimated positions are also associated with a measure of accuracy, a covariance matrix.

The perception subsystem provides the following kinds of information: (1) partial state estimates broadcasted by other robots, (2) feature maps extracted from captured images, and (3) odometric information. The estimates broadcasted by the robots of the own team comprise the estimate of the ball's location. In addition, each robot of the own team provides an estimate of its

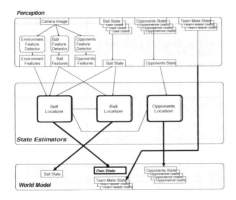 

Fig. 1. (a) Architecture of the state estimator. (b) The figure shows an image captured by the robot and the feature maps that are computed for self, ball, and opponent localization.

own position. Finally, each robot provides an estimate for the position of every opponent. From the captured camera images the feature detectors extract problem-specific feature maps that correspond to (1) static objects in the environment including the goal, the borders of the field, and the lines on the field, (2) a color blob corresponding to the ball, and (3) the visual features of the opponents. The state estimation subsystem consists of three interacting estimators: the self localization system, the ball estimator, and the opponents estimator. State estimation is an iterative process where each iteration is triggered by the arrival of a new piece of evidence, a captured image or a state estimate broadcasted by another robot. The self localization estimates the probability density of the robot's own position based on extracted environment features, the estimated ball position, and the predicted position. The ball localizer estimates the probability density for the ball position given the robot's own estimated position and its perception of the ball, the predicted ball position, and the ball estimations broadcasted by the other robots. Finally, the positions of the opponents are estimated based on the estimated position of the observing robot, the robots' appearances in the captured images, and their positions as estimated by the team mates. Every robot maintains its own global world model, which is constructed as follows. The own position, the position of the ball, and the positions of the opponent players are produced by the local state estimation processes. The estimated positions of the team mates are the broadcasted results of the self localization processes of the corresponding team mates.

3   The Individual State Estimators

3.1   Self- and Ball-Localization

The self- and ball-localization module iteratively estimates, given the observations taken by the robot and a model of the environment and the ball, the probability density over the possible robot and ball positions. A detailed description and analysis of the applied alogrithms can be found in [6,7] or in the long version of this paper enclosed on the CD.

3.2   Opponents Localization

The objective of the opponents localization module is to track the positions of the other team's robots. The estimated position of one opponent is represented by

Fig. 2. (a) The multiple hypotheses framework for dynamic environment modeling. (b) An estimate of the robot's distance is given through the intersection of the viewing ray with the ground plane of the field.

one or more alternative object hypotheses. Thus the task of the state estimator is to (1) detect feature blobs in the captured image that correspond to an opponent, (2) estimate the position and uncertainties of the opponent in world coordinates, and (3) associate them with the correct object hypothesis. In our state estimator we use Reid's Multiple Hypotheses Tracking (MHT) algorithm [10] as the basic method for realizing the state estimation task. In this section we demonstrate how this framework can be applied to model dynamic environments in multi-robot systems. We extend the general framework in that we provide mechanisms to handle multiple mobile sensors with uncertain positions.

Multi Hypotheses Tracking. We will describe the Multiple Hypotheses Tracking method by first detailing the underlying opponents model, then explaining the representation of tracked opponents position estimates, and finally presenting the computational steps of the algorithm.

The Opponents Model. The model considers opponent robots to be moving objects of unknown shape with associated information describing their temporal dynamics, such as their velocity. The number of the opponent robots may vary. The opponent robots have visual features that can be detected as feature blobs by the perception system.

The Representation of Opponent Tracks. When tracking the positions of a set of opponent robots there are two kinds of uncertainties that the state estimator has to deal with. The first one is the inaccuracy of the robot's sensors. We represent this kind of uncertainty using a Gaussian probability density. The second kind of uncertainty is introduced by the data association problem, i.e. assigning feature blobs to object hypotheses. This uncertainty is represented by a hypotheses tree where nodes represent the association of a feature blob with an object hypothesis. A node $H_j(t)$ is a son of the node $H_i(t-1)$ if $H_j(t)$ results from the assignment of an observed feature blob with a predicted state of the hypothesis $H_i(t-1)$. In order to constrain the growth of the hypotheses tree, it is pruned to eliminate improbable branches with every iteration of the MHT.

The MHT Algorithm. Fig. 2a outlines the computational structure of the MHT algorithm. An iteration begins with the set of hypotheses $H(t-1)$ from the previous iteration $t-1$. Each hypothesis represents a different assignment of measurements to objects, which was performed in the past. The algorithm maintains a Kalman filter for each hypothesis. For each hypothesis a position of the dynamic objects is predicted $\widehat{Z}_i(t)$ and compared with the next observed opponent performed by an arbitrary robot of the team. Assignments of measurements to objects are accomplished on the basis of a statistical distance measurement. Each subsequent child hypothesis represents one possible interpretation of the set of observed objects and, together with its parent hypothesis, represents one

---

The Unscented Transformation

The general problem is as follows. Given an n-dimensional vector random variable x with mean $\bar{x}$ and covariance C_x we would like to estimate the mean $\bar{y}$ and the covariance C_y of an m-dimensional vector random variable y. Both variables are related to each other by a non-linear transformation $y = g(x)$. The unscented transformation is defined as follows:

1. Compute the set Z of $2n$ points from the rows or columns of the matrices $\pm\sqrt{nC_x}$. This set is zero mean with covariance C_x. The matrix square root can efficiently be calculated by the Cholesky decomposition.
2. Compute a set of points X with the same covariance, but with mean $\bar{x}$, by translating each of the points as $x_i = z_i + \bar{x}$.
3. Transform each point $x_i \in X$ to the set Y with $y_i = g(x_i)$.
4. Compute $\bar{y}$ and C_y by computing the mean and covariance of the $2n$ points in the set Y.

Fig. 3. Outline of the unscented transformation.

possible interpretation of all past observations. With every iteration of the MHT probabilities describing the validity of an hypothesis are calculated [1]. In order to constrain the growth of the tree the algorithm prunes improbable branches. Pruning is based on a combination of ratio pruning, i.e. a simple lower limit on the ratio of the probabilities of the current and best hypotheses, and the N-scan-back algorithm [10]. The algorithm assumes that any ambiguity at time t is resolved by time $t + N$. Consequently if at time t hypothesis $H_i(t - 1)$ has n children, the sum of the probabilities of the leaf notes of each branch is calculated. The branch with the greatest probability is retained and the others are discarded.

Feature Extraction and Uncertainty Estimation. This section outlines the feature extraction process which is performed in order to estimate the positions and the covariances of the opponent team's robots. Each opponent robots is modeled in world coordinates by a bi-variate Gaussian density with mean Ψ and a covariance matrix C_ψ.

At present it is assumed that the opponent robots are constructed in the same way and have approximately circular shape. All robots are colored black. Friend foe discrimination is enabled through predefined color markers (cyan and magenta, see Fig. 1b) on the robots. Each marker color may be assigned to any of the two competing teams. Consequently it is important that the following algorithms can be parameterized accordingly. Furthermore we assume that (see Fig. 2b) the tracked object almost touches the ground. The predefined robot colors allow a relatively simple feature extraction process.

Step 1: Extraction of Blobs Containing Opponent Robots. From a captured image the black color-regions are extracted through color classification and morphological operators. In order to be recognized as an opponent robot a black blob has to obey several constraints, e.g. a minimum size and a red or green color-region adjacent to the bottom region row. Through this we are able to distinguish robots from black logos and adverts affixed on the wall surrounding the field. Furthermore blobs that contain or have a color-region of the own team color in the immediate neighborhood are discarded.

$$\bar{\omega} = [\Phi, row, col, width]$$

$$C_\omega = \begin{pmatrix} C_\phi & 0 & 0 & 0 \\ 0 & 1 & 0 & 0 \\ 0 & 0 & 1 & 0 \\ 0 & 0 & 0 & 1 \end{pmatrix}$$

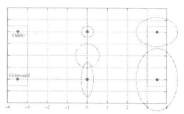

Fig. 4. (a) Intermediate $\bar{\omega}$ mean and covariance C_ω (b) Propagation of uncertainties.

For all remaining regions three features are extracted: The bottom most pixel *row* which exceeds a predefined length, the column *col* representing the center of gravity and a mean blob *width* in pixels. For the latter two features only the three bottom most rows which exceed a certain length are used. In order to determine these rows, we allow also for occlusion through the ball. If the length of these rows exceeds an upper length, we assume that we have detected two opponents which are directly next to each other. In this case two centers of gravity are computed and the width is halfed.

In order to detect cascaded robots, i.e. opponent robots that are partially occluded by other robots, our algorithm also examines the upper rows of the blobs. As soon as the length of a blob row differs significantly from the length of its lower predecessor and the respective world coordinates indicate a height of more than 10 cm above the ground we assume that we have detected cascaded robots. In this case we split the blob into two and apply the above procedure to both blobs. Empirically we have found that this feature extraction procedure is sufficient to determine accurate positions of opponent robots. Mistakenly extracted objects are generally resolved in a fast manner by the MHT algorithm.

Step 2: Estimation of Opponent Position and Uncertainty. In the following we will estimate the position and covariance of an observed robot. For this the pose and the covariance of the observing robots as well as position of the detected feature blob in the image and the associated measurement uncertainties are taken into account.

We define a function *opp* that determines the world coordinates of an opponent robot based on the pose Φ of the observing robot, the pixel coordinates *row,col* of the center of gravity and the width *width* of the opponent robot's blob. Due to rotations and radial distortions of the lenses *opp* is non-linear. First the function *opp* converts the blob's pixel coordinates to relative polar coordinates. On this basis and the width of the observed blob the radius of the observed robot is estimated. Since the polar coordinates only describe the distance to the opponent robot but not the distance to its center, the radius is added to the distance. Finally the polar coordinates are transformed into world coordinates taking the observing robot's pose Φ into account.

In order to estimate the position ψ and the covariance C_ψ of an opponent robot, we will use a technique similar to the unscented transformation [8] (see Fig. 3). First an intermediate mean $\bar{\omega}$ and covariance C_ω describing jointly the observing robot's pose and the observed robot is set up (see Fig. 4a). Φ, *row*, *col* and *width* are assumed to be uncorrelated with a variance of one pixel. To this mean and covariance the unscented transformation using the non-linear mapping *opp* is applied. This yields the opponent robot's position ψ and covariance C_ψ. In Fig. 4b the uncertainties of objects depending on the uncertainty of the

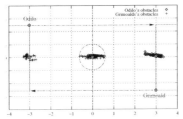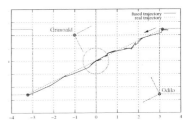

Fig. 5. (a) Two robots are traveling across the field, while they observe three stationary robots of the opponent team. The diamonds and crosses indicate the different measurements performed by the observing robots. (b) The resolved trajectory (continuous line) of an opponent robot, observed by two robots. The real trajectory is displayed as dotted line. The dashed lines indicate the robot's 90 degrees field of view.

observing robot and their relative distances are displayed using 1σ-contours. For illustrative purposes the uncertainty ellipses are scaled by an order of five. Each robot observes two obstacles in 3.5 and 7 meters distance. Robot Odilo is very certain about its pose and thus the covariance of the observed robot depends mainly on its distance. Robot Grimoald has a high uncertainty in its orientation (≈ 7 degrees). Consequently the position estimate of the observed obstacle is less precise and is highly influenced by the orientation uncertainty.

Step 3: Association of Opponents to Object Hypotheses. The association of an opponent robot's position with a predicted object position is currently performed on the basis of the Mahalanobis distance. In future we intent to use the Bhattacharyya distance, which is a more accurate distance measure for probability distributions.

4   Experimental Results

The presented algorithms are applied in our middle-size RoboCup team, the AGILO[1] RoboCuppers. At present, the RoboCup scenario defines a fixed world model with field-boundaries, lines and circles (see Fig. 4). Our approach was successfully applied in 1999 and 2000 during the RoboCup World Soccer Championship in Stockholm and Melbourne and the German Vision Cup. During a RoboCup match, every robot is able to process 15 to 18 frames per second with its on-board Pentium 200 MHz computer. When the robots planning algorithms' are turned off the vision system is easily able to cope with the maximum frame rate of our camera (25 fps). The localization algorithm runs with a mean processing time of 18 msec for a 16-Bit RGB ($384 * 288$) image. Only for 4% of the images the processing time exceeds 25 msec. A detailed analysis of the self- and ball-localization algorithm can be found in [6].

In the following we will present experiments that investigate the capability of tracking multiple opponent robots by our system. In the first experiment we have examined the capability of our algorithms to detect and estimate the opponent robots positions. The robots Odilo and Grimoald are simultaneously traveling in opposite directions from one side of the playing field to the other (see Fig. 5a). While they are in motion they are observing three stationary robots which are set up at different positions in the middle of the field. Diamonds and crosses indicate the observed opponents by Odilo and Grimoald, respectively. The variance in the

---

[1] The name is an homage to the oldest ruling dynasty in Bavaria, the Agilolfinger. The dynasties most famous representatives are Grimoald, Hugibert, Odilo and Tassilo

observation is due to positions estimations over long distances (4 to 7 meters) and minor inaccuracies in the robots self-localization. Furthermore it is noteworthy that the vision system of both robots never mistook their teammate as opponent.

The second experiment examines the tracking and data fusion capability of our system. Odilo and Grimoald are set up at different positions on the field. An opponent robot crosses the field diagonally from the corner of the penalty area at the top right to the corner of the penalty area at the lower left (see Fig. 5b). The first part of the journey is only observed by Grimoald, the middle part of both robots and the final part only by Odilo. The 90 degrees field of view of both robots is indicated through lines.

The opponent robot was tracked using the MHT algorithm with a simple linear Kalman filter. The state transition matrix, described a constant velocity model and the measurement vector provided positional information only. The positions of the opponent robots and their uncertainties were computed according to the algorithm described in section 3.2. Positional variance for the pixel coordinates of the region's center of gravity and region's width was assumed to be one pixel. The process noise was assumed to be white noise acceleration with a variance of 0.1 meters. The Mahalanobis distance was chosen such that $P\{X \leq \chi_2^2\} = 0.95$. N-scan-back pruning was performed from a depth of $N = 3$. In general the update time for one MHT iteration including N-scan-back and hypo pruning was found to be less than 10 msec. This short update time is due to the limited number of observers and observed objects in our experiment. We expect this time to grow drastically with an increasing number of observing and observed robots. However within a RoboCup scenario a natural upper bound is imposed through the limited number of robots per team. A detailed analysis of the hypothesis trees revealed that only at very few occasions new tracks were initiated. All of them were pruned away within two iterations of the MHT. Overall the observed track (see Fig. 5b, continuous line) diverges relatively little from the real trajectory (dotted line).

5   Conclusions

In this paper, we have developed and analyzed a cooperative probabilistic, vision-based state estimation method for individual, autonomous robots. This method enables a team of mobile robots to estimate their joint positions in a known environment and track the positions of autonomously moving objects.

References

1. I. Cox and J. Leonard. Modeling a dynamic environment using a bayesian multiple hypothesis approach. Artificial Intelligence, 66:311–344, 1994.
2. I.J. Cox and S.L. Hingorani. An Efficient Implementation of Reid's Multiple Hypothesis Tracking Algorithm and Its Evaluation for the Purpose of Visual Tracking. IEEE Trans. on PAMI, 18(2):138–150, February 1996.
3. S. Enderle, M. Ritter, D. Fox, S. Sablatnög, G. Kraetzschmar, and G. Palm. Soccer-robot localization using sporadic visual features. In IAS-6, Venice, Italy, 2000.
4. O.D. Faugeras. Three-dimensional computer vision: A geometric viewpoint. MIT Press, page 302, 1993.
5. J.-S. Gutmann, W. Hatzack, I. Herrmann, B. Nebel, F. Rittinger, A. Topor, T. Weigel, and B. Welsch. The CS Freiburg Robotic Soccer Team: Reliable Self-Localization, Multirobot Sensor Integration, and Basic Soccer Skills. In 2nd Int. Workshop on RoboCup, LNCS. Springer-Verlag, 1999.
6. R. Hanek and T. Schmitt. Vision-based localization and data fusion in a system of cooperating mobile robots. In IROS, 2000.
7. R. Hanek, T. Schmitt, M. Klupsch, and S. Buck. From multiple images to a consistent view. In 4th Int. Workshop on RoboCup, LNCS. Springer-Verlag, 2000.
8. S. Julier and J. Uhlmann. A new extension of the kalman filter to nonlinear systems. The 11th Int. Symp. on Aerospace/Defence Sensing, Simulation and Controls., 1997.
9. C. Marques and P. Lima. Vision-Based Self-Localization for Soccer Robots. In IROS, 2000.
10. D. Reid. An algorithm for tracking multiple targets. IEEE Transactions on Automatic Control, 24(6):843–854, 1979.
11. D. Schulz, W. Burgard, D. Fox, and A.B. Cremers. Tracking Multiple Moving Targets with a Mobile Robot using Particle Filters and Statistical Data Association. In ICRA, 2001.
12. S. Thrun. Probabilistic algorithms in robotics. AI Magazine, 2000.
13. S. Thrun, M. Beetz, M. Bennewitz, W. Burgard, A.B. Cremers, F. Dellaert, D. Fox, D. Haehnel, C. Rosenberg, N. Roy, J. Schulte, and D. Schulz. Probabilistic algorithms and the interactive museum tour-guide robot minerva. International Journal of Robotics Research, 2000.

A New Contour-Based Approach
to Object Recognition for Assembly Line Robots

Markus Suing, Lothar Hermes, and Joachim M. Buhmann

Institut für Informatik III, Universität Bonn
Römerstr. 164, D-53117 Bonn
{suing, hermes, jb}@cs.bonn.edu

Abstract. A complete processing chain for visual object recognition is described in this paper. The system automatically detects individual objects on an assembly line, identifies their type, position, and orientation, and, thereby, forms the basis for automated object recognition and manipulation by single-arm robots. Two new ideas entered into the design of the recognition system. First we introduce a new fast and robust image segmentation algorithm that identifies objects in an unsupervised manner and describes them by a set of closed polygonal lines. Second we describe how to embed this object description into an object recognition process that classifies the objects by matching them to a given set of prototypes. Furthermore, the matching function allows us to determine the relative orientation and position of an object. Experimental results for a representative set of real-world tools demonstrate the quality and the practical applicability of our approach.

Keywords: Object Recognition, Shape, Mesh Generation, Model Selection, Robotics

1 Introduction

Object manipulation with assembly line robots is a relatively simple task if the exact type, position and spatial alignment of objects are fixed or at least known in advance. The difficulty of the problem increases significantly if the assembly line transports a large set of various different types of objects, and if these objects appear in arbitrary orientation. In this case, the successful application of robots crucially depends on reliable object recognition techniques that must fulfill the following important requirements:

Reliability: The algorithm should be robust with respect to noise and image variations, i.e. its performance should not degrade in case of slight variations of the object shape, poor image quality, changes in the lightning conditions etc.

Speed: The online scenario of the application implies certain demands on the speed of the image recognition process. It must be able to provide the result of its computations in real time (compared to the assembly line speed) so that the robot can grasp its target from a slowly moving assembly line.

B. Radig and S. Florczyk (Eds.): DAGM 2001, LNCS 2191, pp. 329–336, 2001.
© Springer-Verlag Berlin Heidelberg 2001

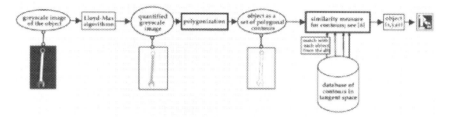

Fig. 1. The process pipeline. The system is trained by processing a single picture of each object and storing its contour in a database. By taking snapshots of the assembly line, it then automatically locates objects and describes their contours by a polygonal mesh. After matching them to the database objects, it is able to determine their type, position, and orientation, which are passed to the robot controller.

Automation: The process should be completely automated, i.e., it should work reliably without any additional user interaction.

In this paper, we describe a combination of algorithms that match the above requirements (fig. 1). It assumes that the robot is equipped with an image database in which a variety of different objects is stored by single prototype images. Using a camera which is mounted above the assembly line, the robot is expected to locate and identify by-passing objects, to pick them up and to put them to their final destination, thereby performing a task like sorting. The object recognition strategy proposed here is a two-stage process. The first stage locates individual objects and describes them by polygonal shapes. It is able to cope with almost all kinds of shapes, including those with holes or strong concavities, which is an important advantage over other contour descriptors such as many active contour approaches [3]. The second stage matches these shapes to the prototypes, detects the type of the objects, and computes their relative orientation.

Alternative approaches to image segmentation combined with polygonization typically depend on an initial edge detection processes and do not offer any strategies to effectively control the precision of the triangular approximation in a statistically well-motivated manner [9,10]. Other object vision systems for assembly line robots require models of each object, which they iteratively fit to 3D information from the scene [2,11]. A similar approach was followed in [12] where 2D contours were used to classify objects based upon [1].

2   Polygonal Image Segmentation

Formally, we describe an image by a function $I(o)$ that assigns each possible position o_i to a pixel value $I(o_i)$. In our current implementation, we just operate on binary images, i.e. $I(o) \in \mathbb{B}$, but the theoretical framework also applies to the multi-valued case. The image is assumed to consist of several areas a_λ, each being characterized by a homogeneous distribution of pixel values. We aim at finding a decomposition of the image $I(o)$ into segments $\hat{a}_\nu$ that are (at least

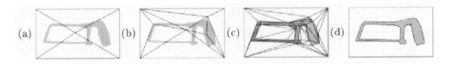

Fig. 2. (a) Binarized input image with superimposed initial mesh. (b) Early optimization stage after few splits. (c) Final triangulation. (d) Corresponding polygonal shape.

after consistent renaming of their indices) in good accordance with the areas a_λ. Thus the desired output of our algorithm is a function $\hat{a}(o)$ that, up to the best possible degree, mirrors the composite structure $a(o)$ of the image.

We assume that the image formation can be described by a simple generative model: First an image site o_i is selected according to a distribution $p(o_i)$ which is assumed to be uniform over all pixel positions. The site o_i is then assigned to an area $a_\lambda = a(o_i)$. Depending exclusively on this area information, the image site is finally provided with a pixel value $I_\mu = I(o_i)$ according to the conditional distribution $p(I_\mu|a_\lambda)$. Replacing a_λ by their estimates $\hat{a}_\nu$ therefore yields

$$p(o_i, I_\mu|a_\lambda) = p(o_i) \cdot p(I_\mu|a_\lambda) = p(o_i) \cdot p(I_\mu|\hat{a}_\nu) \ . \tag{1}$$

According to [6], the latent parameters $\hat{a}(o)$ should maximize the *complete data likelihood*, which – when assuming statistically independent pixel positions – can be written as $\mathcal{L} = \prod_i p(o_i, I(o_i), \hat{a}(o_i)) = \prod_i p(o_i, I(o_i)|\hat{a}(o_i)) \cdot p(\hat{a}(o_i))$. Inserting (1) and dropping constant factors, we obtain

$$\mathcal{L} \propto \prod_{\mu,\nu} \left(p(I_\mu|\hat{a}_\nu)\, p(\hat{a}_\nu) \right)^{n(I_\mu,\hat{a}_\nu)} \ , \tag{2}$$

where $n(I_\mu, \hat{a}_\nu)$ denotes the number of occurrences that the pixel value I_μ is observed in segment $\hat{a}_\nu$. The corresponding negative log likelihood per observation is given by $-\frac{1}{n}\log\mathcal{L} \propto -\sum_{\mu,\nu} p(I_\mu, \hat{a}_\nu) \log\left(p(I_\mu|\hat{a}_\nu) \cdot p(\hat{a}_\nu)\right)$, where $p(I_\mu, \hat{a}_\nu)$ is the probability of a joint occurrence of I_μ and $\hat{a}_\nu$, and n is the total number of observations. $-\frac{1}{n}\log\mathcal{L}$ can be decomposed into two parts. The first part is the *conditional entropy* of the pixel values $I(o_i)$ given their assignments to polygons $\hat{a}(o_i)$. The second part is the *entropy* of the a-priori distribution for the polygons, which is discarded to avoid any prior assumptions on the size of individual polygons. We arrive at the cost function

$$H(\hat{a}) = -\sum_{\mu,\nu} p(I_\mu, \hat{a}_\nu) \log p(I_\mu|\hat{a}_\nu) \ , \tag{3}$$

which is insensitive with respect to consistent renaming of the polygon indices. It can be shown to be minimal for perfect correspondances between the estimated and the true segmentations $\hat{a}(o_i)$ and $a(o_i)$, respectively. Besides it is concave in $p(\hat{a}_\nu, a_\lambda)$, which has the advantage that there are no local minima inside the probability simplex.

We represent the segmentation $\hat{a}(o)$ by a triangular mesh [5], which is refined by a hierarchical optimization strategy. Starting with 4 initial triangles, we iteratively add new vertices to achieve a finer resolution. Once a new vertex v_λ has been added, it is moved to the position where it causes the minimal partial costs with respect to (3). During this optimization, the movement of the vertex has to be restricted to the convex polygon that is formed by the straight lines connecting its adjacent vertices. Under certain preconditions, however, this constraint can be circumvented by *swapping* individual edges, which gives the algorithm additional flexibility. After having found the optimal position for the new vertex, all adjacing vertices are inserted into a queue from which they are extracted for further optimization (fig. 2).

The described algorithm can be implemented as a multiscale variant by downsampling the original image into several resolution levels, optimizing the mesh on a coarse level, mapping the result onto the next finer level, and continuing the optimization there. In this case, however, one has to detect at which granularity the current image resolution is too low to justify any further mesh refinement. For the definition of an appropriate decision criterion, it is important to note that the cost function (3) does not take the exact position of individual pixels into account. Instead, it completely relies on the joint distribution of grey values and image segments. From Sanov's theorem [4], one can thus infer that the probability of measuring a certain cost value H^* is completely determined by the minimal KL-distance between the generating model $p(I_\mu, a_\lambda)$ and the set of all empirical probability distributions $q(I_\mu, \hat{a}_\nu)$ for which the cost value H^* is obtained. It can be shown that, among these distributions, the one with minimal KL divergence has the parametric form

$$q^*(I_\mu, a_\lambda) \propto p(\hat{a}_\nu) \cdot p(I_\mu | \hat{a}_\nu)^\beta \ . \tag{4}$$

The correct value of β can easily be found by an iterated interval bisection algorithm. According to Sanov's theorem, this leads to the probability estimate

$$Pr\{H = H^*\} \approx 2^{-nD(q^*||p)} \ . \tag{5}$$

It can be used to compute the probability that a previous model generates an image with the same costs as the costs measured for the actual image model. If this probability is above a threshold p^{stop}, the optimization algorithm decides that the optimization progress might also be due to noise, and switches to the next finer resolution level in which the respective grey value distributions can be estimated with higher reliability. If it already operates on the finest level, adjacing triangles that share their dominant grey value are fused into larger polygons, which are then passed to the shape matching algorithm.

3   Application to Object Recognition

For the shape matching, we employ the algorithm described in [14], which has been found to feature both high accuracy and noise robustness. It first maps the shapes onto their normalized tangent space representations, which has the advantage of being invariant with regard to position and scale. After smoothing

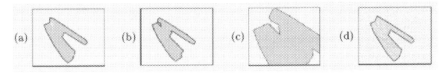

Fig. 3. (a), (b): Stapler segmented with $p^{stop} = 0.75$ and $p^{stop} = 0.99$, respectively. (c) Close-up of the fitted object boundary. (d) Result at a noise level of 40%.

the shapes by an appropriate shape evolution process [13], they are divided into their maximal convex and concave sub-arcs. This is motivated by the fact that visual object parts relate to the convex sub-arcs of the object shape. Based on this decomposition of shapes the similarity of two shapes is defined as a weighted sum over a set of many-to-one and one-to-many matching of consecutive convex and concave sub-arcs.

With this similarity measure, the type of a query object can be determined by retrieving the most similar prototype in the image database. In order to facilitate the subsequent grasp operation, the database also contains an adequate gripper position (*grasp point*) and orientation for each prototype (fig. 4 a). To initiate the grasping of the query object, we thus have to compute its rotation and translation parameters with respect to its prototype. Here we can take advantage of the fact that, to find the optimal matching between two polygonal sub-arcs a_i and b_i in tangent space, the algorithm described in [14] implicitly rotates a_i by the angle ϕ_i which minimizes the squared Euclidian distance $\int_0^1 (a_i(t) - b_i(t) + \phi_i)^2 dt$ between a_i and b_i. The shape similarity measure ignores the angles ϕ_i and is thus able to handle rigid object rotations and flexible joints. Here, however, we propose to compute the α-truncated mean of ϕ_i, which gives us a robust estimate ϕ of the relative orientation of the whole contour. To localize the grasp point on the query shape, the boundary positions of the convex and concave sub-arcs are used as reference points (fig. 4 b). Let p_d denote the grasp point for the database object, x_i the associated reference points, and y_i the reference points on the query shape. In addition define δ_i as the Euclidean distance between x_i and p_d, and d_i as the corresponding distance between y_i and the current grasp position on the query shape, p_q. Our approach is to choose p_q such that the d_i give the best fit to the corresponding δ_i. This problem setting is similar to the problem of multidimensional scaling (MDS), in which you are given pairwise dissimilarity values for a set of objects, which have to be embedded in a low-dimensional space. To find p_q, we therefore adapt the SSTRESS objective function for MDS [7] and minimize $J = \sum_i (\frac{d_i - \delta_i}{\delta_i})^2$, which can be achieved by a standard gradient descent algorithm. Note, however, that each d_i corresponds to a partial contour match and therefore to a rotation angle ϕ_i. If ϕ_i is significantly different from the rotation angle ϕ of the whole object, then the corresponding d_i should not exert a strong influence on the cost function. We, therefore, downweight each term in J by $\exp\left(-\lambda \sin^2(\Delta\phi_i/2)\right)$ with $\Delta\phi_i := \phi_i - \phi$. Besides it is possible to sample additional positions along the sub-arcs to obtain additional reference points, which increases the robustness of the algorithm.

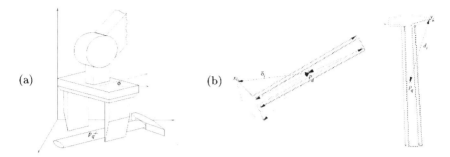

Fig. 4. (a) To adjust the position and orientation of the two-finger gripper, the system adapts the specifications for the prototype in the database. (b) The grasp points of database objects (left) and query (right) objects are defined by their relative distances from a set of control points, which are by-products of the shape matching algorithm.

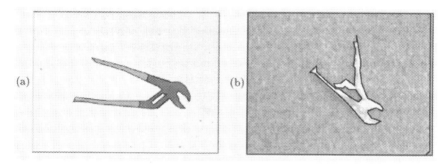

Fig. 5. (a) Segmentation with 3 quantization levels, run on a dithered camera image. (b) Segmentation with a textured background, demonstrating that the segmentation algorithm is not restricted to high contrast situations. Here a Floyd-Steinberg dithering with 32 quantization levels was used for preprocessing.

4 Experimental Results and Discussion

For a first evaluation of the system, a set of 6 different tools was chosen from a standard toolbox, including two rather similar saws, two wrenches, an allen key, and a stapler. From each object, 10 images were taken that showed the object in different positions and orientations. The images were binarized using a variant of the Lloyd-Max-Algorithm [15]. From each object, we randomly selected one image for the prototype database, while the remaining images were joined to form the validation set. The performance was evaluated using 10-fold crossvalidation.

In this scenario, we obtained an object recognition performance of 99.6% with a standard deviation of 0.8%. We also measured the precision of the orientation estimation and measured an average error of 2.2° with a standard deviation of 3.2° compared to visual inspection. The average error for the grasp point estimate was 5 pixels. The polygonization runs on a 1Ghz PC on images with a resolution of 256x256 pixels in less than five seconds. There are still several possibilities to fasten it up significantly, namely stopping the multiscale optimization at a lower stage, finding a better initial mesh and working with areas of interests.

The parameter p^{stop} has been found to be a powerful tool for controlling the accuracy with which the mesh is fitted to the object. See fig. 3 (a), (b) for two results with different p^{stop} values, and fig. 3 (c) for a close-up view of a generated contour. The availability of a reliable tool like this is important to cut down the computational complexity, because the object should not be described with a higher precision than necessary. A too complicated contour has to be simplified afterwards by the curve evolution approach described in [14]. Besides, the algorithm could be shown to remain very robust in the presence of noise. Fig. 3 (d) shows a test image in which 40% of the pixels had been set to random values. It demonstrates that the segmentation result remains nearly unaffected and still produces an accurate result.

With slight modifications, the segmentation algorithm is also capable of processing non-monochrome objects or objects on textured backgrounds (fig. 5). Instead of the Lloyd-Max quantization [15], one can alternatively use the Floyd-Steinberg dithering algorithm [8], which has the additional advantage of avoiding undesirable edges at the boundaries of homogeneously quantized image regions.

5   Conclusion and Future Work

We have presented a new computer vision method for analyzing objects on an assembly line. To automatically extract all information that is necessary to grasp and e.g. sort the objects by a robot, it employs a new fast and robust image segmentation algorithm that locates the objects and describes them by sets of polygons. These object representations are then used to compare the objects to a given set of prototypes, to recognize their type, and also to compute their exact position and orientation. Real-world experiments show that the proposed object recognition strategy produces high-quality results and matches all demands of the application (in terms of speed, robustness, and automation).

Our framework offers several promising starting points for further extensions. In our current implementation, we restrict ourselves to Bernoulli distributions (i.e. binarized images). The generative model, however, is valid for arbitrary discrete probability distributions, and can thus also be applied to images where a larger number of possible grey-values is retained. When applied to these images, the segmentation algorithm is able to describe individual objects as structures with several adjacent or even nested parts. Although we currently use only the outer contour of an object as its descriptor, we expect that there is a generic extension of Latecki's shape similarity concept to compound objects, which will be in the focus of our future research as well as speed improvements and the dependance of the performance of the polygonization on the p^{stop} parameter. Further work will also include the integration of the algorithms into an operational automated production system.

Acknowledgements. This work has been supported by a research grant from Astrium GmbH, Friedrichshafen. The implementation and evaluation of the algorithm were done in cooperation with the mz robotics laboratory, Rheinbach.

References

[1] E. M. Arkin, L. P. Chew, D. P. Huttenlocher, K. Kedem, and J. S. B. Mitchel. An efficiently computable metric for comparing polygonal shapes. *IEEE Transactions on Image Processing and Machine Intelligence*, 13(3):209–215, 1991.

[2] Gernot Bachler, Martin Berger, Reinhard Röhrer, Stefan Scherer, and Axel Pinz. A vision driven automatic assembly unit. In *Proc. Computer Analysis of Images and Patterns (CAIP)*, pages 375–382, 1999.

[3] A. Blake and M. Isard. *Active Contours*. Springer, 1998.

[4] Thomas M. Cover and Joy A. Thomas. *Elements of Information Theory*. John Wiley & Sons, 1991.

[5] Mark de Berg, Marc van Kreveld, Mark Overmars, and Otfried Schwarzkopf. *Computational Geometry: Algorithms and Applications*. Springer, 1997.

[6] A. P. Dempster, N. M. Laird, and D. B. Rubin. Maximum likelihood from incomplete data via the EM algorithm (with discussion). *Journal of the Royal Statistical Society B*, 39:1–38, 1977.

[7] Richard O. Duda, Peter E. Hart, and David G. Stork. *Pattern Classification*. John Wiley & Sons, 2nd ed. edition, 2000.

[8] R. W. Floyd and L. Steinberg. An adaptive algorithm for spatial gray scale. In *Society for Information Display 1975 Symposium Digest of Technical Papers*, page 36, 1975.

[9] Miguel Angel Garcia, Boris Xavier Vintimilla, and Angel Domingo Sapa. Approximation and processing of intensity images with discontinuity-preserving adaptive triangular meshes. In David Vernon, editor, *Computer Vision: ECCV 2000*, volume 1842 of *Lecture Notes in Computer Science*, pages 844–855. Springer, 2000.

[10] T. Gevers and A. W. M. Smeulders. Combining region splitting and edge detection through guided delaunay image subdivision. In J. Ponce D. Huttenlocher, editor, *Proc. of the International Conference on Computer Vision and Pattern Recognition (CVPR)*, pages 1021–1026. IEEE Press, 1997.

[11] F. Keçeci and H.-H. Nagel. Machine-vision-based estimation of pose and size parameters from a generic workpiece description. In *Proc. of the International Conference on Robotics and Automation (ICRA)*, 2001.

[12] S. Kunze and J. Pauli. A vision-based robot system for arranging technical objects. In *Proc. of the International Symposium on Automotive Technology and Automation (ISATA)*, pages 119–124, 1997.

[13] Longin Jan Latecki and Rolf Lakämper. Polygon evolution by vertex deletion. In M. Nielsen, Peter Johansen, Ole Fog Olsen, and Joachim Weickert, editors, *Scale Space 99*, volume 1682 of *Lecture Notes in Computer Science*, pages 398–409. Springer, 1999.

[14] Longin Jan Latecki and Rolf Lakämper. Shape similarity measure based on correspondence of visual parts. *IEEE Transactions on PAMI*, 22(10):1185–1190, October 2000.

[15] S. P. Lloyd. Least squares quantization in pcm. Technical report, Bell Laboratories, 1957.

Where Is the Hole Punch? Object Localization Capabilities on a Specific Bureau Task

E. Michaelsen[*], U. Ahlrichs[◊+], U. Stilla[*], D. Paulus[◊], H. Niemann[◊+]

[*]FGAN-FOM Research Institute for Optronics and Pattern Recognition
Gutleuthausstr. 1, 76275 Ettlingen, Germany
mich@fom.fgan.de, usti@fom.fgan.de (www.fom.fgan.de)
[◊]Lehrstuhl für Mustererkennung (LME, Informatik 5), Universität Erlangen-Nürnberg
Martensstr. 3, 91058 Erlangen, Germany
paulus@cs.fau.de (www5.informatik.uni-erlangen.de)

Abstract. In this paper, knowledge-based recognition of objects in a bureau scene is studied and compared using two different systems on a common data set: In the first system active scene exploration is based on semantic networks and an A*-control algorithm which uses color cues and 2-d image segmentation into regions. The other system is based on production nets and uses line extraction and views of 3-d polyhedral models. For the latter a new probabilistic foundation is given. In the experiments, wide-angle overviews are used to generate hypotheses. The active component then takes close-up views which are verified exploiting the knowledge bases, i.e. either the semantic network or the production net.

1 Introduction

Object localization from intensity images has a long history of research, but has not led to a general solution yet. Approaches proposed differ in objectives, exploited features, constraints, precision, reliability, processing time etc. Although surveys exist on knowledge-based object recognition [8, 6, 1], little has been published on experiments by different groups on a common task. Comparisons mainly exist on data-driven or appearance-based approaches, e.g. on the COIL-data base [7]. We compare two different approaches developed by different groups to solve one common task. We chose the localization of a hole punch from oblique views on an office desk. Fig. 3a,f,g,h below show such frames taken with different focal lengths by a video camera.

In the experiments camera parameters (focal length, pan, tilt) are adjustable and camera actions are controlled by the recognition process. The 3-d position of the hole punch is constrained by a desk. The rotation is restricted to the axis perpendicular to the ground plate (azimuth). The overviews are used to generate hypotheses of the hole

[+] This work was partially supported under grand number NI 191/12 by Deutsche Forschungsgemeinschaft.

B. Radig and S. Florczyk (Eds.): DAGM 2001, LNCS 2191, pp. 337–344, 2001.

punch´s position which result in camera actions to take close-up views. These are the input for final recognition or verification.

In Sect. 2 we outline the structure and interaction of the two systems and present a new probabilistic foundation of the production net system. Results of experiments on a common data-base are given in Sect. 3. In Sect. 4 a discussion of pros and cons of both approaches is given.

2   Architectures of the Two Systems

Initially we describe how the two systems interact on common data.

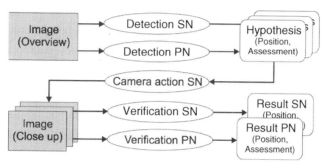

Fig. 1. Overview of the experimental localization setup with semantic network system (SN) and production net system (PN)

Fig. 1 shows the different components of the two localization systems and the data flow between them. Starting with an overview color-image (like the one presented in Fig. 3a) two different algorithms are applied that generate hypotheses for the hole punch´s location. The first system uses a pixel-based color classifier resulting in an interest map (Sect. 2.1), whereas the second system determines the hypotheses with a knowledge-based approach (Sect. 2.2). Both detection systems provide hypotheses as 2-d-coordinates in the image and an assessment value.

Based on the hypotheses, close-up views are then generated by adjusting pan and tilt and increasing the focal length of the active camera. Since close-up views contain objects in more detail, recognition is expected to be more reliable. Results of region segmentation are interpreted by the SN-system providing the center of gravity for each hypothesis. Lines constitute the input for the PN-system yielding a 3-d pose estimate for each hypothesis. This verification utilizes a different parameter setting and finer model compared to the detection phase. Both systems give an assessment value for the results.

2.1 Localization with the Semantic Network System (SN)

The semantic network approach uses the object's color as a cue to hypothesize possible positions of the hole punch in a scene. An interest operator based on histogram back-projection is applied [13], which learns the color distribution of the hole punch and applies this distribution to find pixels of similar color in the overview images. We calculate the color histograms in the normalized rg color space to be insensitive to illumination changes. Since the hole punch is red, the interest operator yields hypotheses for red objects.

The verification of the hypotheses is done by matching the hole punch's model to color regions. These regions are determined by segmenting the close-up views using a split and merge approach. The semantic network represents the 2-d object model by a concept which is linked to a color region concept [2]. The latter concept contains attributes for the region's height, width, and color as well as the allowed value range for each of these attributes. During analysis the expected values for the object are compared to the corresponding feature values calculated for each color region of the close up views. A match is judged according to a probability based optimality criterion [3]. The search for the best matching region is embedded into an A*-search.

2.2 Localization with the Production Net System (PN)

Production nets [12] have been described for different tasks like recognition of roads in maps and aerial images, 3D reconstruction of buildings, and vehicle detection. A syntactic foundation using coordinate grammars is given in [9]. Initially contours are extracted from gray-value images and approximated by straight line segments. The production system works on the set of lines reconstructing according to the production net the model structure of the hole punch. This search process is performed with a bottom-up strategy. Accumulating irrevocable control and associative access is used to reduce the computational load [11, 9].

The view-based localization utilized here for the hole punch search implements accumulation of evidence by means of cycles in the net with recursive productions [10]. The accumulation resembles generalized Hough transform [4]. The hole punch is modeled by a 3-d polyhedron. The 3-d pose space is equidistantly sampled rotating the object in azimuth α in steps of $10°$ and varying the distance d in 5 steps of 10cm. For each of these 180 poses a 2-d model is automatically generated off-line by a hidden line projection assuming perspective projection and internal camera parameters estimated by previous calibration (see Fig. 2). The recognition relies on matching structures formed of straight line segments. Below only L-shaped structures are used, that are 4-d attributed by the location of the vertex and the two orientations. If a L-structure in the image is constructed from two lines, then similar L-structures in each 2-d model are searched, where the two orientations account for the similarity. Matches are inserted as cue instances into an 4-d accumulator of position in the image (x,y), azimuth α, and distance d. Accumulation is performed by recursive productions operating on the associative memory which is discretized in Pixel, $1°$ and 1cm. Values found in the accumulator highly depend on structures and parameters. High values indicate the presence of the object for a corresponding pose.

Fig. 2. Selected set of 2-d models projected from a 3-d polyhedron model ($\Delta\alpha=15°$)

We now replace the accumulator values by an objective function based on probabilistic assessment. For this purpose we modified the theory derived by Wells [14]. But while he uses contour primitives attributed by their location, orientation and curvature our approach matches L-structures; while he operates in the image domain we operate in the accumulator.

Wells´ Theory of Feature-Based Object Recognition

Wells uses a linear pose vector β of dimension 4 (for similarity transform) or 8 (for limited 3-d rotations according to the linear combination of views method), and a correspondence function Γ, mapping the image features to a model feature or to the background. A scaled likelihood

$$\mathbf{L}(\Gamma, \beta) = -\frac{1}{2}(\beta - \beta_0)^{\mathsf{T}}\psi_\beta^{-1}(\beta - \beta_0) + \sum_{i, j: \Gamma_i = M_j}\left[\lambda - \frac{1}{2}(\mathbf{Y}_i - \mathbf{M}_j\beta)^{\mathsf{T}}\psi_{ij}^{-1}(\mathbf{Y}_i - \mathbf{M}_j\beta)\right] \quad (1)$$

of an image-to-model correspondence and a pose is derived from independence and distribution assumptions. The first term in Eq. 1 results from a normal prior distribution on the pose, where ψ_β is the corresponding covariance matrix and β_0 the center. The second term is due to the conditional probability that a set of correspondences between the image features Y_i and model features M_j may be true, given a pose β. Wells gives the model features M_j in a matrix format, that enables linear transformation to the image feature domain. Inside the sum there appears a trade-off rewarding each image-to-model correspondence by a constant λ and punishing the match errors. The punishing term for each correspondence results from the assumption of linear projection and normal distributed error in the mapping of object to image features with covariance ψ. To reduce the complexity of the estimation process, this matrix is independent of the indices i and j. The reward term λ is to be calculated from a representative training-set according to

$$\lambda = \ln\left(\frac{1}{(2\pi)^{\nu/2}\,m}\frac{(1 - \mathbf{B})}{\mathbf{B}}\frac{\mathbf{W}_1 \cdots \mathbf{W}_\nu}{\sqrt{|\psi|}}\right). \quad (2)$$

The middle factor in this product is calculated from the ratio between the probability B that a feature is due to the background, and the probability $(1-B)/m$ that it corresponds to a certain model feature, where m is the number of features in the model. The rightmost factor in the product is given by the ratio between the volume of the whole feature domain $W_1 \ldots W_\nu$ and the volume of a standard deviation ellipsoid of ψ.

Modification for Accumulator-Productions in the PN-System

To apply the theory of Wells to our problem we set $\vec{\beta}=(x,y,\alpha,d)$. The objective funktion L is calculated for each cluster of cues. The pose β is estimated as mean $\hat{\beta}^{\mathsf{T}} = (\hat{\mathbf{x}},\hat{\mathbf{y}},\hat{\alpha},\hat{\mathbf{d}})$ of the poses of the member cues of the cluster. The correspondence Γ is coded as an attribute of the cues. For each model feature j put into correspondence in the cluster the closest cue i to the mean is taken as representative of the set of all cues i corresponding to j. This is done, because we regard multiple cues to the same model feature as not being mutual independent. The attribute values $(x_i, y_i, \alpha_i, d_i)$ directly serve as Y_i for formula (1). There is no need for coding model features in a matrix format, because the projection has been treated off-line in the generation of the 2-d models. We just determine the deviation for each such cue

$$\mathbf{L} = \sum_j \left[\lambda - \underset{\Gamma_i=j}{\mathbf{Min}} \left[\frac{1}{2}(\mathbf{Y}_i - \hat{\beta})^{\mathsf{T}} \psi^{-1}(\mathbf{Y}_i - \hat{\beta}) \right] \right]. \tag{3}$$

The covariance matrix ψ of the cues and the background probability B are estimated from the training-set. These differ in the present bureau application significantly between overviews and close-ups. For the overviews the reward λ is close to the critical value zero indicating that recognition in these data is difficult and not very stable. Recall that the maximization must not take those Γ into account, that include negative terms into the sum. This condition gives a new way to infer the threshold parameters for adjacency in the cluster productions from a training set. In the verification step parameters are set different compared to the detection step, e. g. the accumulator is now sampled in $\Delta\alpha=5°$ and $\Delta d=5$cm. Fig. 2 shows 2-d models used for close-up views, whereas Fig. 3d,e show two coarser 2-d models used for the overviews.

The theory of Wells rejects scenes as non recognizable, if λ turns out to be negative according to Eq. 2. In such situation we still may use a positive reward λ' instead indicating that cues with high values for this objective function will contain more false matches than correct ones with high probability. Still among the set of all cues exciding a threshold, there will be the correct hypothesis with a probability that may be calculated from the difference $\lambda-\lambda'$.

For the close-ups a ML-decision is needed and we have to use the correct reward term λ. For these data the estimation for λ is much bigger. Compared to the Hough-accumulator value used as decision criterion in [10] the likelihood function includes an error measurement on the structures set in correspondence with the model and evaluates the match based on an estimated background probability.

3 Experiments

Each system used its own set of training images for hypothesis generation and object recognition. The training of the SN-system is based on 40 close-up images for model parameter estimation and a histogram for red objects that is calculated using one close-up image of the hole punch. For the PN-system 7 desk scene overview and 7 close-up images were used as training set. The evaluation was done on 11 common scenes disjoint from the training sets. One of these overviews is depicted in Fig. 3a. For each test scene both systems generated their hypotheses (Fig. 3b,c), and corresponding close-up sets were taken by the scene exploration system.

Success and failure was judged manually. In Fig. the highest objective function value L is detected by the PN-system in the correct location. Fig. 3d presents the 2-d model corresponding to this result. The pose is incorrectly determined on this image. Fig. 3e shows 2-d model of a cue cluster with correct pose and location but having a smaller likelihood. On the 11 overview images only two localization results are successful where one gives the correct pose, too. This shows that in this case pure ML is not sufficient. Therefore clusters are sorted according to L and the 1‰-highest-L scoring clusters were taken as hypotheses (see white crosses in Fig. 3b). A successful localization according to the definition is contained in 5 of the 11 hypotheses sets.

The color-based detection of the SN-system does not determine pose. It gives 8 correct ML-localization results in the overview images. In 10 results the hypotheses set contains the correct cue. Fig. 3c shows an interest-map of the overview image. Dark regions correspond to high likelihood of the hole punch´s position. Note that hypotheses sets of the two systems differ substantially, as can be seen comparing Fig. 3b and Fig. 3c. Where the SN-system finds red objects like the glue stick and the adhesive tape dispenser, the PN-system finds rectilinear structures like books.

Fig. 3f,g,h show the three close-up views taken according to the PN-system detection. In the verification step the ML-decision includes all cues from a close-up set resulting from one overview. Fig. 3i,j,k display the result, where the third scores correctly the highest. A successful verification with the PN-system additionally requires the correct pose. This is performed correctly on 3 of the 11 examples. The SN-system succeeds on 9 close-up sets without giving a pose. The PN-system succeeds on one of the two failure examples of the SN-system.

4   Discussion

In this contribution we demonstrated how the difficult problem of object recognition can be solved for a specific task. An office tool is found by two model-based active vision systems. In both cases the object was modeled manually in a knowledge base. A 3-d polyhedral model was used in the PN-system requiring line segmentation for the recognition. 2-d object views were modeled in SN-system using a region based approach. The experiments revealed that color interest maps of the SN-system outperform the line-based hypothesis generation of the PN-system on the considered scenery. We conjecture that this is due to high color saturation and small size of the object in the overview images. Close-up views captured by the active camera increase the recognition stability of both systems; in some cases overview images already yielded the correct result.

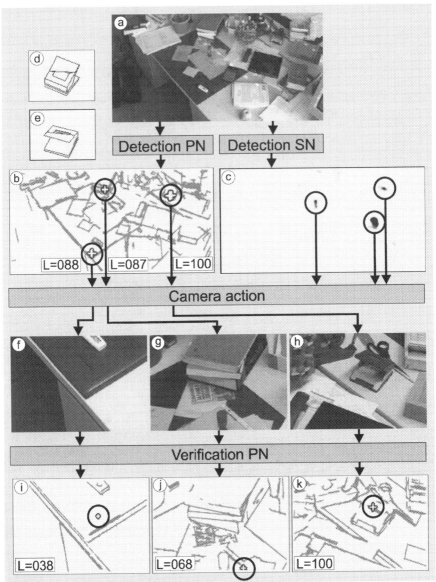

Fig. 3. Localization of the hole punch in a bureau scene; close-up views and verification of the SN-system omitted

For the line-based recognition the process had to be parameterized differently for overview and close-up images. A new probabilistic objective function for the PN-system allows parameter inference from a training set, and opens the way for a better interpretation of the results. Both systems achieved recognition rates that – with respect to the complexity of the task - were satisfactory. It is expected that the combination of line and color segmentation will eventually outperform either approach. This is subject to future work.

The PN-system is designed to work on T-shaped structures as well. Other possibilities like U-shaped structures would be a straight forward extension. Further investigations will include an EM-type optimization of pose and correspondence in the final verification step also following [14].

We proved that one common experimental set-up can be used by two different working groups to generate competitive hypotheses and to verify these hypotheses, even in an active vision system. The image data is publicly available to other groups to allow further comparisons under the web site of the authors.

References

1. Ade F.: The Role of Artificial Intelligence in the Reconstruction of Man-made Objects from Aerial Images. In: Gruen A., Baltsavias E. P., Henricsson O.(eds.): Automatic Extraction of Man-Made Objects from Aerial and Space Images (II), Birkhäuser, Basel (1997). 23-32
2. Ahlrichs U., Paulus D., Niemann H.: Integrating Aspects of Active Vision into a Knowledge- Based System. In: A. Sanfeliu et al. (eds.): 15th International Conference on Pattern Recognition, IEEE, Barcelona, Vol. IV (2000) 579-582
3. Ahlrichs U.: Wissensbasierte Szenenexploration auf der Basis erlernter Analysestrategien. Diss., Uni. Erlangen-Nürnberg, to appear (2001)
4. Ballard D. H., Brown C. M.: Computer Vision. Prentice Hall, Englewood Cliffs, New Jersey, (1982)
5. Binfort T. O., Levitt T. S.: Model-based Recognition of Objects in Complex Scenes. In: ARPA (ed.). Image Understanding Workshop 1994. Morgan Kaufman, San Francisco (1994) 149-155
6. Crevier D., Lepage R.: Knowledge-Based Image Understanding Systems: A Survey. CVIU, 6 (1997) 161-185
7. COIL-100. http://www.cs.columbia.edu/CAVE (confirmed 06.07.2001).
8. Lowe D. G.: Three-dimensional Object Recognition from Single Two-dimensional Images. AI, 31 (1987) 355-395
9. Michaelsen E.: Über Koordinaten Grammatiken zur Bildverarbeitung und Szenenanalyse. Diss., Uni. Erlangen-Nürnberg, (1998)
10. Michaelsen E., Stilla U.: Ansichtenbasierte Erkennung von Fahrzeugen. In: Sommer G., Krüger N., Perwas C. (eds.).: Mustererkennung 2000, Springer, Berlin (2000) 245-252
11. Nilsson N. J.: Principles of Artificial Intelligence. Springer, Berlin (1982)
12. Stilla U.: Map-aided structural analysis of aerial images. ISPRS Journal of Photogrammetry and Remote Sensing, 50, 4 (1995) 3-10
13. Swain M. J., Ballard D. H.: Color indexing. IJCV, 7, 1 (1995) 11-32
14. Wells III W. M.. Statistical Approaches to Feature-Based Object Recognition. IJCV, 21 (1997) 63-98

Phenomenology-Based Segmentation of InSAR Data for Building Detection

Uwe Soergel, Karsten Schulz, and Ulrich Thoennessen

FGAN-FOM Forschungsinstitut für Optronik und Mustererkennung,
Gutleuthausstr. 1, D-76275 Ettlingen, Germany,
soe,schulz,thoe@fom.fgan.de,
WWW home page: http://fom.fgan.de

Abstract. By interferometric SAR measurements digital elevation models (DEM) of large areas can be acquired in a short time. Due to the sensitivity of the interferometric phase to noise, the accuracy of the DEM depends on the signal to noise ratio (SNR). Usually the disturbed elevation data are restored employing statistical modeling of sensor and scene. But in undulated terrain layover and shadowing phenomena occur. Furthermore, especially in urban areas, additional effects have to be considered caused by multi-bounce signals and the presence of dominant scatterers. Unfortunately, these phenomena cannot be described in a mathematically closed form. On the other hand it is possible to exploit them in model-based image analysis approaches. In this paper we propose a method for the segmentation and reconstruction of buildings in InSAR data, considering the typical appearance of buildings in the data.

1 Introduction

The improved ground resolution of SAR suggests to employ this sensor for the analysis of man-made objects [1],[2]. But, due to specific SAR effects, this imagery is difficult to interpret. Particularly in urban areas, phenomena like layover, shadow, multi-path signals and speckle [3] have to be considered.

The phase of interferometric SAR (InSAR) depends on the elevation of objects in the scene. Especially in areas with low (SNR) - respectively poor coherence - the phase information is disturbed. Hence, the noise component has to be removed or at least reduced before further analysis. Often, the noise is decreased by averaging, e.g. low-pass filtering or multi-look processing. However, this leads to reduced spatial resolution and blurred phase jumps at object boundaries.

Other methods base on statistical modeling of sensor and scene [4]. With bayesian inference the data is restored to a configuration which most probably caused the measured data [5]. Scene and sensor are modeled according to the central limit theorem, which requires a large number of independent scatterers per resolution cell, contributing each a small impact to the measured signal only. In case of urban areas this assumptions do not hold anymore, because of the presence of dominant scatterers and the privileged rectangular object alignment. Furthermore, the number of scatterers per resolution cell decreases

B. Radig and S. Florczyk (Eds.): DAGM 2001, LNCS 2191, pp. 345–352, 2001.

with growing resolution of the sensors. Thus, in urban areas the data can not be restored without additional knowledge about the scene.

Recently, approaches for building reconstruction in InSAR elevation data were proposed, which apply either model-based machine-vision methods [6] or take typical phenomena into account, like layover and shadowing [7]. These methods base on the analysis of the geocoded DEM alone. In this approach the entire set of complex InSAR information (phase, intensity and coherence) is analyzed for the segmentation of extended buildings.

2   SAR and InSAR Principle

2.1   Synthetic Aperture Radar (SAR) Principle

An air- or spaceborne sensor illuminates the scene with radar pulses, the runtime of the returned signal is measured. Since the antenna footprint on the ground is large, a side-looking viewing geometry is required to determine the distance between objects in the scene and the sensor from the runtime. The signal is partly either reflected away from the sensor or scattered towards the sensor, depending on the roughness of the scene compared to the signal wavelength (e.g. X-band: 3cm, P-band: 64cm). The object positions in the azimuth direction are obtained by coherently integrating the signal of many pulses along the trajectory of the carrier (synthetic aperture). The resolution of SAR is a function of the impulse bandwidth in range and the length of the synthetic aperture in azimuth.

The illumination geometry and the coherent measurement principle give rise to some phenomena (Fig. 1). Layover occurs always at vertical building walls facing towards the sensor. This leads to a mixture of signal contributions from the building and the ground in the SAR image. On the other side the building casts a shadow which occludes smaller objects behind. The height of a detached building can be derived from the shadow length and the viewing angle θ. Multibounce signals between building walls and the ground or at corners structures lead to strong signal responses. Sloped rooftops which are oriented perpendicular towards the sensor cause very strong reflections as well.

2.2   InSAR Principle

SAR interferometry takes benefit from the coherent SAR measurement principle. Fig. 2 illustrates the principle of airborne single-pass across-track interferometry measurement. Two antennas are mounted above each other on the carrier with geometric displacement B. One of the antennas illuminates the scene and both antennas receive the backscattered complex signals.

The interferogram S is calculated by a pixel by pixel complex multiplication of the master signal s_1 with the complex conjugated slave signal s_2. Due to the baseline B, the distances from the antennas to the scene differ by Δr, which results in a phase difference in the interferogram:

$$S = s_1 \cdot s_2^* = a_1 \cdot a_2 \cdot e^{j\Delta\varphi} \quad with \quad \Delta\varphi = -\frac{2\pi}{\lambda}\Delta r, \tag{1}$$

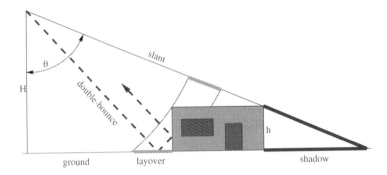

Fig. 1. SAR phenomena at buildings

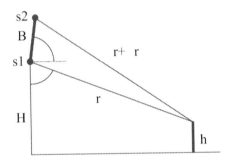

Fig. 2. Geometry of InSAR measurement

where λ denotes the wavelength. The phase difference is unambiguous in the range $-\pi < \Delta\varphi \leq \pi$ only. Thus an phase-unwrapping step is often required before further process. Furthermore, the range dependency of $\Delta\varphi$ has to be removed (flat earth correction). Afterwards, the relative height differences Δh in the scene can be approximated from $\Delta\varphi$:

$$\Delta h \approx \frac{\lambda}{2\pi B} \cdot \frac{r \cdot \sin(\theta)}{\cos(\xi - \theta)} \cdot \Delta\varphi \tag{2}$$

with parameters distance r, wavelength λ, antenna geometry angle ξ and viewing angle θ. The standard deviation of the interferogram phase depends approximately on the SNR and the number of independent looks L:

$$\sigma_\Phi \approx \frac{1}{\sqrt{SNR}} \cdot \left(\frac{1}{\sqrt{L}}\right) \tag{3}$$

With equations 2 and 3, the standard deviation of the elevation is obtained:

$$\sigma_h \approx \frac{\lambda}{2\pi B} \cdot \frac{r \cdot \sin(\theta)}{\cos(\xi - \theta) \cdot \sqrt{SNR} \cdot \sqrt{L}} \tag{4}$$

The coherence γ is a function of the noise impact of the interferogram. It is usually estimated from the data by the magnitude of the complex cross-correlation coefficient of the SAR images:

$$\hat{\gamma} = \frac{\left| \sum_{n=1}^{N} s_1{}^{(n)} \cdot s_2{}^{*(n)} \right|}{\sqrt{\sum_{n=1}^{N} \left| s_1{}^{(n)} \right|^2 \cdot \sum_{n=1}^{N} \left| s_2{}^{(n)} \right|^2}} = \frac{1}{1 + \dfrac{1}{SNR}}. \tag{5}$$

Hence, the local quality of an InSAR DEM can be directly assessed from the data by the related coherence value.

3   Approach

Knowledge about the typical appearance of terrain in the data may be incorporated to discriminate urban from rural areas (Figure 3). For the latter task, classification schemes have been proposed in the literature [1],[2] which base on the statistical properties of SAR imagery. If such a preliminary classification is carried out, the elevation data of natural areas are smoothed with standard methods like averaging. The complementary areas are processed with a phenomenology-based approach described below in more detail.

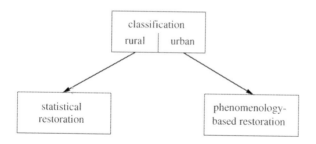

Fig. 3. Suitable restoration of elevation data after classification

3.1   Modeling of Scene and Objects

A section of the test dataset Frankfurt is depicted in Fig. 4. The modeling of the scene is based on the following observations and assumptions:

– Man-made objects often have right-angled or cylindrical structures and appear as regions with similar intensity. Object boundaries in many cases coincide with clearly visible intensity edges.

- The elevation is modeled to be piecewise linear. Steps appear at building walls only.
- Buildings may contain substructures with different height or roof material. Their rooftops are assumed to be flat.
- At the building wall facing towards the sensor, layover and double-bounce occurs. This leads to areas of brighter intensity.
- At the other building wall an area on the ground is occluded (shadow area). This shadow shows low intensity and poor coherence.
- Very flat objects, like roads, ponds or flat roofs without any structure at all, behave very similar to shadow areas, because the signal is totally reflected.

Fig. 4. Test data: intensity, elevation and coherence

3.2 Segmentation and Reconstruction of Buildings

The initial segmentation is carried out by a combined region growing in the intensity and the elevation data. Preprocessing is required to achieve a reasonable segmentation result: The intensity data is de-speckled and the elevation information is smoothed by median filtering. Usually, most of the segments are extracted from the intensity data. The segmentation in the elevation data is mainly required to distinguish rooftops from adjacent ground which sometimes appear very similar in the intensity channel. It is crucial to detect as many object boundaries as possible. Hence, the adaptive region growing threshold th_{rg} can be set to a small maximum value. As a consequence, over-segmentation occurs, which is corrected in a subsequent post-processing step described below.

For each segment an average height is calculated independently. Considering the noise influence, the elevation values are weighted with the coherence in the averaging step. This results in preliminary depth map with prismatic objects. Segments with low average intensity or coherence are regarded as unreliable. These segments are assumed to coincide with shadow areas or roads, and are considered later to check the consistency of the results.

Two types of building parts are discriminated. Mayor building parts have a significantly larger average height than at least one adjacent segment. They are found at boundaries between buildings and ground. Minor building parts are surrounded by mayor building parts and correspond to superstructures. Adjacent building segments are joint and form a set of more complex structures. Furthermore, the segments in question have to match the building model with respect to area, shape and compactness.

Shadow cast from a building leads to either stripe or L-shaped segments, depending on the aspect. Their width is a function of viewing angle and object elevation. Hence, for each building candidate an expectation area for a shadow stripe is predictable. Unfortunately, shadow cannot always be distinguished from objects which appear similar in the data, like roads. Therefore, as a minimum requirement, an area of the set of unreliable segments is expected to be found at the predicted shadow location. If so, the candidate segment is labeled to be a building. In case shadow does not interfere with roads, a more subtle analysis is carried out. Shadow stripes are extracted in the intensity data with a simple structural image analysis algorithm. Starting with short lines as primitives, stripes are built-up, which enclose regions of low intensity.

Shadow areas are used as well to overcome under-segmentation. Segments, which contain a possible shadow area,, are further investigated in a post processing step [8]. Under-segmentation is corrected in two different ways. If the histogram of the original elevation values shows a bimodal curve, the segment is split in two closed segments, if possible. In a second approach a region growing step in the median filtered elevation data is performed. In contrast to the initial segmentation, the border towards the shadow region is used as seed and the threshold is smaller [9]. Over-segmentation is corrected by merging adjacent segments with similar heights. After post-processing, the depth map is recalculated in the manner described above.

4   Results

The test data (Fig. 4) was acquired with the airborne AER-II sensor of FGAN [10]. Range direction is from left to right, ground resolution is approximately one meter. From the sensor configuration the standard deviation of the elevation measurement is estimated to be about two meter in the best case. Several extended buildings are present in the scene at the airport Frankfurt. The rooftops are generally flat with small elevated superstructures, mostly required for illumination and air-conditioning inside the building (Fig. 5a).

Thresholds are related to a maximum value of 255, except coherence which is defined to be in the range $[0, 1]$. The threshold th_{rg} for the initial region growing was set to 10. In Fig. 5b possible layover segments (high intensity) and unreliable segments (low average intensity or coherence, $th_{int} = 70$ and $th_{coh} = 0.75$) are shown. The layover candidates coincide as expected with building walls towards the sensor. The superstructures on the rooftops show bright intensity as well. However, closed layover candidate segments could not be detected at every suitable location. The area considered as unreliable covers the roads and is found at the building walls facing away from the sensor. It turned out that especially shadow cast from objects with small height difference to the ground could not be segmented from the average intensity data alone. This behavior is probably caused from multi-bounce effects. The extracted shadow stripes (Fig. 5c) correspond well with the unreliable segments.

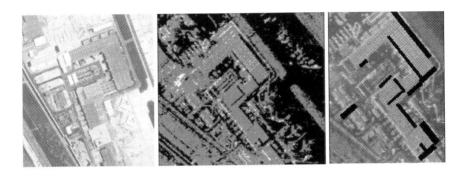

Fig. 5. a) Aerial image, b) Segmentation: layover (bright) and unreliable areas (dark), c) shadow stripes

In Fig. 6a the extracted mayor and minor building segments are depicted. The depth map in Fig. 6b shows all details. Especially at layover areas over-segmentation occurs. In Fig. 6c the minor objects are neglected to give a more general overview of the scene. This result is superimposed with building foot-prints extracted from the aerial image. The missing part of the large building was rejected because of poor coherence. One building was not detected, probably caused by interference with the large building nearby. This behavior is subject to further studies. The forest in the lower left showed similar properties and could not be distinguished from the buildings. The remaining buildings match well with the reference data. Note the building in the middle left, missing in the aerial image. It was erected in the period between the acquisition of the aerial image and the InSAR measurement campaign. The accuracy of the averaged elevation data was in the order of the standard deviation of the measurement.

5   Conclusion and Future Work

A model-based approach for the segmentation of buildings in InSAR data was proposed. The results are useful for an improved interpretation of the scene. In case information about vast areas has to be acquired very fast, for example in a disaster scenario like an earthquake, the approach may be employed for change detection. However, the method is limited to extended, detached and flat roofed buildings. In future work a subsequent reconstruction step will be carried out, which yields a generalized vector description of the buildings. Additionally, the object model will be expanded to sloped objects like gable roofs.

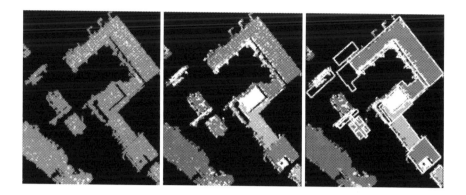

Fig. 6. Results: Building segments, detailed depth map, depth map with reference data

Acknowledgment. We want to thank Dr. Ender (FGAN-FHR Research Institute for High Frequency Physics and Radar Techniques) for providing the InSAR data [10].

References

1. Carlotto, M.: Detecting Man-Made Features in SAR Imagery. Proc. IGARSS (1996) 34–36
2. Gouinaud, C., Tupin, F., Maître, H.: Potential and Use of Radar Images for Characterization and Detection of Urban Areas. Proc. IGARSS (1996) 474–476
3. Schreier, G.: Geometrical Properties of SAR Images. In Schreier, G., editor, SAR Geocoding: Data and Systems. Wichmann, Karlsruhe. (1999) 103–134
4. Lee, J. S., Hoppel, K. W., Mange, S. A., Miller A. R.: Intensity and Phase Statistics of Multilook Polarimetric and Interferometric SAR Imagery. IEEE Trans. Geosci. Remote Sensing **32(5)** (1994) 1017–1028
5. Walessa, M., Datcu, M.: Enhancement of Interferometric DEMs by Spatially Adaptive Model-Based Filtering of Non-Stationary Noise. Proc. EUSAR (2000) 695–698
6. Gamba, P., Houshmand, B., Saccini, M.: Detection and Extraction of Buildings from Interferometric SAR Data. IEEE Trans. Geosci. Remote Sensing **38(1)** (2000) 611–618
7. Bolter, R., Leberl F.: Phenomenology-Based and Interferometry-Guided Building Reconstruction from Multiple SAR Images. Proc. EUSAR (2000) 687–690
8. Soergel, U., Schulz, K., Thoennessen, U.: Segmentation of Interferometric SAR Data in Urban Areas. Proc. of AeroSense (2001) in press
9. Soergel, U., Schulz, K., Thoennessen, U.: Segmentation of Interferometric SAR Data for Building Detection. IAPRS **33(B1)** (2000) 328–335
10. Ender, J. H. G.: Experimental Results Achieved with the Airborne Multi-Channel SAR System AER-II. Proc. EUSAR (1998) 315-318

Convex Relaxations for Binary Image Partitioning and Perceptual Grouping

Jens Keuchel, Christian Schellewald, Daniel Cremers, and Christoph Schnörr

Computer Vision, Graphics, and Pattern Recognition Group
Department of Mathematics and Computer Science;
University of Mannheim, D-68131 Mannheim, Germany
Email: {jkeuchel,cschelle,cremers,schnoerr}@ti.uni-mannheim.de;
fax: +49 621 181 2744; http://www.cvgpr.uni-mannheim.de

Abstract. We consider approaches to computer vision problems which require the minimization of a global energy functional over binary variables and take into account both local similarity and spatial context. The combinatorial nature of such problems has lead to the design of various approximation algorithms in the past which often involve tuning parameters and tend to get trapped in local minima.

In this context, we present a novel approach to the field of computer vision that amounts to solving a convex relaxation of the original problem without introducing any additional parameters. Numerical ground truth experiments reveal a relative error of the convex minimizer with respect to the global optimum of below 2% on the average.

We apply our approach by discussing two specific problem instances related to image partitioning and perceptual grouping. Numerical experiments illustrate the quality of the approach which, in the partitioning case, compares favorably with established approaches like the ICM-algorithm.

1 Introduction

The minimization of energy functionals plays a central role in many computer vision problems. When additionally discrete decision variables are involved, this task becomes intrinsically combinatorial and hence not easy to tackle. This fact motivated the development of various optimization approaches, like simulated annealing for binary image restoration [1], the ICM-algorithm for Markov Random Field based estimates [2], deterministic annealing for perceptual grouping [3], and many more (see [4]).

However, two crucial requirements from the optimization point-of-view continue to challenge these results: The quality of suboptimal solutions that can be achieved and the presence of additional parameters that have to be tuned by the user. Concerning quality, only simulated annealing can guarantee to find the optimal solution (see [5]) at the cost of unpractically slow annealing schedules. Other approaches are not immune against being trapped in an – eventually bad – local minimum. On the other hand, additional algorithmic tuning parameters

B. Radig and S. Florczyk (Eds.): DAGM 2001, LNCS 2191, pp. 353–360, 2001.
© Springer-Verlag Berlin Heidelberg 2001

for controlling search heuristics, annealing schedules, etc., often critically influence the quality of a solution despite having nothing to do in the first place with the original problem to be solved.

One possibility to overcome this latter point is to consider the mathematically well-understood class of convex optimization problems: They only have one global minimum which can be determined by established numerical algorithms without using additional parameters. In order to tackle a highly non-convex combinatorial optimization problem in this way, it is relaxed by mapping it into a higher dimensional space where the feasible solutions are contained in a convex set (see [6]). Minimization in that space and mapping back yields a suboptimal solution of the original problem, which usually is of a good quality. For special combinatorial problems it is even possible to give an optimality bound: Goemans and Williamson [7] proved the remarkable result that suboptimal solutions computed by convex optimization for the well known max-cut problem are at most 14% worse than the global optimum.

These favorable properties of convex optimization approaches have motivated our work. In the following sections we show how problems from the general class of binary quadratic functionals may be relaxed and solved by convex optimization. We next apply our approach to two specific computer vision problems (binary image partitioning and perceptual grouping) that fit into this class and present numerical results. Additionally, we show the quality of our approach by checking it using one-dimensional signals for which the optimal solution (ground truth) can be easily computed, and by comparing the image partitioning results with those of the ICM-algorithm.

2   Problem Statement: Minimizing Binary Quadratic Functionals

In this paper, we consider the problem of minimizing binary quadratic functionals which have the following general form:

$$J(x) = x^t Q x + 2b^t x + const , \quad x \in \{-1, 1\}^n, \ Q \in \mathcal{S}^n, \ b \in \mathbb{R}^n . \tag{1}$$

As no constraints are imposed on the matrix Q (apart from being in the class of symmetric matrices $\mathcal{S}^n$), such a functional is generally not convex. Furthermore, the integer constraint $x_i \in \{-1, 1\}$, $i = 1, \ldots, n$, makes the minimization problem (1) intrinsically difficult.

Computer vision problems with quadratic functionals like (1) arise in various contexts; in this paper, we will consider two representatives that are briefly illustrated in the following sections.

2.1   Binary Image Partitioning

Suppose that for each pixel position i of an image, a feature value $g_i \in \mathbb{R}$ has been measured that originates from either of two known prototypical values u_1, u_2[1].

---

[1] Besides the case of gray-values considered in this paper, local features related to motion, texture, etc., could also be dealt with.

Fig. 1. A binary image, heavily corrupted by (real-valued) noise.

Figure 1 shows an example, where g gives the gray-values of the noisy image that originally was black and white.

To restore the discrete-valued image function x that represents the original image, we wish to minimize the following functional which has the form of (1):

$$J(x) = \tfrac{1}{4} \sum_i \left((u_2 - u_1) x_i + u_1 + u_2 - 2g_i \right)^2 + \tfrac{\lambda}{2} \sum_{\langle i,j \rangle} (x_i - x_j)^2, \; x_i \in \{-1, 1\}, \; \forall i \,. \tag{2}$$

Here, the second term sums over all pairwise adjacent variables in vertical and horizontal direction on the regular image grid.

Functional (2) comprises two terms familiar from many regularization approaches [8]: A data-fitting term and a smoothness term modeling spatial context. However, due to the integer constraint $x_i \in \{-1, 1\}$, the optimization problem considered here is much more difficult than standard regularization problems.

In comparison to the ICM-algorithm [2], which minimizes a similar objective function, there are two main differences: Whereas the functional (2) sums over all pixels and hence is a global approach, the ICM-algorithm optimizes the objective function locally for each pixel in turn, which results in a much smaller complexity. The second difference is that the ICM-algorithm also uses the diagonally adjacent variables in the smoothness term for each pixel.

2.2 Perceptual Grouping

The task in perceptual grouping is to separate familiar configurations from the (unknown) background. Figure 2 shows an example: The instances of a given object consisting of three edge-elements are to be found in a noisy image.

To describe this problem mathematically, let $g_i, i = 1, \dots, n$, denote a feature primitive (e.g. an edgel computed at location i) in the image plane. We suppose that for each pair of primitives g_i, g_j a similarity measure d_{ij} can be computed corresponding to some given specific object properties (e.g. the difference between the relative angle of the edgels and the expected one according to the given object). Using the spatial context modeled by the values d_{ij}, each primitive g_i is labeled with a decision variable $x_i \in \{-1, 1\}$ ("1" corresponding to figure, "-1" corresponding to background and noise) by minimizing a functional

Fig. 2. Left: An object. **Right:** The object was rotated by a fixed arbitrary angle, and translated and scaled copies have been superimposed by noise.

of the form (1):

$$J(x) = \sum_{\langle i,j \rangle} (\lambda - d_{ij}) x_i x_j + 2 \sum_i (\lambda n - \sum_j d_{ij}) x_i, \ x_i \in \{-1, 1\}, \ \forall i , \quad (3)$$

where the first term sums over all pairs of feature primitives (see [3] for further details).

3   Convex Problem Relaxation and Algorithm

To overcome the hard integer constraints, problem (1) is relaxed to arrive at a less restricted, convex optimization problem of real variables, which can be tackled by using known methods like interior point algorithms that lead to an approximate solution for the original problem.

By dropping the constant and homogenizing the objective function, we rewrite the original functional (1) as follows:

$$x^t Q x + 2 b^t x = \begin{pmatrix} x \\ 1 \end{pmatrix}^t L \begin{pmatrix} x \\ 1 \end{pmatrix} , \quad L = \begin{pmatrix} Q & b \\ b^t & 0 \end{pmatrix} . \quad (4)$$

With slight abuse of notation, we denote the vector $(x \ 1)^t$ again by x. Then the minimization problem (4) can be rewritten:

$$\inf_{x \in \{-1,1\}^{n+1}} x^t L x = \inf_{x \in \{-1,1\}^{n+1}} L \bullet xx^t ,$$

where $X \bullet Y = \text{trace}(XY)$ denotes the standard matrix inner product for two symmetric matrices X, Y.

The convex relaxation is now achieved be replacing the rank-one matrix $xx^t \in \mathcal{K}$ by an arbitrary matrix $X \in \mathcal{K}$, where $\mathcal{K}$ denotes the cone of symmetric, positive semidefinite $(n+1) \times (n+1)$-matrices. Additionally, the integer constraint

$x_i \in \{-1, 1\}$ is *weakly* replaced by the according constraint $x_{ii} = 1$, so that we get:

$$\inf_{X \in \mathcal{K}} L \bullet X , \quad x_{ii} = 1, \forall i . \tag{5}$$

The optimization problem (5) belongs to the class of conic programs, which can be solved approximately with iterative interior-point algorithms (see [9]). To finally get back the solution x to (1) from the computed solution X to (5), we used the randomized-hyperplane technique described in [7].

4   Numerical Experiments

4.1   Restoration of 1D Noisy Signals Comprising Multiple Scales

To investigate the performance of the convex relaxation approach (5), we chose a one-dimensional synthetic signal x' (see Figure 3) that was superimposed with Gaussian white noise with standard deviation $\sigma = 1.0$, and tried to restore the original signal by using the one-dimensional version of functional (2). Since it is possible to compute the global optimum x^* of (1) for one-dimensional signals by using dynamic programming, we were able to compare the resulting suboptimal solution x to the optimal solution x^*. This experiment was repeated 1000 times for different noisy signals and varying values of λ. The results revealed an average relative error of below 2% for both the objective function value and the number of correctly classified pixels (see Figure 4). A representative example of the restoration is given in Figure 5.

4.2   2D-Images and Grouping

The results of applying the algorithm to restoration problems in the context of two-dimensional images are shown in Figures 6 – 8. The quality of the restorations using convex optimization is encouraging. Small errors that occur at the corners of connected regions as in Figure 8 (b) are due to the fact that the homogeneity constraint is less restrictive there as the local structure resembles noise.

We also implemented the locally classifying ICM-algorithm (see [2]), and applied it for different values of the parameter $\kappa\beta$, which plays a similar role as the parameter λ in (2). The comparison reveals the power of our global approach: Whereas the ICM-algorithm leaves some local holes within the structure (see Figures 6(d), 7(c), 8(c)), convex optimization is able to close these holes and yield a better piecewise-smooth result.

Concerning the grouping problem, the results of convex optimization are equally good (see Figure 9): Besides a small number of misclassified edgels that couldn't be identified as background by the chosen similarity measure, the original structure is clearly visible.

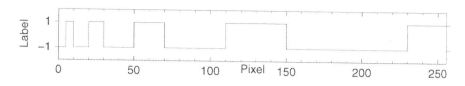

Fig. 3. Signal x' comprising multiple spatial scales.

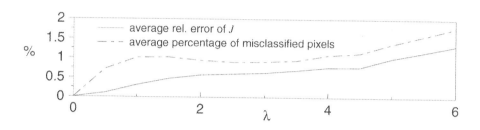

Fig. 4. Average relative error of the objective function J and average percentage of misclassified pixels of the suboptimal solution x compared to the optimal solution x^* for different values of the scale parameter λ.

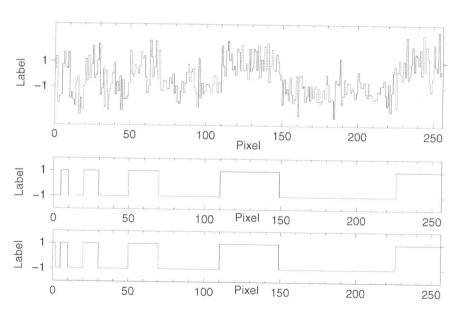

Fig. 5. A representative example illustrating the statistics shown in Fig. 4. **Top:** Noisy input signal. **Middle:** Optimal Solution x^*. **Bottom:** Suboptimal solution x.

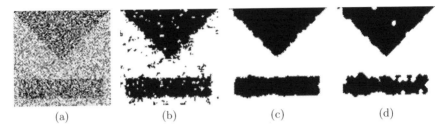

Fig. 6. Arrow and bar real image. **(a)** Noisy original. **(b)**, **(c)**: Suboptimal solutions computed with convex optimization for $\lambda = 0.8, 3.0$. **(d)** Solution computed with the ICM-algorithm for $\kappa\beta = 0.99$.

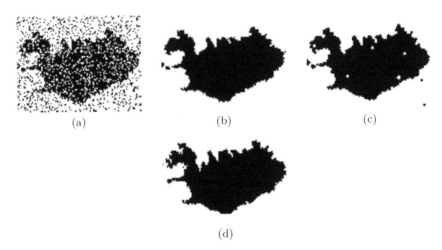

Fig. 7. Iceland image. **(a)** Binary noisy original. **(b)** Suboptimal solution computed with convex optimization for $\lambda = 2.0$. **(c)** Solution computed with the ICM-algorithm for $\kappa\beta = 0.9$. **(d)** Original before adding noise.

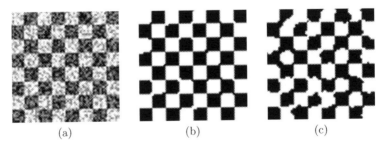

Fig. 8. Checkerboard image. **(a)** Noisy original. **(b)** Suboptimal solution computed with convex optimization for $\lambda = 1.5$. **(c)** Solution computed with the ICM-algorithm for $\kappa\beta = 0.4$.

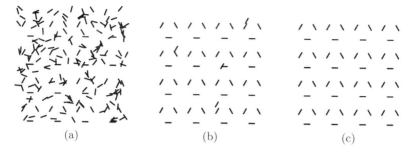

Fig. 9. Grouping. (**a**) Input data (see Section 2.2). (**b**) Suboptimal solution computed with convex optimization for $\lambda = 0.9$. (**c**) The true solution.

5   Conclusion

The quality of the results of the numerical experiments approves the wide range of applicability of the convex optimization approach. Many other problems with objective functions from the large class of binary quadratic functionals could be tackled. This fact, together with the nice mathematical property that no additional tuning parameters are necessary encourages us to extend our work on the convex optimization approach.

References

1. S. Geman and D. Geman. Stochastic relaxation, gibbs distributions, and the bayesian restoration of images. *IEEE Trans. Patt. Anal. Mach. Intell.*, 6(6):721–741, 1984.
2. J.E. Besag. On the analysis of dirty pictures (with discussion). *J. R. Statist. Soc. B*, 48:259–302, 1986.
3. L. Herault and R. Horaud. Figure-ground discrimination: A combinatorial optimization approach. *IEEE Trans. Patt. Anal. Mach. Intell.*, 15(9):899–914, 1993.
4. C. Schellewald, J. Keuchel, and C. Schnörr. Image labeling and grouping by minimizing linear functionals over cones. In *Proc. Third Int. Workshop on Energy Minimization Methods in Computer Vision and Pattern Recognition (EMM-CVPR'01)*, Lect. Notes Comp. Science, INRIA, Sophia Antipolis, France, Sept. 3–5 2001. Springer. *in press.*
5. E. Aarts and J.K. Lenstra, editors. *Local Search in Combinatorial Optimization*, Chichester, 1997. Wiley & Sons.
6. L. Lovász and A. Schrijver. Cones of matrices and set–functions and 0–1 optimization. *SIAM J. Optimization*, 1(2):166–190, 1991.
7. M.X. Goemans and D.P. Williamson. Improved approximation algorithms for maximum cut and satisfiability problems using semidefinite programming. *J. ACM*, 42:1115–1145, 1995.
8. M. Bertero, T. Poggio, and V. Torre. Ill-posed problems in early vision. *Proc. IEEE*, 76:869–889, 1988.
9. S.J. Benson, Y. Ye, and X. Zhang. Mixed linear and semidefinite programming for combinatorial and quadratic optimization. *Optimiz. Methods and Software*, 11&12:515–544, 1999.

Evaluation of Convex Optimization Techniques for the Weighted Graph-Matching Problem in Computer Vision

Christian Schellewald, Stefan Roth, Christoph Schnörr

Computer Vision, Graphics, and Pattern Recognition Group
Dept. Mathematics and Computer Science
University of Mannheim, D-68131 Mannheim, Germany
{cschelle,roths,schnoerr}@ti.uni-mannheim.de

Abstract. We present a novel approach to the weighted graph-matching problem in computer vision, based on a convex relaxation of the underlying combinatorial optimization problem. The approach always computes a lower bound of the objective function, which is a favorable property in the context of exact search algorithms. Furthermore, no tuning parameters have to be selected by the user, due to the convexity of the relaxed problem formulation.

For comparison, we implemented a recently published deterministic annealing approach and conducted numerous experiments for both established benchmark experiments from combinatorial mathematics, and for random ground-truth experiments using computer-generated graphs. Our results show similar performance for both approaches. In contrast to the convex approach, however, four parameters have to be determined by hand for the annealing algorithm to become competitive.

1 Introduction

Motivation. Visual object recognition is a central problem of computer vision research. A key question in this context is how to represent objects for the purpose of recognition by a computer vision system. Approaches range from view-based to 3D model-based, from object-centered to viewer-centered representations [1], each of which may have advantages under constraints related to specific applications. Psychophysical findings provide evidence for *view-based* object representations [2] in human vision.

A common and powerful representation format for object views is a set of local image features V along with pairwise relations E (spatial proximity and (dis)similarity measure), that is an undirected graph $G = (V, E)$. In this paper, we will discuss the application of a novel convex optimization technique to the problem of matching relational representations of object views.

Relations to previous work. There are numerous approaches to graph-matching in the literature (e.g., [3–8]). Our work differs from them with respect to the following points:

B. Radig and S. Florczyk (Eds.): DAGM 2001, LNCS 2191, pp. 361–368, 2001.
© Springer-Verlag Berlin Heidelberg 2001

1. We focus on *problem relaxations*, i.e. the optimization criterion equals the original one but is subject to weaker constraints. As a consequence, such approaches compute a *lower bound* of the original objective function which has to be minimized.
2. The *global* optimum of the *relaxed* problem can be computed with polynomial-time complexity.

Fig.1 A graph based on features described in [9] using corresponding public software (http://www.ipb.uni-bonn.de/ipb/projects/fex/fex.html). This graph has $|V| = 38$ nodes.

The first property above is necessary for combining the approach with an exact search algorithm where lower bounds of the original objective function are needed. Furthermore, it allows to compare different approaches by simply ranking the corresponding lower bounds.

The second property is important since graph-matching belongs to the class of NP-hard combinatorial problems. Matching two graphs with, say, $|V| = 20$ nodes gives $\sim 10^{18}$ possible matches. Typical problem instances however (see Fig. 1) comprise $|V| > 20$ nodes and thus motivate to look for tight problem relaxations to compute good suboptimal solutions in polynomial time.

Contribution. We discuss the application of novel convex optimization techniques to the graph-matching problem in computer vision.

First, we sketch a recently published deterministic annealing approach [6, 10] which stimulated considerable interest in the literature due to its excellent performance in numerical experiments. Unfortunately, this approach cannot be interpreted as a relaxation of the graph-matching problem and requires the selection of (at least) four parameters to obtain optimal performance (Section 3).

Next we consider the relaxed problems proposed in [11, 3] and show that, by using convex optimization techniques based on the work [12], a relaxation of the graph-matching problem is obtained with equal or better performance than the other approaches (Section 4). Moreover, due to convexity, no parameter selection is required.

In Section 5, we report extensive numerical results with respect to both benchmark-experiments [13] from the field of combinatorial mathematics, and random ground-truth experiments using computer-generated graphs.

Remark. Note that, in this paper, we are exclusively concerned with the *optimization procedure* of the graph-matching problem. For issues related to the *design of the optimization criterion* we refer to, e.g., [4, 14].

Notation.

X^t: transpose of a matrix X

$\mathcal{O}$:   set of orthogonal $n \times n$-matrices X, i.e. $X^t X = I$ (I: unit matrix)

$\mathcal{E}$:   matrices with unit row and column sums

$\mathcal{N}$:   set of non-negative matrices

Π: set of permutation matrices $X \in \mathcal{O} \cap \mathcal{E} \cap \mathcal{N}$

e: one-vector $e_i = 1, \quad i = 1, \ldots, n$

vec $[A]$: vector obtained by stacking the columns of some matrix A

$\lambda(A)$:   vector of eigenvalues of some matrix A

2   Problem statement

Let $G = (V, E)$, $G' = (V', E')$ denote two weighted undirected graphs with $|V| = |V'| = n$, weights $\{w_{ij}\}, \{w'_{ij}\}$, and adjacency matrices $A_{ij} = w_{ij}$, $A'_{ij} = w'_{ij}$, $i, j = 1, \ldots, n$. Furthermore, let ϕ denote a permutation of the set $\{1, \ldots, n\}$ and $X \in \Pi$ the corresponding permutation matrix, that is $X_{ij} = 1$ if $\phi(i) = j$ and $X_{ij} = 0$ otherwise. The weight functions $w, w' : E \subset V \times V \to \mathbb{R}_0^+$ encode (dis)similarity measures of local image features V_i, $i = 1, \ldots, n$, which we assume to be given in this paper. We are interested in matching graphs G and G' by choosing a permutation ϕ^* such that

$$\phi^* = \arg\min_\phi \sum_{i,j} (w_{\phi(i)\phi(j)} - w'_{ij})^2 \ .$$

By expanding and dropping constant terms, we obtain the equivalent problem:

$$\min_\phi \left(- \sum_{i,j} w_{\phi(i)\phi(j)} w'_{ij} \right) = \min_X (-\text{tr}(A'XAX^t)) \ ,$$

with $\text{tr}(\cdot)$ denoting the trace of a matrix. Absorbing the minus sign, we arrive at the following *Quadratic Assignment Problem (QAP)* with some arbitrary, symmetric matrices A, B:

$$(QAP) \qquad \min_{X \in \Pi} \text{tr}(AXBX^t) \ . \tag{1}$$

3   Graduated assignment

Gold and Rangarajan [6] and Ishii and Sato [10] independently developed a technique commonly referred to as *graduated assignment* or *soft assign* algorithm. The set of permutation matrices Π is replaced by the convex set $\mathcal{D} = \mathcal{E} \cap \mathcal{N}^+$ of positive matrices with unit row and column sums (doubly stochastic matrices). In contrast to previous mean-field annealing approaches, the graduated assignment algorithm enforces hard constraints on row *and* column sums, making it usually superior to other deterministic annealing approaches. The core of the algorithm is the following iteration scheme, where $\beta > 0$ denotes the annealing parameter and the superscript denotes the iteration time step (for β fixed):

$$X_{ij}^{(r+1)} = g_i h_j y_{ij}^{(r)} \ , \quad \text{with } y_{ij}^{(r)} = \exp\left(-\beta \sum_{k,l} A_{ik} B_{jl} X_{kl}^{(r)}\right) \tag{2}$$

The scaling coefficients g_i, h_j are computed so that $X^{(r+1)}$ is projected on the set $\mathcal{D}$ using Sinkhorn's algorithm [6] as inner loop.

This scheme locally converges under mild assumptions [15]. Several studies revealed excellent experimental results. In our experiments, we improved the obtained results with a local 2opt heuristics which iteratively improve the objective function by exchanging two rows and columns of the found permutation matrix until no improvement in the objective function is possible, as proposed in [10].

A drawback of this approach is that the selection of several "tuning"-parameters is necessary to obtain optimal performance, namely:

- the parameter β related to the annealing schedule,
- a "self-amplification" parameter enforcing integer values, and
- two stopping criteria with respect to the two iteration loops in (2).

Furthermore, the optimal parameter values vary for different problem instances (cf. [10]). For more details, we refer to [16].

4 Convex Approximations

In this section, we discuss a *convex* approximation to the weighted graph-matching problem (1). For more details and proofs, we refer to [16].

As explained in Section 1, our motivation is twofold: Firstly, the need to select parameter values (cf. previous section) is quite inconvenient when using a graph-matching approach as a part within a computer vision system. Convex optimization problems admit algorithmic solutions without any further parameters. Secondly, we focus on problem relaxations providing lower bounds of the objective criterion (1), which then can be used in the context of exact search algorithms.

4.1 Orthogonal relaxation and eigenvalue bounds

Replacing the set Π by $\mathcal{O} \supset \Pi$, Finke et al. [11] proved the following so called *Eigenvalue Bound* (*EVB*) as a lower lower bound of (1):

$$(EVB) \qquad \min_{X \in \mathcal{O}} \operatorname{tr}(AXBX^t) = \left(\lambda(A)\right)^t \lambda(B) \ , \tag{3}$$

with $\lambda(A), \lambda(B)$ sorted such that $\lambda_1(A) \geq \cdots \geq \lambda_n(A)$ and $\lambda_1(B) \leq \cdots \leq \lambda_n(B)$. This bound can be improved to give the *Projected Eigenvalue Bound* (*PEVB*) by further constraining the set of admissible matrices [17], but in contrast to the approach sketched in Section 4.3 this does not produce a matrix X for which the bound (*PEVB*) is attained.

4.2   The approach by Umeyama

Based on (3), Umeyama [3] proposed the following estimate for the solution of (1):

$$\hat{X}_{Ume} = \arg\max_{X \in \Pi} \operatorname{tr}(X^t \, |U| \, |V|^t) \,. \tag{4}$$

Here, U and V diagonalize the adjacency matrices A and B, respectively with the eigenvalues sorted according to (EVB), and $|\cdot|$ denotes the matrix consisting of the absolute value taken for each element. (4) is a linear assignment problem which can be efficiently solved by using standard methods like linear programming.

4.3   Convex relaxation

Anstreicher and Brixius [12] improved the projected eigenvalue bound $(PEVB)$ introduced in Section 4.1 to the *Quadratic Programming Bound* (QPB):

$$(QPB) \qquad \left(\lambda(\tilde{A})\right)^t \lambda(\tilde{B}) + \min_{X \in \mathcal{E} \cap \mathcal{N}} \operatorname{vec}[X]^t Q \operatorname{vec}[X] \,, \tag{5}$$

where $\tilde{A} = P^t A P$, $\tilde{B} = P^t B P$, with P being the orthogonal projection onto the complement of the 1D-subspace spanned by the vector e, and where the matrix Q is computed as solution to the Lagrangian dual problem of the minimization problem (3) (see [12, 16] for more details). Notice that both the computation of Q and minimizing (QPB) are *convex* optimization problems. Let $\hat{X}$ denote the global minimizer of (5). Then we compute a suboptimal solution to (1) by solving the following linear assignment problem:

$$\hat{X}_{QPB} = \arg\min_{X \in \Pi} \operatorname{tr}(X^t \tilde{X}). \tag{6}$$

The bounds presented so far can be ranked as follows:

$$(EVB) \le (PEVB) \le (QPB) \le (QAP) = \min_{X \in \Pi} \operatorname{tr}(AXBX^t) \,. \tag{7}$$

We therefore expect to obtain better solutions to (1) using (6) than using (4). This will be confirmed in the following section.

5   Experiments

We conducted extensive numerical experiments in order to compare the approaches sketched in Sections 3 and 4. The results are summarized in the following. Two classes of experiments were carried out:

- We used the QAPLIB-library [13] from combinatorial mathematics which is a collection of problems of the form (1) which are known to be "particularly difficult".

- Furthermore, we used large sets of computer-generated random graphs with sizes up to $|V| = 15$ such that (i) the global optimum could be computed as ground-truth by using an exact search algorithm, and (ii) significant statistical results could be obtained with respect to the quality of the various approaches.

QAPLIB benchmark experiments.

Table 1 shows the results computed for several QAPLIB-problems. The following abbreviations are used:

QAP: name of the problem instance (1) taken from the library
X^*:   value of the objective function (1) at the global optimum
QPB: the quadratic programming bound (5)
$\hat{X}_{QPB}$:   value of the objective function (1) using $\hat{X}_{QPB}$ from (6)
$\hat{X}_{QPB}+$: $\hat{X}_{QPB}$ followed by the 2opt greedy-strategy
$\hat{X}_{GA}$:   value of the objective function (1) using $\hat{X}$ from (2)
$\hat{X}_{GA}+$: $\hat{X}_{GA}$ followed by the 2opt greedy-strategy
$\hat{X}_{Ume}$:   value of the objective function (1) using (4)
$\hat{X}_{Ume}+$: $\hat{X}_{Ume}$ followed by the 2opt greedy-strategy

The 2opt greedy-strategy amounts to iteratively exchanging two rows and columns of the matrix $\hat{X}$ as long as an improvement of the objective function is possible [10].

By inspection of table 1, three conclusions can be drawn:

- The convex relaxation approach $\hat{X}_{QPB}$ and the soft-assign approach $\hat{X}_{GA}$ have similarly good performance, despite the fact that the latter approach is much more intricate from the optimization point-of-view and involves a couple of tuning parameters which were optimized by hand.
- The approach of Umeyama $\hat{X}_{Ume}$ based on orthogonal relaxation is not as competitive.
- Using the simple 2opt greedy-strategy as post-processing step significantly improves the solution in most cases.

In summary, these results indicate that the convex programming approach $\hat{X}_{QPB}$ embedded in a more sophisticated search strategy (compared to 2opt) is an attractive candidate for solving the weighted graph-matching problem.

Random ground-truth experiments.

We created many problem instances of (1) by randomly computing graphs. The probability that an edge is present in the underlying complete graph was about 0.3. For each pair of graphs, the global optimum was computed using an exact search algorithm.

Table 2 summarizes the statistics of our results. The notation explained in the previous Section was used. The first column on the left shows the problem size n together with the number of random experiments in angular brackets. The number pairs in round brackets denote the number of experiments for which the global optimum was found with/without the 2opt greedy-strategy as a post-processing step. Furthermore the worst case, the best case, and the average case

QAP	X^*	QPB	$\hat{X}_{QPB}$	$\hat{X}_{QPB}+$	$\hat{X}_{GA}$	$\hat{X}_{GA}+$	$\hat{X}_{Ume}$	$\hat{X}_{Ume}+$
chr12c	11156	-22648	20306	15860	19014	11186	40370	11798
chr15a	9896	-48539	26132	14454	30370	11062	60986	17390
chr15c	9504	-47409	29862	17342	23686	13342	76318	13338
chr20b	2298	-7728	6674	2858	6290	2650	10022	3294
chr22b	6194	-20995	9942	6848	9658	6732	13118	7418
esc16b	292	250	296	292	298	292	306	292
rou12	235528	205461	278834	246712	273438	246282	295752	251848
rou15	354210	303487	381016	371480	457908	359748	480352	384018
rou20	725522	607362	804676	746636	840120	738618	905246	765872
tai10a	135028	116260	165364	143260	168096	135828	189852	147838
tai15a	388214	330205	455778	399732	451164	400328	483596	405442
tai17a	491812	415578	550852	513170	589814	505856	620964	526814
tai20a	703482	584942	799790	740696	871480	724188	915144	775456
tai30a	1818146	1517829	1996442	1883810	2077958	1886790	2213846	1875680
tai35a	2422002	1958998	2720986	2527684	2803456	2496524	2925390	2544536
tai40a	3139370	2506806	3529402	3243018	3668044	3249924	3727478	3282284

Table 1. Results of the QAPLIB benchmark experiments (see text).

for the relative values for each of the three estimates presented in Sections 3 and 4 are shown (note that these values are smaller than 1 because the value of the objective function (1) is negative for this class of experiments). In summary, the conclusions with respect to the QAPLIB-experiments are confirmed.

	$\hat{X}_{QPB}/X^*$			$\hat{X}_{Ume}/X^*$			$\hat{X}_{GA}/X^*$		
	mean	worst case	best case	mean	worst case	best case	mean	worst case	best case
n=9 [128]	(22/53)			(7/29)			(31/55)		
2opt	0.87607	0.43552	1	0.638244	0.0651729	1	.948342	.7756129	1
	0.966155	0.79256	1	0.928304	0.753007	1	.9699138	.843046	1
n=11 [42]	(3/11)			(0/7)			(7/10)		
2opt	0.824023	0.514964	1	0.636159	0.295194	0.998591	.940740	.8338586	1
	0.962258	0.842204	1	0.933206	0.811326	1	.9588626	.8434407	1
n=15 [99]	(0/5)			(0/1)			(4/11)		
2opt	0.741563	0.232741	0.938917	0.131333	0.225983	0.863508	.916225	.105164	1
	0.925801	0.777494	1	0.890131	0.74688	1	.9576297	.8205957	1

Table 2. Statistics of the results of random ground-truth experiments (see text).

6   Conclusion

We have shown that, based on advanced techniques from convex optimization theory, suboptimal solutions to the weighted graph-matching problem can be computed which are competitive with respect to recent deterministic annealing approaches. In contrast to annealing approaches, however, the convex approach exhibits two favorable properties: Firstly, no tuning parameters are needed. Secondly, it computes a lower bound and thus can be used as a subroutine within an exact search strategy like branch-and-bound, for example. As a result, it is an attractive candidate for solving matching problems in the context of view-based object recognition.

Acknowledgment: We are thankful for discussions with Prof. Dr.-Ing. W. Förstner, D. Cremers and J. Keuchel.

References

1. M. Herbert, J. Ponce, T. Boult, and A. Gross, editors. *Object Representation in Computer Vision*, volume 994 of *Lect. Not. Comp. Sci.* Springer-Verlag, 1995.
2. H.H. Bülthoff and S. Edelman. Psychophysical support for a two-dimensional view interpolation theory of object recognition. *Proc. Nat. Acad. Science,*, 92:60–64, 1992.
3. S. Umeyama. An eigendecomposition approach to weighted graph matching problems. *IEEE Trans. Patt. Anal. Mach. Intell.*, 10(5):695–703, 1988.
4. G. Vosselmann. *Relational matching*, volume 628 of *Lect. Not. Comp. Sci.* Springer, 1992.
5. W.K. Konen, T. Maurer, and C. von der Malsburg. A fast dynamic link matching algorithm for invariant pattern recognition. *Neural Networks*, 7(6/7):1019–1030, 1994.
6. S. Gold and A. Rangarajan. A graduated assignment algorithm for graph matching. *IEEE Trans. Patt. Anal. Mach. Intell.*, 18(4):377–388, 1996.
7. A.D.J. Cross, R.C. Wilson, and E.R. Hancock. Inexact graph matching using genetic search. *Pattern Recog.*, 30(6):953–970, 1997.
8. A.D.J. Cross and E.R. Hancock. Graph-matching with a dual-step em algorithm. *IEEE Trans. Patt. Anal. Mach. Intell.*, 20(11):1236–1253, 1998.
9. W. Förstner. A framework for low level feature extraction. In J.O. Eklundh, editor, *Computer Vision - ECCV '94*, volume 801 of *Lect. Not. Comp. Sci.*, pages 61–70. Springer-Verlag, 1994.
10. S. Ishii and M. Sato. Doubly constrained network for combinatorial optimization. *Neurocomputing*, 2001. to appear.
11. G. Finke, R.E. Burkard, and F. Rendl. Quadratic assignment problems. *Annals of Discrete Mathematics*, 31:61–82, 1987.
12. K.M. Anstreicher and N.W. Brixius. A new bound for the quadratic assignment problem based on convex quadratic programming. Technical report, Dept. of Management Sciences, University of Iowa, 1999.
13. R.E. Burkard, S. Karisch, and F. Rendl. Qaplib – a quadratic assignment problem library. *J. Global Optimization*, 10:391–403, 1997.
14. H. Bunke. Error correcting graph matching: On the influence of the underlying cost function. *IEEE Trans. Patt. Anal. Mach. Intell.*, 21(9):917–922, 1999.
15. A. Rangarajan, A. Yuille, and E. Mjolsness. Convergence properties of the softassign quadratic assignment algorithm. *Neural Computation*, 11(6):1455–1474, 1999.
16. C. Schellewald, S. Roth, and C. Schnörr. Evaluation of spectral and convex relaxations to the quadratic assignment of relational object views. Comp. science series, technical report, Dept. Math. and Comp. Science, University of Mannheim, Germany, 2001. in preparation.
17. S.W. Hadley, F. Rendl, and H. Wolkowicz. A new lower bound via projection for the quadratic assignment problem. *Math. of Operations Research,*, 17:727–739, 1992.

Learning Shape Models from Examples

D.M. Gavrila[1], J. Giebel[1], and H. Neumann[2]

[1] Image Understanding Systems, DaimlerChrysler Research,
Wilhelm Runge St 11, 89081 Ulm, Germany
dariu.gavrila, jan.giebel@DaimlerChrysler.com, www.gavrila.net
[2] Department of Neuro-informatics, University of Ulm,
89069 Ulm, Germany
hneumann@neuro.informatik.uni-ulm.de

Abstract. This paper addresses the problem of learning shape models from examples. The contributions are twofold. First, a comparative study is performed of various methods for establishing shape correspondence - based on shape decomposition, feature selection and alignment. Various registration methods using polygonal and Fourier features are extended to deal with shapes at multiple scales and the importance of doing so is illustrated. Second, we consider an appearance-based modeling technique which represents a shape distribution in terms of clusters containing similar shapes; each cluster is associated with a separate feature space. This representation is obtained by applying a novel simultaneous shape registration and clustering procedure on a set of training shapes. We illustrate the various techniques on pedestrian and plane shapes.

1 Introduction

For many interesting object detection tasks there are no explicit prior models available to support a matching process. This is typically the case for the detection of complex non-rigid objects under unrestricted viewpoints and/or under changing illumination conditions. In this paper we deal with methods for acquiring (i.e. "learning") shape models from examples. Section 2 reviews existing methods for establishing shape correspondence and modeling shape variation. Shape registration methods bypass the need for tedious manual labeling and establish point correspondences between shapes in a training set automatically. Although a sizeable literature exists in this area (e.g. [1] [2] [3] [5] [9]), there has been little effort done so far in comparing various approaches. We perform a comparative study on various shape registration methods in Section 3 and demonstrate the benefit of describing shapes at multiple scales for this purpose. The best performing registration method is combined with a clustering algorithm to describe arbitrary shape distributions in terms of clusters containing similar shapes; each cluster is associated with a separate feature space, see Section 4. Benefits of such representation are discussed in Section 5, after which we conclude in Section 6.

B. Radig and S. Florczyk (Eds.): DAGM 2001, LNCS 2191, pp. 369–376, 2001.
© Springer-Verlag Berlin Heidelberg 2001

2   Review

2.1   Shape Registration

A review of previous work on shape registration shows that a typical procedure follows a similar succession of steps: shape decomposition, feature selection, point correspondence and finally, alignment.

The first step, shape decomposition, involves determining control ("land-mark") points along a contour and breaking the shape into corresponding segments. One way of doing this is to consider the curvature function along the object's contour and to determine the locations of the minima and maxima. The curvature function is computed by convolving the edge direction function of a contour point with the first derivative of a Gaussian function. The parameter σ in the Gaussian function determines the smoothing of a shape, see for example [11] [12] [13]. A different method for determining control points is described in [14], where points are removed according to a criticality measure based on the area of three successive points.

Once shape segments have been determined, the next step involves selecting features that are transformation invariant (e.g. translation, rotation and scale). These features are usually selected based on an approximation of the shape segments; most common are straight-line (i.e. polygonal) [3] [5] [9] [11] and Fourier approximations [7]. Similarity measures are typically based on length ratios and angles between successive segments for the polygonal case (e.g. [11]) and weighted Euclidean metrics on the low-order Fourier coefficients, for the Fourier approximations (e.g. [7]).

At this point, correspondence between the control points of two shapes can be established by means of either combinatoric approaches or sequential pattern matching techniques. Each correspondence is evaluated using match measures on the local features discussed earlier. Combinatoric approaches [3] [11] select iteratively a (e.g. minimal) set of initial correspondences and use various greedy methods to assign the remaining points. The advantage of this approach is that the overall goodness of a match can be based on all contour points simultaneously. Additional effort is necessary, though, to account for ordering constraints. Sequential pattern matching techniques, on the other hand, inherently enforce ordering constraints. Dynamic programming is widely used [5] [7] since it is an efficient technique to come up with optimal solutions for the case of an evaluation measure which has the Markov property.

Finally, after correspondence between control points has been established (and possibly, between interpolated points), alignment with respect to similarity transformation is achieved by a least-squares fit [2]. The above techniques for shape registration have important applications for partial curve matching in object recognition tasks [5] [7] [11]. Next subsection deals with their use for modeling shape variation.

2.2   Modeling Shape Variation

Registration establishes point correspondence between a pair of shapes. The straightforward way to account for N shapes is to embed all N shapes in a single feature vector space, based on the x and y locations of their corresponding points. This is done either by selecting one shape (typically, the "closest" to the others) and aligning all others to it, or by employing a somewhat more complex hierarchical procedure [9]. The resulting vector space allows the computation of various compact representations for the shape distribution, based on radial (mean-variance) [6] or modal (linear subspace) [1] [2] [9] decompositions. Combinations are also possible [8].

The assumption that point correspondence can be established across all training shapes of a particular object class by means of automatic shape registration is in many cases problematic, however. For example, none of the shape registration methods we analyzed were able to correctly register a pedestrian shape with the two feet apart with one with the feet together, without operator input or prior knowledge. A more general registration approach does not forcibly embed all N shapes into the same feature vector space. Instead, it combines shape clustering and registration, embedding only the (similar) shapes within a cluster into the same vector space. This is the approach pursued in Section 4, adapted from earlier work [3].

Finally, some approaches [4] [5] do not try to embed shapes into a vector space altogether; a hierarchical representation is built solely on the basis of pairwise dissimilarity values. See also Section 5 and [10].

3   Shape Registration

In this study, we jointly compare the performance of control point detection, feature extraction and matching algorithms for the purpose of shape registration. Under consideration are two techniques for control point detection, the first is the Gaussian-based filtering of the curvature function [11] and the second is the critical point detection algorithm described in [14]. We furthermore compare two techniques for feature selection and similarity measurement: one based on polygonal approximations [11] and one based on piecewise Fourier decompositions [7]. We choose as matching algorithm invariably dynamic programming, because of its efficiency and optimality property. This leads to a total of four methods under consideration. The experiments involve computing pairwise alignments between all elements of a particular shape data set and recording the mean Euclidean distance between corresponding contour points after alignment, i.e. the mean alignment error. Dense point correspondences are inferred by interpolating the correspondences between the control points.

Our study furthermore extends previous shape registration work [7] [11] by representing shapes at multiple scales. For the method of [11], this is achieved by using multiple Gaussian σ values (e.g. [12] [13]), whereas in [14] this involves using different area criteria. In the experiments, we compute shape registrations for all scales and consider the one which minimizes the mean alignment error.

Two data sets were used to evaluate the four method combinations, a set of 25 plane contours (height 100 - 200 pixels) and a set of 50 pedestrian contours (height 80 pixels). See Figure 1. Figure 2b illustrates the multi-scale shape representation resulting from the Gaussian filtering of the curvature function. Figure 2c shows the effects of varying the number of Fourier coefficients, at one particular scale.

The importance of maintaining shape representations at multiple scales is demonstrated in Figure 3. The histogram shows the number of alignments (y-axis) at which a particular scale σ-interval (x-axis) results in the best pairwise alignment in terms of minimizing the mean alignment error. This particular data pertains to the registration method that combines control point detection by Gaussian curvature filtering and the use of Fourier features for the pedestrian data set. From the Figure one observes that a wide range of scales are utilized for the "best" alignment; a registration approach that would only use a single scale representation (i.e. choosing a single bar of the histogram) would be non-optimal for most of the shape alignments considered.

Some typical point correspondences and alignments are shown in Figure 4. As can be seen, the registration method is quite successful in pairing up the physically corresponding points (e.g. the tip and wings of the planes, the heads and feet of the pedestrians).

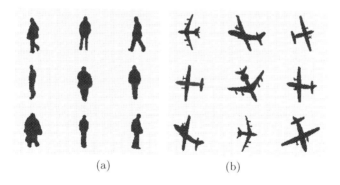

(a)   (b)

Fig. 1. Example (a) pedestrian shapes (b) plane shapes.

Figure 5 summarizes the results of the shape registration experiments. It shows the cumulative distribution of the mean alignment error for the plane (Figure 5a) and pedestrian (Figure 5b) data sets, for the four combinations analyzed and based on 600 and 2450 pairwise alignments, respectively. For example, about 80% of the pedestrian alignments resulted in a mean alignment error smaller than 9 pixels (on a pedestrian size of 80 pixels) for method **c-**, Gaussian curvature filtering with polygonal features. More revealing is relative performance of the methods. From the Figure one observes that Gaussian filtering of the curvature function provides a better multi-scale shape representation

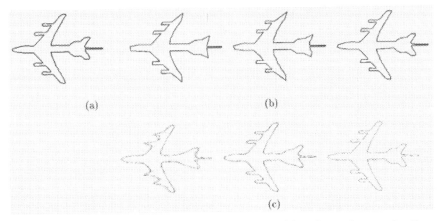

Fig. 2. Multi scale representation (a) original shape (b) polygonal approximations (decreasing σ value from left to right) (c) Fourier approximations (increasing number of coefficients used from left to right)

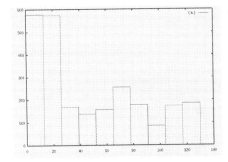

Fig. 3. Histogram showing number of alignments (y-axis) at which a particular scale σ-interval (x-axis) results in the best pairwise alignment, using Gaussian curvature filtering [11]

than that derived from the critical point detection algorithm (compare graphs **a-** and **c-** versus graphs **b-** and **d-**), at least as far as our implementation is concerned. Also, the Fourier features proved to be more suitable in dealing with the curved shapes of our data sets (compare graphs **a-** and **b-** versus graphs **c-** and **d-**).

4   Shape Clustering

After the comparative study on shape registration, we used the best performing method (i.e. Gaussian curvature filtering for control point detection and Fourier coefficients as features) to embed the N shapes of the training set into feature spaces. As mentioned in Subsection 2.2, for many datasets it is not feasible

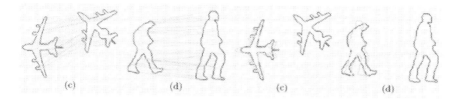

Fig. 4. Established point correspondences between two (a) planes and (b) pedestrians and their pairwise alignment, (c) and (d). Aligned shapes are superimposed in grey.

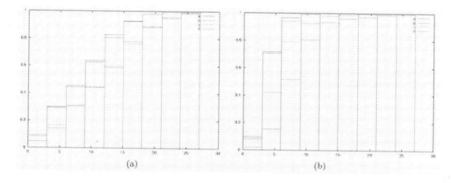

Fig. 5. Cumulative distribution of the mean alignment error for the (a) plane and (b) pedestrian data of the four methods analyzed (**a-** Gaussian curvature filtering [11] multi-scale with Fourier features [7], **b-** "critical point" [14] multi-scale with Fourier features [7], **c-** Gaussian curvature filtering [11] multi-scale with polygonal features [11], and **d-** "critical point" [14] multi-scale with polygonal features [11]). The horizontal axis is in units of pixels. Object size 100 - 200 pixels for (a) and 80 pixels for (b)

to map all N shapes onto a single feature space because of considerable shape differences. Therefore, we follow a combined clustering and registration approach which establishes shape correspondence only between (similar) shapes within a cluster. The clustering algorithm is similar to the classical K-means approach:

0. pick an initial shape S_1 and add it to cluster C_1
    as prototype: $C_1 = \{S_1\}$, $P_1 = S_1$
while there are shapes left do
    1. select one of remaining shapes: S_k
    2. compute mean alignment error $d(S_k, P_i)$ from
        element S_k to the existing prototypes P_i,
        where i ranges over the number of clusters
        created so far
    3. Compute $d_{min} = d(S_k, P_j) = min_i d(S_k, P_i)$.
        if $d(S_k, P_j) > \theta$

then assign S_k to a new cluster C_{n+1}:
$$C_{n+1} = \{S_k\}, P_{n+1} = S_k$$
else assign S_k to existing cluster
$$C_j = \{S_{j1}, ...S_{jn}\} \text{ and update its prototype:}$$
$$C_j = C_j \cup \{S_k\}$$
$$P_j = \text{Mean}(S_{j1}, ..., S_{jn}, S_k)$$
end

In the above, Step 2 consists of applying our best performing shape registration method (see previous Section) to establish point correspondences and compute alignment errors. The resulting point correspondences are used for the prototype computation in Step 3. See Figure 6a. Parameter θ is a user-defined dissimilarity threshold that controls the number of clusters to be created. Compared to [3], the above formulation has the advantage that it does not require the computation of the full dissimilarity matrix $d(S_i, S_j)$. It furthermore adjusts the prototype whenever new elements are assigned to a group. Figure 6b illustrates some typical clustering results.

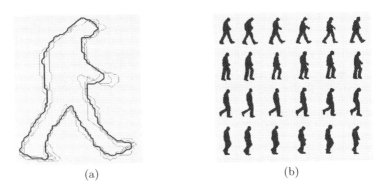

(a)   (b)

Fig. 6. (a) Computing a "mean" or prototype shape (in black) from aligned shape samples (in grey) (b) Shape clustering: each row contains the elements of a different cluster

5   Outlook

Learned shape models can be used for matching and tracking purposes. We are currently utilizing the approach described in previous Section for learning pedestrian shapes and improving the performance of the Chamfer System [4], a system for shape-based object detection. At its core, the system performs template matching using distance transforms. It has an off-line phase where a template hierarchy is built by clustering shapes recursively; clustering is solely based on dissimilarity values [4]. Here, the followed shape registration and modeling approach establishes feature spaces which facilitate the computation of improved shape prototypes, i.e. the arithmetic mean of the shape cluster elements. Furthermore, the presence of a feature space enables standard data dimensionality reduction techniques which can used for the generation of "virtual" shapes, enriching the training set of the Chamfer System.

6   Conclusions

This paper performed a comparative study of various methods for shape registration and identified a multi-scale method based on Gaussian curvature filtering and Fourier features as best performing one. This registration step was incorporated in a shape clustering algorithm which allows the representation of arbitrary shape distributions in terms of clusters of similar shapes, embedded in separate feature spaces.

References

1. A. Baumberg and D. Hogg. Learning flexible models from image sequences. In *Proc. of the ECCV*, pages 299–308, 1994.
2. T. Cootes, C. Taylor, D. Cooper, and J. Graham. Active shape models - their training and applications. *CVIU*, 61(1):38–59, 1995.
3. N. Duta, A. Jain, and M.-P. Dubuisson-Jolly. Learning 2d shape models. In *Proc. of the ICCV*, pages 8–14, Kerkyra, Greece, 1999.
4. D. M. Gavrila and V. Philomin. Real-time object detection for "smart" vehicles. In *Proc. of the ICCV*, pages 87–93, Kerkyra, Greece, 1999.
5. Y. Gdalyahu and D. Weinshall. Flexible syntatic matching of curves and its application to automatic hierarchical classification of silhouettes. *IEEE Trans. on PAMI*, 21(12):1312–1328, December 1999.
6. C. Goodall. Procrustes methods in the statistical analysis of shape. *J. Royal Statistical Soc. B*, 53(2):285–339, 1991.
7. J. Gorman, R. Mitchell, and F. Kuhl. Partial shape recognition using dynamic programming. *IEEE Trans. on PAMI*, 10(2):257–266, 1988.
8. T. Heap and D. Hogg. Improving the specificity in PDMs using a hierarchical approach. In *Proc. of the BMVC*, Colchester, UK, 1997. BMVA Press.
9. A. Hill, C. Taylor, and A. Brett. A framework for automatic landmark identification using a new method of nonrigid correspondence. *IEEE Trans. on PAMI*, 22(3):241–251, March 2000.
10. D. Jacobs, D. Weinshall, and Y. Gdalyahu. Condensing image databases when retrieval is based on non-metric distances. In *Proc. of the IEEE CVPR Conf.*, pages 596–601, Ft. Collins, U.S.A., 1999.
11. H.-C. Liu and M. Srinath. Partial shape classification using contour matching in distance transformation. *IEEE Trans. on PAMI*, 12(11):1072–1079, November 1990.
12. F. Mokhtarian and A. K. Mackworth. A theory of multiscale, curvature-based shape representation for planar curves. *IEEE Trans. on PAMI*, 14(8):789–805, 1992.
13. A. Rattarangsi and R. T. Chin. Scale-based detection of corners of planar curves. *IEEE Trans. on PAMI*, 14(4):430–449, 1992.
14. P. Zhu and P. Chirlian. On critical point detection of digital shape. *IEEE Trans. on PAMI*, 17(8):737–748, 1995.

Shape from 2D Edge Gradients

S. Winkelbach and F.M. Wahl

Institute for Robotics and Process Control,
Technical University of Braunschweig
Hamburger Str. 267, D-38114 Braunschweig, Germany
{S.Winkelbach, F.Wahl}@tu-bs.de

Abstract. This paper presents a novel strategy for rapid reconstruction of 3d surfaces based on 2d gradient directions. I.e., this method does not use triangulation for range data acquisition, but rather computes surface normals. These normals are 2d integrated and thus yield the desired surface coordinates; in addition they can be used to compute robust 3d features of free form surfaces. The reconstruction can be realized with uncalibrated systems by means of very fast and simple table look-up operations with moderate accuracy, or with calibrated systems with superior precision.

1. Introduction

Many range finding techniques have been proposed in the open literature, such as stereo vision [1], structured light [2,3,4,5], coded light [6], shape from texture [7,8], shape from shading [9], etc.. Similar to some structured light methods, our suggested novel approach for 3d surface reconstruction requires one camera and two light stripe projections onto an object to be reconstructed (Fig. 1). However: *Our reconstruction technique is based on the fact, that angles of stripes in the captured 2d image depend on the orientation of the local object surface in 3d. Surface normals and range data are <u>not</u> obtained via triangulation, like in the case of most structured light or coded*

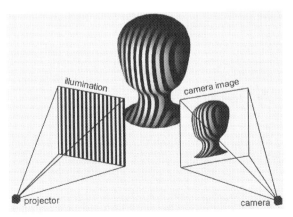

Fig. 1. System setup with light projector and camera

B. Radig and S. Florczyk (Eds.): DAGM 2001, LNCS 2191, pp. 377–384, 2001.

light approaches, but rather by computing the stripe angles of the 2d stripe image by means of gradient directions. Each stripe angle determines one degree of freedom of the local surface normal. Therefore, the total reconstruction of all visible surface normals requires at least two projections with rotated stripe patterns relative to each other. At first glance, an almost similar method using a square pattern has been presented in [10]; in contrast to our approach it requires complex computation, e.g. for detection of lines and line crossing and for checking of grid connectivity. Moreover, it utilizes a lower density of measurement points yielding a lower lateral resolution.

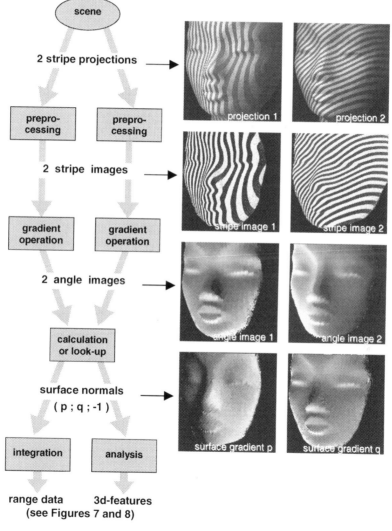

Fig. 2. Processing steps of the 'Shape form 2D Edge Gradients' approach

2. Measurement Principle

The surface reconstruction can be subdivided into several functional steps (see Fig. 2). First, we take two grey level images of the scene illuminated with two differently rotated stripe patterns. Undesired information, like inhomogeneous object shadings and textures are eliminated by an optional appropriate preprocessing (Section 3). Subsequently, local angles of stripe edges are measured by a gradient operator. This leads to two angle images, which still contain erroneous angles and outliers which have to be extracted and replaced by interpolated values in an additional step (Section 4). On the basis of two stripe angles at one image pixel we calculate the local 3d surface slope or surface normal (Section 5). The surface normals can be used to reconstruct the surface itself, or they can be utilized as basis for 3d feature computation (Section 6).

3. Preprocessing

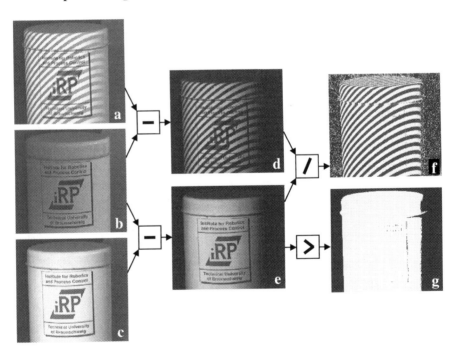

Fig. 3. Preprocessing steps of a textured test object. (a) object illuminated with stripe pattern; (b) object with ambient light; (c) object with homogeneous projector illumination; (d) absolute difference between (a) and (b); (e) absolute difference between (b) and (c); (f) normalized stripe image; (g) binary mask

In order to be able to detect and analyse the illumination stripe patterns in grey level images, we apply an adapted optional preprocessing procedure, which separates the stripe pattern from arbitrary surface reflection characteristics of the object (color, texture, etc.). Fig. 3 illustrates this procedure: After capturing the scene with stripe illumination (a) we acquire a second image with ambient light (b) and a third one with homogenous illumination by the projector (c). Using the absolute difference   (d = |a-b|) we scale the dark stripes to zero value and separate them from object color. However, shadings and varying reflections caused by the projected light still are retained in the bright stripes. For this reason we normalize the stripe signal (d) to a constant magnitude by dividing it by the absolute difference (e) between the illuminated and non-illuminated image (f = d / e). As can be seen from Fig. 3f, noise is intensified as well by this division; it gets the same contrast as the stripe patterns. This noise arises in areas, where the projector illuminates the object surface with low intensity. Therefore we eliminate it by using the mask (g = 1 <u>if</u> (e > threshold), g = 0 <u>else</u>).

4.   Stripe Angle Determination

After preprocessing the stripe images, determination of stripe angles can take place by well-known gradient operators. We evaluated different gradient operators like Sobel, Canny, etc. to investigate their suitability. Fig. 4 shows the preprocessed stripe image of a spherical surface in (a), gradient directions in (b) (angles are represented by different grey levels); in this case the Sobel operator has been applied. Noisy angles arise mainly in homogenous areas where gradient magnitudes are low. Thus low gradient magnitudes can be used to eliminate erroneous angles and to replace them by interpolated data from the neighborhood. For angle interpolation we propose an efficient data-dependent averaging interpolation scheme: A homogeneous averaging-filter is applied to the masked grey level image and the result is divided by the likewise average-filtered binary mask (0 for invalid and 1 for valid angles). In this way one obtains the average value of *valid* angles within the operator window. Finally, erroneous angles are replaced by the interpolated ones.

Fig. 4. Computation of angle images. (a) Stripe image; (b) Sobel gradient angles (angle image); (c) masked angle image by means of gradient magnitude; (d) interpolated angle image

5.   Surface Normal Computation

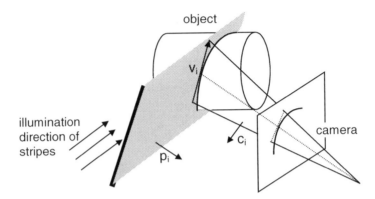

Fig. 5. Projection of a stripe on an object

We investigated two methods to compute surface slopes (or normals) from stripe angles: A mathematical correct computation with calibrated optical systems (camera and light projectors) on the one hand and on the other hand a simple table look-up method which maps two stripe angles to one surface normal. Due to the limited space of this paper, we only will give a general idea of the mathematical solution: The angle values ω_1, ω_2 of both rotated stripe projections and their 2d image coordinates specify two "camera planes" p_1, p_2 and corresponding normals c_1, c_2 (see Fig. 5). The tangential direction vector v_i of a projected stripe on the object surface is orthogonal to c_i and orthogonal to the normal p of the stripe projection plane. So we can use the following simple equation to calculate the surface normal: $n = (c_1 \times p_1) \times (c_2 \times p_2)$

Generation of the look-up table in the second approach works in a similar way like the look-up table based implementation of photometric stereo [9]:

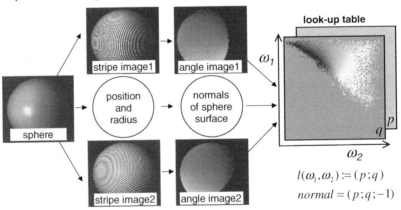

$$l(\omega_1, \omega_2) := (p;q)$$
$$normal = (p;q;-1)$$

Fig. 6. Computation of the look-up table with use of stripe projections onto a spherical surface

By means of the previously described processing steps, we first estimate the stripe angles of two stripe projections rotated relatively to each other onto a spherical surface (see Fig. 6). As the surface normals of a sphere are known, we can use the two angle values ω_1, ω_2 at each surface point of the sphere to fill the 2d look-up table with ω_1 and ω_2 as address. Subsequently, missing values in the table are computed by interpolation. Now the look-up table can be used to map two stripe angles to one surface normal. To compute range data from surface slopes we applied the 2d integration method proposed by Frankot/Chellappa [11].

6.   Experimental Results and Conclusions

The following images illustrate experimental results of the look-up table approach proposed above.

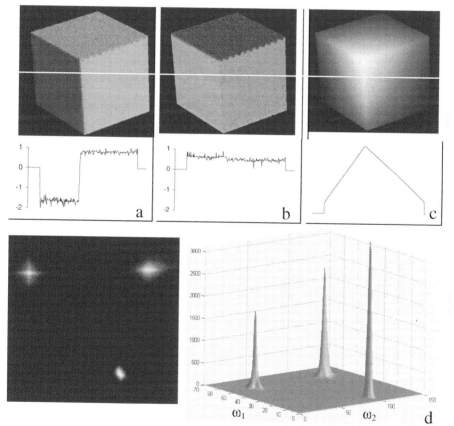

Fig. 7. Depths data and plane features of a test cube: (a) surface x-gradient, (b) surface y-gradient, (c) range map with corresponding line profiles; (d) histograms of (ω_1, ω_2)-tuples

Fig. 7 shows the gradients of a cube and plots of sample lines. The ideal surface gradients are constant within every face of the cube. Thus, accuracy of measurement can be evaluated by the standard derivation within a face, which in our first experiments shown here is approximately 0.4109 degree. Errors are reduced after integration (see Fig.7(c)). Fig.7(d) shows the 2d histogram of the gradient direction tuples ω_1, ω_2, corresponding to the three faces of the cube.

Fig. 8 shows the 2d grey level image of a styrofoam head, its reconstructed range map and its corresponding rendered grey level images from two different viewing directions. Using more than two stripe projections from different illumination directions can improve the reconstruction result.

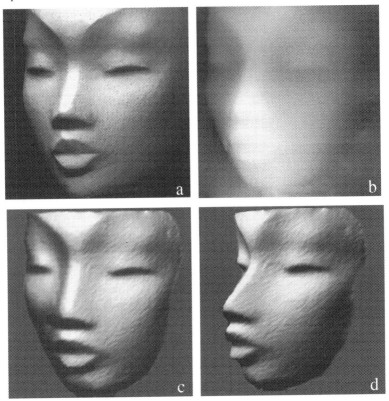

Fig. 8. Reconstruction of a styrofoam head: (a) grey level image; (b) reconstructed range map; (c and d) corresponding rendered grey level images from two different viewing directions obtained by virtual illumination in 3d

In many applications surface normals are an important basis for robust 3d features, as for example surface orientations, relative angles, curvatures, local maxima and saddle points of surface shape. An advantage of our approach is, that it is very efficient and directly generates surface normals without the necessity deriving them subsequently from noisy range data. In case of textured and inhomogeneously reflecting objects our technique offers a higher robustness in comparison to most other methods.

Due to the limited space of this paper, we only have been able to present a rough outline of our new approach. Discussions about important aspects like a detailed error analysis, applications of our technique, etc. are subject of further publications [12]. Regarding accuracy, we should mention, that in the experiments shown above, we used optical systems with long focal lengths. Although our experiments are very promising, the new technique is open for improvements. E.g., the reconstruction time can be reduced by color-coding the two stripe patterns and projecting them simultaneously. Acquiring serveral stripe images with phase shifted stripe patterns could increase the number of gradients with high magnitudes, thus reducing the need for replacing erroneous gradient directions by interpolation. An alternative augmented technique uses only one stripe projection for full 3d surface reconstruction [13]. This is possible by determining the stripe angles and the stripe widths as source of information to estimate surface orientations.

References

1. D. C. Marr, T. Poggio: A computational theory of human stereo vision, Proc. Roy. Soc. London 204, 1979
2. 2. T. Ueda, M. Matsuki: Time Sequential Coding for Three-Dimensional Measurement and Its Implementation, Denshi-Tsushin-Gakkai-Ronbunshi, 1981
3. M. Oshima, Y. Shirai: Object recognition using three dimensional information, IEEE Transact. on PAMI, vol. 5, July 1983
4. K. L. Boyer and A. C. Kak: Color-Encoded Structured Light for Rapid Active Ranging, IEEE Transact. on PAMI, vol. 9, no. 1, Januar 1987
5. Vuylsteke, A. Oosterlinck: Range Image Acquisition with a Single Binary-Encoded Light Pattern, IEEE Transact. on PAMI, vol. 12, no. 2, 1990
6. F. M. Wahl: A Coded Light Approach for 3-Dimensional (3D) Vision, IBM Research Report RZ 1452, 1984
7. J.J. Gibson, The Preception of the Visiual Worl, MA: Reverside Press, Cambridge, 1950
8. J.R. Kender, Shape from texture, Proc. DARPA IU Workshop, November 1978
9. B. K. P. Horn and M. J. Brooks: Shape from Shading, M.I.T., Cambridge 1989
10. M. Proesmans, L. Van Gool and A. Oosterlinck: One-Shot Active Shape Acquisition, IEEE Proc. of ICPR, 1996
11. Robert T. Frankot, Rama Chellappa: A Methode for Enforcing Integrability in Shape from Shading Algorithms, IEEE Transact. on PAMI, vol. 10, no. 4, July 1988
12. S. Winkelbach. F. M. Wahl: 3D Shape Recovery from 2D Edge Gradients with Uncalibrated/Calibrated Optical Systems, to be published elsewhere
13. S. Winkelbach, F. M. Wahl: Efficient Shape Recovery of Objects Illuminated with one Single Bar Pattern , to be published elsewhere

Robust Obstacle Detection from Stereoscopic Image Sequences Using Kalman Filtering

Alexander Suppes, Frank Suhling, and Michael Hötter

Fachhochschule Hannover Ricklinger Stadtweg 120 30459 Hannover
alexander.suppes@etech.fh-hannover.de

Abstract. In this paper a new approach for video based obstacle detection for a mobile robot is proposed, based on probabilistic evaluation of image data. Apart from the measurement data, also their uncertainties are taken into account. Evaluation is achieved using Kalman filter technique combining the results of video data processing and robot motion data. Obstacle detection is realised by computing obstacle probability and subsequent application of a threshold operator. The first experiments show remarkably stable obstacle detection.

Keywords: Kalman filter, obstacle detection, stereo based vision.

1. Introduction

Mobile service robots can be used for different tasks in industrial environments where highly reliable and robust navigation is required. One of the main tasks of such a mobile robot system is to detect moving and non-moving obstacles even if the (lighting) conditions around the robot change.

Kalman filter is a popular method to solve localisation tasks for mobile robots. An overview is given e.g. in [3]. In [1] the Kalman filter performs the data fusion of results of image processing algorithms and the laser scanner data, dependent on their accuracies, which allows to determine the robot position more accurately. A relatively new method is proposed in [3]: The authors used a robust probabilistic approach called Markov localisation to determine the robot position utilising sonar sensor data or laser scanner data.

In previous work [6] a stereo based vision system was presented, which enables obstacle detection using a robust method for disparity estimation. Even if the system yields good results, there could be situations, where some phantom objects appear, that is, objects, which do not exist in reality. This can have different reasons: e.g. reflections on the ground where the robot moves, camera blinding by a light beam, or noise. Because these objects do not exist in reality, they normally disappear in the next image pair after the robot moves. It seems possible to eliminate these effects by using information about robot movement and by evaluation of subsequent images.

In this paper we present a method that uses Kalman filter techniques to robustly combine results of 3D-reconstruction from different image pairs, taken at different robot positions. Hereby the uncertainties of robot motion are taking into account as

B. Radig and S. Florczyk (Eds.): DAGM 2001, LNCS 2191, pp. 385–391, 2001.
© Springer-Verlag Berlin Heidelberg 2001

well as the uncertainties of the 3D-points that are measured from different image pairs. The description of this method including error propagation can be found in chapter 2.

In chapter 3, a probabilistic interpretation of each 3D-point including its uncertainty in form of the covariance matrix is made to determine the probability that at a certain area in front of the robot is an obstacle, whereby a similar idea is used as described in [3]. The difference is that in [3] the probabilistic interpretation of the sensor data was performed to determine the position of a mobile robot.

The experimental results are given in chapter 4. Finally the paper will conclude with a short summary in chapter 5.

2. Kalman Filter

The well-known equations of the Kalman filter are not given here, the interested reader is referred to introductory paper [8] or to book [4].

First, the prediction step will be considered (see Fig. 1). Given an estimate of a

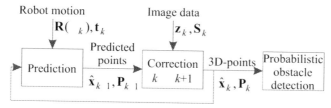

Fig. 1. Block diagram of Kalman filtering and probabilistic obstacle detection

3D-point computed after the image pair k was evaluated, the prediction of $\hat{\mathbf{x}}_k = (\hat{x}_k, \hat{y}_k, \hat{z}_k)^T$ to the robot position where the image pair $k+1$ is grabbed, is done as follows (process equation):

$$\hat{\mathbf{x}}^-_{k+1} = \mathbf{R}(\beta_k)(\hat{\mathbf{x}}_k - \mathbf{t}_k),\qquad(1)$$

with the rotation matrix $\mathbf{R}(\beta_k)$ that describes the change of robot orientation by an angle β_k (rotation around the robot y-axis) and the translation vector $\mathbf{t}_k = (t_{xk}, t_{yk}, t_{zk})^T$ (see Fig. 2). It is assumed that the robot moves on the xz-plane, so the motion does not change the y-coordinate ($t_{yk} = 0$).

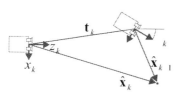

Fig. 2. Representation of robot motion

Both, the rotation angle β_k and the translation vector $\mathbf{t}_k$ are assumed to be affected by normally distributed non-correlated errors. The error variance of β_k is denoted by $\sigma^2_{\beta k}$; the error of $\mathbf{t}_k$ is described by its 3×3 covariance matrix $\mathbf{C}_{tk}$

and the uncertainty of the point $\hat{\mathbf{x}}_k$ by the 3×3 covariance matrix $\mathbf{P}_k$. Because $t_{yk} = 0$, the variances and covariances in $\mathbf{C}_{tk}$ that are related to t_{yk} are 0.

To determine the covariance matrix $\mathbf{P}_{k+1}^-$ of $\hat{\mathbf{x}}_{k+1}^-$, the prediction (1) is considered as a function of 7 parameters: $\hat{\mathbf{x}}_{k+1}^- = \hat{\mathbf{x}}_{k+1}^-(\beta_k, t_{xk}, t_{yk}, t_{zk}, \hat{x}_k, \hat{y}_k, \hat{z}_k)$. Then, $\mathbf{P}_{k+1}^-$ is computed by means of Gaussian error propagation technique: $\mathbf{P}_{k+1}^- = \mathbf{TCT}^T$ [2] with the covariance matrix $\mathbf{C}$ of the parameter vector and the Jacobian matrix $\mathbf{T}$:

$$\mathbf{C} = \begin{pmatrix} \sigma_{\beta k}^2 & \mathbf{0} & \mathbf{0} \\ \mathbf{0} & \mathbf{C}_{tk} & \mathbf{0} \\ \mathbf{0} & \mathbf{0} & \mathbf{P}_k \end{pmatrix}; \quad \mathbf{T} = \begin{pmatrix} \partial\hat{x}_{k+1}^-/\partial\beta_k & \cdots & \partial\hat{x}_{k+1}^-/\partial\hat{z}_k \\ \partial\hat{y}_{k+1}^-/\partial\beta_k & \cdots & \partial\hat{y}_{k+1}^-/\partial\hat{z}_k \\ \partial\hat{z}_{k+1}^-/\partial\beta_k & \cdots & \partial\hat{z}_{k+1}^-/\partial\hat{z}_k \end{pmatrix}.$$

Further simplification can be made: because of assumed independence of errors and the assumption that $\hat{y}_{k+1}^-$ depends only on $\hat{y}_k$, it can be shown that the influence of $\sigma_{\beta k}^2$, $\mathbf{C}_{tk}$, and $\mathbf{P}_k$ on the covariance matrix of prediction can be considered separately:

$$\mathbf{P}_{k+1}^- = \frac{\partial\hat{\mathbf{x}}_{k+1}^-}{\partial\beta_k} \sigma_{\beta k}^2 \left(\frac{\partial\hat{\mathbf{x}}_{k+1}^-}{\partial\beta_k}\right)^T + \mathbf{R}(\beta_k) \cdot (\mathbf{C}_{tk} + \mathbf{P}_k) \cdot \mathbf{R}^T(\beta_k).$$

In the correction step (see Fig. 1), the actual measurement $\mathbf{z}_k$ is used to correct the prediction $\hat{\mathbf{x}}_k^-$. Here, the index $k+1$ is replaced by k to simplify the notification and to underline the iterative nature of the process. To get $\mathbf{z}_k$ from the actual image pair, the disparity estimation is performed using a stochastical method as described in [5]. The advantage of this method is that beyond the disparity itself, its reliability can be estimated as the variance of disparity. From the disparity, the 3D-point $\mathbf{z}_k$ is computed using parameters of the calibrated stereo camera rig. The correspondent covariance matrix $\mathbf{S}_k$ is computed by means of the covariance propagation using the variances and covariances of the camera parameters and the disparity variance, see [2]. Using the actual measurement $\mathbf{z}_k$ and its covariance matrix, the measurement update is computed as follows [8]:

- compute Kalman gain: $\mathbf{K}_k = \mathbf{P}_k^-(\mathbf{P}_k^- + \mathbf{S}_k)^{-1}$,
- correct the prediction $\hat{\mathbf{x}}_k^-$ using measurement $\mathbf{z}_k$: $\hat{\mathbf{x}}_k = \hat{\mathbf{x}}_k^- + \mathbf{K}_k(\mathbf{z}_k - \hat{\mathbf{x}}_k^-)$, (2)
- update the covariance matrix of estimate: $\mathbf{P}_k = (\mathbf{I} - \mathbf{K}_k)\mathbf{P}_k^-$

   ($\mathbf{I}$ denotes the unity matrix).

As already mentioned, each 3D-point as well as its covariance matrix have to be „tracked" over an image pair sequence separately from other points. The „tracking" is achieved in the following way: Assume that for image pair k at some position a disparity was measured, that results in 3D-point $\mathbf{z}_k$. After computing the point $\hat{\mathbf{x}}_k$ with equations (2), the prediction $\hat{\mathbf{x}}_{k+1}^-$ is made using the robot movement data, equation (1). This predicted 3D-point is then projected into image pair $k+1$, which results in a certain predicted disparity. The actual disparity is measured at the projected position and the correspondent 3D-point is reconstructed. The next estimate $\hat{\mathbf{x}}_{k+1}$ is then calculated dependent on the uncertainty of the prediction $\hat{\mathbf{x}}^-_{k+1}$ and on the uncertainty of the actual measurement.

3. Probabilistic Obstacle Detection

The goal of obstacle detection for a mobile robot that moves on a plane is to detect obstacles and to determine their position on the plane. For this purpose a grid is laid on the xz-plane where the robot moves. The task of the obstacle detection procedure is to mark those elements of the grid where an obstacle is detected. In the following, a probabilistic method for marking of obstacle areas is proposed.

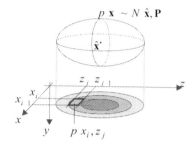

Fig. 3. Probabilistic obstacle detection

The described Kalman filtering requires Gaussian probability distribution of errors. In this case, the probability distribution of a point $\mathbf{x} = (x, y, z)^T$ is completely determined by its estimated value $\hat{\mathbf{x}} = (\hat{x}, \hat{y}, \hat{z})^T$ and the covariance matrix $\mathbf{P}$. The probability density function (PDF) is given by

$$p(\mathbf{x}) = N(\mathbf{x}, \mathbf{P}) = \frac{1}{(2\pi)^{3/2} (\det \mathbf{P})^{1/2}} \exp[-\frac{1}{2}(\mathbf{x} - \hat{\mathbf{x}})^T \mathbf{P}^{-1}(\mathbf{x} - \hat{\mathbf{x}})].$$

Normally, an obstacle edge consists of many 3D points that are found over a comparable small area on the plane. Each point is detected with its own uncertainty in image data. For some points this results in PDFs, that are broadly distributed over many grid elements, and for other points in PDFs that are distributed over only a few grid elements. The problem is to combine these different PDFs in an appropriate way to make the marking of obstacle areas possible.

In a first step, only one point, tracked as described above and the corresponding PDF will be considered (Fig. 3). The PDF with the expected value $\hat{\mathbf{x}}$ and the covariance matrix $\mathbf{P}$ is shown with an ellipsoid. The projection of this PDF on the xz-plane is represented by ellipses on this plane and gives an idea where the obstacle area should lie. The projection is done by integration of the PDF:

$$p(x_i, z_j) = \int_{\hat{y}-\delta_y}^{\hat{y}+\delta_y} \int_{x_i}^{x_{i+1}} \int_{z_j}^{z_{j+1}} p(x, y, z) dx \, dy \, dz .$$

Here, $p(x_i, z_j)$ denotes the probability, that the estimated point $\hat{\mathbf{x}}$ lies over the grid element between $[x_i, x_{i+1}]$ and $[z_j, z_{j+1}]$. Using the threshold δ_y, the influence of the points that could be estimated with small certainty is reduced.

If there are altogether N points, lying over the grid element, the probabilities $p_n(x_i, z_j)$, $n = 1, ..., N$ of all points are accumulated. With this method, the number of the points over a grid element becomes important as well as their precision is taken into account.

4. Experimental Results

The presented algorithm have been implemented on a standard PC using the C programming language. The experiments were carried out with a mobile robot from the company „Götting KG" which is equipped with odometry sensors that are mounted on the driving shaft. From the odometric data the robot motion is computed and transmitted to the PC. To determine the uncertainty of the robot motion, the robot was moved and its actual position and orientation were compared with odometric data. The uncertainties of translation were measured as 5% in perpendicular direction of robot motion and 2% parallel to it; the uncertainty of rotation was 0.05 radian.

As stereoscopic video sensor two synchronised monochrome CCD-cameras have been used. They are mounted 60 cm over the floor plane and have a distance of about 12 cm from each other. The cameras were calibrated using the Tsai-method [7] with a precision of 3D-reconstruction of 3-5 % up to a distance of 5 m. The processing of the video data has been performed as described in [6] with the goal to perform the 3D-reconstruction of the scene.

To investigate the results of 3D-points tracking by means of Kalman filtering, the video sensor has been applied in a static environment. In each image pair at the same image position, the disparities were estimated with slightly different disparity variances due to image noise. Using the variances and covariances of camera parameters and the disparity variance, the covariance matrices $\mathbf{S}_k$ of corresponding 3D-points are computed (k denotes the image number). Due to relatively short distance between the cameras, the resulting uncertainty in the z-direction, σ_{zk}, is much bigger than the uncertainties in x- and y-direction, σ_{xk} and σ_{yk}. To simplify the interpretation of the results, it was assumed that the values of σ_{xk} and σ_{yk} are equal to the value of σ_{zk} (worst case) and non-diagonal elements are set to 0. This also results in diagonal shape of $\mathbf{K}_k$ and $\mathbf{P}_k$ after performing the Kalman filtering, formulas (2), so that the PDFs of corresponding 3D-points are radial-symmetric. Fig. 4 shows the computed variances (diagonal elements of matrices $\mathbf{P}_k$) and the Kalman gain from 10

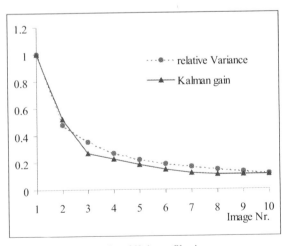

Fig. 4. Results of Kalman filtering

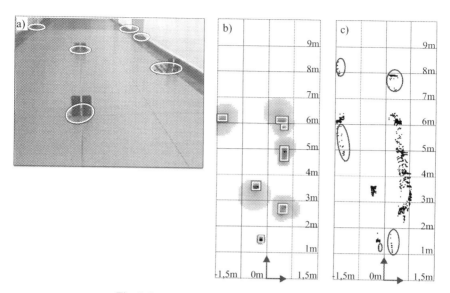

Fig. 5. Results of probabilistic obstacle detection

image pairs. Because the 3D-point was not disturbed by the robot motion, the 3D-variance as well as the Kalman gain decreases continuously, as expected.

Fig. 5 a) shows the left image of an image pair. The results of the projection of PDFs of single 3D-points with subsequent accumulation as described in chapter 3 are represented in Fig. 5 b). The figure shows the „bird's-eye view" of the scene in front of the robot, which is placed at the position denoted by the coordinate cross. The grey scale value of a point in the picture represents the logarithm of the probability, that there is an obstacle. The dark pixels represent higher probability compare to the light ones. Fig. 5 c) shows the results of the 3D-reconstruction without any probabilistic data interpretation. Comparing Fig. 5 b) and 5 c), it can be seen that most outliers could be successfully suppressed (some outliers are marked by ellipses in Fig. 5 c). The final step of obstacle detection has been made by marking those points whose probability exceeds a certain threshold (in the Fig. 5 b) denoted by rectangles). For testing purposes the obstacles were projected back in the left image (in Fig. 5 a) denoted by ellipses).

5. Summary

Mobile robot applications require robust and reliable 3D-reconstruction and obstacle detection. In the presented paper, the Kalman filter technique was used to robustly combine measurements from different image pairs. The experimental results show the ability of the described method to perform the fusion of robot motion data with results of stereoscopically based 3D-reconstruction.

Furthermore, a stochastically motivated method was developed to carry out the obstacle detection. It could be shown experimentally that this method can be used for the outlier elimination in reconstructed 3D-data and in this way for suppression of the phantom objects.

Further developments will concentrate on course generation to allow the robot to move around obstacles. Another future task is to develop land mark based global localisation technique for mobile robot using odometry and video data. A promising approach for this is to apply the Markov localisation procedure used in [3].

Acknowledgments. The authors would like to thank AMIS-team of the Fachhochschule Hannover for support while implementing and testing of described algorithms. We would also like to thank the company "Götting KG" for providing us with a mobile robot test platform.

References

[1] Arras K.O., Tomatis N., „Sensordatenfusion zur Robusten und Präzisen EKF Lokalisierung von Mobilen Robotern", in *Autonome Mobile Systeme (AMS'99), 15. Fachgespräch*, München, 26.-27. November 1999, SpringerVerlag 1999.

[2] Olivier Faugeras: *Three-dimensional computer vision : a geometric viewpoint* -Cambridge, Mass. [u.a.] : MIT Press, 1993.

[3] D. Fox, W. Burgard and S. Thrun, „Markov Localisation for Mobile Robots in Dynamic Environments", *Journal of Artificial Intelligence Research (JAIR)*, 11, 1999.

[4] M.S. Grewal, A.P. Andrews, *Kalman Filtering: Theory and Practice*, Prentice Hall, 1993

[5] R. Mester, M. Hötter, „Robust Displacement Vector Estimation Including a Statistical Error Analysis", in *Image Processing and its Applications*, 4-6 July, 1995, Conference Publication, pp 168-172.

[6] A. Suppes, S. Niehe, M. Hötter, E. Kunze, „Stereobasierte Videosensorik unter Verwendung einer stochastischen Zuverlässigkeitsanalyse", in G. Sommer, N. Krüger, C. Perwass, (Hrsg.): *Mustererkennung 2000*, 22. DAGM-Symposium. Kiel, 13.-15. September 2000.

[7] R.Y. Tsai, „A Versatile Camera Calibration Technique for High-Accuracy 3D Machine Vision Metrology Using off-the-Shelf TV Cameras and Lenses" in *IEEE Journal of Robotics and Automation*, Vol. RA-3, No.4, August 1987, pp. 323-344.

[8] G. Welch, G. Bishop (1995). *An Introduction to the Kalman Filter*, University of North Carolina at Chapel Hill, Department of Computer Science, Chapel Hill, NC, USA. TR95-041. Available at http://www.cs.unc.edu/~welch/publications.html.

3D Model Retrieval with Spherical Harmonics and Moments

Dietmar Saupe and Dejan V. Vranić

Institut für Informatik, Universität Leipzig

Abstract. We consider 3D object retrieval in which a polygonal mesh serves as a query and similar objects are retrieved from a collection of 3D objects. Algorithms proceed first by a normalization step in which models are transformed into canonical coordinates. Second, feature vectors are extracted and compared with those derived from normalized models in the search space. In the feature vector space nearest neighbors are computed and ranked. Retrieved objects are displayed for inspection, selection, and processing. Our feature vectors are based on rays cast from the center of mass of the object. For each ray the object extent in the ray direction yields a sample of a function on the sphere. We compared two kinds of representations of this function, namely spherical harmonics and moments. Our empirical comparison using precision-recall diagrams for retrieval results in a data base of 3D models showed that the method using spherical harmonics performed better.

1 Introduction

Currently methods for retrieving multimedia documents using audio-visual content as a key in place of traditional textual annotation are developed in MPEG-7 [6]. Many similarity-based retrieval systems were designed for still image, audio and video, while only a few techniques for content-based 3D model retrieval have been reported [2,5,6,7,8,9,10,11]. We consider 3D object retrieval in which a 3D model given as a triangle mesh serves as a query key and similar objects are retrieved from a collection of 3D objects. Content-based 3D model retrieval algorithms typically proceed in three steps:

1. *Normalization (pose estimation).* 3D models are given in arbitrary units of measurement and undefined positions and orientations. The normalization step transforms a model into a canonical coordinate frame. The goal of this procedure is that if one chose a different scale, position, rotation, or orientation of a model, then the representation in canonical coordinates would still be the same. Moreover, since objects may have different levels-of-detail (e.g., after a mesh simplification to reduce the number of polygons), their normalized representations should be similar as much as possible.
2. *Feature extraction.* The features capture the 3D shape of the objects. Proposed features range from simple bounding box parameters [8] to complex image-based representations [5]. The features are stored as vectors of fixed dimension. There is a tradeoff between the required storage, computational complexity, and the resulting retrieval performance.
3. *Similarity search.* The features are designed so that similar 3D-objects are close in feature vector space. Using a suitable metric nearest neighbors are

B. Radig and S. Florczyk (Eds.): DAGM 2001, LNCS 2191, pp. 392–397, 2001.
© Springer-Verlag Berlin Heidelberg 2001

computed and ranked. A variable number of objects are thus retrieved by listing the top ranking items.

We present an empirical study extending our contribution [11] in which we introduced a modification of the Karhunen-Loeve transform and the application of spherical harmonics to the problem of 3D object retrieval. We first review the 3D model retrieval problem and previous work. Then we recall our approach based on spherical harmonics and present an alternative using moments. We describe our experiments that we designed to evaluate and contrast the two competing methods. Finally, the results and conclusions are presented.

2 Previous Work

The normalization step is much simpler than the pose estimation deeply studied in computer vision where a 3D pose must be inferred from one or more images, i.e., projections of a 3D object. Here, the 3D models for the retrieval problem are already given in 3D space, and, thus, the most prominent method for normalization is the *principle component analysis* (PCA) also known as the Karhunen-Loeve transform. It is an affine transformation based on a set of vectors, e.g., the set of vertices of a 3D model. After a translation of the set moving its center of mass to the origin a rotation is applied so that the largest variance of the transformed points is along the x-axis. Then a rotation around the x-axis is carried out so that the maximal spread in the yz-plane occurs along the y-axis. Finally, the object is scaled to a certain unit size. A problem is that differing sizes of triangles are not taken into account which may cause widely varying normalized coordinate frames for models that are identical except for finer triangle resolution in some parts of the model. To address this issue we introduced appropriately chosen vertex weights for the PCA [10], while Paquet et al. [8] used centers of mass of triangles as vectors for the PCA with weights proportional to triangle areas. Later we generalized the PCA so that *all* of the (infinitely many) points in the polygons of an object are equally relevant for the transformation [11].

Feature vectors for 3D model retrieval can be based on Fourier descriptors of silhouettes [1,5], on 3D moments [8], rendered images or depth maps [5], or on volumetric representation of the model surface [2] or the corresponding volume (if the surface bounds a solid) [7,6,8].

Using special moments of 3D objects the normalization step may be joined with the feature extraction. In [3] a complete set of orthogonal 3D Zernike polynomials provides spherical moments with advantages regarding noise effects and with less information suppression at low radii. The normalization is done using 3D moments of degree not greater than 3. There were no examples demonstrating the performance of these feature vectors in 3D model retrieval.

In this paper we consider a particular method to generate feature vectors for 3D object retrieval. In a first step the 3D shape is characterized by a function on the sphere. For this function we empirically compare two kinds of representation, one using spherical harmonics and the other by computing moments.

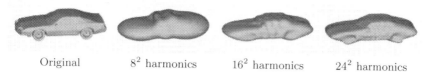

Original 8^2 harmonics 16^2 harmonics 24^2 harmonics

Fig. 1. Multi-resolution representation of the function $r(\mathbf{u}) = \max\{r \geq 0 \mid r\mathbf{u} \in I \cup \{\mathbf{0}\}\}$ used to derive feature vectors from Fourier coefficients for spherical harmonics.

3   Functions on the Sphere for 3D Shape Feature Vectors

In this section we describe the feature vectors used in our comparative study. As 3D models we take triangle meshes consisting of triangles $\{T_1, \ldots, T_m\}$, $T_i \subset \mathbb{R}^3$, given by vertices (geometry) $\{\mathbf{p}_1, \ldots, \mathbf{p}_n\}$, $\mathbf{p}_i = (x_i, y_i, z_i) \in \mathbb{R}^3$ and an index table with three vertices per triangle (topology). Then our object is $I = \bigcup_{i=1}^{m} T_i$, the point set of all triangles. We may assume that our models are normalized by a modified PCA as outlined in Section 1. For details we refer to [11].

Some feature vectors can be considered as samples of a function on the sphere S^2. For example, for a (normalized) model I define

$$r : S^2 \to \mathbb{R}$$
$$\mathbf{u} \mapsto \max\{r \geq 0 \mid r\mathbf{u} \in I \cup \{\mathbf{0}\}\}$$

where $\mathbf{0}$ is the origin. This function $r(\mathbf{u})$ measures the extent of the object in directions given by $\mathbf{u} \in S^2$. In [10] we took a number of samples $r(\mathbf{u})$ as a feature vector, which, however, is sensitive to small perturbations of the model. In this paper we improve the robustness of the feature vector by sampling the spherical function $r(\mathbf{u})$ at many points but characterizing the map by just a few parameters, using either spherical harmonics or moments. Other definitions of features as functions on the sphere are possible. For example, one may consider a rendered perspective projection of the object on an enclosing sphere, see [5].

The Fourier transform on the sphere uses the spherical harmonic functions Y_l^m to represent any spherical function $r \in L^2(S^2)$ as $r = \sum_{l \geq 0} \sum_{|m| \leq l} \hat{r}(l, m) Y_l^m$. Here $\hat{r}(l, m)$ denotes a Fourier coefficient and the spherical harmonic basis functions are certain products of Legendre functions and complex exponentials. The (complex) Fourier coefficients can be efficiently computed by a spherical FFT algorithm applied to samples taken at points $\mathbf{u}_{ij} = (x_{ij}, y_{ij}, z_{ij}) = (\cos \varphi_i \sin \theta_j, \sin \varphi_i \sin \theta_j, \cos \theta_j)$, where $\varphi_i = 2i\pi/n$, $\theta_j = (2j + 1)\pi/2n$, $i, j = 0, \ldots, n - 1$, and n is chosen sufficiently large. We cannot give more details here and refer to the survey and software in [4]. One may use the spherical harmonic coefficients to reconstruct an approximation of the underlying object at different levels, see Figure 1. An example output of the absolute values of the spherical Fourier coefficients (up to $l = 3$) is given here:

			1.161329			
		0.063596	0.162562	0.063596		
	0.213232	0.037139	0.373217	0.037139	0.213232	
0.016578	0.008051	0.009936	0.008301	0.009936	0.008051	0.016578

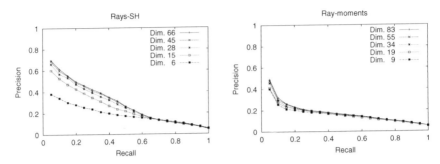

Fig. 2. Precision vs. recall results for varying dimensions in spherical harmonics (left) and moments (right). Results were averaged over all retrieval results in the class of airplane models.

Feature vectors can be extracted from the first $l + 1$ rows of coefficients. This implies that such a feature vector contains all feature vectors of the same type of smaller dimension, thereby providing an embedded multi-resolution approach for 3D shape feature vectors. We have chosen to use only the absolute values as components of our feature vectors. Because of the symmetry in the rows of the coefficients (for real functions on the sphere coefficients in rows are pairwise complex conjugate) we therefore obtain feature vectors of dimension $\sum_1^{l+1} k = (l+1)(l+2)/2$ for $l = 0, 1, 2, \ldots$, i.e., 1, 3, 6, 10, 15, an so forth.

An alternative to the representation of a spherical function by spherical harmonics is given by moments. To be consistent we sample the spherical function $r(\mathbf{u})$ at the same n^2 points $\mathbf{u}_{ij}$, $i, j = 0, \ldots, n-1$, as for the representation by spherical harmonics. As moments we define

$$M^{q,r,s} = \sum_{i,j=0}^{n-1} r(\mathbf{u}_{ij})\, \Delta s_{ij}\, x_{ij}^q\, y_{ij}^r\, z_{ij}^s$$

for $q, r, s = 0, 1, 2, \ldots$ The factor Δs_{ij} represents the surface area on the sphere corresponding to the sample point $\mathbf{u}_{ij} = (\cos\varphi_i \sin\theta_j, \sin\varphi_i \sin\theta_j, \cos\theta_j)$ and compensates for the nonuniform sampling. For example, when $n = 128$ we have $\Delta s_{ij} = \frac{\pi}{64}(\cos(\theta_i - \frac{\pi}{256}) - \cos(\theta_i + \frac{\pi}{256}))$. For the feature vector we ignore $M^{0,0,0}$, and use $1 \leq q + r + s \leq m$. As m grows from 2 to 6 the dimension of the corresponding feature vectors increases from 9 to 19, 34, 55, and 83 (the dimension is $(m+1)(m+2)(m+3)/6 - 1$).

4   Results and Conclusion

For our tests we collected a data base of 1829 models which we manually classified. For example, we obtained 52 models of cars, 68 airplanes, 26 bottles, and 28 swords. On average a model contains 5667 vertices and 10505 triangles. We

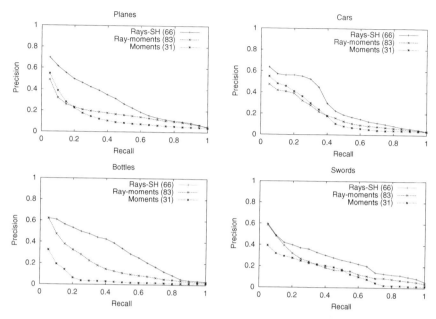

Fig. 3. Precision vs. recall results for four classes (airplanes, cars, bottles, and swords) using three methods, the ray-based feature vectors with spherical harmonics (Rays-SH), with moments (Ray-moments), and a method based on statistical moments [8] (Moments). The dimensions of the feature vectors are shown in the legends in brackets.

used $n^2 = 128^2 = 16384$ samples $r(\mathbf{u}_{ij})$ of the spherical function for the computation of the spherical harmonics and the moments. For the nearest neighbor computation in feature vector space we used the l_1-distance.

The retrieval performance can be expressed in so-called precision-recall diagrams. Briefly, *precision* is the proportion of retrieved models that are relevant (i.e., in the correct class) and *recall* is the proportion of the relevant models actually retrieved. By increasing the number of nearest neighbors in the retrieval the recall value increases while the precision typically decreases. By examining the precision-recall diagrams for different queries (and classes) we obtained a measure of the retrieval performance. For our tests we selected one class of objects (e.g., cars) and used each of the objects in the class as a query model. The precision-recall values for these experiments were averaged and yielded one curve in the corresponding diagram.

In our first test series we studied the dependency of the retrieval performance on the dimensionality of the feature vectors. The class of objects was given by the 68 airplanes. We conclude that both types of ray-based feature vectors yield a better performance when the dimension is increased.

In our second test series we compared the performance of the feature vectors for retrieving 3D models in four classes. In all cases the representation of the ray-based feature vector using spherical harmonics performed best, see Figure 3.

The graphs also include results for feature vectors based on statistical moments from [8], defined as $M^{q,r,s} = \sum_i S_i\, x_i^q\, y_i^r\, z_i^s$ where the point (x_i, y_i, z_i) is the centroid of the i-th triangle and S_i is the area of that triangle. Due to the normalization the moments with $q + r + s \leq 1$ are zero and can be omitted in the moment feature vectors. The retrieval performance was tested for several dimensions, and we found that the performance decreased for dimensions larger than 31. As shown in Figure 3 the retrieval performance of these feature vectors was inferior to that produced by the ray-based feature vectors.

To conclude we summarize that the Fast Fourier Transform on the sphere with spherical harmonics provides a natural approach for generating embedded multi-resolution 3D shape feature vectors. In tests using a ray-based feature vector the representation with spherical harmonics performed better than a representation using moments.

References

1. K. Arbter, W.E. Snyder, H. Burkhardt, G. Herzinger, "Application of affine-invariant Fourier descriptors to recognition of 3-D objects", *IEEE Trans. on Pattern Analysis and Machine Intelligence*, 12 (1990) 640–647.
2. M. Ankerst, G. Kastenmüller, H.-P. Kriegel, T. Seidl, "3D shape histograms for similarity search an classification in spatial databases", *Proc. 6th Intern. Symp. on Spatial Databases (SSD'99).*, Hong Kong, China, Springer-Verlag, 1999.
3. N. Canterakis, "3D Zernike moments and Zernike affine invariants for 3D image analysis and recognition", *Proc. 11th Intern. Conf. on Image Analysis.*, Kangerlussuaq, Greenland, June 1999.
4. D.M. Healy, D. Rockmore, P. Kostelec, and S. Moore, "FFTs for the 2-sphere — Improvements and variations," *Advances in Applied Mathematics*, (to appear). Preprint and corresponding software, *SpharmonicKit,* are available at: http://www.cs.dartmouth.edu/~geelong/sphere/.
5. M. Heczko, D. Keim, D. Saupe, and D.V. Vranić, "A method for similarity search of 3D objects", *Proc. of BTW 2001*, Oldenburg, Germany, pp. 384–401, 2001.
6. MPEG Video Group, "MPEG-7 Visual part of eXperimetation Model (version 9.0)," Doc. ISO/MPEG N3914, Pisa, January, 2001.
7. M. Novotni and R. Klein, "A geometric approach to 3D object comparison," *Proc. of Shape Modelling International (SMI 2001)*, Genova, Italy, 2001, (to appear).
8. E. Paquet, A. Murching, T. Naveen, A. Tabatabai, and M. Rioux, "Description of shape information for 2-D and 3-D objects," *Signal Processing: Image Communication*, 16:103–122, 2000.
9. M.T. Suzuki, T. Kato, and N. Otsu, "A similarity retrieval of 3D polygonal models using rotation invariant shape descriptors," *IEEE Int. Conf. on Systems, Man, and Cybernetics (SMC2000)*, Nashville, Tennessee, pp. 2946–2952, 2000.
10. D.V. Vranić and D. Saupe, "3D model retrieval," *Proc. of Spring Conf. on Comp. Graph. and its Appl. (SCCG2000)*, Budmerice, Slovakia, pp. 89–93, May 2000.
11. D.V. Vranić and D. Saupe, "Tools for 3D-object retrieval: Karhunen-Loeve Transform and spherical harmonics," to appear, *IEEE Workshop on Multimedia Signal Processing (MMSP'2001)*, Cannes, France, Oct. 2001.

Least Squares Orthogonal Distance Fitting of Implicit Curves and Surfaces

Sung Joon Ahn, Wolfgang Rauh, and Matthias Recknagel

Fraunhofer Institute for Manufacturing Engineering and Automation (IPA)
Nobelstr. 12, 70569 Stuttgart, Germany
{sja, wor, mhr}@ipa.fhg.de
http://www.ipa.fhg.de/english/600/Informationstechnik_e.php3

Abstract. Curve and surface fitting is a relevant subject in computer vision and coordinate metrology. In this paper, we present a new fitting algorithm for implicit surfaces and plane curves which minimizes the square sum of the orthogonal error distances between the model feature and the given data points. By the new algorithm, the model feature parameters are grouped and simultaneously estimated in terms of form, position, and rotation parameters. The form parameters determine the shape of the model feature, and the position/rotation parameters describe the rigid body motion of the model feature. The proposed algorithm is applicable to any kind of implicit surface and plane curve.

1 Introduction

Fitting of curve or surface to a set of given data points is a very common task carried out with applications of image processing and pattern recognition, e.g. edge detection, information extraction from 2D-image or 3D-range image. In this paper, we are considering least squares fitting algorithms for implicit model features. *Algebraic fitting* is a procedure whereby model feature is described by implicit equation $F(\mathbf{a}, \mathbf{X}) = 0$ with parameters $\mathbf{a} = (a_1, \dots, a_q)^T$, and the error distances are defined with the deviations of functional values from the expected value (i.e. zero) at each given point. If $F(\mathbf{a}, \mathbf{X}_i) \neq 0$, the given point $\mathbf{X}_i$ does not lie on the model feature (i.e. there is some error-of-fit). Most publications about LS-fitting of implicit features have been concerned with the square sum of algebraic distances or their modifications [5,9,10,12]

$$\sigma_0^2 = \sum_i^m F^2(\mathbf{a}, \mathbf{X}_i) \qquad \text{or} \qquad \sigma_0^2 = \sum_i^m [F(\mathbf{a}, \mathbf{X}_i)/\nabla F(\mathbf{a}, \mathbf{X}_i)]^2 \ .$$

In spite of advantages in implementation and computing costs, the algebraic fitting has drawbacks in accuracy, and is not invariant to coordinate transformation. In *geometric fitting*, also known as best fitting or orthogonal distance fitting, the error distance is defined as the shortest distance (geometric distance) of a given point to the model feature. Sullivan et al. [11] have presented a geometric

B. Radig and S. Florczyk (Eds.): DAGM 2001, LNCS 2191, pp. 398–405, 2001.
© Springer-Verlag Berlin Heidelberg 2001

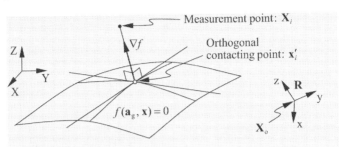

Fig. 1. Implicit surface, and the orthogonal contacting point $\mathbf{x}'_i$ in frame xyz from the given point $\mathbf{X}_i$ in frame XYZ.

fitting algorithm for implicit algebraic features

$$F(\mathbf{a}, \mathbf{X}) = \sum_{j}^{q} a_j X^{k_j} Y^{l_j} Z^{m_j} = 0 \; ,$$

minimizing the square sum of the geometric distances $d(\mathbf{a}, \mathbf{X}_i) = \|\mathbf{X}_i - \mathbf{X}'_i\|$, where $\mathbf{X}_i$ is a given point, and $\mathbf{X}'_i$ is the nearest point on the model feature F from $\mathbf{X}_i$. A weakness of Sullivan's algorithm, the same as in the case of algebraic fitting, is that the physical parameters are combined into an algebraic parameters vector.

We will now introduce a universal and very efficient orthogonal distance fitting algorithm for implicit surfaces and plane curves. Our algorithm is a generalized extension of an orthogonal distance fitting algorithm for implicit plane curves [1,2]. The new algorithm consists of two *nested iteration* parts. The inner iteration finds the orthogonal contacting point on the model feature from the given point (Section 2), and, the outer iteration updates the estimation parameters (Section 3). By the new algorithm, the estimation parameters $\mathbf{a}$ are grouped in three categories and simultaneously estimated.

First, the *form parameters* $\mathbf{a}_g$ describe the shape of the standard model feature f defined in *model coordinate system* xyz (Fig. 1)

$$f(\mathbf{a}_g, \mathbf{x}) = 0 \qquad \text{with} \qquad \mathbf{a}_g = (a_1, \dots, a_l)^T \; . \tag{1}$$

The form parameters are invariant to the rigid body motion of the model feature. The second and the third parameters group (the *position parameters* $\mathbf{a}_p$ and the *rotation parameters* $\mathbf{a}_r$) describe the rigid body motion of the model feature f in machine coordinate system XYZ

$$\mathbf{X} = \mathbf{R}^{-1}\mathbf{x} + \mathbf{X}_o \qquad \text{or} \qquad \mathbf{x} = \mathbf{R}(\mathbf{X} - \mathbf{X}_o) \; , \qquad \text{where} \tag{2}$$

$$\mathbf{R} = \mathbf{R}_\kappa \mathbf{R}_\varphi \mathbf{R}_\omega \; , \qquad \mathbf{R}^{-1} = \mathbf{R}^T \; ,$$

$$\mathbf{a}_p = \mathbf{X}_o = (X_o, Y_o, Z_o)^T \; , \qquad \text{and} \qquad \mathbf{a}_r = (\omega, \varphi, \kappa)^T \; .$$

In this paper, we intend to simultaneously estimate all these parameters

$$\mathbf{a}^T = (\mathbf{a}_g^T, \, \mathbf{a}_p^T, \, \mathbf{a}_r^T) = (a_1, \dots, a_l, X_o, Y_o, Z_o, \omega, \varphi, \kappa) = (a_1, \dots, a_q) \; .$$

For plane curve fitting, we simply ignore all terms concerning z, Z, ω, and φ.

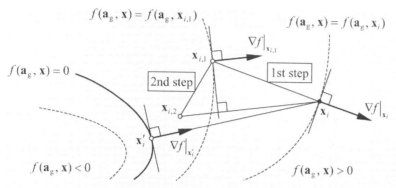

Fig. 2. Iterative search of the orthogonal contacting point $\mathbf{x}'_i$ on $f(\mathbf{a}_g, \mathbf{x})=0$ from the given point $\mathbf{x}_i$. The points $\mathbf{x}_{i,1}$ and $\mathbf{x}_{i,2}$ are the first and the second approximation of $\mathbf{x}'_i$, respectively.

2 Orthogonal Contacting Point

For each given point $\mathbf{x}_i = \mathbf{R}(\mathbf{X}_i - \mathbf{X}_o)$ in frame xyz, we determine the orthogonal contacting point $\mathbf{x}'_i$ on the standard model feature (1). Then, the orthogonal contacting point $\mathbf{X}'_i$ in frame XYZ to the given point $\mathbf{X}_i$ will be obtained through a backward transformation of $\mathbf{x}'_i$ into XYZ. From the fact that the connecting line of $\mathbf{x}_i$ with $\mathbf{x}'_i$ on $f(\mathbf{a}_g, \mathbf{x}) = 0$ is parallel to the surface normal ∇f at $\mathbf{x}'_i$ (Fig. 1), we build the orthogonal contacting equation (3) defined in *model coordinate system* xyz, and directly solve it for $\mathbf{x}$ by using a generalized Newton method starting from the initial point of $\mathbf{x}_0 = \mathbf{x}_i$ (Fig. 2). (How to derive $\partial \mathbf{f}/\partial \mathbf{x}$ is shown in Section 3):

$$\mathbf{f}(\mathbf{a}_g, \mathbf{x}_i, \mathbf{x}) = \begin{pmatrix} f \\ \nabla f \times (\mathbf{x}_i - \mathbf{x}) \end{pmatrix} = \mathbf{0} \ , \qquad \left. \frac{\partial \mathbf{f}}{\partial \mathbf{x}} \right|_k \Delta \mathbf{x} = -\mathbf{f}(\mathbf{x}_k) \ . \qquad (3)$$

Alternatively, we can find $\mathbf{x}'_i$ minimizing the Lagrangian [6,11] as follows:

$$L(\lambda, \mathbf{x}) = (\mathbf{x}_i - \mathbf{x})^{\mathrm{T}}(\mathbf{x}_i - \mathbf{x}) + \lambda f \ ,$$

$$\begin{pmatrix} 2\mathbf{I} + \lambda \mathbf{H} & \nabla f \\ \nabla^{\mathrm{T}} f & 0 \end{pmatrix} \begin{pmatrix} \Delta \mathbf{x} \\ \Delta \lambda \end{pmatrix} = \begin{pmatrix} 2(\mathbf{x}_i - \mathbf{x}) - \lambda \nabla f \\ -f \end{pmatrix} \ , \quad \text{where} \quad \mathbf{H} = \frac{\partial}{\partial \mathbf{x}} \nabla f \ . \qquad (4)$$

The iteration with (4) converges relatively fast. Nevertheless, if it fails to converge, we catch it using the direct method (3).

3 Orthogonal Distance Fitting

The goal of the orthogonal distance fitting of a model feature to a set of given data points is the estimation of the feature parameters $\mathbf{a}$ minimizing the performance index

$$\sigma_0^2 = (\mathbf{X} - \mathbf{X}')^{\mathrm{T}} \mathbf{P}^{\mathrm{T}} \mathbf{P} (\mathbf{X} - \mathbf{X}') \ , \qquad (5)$$

where $\mathbf{X}$ and $\mathbf{X}'$ are coordinate column vectors ($\mathbf{X}^{\mathrm{T}} = (\mathbf{X}_1^{\mathrm{T}}, \ldots, \mathbf{X}_m^{\mathrm{T}})$), and $\mathbf{P}^{\mathrm{T}}\mathbf{P}$ is the weighting matrix or the error covariance matrix. The nearest point $\mathbf{X}_i'$ on the model feature from the given point $\mathbf{X}_i$ is to have been found by the algorithms described in Section 2 in a nested iteration scheme (inner iteration). In this section, we are describing the update of the parameters $\mathbf{a}$ (outer iteration).

The first order necessary condition for the minimum of the performance index (5) as a function of the parameters $\mathbf{a}$ is

$$\left(\frac{\partial}{\partial \mathbf{a}}\sigma_0^2\right)^{\mathrm{T}} = \mathbf{0} = -2\mathbf{J}^{\mathrm{T}}\mathbf{P}^{\mathrm{T}}\mathbf{P}(\mathbf{X} - \mathbf{X}') \ , \quad \text{where} \quad \mathbf{J} = \frac{\partial \mathbf{X}'}{\partial \mathbf{a}} \ . \tag{6}$$

In this paper, we iteratively solve (6) for $\mathbf{a}$ by using the Gauss-Newton method

$$\mathbf{P}\mathbf{J}\Delta\mathbf{a} = \mathbf{P}(\mathbf{X} - \mathbf{X}') \ , \qquad \mathbf{a}_{k+1} = \mathbf{a}_k + \alpha\Delta\mathbf{a} \ , \tag{7}$$

with the Jacobian matrices of each orthogonal contacting points $\mathbf{X}_i'$, directly derived from (2),

$$\mathbf{J}_{\mathbf{X}_i',\mathbf{a}} = \frac{\partial \mathbf{X}}{\partial \mathbf{a}}\bigg|_{\mathbf{X}=\mathbf{X}_i'} = \left(\mathbf{R}^{-1}\frac{\partial \mathbf{x}}{\partial \mathbf{a}} + \frac{\partial \mathbf{R}^{-1}}{\partial \mathbf{a}}\mathbf{x} + \frac{\partial \mathbf{X}_o}{\partial \mathbf{a}}\right)\bigg|_{\mathbf{x}=\mathbf{x}_i'}$$

$$= \mathbf{R}^{-1}\frac{\partial \mathbf{x}}{\partial \mathbf{a}}\bigg|_{\mathbf{x}=\mathbf{x}_i'} + \left(\begin{array}{c|c|c} \mathbf{0} & \mathbf{I} & \dfrac{\partial \mathbf{R}^{-1}}{\partial \mathbf{a}_r}\mathbf{x}_i' \end{array}\right) \ . \tag{8}$$

The derivative matrix $\partial \mathbf{x}/\partial \mathbf{a}$ at $\mathbf{x}=\mathbf{x}_i'$ in (8) describes the variational behavior of the orthogonal contacting point $\mathbf{x}_i'$ in frame xyz relative to the differential changes of the parameters vector $\mathbf{a}$. Purposefully, we obtain $\partial \mathbf{x}/\partial \mathbf{a}$ from the orthogonal contacting equation (3). Because (3) has an implicit form, its derivatives lead to

$$\frac{\partial \mathbf{f}}{\partial \mathbf{x}}\frac{\partial \mathbf{x}}{\partial \mathbf{a}} + \frac{\partial \mathbf{f}}{\partial \mathbf{x}_i}\frac{\partial \mathbf{x}_i}{\partial \mathbf{a}} + \frac{\partial \mathbf{f}}{\partial \mathbf{a}} = \mathbf{0} \quad \text{or} \quad \frac{\partial \mathbf{f}}{\partial \mathbf{x}}\frac{\partial \mathbf{x}}{\partial \mathbf{a}} = -\left(\frac{\partial \mathbf{f}}{\partial \mathbf{x}_i}\frac{\partial \mathbf{x}_i}{\partial \mathbf{a}} + \frac{\partial \mathbf{f}}{\partial \mathbf{a}}\right) \ , \tag{9}$$

where, $\partial \mathbf{x}_i/\partial \mathbf{a}$ is, from $\mathbf{x}_i = \mathbf{R}(\mathbf{X}_i - \mathbf{X}_o)$,

$$\frac{\partial \mathbf{x}_i}{\partial \mathbf{a}} = \frac{\partial \mathbf{R}}{\partial \mathbf{a}}(\mathbf{X}_i - \mathbf{X}_o) - \mathbf{R}\frac{\partial \mathbf{X}_o}{\partial \mathbf{a}} = \left(\begin{array}{c|c|c} \mathbf{0} & -\mathbf{R} & \dfrac{\partial \mathbf{R}}{\partial \mathbf{a}_r}(\mathbf{X}_i - \mathbf{X}_o) \end{array}\right) \ .$$

The other three matrices $\partial \mathbf{f}/\partial \mathbf{x}$, $\partial \mathbf{f}/\partial \mathbf{x}_i$, and $\partial \mathbf{f}/\partial \mathbf{a}$ in (9) are to be directly derived from (3). The elements of these three matrices are composed of simple linear combinations of components of the error vector $(\mathbf{x}_i - \mathbf{x})$ with elements of the following three vector/matrices ∇f, $\mathbf{H}$, and $\mathbf{G}$ (FHG matrix):

$$\nabla f = \left(\frac{\partial f}{\partial x}, \frac{\partial f}{\partial y}, \frac{\partial f}{\partial z}\right)^{\mathrm{T}} \ , \qquad \mathbf{H} = \frac{\partial}{\partial \mathbf{x}}\nabla f \ , \qquad \mathbf{G} = \frac{\partial}{\partial \mathbf{a}_g}\left(\frac{f}{\nabla f}\right) \ , \tag{10}$$

$$\frac{\partial \mathbf{f}}{\partial \mathbf{x}} = \begin{pmatrix} 0 & 0 & 0 \\ y_i - y & -(x_i - x) & 0 \\ -(z_i - z) & 0 & x_i - x \\ 0 & z_i - z & -(y_i - y) \end{pmatrix} \mathbf{H} + \begin{pmatrix} \frac{\partial f}{\partial x} & \frac{\partial f}{\partial y} & \frac{\partial f}{\partial z} \\ \frac{\partial f}{\partial y} & -\frac{\partial f}{\partial x} & 0 \\ -\frac{\partial f}{\partial z} & 0 & \frac{\partial f}{\partial x} \\ 0 & \frac{\partial f}{\partial z} & -\frac{\partial f}{\partial y} \end{pmatrix} \ ,$$

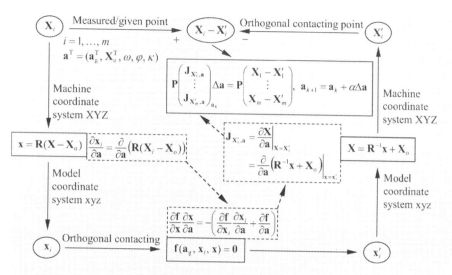

Fig. 3. Information flow for orthogonal distance fitting of implicit features.

$$\frac{\partial \mathbf{f}}{\partial \mathbf{x}_i} = \begin{pmatrix} 0 & 0 & 0 \\ -\frac{\partial f}{\partial y} & \frac{\partial f}{\partial x} & 0 \\ \frac{\partial f}{\partial z} & 0 & -\frac{\partial f}{\partial x} \\ 0 & -\frac{\partial f}{\partial z} & \frac{\partial f}{\partial y} \end{pmatrix} \quad ,$$

$$\frac{\partial \mathbf{f}}{\partial \mathbf{a}} = \begin{pmatrix} 1 & 0 & 0 & 0 \\ 0 & y_i - y & -(x_i - x) & 0 \\ 0 & -(z_i - z) & 0 & x_i - x \\ 0 & 0 & z_i - z & -(y_i - y) \end{pmatrix} (\ \mathbf{G} \ | \ \mathbf{0} \ | \ \mathbf{0} \ ) \quad .$$

For the sake of a common practice of program source coding for curve and surface, we have interchanged, without loss of generality, the second and the fourth row of (3). Then, for plane curve fitting, we consider only the first two rows of the modified equation (3). Now, equation (9) can be solved for $\partial \mathbf{x}/\partial \mathbf{a}$ at $\mathbf{x} = \mathbf{x}'_i$, and consequently, the Jacobian matrix (8) and the linear system (7) can be completed. The Jacobian matrix in (7) will be decomposed by SVD [8]:

$$\mathbf{PJ} = \mathbf{UWV}^\mathrm{T} \qquad \text{with} \qquad \mathbf{U}^\mathrm{T}\mathbf{U} = \mathbf{V}^\mathrm{T}\mathbf{V} = \mathbf{I} \ , \quad \mathbf{W} = [\mathrm{diag}(w_1, \dots, w_q)] \ ,$$

then the linear system (7) can be solved for $\Delta \mathbf{a}$. After a successful termination of iteration (7), along with the performance index σ_0^2 of (5), the Jacobian matrix $\mathbf{J}$ provides useful information about the quality of parameter estimations as follows:

Covariance matrix: $\qquad \mathrm{Cov}(\hat{\mathbf{a}}) = (\mathbf{J}^\mathrm{T}\mathbf{P}^\mathrm{T}\mathbf{PJ})^{-1} = \mathbf{VW}^{-2}\mathbf{V}^\mathrm{T} \ ;$

Parameter covariance: $\qquad \mathrm{Cov}(\hat{a}_j, \hat{a}_k) = \sum_{i=1}^{q} \left(\frac{V_{ji}V_{ki}}{w_i^2} \right) \ ;$

Variance of parameters: $\sigma^2(\hat{a}_j) = \dfrac{\sigma_0^2}{m-q}\mathrm{Cov}(\hat{a}_j, \hat{a}_j)$;

Correlation coefficients: $\rho(\hat{a}_j, \hat{a}_k) = \dfrac{\mathrm{Cov}(\hat{a}_j, \hat{a}_k)}{\sqrt{\mathrm{Cov}(\hat{a}_j, \hat{a}_j)\mathrm{Cov}(\hat{a}_k, \hat{a}_k)}}$.

Using above information, we can test the reliability of the estimated parameters
â and the propriety of the model selection (object classification). For example,
we would try to fit an ellipsoid to a set of measurement points of a sphere-
like object surface. Then, besides $a \approx b \approx c$ and existence of strong correlations
between the rotation parameters and the other parameters, we get very large
variances of the rotation parameters. In this case, the rotation parameters are
redundant here (over-parameterized), and, although the fitting of an ellipsoid to
the points set has a better performance than a sphere fitting according to (5),
the proper model feature for the points set is a sphere.

We would like to stress that only the standard model feature equation (1),
without involvement of the position/rotation parameters, is required in (10).
The overall structure of our algorithms remains unchanged for all dimensional
fitting problems of implicit features. All that is necessary for a new implicit
feature is to derive the FHG matrix of (10) from (1) of the new model feature, and to supply a proper set of initial parameter values $\mathbf{a}_0$ for iteration (7).
This fact makes possible the realization of a universal and very efficient orthogonal distance fitting algorithm for implicit surfaces and plane curves. An overall
schematic information flow is shown in Fig. 3.

In order to demonstrate the capabilities of our algorithm, we give a not easy
fitting example, a superquadric fitting. A superquadric [4] is a generalization of
an ellipsoid, and is described in implicit form as below:

$$f(a, b, c, \varepsilon_1, \varepsilon_2, \mathbf{x}) = \left((|x|/a)^{2/\varepsilon_1} + (|y|/b)^{2/\varepsilon_1} \right)^{\varepsilon_1/\varepsilon_2} + (|z|/c)^{2/\varepsilon_2} - 1 = 0 ,$$

where a, b, c are the axis lengths, and exponents ε_1, ε_2 are the shape coefficients.
In comparison with the algebraic fitting algorithm [10], our algorithm can also
fit extreme shapes of a superquadric (e.g. a box with $\varepsilon_{1,2} \ll 1$, or a star with
$\varepsilon_{1,2} > 2$). We obtain the initial parameter values set from a sphere fitting and an
ellipsoid fitting, successively, with $\varepsilon_1 = \varepsilon_2 = 1$ (Table 2). Superquadric fitting to
the 30 points in Table 1 representing a box is terminated after 18 outer iteration
cycles for $\|\Delta\mathbf{a}\| = 7.9 \times 10^{-7}$ (Fig. 4).

4   Summary

Dimensional model fitting finds its applications in various fields of science and
engineering, and, is a relevant subject in computer vision and coordinate metrology. In this paper, we have presented a new algorithm for orthogonal distance
fitting of implicit surfaces and plane curves, by which the estimation parameters are grouped in form/position/rotation parameters, and simultaneously estimated. The new algorithm is universal, and very efficient, from the viewpoint

Table 1. Thirty coordinate triples representing a box

X	−4	1	4	20	−11	−26	−3	−7	6	11
Y	3	16	−11	−17	1	7	−13	−26	19	24
Z	13	29	10	22	4	−8	1	−15	9	19
X	3	15	18	−21	−4	−2	−14	20	4	6
Y	−18	9	−3	3	−14	19	14	−17	−20	20
Z	−25	21	22	−13	−22	11	1	15	−18	24
X	22	30	−8	−16	8	26	−22	−2	−3	7
Y	−8	−9	15	15	−13	−14	12	−22	−3	1
Z	4	12	−9	−18	−15	17	−13	−20	9	−5

Table 2. Results of the orthogonal distance fitting to the points set in Table 1

Parameters $\hat{a}$	σ_0	a	b	c	ε_1	ε_2
Sphere	33.8999	46.5199	−−	−−	−−	−−
Ellipsoid	14.4338	46.3303	25.5975	9.3304	−−	−−
Superquadric	0.9033	24.6719	20.4927	8.2460	0.0946	0.0374
$\sigma(\hat{a})$	−−	0.1034	0.1026	0.0598	0.0151	0.0197

Parameters $\hat{a}$	X_0	Y_0	Z_0	ω	φ	κ
Sphere	27.3955	18.2708	−20.8346	−−	−−	−−
Ellipsoid	1.6769	−1.2537	0.8719	0.7016	−0.7099	0.6925
Superquadric	1.9096	−1.0234	2.0191	0.6962	−0.6952	0.6960
$\sigma(\hat{a})$	0.0750	0.0690	0.0774	0.0046	0.0031	0.0059

of implementation and application to a new model feature. Memory space and computing time costs are proportional to the number of the given points. Our algorithm converges very well, and does not require a necessarily good initial parameter values set, which could also be internally provided (e.g. gravitational center and RMS central distance of the given points set for sphere fitting, sphere parameters for ellipsoid fitting, and ellipsoid parameters for superquadric fitting, etc.). If there is a danger of local minimum estimation, we apply the random walking technique along with the line search [6]. For practical applications, we can individually weight each coordinate of the given data points with the reciprocals of the axis accuracy of the measuring machine (see Eq. (5)). Together with other algorithm for orthogonal distance fitting of parametric features [3], our algorithm is certified by the German authority PTB [7], with a certification grade that the parameter estimation accuracy is higher than 0.1 μm for length unit, and 0.1 μrad for angle unit for all parameters of all tested model features.

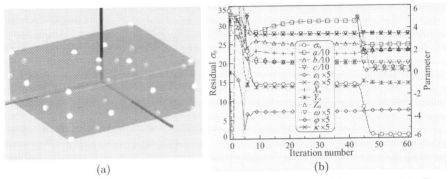

(a)   (b)

Fig. 4. Orthogonal distance fit to the points set in Table 1: (a) Superquadric fit; (b) Convergence. Iteration number 0–42: ellipsoid, and 43–: superquadric fit ($a \geq b \geq c$).

References

1. S.J. Ahn and W. Rauh, Geometric least squares fitting of circle and ellipse, Int. J. of Pattern Recognition and Artificial Intelligence, **13**(7) (1999) 987–996
2. S.J. Ahn, W. Rauh, and H.-J. Warnecke, Least-squares orthogonal distances fitting of circle, sphere, ellipse, hyperbola, and parabola, Pattern Recognition, to appear
3. S.J. Ahn, E. Westkämper, and W. Rauh, Orthogonal Distance Fitting of Parametric Curves and Surfaces, *Int. Symp. Algorithms for Approximation IV*, July 16–20, 2001, The University of Huddersfield, West Yorkshire, UK
4. A.H. Barr, Superquadrics and Angle-Preserving Transformations, IEEE Computer Graphics and Applications, **1**(1) (1981) 11–23
5. F.L. Bookstein, Fitting conic sections to scattered data, Comp. Graphics and Image Proc., **9** (1979) 56–71
6. R. Fletcher, Practical methods of optimization, John Wiley, New York (1987)
7. ISO/DIS 10360-6, Geometrical Product Specification (GPS) - Acceptance test and reverification test for coordinate measuring machines (CMM) - Part 6: Estimation of errors in computing Gaussian associated features, Draft International Standard, ISO, Geneva (1999)
8. W.H. Press, B.P. Flannery, S.A. Teukolsky, and W.T. Vetterling, Numerical Recipes in C: The Art of Scientific Computing, Cambridge University Press, Cambridge, UK (1988)
9. P.D. Sampson, Fitting conic sections to "very scattered" data: An iterative refinement of the Bookstein algorithm, Comp. Graphics and Image Proc., **18** (1982) 97–108
10. F. Solina and R. Bajcsy, Recovery of Parametric Models from Range Images: The Case for Superquadrics with Global Deformations, IEEE Trans. Pattern Analysis and Machine Intelligence, **12**(2) (1990) 131–147
11. S. Sullivan, L. Sandford, and J. Ponce, Using Geometric Distance Fits for 3-D Object Modeling and Recognition, IEEE Trans. Pattern Analysis and Machine Intelligence, **16**(12) (1994) 1183–1196
12. G. Taubin, Estimation of Planar Curves, Surfaces, and Nonplanar Space Curves Defined by Implicit Equations with Applications to Edge and Range Image Segmentation, IEEE Trans. Pattern Analysis and Machine Intelligence, **13**(1) (1991) 1115–1138

Segmentation of Tubular Structures in 3D Images Using a Combination of the Hough Transform and a Kalman Filter

Thorsten Behrens[1], Karl Rohr[2], and H. Siegfried Stiehl[1]

[1] Universität Hamburg, FB Informatik, AB KOGS, Vogt-Kölln-Straße 30, D-22527 Hamburg, {behrens,stiehl}@kogs.informatik.uni-hamburg.de

[2] International University in Germany, D-76646 Bruchsal, rohr@i-u.de

Abstract. In this paper, we present a new approach for coarse segmentation of tubular anatomical structures in 3D image data. Our approach can be used to initialise complex deformable models and is based on an extension of the randomized Hough transform (RHT), a robust method for low-dimensional parametric object detection. In combination with a discrete Kalman filter, the object is tracked through 3D space. Our extensions to the RHT feature adaptive selection of the sample size, expectation-dependent weighting of the input data, and a novel 3D parameterisation for straight elliptical cylinders. For initialisation, only little user interaction is necessary. Experimental results obtained for 3D synthetic as well as for 3D medical images demonstrate the robustness of our approach w.r.t. image noise. We present the successful segmentation of tubular anatomical structures such as the aortic arc or the spinal chord.

Keywords: 3D medical images, 3D tubular structure segmentation, minimal user interaction, randomized Hough transform (RHT), Kalman filter-based tracking

1 Introduction

Deformable models are often used to segment objects in complex 2D and 3D images (e.g. [10]). Since usually local optimisation methods are employed for deformable model fitting, model initialisation is generally required to be close to the real object to obtain reasonable fitting results. In particular, initialisation becomes a major problem for elongated and complicately shaped objects (such as long blood vessels), which are generally described by a large set of parameters. Typically, these model parameters have to be initialised manually. Thus, there is a clear need for automated methods, yielding an approximate segmentation of complex shaped tubular objects, while requiring *minimal* user interaction.

Only a few approaches (e.g. [14,3]) consider the segmentation of tubular structures in 3D medical image data with minimal user interaction. However, their drawbacks are that either an ad-hoc slice-tracking procedure is used in

B. Radig and S. Florczyk (Eds.): DAGM 2001, LNCS 2191, pp. 406–413, 2001.
© Springer-Verlag Berlin Heidelberg 2001

conjunction with threshold-based determination of the tube wall [14], or the method works only for a previously given scale of the tube diameter [3].

In this contribution, we introduce a new approach for segmentation of tubular structures in 3D image data. To detect objects in 3D image data, we extend in Sect. 2 the randomized Hough transform (RHT), a robust method for low-dimensional parametric object detection, while in Sect. 3 we describe how this method can be combined with a discrete Kalman filter to track the objects through 3D space. Segmentation is achieved by detecting elliptical cross sections or straight elliptical cylinder segments that are subsequently tracked through the 3D image. Our algorithm has been applied to both 3D synthetic and 3D medical images (Sect. 4).

2   Extensions of the Randomized Hough Transform

The Hough transform is a well-known method for parametric object detection, where detected pixels in the input image are mapped to a discrete parameter space, whose maxima represent object candidates. In order to detect ellipses or straight elliptical cylinders, which have a relatively large number of parameters (leading to *excessive* space/time complexity for the conventional Hough transform), we build upon the so-called randomized Hough transform (RHT) [16].

The RHT uses a randomly chosen subset of the input data, together with a so-called many-to-one sampling scheme that maps input point sets to zero-dimensional point sets in the parameter space. Thus, parameter spaces of higher dimensions remain tractable, if a dynamic accumulation scheme is used. Several drawbacks inherent to coarse-to-fine and parameter-space decomposition Hough transforms, such as increased noise sensitivity and projection artifacts [4,9], can be alleviated by the RHT, because the parameter space can always have both full dimension and resolution. Our proposed extensions include a new object parameterisation for straight elliptical cylinders, new derivations for an adaptive sample size, and a novel input weighting scheme.

2.1   Object Parameterisations

For the object parameterisation of an *ellipse*, we apply an approach proposed for the Hough transform in [8, p. 151], which determines a unique ellipse (if there is any) that passes through a set of five coplanar points. The advantages over other methods are that no additional information (such as local edge direction) is needed, and because the problem is reduced to linear equations, standard numerical methods can be applied. As discussed in Sect. 3, the plane from which the samples are taken should be orthogonal to

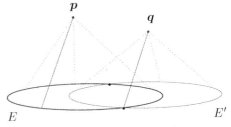

Fig. 1: Determining the cylinder axis

the tube axis. The *straight elliptical cylinder* is a degenerate quadric, so that a direct approach in the above sense leads to a rather complex non-linear algebraic problem. For the sake of speed, we therefore devised the following two-step algorithm for straight elliptical cylinder parameter calculation, using the fact that it is a ruled surface, but still avoiding the use of local edge direction (which is hard to estimate in a robust way with the required accuracy):

1. Select randomly five coplanar points and determine the ellipse E through them (if there is any).
2. Select randomly two distinct points p and q outside the plane containing E. Sweep a line through p and points along ellipse E, and calculate the ellipse E' in the same plane generated by sweeping simultaneously a parallel line through q (see Fig. 1). The intersection points of these two ellipses (it can be shown that there are at maximum two) determine the possible cylinder axes: A line through one of those intersections and q (solid line in Fig. 1) is parallel to the cylinder axis, which of course intersects the two ellipses' plane at the center of E. Having determined the axis, the remaining cylinder parameters can easily be calculated.

2.2   Adaptive Sample Size

When using random sampling schemes for the Hough transform, it is normally no longer necessary to consider *all* points of the input data set. Usually, a subset will suffice, whose size depends on the input data quality. This subset is typically generated by drawing a sample of a given size from the input data points. Instead of the formulas given in [15], which are only hints to sample size selection, we suggest a different way to derive an estimation of an appropriate (data-dependent) sample size. This enables us to state an upper bound for the probability of false detections. Although the derivation is strictly correct only for an unlimited sample size, in practice the given error limit is almost always valid.

Because the counts in the accumulator cells are binomially distributed [15], we can approximate an individual cell's count for large sample sizes by the normal distribution. Thus, if we know *a priori* the probability p_s for sampling points from a significant object and the probability p_{ns} for sampling points from a non-significant object, it can be shown that if the sample size satisfies

$$n \geq \frac{z^2 \left(\sqrt{p_s\,(1 - p_s)} + \sqrt{p_{ns}\,(1 - p_{ns})} \right)^2}{(p_s - p_{ns})^2} \;, \tag{1}$$

then with probability of at least $1 - \mathrm{erf}(z/2)$ the counts of significant cells are larger than those of non-significant ones. This actually prevents non-significant objects from being erroneously detected, because for the RHT, the detected object coincides with the maximal accumulator count. The value z thus parameterises the sample size and the remaining error probability.

We can refine this a priori sample size estimate by calculating the probability p_s', which denotes the *actual* probability for sampling points from an object corresponding to a given cell, using the theorem of the iterated logarithm by Khintchine (e.g. [2, pp. 204]):

$$p'_s \geq \frac{nk + n\log(\log(n)) - \sqrt{n\log(\log(n))\,(2nk - 2k^2 + n\log(\log(n)))}}{n^2 + 2n\log(\log(n))} \quad , \quad (2)$$

where n denotes the current sample size and k the current cell count. As it is only required for the most significant object's cell count to be larger than non-significant cells, we can substitute for p_s in (1) the estimate p'_s calculated from the maximum accumulator cell count to determine a data-dependent sample size.

2.3 Windowing the Hough Transform

In images from cluttered environments, non-relevant image structures often distract the RHT from the relevant features, especially when the objects to be detected are tiny compared to the image size. Therefore, masking out all but small areas around the features has proven to be advantageous [6,7], where usually rectangular, binary-valued windows are used. We extend masking towards arbitrary discrete functions that are adapted to the problem at hand: As the input pixels are selected randomly for the RHT, we have to induce an appropriate discrete probability density function onto the input image, with high values at the most possible object locations. These arbitrary discrete probability functions can be realised by employing the so-called alias method described in [13].

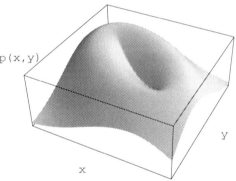

Fig. 2: Example of a continuous window function for ellipse detection

As the Kalman filter (explained below) yields estimates of the expected position, size, and shape of the input object in the next slice, the image can be windowed appropriately. Assuming a Gaussian distribution of the ellipse's main axes errors and exact estimates of the center position and the rotation angle, the window function in Fig. 2 shows the incorporation of Kalman prediction into the RHT.

3 Kalman Filter Approach

In order to track the detected objects (either ellipses or straight elliptical cylinders) through 3D image data, we apply a discrete Kalman filter [5]. Apart from the useful prediction information which can be exploited as mentioned in Sect. 2.3, this approach allows to include an explicit model of the tubular structure's axis curve. For modeling this axis, we used both a linear and a quadratic Taylor approximation.

If $\boldsymbol{x}_k$ is a point on the tube axis at time $k\Delta t$, an estimate at instant $(k+1)\Delta t$ can be calculated as follows (quadratic model):

$$\boldsymbol{x}_{k+1} = \boldsymbol{x}_k + \Delta t \boldsymbol{x}'_k + \frac{1}{2}\Delta t^2 \boldsymbol{x}''_k, \quad \boldsymbol{x}'_{k+1} = \boldsymbol{x}'_k + \Delta t \boldsymbol{x}''_k, \quad \boldsymbol{x}''_{k+1} = \boldsymbol{x}''_k , \qquad (3)$$

where Δt denotes the time interval and $\boldsymbol{x}'_k$, $\boldsymbol{x}''_k$ the first and second derivative w.r.t. time, resp.

Therefore, taking together the results from the previous sections, we were able to implement a tube tracker that adapts itself to the input data quality and restricts random sampling effectively to the Kalman-predicted area. Furthermore, the Kalman prediction of the axis curve offers an additional advantage: If the intersection plane is not orthogonal to the cylinder axis, even tubular structures with elliptical cross sections generally do not yield ellipses when intersected by a plane (see e.g. [12] or [11] for a more in-depth discussion). Thus, when employing the detection of elliptical cross sections, it is essential to re-slice the 3D input data locally, orthogonal to the Kalman prediction of the axis curve. Otherwise, when tracking highly curved structures, the plane intersection curve will differ significantly from an ellipse after a few steps. This can lead to inaccuracies due to model mismatch.

4   Experimental Results

We performed about 20,000 experiments using 3D synthetic binary data with varying object sizes and noise levels to assess the performance and robustness for all four possible combinations of the described object parameterisations (ellipse and straight elliptical cylinder) and the axis approximation (linear and quadratic). It turned out that the detection of elliptical cross sections and the tracking with the quadratic model in (3) performed best. For this variant we show in Fig. 3 one of the binary input images used (slices of a torus), which was degraded with 10% shot noise, and the rendered segmentation result. The plot on the right hand side of Fig. 3 depicts the mean fraction of successfully segmented 3D input images (solid line). This means that the whole arch was tracked and the detected axis was never farther away from the real axis than twice the radius. The mean of that distance from the true arch axis is depicted by the dashed line, whereas the vertical error bars for both plots denote the standard deviation from the corresponding mean. The results are promising, especially regarding noise insensitivity. Up to a noise level of 15%, the test structures were always fully tracked. The small systematic error w.r.t. the true torus axis (≈ 0.5 pixel) is due to discretisation artifacts in the RHT accumulator. In comparison, the other variants were more sensitive to noise. However, for small noise levels, tracking elliptical cylinder segments was significantly more accurate than tracking elliptical cross-sections.

We also conducted experiments using 3D Magnetic Resonance (MR) data, applying the same approach as above (detection of elliptical cross sections and tracking with the quadratic model). To generate the binary data sets necessary

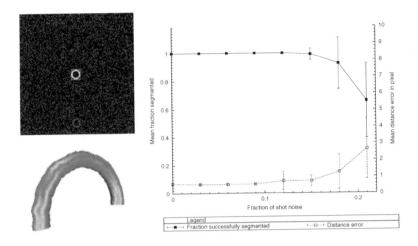

Fig. 3. Experiments using 3D synthetic data. The two images on the left hand side show at the top a slice of a 3D input data set (torus, degraded with 10% shot noise) and below the segmentation result. On the right hand side, a plot of two statistics for the experiments with the method using detection of elliptical cross sections and the quadratic axis model is given, where every point is the mean value of 20 to 40 separate experiments.

for the algorithm, we used a 3D extension of the edge detection method described in [1]. Figure 4 shows the segmentation result of the human aorta in a thorax MR angiography after 3D edge detection. The only initial parameters required for the algorithm were the start point of the aorta axis, the initial radius, and an approximate initial direction. The algorithm then continued segmentation through 3D space until the bottom of the image data volume was reached.

Using the same approach, Fig. 5 shows the result for a 3D MR image of the human head, where the spinal chord was segmented, starting from the bottom of the image up to the medulla oblongata.

5 Summary

We have proposed a new segmentation method for tubular structures in 3D image data, which is based on an extension of the randomized Hough Transform and a discrete Kalman filter. Experimental results obtained for both 3D synthetic and 3D MR image data showed promising results, especially regarding the robustness w.r.t. noise. Out of the four variants we investigated, the one using a quadratic axis model and the detection of elliptical cross sections performed best. Because of its robustness and the small number of required initial values, we characterize our novel algorithm to be well suited for coarse segmentation as well as for initialisation of complex deformable model fitting.

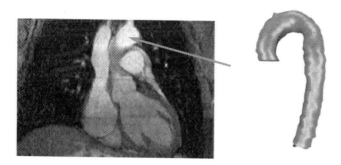

(a) Coronal slice of the thorax   (b) 3D segmentation of the aorta

Fig. 4. Experiments using real 3D MR-angiography data of the thorax. CPU time (without prior 3D edge detection) for segmentation of the aorta was 347.29 sec on a 300 MHz Sun Ultra 2 workstation. The arrow marks the position of the aorta when crossing the image plane.

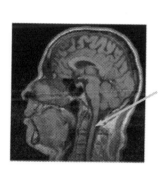

(a) Sagittal slice of the   (b) 3D segmentation of the spinal chord
human head

Fig. 5. Experiments using real 3D MR data of the human head. CPU time (without prior 3D edge detection) for segmentation of the spinal chord (see arrow) was 108.46 sec on a 300 MHz Sun Ultra 2 workstation.

Acknowledgement. The 3D MR and MRA image data has been kindly provided by Dr. T. Schäffter from Philips Research Laboratories Hamburg. Many helpful comments by Sönke Frantz are gratefully acknowledged.

References

1. J. F. Canny. A computational approach to edge detection. *IEEE Trans. Pattern Analysis and Machine Intelligence*, 8(6):679–697, 1986.
2. W. Feller. *An Introduction to Probability Theory and Its Applications*, volume 1. John Wiley & Sons, Inc., New York, 3rd edition, 1968.
3. M. Hernández-Hoyos, A. Anwander, M. Orkisz, J.-P. Roux, P. Douek and I. E. Magnin. A deformable vessel model with single point initialization for segmentation, quantification and visualization of blood vessels in 3D MRA. In *Proc. MICCAI 2000*, LNCS 1935, pp. 735–745. Springer-Verlag, 2000.
4. J. Illingworth and J. Kittler. A survey of the Hough transform. *Computer Vision, Graphics and Image Processing*, 44(1):87–116, 1988.
5. R. E. Kalman. A new approach to linear filtering and prediction problems. *Trans. ASME, Journal of Basic Engineering*, (82):35–45, 1960.
6. H. Kälviäinen, P. Hirvonen, L. Xu and E. Oja. Comparisons of probabilistic and non-probabilistic Hough transforms. In *Proc. 3rd ECCV*, LNCS 800, pp. 351–360. Springer-Verlag, 1994.
7. V. Kyrki and H. Kälviäinen. Combination of local and global line extraction. *Real-Time Imaging*, 6:79–91, 2000.
8. V. F. Leavers. *Shape Detection in Computer Vision Using the Hough Transform*. Springer-Verlag, London, 1992.
9. V. F. Leavers. Survey: Which Hough transform? *Computer Vision, Graphics and Image Processing: Image Understanding*, 58(2):250–264, 1993.
10. T. McInerney and D. Terzopoulos. Deformable models in medical image analysis: A survey. *Medical Image Analysis*, 1(2):91–108, 1996.
11. T. O' Donnell, A. Gupta, and T. Boult. A new model for the recovery of cylindrical structures from medical image data. In *Proc. CVRMed-MRCAS'97*, LNCS 1205, pp. 223–235. Springer-Verlag, 1997.
12. B. I. Soroka, R. L. Andersson, and R. K. Bajcsy. Generalised cylinders from local aggregation of sections. *Pattern Recognition*, 13(5):353–363, 1981.
13. A. J. Walker. An efficient method for generating discrete random variables with general distributions. *ACM Trans. on Mathematical Software*, 3(3):253–256, 1977.
14. O. Wink, W. J. Niessen, and M. A. Viergever. Fast quantification of abdominal aortic aneurysms from CTA volumes. In *Proc. MICCAI 1998*, LNCS 1496, pp. 138–145. Springer-Verlag, 1998.
15. L. Xu and E. Oja. Randomized Hough transform (RHT): Basic mechanisms, algorithms, and computational complexities. *Computer Vision, Graphics and Image Processing: Image Understanding*, 57(2):131–154, 1993.
16. L. Xu, E. Oja, and P. Kultanen. A new curve detection method: Randomized Hough transform (RHT). *Pattern Recognition Letters*, 11(5):331–338, 1990.

Pros and Cons of Euclidean Fitting*

P. Faber and R.B. Fisher

Division of Informatics, University of Edinburgh,
5 Forrest Hill, Edinburgh EH1 2QL, SCOTLAND
npf|rbf@dai.ed.ac.uk

Abstract. The purpose of this paper is to discuss pros and cons of fitting general curves and surfaces to 2D and 3D edge and range data using the Euclidean distance. In the past researchers have used approximate distance functions rather than the Euclidean distance. But the main disadvantage of the Euclidean fitting, computational cost, has become less important due to rising computing speed. Experiments with the real Euclidean distance show the limitations of suggested approximations like the Algebraic distance or Taubin's approximation. We compare the performance of various fitting algorithms in terms of efficiency, correctness, robustness and pose invariance.

1 Introduction

The ability to construct CAD or other object models from edge and range data has a fundamental meaning in building a recognition and positioning system. While the problem of model fitting has been successfully addressed, the problem of a high accuracy and stability of the fitting is still an open problem. On the one hand it is imperative to solve the problem of how curves and surfaces can be fitted to a given data set. But on the other hand it is obvious that accuracy and stability of the fitting has a substantial impact on the recognition performance especially in reverse engineering where we desire an accurate reconstruction of 3D geometric models of objects from range data. Thus it is very important to get good shape estimates from the data.

Implicit polynomial curves and surfaces are potentially among the most useful object or data representations for use in computer vision and image analysis. Their power appears by their ability to smooth noisy data, to interpolate through sparse or missing data, their compactness and their form being commonly used in numerous constructions. An implicit curve or surface is the zero set of a smooth function $f : \mathbb{R}^n \to \mathbb{R}^m$ of the n variables: $\mathcal{Z}(f) = \{\boldsymbol{x} : f(\boldsymbol{x}) = 0\}$. Let $f(\boldsymbol{x})$ be an *implicit polynomial* of degree d given by

$$f(\boldsymbol{x}) = \sum_{\substack{(i+j+k) \leq d \\ \{i,j,k\} \geq 0}} a_{ijk} \cdot x^i \cdot y^j \cdot z^k = 0 \ . \tag{1}$$

Then, we only have to determine the parameter set $\{a_{ijk}\}$ that describes the given data best.

---

* The work was funded by the CAMERA (*CA*d *M*odelling of Built *E*nvironments from *R*ange *A*nalysis) project, an EC TMR network (ERB FMRX-CT97-0127).

B. Radig and S. Florczyk (Eds.): DAGM 2001, LNCS 2191, pp. 414–420, 2001.
© Springer-Verlag Berlin Heidelberg 2001

2 Least Squares Fitting of General Curves and Surfaces

Parameter estimation, usually cast as an optimization problem, can be divided into three general techniques: least-squares fitting (e.g. [1,3,9,10,12]), Kalman filtering (e.g. [4,5]), and robust techniques (e.g. [2,6]). Given a finite set of data points $\mathcal{D} = \{\boldsymbol{x}_p\}$, $p \in [1, P]$, the problem of fitting a general curve and surface $\mathcal{Z}(f)$ to $\mathcal{D}$ by a least-squares method is to minimize a distance measure

$$\frac{1}{P} \sum_{p=1}^{P} \text{dist}\,(\boldsymbol{x}_p, \mathcal{Z}(f)) \rightarrow \text{Minimum} \tag{2}$$

from the data points $\boldsymbol{x}_p$ to the curve or surface $\mathcal{Z}(f)$, a function of the parameter set $\{a_{ijk}\}$. The distance from the point $\boldsymbol{x}_p$ to the zero set $\mathcal{Z}(f)$ is defined as the minimum of the distances from $\boldsymbol{x}_p$ to points $\boldsymbol{x}_t \in \mathcal{Z}(f)$:

$$\text{dist}(\boldsymbol{x}_p, \mathcal{Z}(f)) = \min \{ \| \boldsymbol{x}_p - \boldsymbol{x}_t \| : f(\boldsymbol{x}_t) = 0 \} \ . \tag{3}$$

In the past researchers have often replaced the real Euclidean distance by an approximation. But it is well known that a different performance function can produce biased results, and for a lot of primitive curves and surfaces a closed form expression exists for the Euclidean distance. In the following we summarize the Algebraic fitting, Taubin's fitting [13,14] and an Euclidean fitting [7,8].

Algebraic fitting ($\boldsymbol{AF}$) is based on the approximation of the Euclidean distance by the algebraic distance $\text{dist}_A\,(\boldsymbol{x}_p, \mathcal{Z}(f)) = f(\boldsymbol{x}_p)$. Given the Algebraic distance for each point, Eq.(2) can be formulated as an Eigenvector problem. To avoid the trivial solution $\{a_{ijk}\} = \boldsymbol{0}$ and any multiple of a solution, the parameter set $\{a_{ijk}\}$ may be constrained in some way. The *pros and cons* of using algebraic distances are the gain in computational efficiency, because closed form solutions can usually be obtained, but often the results are unsatisfactory.

Taubin's fitting ($\boldsymbol{TF}$) uses the first order approximation of Eq. (1) to estimate $\text{dist}_T(\boldsymbol{x}_p, \mathcal{Z}(f))$ [13].

$$\text{dist}_T\,(\boldsymbol{x}_p, \mathcal{Z}(f)) = \frac{|f(\boldsymbol{x}_p)|}{\|\nabla f(\boldsymbol{x}_p)\|} \tag{4}$$

The *pros and cons* of using Taubin's distance are no iterative procedures are required and it is a first order approximation to the exact distance, but the approximate distance is also biased in some sense. If, for instance, a data point $\boldsymbol{x}_p$ is close to a critical point of the polynomial, i.e., $\|\nabla f(\boldsymbol{x}_p)\| \approx 0$, but $f(\boldsymbol{x}_p) \neq 0$, the distance becomes large which is certainly a limitation. To minimize Eq.(2) the usage of the Levenberg-Marquardt ($\boldsymbol{LM}$) algorithm is proposed.

Euclidean fitting ($\boldsymbol{EF}$) replaces the approximated distances again by the Euclidean distance, which is invariant to transformations in Euclidean space and not biased. For primitive curves and surfaces like straight lines, ellipses

[15,16], planes, cylinders, cones, and ellipsoids, a closed form expression exists for the Euclidean distance from a point to the zero set and we use these. However, as the general expression of the Euclidean distance is more complicated and there exists no known closed form expression, an iterative optimization procedure must be carried out. Given the Euclidean distance $\text{dist}_E(\boldsymbol{x}_p, \mathcal{Z}(f))$ for each point the following simple algorithm can be used:

1. The Euclidean fitting requires an initial estimate for the parameters $\{a_{ijk}\}$ and we have found that the result of Taubin's fitting method is more suitable than others. We get the initial parameter set $\{a_{ijk}\}^{[0]}$.
2. In the second step $\{a_{ijk}\}^{[s]}, s = 0, 1, \ldots$, is updated using the LM algorithm, minimizing the sum of Euclidean distances for all data points.
3. Finally, each $\{a_{ijk}\}^{[s+1]}$ is evaluated by a M-*estimator* $\mathcal{L}$ on the basis of $\text{dist}_E(\boldsymbol{x}_p, \mathcal{Z}(f))$. If $\mathcal{L}(\{a_{ijk}\}^{[s+1]}) < \mathcal{L}(\{a_{ijk}\}^{[s]})$, $\{a_{ijk}\}^{[s+1]}$ is accepted and the fitting will be continued with step 2. Otherwise the fitting is terminated and $\{a_{ijk}\}^{[s]}$ is the desired solution.

3   Evaluating the Euclidean Fitting

To work out the pros and cons of Euclidean fitting we compare the performance of the EF method with the performance of AF and TF in terms of efficiency, correctness and robustness for both simulated and real data. In case of simulated data we have generated data sets which describe (elliptical) cylinders and cones. The 3D data were generated by adding isotropic Gaussian noise $\sigma = \{1\%, 5\%, 10\%, 20\%\}$. Additionally the surfaces were partially occluded. The visible surfaces were varied between $1/2$ (maximal case) and $1/6$ of the full 3D cylinder. To show that the EF works even for real data we have used several range data sets. For all experiments we include in all three fitting methods the same constraints which describe the expected surface type to enforce the fitting of a special surface type. Finally, we look to the pose invariance of the fitting methods.

3.1   Efficiency

A good fitting algorithm has to be efficient as possible in terms of run time and formal complexity. While the problem of computational cost is no longer a really hard problem because of the rapidly increasing machine speed, we should guarantee the fitting with acceptable computational cost as well as the algorithm with relatively low complexity. All algorithms have been implemented in C and the computation was performed on a Pentium III 466 MHz. The average computational costs for the AF, TF and EF are in Tab. 1. As expected the AF and TF supply the best performance. The EF algorithm requires a repeated search for the point x_t closest to x_p and the calculation of the Euclidean distance. A quick review of the values in Tab.1 shows that the computational costs increase if we fit an elliptical cylinder, a circular or an elliptical cone respectively a general quadric, because the distance estimation is more complicated. In summary

Table 1. Average computational costs in milliseconds per 1000 points.

	AF	TF	EF
Plane	0.958	1.042	2.417
Sphere	1.208	1.250	3.208
Circular cylinder	3.583	3.625	12.375
Elliptical cylinder	13.292	13.958	241.667
Circular cone	15.667	15.833	288.375
Elliptical cone	15.042	15.375	291.958
General quadric	18.208	18.458	351.083

the efficiency is a *con* of *EF*, but is bounded by a factor of about 20 times the performance of the other algorithms and is still computationally reasonable for up to 10^6 data points if real-time performance is not needed.

3.2 Correctness

It is obvious that the fitting result should describe the data set by the correct curve or surface type. That means that it should not fit a false type to the data. To verify the correctness we tested if the fitting result of the (constrained) eigenvalue analysis corresponds to the general curve or surface invariants. If one solution satisfies the conditions for one curve or surface type, it is assumed that the fitting is correct in sense of an interpretable real curve or surface. Otherwise, the fitting will be defined as failure. In our experiments AF failed sometimes (up to 23 percent) respecting our expectations, especially with higher noise levels or a sparse data set (see Sec. 3.3). For TF and EF we had no failures in our experiments. In summary the correctness is a *pro* of *EF*.

3.3 Robustness

A fitting method must degrade gracefully with increasing noise in the data, with a decrease in the available relevant data, and with an increase in the irrelevant data. To evaluate the robustness of the proposed EF, we use synthetic generated data describing an elliptical cylinder by adding isotropic Gaussian noise $\sigma = \{1\%, 5\%, 10\%, 20\%\}$ and partially occlusion varied between $1/2$ (maximal case) and $1/6$ of the full 3D cylinder. In the first experiment the number of 3D points for the simulated cylinder was $n = 100$ and to measure the average fitting error each experiment runs 100 times. The reported error is the Euclidean geometric distance between the 3D data points and the estimated surfaces. The mean squares errors (MSE's) and standard deviations of the different fittings are in Fig. 1. As expected, TF and EF yield the best results respect with to the mean and standard deviation, and the mean for EF is always lower than for the other two algorithms. The results of AF are only partially acceptable, because of the mean and the standard deviation. In the direct comparison of TF with EF the results of EF are much better and the mean of EF is always lower than the mean

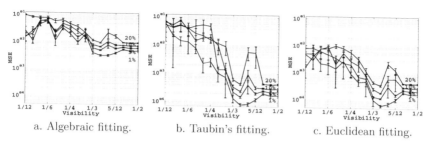

a. Algebraic fitting.   b. Taubin's fitting.   c. Euclidean fitting.

Fig. 1. Average least squares error fitting a synthetic generated cylinder with added Gaussian noise $\sigma = \{1\%, 5\%, 10\%, 20\%\}$. The visible surfaces were varied between $1/2$ (maximal case) and $1/6$ of the full 3D cylinder. The number of trials was 500.

of the other two algorithms. As mentioned in Sec.3.2, AF can give sometimes wrong results which means that the fitted curve or surface types does not come up with our expectations. We removed all failed fittings out of the considerations.

In the second experiment, the number of 3D points was stepwise decreased from $n = 1000$ down to $n = 10$ 3D data points to evaluate the behaviour of the several fitting methods. Each experiment runs 100 times. The mean squares errors (MSE's) and standard deviations of the different fittings are in Fig. 2. As expected, TF and EF yield also the best results in this experiment. With

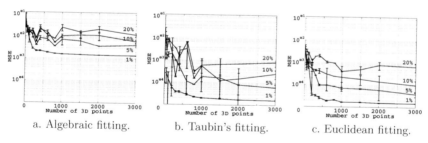

a. Algebraic fitting.   b. Taubin's fitting.   c. Euclidean fitting.

Fig. 2. Average least squares error fitting a synthetic generated cylinder with added Gaussian noise $\sigma = \{1\%, 5\%, 10\%, 20\%\}$. The number of 3D points was stepwise decreased from 1000 up to 10. The visible surfaces was $5/12$ of the full 3D cylinder. The number of trials was 500.

decreased point density especially the AF becomes more and more unstable which is reflected in the mean and standard deviation. Unexpectedly, the EF is very stable even with only $n = 10$ 3D data points. This underlines once more the outstanding performance of the EF. In summary the robustness is clearly a *pro* of EF.

3.4   Pose Invariance

It is obvious that the fitting results should be pose invariant. But, it is well known that this reasonable and necessary requirement cannot be always guaranteed by all three fitting methods. To evaluate the pose invariance we use a real data set (see Fig. 3a.) describing an elliptical cylinder. The normalized data set was a) shifted, b) rotated, and c) both rotated and shifted. A quick review of the residuals (MSE) in Tab. 2 shows AF and TF are not pose invariant while the EF is pose invariant. To illustrate the pose dependency, the fitting results for position 3 are visualized in Fig. 3. In summary the pose invariance is clearly a *pro* of EF.

Table 2. Residuals fitting an elliptical cylinder (see Fig. 3). The normalized cylinder was shifted by $t = [0.3, 0.2, 0.1]$ (pos. 1), rotated by $\vartheta = \pi/12$ and $n = [0.5, 1.0, 0.5]$ (pos. 2), shifted and rotated (pos. 3).

		normal pos	position 1	position 2	position 3
AF	$[10^{-3}]$	0.5242	2.0181	2.6950	1.8271
TF	$[10^{-3}]$	0.5024	1.5143	2.0277	1.3817
EF	$[10^{-3}]$	0.4021	0.4152	0.8634	0.6088

4   Conclusion

The focus was on the pros and cons of Euclidean fitting compared with the commonly used Algebraic fitting and Taubin's fitting. Referring to our objective we can finally conclude that we have more pros than cons for the Euclidean fitting. While the main disadvantage of the Euclidean fitting, computational cost, has become less important due to rising computing speed, robustness and accuracy increases sufficiently compared to both other methods. Additionally, the Euclidean fitting is pose invariant.

References

1. Allan, F. E. The general form of the orthogonal polynomial for simple series with proofs of their simple properties. In *Proc. Royal Soc. Edinburgh*, pp. 310–320, 1935.
2. Besl, P. J. and R. C. Jain. Three-dimensional object recognition. *Computing Survey*, 17(1):75–145, 1985.
3. Bookstein, F. L. Fitting conic sections to scattered data. *CGIP*, 9:56–71, 1979.
4. Chui, C. K. and G. Chen. *Kalman filtering with real time applications*. Springer, Berlin-Heidelberg-New York, 1987.
5. Dickmanns, E. D. and V. Graefe. *Dynamic monocular machine vision*. MVA, 1:223–240, 1988.

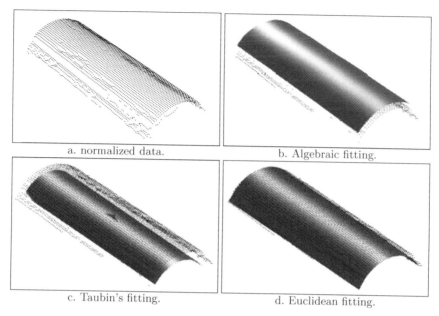

a. normalized data.   b. Algebraic fitting.

c. Taubin's fitting.   d. Euclidean fitting.

Fig. 3. Fitting results for a real range data ($\approx$ 3300 points). The normalized data set was shifted by $t = [0.3, 0.2, 0.1]$ and rotated by $\vartheta = \pi/12$ and $n = [0.5, 1.0, 0.5]$.

6. Duda, R. O. and P. E. Hart. The use of Hough transform to detect lines and curves in pictures. *Comm. Assoc. Comp. Machine*, 15:11–15, 1972.
7. Faber, P. and R. B. Fisher. Euclidean fitting revisited. In *4th IWVF*, pp. 165–175, 2001.
8. Faber, P. and R. B. Fisher. Estimation of General Curves and Surfaces to Edge and Range Data by Euclidean Fitting. *submitted to the MVA*.
9. Fitzgibbon, A. W. and R. B. Fisher. A buyer's guide to conic fitting. In *6th BMVC*, pp. 513–522, 1995.
10. Kanatani, K. Renormalization for biased estimation. In *4th ICCV*, pp. 599–606, 1993.
11. Ray, W.J.J. *Introduction to Robust and Quasi-Robust Statistical Methods*. Springer, Berlin-Heidelberg-New York, 1983.
12. Rosin, P. L. A note on the least square fitting of ellipses. *PRL*, 14:799–808, 1993.
13. Taubin, G. Estimation of planar curves, surfaces and non-planar space curves defined by implicit equations, with applications to edge and range image segmentation. *IEEE Trans. on PAMI*, 13(11):1115–1138, 1991.
14. Taubin, G. An improved algorithm for algebraic curve and surface fitting. In *4th ICCV*, pp. 658–665, 1993.
15. Voss, K. and H. Süße. *Adaptive Modelle und Invarianten für zweidimensionale Bilder*. Shaker, Aachen, 1995.
16. Zhang, Z. Parameter estimation techniques: a tutorial with application to conic fitting. *IVC*, 15:59–76, 1997.

Placing Arbitrary Objects in a Real Scene Using a Color Cube for Pose Estimation

Jochen Schmidt, Ingo Scholz*, and Heinrich Niemann

Lehrstuhl für Mustererkennung, Universität Erlangen-Nürnberg
Martensstr. 3, 91058 Erlangen, Germany
jschmidt@informatik.uni-erlangen.de,
http://www5.informatik.uni-erlangen.de

Abstract. We describe an Augmented Reality system using the corners of a color cube for camera calibration. In the augmented image the cube is replaced by a computer generated virtual object. The cube is localized in an image by the CSC color segmentation algorithm. The camera projection matrix is estimated with a linear method that is followed by a nonlinear refinement step. Because of possible missclassifications of the segmented color regions and the minimum number of point correspondences used for calibration, the estimated pose of the cube may be very erroneous for some frames; therefore we perform outlier detection and treatment for rendering the virtual object in an acceptable manner.

Keywords: Augmented Reality, camera calibration, color segmentation

1 Introduction

In this paper a system is introduced which is an application of Augmented Reality, a visual enhancement of real environments. Unlike many other applications in this field the system described here uses no independent tracking device, but follows a so-called vision-based approach, i. e. calibration information is derived solely from camera input. Many common vision-based systems [10] use some kind of calibration pattern or fiducials still visible in the scene even after augmentation, e. g. [8,16]. Other methods require manually selected control points [2], but do not use fiducials. In our approach, a metal cube with a side length of 6 cm is used that is painted with a different color on each side such that its position and orientation can be determined unambiguously. A real scene can be augmented by rendering a virtual object in the same pose, thus replacing the cube. A possible application of this system is the usage of a head-mounted display for the visualization of three-dimensional objects that do not yet exist or only at distant locations. The system works without human intervention, and no explicit calibration step is required before using it. The main advantages of our approach comprise the usability in indoor and outdoor applications, easy interaction with the user, and the possibility of illumination estimation by exploiting the knowledge about the colors used on the cube.

---

* This work was partially funded by the German Science Foundation (DFG) under grant SFB 603/TP C2. Only the authors are responsible for the content.

B. Radig and S. Florczyk (Eds.): DAGM 2001, LNCS 2191, pp. 421–428, 2001.

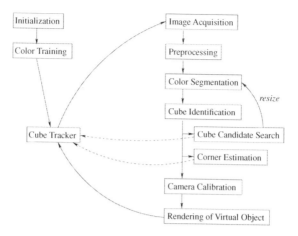

Fig. 1. Overview of system structure with special focus on detection of cube corners.

2   System Overview

The first – and most time-consuming – task of the system is to detect the cube in the image and to determine its corners, thus establishing a correspondence between 2-D image and 3-D world points. In order to get a correct calibration of the camera, the identification of the corners must be as accurate as possible. Details on the method described here can be found in [15].

The system is basically structured as shown in Fig. 1. After an initialization phase and the training of the color classificator, the main loop of the cube tracker is started. This is the manager of the whole system: it contains general information, like the image size and previously known positions of the cube, and it executes the subsequent phases.

In each loop the tracker reads the current image and preprocesses it as described in Sect. 3. Color segmentation is done in two steps: first a version of the image that was reduced in size is segmented and checked for cube canditates. If one or more candidates are found, the corresponding image regions are segmented once more, this time in normal resolution. The color segmentation yields a number of uniformely colored regions. Cube candidates are identified out of these regions by applying a number of restrictions on sets of three or two regions. That is, their colors have to correspond to those of the cube and they must fulfill some geometric properties. If none of the region sets fits these qualities, the tracker discards this image and proceeds with the next one. After that, a set of one or more cube candidates remains, each of which is given a score depending on how well it fits the conditions above. The corner estimator then tries to find the corners of the cubes with the highest scores. If this step fails, the candidate is rejected and the next one is tried. If no candidate remains, the tracker continues with the next image as well.

With the corner points identified, it is now possible to do camera calibration. Details on that part are given in Sect. 4. The final step in the cycle is to render the virtual object that is to replace the cube in the image. From this point on the sequence starts again with the acquisition of the next image frame. If a cube was recognized, its position is taken as a cue for where to start the search in the next image.

3   Finding the Cube

For locating the corners of the cube, two of its properties are used: its color and its geometry. In order to distinguish the cube from the background it was painted in luscious, matte colors. Each side received a unique color such that the system can identify the cube's correct orientation. Of course, in a natural scene it is very likely that other objects are colored similarly. Therefore the geometric appearance of the objects in consideration has to fit that of a cube as well. The input of the cube detector is a stream of RGB images. An enhancement of quality is reached by applying a Symmetric Nearest Neighbour (SNN) filter as suggested in [12] which reduces noise like a mean filter, but preserves edges. Each side of the cube is a region of almost uniform color, except for shadows cast onto it. By choosing matte colors the problem of highlights reflected from a light source was mostly eliminated. Therefore the first step in identifying the cube is a color segmentation of the image. The algorithm used for this is the Color Structure Code (CSC) as described in [12], which is based on an earlier method [5].

It is assumed that each visible side of the cube can be segmented as exactly one region, given that a coarse enough parameterization for the CSC is used. A division of a side happens only in extreme cases, e. g. if a shadow is partially cast over it. Thus each region in the image is classified for being a possible cube side or not, according to its mean color. The numerical classifier applied here uses two feature vectors, the RGB values of a region's color and its hue and saturation values, taken from HSV color space. The distance between a region's mean color and a cube side color class is calculated by the Mahalanobis distance measure. As the color segmentation is costly, the image is first shrunk to a fifth of its size and possible cubes are localized herein. The corresponding windows are cut out of the full-size image, where the cube detection is performed again. After color classification a set of regions remains containing all the regions that possibly are part of the cube. From these the ones truly belonging to the cube have to be filtered out. The subsequent processing of the image requires that at least two sides of the cube are visible – a criterion which reduces the number of cube side candidates, because the knowledge of adjacent colors on the cube can be exploited. In addition, the regions must have the correct appearance: their edges have to be straight lines, forming a parallelogram. Each of the remaining regions gets a score measuring the regions' affinity to the cube. Corners are determined for the regions with the highest scores. This is done by approximating the edges of each side with straight lines using the Hough transform. The intersections of these lines are taken as the corners of the side. In cases where lines are missing due to occlusion, the corners are approximated using information from neighboring sides or the original image in Cartesian coordinates.

The algorithms for camera calibration applied in the following sections need at least six or seven point correspondences, depending on the method. With one side of the cube visible only four points can be obtained, so that two or three sides have to be visible, providing six or seven point pairs respectively. In the case where only one side is visible, the method described in Sect. 4.4 can be applied.

4   Camera Calibration

Camera calibration is done in the following steps, which are described in detail afterwards: Computation of additional point correspondences (Sect. 4.1), linear calibration of all camera parameters (Sect. 4.2), maximum-likelihood estimation of the focal lengths (Sect. 4.2), nonlinear refinement of extrinsic camera parameters (Sect. 4.3), and test of the validity of the computed parameters (Sect. 4.4).

4.1   Computing Additional Point Correspondences

Either six or seven 2-D/3-D point correspondences are established by the algorithm described in the previous section. While six points are enough for one of the methods described below, at least seven are needed for applying the algorithm of Tsai.

Since we use an object of known shape we can compute one additional point correspondence for each side where all four corners have been detected by using the intersection of the two diagonals of a cube side. These additional points are easy to compute in the image and in 3-D and are valid correspondences because the perspective projection preserves intersections. Using projective geometry (see [4] for an introduction) the intersection q_S of the diagonals in the image plane can be computed by

$$q_S = (q_1 \times q_3) \times (q_2 \times q_4) \quad , \tag{1}$$

where q_S, q_i $(i = 1, \ldots, 4)$ are 3-vectors representing image points in homogeneous coordinates, q_1 is opposite to q_3, q_2 is opposite to q_4.

4.2   Linear Calibration

For calibration we assume a perspective camera model. A homogeneous 3-D point w_i is projected onto a homogeneous 2-D point q_i in the image plane using the following equation:

$$q_i = Pw_i = KR^T(I_3| - t)w_i \quad , \tag{2}$$

where K is a 3×3 matrix containing the intrinsic parameters f_x, f_y, u_0, and v_0, R is a rotation matrix whose columns correspond to the axes of the camera coordinate system, t is a translation vector giving the position of the camera's optical center, and I_3 is the 3×3 identity matrix.

After the previous steps there are enough point correspondences to apply a linear calibration method. For this purpose we use either the algorithm of Tsai that can be found in [18,17], or the algorithm described in [17] for estimating the projection matrix. Radial distortions are neglected, the angle between the axes of the image reference frame is assumed to be $90°$. Tsai's method assumes that the principal point is known and the camera parameters are computed directly, in contrast to the second method used which estimates the projection matrix first and makes no assumptions about the principal point. Both methods require non-coplanar point correspondences and the orthogonalization of the resulting rotation matrix which can be done by applying a singular value decomposition (SVD) [11].

Since f_x, f_y are assumed to be constant over the whole sequence, we can get maximum-likelihood estimates $\hat{f}_x$, $\hat{f}_y$ of these parameters at frame t ($t = 1, 2, \dots$) under the assumption of normally distributed, isotropic, and zero-mean noise by the following recursive equation (given here for $\hat{f}_x$ only):

$$\hat{f}_{x,t} = \frac{1}{t+1}\left(t\hat{f}_{x,t-1} + \tilde{f}_{x,t}\right) = \hat{f}_{x,t-1} + \frac{1}{t+1}\left(\tilde{f}_{x,t} - \hat{f}_{x,t-1}\right) \quad , \qquad (3)$$

where $\tilde{f}_{x,t}$ is the result of the linear calibration at time step t. For $t = 0$ the initialization $\hat{f}_{x,0} = \tilde{f}_{x,0}$ is used.

4.3 Nonlinear Refinement

Since we use only slightly more points than the minimum number required for calibration, nonlinear refinement of camera parameters with the linear estimation as initialization is absolutely essential. Optimization is done here for the extrinsic parameters only, while the intrinsic parameters from the previous maximum-likelihood estimation are used and held constant during nonlinear refinement. For this purpose the Gauss-Newton algorithm with Levenberg-Marquardt extension (see [3] for details) is utilized which computes a new estimate of a parameter vector a using a local parametrization Δa by $\hat{a}_{k+1} = \hat{a}_k + \Delta a$ where

$$\Delta a = -\left(\lambda I + J^T J\right)^{-1} J^T \epsilon(\hat{a}_k) \quad . \qquad (4)$$

This method minimizes the mean square error $\epsilon^T \epsilon$, where ϵ is a residual function that computes in our case the (non-squared) back-projection error between each image point (x_i, y_i) and the projection $q_i = (q_{ix}, q_{iy}, q_{iw})^T$ of its corresponding 3-D point w_i obtained by equation (2):

$$\epsilon = \left(x_1 - \frac{q_{1x}}{q_{1w}}, y_1 - \frac{q_{1y}}{q_{1w}}, \dots, x_n - \frac{q_{nx}}{q_{nw}}, y_n - \frac{q_{ny}}{q_{nw}}\right)^T \quad . \qquad (5)$$

J is the Jacobian of the first derivatives of ϵ evaluated at $\hat{a}_k$: $J = \frac{\partial \epsilon}{\partial a}(\hat{a}_k)$. Since the matrix inversion in equation (4) may be numerically instable due to a nearly singular matrix $J^T J$, the factor λ is introduced in the Levenberg-Marquardt algorithm and adapted during each iteration. One Levenberg-Marquardt iteration comprises the following actions: Computation of a parameter update using equation (4) as well as the resulting back-projection error, acceptance of the new parameters if the error is smaller than the error after the last iteration and division of λ by a factor of 10, or rejection of the computed parameters and muliplication of λ by a factor of 10. Since the error may increase during one iteration due to instabilities in matrix inversion, the preceding steps are done until the new parameters yield a smaller error than at the end of the last iteration. The parameter vector a contains the 3 components of the translation t plus 3 components parametrizing the rotation matrix R, which has 9 elements but only 3 degrees of freedom (DOF). A numerically stable parametrization should be used, i. e. either the axis/angle representation or quaternions which are both a fair parametrization of rotations in the sense of [6], while Euler angles are not. A rotation matrix can be represented by a 3-vector $r = (r_1, r_2, r_3)^T$ giving the direction of the rotation axis with 2 DOF plus the rotation angle θ encoded as the norm of r. The corresponding rotation matrix R can be calculated by Rodrigues' formula [4]:

$$R = I_3 + \frac{\sin\theta}{\theta} \begin{pmatrix} 0 & -r_3 & r_2 \\ r_3 & 0 & -r_1 \\ -r_2 & r_1 & 0 \end{pmatrix} + \frac{1 - \cos\theta}{\theta^2} \begin{pmatrix} 0 & -r_3 & r_2 \\ r_3 & 0 & -r_1 \\ -r_2 & r_1 & 0 \end{pmatrix}^2 . \qquad (6)$$

When using quaternions for nonlinear optimization it is necessary to consider that a quaternion representing a rotation has 4 elements but only 3 DOF, since it must be normalized to 1. The Levenberg-Marquardt algorithm cannot deal with constraints on the parameters and it must be guaranteed that the norm of a quaternion is always 1 during optimization. In order to accomplish this goal a quaternion parametrization at the operating point using only 3 elements was introduced in [13,14].

4.4   Detection and Treatment of Outliers

For different reasons the virtual object in the resulting augmented image may be rendered in a completely different pose than the cube. Most of the time this is not due to calibration errors or badly localized cube corners, but to missclassification of the colors painted on the sides of the cube. Additionally there are images where no cube could be found at all. Both cases lead to visually inacceptable results and hence have to be dealt with in an appropriate way. For detection of a non-valid pose, we use thresholds for change in rotation (measured in distance between vectors in axis/angle representation) and translation with respect to the last valid frame.

The easiest solution is to keep the pose of the last valid frame. This is acceptable when only a few frames have to be dropped. Otherwise a prediction of the cube's movement would yield a better result for the human observer. For this purpose we use linear prediction, a technique classically applied in speech recognition [9]. Linear prediction estimates the n-th value of a sequence of discrete values g_j using a combination of the preceding k values as follows:

$$\hat{g}_n = -\sum_{i=1}^{k} \alpha_i g_{n-i} \quad . \qquad (7)$$

Having a long enough sequence, one can estimate the unknowns α_i from a linear system of equations using e. g. the SVD which minimizes the mean square error. The α_i are in turn used for predicting new values of the sequence. In our case we predict the elements of the translation vector and of the rotation matrix in axis/angle representation.

5   Experiments

In our experiments we used images of size 360×288 pixels. Two results of augmentation are shown in Fig. 2. More images and video-sequences are available at [1].

Fig. 2. Two examples of augmentation: Original (top left), CSC segmented cut-out (top middle), and augmented image (top right) on a turntable; original (bottom left) and augmented image (bottom right) of cube held in hand.

We found that the part most prone to errors is the color classification due to different lighting conditions. Missclassification of a cube side leads to wrong 2-D/3-D assignment and thus to unusable calibration results. The color classifier was trained using 577 to 885 samples per color. The recognition rate for the whole cube ranges from 74% - 93%, depending on the illumination of the scene. The mean detection accuracy (measured by hand) of the cube's corners is about 1.3 pixels. If Tsai's calibration method is to be used, additional point correspondences must be computed when only six points have been detected which leads to fairly good visual results. When using the other method, simulations showed that calibration can be done accurately enough even with only six point correspondences, while computation of additional points yields a worse back-projection error and worse camera parameters.

The system is still working off-line, but since we have a real-time system in mind we want to give an impression of the computation times needed for one frame on a 800 MHz Pentium III. Using the Windows program of [12], the CSC took 40 to 130 msec for two passes, one on the reduced size image and one on the cube cut-out, the given time depending on the number of possible cube-regions found in the reduced-size image. Additional 150 to 250 msec are needed for color classification of the segmented regions and computing the corners. The time needed for calibration is dominated by non-linear optimization; depending on the number of Levenberg-Marquardt iterations done, computation time varied from 10 msec (5 iterations) to about 30 msec (20 iterations). OpenGL rendering takes additional 30 msec.

6   Conclusion and Future Work

In this contribution we present an Augmented Reality system using a color segmentation approach for localizing a metal cube in an image which can be replaced by an arbitrary computer-generated object. Camera calibration with a minimum number of point correspondences works well and is fast enough for real-time applications even when nonlinear refinement is done. Topics for further improvement are the speed and accuracy of cube localization and corner detection. We also want to consider illumination estimation using information on the cube's colors in the future.

References

1. http://www5.informatik.uni-erlangen.de/~ar.
2. C.-S. Chen, C.-K. Yu, and Y.-P. Hung. New calibration-free approach for augmented reality based on parameterized cuboid structure. In ICCV 99 [7], pages 30–37.
3. J. E. Dennis and R. B. Schnabel. *Numerical Methods for Unconstrained Optimization and Nonlinear Equations*. Prentice-Hall, Englewood Cliffs, NJ, 1983.
4. Oliver Faugeras. *Three-Dimensional Computer Vision: A Geometric Viewpoint*. MIT Press, Cambridge, MA, 1993.
5. G. Hartmann. Recognition of hierarchically encoded images by technical and biological systems. *Biological Cybernetics*, 57:73–84, 1987.
6. J. Hornegger and C. Tomasi. Representation issues in the ML estimation of camera motion. In ICCV 99 [7], pages 640–647.
7. *Proceedings of the 7th International Conference on Computer Vision (ICCV)*, Corfu, September 1999. IEEE Computer Society Press.
8. D. Koller, G. Klinker, E. Rose, D. Breen, R. Whitaker, and M. Tuceryan. Automated camera calibration and 3D egomotion estimation for augmented reality applications. In *Computer Analysis of Images and Patterns (CAIP)*, pages 199–206, Kiel, September 1997. Springer.
9. J. D. Markel and A. H. Gray Jr. *Linear Prediction of Speech*, volume 12 of *Communications and Cybernetics*. Springer Verlag, Berlin, Heidelberg, New York, 1976.
10. Y. Ohta and H. Tamura, editors. *Mixed Reality – Merging Real and Virtual Worlds*. Springer-Verlag, Berlin, 1999.
11. W. H. Press, S. A. Teukolsky, W. T. Vetterling, and B. P. Flannery. *Numerical Recipes in C: The Art of Scientific Computing*. Cambridge University Press, Cambridge, 2nd edition, 1992.
12. V. Rehrmann and L. Priese. Fast and robust segmentation of natural color scenes. In *Proceedings of the 3rd Asian Conference on Computer Vision*, volume 1, pages 598–606, HongKong, January 1998.
13. J. Schmidt. Erarbeitung geeigneter Optimierungskriterien zur Berechnung von Kameraparametern und Szenengeometrie aus Bildfolgen. Diplomarbeit, Lehrstuhl für Mustererkennung, Universität Erlangen-Nürnberg, 2000.
14. J. Schmidt and H. Niemann. Using quaternions for parametrizing 3–D rotations in unconstrained nonlinear optimization. In T. Ertl, B. Girod, G. Greiner, H. Niemann, and H.-P. Seidel, editors, *Vision, Modeling, and Visualization 2001*, Stuttgart, Germany, November 2001. Submitted.
15. I. Scholz. Augmented Reality: A System for the Visualization of Virtual Objects Using a Head-mounted Display by Localization of a Real Object of Known Geometry and Color. Diplomarbeit, Lehrstuhl für Mustererkennung, Universität Erlangen-Nürnberg, 2000.
16. Y. Seo and K. Sang Hong. Calibration-free augmented reality in perspective. *IEEE Transactions on Visualization and Computer Graphics*, 6(4):346–359, 2000.
17. E. Trucco and A. Verri. *Introductory Techniques for 3–D Computer Vision*. Prentice Hall, New York, 1998.
18. R. Y. Tsai. A versatile camera calibration technique for high-accuracy 3D machine vision metrology using off-the-shelf TV cameras and lenses. *IEEE Journal of Robotics and Automation*, Ra-3(3):323–344, August 1987.

Detecting, Tracking, and Interpretation of a Pointing Gesture by an Overhead View Camera

Marina Kolesnik and Thomas Kuleßa

Institute for Media Communication, GMD-IMK, Schloss Birlinghoven,
D-53754 Sankt-Augustin, Germany.

Abstract. In this work we describe a set of visual routines, which support a novel sensor free interface between a human and virtual objects. The visual routines detect, track and interpret a gesture of pointing in real time. This is solved in the context of a scenario, which enables a user to activate virtual objects displayed on a projective screen. By changing a direction of pointing with an extended towards the screen arm, the user controls the motion of virtual objects. The vision system consists of a single overhead view camera and exploits a *priori* knowledge of the human body appearance, interactive context and environment. The system operates in real time on a standard Pentium-PC platform.

1. Introduction

At the beginning of the 1990's there was an explosion in creating physically interactive environments where users could explore a virtual environment or interact with a character. A key task for vision systems supporting such interaction is to detect and interpret human actions as they appear in imaging data. In this paper we focus on the visual analysis of a gesture of pointing.

A number of systems have been developed that use interactive gesture recognition. These are relevant for the present work in that the system has to recognise that the gesture occurred and extract a parameter important to the interaction. The ALIVE [4] and Perseus [10] systems are examples. The approach of these systems is first to identify the static configurations of the user's body that are diagnostic of the gesture, and then use a separate method to extract the gesture parameters. In the present work we refer to the notion of *parameterised movements* [15], meaning the movements that exhibit meaningful, systematic variation.

The ability to follow people's action in real time is an important component of all these systems. Progress in tracking of human movements was reported in [1], [3], [8], [14] for various conditions, such as static background, periodic motion, stereovision, and gesture-initialisation. The main principle of all these schemes, which is also used in the present work, is that the body is segmented into parts, which are tracked independently. The visual tracking often exploits the knowledge of the context of the specific tracking task [13] or enforces the kinematics constraint on the body motion [7]. Statistical models associated with different body parts are often used for their

B. Radig and S. Florczyk (Eds.): DAGM 2001, LNCS 2191, pp. 429–436, 2001.

tracking [16]. In this work we use a *closed-world* assumption [8], which means a region of space and time in which the specific context of what is happening in the region assumed to be known.

The vision system presented here supports specific interaction between a person and virtual objects. In the scenario a person observes a 3-D virtual environment projected onto the screen, selects a particular object by pointing at it with an extended arm and controls its motion by changing direction of pointing. Our philosophy has been to integrate those complementary and inexpensive vision modules into an integrated system, which is likely to perform well in the given context and environment constraints.

2. Visually Driven Interface and the Environment

One of the most frequently used and expressively powerful gestures is pointing. In the scenario a user can move and rotate an object across the screen. The object would follow the motion of the extended toward the screen arm as it points in different directions. We are only interested in the horizontal coordinate of pointing as virtual objects could move and rotate either to the left or to the right depending on the side of the screen the user pointed at. This consideration allows using a single, overhead view, greyscale camera for the vision system supporting the interaction. The pointing gesture, viewed by the overhead camera, generates salient visual cues, which are easy to detect and interpret.

In the system the user moves freely in a real-world space of approximately 6 by 3 meters. A virtual scene is projected on a wall of 3m bright and 2m height. A monochrome CCD camera, which is placed at the ceiling of the space, captures the top image of the user with the standard video frequency rate of 25 frames per second. The pointing gesture is defined to occur when the user extends either of arms towards the screen. Due to the context and space geometry, direction of pointing is restricted to one hemisphere in front of the user and it is parameterised relative to the projective screen. Pointing is modelled by a 3-D line connecting a middle point on the user's head and the tip of the pointing hand. Reconstruction of the pointing gesture is then equivalent to finding the horizontal and the vertical coordinates of a point where this line meets the screen. In this work we find only the horizontal coordinate that parameterises pointing.

3. Segmentation of a Human Body

The first task to be solved by the system is segmentation of the user in the camera image. This task is normally difficult, but the static room environment that is valid in our case and the fixed camera allows using *background subtraction*. However, due to non-uniform lighting, a shadow cast by the user on the floor may cause problems. Previous attempts at segmenting people from a known background have taken advantage either of colour cameras [2] or multiple cameras [9]. Having a single greyscale camera, segmentation of the user is done by background subtraction, followed by morphological operations to remove noise.

Background subtraction. We have observed that for robust segmentation of a human body a dark colour of the floor has an advantage over a bright one. Firstly, it suppresses the user's shadow; secondly, it significantly diminishes random brightness variations of those pixels that contribute to isolated noise in the segmented image. Segmentation tends to be more stable if threshold values applied to the difference are attuned to overtime brightness variations at each image pixel. A threshold array of the size of the image is computed off-line. Typical brightness variations are observed at each pixel during live image acquisition. The threshold values are set to the maximum variation recorded at each pixel during about 15 minutes of acquisition. Segmentation process starts by acquiring the static background of the room. Smoothing this background image with the averaging operator in a local 3x3-pixel window generates a reference image. The same local smoothing is applied to all frames. The difference between the reference image and each smoothed image from the frame sequence is computed. Final segmentation is obtained by thresholding the difference using the threshold array.

Morphological analysis. Human body segmentation is followed by a morphological analysis, to ensure that all noisy areas are removed, and only the body segment remains in the segmented image. The morphological operator is applied to the binary-segmented image in order to extract all of its connected components. Each component is then labelled and its size is recorded. Final segmentation is obtained by eliminating all but the largest connected component, what we consider to be the human body segment. The process of extraction of connected components in the binary image consists of the two steps. The first *Run length encoding of a binary image* step, transforms the binary-pixel values of the image into a list of encoded line segments that contain only non-zero pixels. The second step, called *Neighbourhood analysis of line segment* uses the list to identify all connected components in the binary image and label them by its unique *Identification number*. The algorithm has an $O(n)$ complexity, where n is the number of encoded line segments. This method gives reasonably stable segmentation of a person without shadow.

4. Modelling the Gesture of Pointing

Once the body segment has been isolated from the background, we label critical body parts. We use explicit *a priori* knowledge of a human body appearance in the overhead view image, and also the given context and room geometry. As we know to which side the screen appears in the image, the pointing arm is restricted to a certain angular sector centred at user location. We proceed by drawing a bounding box around the isolated body segment. The overhead view of the body segment in the box has specific features: a) A prominent head crowns the shoulders while leaving the rest of the body being almost occluded. b) This typical body shape changes dramatically if the user extends one of his arms towards the screen: the body size increases about twice in the direction of the screen. We use the size of the bounding box to classify the current activity of the user, which is either "non-pointing" or "pointing". If the box increases by more than 50% relative to its original size, the gesture of pointing is detected and the human body is segmented into two parts: 1) the arm/hand segment, and 2) the head/shoulders segment. Next, both segments are enclosed into a separate bounding box. The pointing gesture is modelled by a *line of sight* connecting the middle pixel on the user's head and the tip of the pointing hand. Taking into account real time processing requirements we compute a centre of gravity of the head/shoulders segment to approximate the most probable location of the middle pixel on the head. The above process is illustrated in Fig. 1.

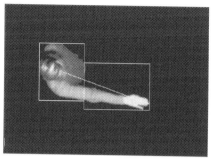

Fig. 1. Classification of the body parts and construction of the line of sight in the image.

5. Tracking of the Gesture of Pointing

Real time interaction ought to trigger immediate modifications in the virtual scene in response to motion of the gesturing arm. We use tracking to follow the gesture of pointing over time. We track two points of interest, which define the line of sight, i.e. the middle pixel of the head and the tip of the hand used for pointing. It is faster to track these two points in the image sequence than to segment each frame. We extend a Hierarchical Feature Vector Matching (HFVM) [11] algorithm, by computing an object associated *feature vector* of a pixel. A *feature* is a real number, which numerically describes statistical information of the neighbourhood of pixel location. Each object in the image has a data structure that characterises its estimated size, shape, directional intensity distribution, shape of edges, etc. We collect this statistical data into the *object feature vector* of the pixel associated with this object. These feature vectors are then compared during the matching process. Here we exploit *closed-world* assumption i.e. no new objects are expected to appear in the search area. We match feature vectors in images with original resolution in rather restricted *search area*. If the search area is too small for the successful match of the head or the hand object, the vision system aborts the tracking mode and returns to full frame segmentation.

6. Reconstruction of the Direction of Pointing

3-D interpretation of the pointing gesture is based on the knowledge of the internal camera parameters and room geometry. Below we describe off-line calibration of the vision system followed by real time reconstruction of the user's pointing.

Offline calibration of the vision system. There are two independent steps in calibration of the vision system: 1) obtaining the camera internal parameters and 2) finding camera location and orientation (camera pose) relative to the screen. We use a pinhole camera model, which is described by the perspective projection matrix $\tilde{P}$ in the *normalised coordinate system* of the camera (see [5], page 57). We use the DLT

calibration method [5] to find internal camera parameters that define the matrix $\tilde{\mathbf{P}}$.
Camera pose is defined by the 6 parameters: 3 for rotation and 3 for translation. As we do not explicitly need all 3 angular values of camera rotation, we only find an optical ray, which is vertical to the room's floor. To do that, a mirror is placed on the floor in such a way that enables to view the reflected image of the camera in the mirror. If pixel v (Fig.2) is the middle pixel of the camera in its reflected image, then the optical ray $<Cv>$ spanned by the camera centre C and pixel v is the vertical to the floor optical ray.

Camera translation is defined relative to room geometry. The following parameters are either measured or computed off-line (Fig.2):

1. The altitude of the camera above the floor $|CV|$.
2. The image line l, which is the image of the 3-D line of intersection between the screen and the floor. Note that l can extend beyond the image boundaries.
3. The pixel w, which is the image of the 3-D point W such that a) it belongs to the lower screen boundary, and b) the line segment $<WV>$ on the floor is perpendicular to the screen.
4. The distance $|WV|$ between the points V and W on the floor.

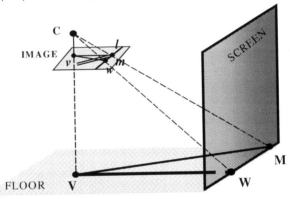

Fig. 2. 3-D model of the pointing gesture. The double line in the image illustrates the line of sight. Pixel m is the point selected by the user on the screen.

3-D Interpretation of the direction of pointing. To determine the horizontal screen coordinate that parameterises the direction of pointing, a two-step algorithm is applied. First, the pointing line in 2-D is constructed. In the second 3-D step we compute both perspective projection of the pointing line onto the room floor, and its intersection with the screen. These two steps are also illustrated in Fig. 2:

2-D step. Direction of pointing is modelled by the line of sight (Section 4). The intersection point m of the line of sight and the line l is found.

3-D step. The perspective projections of the image points' v and m onto the floor are computed. These points are denoted by the capital letters V and M, respectively. The end point of the vector $\mathbf{V}$ on the optical ray $<Cv>$ in the normalised coordinate system is given by: $\mathbf{V} = \lambda \mathbf{P}^{-1} \tilde{\mathbf{v}}$. Here $\mathbf{P}$ is the 3x3 leftmost sub-matrix of $\tilde{\mathbf{P}}$ and $\mathbf{v} = \lfloor v_x, v_y, 1 \rfloor$ is the homogeneous vector of v, and λ is a scalar. Given a similar expression for the vector $\mathbf{M}$, the angle γ between the optical rays $<Cv>$ and $<Cm>$ is given by: $\cos\gamma = \mathbf{M} \cdot \mathbf{V}/|\mathbf{M}||\mathbf{V}|$. As $\gamma < 180^{\circ}$, this definition is unique. The distance between the points V and M on the floor is obtained from the right triangle CVM and the measured altitude $|CV|$. Finally, the direction of pointing is defined by the distance $|WM|$ computed from the right triangle VWM.

7. Experiments

Many people have tested the interactive interface by pointing at virtual objects from different locations. The distance to the screen varied within the range of about 1m to 5m. Before entering the room subjects were only told that pointing with either of arms activates manipulation with virtual objects. We have observed that it takes about 1-2 minutes before a naïve user accommodates to the interface. The visual routines performing detection, tracking and interpretation of pointing run on a Pentium processor under GNU/Linux operation system. If images are digitised at a size of 384x288 pixels the system is able to follow events at a rate of 15 Hz.

Typically, background subtraction resulted in a binary image with about 20-30 scattered segments with the average size of about 15 pixels. After all smaller segments were discarded, we obtained stable segmentation of the user body. Failures, such as fragmented body segmentation, have occurred for those users whose dark clothes looked similar to the floor background. Standard random noise did not disrupt final segmentation because it does not affect much the shape of the biggest segment. We have observed stable tracking both for the tip of the hand and the middle point of the head. The search area used for tracking of the head object was 3 times smaller than the one used for tracking of the hand tip. However, tracking of the head was lost in those cases when the user rotated the head noticeably. It is due to the fact that HFVM matching is not invariant to rotations above 15 degrees. Tracking of the tip point of the hand was stable as long as the user kept his arm pointing.

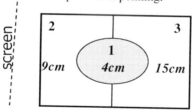

Fig. 3. Accuracy of reconstruction of pointing for the three areas in the camera image. Area 2 lies at about 1m from the screen. Area 3 extends within distance range of about 3m to 6m from the screen. Best accuracy of reconstruction of about 4cm (1% of the screen size) is achieved for pointing from the central area 1. The accuracy decreases for the peripheral areas 2 and 3 due to poor estimation of the middle pixel on the head:

A vertical strip was projected onto the screen in position defined by the reconstructed horizontal coordinate. The accuracy of interpretation of pointing depends on position of the user in the camera image (Fig.3). Main source of inaccurate reconstruction comes from the unstable modelling of the line of sight. It occurs when the head occludes either of the user shoulders in the image. Table 1 presents results on system performance and Fig. 4 exemplifies the process of interaction.

Table 1. Performance of the system recorded over time in experiments with 12 subjects. Segmentation failed in 13% of the time. Given successful segmentation, failures for modelling of the line of sight were recorded in 3% of the time for the area 1 and in 7% of the time for the peripheral areas 2 and 3. We recorded failure if the line deviated from the correct direction by more than 5 degrees. Tracking failures were attributed only to head rotation. Overall performance of reconstruction shown in the last row was mainly affected by unstable segmentation.

	Area 1	Area 2	Area 3
Segmentation	87%	87%	87%
Line of sight	97%	93%	93%
Tracking	96%	95%	96%
Overall	85%	83%	83%

Fig. 4. Three frames from the video sequence illustrating pointing driven rotation of the virtual printer. The vertical stripe indicates horizontal position pointed at the screen.

8. Conclusions and Future Work

We have presented a set of visual routines for perceiving the gesture of pointing in the novel sensor free interface between a human and virtual object. A user can move freely in the real space and activate motion of virtual objects by pointing towards the screen with an extended arm. The visual routines perform detection, tracking and reconstruction of horizontal direction of pointing in real time. The vision system consists of an overhead view greyscale camera. Camera calibration is obtained off-line by classical means using a 3-D calibration target.

Our experiments have shown that the interactive environment provides its users with an easy insight on how to activate and control virtual objects. Detection of pointing operates well regardless of the size of the user's body, because we use relative increase in the size of the bounding box as a sign that pointing occurred. Pointing is detected successfully in cases it is performed by half-bent arm. The accuracy of reconstruction of horizontal location on the screen is enough to provide comfortable interaction.

Major limitation of the current implementation is that segmentation of the user's body from the background is sensitive to the colour of clothes and hair. These weakness results from intensity based segmentation of grey scale images. Another limitation arises from simplistic computation of the middle pixel on the user's head, which leads to somewhat unstable modelling of the line of sight in the peripheral areas of the camera image. Both limitations are the price paid for the simplicity of the setup of the vision system, which includes one monochrome camera. In the future work we will use a stereo technique to reconstruct both the horizontal and the vertical coordinates of the direction of pointing. It will also improve the robustness of human body segmentation and the modelling of the line of sight.

References

1. C. Bregler and J. Malik. Tracking people with twists and exponential maps. In Proc. IEEE CVPR'98, pp. 8-15.
2. I. Cohen, A. Garg and T. S. Huang. Vision-Based Overhead View Person Recognition. In Proc. Int. Conf on Pattern Recognition, Barcelona, Spain, September 2000, Vol. 1, pp. 1119-1124.
3. L. Concalves, E.D. Bernardo, E. Ursella and P. Perona. Monocular tracking of the human arm in 3D. In Proc. of 5th Int. Conf. Computer Vision, Cambridge, Mass, June 1995, pp. 764-770.
4. T. Darrel, P. Maes, B.Blumberg and A. Pentland. A novel environment for situated vision and behavior. In Proc. of CVPR-94 Workshop for Visual Behaviors, Seattle, Washington, June 1994, pp. 68-72.
5. O. Faugeras. Three-Dimensional Computer Vision. A Geometric Viewpoint. MIT Press, Cambridge, MA, pages 55-65, 1993.
6. D. M. Gavrila and L.S. Davis. 3-D model-based tracking of humans in action: a multi-view approach. In Proc. IEEE Computer Vision and Pattern Recognition, San Francisco, 1996.
7. Haritaoglu, D. Harwood and L. Davis. Who, when, where, what: A real time system for detecting and tracking people. In Proc. Third Face and Gesture Recognition Conference, 1998, pp. 222-227.
8. S. S. Intille, J. W. Davis and A. F. Bobick. Real-Time Closed-World Tracking. M.I.T. Media Laboratory Perceptual Computing, technical Report No. 403. 1996.
9. Y. Ivanov, A. Bobick and J. Liu. Fast Lighting Independent Background Subtraction. M.I.T. Media Laboratory Perceptual Computing, technical Report No. 437.
10. R.E.Kahn and M.J.Swain. Understanding people pointing: The Perseus system. In Proc. IEEE Int. Symposium on Computer Vision, Coral Gables, Florida, November 1995, pp. 569-574.
11. M. Kolesnik, G. Paar, A. Bauer and M. Ulm. Algorithmic Solution for Autonomous Vision-Based Off-Road Navigation. In Proc. of SPIE: Enhanced and Synthetic Vision, April 1998, Orlando, Florida.
12. P. N. Prokopowicz, M. J. Swain and R. E. Kahn. Task and environment-sensitive tracking. In Proc. Work. Visual Behaviors, Seattle, June 1994, pp. 73-78.
13. J. Rehg and T. Kanade. Digit eyes: Vision-based hand tracking for human-computer interaction. In Proc. of the workshop on Motion of Non-Rigid and Articulated Bodies. 1994, pp. 16-24.
14. K.Rohr. Incremental recognition of pedestrians from image sequences. In Proc. IEEE Conf. Computer Vision and Pattern Recognition, New York City, June 1993, pp. 8-13.
15. A.D.Wilson and A.F.Bobick. Parametric Hidden Markov Models for Gesture Recognition. IEEE Trans. Pattern Analysis and Machine Intelligence. Vol. 21, No. 9, September 1999, pp. 884-900.
16. C. Wren, A. Azarbayejani, T. Darrel and A. Pentland. Pfinder: real Time Tracking of the Human Body. IEEE Trans. Pattern Analysis and Machine Intelligence, July 1997, Vol. 19, No. 7, pp. 780-785.

Recognition of the German Visemes Using Multiple Feature Matching

Islam Shdaifat[1], Rolf-Rainer Grigat[1], and Stefan Lütgert[2]

[1] Technische Universität Hamburg-Harburg,
shdaifat@tu-harburg.de, http://www.tuvision.de
[2] Philips Semiconductors
Systems Laboratory Hamburg, http://www.philips.com

Abstract. In this paper, we present a technique for the extraction of the main five visemes for German spoken language analysis from images. The intensity, the edges, and the line segments are used to locate the lips automatically, and to discriminate between the desired viseme classes. Good recognition rate has been achieved on different speakers.

1 Introduction

Automated speech perception systems are very sensitive to background noise. They fail totally when multiple speakers are talking simultaneously (cocktail party effect). Besides the acoustic signals from both ears, visual information, mostly lip movements, are subconsciously involved in the recognition process of human beings [1,2].

Tracking of the lips in image sequences and relating the features of the lips to the speech are two challenging problems. This is due to the lack of dominant image features defining the lips [8]. For lip location and visual features extraction, several methods were proposed in the literature. Deformable templates [5] [9] are effective in lip tracking, though quite computationally expensive [8]. Principal component analysis (PCA) was used [3]. But not each form of lips can be described by PCA, and a large data base of objects is needed [4]. A 3D model of the lips using two calibrated cameras was proposed [10]. However, the human being can read the speech even from still 2D images.

Here, we present a method for lips tracking and viseme classification using feature templates matching. Given a number of independent features of the sample data, a linear combination of these is created which yields the largest mean difference between the desired classes [4]. For a certain speaker, the system is trained with five different visemes. The different features of the visemes are stored in templates. These templates are used to track the lips and to recognize the viseme.

The paper is organized as follows. In sec. 2 we describe how the phonemes are related to mouth shape, and how they are divided into classes of visemes similar to the perception of the human being. In sec. 3 the use of the feature templates in locating the lips from the face of the speaker is illustrated. In sec. 4,

B. Radig and S. Florczyk (Eds.): DAGM 2001, LNCS 2191, pp. 437–442, 2001.

the classification of the features into the viseme classes is illustrated. In sec. 5 a comparison between different sequences and the results are presented.

2   Grouping Phonemes into Visemes

The human being can relate the lip shape to groups of phonemes. This can be noticed especially when the lips are mainly used to produce a certain phoneme. For example, in the phonemes **m p b** the mouth must be closed.

Dodd [7] divided the sounds or phonemes into 14 groups of visemes for English. A reasonable grouping was supposed by Abry [6]. The phonemes in French were subdivided into six groups according to the lips' shapes. We subdivided the phonemes into five groups depending on the lip shape. These are

1. **C**: closed lips m, b, p, ...
2. **O**: open lips a, h, ...
3. **H**: half open lips t, d, k, g, s, ...
4. **L**: long lips i, e, ...
5. **R**: rounded lips o, u, $ü$, $ö$ ... .

We noticed that this is not always the case for all the speakers. The boundaries between the visemes are not always clearly defined for each speaker. Thus, the number of the viseme classes can be even less than 5. Fig. 1 shows an example of five distinguishable viseme classes.

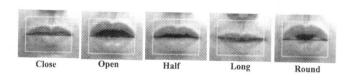

| Close | Open | Half | Long | Round |

Fig. 1. An example of images of five viseme classes.

3   Tracking of the Lips

A pattern image representing the lips is correlated with the speaker's image pixel by pixel, see Fig. 2. The speaker's image and the pattern image are scaled down to speed up the search.

The areas where the correlation is greater than a certain threshold are marked. Due to the scale and rotation in the lips' image and the variable lighting condition, the position of the absolute maximum correlation is not always the correct position of the lips. The eyes sometimes have correlation coefficients larger than that of the lips.

To avoid getting stuck with non lips' locations, we inspect additional features of the lips. The edge image is calculated and fitted with 10 pixel line segments. Distinguished features of the lips are the corners of the mouth. Along the line segments, we search for the corners of the mouth pattern the same way that was used for the lip pattern. Using these two corners, we rotate and scale the image of the lips to be in the standard position for further viseme recognition. Fig. 3 illustrates this procedure. In sec. 4 further refinement will be described.

The region of interest ROI is defined as 150% of the lip size at the current lips' location. The process is restricted to the ROI if the correlation coefficient ρ is less than a certain threshold value at least every 20 images.

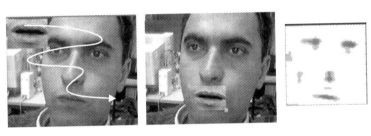

Fig. 2. Searching for the lips, left the searched pattern, middle the pattern matched, right regions where $\rho >$ threshold.

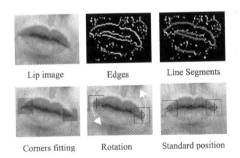

Fig. 3. Searching for the corners of the mouth in ROI, and putting the lip in standard position

4   Viseme Recognition

Different visemes are very close to each other in feature space. Only very small variations exist between them. This makes the recognition a non-trivial task.

Fig. 4 shows a diagram of the five viseme classes and the large overlap between them.

In sec 3, the image of the lips was detected, and transformed into the standard position. The resulting image of the lips is compared with each viseme template. Fig 5 shows an image of closed lips and the basic features that are used in the recognition.

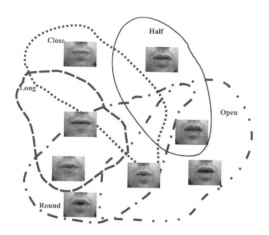

Fig. 5. Features used to discriminate between the visemes.

Fig. 4. A hypothetical representation of the overlap between the different viseme classes.

For intensity comparison the intensity correlation ρ_i is used. Given two images I_1 and I_2, with N pixels each, and let $\overline{I_1}$ and $\overline{I_2}$, σ_1, σ_2 be the averages and the standard deviations of I_1 and I_2, respectively, then $\rho_i = \frac{\sum (I_1 - \overline{I_1})(I_2 - \overline{I_2})}{\sigma_1 \sigma_2 N^2}$

For the edges ρ_e

    for each edge point in image I_1 **do**
        if edge point exists in $w_e \times w_e$ window in I_2 **then**
            counter = counter + 1
        end if
    end for
    $\rho_e = \frac{counter}{N \ edge \ points \ of \ I_1}$

For the lines ρ_l

    for each line segment in image I_1 **do**
        if line segment exists in $w_l \times w_l$ window in I_2 **then**
            if angle of line segment in I_1 and in I_2 are equal **then**
                counter = counter + 1
            end if
        end if
    end for
    $\rho_l = \frac{counter}{N \ line \ segments \ of \ I_1}$

The total recognition rate ρ_t is the linear combination of ρ_i, ρ_e, and ρ_l. ρ_t is calculated for each viseme template. The output viseme is the one with maximum ρ_t. If ρ_t is less than a certain threshold value the search for lips is repeated again for the whole image. If ρ_t is again below the threshold the the classification is rejected.

5 Results

We tested our method for four speakers. Every speaker read a German text. The duration of each sequence is 20 sec at 10 frames per sec *(fps)*. The image size was 352×288, the output frame rate was about 5 *fps* on Pentium III 700 MHz using a desktop camera. The system was trained using representative phonemes of the five visemes. The normalized recognition rate is shown in the tables. The location of the lips was incorrect only for few frames less than 1% of the number of the whole frames.

The quality of a lip tracking algorithm is indicative of how well it performs in the recognition of visemes or words [11]. Table 1 shows the percentage of the correctly estimated visemes for each sequence. For sequence 2, Table 2 shows the recognition of each viseme separately in detail.

Table 1. Ratio of correctly classified visemes using a single feature and combined features

Sequence	1	2	3	4
Only Intensity	55 %	64 %	40 %	39 %
Only Edges	46 %	43 %	33 %	30 %
Only Lines	21 %	31 %	25 %	21 %
Altogether	61 %	73 %	59 %	43 %

Table 2. Viseme recognition for sequence 2. The visemes in horizontal direction are expected (top row), in vertical direction they are the estimated (left column)

Visemes	C	O	R	L	H
C	55 %	0 %	0 %	0 %	0 %
O	5 %	84 %	0 %	7 %	35%
R	15 %	0 %	84 %	4 %	4 %
L	15 %	12 %	5 %	60 %	22 %
H	10 %	4 %	16 %	30 %	37 %

For some of the speakers, it was difficult to distinguish between very close visemes e.g. **L** and **H**, or between **C** and **L**. This was the case in e.g sequence 3, where the **L** viseme was difficult to be detected.

The speaker in sequence 4 has beard and moustache. This reduced the recognition rate, the viseme **H** was always classified as **R** or **L**. Table 3 shows the recognition rate after reducing the image size to 75%. This simulates the case when the speaker is moving away from the camera. The recognition rate was reduced due to the insufficiency of the lips features.

Table 3. Recognition rate for 75% zoomed image.

Sequence	1	2	3	4
Correct visemes	41 %	49 %	34 %	29 %

6   Conclusion & Future Work

We have presented a method for lip tracking and recognition of the five main visemes in German. This can also be applied to other languages, however. The visemes were divided into five groups according to the shape of the lips in natural speaking. Three features of the lips were used for the recognition, which made the location of the lips and the viseme recognition robust.

The method has been tested for different speakers, and has achieved a good recognition rate of the visemes of about 60%. The frame rate was 5 *fps*.

Currently, visemes are extracted only from one image at a time. As the speech is determined by the absolute shape and the transition between the visemes, this will be taken into account in our future work, as well as the combination with a speech recognition system.

Acknowledgment. This work is supported by Philips Semiconductors, Systems Laboratory Hamburg Germany.

References

1. C. Bregler, H. Hild, S. Manke, and W. A. "Improving connected letter recognition by lipreading". In International Joint Conference of Speech and Signal Processing, volume 1, pages 557–560, Mineapolis, MN, 1993.
2. Tsuhan Chen. "Audiovisual Speech Processing Lip Reading and Lip Synchronization". IEEE Signal Processing Magazine, Vol. 18, No. 1, pages 9–21, January 2001.
3. C. Bregler and Y. Konig "'Eigenlips' for robust speech recognition", Proc. Int. Conf. Acoust. Speech Signal Process. Vol. 75, 1994, pp 669-672.
4. Aleix M. and Avinash K. " PCA versus LDA", IEEE Transaction on Pattern Analysis and Machine Intelligence, Vol. 23, No 2, Feb. 2001, pp 228-233.
5. Marcus E. Hennecke, David G. Stork, and K. Venkatesh Prasad. "Visionary speech: Looking ahead to practical speechreading systems". Speechreading by Humans and Machines, volume 150 of NATO ASI Series, Series F: Computer and Systems Sciences, Berlin, 1995. Springer Verlag.
6. Abry, C. and Boe L.-J. "Laws for Lips", J. Speech Communication, Vol. 5, 1986, p 97-104.
7. B. Dodd and R. Cambell, Eds, "Hearing by Eye: The Psychology of Lipreading". London: Lawrence Erlbaum, 1987.
8. Lucey, S., Srindharan, S. and Chandran, V., "Initialized Eigenlip Estimator for Fast Lip Tracking Using Linear Regression", ICPR'2000, Barcelona, Spain.
9. M. U. Ramos Sanchez, J. Matas, and J. Kittler. Statistical chromaticity models for lip tracking with B-splines. In Proceedings of the First International Conference on Audio- and Video-based Biometric Person Authentication, Lecture Notes in Computer Science, pages 69–76. Springer Verlag, 1997.
10. L. Revéret, C. Benoît. A New 3D Lip Model for Analysis and Synthesis of Lip Motion in Speech Production. Proc. 2nd ESCA Workshop on Audio-Visual Speech Processing, Terrigal, Australia, Dec. 4-6, 1998.
11. J. Luettin, N. Thacker, and S. Beet. Statistical lip modelling for visual speech recognition. In VIII European Signal Processing Conference, Trieste Italy, 1996.

Medical & Industrial Augmented Reality: Challenges for Real-Time Vision, Computer Graphics and Mobile Computing

Keynote Speech by Dr. Nassir Navab

Siemens Corporate Research, 755 College Road East, Princeton, NJ 08540, USA
`nassir.navab@scr.siemens.com`

Abstract. This paper is an extended abstract for a keynote speech at DAGM 2001. The talk aims at describing different Augmented Reality (AR) applications and some of the challenges they bring for the researchers in computer vision, computer graphics and mobile computing. Different applications developed at Siemens Corporate Research (SCR)[1] are used to illustrate both advantages and shortcomings of the existing AR systems[2].

Augmented Reality (AR) is a relatively new field. Before 90's the idea of real-time augmentation of one's view of the world had come up mostly in terms of wishful and futuristic thoughts and/or science fiction. In different movies the imaginary characters were able to see location based information, messages or other information superimposed onto their view of the real world. The scientific community had to wait until early 90's to see some of the first implementations of such ideas. In the following years, the more Virtual Reality (VR) failed to fulfill its promise of changing the way people were doing their tasks, the more AR was considered as a serious alternative. AR started to define itself as the solution to problems, which prevented VR to become as popular as expected. Virtual Reality failed to satisfy its users for many reasons including the high cost for: a) building the virtual model of the world, b) keeping the model up to date, and c) training the users to work in such unfamiliar and non intuitive environment. VR required its industrial users to create detailed models of the environment and to radically change their workflow. By definition, VR aims at integrating or immersing the user into the virtual world. In contrast, AR aims at integrating virtual elements into the real world of its users. This seems more attractive, since it does not require the user to build the whole world in order to be able to work. The working environment does not need to change dramatically.

---

[1] Other than the author, the following researchers also work on Augmented Reality at or in collaboration with SCR: Mirko Appel, Benedicte Bascle, Yakup Genc, Ali Khamene, Erin Mcgarrity, Matthias Mitschke, Frank Sauer, Mihran Tuceryan and Xiang Zhang.

[2] This extended abstract is not intended to be a review paper on augmented reality literature. The references provide the readers only with publications of Siemens corporate Research on or related to Augmented Reality.

B. Radig and S. Florczyk (Eds.): DAGM 2001, LNCS 2191, pp. 443–451, 2001.
© Springer-Verlag Berlin Heidelberg 2001

The virtual element can be added incrementally in order to give user the time to adopt to the new workflow. In addition the user can often continue to work in a modified environment without explicitly modeling the modifications. However, Augmented Reality poses new challenges and needs dramatic progress in multiple research fields before achieving its ultimate goals.

Augmented Reality attracts researchers from many scientific and technical communities. Other than software design and software engineering aspects of an AR system that I decided not to talk about in this short presentation, real-time pose estimation, rendering and tracking are three major aspects of any AR system. Therefore, researchers from computer vision and computer graphics background form a majority of the AR scientific community. In order to augment users view of the surrounding world one can choose one of the following four options:

- project the virtual components onto the real world,
- project the virtual components onto user's retina,
- observe the real world through a semi-transparent display visualizing the virtual components,
- observe the world through video cameras and integrate the virtual components into the camera images.

The first two options are quite interesting but less common than the last two. The first option is well studied and experimented in particular at University of North Carolina, Chapel Hill. The second option is provided by MicroVision Virtual Retinal Scan Display (VRD). This system projects low energy laser onto user's retina. The third and forth options are available in different formats and are used in many academic and industrial research laboratories.

Computer vision can play an important role in AR applications. Its primary role is probably in automatic real-time detection, tracking and pose estimation. A tracking camera can be attached to all different types of augmentation devices described in the previous paragraph. For the forth option, i.e. the camera see-through devices, sometimes same camera can be used for tracking and pose estimation as well as view augmentation.

The Augmented Reality Group at Siemens Corporate Research was formed by a collection of researchers all coming from a computer vision background. Industrial as-built reconstruction for update of the CAD data and revamp and maintenance planning was the first motivation for our image augmentation activities. Fig. 1 shows some of the results of CyliCon, our off-line calibration, reconstruction and augmentation software [13,11,14,20,10,1]. Once the industrial customers gets exposed to such results, their first question is "could we have these augmentations in real-time?". This has a lot of applications. For example, power plants need to be inspected both on regular basis and after each plant modification and update. The inspectors need to get to the right components in large plants and access the necessary data. This brings new challenges for both computer vision and mobile/wearable computing. In this talk I will discuss these challenges in detail. I use our vision based real-time localization, navigation and augmented reality data access [23,22], see Fig. 3 for illustration. This system uses the real-time marker-based pose estimation and image augmentation, which we had previously developed for electronic sales support [24, 5], see Fig. 2. The system runs on different mobile and wearable computers all equipped with optical cameras. I will talk about advantages and shortcomings of the currently available mobile and wearable computers in regard to their use for mobile AR applications.

The majority of optical and video see-through augmented reality systems, which use cameras for tracking and localization, are using specially designed markers. In spite of many years of research on self calibration and structure from motion in both photogrammetry and computer vision, none of the existing AR systems can rely on this technology for robust and consistent feature-based pose estimation in real environment and in real-time. In this talk, I will describe this problem and the challenges it brings to the computer vision community in more details. Examples of the computer vision algorithms which are currently used in AR system will be given and their shortcomings and some possible solutions will be discussed.

For calibration of optical see-through systems one of the challenges is to recover the projection geometry of each user's eye. In these systems as well as in VRD systems there is no camera and the image is formed only on the user's retina. In order to calibrate these systems one needs to model and recover the projection geometry of users eyes. We developed the Single Point Active Alignment Method (SPAAM) [21] to calibrate optical see-through HMDs (this method is also applicable to the stereo case [3] and can be made more robust when a vision-based tracker is used [4]). The first version of our optical see-through system used magnetic trackers to estimate users head position. Our latest version uses optical and infra-red tracking for this purpose (see Fig. 4 for details of the our latest see-through systems). Since these systems augment users view of the world and not images, evaluation of such systems also poses new challenges. We describe a first proposal for evaluation of such AR systems in [2,7,6].

The most precise and reliable augmentation of video see-through HMD systems, to our knowledge, is developed for medical applications. One of these systems is designed and developed at Siemens Corporate Research [19,17,18]. This system allows the physician to see CT, MR or Ultrasound images overlaid on patient during operation, see Fig. 5. This provides physician with a whole new way of visualizing medical images and relating them to the patient during the surgery. The physician can move his head freely and observe the augmentation with no jitter. However, this impressive system cannot be used in practice unless computer vision and computer graphics can face the challenges this application poses for them. The main problem is the correct perception of the virtual objects behind or inside real objects. The first part of the problem is simple occlusion. For example, the physician should not see the medical image overlaid on his/her hand or instruments during the surgery. This is a difficult challenge for computer vision research. There is a need for precise and real-time detection of physician's hands and instruments. Note that both hands and instruments change shape and color during the surgery. The second part of the problem concerns the correct perception of virtual objects inside real objects. This poses even more difficult challenges for researchers in computer vision and in particular in computer graphics. How should we render a virtual medical data such as CT, MR or Ultrasound on top of optical views of the patients anatomy such that the viewer perceives them at the right depth? This is a difficult problem and it becomes much harder as the physician cuts the surface and open the patients during invasive surgeries. These are beautiful open problems that need to be addressed by computer visions and computer graphics communities [3].

References

1. M. Appel and N. Navab. Registration of technical drawings and calibrated images for industrial augmented reality. In *WACV*, pages 48–55, Palm Springs, CA, December 2000.
2. Y. Genc, N. Navab, M. Tuceryan, and E. McGarrity. Evaluation of optical see-through systems. Technical Report SCR-01-TR-688, Siemens Corporate Research, Inc., January 2001.
3. Y. Genc, F. Sauer, F. Wenzel, M. Tuceryan, and N. Navab. Stereo optical see-through hmd calibration: A one step method validated via a video see-through system. In *International Symposium for Augmented Reality*, pages 165–174, Munich, Germany, October 2000.
4. Y. Genc, M. Tuceryan, A. Khamene, and N. Navab. Optical see-through calibration with vision-based trackers: Propagation of projection matrices. In *International Symposium for Augmented Reality*, New York, USA, October 2001. To appear.
5. S. P. Liou, T. Goradia, and N. Navab. An integrated customer center approach to e-business. In *Proc. of the Int. Conf. on Advances in Infrastructure for Electronic Business, Science, and Education on the Internet*, Italy, 2000.
6. E. McGarrity, Y. Genc, M. Tuceryan, C. Owen, and N. Navab. A new system for online quantitative evaluation of optical see-through augmentation. In *International Symposium for Augmented Reality*, New York, USA, October 2001. To appear.
7. E. McGarrity, M. Tuceryan, C. Owen, Y Genc, and N. Navab. Evaluation of optical see-through systems. In *International Conference on Augmented, Virtual Environments and 3D Imaging*, pages 18–21, Mykonos, Greece, May 2001.
8. M. Mitschke, A. Bani-Hashemi, and N. Navab. Interventions under video-augmented X-ray guidance: Application to needle placement. In *MICCAI*, pages 858–868, Pittsburgh, PA, USA, 2000.

---

[3] For the moment the alternative is to use augmented reality only for better visualization during interventions. In this case, one may not need to augment the exact view of the physician. For example, we have proposed a new system for real-time integration of video and X-ray images. This systems uses a double mirrors system to align the X-ray and optical images taken by a camera augmented C-arm (CAMC) [16,15,9], see Fig 6. Such system can be used in many medical applications including the precise needle placement [12,8]

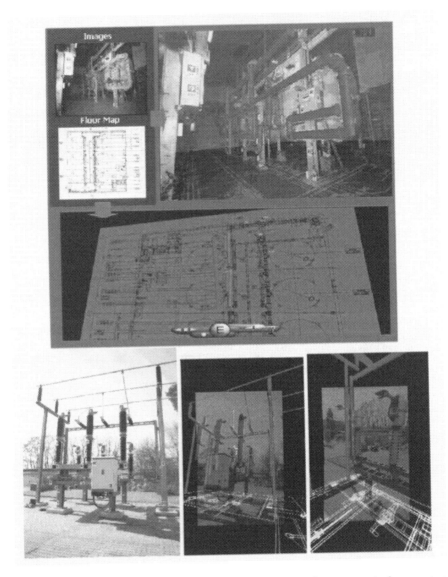

Fig. 1. Example augmentations from several reconstructed components for a water treatment plant and a power transmission installation. The floorplan drawing, the images, and the reconstructions are all registed in 3D and two snapshots of the viewer are shown along with the one of the original images.

Fig. 2. A snapshot from the E-Commerce application where a user is demonstrating a product.

9. M. Mitschke and N. Navab. Optimal configuration for dynamic calibration of projection geometry of x-ray c-arm systems. In *MMBIA*, pages 204–209, Hilton Head, SC, USA, 2000.

10. N. Navab, M. Appel, Y. Genc, B. Bascle, V. Kumar, and M. Neuberger. As-built reconstruction using images and industrial drawings. In *Mustererkennung 2000 - 22nd DAGM Symposium*, pages 1–8, Kiel, Germany, September 2000.

11. N. Navab, B. Bascle, M. Appel, and E. Cubillo. Scene augmentation via the fusion of industrial drawings and uncalibrated images with a view to marker-less calibration. In *Proc. IEEE International Workshop on Augmented Reality*, San Francisco, CA, USA, October 1999.

12. N. Navab, B. Bascle, M. H. Loser, B. Geiger, and R. H. Taylor. Visual servoing for automatic and uncalibrated needle placement for percutaneous procedures. In *CVPR*, Hilton Head Island, SC, June 2000.

13. N. Navab, N. Craft, S. Bauer, and A. Bani-Hashemi. CyliCon: software package for 3d reconstruction of industrial pipelines. In *WACV*, October 1998.

14. N. Navab, Y. Genc, and M. Appel. Lines in one orthographic and two perspective views. In *CVPR*, Hilton Head Island, SC, June 2000.

15. N. Navab, M. Mitschke, and A. Bani-Hashemi. Merging visible and invisible: Two camera-augmented mobile C-arm (CAMC) applications. In *Proc. IEEE International Workshop on Augmented Reality*, pages 134–141, San Francisco, CA, USA, October 1999.

16. N. Navab, M. Mitschke, and O. Schütz. Camera augmented mobile C-arm (CAMC) application: 3D reconstruction using a low-cost mobile C-arm. In *MICCAI*, pages 688–697, Cambridge, England, 1999.

17. F. Sauer, A. Khamene, B. Bascle, and G. J. Rubino. A head-mounted display system for augmented reality image guidance: Towards clinical evaluation for imri-guided neurosurgery. In *MICCAI*, Utrecht, The Netherlands, October 2001. To appear.

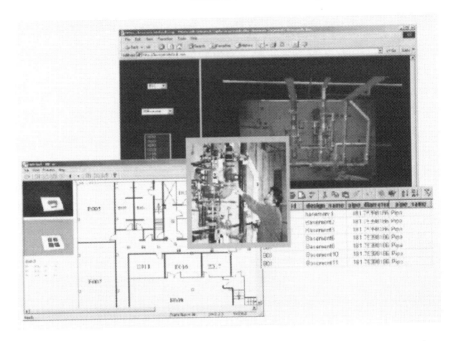

Fig. 3. Wearable computers such as Xybernaut MAIV or mobile computers such as Sony VAIO with wireless network connections and built-in cameras are used to locate the user in a large industrial environment and allow him/her to access location dependent information from a database.

18. F. Sauer, A. Khamene, B. Bascle, L. Schimmang, F. Wenzel, and S. Vogt. Augmented reality visualization of ultrasound images: System description, calibration, and featur. In *International Symposium for Augmented Reality*, New York, USA, October 2001. To appear.

19. F. Sauer, F. Wenzel, S. Vogt, Y. Tao, Y. Genc, and A. Bani-Hashemi. Augmented workspace: Designing an AR testbed. In *International Symposium for Augmented Reality*, pages 165–174, Munich, Germany, October 2000.

20. B. Thirion, B. Bascle, V. Ramesh, and N. Navab. Fusion of color, shading and boundary information for factory pipe segmentation. In *CVPR*, pages 349–358, Hilton Head Island, SC, June 2000.

21. M. Tuceryan and N. Navab. Single point active alignment method (spaam) for optical see-through hmd calibration for ar. In *International Symposium for Augmented Reality*, pages 149–158, Munich, Germany, October 2000.

22. X. Zhang, Y. Genc, and N. Navab. Taking AR into large scale industrial environments: Localization and data navigation with mobile computers. In *International Symposium for Augmented Reality*, New York, USA, October 2001. To appear.

23. X. Zhang and N. Navab. Tracking and pose estimation for computer assisted localization in industrial environments. In *WACV*, pages 214–221, Palm Springs, CA, December 2000.

24. X. Zhang, N. Navab, and S. Liou. E-commerce direct marketing using augmented reality. In *Proc. of IEEE International Conference on Multimedia & Expo.*, 2000.

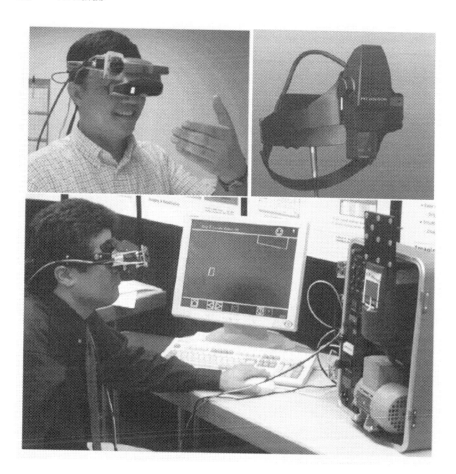

Fig. 4. The various components of our see-through system. A Sony XC-55BB camera with an infra-red filter is attached to one of the head-mounted displays (the video see-through display from Mixed Reality Labs and the two optical see-through devices the Virtual Retinal Scan Display (VRD) from Microvision and the I-glasses. The attached camera observes a set of retro-reflective markers for tracking. The camera is surrounded by a set of infra-red LEDs to illuminate the scene for optimal real-time tracking.

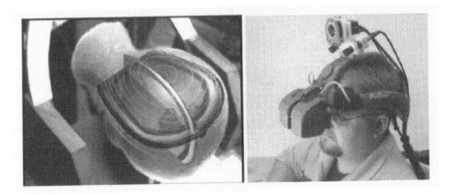

Fig. 5. Left image: video view of head phantom augmented with skull contour lines and the model of a tumor, segmented from a set of magnetic resonance (MR) images. Two of the MR slices are also shown. Right image: Video-see-through head-mounted display with additional tracker camera.

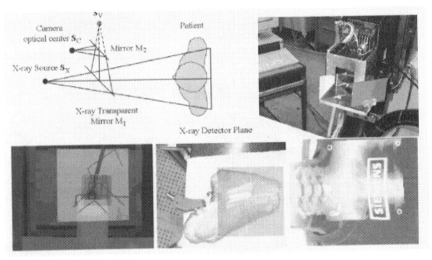

Fig. 6. The top images illustrate the CAMC concept for real-time alignment of X-ray ad video images as well as our first prototype with the camera attached to housing of the X-ray source and the double mirror system. The bottom images show three examples of real-time merger of X-ray and video images. The precise alignment of visible and invisible lines on the left image demonstrate the accuracy of the overlay, while the other two images show the clear advantage of this new visualization for image guided surgery.

Author Index

Lecture Notes in Computer Science

For information about Vols. 1–2084
please contact your bookseller or Springer-Verlag

Vol. 2124: W. Skarbek (Ed.), Computer Analysis of Images and Patterns. Proceedings, 2001. XV, 743 pages. 2001.

Vol. 2125: F. Dehne, J.-R. Sack, R. Tamassia (Eds.), Algorithms and Data Structures. Proceedings, 2001. XII, 484 pages. 2001.

Vol. 2126: P. Cousot (Ed.), Static Analysis. Proceedings, 2001. XI, 439 pages. 2001.

Vol. 2127: V. Malyshkin (Ed.), Parallel Computing Technologies. Proceedings, 2001. XII, 516 pages. 2001.

Vol. 2129: M. Goemans, K. Jansen, J.D.P. Rolim, L. Trevisan (Eds.), Approximation, Randomization, and Combinatorial Optimization. Proceedings, 2001. IX, 297 pages. 2001.

Vol. 2130: G. Dorffner, H. Bischof, K. Hornik (Eds.), Artificial Neural Networks – ICANN 2001. Proceedings, 2001. XXII, 1259 pages. 2001.

Vol. 2132: S.-T. Yuan, M. Yokoo (Eds.), Intelligent Agents. Specification. Modeling, and Application. Proceedings, 2001. X, 237 pages. 2001. (Subseries LNAI).

Vol. 2136: J. Sgall, A. Pultr, P. Kolman (Eds.), Mathematical Foundations of Computer Science 2001. Proceedings, 2001. XII, 716 pages. 2001.

Vol. 2138: R. Freivalds (Ed.), Fundamentals of Computation Theory. Proceedings, 2001. XIII, 542 pages. 2001.

Vol. 2139: J. Kilian (Ed.), Advances in Cryptology – CRYPTO 2001. Proceedings, 2001. XI, 599 pages. 2001.

Vol. 2141: G.S. Brodal, D. Frigioni, A. Marchetti-Spaccamela (Eds.), Algorithm Engineering. Proceedings, 2001. X, 199 pages. 2001.

Vol. 2142: L. Fribourg (Ed.), Computer Science Logic. Proceedings, 2001. XII, 615 pages. 2001.

Vol. 2143: S. Benferhat, P. Besnard (Eds.), Symbolic and Quantitative Approaches to Reasoning with Uncertainty. Proceedings, 2001. XIV, 818 pages. 2001. (Subseries LNAI).

Vol. 2146: J.H. Silverman (Eds.), Cryptography and Lattices. Proceedings, 2001. VII, 219 pages. 2001.

Vol. 2147: G. Brebner, R. Woods (Eds.), Field-Programmable Logic and Applications. Proceedings, 2001. XV, 665 pages. 2001.

Vol. 2149: O. Gascuel, B.M.E. Moret (Eds.), Algorithms in Bioinformatics. Proceedings, 2001. X, 307 pages. 2001.

Vol. 2150: R. Sakellariou, J. Keane, J. Gurd, L. Freeman (Eds.), Euro-Par 2001 Parallel Processing. Proceedings, 2001. XXX, 943 pages. 2001.

Vol. 2151: A. Caplinskas, J. Eder (Eds.), Advances in Databases and Information Systems. Proceedings, 2001. XIII, 381 pages. 2001.

Vol. 2152: R.J. Boulton, P.B. Jackson (Eds.), Theorem Proving in Higher Order Logics. Proceedings, 2001. X, 395 pages. 2001.

Vol. 2153: A.L. Buchsbaum, J. Snoeyink (Eds.), Algorithm Engineering and Experimentation. Proceedings, 2001. VIII, 231 pages. 2001.

Vol. 2154: K.G. Larsen, M. Nielsen (Eds.), CONCUR 2001 – Concurrency Theory. Proceedings, 2001. XI, 583 pages. 2001.

Vol. 2157: C. Rouveirol, M. Sebag (Eds.), Inductive Logic Programming. Proceedings, 2001. X, 261 pages. 2001. (Subseries LNAI).

Vol. 2158: D. Shepherd, J. Finney, L. Mathy, N. Race (Eds.), Interactive Distributed Multimedia Systems. Proceedings, 2001. XIII, 258 pages. 2001.

Vol. 2159: J. Kelemen, P. Sosík (Eds.), Advances in Artificial Life. Proceedings, 2001. XIX, 724 pages. 2001. (Subseries LNAI).

Vol. 2161: F. Meyer auf der Heide (Ed.), Algorithms – ESA 2001. Proceedings, 2001. XII, 538 pages. 2001.

Vol. 2162: Ç. K. Koç, D. Naccache, C. Paar (Eds.), Cryptographic Hardware and Embedded Systems – CHES 2001. Proceedings, 2001. XIV, 411 pages. 2001.

Vol. 2164: S. Pierre, R. Glitho (Eds.), Mobile Agents for Telecommunication Applications. Proceedings, 2001. XI, 292 pages. 2001.

Vol. 2165: L. de Alfaro, S. Gilmore (Eds.), Process Algebra and Probabilistic Methods. Proceedings, 2001. XII, 217 pages. 2001.

Vol. 2166: V. Matoušek, P. Mautner, R. Mouček, K. Taušer (Eds.), Text, Speech and Dialogue. Proceedings, 2001. XIII, 452 pages. 2001. (Subseries LNAI).

Vol. 2170: S. Palazzo (Ed.), Evolutionary Trends of the Internet. Proceedings, 2001. XIII, 722 pages. 2001.

Vol. 2172: C. Batini, F. Giunchiglia, P. Giorgini, M. Mecella (Eds.), Cooperative Information Systems. Proceedings, 2001. XI, 450 pages. 2001.

Vol. 2176: K.-D. Althoff, R.L. Feldmann, W. Müller (Eds.), Advances in Learning Software Organizations. Proceedings, 2001. XI, 241 pages. 2001.

Vol. 2177: G. Butler, S. Jarzabek (Eds.), Generative and Component-Based Software Engineering. Proceedings, 2001. X, 203 pages. 2001.

Vol. 2181: C. Y. Westort (Eds.), Digital Earth Moving. Proceedings, 2001. XII, 117 pages. 2001.

Vol. 2184: M. Tucci (Ed.), Multimedia Databases and Image Communication. Proceedings, 2001. X, 225 pages. 2001.

Vol. 2186: J. Bosch (Ed.), Generative and Component-Based Software Engineering. Proceedings, 2001. VIII, 177 pages. 2001.

Vol. 2188: F. Bomarius, S. Komi-Sirviö (Eds.), Product Focused Software Process Improvement. Proceedings, 2001. XI, 382 pages. 2001.

Vol. 2189: F. Hoffmann, D.J. Hand, N. Adams, D. Fisher, G. Guimaraes (Eds.), Advances in Intelligent Data Analysis. Proceedings, 2001. XII, 384 pages. 2001.

Vol. 2190: A. de Antonio, R. Aylett, D. Ballin (Eds.), Intelligent Virtual Agents. Proceedings, 2001. VIII, 245 pages. 2001. (Subseries LNAI).

Vol. 2191: B. Radig, S. Florczyk (Eds.), Pattern Recognition. Proceedings, 2001. XVI, 452 pages. 2001.

Vol. 2193: F. Casati, D. Georgakopoulos, M.-C. Shan (Eds.), Technologies for E-Services. Proceedings, 2001. X, 213 pages. 2001.